SQL Server 2019 Administration

Randolph West
Melody Zacharias
William Assaf
Sven Aelterman
Louis Davidson
Joseph D'Antoni

SQL Server 2019 Administration Inside Out
Published with the authorization of Microsoft Corporation by:
Pearson Education, Inc.

ISBN-13: 978-0-13-556108-9
ISBN-10: 0-13-556108-6

Library of Congress Control Number: 2020930782

1 2020

Trademarks
Microsoft and the trademarks listed at http://www.microsoft.com on the "Trademarks" webpage are trademarks of the Microsoft group of companies. All other marks are property of their respective owners.

Warning and Disclaimer
Every effort has been made to make this book as complete and as accurate as possible, but no warranty or fitness is implied. The information provided is on an "as is" basis. The author, the publisher, and Microsoft Corporation shall have neither liability nor responsibility to any person or entity with respect to any loss or damages arising from the information contained in this book or from the use of the programs accompanying it.

Special Sales
For information about buying this title in bulk quantities, or for special sales opportunities (which may include electronic versions; custom cover designs; and content particular to your business, training goals, marketing focus, or branding interests), please contact our corporate sales department at corpsales@pearsoned.com or (800) 382-3419.
For government sales inquiries, please contact governmentsales@pearsoned.com.
For questions about sales outside the U.S., please contact intlcs@pearson.com.

Editor-in-Chief: Brett Bartow
Executive Editor: Loretta Yates
Development Editor: Troy Mott
Managing Editor: Sandra Schroeder
Senior Project Editor: Tracey Croom
Copy Editor: Liv Bainbridge
Editorial Assistant: Cindy Teeters
Proofreader: Liv Bainbridge
Cover Designer: Twist Creative, Seattle
Compositor: MAP Systems, Bangalore
Graphics: Vived Graphics

To Marinus (obviously), but also Larry Toothman, Robert Davis, and Ian van Schalkwyk, because I miss you.

– Randolph West

To my husband Chris and daughters Jessica and Chloe for all your patience and understanding.

– Melody Zacharias

To Christine from her biggest fan

– William Assaf

In Memory of Erick Aelterman
Your example of hard work and perseverance made this possible

– Sven Aeleterman

To the rest of the writing and tech editing team. This edition of the book has been so much more of a joy due to everyone's hard work and commitment to the project. I am very proud to have been chosen to not only tech-edit half of this book, but to also take charge of revising two chapters.

– Louis Davidson

I'd like to thank the SQL Server Product Group for their hard work on the product.

– Joseph D'Antoni

To my dog Buster. Thanks for being patient and dealing with fewer dog park visits while I edited this book.

– Meagan Longoria

Contents at a Glance

Table of Contents

Part III	**SQL Server management** **305**
Chapter 8	**Maintaining and monitoring SQL Server** **307**

About the authors

Randolph West (they / them) is a technologist and Data Platform MVP from Calgary, Alberta, Canada, and hates writing in the third person because pronouns suck. Randolph is the founder of the Calgary Data User Group, and leader of the Calgary PASS User Group. You can see Randolph presenting at various conferences around the world, and acting on stage and screen. Randolph specializes in implementing best practices, performance tuning, disaster recovery, cloud migrations, software development, and yelling at Microsoft Word. If you're interested in becoming a public speaker, check out SpeakingMentors.com. Blog: bornsql.ca/blog. Twitter: @_randolph_west. Not to be trusted around chocolate.

Melody Zacharias has worked with SQL Server since version 7, and she is very passionate about all things data! As a Microsoft MVP Melody loves to share her passion with users around the world by teaching at events, working within the SQL community, and mentoring. When not working with data she loves to hike with her dog in the Canadian Rockies. You can find her on her blog at SQLMelody.com where she shares musings on how to make SQL sing, or sometimes just carry a tune, or on Twitter @SQLMelody.

William Assaf (he/him) is a Microsoft SQL Server consultant, speaker, and manager, and blogs about SQL at sqltact.com. William has been a developer, admin, and consultant for databases around the world, having launched from in-house DBA to consulting DBA thanks to the recession. He has helped develop Microsoft SQL Server certification exams since 2012, has been a Regional Mentor for PASS since 2015, and just stepped down from being the lead organizer of SQLSaturday Baton Rouge after a decade leading one of the largest SQLSat events in the world, and the only one with jambalaya. William enjoys volunteering for STEM initiatives as well as guest lecturing at LSU and SELU, where he gives a shoutout to all the ISDS and CIS students. William lives in continuous awe of his far more accomplished high school sweetheart Christine, and they would like to say that empty nesting is pretty great. Both of them hope to see you at PASS Summit and a future SQLSaturday event.

Sven Aelterman started with SQL Server when he first deployed version 2000 in a failover cluster scenario. Since then, he has worked as IT manager, principal consultant, and IT director. He currently serves the Trojans (students) of Troy University as a lecturer in information systems in the Sorrell College of Business and as director of IT for the College. In addition, he is cloud software architect for Sorrell Solutions, a business services nonprofit through which Trojans can gain real-world business and IT experience. In a fledgling attempt to give back to the community, he has spoken at many SQL Saturdays and code camps in the southeastern United States since 2005. He spoke about SSIS 2012 at Microsoft TechEd 2012. In 2012, he co-authored a book dedicated to SQL Server FILESTREAM. He was a co-author on the 2017 edition of this text. His involvement with Microsoft Azure resulted in the organization of four Global Azure Bootcamp events at Troy University. Sven blogs about a variety of Microsoft technologies at blog.aelterman.com and tweets and retweets about technology @svenaelterman.

Louis Davidson is a data architect for CBN in Virginia Beach, VA; telecommuting from Cleveland, TN (which is not even as glamourous as it sounds.) Louis has written and contributed to many books on SQL Server topics over the past 20 years. His most prominent work has been five editions of his book entitled: "Pro SQL Server Relational Database Design and Implementation" for Apress in 2016, with a new version forthcoming in 2020. Louis has been a speaker at many SQL Saturday events, and has helped organize events in Nashville and Chattanooga, TN. He blogs on Red-Gate's Simple-Talk website here: https://www.red-gate.com/simple-talk/author/louis-davidson/ and you can visit his website at http://drsql.org.

 Joseph D'Antoni is a Principal Consultant and Microsoft Data Platform MVP with over 20 years of experience working in both Fortune 500 and smaller firms. He has worked with SQL Server and Oracle since version 7 of each database and has specific expertise in performance tuning, infrastructure, and disaster recovery.

 Meagan Longoria is a Microsoft Data Platform MVP living in Denver, Colorado. She is an experienced consultant who has worked in business intelligence, data warehousing, and database development for over a decade. She enjoys creating solutions in Azure and SQL Server that make data useful for decision makers. Meagan enjoys sharing her knowledge with the technical community by speaking at conferences, blogging (Datasavvy.me), and sharing tips and helpful links on twitter (@mmarie).

Introduction

Much has changed in the months leading up to the publishing of Microsoft SQL Server 2019 Administration Inside Out, a follow-up edition to this team's successful and well-reviewed Microsoft SQL Server 2017 Administration Inside Out. Among just our writing and editing team, one became an empty nester, another got a new knee, another two new hips. One was evacuated because of forest fires, another left powerless under a hurricane, another twice moved houses, others got new jobs and job roles. Countless naming conventions and product names were changed in the Microsoft data platform, too, causing many late edits to this book. Azure SQL Database managed instance was made generally available, as well as the concepts of Big Data Clusters, Azure DevOps, Azure SQL Database Hyperscale and Azure SQL Database serverless tier, Azure Arc, Azure Cosmos DB, and more. SQL Server 2008 and 2008 R2 hit their end of life support dates and are no longer supported by Microsoft*, new streaming services were launched, the Washington Nationals won the World Series, LSU beat Alabama in football, and Avengers: Endgame finally beat Avatar as the highest grossing film of all time... so yeah, a lot of long-standing states of information have changed.

While no book can keep up with all the changes Microsoft has made even to just the data platform and supporting technologies in Azure, this book does its best to fully outer join the latest guidance on modern data platform solutions with long-standing database administrator wisdom. We'll cover both columnstore and rowstore indexes. Both Linux and Windows. Both Azure and on-prem solutions (and hybrid). Both memory-optimized tables and disk-based tables, with optimistic and pessimistic isolation. This book aims to be a reference, inspiration, early radar warning, or at least a launch pad, for your continued education and data platform solutions development.

Data warehousing has changed, with the traditional extract-transform-load (ETL) strategies giving way to extract-load-transform on-demand (ELT) strategies. SQL Server 2019 has new features and tools to develop these solutions while leveraging your existing Transact-SQL skillset. Features like Big Data Clusters and PolyBase external tables are helping you design fast, scalable, modern solutions where once you had to rely on external products, custom solutions in SQL Server Integration Services (SSIS), or linked server objects. All these solutions have their place, and all will continue to be in the inventory of your DBA utility belt, but your ensured success as a modern, relevant DBA requires adding tools. This book, and its large accompanying repository of sample scripts, aims to be that reference to DBAs as they add modern tools to their skill set.

Threat vectors and regulatory requirements have also changed. That's why SQL Server 2019 has vastly improved data classification capabilities leveraging a new dedicated schema, as well as Always Encrypted now with secure enclaves. There's also a new certificate manager built-in to SQL Server Configuration Manager, and new integrations with Azure Key Vault. We've expanded the SQL Server security and protecting data chapters greatly from the last book, recognizing the DBA's role as key to an enterprise data security team.

This book's content, and especially the Inside OUT features, are derived directly from the skills and experience of a group of seasoned database professionals with many decades of experience in designing, optimizing, developing, and teaching complex modern data platform solutions. It is written for experienced DBAs and developers.

After reading this book, you will be able implement a cloud-based, hybrid, and on-premises data solution using SQL Server 2019.

The velocity of change for the Microsoft SQL Server DBA has increased this decade. Gone are the days when DBAs had between three and five years to soak in and adjust to new tools and tricks in the Database Engine and surrounding features. We had less than a calendar year between the release of SQL Server 2017 and the first technical previews of SQL Server 2019.

This book is written and edited by SQL Server experts with two goals in mind: to deliver a solid foundational skillset for all of the topics covered in SQL Server configuration and administration, and also to deliver awareness and functional, practical knowledge for the dramatic number of new features introduced in SQL Server 2019. We haven't avoided late-breaking content—even content that stretched the boundaries of writing deadlines with late-breaking new releases. You will be presented with not only the "how" of new features, but also the "why" and the "when" for their use.

There are still a couple ways to get support for SQL Server 2008 / 2008 R2. One involves paying a lot of money, the other involves migrating it all to Azure VMs. Neither are as good an option as just upgrading it already!

Who this book is for

SQL Server administration was never the narrow niche skillset that our employers might have suspected it was. Even now it continues to broaden, with support for new operating systems and platforms: cloud-based and serverless in addition to on-premises, or maybe, a little of all three. This book is for the DBAs who are unafraid to add these new skillsets and features to their utility belt, and to give courage and confidence to those who are still hesitant. SQL Server administrators should read this book to become more prepared and aware of features when talking to their colleagues in application development, data analytics, and system administration.

How this book is organized

This book gives you a comprehensive look at the various features you will use. It is structured in a logical approach to all aspects of SQL Server Administration, whether you are implementing, developing, or supporting development.

Part I: Introduction

Chapter 1, "Getting started with SQL Server tools" gives you a tour of modern tooling for SQL Server administrators, from the installation media to the free downloads, not the least of which is the rapidly evolving SQL Server Management Studio and Azure Data Studio, as well as the newly enhanced Configuration Manager, performance and reliability monitoring tools, tools for writing PowerShell, and more.

Chapter 2, "Introducing database server components" introduces the working vocabulary and concepts of database administration, starting with hardware-level topics such as memory, processors, storage, and networking. We then move into high availability basics (much more on those later), security, and hardware and OS virtualization.

Chapter 3, "Designing and implementing an on-premises database infrastructure" introduces the architecture and configuration of SQL Server, including deep dives into transaction log virtual log files (VLFs), data files, in-memory Online Transaction Processing (OLTP), and the new Accelerated Database Recovery feature, one of many new features of SQL Server 2019. We spend time with TempDB and its optimal configuration, and server-level configuration options. Finally, we introduce you to Kubernetes.

Part II: Deployment

Chapter 4, "Installing and configuring SQL Server instances and features" reviews installation of SQL Server for Windows platforms when SQL Server Setup is needed to install SQL Server. We discus volume settings and layout for a SQL Server instance, editions, Smart Setup and unattended setup configuration, and setup logging. Look here also for post-installation checklists and configuration guidance, as well as configuration and guidance for other features including SSIS, SSAS, and SSRS, as well as PolyBase.

Chapter 5, "Installing and configuring SQL Server on Linux" reviews configuration of SQL Server on Linux instances, including feature differences between Windows and Linux. We'll provide guidance and caveats on Linux distributions, Linux-specific monitoring and storage considerations, and tooling for setup and administration.

Chapter 6, "Provisioning and configuring SQL Server databases" reviews creation and configuration of SQL Server databases on any SQL Server platform, including strategies for migrating and moving databases. Database options and properties are discussed, as well as database collations.

Chapter 7, "Understanding table features" completes the drill down from instances to databases to tables, covering table design, data types, keys and constraints. Use of IDENTITY and sequences, computed columns and other column properties, as well as special table types are discussed. We'll review special types of tables including temporal tables, introduce memory-optimized tables (more on these in Chapter 14), and graph tables. Finally, we're reviewing FILESTREAM and FileTable for storing blobs, table partitioning for storing and switching large amounts of data, and strategies for tracking data changes.

Part III: SQL Server management

Chapter 8, "Maintaining and monitoring SQL Server" covers the care and feeding of SQL Server instances on both Windows and Linux, including monitoring for database corruption, monitoring index activity and fragmentation, and maintaining and monitoring indexes and index statistics. We dive into extended events, the superior alternative to traces, and also cover Resource Governor, used for insulating your critical workloads. We review monitoring and data collection strategies based in Windows, Linux, and Azure, as well as the new SQL Assessment API. We'll finally discuss the current Microsoft servicing model for SQL Server.

Chapter 9, "Automating SQL Server administration" includes an introduction to automating activities for SQL Server, including maintenance plans, but also custom solutions involving PowerShell, including the latest features available in PowerShell. We also review built-in tools and features needed to automate tasks to your SQL Server, including database mail, SQL Server Agent jobs, Master/Target Agent jobs, proxies, SQL Agent alerts, event forwarding and Policy-Based Management.

Chapter 10, "Developing, deploying, and managing data recovery" covers the fundamentals of SQL Server database backups in preparation for disaster recovery scenarios, including a backup and recovery strategy appropriate for your environment. Backups and restores in a hybrid environment, Azure SQL Database recovery, and geo-replication are important assets for the modern DBA.

Chapter 11, "Implementing high availability and disaster recovery" then goes beyond backups and into strategies for disaster recovery from the old (log shipping and replication) to the new (availability groups), as well as monitoring and troubleshooting availability groups. We'll compare HA and DR strategies and dive into proper architecture for maximizing SQL Server uptime.

Part IV: Security

Chapter 12, "Administering security and permissions" begins with the basics of authentication, the configuration, management, and troubleshooting of logins and users. Then, we dive into permissions, including how to grant and revoke server and database-level permissions and role membership, with a focus on moving security from server to server.

Chapter 13, "Protecting data through encryption, privacy and auditing" takes the security responsibilities of the SQL Server DBA past the basics of authentication and permissions and discusses advanced topics including the various features and techniques for encryption including Transparent Data Encryption (TDE) and Always Encrypted, as well as protecting data in motion with TLS. The new Certificate Management feature of SQL Server 2019 Configuration Manager is reviewed, as well as modern strategies for row-level security and protection of sensitive data. We discuss security measures to be taken for SQL Server instances and Azure SQL databases as well as the SQL Server Audit feature.

Part V: Performance

Chapter 14: "Performance tuning SQL Server" dives deep into isolation and concurrency options, including Read Committed Snapshot Isolation (RCSI), and why your developers shouldn't be using NOLOCK. We'll discuss various strategies for memory-optimized data including delayed durability. We review graphical execution plans analysis, the important Query Store feature, and automatic plan correction. We review important performance-related Dynamic Management Objects (DMOs) and several new SQL Server 2019 performance features, most notably in the Intelligent Query Processing family.

Chapter 15: "Understanding and designing indexes" tackles performance from the angle of indexes, from their creation, monitoring, and tuning. We review all the various forms of indexes at our disposal, past rowstore clustered and nonclustered indexes and into other types of indexes including columnstore and memory-optimized hash. We review statistics and statistics options, including understanding how they work on a variety of index and table types.

Part VI: Cloud

Chapter 16, "Designing and implementing hybrid and Azure database infrastructure" discusses the infrastructure options for Azure-based SQL Server databases, including Platform-as-a-Service (PaaS) options of Azure SQL Database, Azure SQL managed instance, and also Infrastructure-as-a-Service options of Azure VMs running SQL Server instances. We discuss the resource scalability options for Azure SQL Database, which have dramatically expanded recently. We discuss management and governance in the Azure SQL data platform using the Azure Portal or PowerShell.

Chapter 17, "Provisioning Azure SQL Database" covers the cloud-first database service with a very high degree of compatibility with SQL Server 2019. This platform powers many web-based applications and services, scalable from basic $5/month to 80-vCore and 100 TB. You will learn about the Azure SQL database platform, compatibility, security, and availability. You will learn how to create servers, databases, and elastic pools, and how to perform important management tasks for your databases.

Chapter 18, "Provisioning Azure SQL Database managed instance" details the powerful Azure SQL Database managed instance offering, including provisioning, managing, and scaling the instance. We review the service objectives, limitations and advantages, and security features of the managed instance.

Chapter 19, "Migrating to SQL Server solutions in Azure" covers various strategies for Azure migrations, including the Microsoft tools provided for testing and migrating SQL Server workloads. We review differences and limitations for on-prem feature migration strategies to Azure platforms, including how to migrate SSIS packages to the Integration Runtime. We review post-migration steps, best practices for security and resiliency during migration, and the common causes for migration failures.

Part VII: Big Data and Machine Learning

Chapter 20, "Leveraging Big Data and Machine Learning" starts with a primer on big data features in SQL Server, including an introduction to Big Data Clusters. We're review how to operationalize analytics with machine learning services and the benefits of PolyBase external tables for direct access to external data sources, even non-relational data sources.

Acknowledgments

Randolph West They say it's easier the second time around. They are liars. Fortunately, I managed to rope in Melody Zacharias as payback for getting me involved in the last book. Cue evil laugh. After sitting at the kitchen counter for most of the last book, my husband bought me a desk which I never sit at. Thanks anyway! And thank you to my dog Trixie for taking me on long walks to think about better phrasing to keep Meagan happy. I would also like to give special thanks to Anthony Nocentino, Argenis Fernandez, and Glenn Berry for their help, technical advice, and support. Since we're naming names, here's a shout-out to the book team: Meagan, Melody (again), Loretta, Liv, Louis, William, Sven, and Joey. Each of you deserves a medal. This book would not be possible without the contributions of everyone involved.

Melody Zacharias I really want to thank the #SQLFamily for their inspiration, support, friendship and guidance. Particularly Argenis Fernandez who was my PASS Summit big buddy and introduced me to the community in 2011. Because of that experience, my life was forever changed for the better. No family is perfect, but my #SQLFamily is an amazingly supportive and inclusive family, and I am so proud to be a member.

William Assaf I'd like to thank the mentors and managers and colleagues in my professional career heretofore, who affected my trajectory, and to whom I remain grateful for technical and nontechnical lessons learned. I'd like to thank Connie Murla, David Alexander, Darren Schumaker, Ashagre Bishaw, Charles Sanders, Todd Howard, Chris Kimmel, Richard Caronna, Mike Huguet, Mike Carter, Jason Prell, James Sampson, my personal dream team of coauthors on this very book, and finally Patrick Leblanc, a fellow Baton Rouge native, whose friendship has repeatedly challenged and furthered me and my career. I'd also like to thank my father, a rare mechanical and electrical engineer (and a HAM), and both my older brothers who are brilliant software engineers, for repeatedly letting me play games on their computers. I'd finally like to thank Kim Fossey, Casey Phillips, Kristen Reeves, Helena Williams, Cheryl Cummings, Ajayi Anwansedo, Quinton Jason Jr, and other heroes of the STEM education in Baton Rouge, La., and all over. They are doing the hard work of developing our future coworkers and coauthors in my home state's perpetually underfunded, underappreciated, and underestimated public school youth.

Sven Aelterman There are a lot of people who have made my contributions to this book possible. They include those who have given me chances early in my career, enabled me to study abroad, and encouraged career development and growth. In no particular order, I want to recognize Walter Weyne, Yves Sucaet, Judson Edwards, Bill Belcher, Hank Findley, David Phelps, Janet and Jeff Kervin, and the late Don Hines. This "old" and expanded group of co-authors have held me to high standards, as have the editors. Speaking of editors, they're an odd breed. During the writing process: entirely unnecessary; my initial draft is perfect, of course. After the first review round, they're know-it-all, nit-picky experts who just don't see it the way it is. By the second review round, they're usually correct. And when the book is finished, it turns out they were invaluable. Thanks, Meagan and Louis! Most importantly, my family continues to be the driving force behind what I do every day. It's not easy for Ebony, Edward, and Sofia to put up with the late nights of learning and writing. But they do it, with love and a smile (most of the time). I want them to know their support and love are valuable, valued, and acknowledged

Louis Davidson Acknowledgements are super hard, not because I am so great and have no need for others, but rather because I have been surrounded by scores of people who are amazing for so long. The authors of this and the previous edition have taught me a ton along the way. I could not have survived the writing and tech editing processes without the writers on the docs.microsoft.com site and the many blogs in the #sqlfamily community. Additionally, I must acknowledge the PASS and the Microsoft MVP program, because they have helped me to expand my horizons throughout the past 20 years, helping me to get to the point I have reached in my career.

Meagan Longoria I'd like to thank my coworkers at Denny Cherry & Associates Consulting. I learn about the Microsoft Data Platform from them every day, and I enjoy them as humans. Thanks to Melissa Coates for giving me my first technical editing opportunity, as well as for all the friendship and data platform knowledge she has shared over the years. Thanks to Melody Zacharias and Rie Irish, who gave me the opportunity to become a published author and set me on the path to more editing opportunities. Thank you to Bill Fellows, for helping me get involved in the SQL Server community, which changed my life in so many ways, and for being my friend. And of course, I'd like to thank the authors of this book: William Assaf, Randolph West, Sven Aelterman, Melody Zacharias, Louis Davidson, and Joey D'Antoni. I'm so glad to know them and thankful for everything they do in the SQL Server community.

Errata, updates, & book support

We've made every effort to ensure the accuracy of this book and its companion content. You can access updates to this book—in the form of a list of submitted errata and their related corrections—at:

MicrosoftPressStore.com/SQLServer2019InsideOut/errata

If you discover an error that is not already listed, please submit it to us at the same page.

For additional book support and information, please visit:

MicrosoftPressStore.com/Support

Please note that product support for Microsoft software and hardware is not offered through the previous addresses. For help with Microsoft software or hardware, go to *https://support.microsoft.com*.

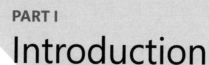

PART I

Introduction

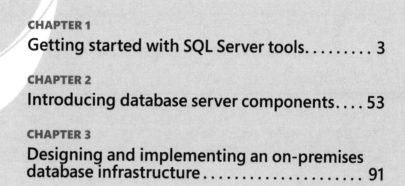

Getting started with SQL Server tools

This chapter provides information about where to find many of the Microsoft tools used to manage and work with the Microsoft SQL Server platform. It also walks you through the installation, configuration, and basic utility of each tool, including an overview of the two main tools for working with SQL Server, namely SQL Server Management Studio (SSMS) and Azure Data Studio.

The chapter is divided into the following sections:

- Installation Center

    - The Planning Tab

    - The Installation Tab

- Tools installed with the Database Engine

- SQL Server Management Tools

- SQL Server Data Tools

NOTE
Although SQL Server 2019 also runs on Linux, many of the administration tools that work with the Windows Server version will work with the Linux version. We note the specific cases for which platform-specific tools are available.

SQL Server setup

You can install SQL Server 2019 natively on Windows and Linux. For development and testing environments, you can install SQL Server with Docker container images on Windows, Linux, and macOS.

The following section covers installing SQL Server natively on Microsoft Windows.

> ➤ **For more details on how to set up and configure SQL Server, read Chapter 4, "Installing and configuring SQL Server instances and features."**

Installing SQL Server by using the Installation Center

SQL Server Installation Center is the application that you use to install and add features to an instance of SQL Server. As illustrated in Figure 1-1, it can also serve as a launch point for downloading the installation packages for SQL Server Upgrade Advisor, SQL Server Management Tools, SQL Server Reporting Services, and SQL Server Data Tools.

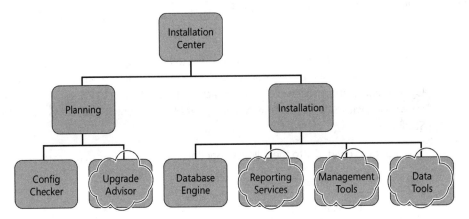

Figure 1-1   Installation Center components; downloadable tools have a cloud outline.

It might seem a bit confusing, but on the Installation tab, the installers for SQL Server Reporting Services, SQL Server Management Tools, and SQL Server Data Tools, are merely links that redirect to a download location on the Microsoft website for each of these components' installation files. You also can download and install the tools independently without using Installation Center.

NOTE

As a best practice, you should install SQL Server Management Studio and Data Tools only on client machines, not the production instance. This ensures a smaller installation and administration footprint on the server. It is therefore uncommon to use the Installation Center on client machines.

This is also true for the Planning tab, found on the Upgrade Advisor (also known as the Data Migration Assistant), which is simply a launch point for a continuously updated .MSI file that you can download.

Inside OUT

How do you install SQL Server 2019 on Linux?

SQL Server is fully supported on Red Hat Enterprise Linux (RHEL), SUSE Linux Enterprise Server (SLES), and Ubuntu, using the built-in package manager for each distribution.

The main SQL Server package is the Database Engine. You can install the command-line tools, SQL Server Agent, Full-Text Search, and SQL Server Integration Services as optional packages.

For more information about installing SQL Server on Linux, see Chapter 5, "Installing and configuring SQL Server on Linux," or visit Microsoft Docs at *https://docs.microsoft.com/sql/linux/sql-server-linux-setup.*

Planning before an upgrade or installation

When you first start the SQL Server Installation Center, it opens with the Planning tab preselected. This tab has two tools that you might find useful before installing or upgrading a SQL Server instance to SQL Server 2019: Configuration Checker and Upgrade Advisor.

Configuration Checker

The Configuration Checker tool checks for conditions that might prevent a successful SQL Server 2019 installation. When you click the Configuration Checker, a wizard runs against the local computer. There is no option to choose an alternate computer location. The wizard returns an HTML report listing all of the installation requirement rules (facets) and the results of each test. Nine of these rules are universal to all Windows Configurations, and you can easily remedy most of them.

1. **FacetDomainControllerCheck.**   We recommend that you do not install SQL Server 2019 on a Domain Controller. There are two reasons for this. First, it can compromise the security of both Active Directory and the SQL Server instance. Second, it can cause resource contention between the two services.

2. **FacetWOW64PlatformCheck.**   Windows operating systems must be 64-bit to support a SQL Server 2019 installation.

3. **MediaPathLength.**   The path for the location from which SQL Server 2019 is being installed must be fewer than 260 characters in length.

4. **NoRebootPackage.**   The correct .NET Framework must already be installed.

5. **RebootRequiredCheck.**   No installation reboots can be pending.

6. **SetupCompatibilityCheck.**   No subsequent incompatible versions of SQL Server can be installed on the computer.

7. **SSMS_IsInternetConnected.**   Verifies that the computer is connected to the Internet. This is required for validating a certificate when a .NET application starts.

8. **ThreadHasAdminPrivilegeCheck.**   The account running the setup file must have Local Administrator rights on the computer.

9. **WmiServiceStateCheck.**   Checks whether the Windows Management Instrumentation (WMI) service is started and running on the computer.

➤ You can find the most up-to-date Rules Documentation at *https://docs.microsoft.com/sql/ sql-server/sql-server-version-15-release-notes*.

NOTE

The minimum version of Windows Server for SQL Server 2019 is Windows Server 2016.

Data Migration Assistant (DMA)

There is a link on the Planning tab of Installation Center to download the Data Migration Assistant installation package.

NOTE

The Data Migration Assistant is now continually updated by Microsoft. You can download the most recent version from *https://www.microsoft.com/download/details. aspx?id=53595*.

This application is really two tools in one, which you can use to create two project types:

- An assessment of upgrade or migration readiness

- A migration of data between versions of SQL Server and/or Microsoft Azure SQL Database

For the assessment project type, the Source Server can be either a SQL Server instance, or Amazon Web Services (AWS) Relational Database Service (RDS) for SQL Server instance. For the Migration project type, the Source Server must be a SQL Server instance. The target server choices for all Target Server Types accommodate both Assessment and Migration, as shown in Table 1-1.

Table 1-1 **Data Migration Assistant assessment matrix**

Target server type	Assessment	Migration
Azure SQL Database	✓	✓
Azure SQL Database Managed Instance	✓	✓
SQL Server on Azure Virtual Machines	✓	✓
SQL Server	✓	✓

Assessment

The Assessment project type of the Data Migration Assistant detects database-specific compatibility issues between origin and destination SQL Server versions in the course of pre-upgrade discovery. It is common between versions for there to be deprecation and feature differences, and this is especially true if the Target Server Type is an Azure SQL Database. If not addressed, some of these items might affect database functionality during or post upgrade. The tool neatly outlines all findings and makes recommendations.

The Assessment project type examines the following aspects of upgrading SQL Server:

- **Database compatibility.**   Looks at deprecated features and functionality issues that could be "showstoppers."

- **Feature parity.**   Identifies unsupported or partially supported features and functions that applications using the database might rely on. For example, if you plan to move to Azure SQL Database, these include Cross Database Queries, Server-Scoped Logon Triggers, and Trace Flags.

- **Benefits from new features.**   This option is expected sometime in the future and is not currently available.

- ➤ You can find more information online by searching for "Discontinued Database Engine Functionality in SQL Server XXXX," where XXXX is your Source SQL Server platform.

NOTE
You can find a list of SQL Server database features that are not supported in Azure SQL Database at *https://docs.microsoft.com/azure/sql-database/sql-database-transact-sql-information*.

Migration

Using the Migration project type of the Data Migration Assistant, an administrator can move a database's schema, data, and non-contained objects from a source server to a destination server. The wizard works by providing a user with the option to select a Source and Destination Server and to choose one or more databases for migration.

The Migration Scope allows you to choose what to migrate. You can choose between the database schema only, the data only, or both the schema and data.

Moving to SQL Server

For SQL Server migrations, there must be a backup location that is accessible by both the source and destination servers, generally a UNC path. If this is a network location, the service running the source SQL Server instance must have write permissions for the directory. In addition, the service account running the destination SQL Server instance must have read permissions to the same network location.

If this poses a challenge, there is a check box labeled Copy The Database Backups To A Different Location That The Target Server Can Read And Restore From that you can select to break up the process into steps and utilize the (hopefully) elevated permissions of the administrator running the wizard.

When you select this option, the security privileges of the account of the individual running the Data Migration Assistant are used to perform the copy of the file from the backup location to the restore location. The user must have access to each of these locations with the needed read and write permissions for this step to succeed.

The wizard gives the user the option to specify the location to restore the data files and log files on the destination server.

As a final step, the wizard presents the user with a list of logins for migration consideration, with conflicting login names or logins that already exist identified. Where possible, the wizard attempts to map orphaned logins and align login security IDs (SIDs).

Moving to Azure SQL Database

The Data Migration Assistant tool performs an Azure SQL Database migration in two phases:

- **Schema.**   First, it generates a script of the database schema (you can save this script before deployment, for archival and testing purposes), which you deploy to the destination database.

- **Data.**   If you choose to move the data, another step is added after the creation of the tables on the destination database. This gives you the opportunity to verify that all of the tables exist in the destination database after the initial schema migration. Data migration makes use of Bulk Copy Program (BCP) under the hood.

The schema migration is required; the data migration is optional.

Installing or upgrading SQL Server

When it comes to administration and development tools used to work with SQL Server, the other important tab in Installation Center is the Installation tab. This tab contains a link to install the SQL Server Database Engine (the SQL Server service). A few of the utilities discussed in this chapter are installed as options only during a full SQL Server Database Engine installation and cannot be downloaded and installed independently.

During an in-place upgrade of an existing SQL Server instance, you can neither add nor remove components. The process will simply upgrade existing components.

CAUTION

An in-place upgrade to SQL Server 2019 will uninstall SQL Server Reporting Services if it is installed.

If you have multiple versions installed on the same server (instance stacking), a number of shared components will be upgraded automatically, including SQL Server Browser and SQL Server VSS Writer.

➤ You can read more about multiple instances and versions of SQL Server on Microsoft Docs at *https://docs.microsoft.com/sql/sql-server/install/work-with-multiple-versions-and-instances-of-sql-server*.

Tools and services installed with the SQL Server Database Engine

SQL Server 2019 provides a number of optional tools and services that you can select during the installation process. We'll take a look at some of them in the sections that follow. (Note that this list is not exhaustive and that some of these components might not be available in SQL Server 2019 on Linux.)

Inside OUT

What other feature improvements should you know about?

In SQL Server 2019, the Master Data Services (MDS) user interface has been significantly improved, by switching controls from Silverlight to HTML. You can also host MDS on a managed instance. See more about installing MDS at *https://docs.microsoft.com/sql/master-data-services/master-data-services-installation-and-configuration*.

> Additionally, SQL Server Analysis Services (SSAS) has some improvements in calcula-
> tion groups, as well as many-to-many relationships in tabular models. You can find
> out more about SSAS by visiting *https://docs.microsoft.com/sql/analysis-services/*
> *analysis-services*.

➤ For more information about configuring features, see Chapter 4.

Machine Learning Services

Starting with SQL Server 2016, Microsoft has created an extensibility framework for executing
external code on SQL Server. Machine Learning Services now support the following external
languages: R (introduced in SQL Server 2016), Python (introduced in SQL Server 2017), and Java
(introduced in SQL Server 2019).

NOTE

Java support in SQL Server 2019 is provided free of charge through the Zulu Embedded runtime from Azul Systems, for all scenarios where Java is used. For more
information you can visit *https://cloudblogs.microsoft.com/sqlserver/2019/07/24/*
free-supported-java-in-sql-server-2019-is-now-available.

You can install these extensions independently or together. What's more, you can install these
Machine Learning services directly in the Database Engine (in-database) or as standalone
components.

The in-database option creates a secure integration between the Database Engine and the
external runtimes containing the Machine Learning libraries. You run queries using Transact-SQL
(T-SQL) and make use of the Database Engine as the compute context.

If you decide to use R, Python, or Java without installing SQL Server, you must choose the standalone option. Each service will then run in its own independent compute context.

NOTE

Installing any of the Machine Language Services requires agreeing to an additional
license for each language option.

➤ You can read more about Machine Learning Services on Microsoft Docs at
https://docs.microsoft.com/sql/advanced-analytics/what-is-sql-server-machine-learning.

CHAPTER 1

Data Quality Services

The standardization, cleaning, and enhancement of data is critical to validity when performing analytical research. SQL Server Data Quality Services allows for both homegrown knowledge-base datasets and cloud-based reference data services by third-party providers.

Data Quality Services is a product that makes possible important data quality tasks, including the following:

- Knowledgebase-driven correction

- De-duplication

- Additional metadata enrichment

Data Quality Services has two parts: the Data Quality Server and the Data Quality Client. Data Quality Server has a dependency on the SQL Server Database Engine. Apart from that, you can install these two components on the same computer or on different computers. The tools are completely independent, and you can install one without having to install the other previously (i.e., the order doesn't matter).

To be functional, the Data Quality Client tool needs only to be able to connect to a Data Quality Server. There are certain operations the Data Quality Client can perform that require an installation of Microsoft Excel local to the client installation. It is commonplace to have the Data Quality Client on one or more workstations, but not the computer running SQL Server.

Data Quality Server

To install Data Quality Server, you must select its check box during SQL Server 2019 setup, which copies an installer file to a drive you specify. After you have installed SQL Server 2019, to use Data Quality Server you must install it. In your Windows Start Menu, expand Microsoft SQL Server 2019, and then click SQL Server 2019 Data Quality Server Installer. This runs the DQSInstaller.exe file. The installation asks you to type and confirm a database master key password and creates three new databases into the SQL Server instance chosen to be host Server: DQS_Main, DQS_Projects, and DQS_Staging_Data.

Data Quality Client

The Data Quality Client is an application most commonly used in conjunction with master data management (not to be confused with Master Data Services), data warehousing, or just plain data cleaning. It is typically used by a data steward who has a deep understanding of the business and domain knowledge about the data itself. You can use this tool to create knowledgebases surrounding data element rules, conversions, and mappings to help manage and align data elements. You also can use it to create and run data quality projects and to perform administrative tasks.

To sign in to a Data Quality Server using the Data Quality Client tool, you must be either a member of the sysadmin server role or one of these three roles in the DQS_Main database:

- dqs_administrator

- dqs_kb_editor

- dqs_kb_operator

line interface

You can use and administer SQL Server from a command line, which is especially relevant with Linux as a supported operating system (OS) for SQL Server. Utilities such as SQLCMD and BCP run on Windows, Linux, and macOS, with some minor differences.

SQLCMD

The SQLCMD utility is used to run T-SQL statements, stored procedures, or script files, using an ODBC connection to a SQL Server instance.

Inside OUT

What does ODBC mean?

ODBC stands for Open Database Connectivity, which is an open-standard application programming interface (API) for communicating from any supported OS to any supported database engine.

Although some people might consider the SQLCMD utility "old school" because it has been around since SQL Server 2005, it is still very popular because of its versatility. You can invoke SQLCMD from any of the following:

- Windows, Linux, or macOS command line

- Windows, Linux or macOS script files

- SQL Server Agent job step

- Using PowerShell with the command line

NOTE

Both SQL Server Management Studio and Azure Data Studio can invoke SQL-CMD mode, which makes a lot of very useful functionality possible. Although it's

technically part of SQLCMD, it is not strictly a command-line tool. You can read more about it at *https://docs.microsoft.com/sql/relational-databases/scripting/edit-sqlcmd-scripts-with-query-editor*.

Inside OUT

Is there a more modern command-line interface for SQL Server?

The mssql-cli utility provides significant enhancements over SQLCMD, however it is not installed with SQL Server by default. Some features include:

- IntelliSense for T-SQL
- Syntax highlighting
- Improved formatting for query results
- Multi-line editing
- Support for configuration files

➤ You can read more about mssql-cli at *https://docs.microsoft.com/sql/tools/mssql-cli*.

BCP

If you thought that SQLCMD is "old school," hold on to your hat. The Bulk Copy Program (BCP) makes SQLCMD look like the new kid on the block. First introduced in 1992 with the release of the very first edition of SQL Server, it is quite a testament that to this day BCP is still a practical way to work with SQL Server as a means to insert or export large quantities of data. It uses minimal logging techniques and bulk data flows to its advantage.

If that reminds you of SQL Server Integration Services, be aware that BCP is not nearly as powerful. You use BCP to move data between data files (text, comma-delimited, or other formats) and a SQL Server table.

You can use BCP to import files into SQL Server tables or to export data from SQL Server tables into data files. BCP requires the use of a format file to designate the structure of the receiving table and the data types allowed in each column. Fortunately, BCP helps you to create this format file quite easily.

There are a few things about BCP that you must understand and do for the tool to optimally perform:

- Use SELECT INTO syntax

- Put the database into the simple or bulk-logged recovery model

- Drop any nonclustered indexes on the destination table

- Insert sorted data and use the `sorted_data` option if a clustered index exists

- Run BCP on the same machine as the SQL Server

- Place source and destination files on separate physical drives

- Manually grow SQL data files in advance if growth is expected

- Take advantage of Instant File Initialization

- Use `sp_tableoption` to set table lock on bulk load (TABLOCK) to ON

➤ **For more information, go to**
https://docs.microsoft.com/previous-versions/sql/sql-server-2008-r2/ms177445(v=sql.105).

Inside OUT

How do you download the most recent command-line tools?

The versions of SQLCMD and BCP installed with SQL Server 2019 on Windows are updated through a separate package called Line Utilities for SQL Server, available at *https://docs.microsoft.com/sql/tools/sqlcmd-utility.*

For features like Always Encrypted and Azure Active Directory authentication, SQLCMD requires a minimum of version 13.1. It is entirely possible (and likely) to have more than one version of SQLCMD installed on a server, so be sure to check that you are using the correct version by running `sqlcmd -?`.

Separate installers for Linux and macOS versions of these command-line tools are available and regularly updated.

SQL Server PowerShell Provider

If you love to use a command line or if you have begun to use PowerShell to help manage and maintain your SQL Servers, Microsoft offers the PowerShell Provider for SQL Server. It can be installed with Windows PowerShell and PowerShell Core.

NOTE

There are two PowerShell modules for SQL Server, namely `SQLPS` and `SQLServer`. `SQLPS` is an older module included in SQL Server for backward compatibility but is no longer being updated. Instead you should use the Sql Server module, which is installed separately via the PowerShell Gallery, and is regularly updated.

Inside OUT

What's the difference between Windows PowerShell and PowerShell Core?

Windows PowerShell (based on the .NET Framework) is installed by default on all versions of Windows Server from 2008 R2 with Service Pack 1 onwards. PowerShell Core (based on .NET Core) is a separate download, and runs cross-platform on Windows, Linux, and macOS. To complicate matters, both Windows PowerShell and PowerShell Core can be installed side-by-side on Windows Server.

Many of the PowerShell modules for Windows PowerShell can be installed on PowerShell Core, with some limitations caused by dependencies on the .NET Framework, which may not be available on .NET Core.

To find out more about these differences, visit Microsoft Docs at *https://docs.microsoft.com/powershell/scripting/install/installing-powershell.*

The SQL Server PowerShell Provider uses SQL Server Management Objects (SMO), which are included when you install the Sql Server PowerShell module. These objects were designed by Microsoft to provide for the management of SQL Server programmatically. There are many ways that developers and administrators can use PowerShell to automate their work in SQL Server, especially when dealing with multiple server environments.

➤ To learn more about automation in SQL Server using PowerShell, see Chapter 8, "Maintaining and monitoring SQL Server."

SQL Server Configuration Manager

SQL Server Configuration Manager is a tool that uses the Microsoft Management Console as a shell. Because it is not a freestanding program, finding and opening the application can be a little tricky. To launch SQL Server Configuration Manager, on the Windows Start Menu, under Apps, search for SQLServerManager15.msc.

NOTE

SQL Server on Linux has its own set of configuration tools, which you can read about in Chapter 5.

Administrators use SQL Server Configuration Manager to manage SQL Server Services. These services include the SQL Server Database Engine, the SQL Server Agent, SQL Server Integration

Services, the PolyBase Engine, and others. SQL Server Configuration Manager provides a GUI to perform the following tasks associated with SQL Server–related services:

- Start or stop a service

- Alter the start mode (manual, automatic, disabled)

- Change startup parameters, including trace flags

- Create server aliases

- Change the Log On As accounts

- Manage client protocols, including TCP/IP default port, keep alive, and interval settings

- Manage FILESTREAM behavior

Inside OUT

Can you manage SQL Server services from Windows Services Manager?

Although you can perform most of these same tasks using the default Windows Services Manager (Control Panel > Administrative Tools > Services), we do not recommend doing so.

The Windows Services Manager (services.msc) does not provide all of the various configuration options found in the SQL Server Configuration Manager. More importantly, it can omit adjusting important registry settings that need to be changed, which will compromise the stability of your SQL Server environment.

You must always change SQL Server services using the SQL Server Configuration Manager. This is especially true for managing SQL Server Service Accounts.

Performance and reliability monitoring tools

The Database Engine Tuning Advisor, Extended Events, and Profiler tools are installed with the SQL Server Database Engine and do not require additional installation steps. This next section explores each tool in more detail.

Database Engine Tuning Advisor

Among the many administrative tools Microsoft provides to work with SQL Server is the Database Engine Tuning Advisor. You can start it either from the Start menu or from within SQL

Server Management Studio (SSMS) by clicking **Tools** and then **Database Engine Tuning Advisor**. Using this tool, you can analyze a server-side trace captured by SQL Server Profiler. It will analyze every statement that passes through the SQL Server and present various options for possible performance improvement.

NOTE

The Database Engine Tuning Advisor is not supported in Azure SQL Database, including managed instance.

The suggestions that Database Engine Tuning Advisor makes, focus solely on indexing, statistics, and partitioning strategies. The Database Engine Tuning Advisor simplifies the implementation of any administrator-approved changes it suggests. You need to scrutinize these changes to ensure that they will not negatively affect the instance.

CAUTION

You should not run the Database Engine Tuning Advisor directly against a production server, because it can leave behind hypothetical indexes and statistics that can persist without a DBA's knowledge. These will require additional resources to maintain. Use the `is_hypothetical` column in the `sys.indexes` system view to find hypothetical indexes for manual removal.

Extended events

Technically, the Extended Events GUI (client only) is installed with and is a built-in part of SSMS, but we discuss it here with the other performance-specific tools for categorical reasons.

> ➤ **You can read more about how extended events are supported in Azure SQL Database, with some differences, at** *https://docs.microsoft.com/azure/sql-database/sql-database-xevent-db-diff-from-svr*.

SQL Server Extended Events is an event-handling system created to replace SQL Server Profiler. Think of it as the "new and improved" version of Profiler. It is more lightweight, full-featured, and flexible, all at once. Extended events offer a way of monitoring what's happening in SQL Server, with much less overhead than an equivalent trace run through the SQL Profiler, because extended events are asynchronous.

You access extended events through SSMS by connecting to a SQL Server instance, navigating to the **Management** folder, then expanding the **Extended Events** node to display **Sessions**. Right-click on **Sessions**, and then, on the shortcut menu that opens, select the **New Session Wizard**. You can then use this wizard to schedule events to run at server startup or immediately after the event has been created.

CHAPTER 1

> **NOTE**
>
> **SQL Server Management Studio provides a simple extended events viewer called XEvent Profiler, which is meant to replace the standalone Profiler tool for monitoring activity in real time on a SQL Server instance.**

Scripting extended events sessions via T-SQL can be a much quicker and consistent way to create a library of extended event sessions for reuse in multiple environments. This gives you the flexibility to start and stop them as needed, even as a job in SQL Server Agent.

Components

The following subsections describe the extended events components.

Events

Because Profiler has been deprecated, a number of new features in SQL Server have matching extended events, but not Profiler events. This means that using extended events to capture diagnostic and performance visibility (rather than Profiler) provides a much larger library of events to choose from than Profiler. Each event has its own set of default fields. In addition, there are global fields (known as actions) that you can add to the collection of any event, for example, `database_name`, `database_id`, `sql_text`, and `username`.

Targets (Data Storage Options)

Targets are basically the consumers, or recipients of events. Targets can log additional event context upon receipt of an event. The target options allow for different ways to view or even save event data. Although users can observe data during collection with extended events (watching the target in action), we do not recommend that you do so on a production machine. Targets come in two flavors:

- **File (`event_file` target).**   This is best for large datasets, later analysis, remote analysis for retrieval by a consultant or tool, or historical record keeping/baselines. Options with this target setting are where to save the file, what to name it, what the maximum file size should be, whether the file should roll over, and how many files should be saved in total.

- **Memory (`ring_buffer` target).**   This is best for smaller datasets or long sessions. With this option, the user can specify how many events to keep, how much memory to use (max), or how many events (per type) to keep.

Actions

These are instructions that specify what to do when an event fires. Actions are associated with events.

Predicates

These are filters that limit event firing and provide a more concise view of the issue being reviewed. Some examples are `LoginName`, `ApplicationName`, or `SPID`.

Scenarios for use

You can use extended events for a wide range of scenarios. As of SQL Server 2019, you can choose from more than 1,700 events. Here are some of the most common uses for extended events:

- Troubleshooting

- Diagnosing slowness

- Diagnosing deadlocks

- Diagnosing recompiles

- Debugging

- Login auditing

- Baselining

By scripting out an event session and using automation, you have a stock set of sessions that you can use to troubleshoot depending on the problem. You can deploy these solutions on any server that needs a closer examination into performance issues.

You can also use extended event trace to provide a baseline from which you can track code improvements or degradation over time.

Management data warehouse

The management data warehouse (MDW), introduced in SQL Server 2008, collects data about the performance of a SQL Server instance, and feeds the information back to an administrator in a Visual Analytic style format. MDW has its own relational database containing tables that are the recipient (target) of specific extended events collection activities.

Upon installation, MDW provides three reports: Server Active History, Query Statistics History, and System Disk Usage. You can create additional reports and add them to the data warehouse collection.

Using the three-report configuration of MDW makes it possible for a database administrator to do basic performance baselining and to plan for growth. It also allows for proactive tuning activities. If you plan on using MDW, you should set it up when you install a new instance of SQL Server.

Installing a management data warehouse

Perform the following steps to install your MDW:

1. In SSMS, in Object Explorer, expand the Management node, and then right-click **Data Collection**. On the shortcut menu that opens, point to **Tasks**, and then select **Configure Management Data Warehouse**, as shown in Figure 1-2.

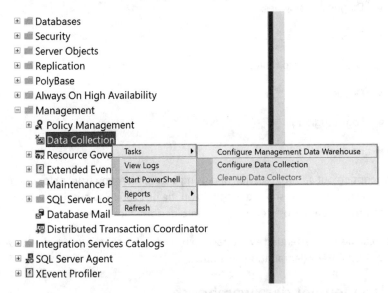

Figure 1-2   Navigating to the Management Data Warehouse menu item.

2. In the Configure Management Data Warehouse Wizard, Select Create Or Upgrade A Management Data Warehouse, and then click **Next**.

3. The server name is already populated, so either select the Management Data Warehouse database you are already using for collection by clicking it in the Database Name list box, or, to the right of the list box, click **New**. If you click **New**, in the **New Database** dialog box that opens, type the database name to which you want to store the information collected by the management data warehouse, as demonstrated in Figure 1-3.

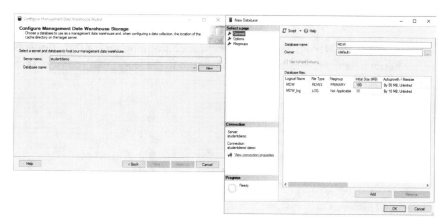

Figure 1-3   Creating a new database for collecting management data warehouse data.

4.   Select a user to map to the Management Data Warehouse role.

Setting up a data collection

After you install MDW, you need to set up a data collection to collect data from the server and databases of interest. Here's how to do that:

1.   In Object Explorer, expand the Management node, right-click **Data Collection**, point to Tasks, and then click **Configure Data Collection**.

2.   In the wizard that opens, select the Server Name and Database Name specified during the installation. Finish by choosing any other needed settings.

Go back and view Data Collection node. Things look different now: The Data Collection Sets in Object Explorer as well as the Data Collection node itself no longer displays a red down-arrow icon, as depicted in Figure 1-4.

Figure 1-4   Active data collection sets.

CHAPTER 1

Accessing reports

To access the Management Data Warehouse reports, right-click **Data Collection**, point to **Reports**, and then move through the menus to the report that you would like to view, as shown in Figure 1-5.

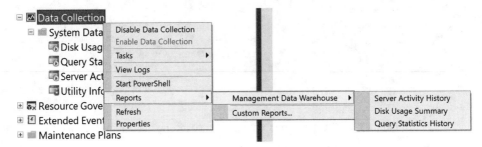

Figure 1-5   Accessing the management data warehouse reports.

SQL Server Reporting Services

Starting with SQL Server 2017, SQL Server Reporting Services is a separate download outside of the SQL Server installer. You can use SQL Server Reporting Services to create reports against a variety of data sources. It includes a complete set of tools for creating, managing, scheduling, and delivering reports. The reports can include charts, maps, data matrixes, and, with the addition of R, Python, and Java, almost unlimited data visualizations that are rich and limited only by creativity.

SQL Server Reporting Services provides a web portal interface to manage and organize reports and other items. Internet Information Services (IIS) is not required to use SQL Server Reporting Services.

Installation

You must download SQL Server Reporting Services separately, either by following the stub on the Installation Center screen or by going to *https://docs.microsoft.com/sql/reporting-services/install-windows/install-reporting-services*.

Completing the installation of SQL Server Reporting Services sets up and configures the following services and features:

- Installs the Report Server Service, which consists of the following:

  - Report Server Web Service

  - Web Portal for viewing and managing reports and report security

- Report Services Configuration Manager

- Configures the Report Service and Web Portal URLs

- Establishes the Service accounts needed for SQL Server Reporting Services to operate

➤ **You can read more about configuring SQL Server Reporting Services in Chapter 4.**

After the installation is complete, using administrative rights, browse to the following directories to verify that the installation was successful and that the service is running:

- *localhost/Reports*

- *localhost/ReportServer*

If you are running a named instance of SQL Server, you need to use the Web Portal URL tab in the Report Services Configuration Manager dialog box to determine the exact path of both the Web Service URL and the Web Portal URL, as illustrated in Figure 1-6.

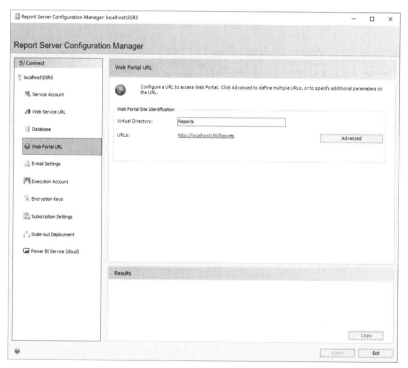

Figure 1-6   Web Portal URL setting in Reporting Services Configuration Manager.

Report Services Configuration Manager

The Report Services Configuration Manager simplifies customization of the behavior of features and capabilities offered by SQL Server Reporting Services. You can use it to perform the following tasks and more:

- Create or select existing Report Server databases

- Define the URLs used to access the Report Server and Report Manager

- Configure the Report Server Service Account

- Modify the connection string used by the Report Server

- Set up email distribution capability

- Integrate with a Power BI service

Inside OUT

How do you configure SQL Server Reporting Services?

The Configuration Manager in SQL Server Reporting Services (SSRS) comes with no shortage of customization options. Beyond the default, you can alter the configuration of almost any setting using the GUI, through SSMS, directly via `web.config` files, and even in some cases the Windows registry. Customizing accounts, IP addresses, ports, or behaviors can be quite an endeavor, the scope of which is far beyond what we can cover in this chapter.

You can find more information at *https://docs.microsoft.com/sql/reporting-services/ install-windows/reporting-services-configuration-manager-native-mode*.

To configure an SSL certificate to secure your SSRS installation, you can read more at *https://docs.microsoft.com/sql/reporting-services/ security/configure-ssl-connections-on-a-native-mode-report-server*.

SQL Server Management Studio (SSMS)

SSMS is the *de facto* standard SQL Server database development and management tool. It provides a rich graphical interface and simplifies the configuration, administration, and development tasks associated with managing SQL Server and Azure SQL Database environments. SSMS also contains a robust script editor and comes stocked with many templates, samples, and script-generating features.

Inside OUT

Does SQL Server Management Studio support other operating systems?

SQL Server Management Studio is a Windows-only application; it does not work in Linux and macOS environments. Instead, you can use the free cross-platform Azure Data Studio to connect to SQL Server, Azure SQL Database, and Azure Synapse Analytics (formerly Azure SQL Data Warehouse) from Windows, Linux, and macOS.

You can read the section later in this chapter for more about this exciting addition to your toolkit.

Releases and versions

Since the release of SQL Server 2016, SSMS is a freestanding toolset that you can download and install independent of the Database Engine.

Installing SQL Server Management Studio

As of this writing, the latest major version of SQL Server Management Studio (SSMS) is 18.x. It can be installed alongside previous major versions of SSMS, including those bundled with earlier versions of SQL Server.

CAUTION

We recommend that you do not install SSMS on a computer running a production instance of SQL Server. Instead, you can install SSMS on a workstation and connect to the production instance through a secure connection. Aside from reducing the temptation to connect remotely to a production instance, it has the added benefit of limiting the attack surface area.

To install SSMS, download the latest version of the product by visiting *https://docs.microsoft.com/sql/ssms/download-sql-server-management-studio-ssms*.

After you download the executable file, install and then watch the Package Progress and Overall Progress meter bars do their thing. There's not much more to it than that. The installation finishes with a Setup Completed message. In some cases, you may be prompted to restart your computer.

At this point, you can start the application by browsing through your Start Menu to **Microsoft SQL Server Tools 18** > **Microsoft SQL Server Management Studio 18**. For ease of access, you might want to pin the program to your Start Menu or copy the icon to your desktop.

CHAPTER 1

If you also have Azure Data Studio installed on the same computer, you can invoke Azure Data Studio features, such as queries or notebooks, from inside SQL Server Management Studio.

➤ **You can read about integration between SSMS and Azure Data Studio in the "Azure Data Studio" section later in this chapter.**

Upgrading SQL Server Management Studio

SSMS will notify you if an update is available. You can also manually check whether one is available. To do so, select **Tools** from the menu, and then choose **Check For Updates**. The different versions of the SSMS components—the installed version and the latest available version—will display. If any updates are available, you can click the **Update** button to bring you to a webpage from which you can download and install the latest recommended version.

Now that the tools used to manage SQL Server are completely independent of the Database Engine, upgrading these components has become very easy. It has also become much safer to upgrade: there is no longer any concern about accidentally affecting your production environment (SQL Server Database Engine) because you upgraded your SSMS toolset.

Features of SQL Server Management Studio

The power of SSMS is in the many ways in which you can interact with one or more SQL Server instances. This section highlights some useful features.

Object Explorer and Object Explorer Details

Object Explorer is the default SSMS view, providing both a hierarchical and tabular view of each instance of SQL Server and the child objects within those instances (including databases, tables, views, stored procedures, functions, and so on).

> NOTE
> **Object Explorer uses its own connection to the database server, and can block certain database-level activities, just like any other SSMS query.**

Object Explorer presents two panes (see Figure 1-7): the Object Explorer pane (left) and the Object Explorer Details pane (right). The Object Explorer pane is strictly hierarchical, whereas the Object Explorer Details pane is both hierarchical and tabular. As such, the latter provides additional functionality over its companion pane; for example, object search, and selection and scripting of multiple, noncontiguous objects. To display the Object Explorer Details pane, click **View** > **Object Explorer Details**, or press **F7**.

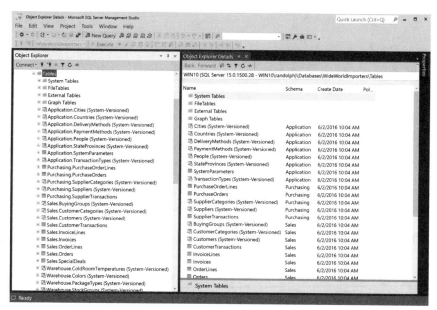

Figure 1-7   The Object Explorer view in SQL Server Management Studio.

Server Registration

The Server Registration feature within SSMS can save time and make it easier to manage a complex environment by saving a list of commonly accessed instances. Registering connections in advance for future reuse provides the following benefits:

- Preservation of connection information

- Creation of groups of servers

- Aliasing of servers with more meaningful names

- Ability to add detailed descriptions to both servers and server groups

- Import and export of registered server groups for sharing between machines or teammates

To access the Server Registration feature within SSMS, click **View** > **Registered Servers**, or press **Ctrl+Alt+G**. You can use SSMS to manage four different types of servers and services:

- Database Engine

- Analysis Services

- Reporting Services

- Integration Services

NOTE

Server registration of SQL Server Integration Services is included for backward compatibility for versions prior to SQL Server 2012.

Database Engine

When you use the Registered Servers feature to work with Database Engines, two nodes appear: Local Server Groups and Central Management Servers. Each of these has some very useful features:

- **Local Server Groups.**   The Local Server Groups node allows for the addition of either freestanding individual server registrations or the creation of server groups. Think of server groups as "folders" within the Local Server Groups node. Each of these folders can contain one or more individual servers. Figure 1-8 shows one of the many ways in which you can use the Local Server Groups feature to organize and save frequently used Database Engine connections.

Figure 1-8   The Local Server Group.

- **Exporting Registered Servers.**   To access the Export Registered Servers Wizard, right-click the **Local Server Groups** folder node or any folder or server nested within this node. On the shortcut menu, point to **Tasks**, and then click **Export**. From there, you have quite a bit of freedom; you can choose to export from any level within the tree structure and whether to include user names and passwords. In the preceding case, if you want to export only the Development Servers node and those servers within it, you can do so with the wizard by choosing where to save the created file and then build out an XML document with the extension .regsrvr.

- **Importing Registered Servers.**   To access the Import Registered Servers Wizard, right-click the **Local Server Groups** folder node or any folder or server nested within this node. On the shortcut menu, point to **Tasks**, and then click **Import**. Browse to and select a previously created .regsrvr file, as demonstrated in Figure 1-9.

Figure 1-9   Importing registered servers.

- From here you can choose in which folder you would like the imported object or object tree to reside. If you select a folder that already contains the same structures you are attempting to import, a message will appear asking you to approve or disapprove an update/overwrite to the existing object structure.

- **Central Management Servers.**   The second node available in the Database Engine feature is Central Management Servers. At first glance, this might appear to be almost the same thing as Local Server Groups: you're able to add servers and create folders with descriptive names to which you can add servers. And, yes, in this way, it is much the same. However, Centralized Management Servers includes some very significant differences.

First, when using this feature, you must choose a SQL Server Database Engine to play the role of a Central Management Server (CMS). You can alias the server with a new name, but the server itself must exist. After you have chosen a server to play this role and have created a CMS, you can create new Server Groups or individual Server Registrations using the same methods explained in the Local Server Groups section.

Here is where things become interesting. If you right-click any level (a server, a group, or the CMS itself), you are presented with multiple options:

- New Query

- Object Explorer

- Evaluate Policies

- Import Policies

Anything that is run will be run against each of the servers in the chosen group's tree. Running a query against the CMS itself will result in the query being run against every server hierarchically present in all trees within the CMS. This is a very handy feature, but with great power comes great responsibility!

The default behavior of CMS is that multiple server results are merged into one result set. You can change and customize this behavior by going to **Tools** > **Options** > **Query Results** > **SQL Server** > **Multiserver Results**, and then turn on the **Merge Results** setting. Other behavior options available here include Add Login Name and Add Server Name to the result set from a CMS query.

When you create a CMS on an existing SQL Server, others can access and use the structure setup, so there is no need to Export or Import and keep folders and structures synchronized. This is great for team collaboration and efficiency.

Filtering objects

In the default Object Explorer view, SSMS lists objects within each category in alphabetical order. There are several main groups, or tree categories, that are common across all versions of SQL Server. These include the following:

- **Databases.**   This provides a full list of databases (including system databases) on the SQL Server instance. Database snapshots also appear here.

- **Security.**   This contains a diverse list of object types including Logins, Server Roles, Credentials, Cryptographic Providers, and Audits.

- **Server Objects.**   These include Backup Devices, Endpoints, Linked Servers, and Triggers (server-level triggers).

- **Replication.**   This provides information about Publishers and Subscriptions.

- **Always On High Availability.**   This includes Failover Clustering and Availability Groups.

- **Management.**   This category covers a number of diverse features and tools, including Policy Management, Data Collection, Resource Governor, Extended Events, Maintenance Plans, Database Mail, DTC (Distributed Transaction Coordinator), and SQL Server error logs.

- **SQL Server Agent.**   Covers jobs, alerts, operators, proxies, and error logs of its own.

- **Integration Services Catalogs.**   The SQL Server Integration Services package catalog, depending on the SQL Server version.

By default, SSMS lists all objects alphabetically beneath each tree category. When working with databases that have a large quantity of objects, this can become quite aggravating while the user waits through potentially long list load times and expends energy scrolling and watching the screen very closely for the object in question.

Fortunately, SSMS has a filtering feature. You can apply filters to many object categories; such as user databases, tables, views, stored procedures, table-valued functions, user-defined functions, and even database users.

You can independently configure filter settings in either the Object Explorer pane or the Objects Explorer Details pane. Table 1-2 lists the available filtering options.

Table 1-2 SQL Server Management Studio Filters and Options

Filter	Options
Name	Contains Equals Does Not Contain
Schema	Contains Equals Does Not Contain
Owner	Equals Does Not Equal
Is Natively Compiled	True False
Creation Date	Equals Less Than Less Than or Equal More Than More Than or Equal Between Not Between

After you have selected a filter, the suffix "(filtered)" appears in the Object Explorer or Object Explorer Details tree above your filtered list.

To clear an applied filter and display all objects in a tree again, right-click a filtered category, select **Filter**, and then click **Remove Filter**.

CHAPTER 1

Multi-Select

In the Object Explorer pane, you can select only one object at a time. The Object Explorer Details pane, however, provides a Multi-Select feature with which you can work on multiple objects at the same time (tables, views, jobs, and so on). Following the standard in the Windows environment, the Shift key allows for the selection of contiguous objects, whereas the Ctrl key allows for noncontiguous selection. You can specify actions against multiple objects using the GUI or choose to script multiple objects at once. Scripting each object into its own file or merging all object scripting into one larger file are both available options.

Additional tools in SQL Server Management Studio

SSMS provides a number of time-saving tools and techniques for making you more productive. The following subsections provide just a few highlights.

IntelliSense tools

IntelliSense is a ubiquitous Microsoft technology found in many of its products that helps you with code completion. IntelliSense effectively reduces the amount of typing you do by offering shortcuts and autocompletion of keywords and object names, which also makes your code more accurate.

Additionally, SSMS comes with snippets to help you code more easily. Snippets are preconfigured code fragments that you can quickly drop into or around an existing block of code. The two options for using them are Insert Snippet and Surround With Snippets. You also can create your own snippets (you build them using XML), but that is beyond the scope of this discussion.

> NOTE
> **You can manage code snippets from the Tools menu, via the Code Snippets Manager option.**

Let's take a look at some use cases for snippets.

One of the options for SQL Server 2012 and later includes a snippet for an IF statement. After testing a block of code, you can quickly add the IF statement (including the BEGIN/END statements) by highlighting your code and choosing a snippet.

There are three ways to access snippets:

- Use a keyboard shortcut.

- Right-click and use the option from the context menu that opens.

- On the Edit menu, point to **IntelliSense**, and then click the snippets option you want—**Surround With**, in the example shown in Figure 1-10.

Figure 1-10   Accessing the Surround With snippet from the Edit menu.

Clicking a snippet surrounds the highlighted code with the snippet template code. You can even insert "placeholder" text for replacing later.

There are only a few stock Surround With snippets, but many Insert Snippets. You can find these by going to the **Edit** menu, pointing to **IntelliSense**, and then clicking **Insert Snippet**. You can double-click the **Function** folder to see the available snippets, and use them in the same manner you do for Surround With snippets, except that the code is placed at the current location of the cursor within a block of code. There are also keyboard shortcuts to use this feature. You can use **Ctrl+K**, **Ctrl+S** for Surround With snippets, and **Ctrl+K**, **Ctrl+X** for Insert Snippets.

Inside OUT

Did someone say keyboard shortcuts?

SQL Server Management Studio offers a large range of keyboard shortcuts for increasing productivity.

For example, you can show and hide the results pane of a query by using **Ctrl+R**. Accessing the Code Snippets Manager is as easy as using the combination **Ctrl+K**, **Ctrl+B**. Do you want to include the Actual Query Plan in a query? Use **Ctrl+M**. **Ctrl+F5** parses a

> query before you run it to ensure that the syntax is correct. By far the most popular one is **F5**, which runs a query, but you can also use **Ctrl+E** to do that.

Guided upgrades using the Query Tuning Assistant

SSMS 18.0 introduced the Query Tuning Assistant (QTA), which works with the Query Store to help guide SQL Server upgrades from SQL Server 2016 and SQL Server 2017 to SQL Server 2019.

The Query Tuning Assistant will be covered in more detail in Chapter 9, "Performance tuning SQL Server", and you can read the official documentation at *https://docs.microsoft.com/sql/relational-databases/performance/upgrade-dbcompat-using-qta*.

Customizing menus and shortcuts

SSMS is based on the Visual Studio integrated development environment (IDE), which means that it is customizable and extensible. Adding extensions is beyond the scope of this book, but the next few sections describe how to customize elements such as the toolbars and keyboard shortcuts.

Customize toolbars

SSMS installs with only the standard toolbar as the default. There are many other toolbars available for use. To access these options, on the toolbar, click **Tools**, and then click **Customize**. In the Customize dialog box, there are two tabs. On the first tab, **Toolbars**, you can select the toolbars that are useful in your work environment. Among the many choices are toolbars for working with Database Diagrams, extended events, and XML. On the second tab, the **s** tab, you can set up a custom toolbar or edit the drop-down menus and functionality of the existing toolbars.

Tool options

You also can customize the appearance of your SSMS interface. Click **Tools** and then **Options** to adjust color, font, keyboard hotkeys, length of strings in results, location of results, scripting preferences, international settings, theme, autorecovery timeframe, and more.

One very handy option is the **Keyboard, Query Shortcuts** feature. SSMS comes with several shortcuts already turned on (see Figure 1-11), but you can tailor these to your needs. Many longtime DBAs make heavy use of this feature to reduce the number of keystrokes to carry out commonly stored procedures.

Using shortcuts in SSMS, you can highlight text and then press the shortcut to run the associated stored procedure, supplying a parameter of the highlighted text. For instance, to see the text of a stored procedure or view, you can use the system procedure `sp_helptext`. By adding this stored procedure to the shortcut **Ctrl+0** (which you can see in Figure 1-11), you can display the data definition language (DDL) of any scripted object within a database by highlighting the name and using the appropriate key combination.

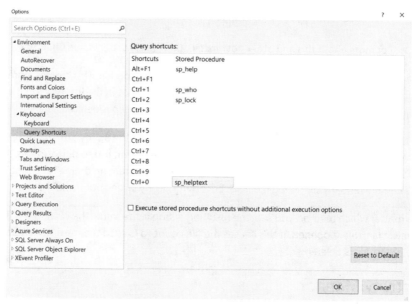

Figure 1-11   Managing query shortcuts.

Error logs

Each SQL Server instance maintains a distinct set of relevant error log messages that are accessible in two places: in the Management > Error Logs node, and in a context menu when you right-click an instance in the Registered Servers window. By default, these log files contain information about the SQL Server instance when coming online, what configuration settings were applied (or failed to apply), when backups occurred, when corruption is detected, when I/O is taking too long, partial stack dumps, and lots of other useful pieces of information. It's a great place to go to when troubleshooting stability or performance problems and to look for things that might cause trouble in the future.

To keep the log information to a reasonable and searchable size, the information is kept in a series of files rather than a single file. It is possible to close one file and start a new, blank file. Unfortunately, the default settings for cycling the log are not very useful.

By default, SQL Server keeps the six most-recent error log files. To configure the number of log files to maintain, in. the SSMS Object Explorer, open the **Management** folder, right-click **SQL Server Logs**, and then select **Configure**. In the dialog box that opens, select the check box labeled **Limit The Number Of Error Log Files Before They Are Recycled**, and then, in the **Maximum Number Of Error Log Files** box, type a value. The value must be between 6 and 99.

NOTE

It is not currently possible to change the number of error log files in SQL Server on Linux.

➤ For more about this and other post-installation checklist items, see Chapter 4.

Every time the SQL Server service is restarted, it cycles the log file. This creates a brand new, empty log file and moves the previous log file down one spot in the list. Any log file older in sequence than the maximum specified number of files to keep is deleted.

You also can choose to manually cycle the log file by using the `sp_cycle_errorlog` command, or you can automate this process by using a SQL Server Agent job to perform this task. When working with SQL Server instances that are quite large and remain online for a long timeframe, this can prevent any single log file from becoming overly large and unwieldy.

No matter which method you use, the resulting action is the same: the current file is closed and a new, blank file is opened. If this causes the file count to exceed the maximum number of files, the oldest file is deleted.

Activity Monitor

Activity Monitor is a tool that provides information about what is currently running on the SQL Server and how that code might be affecting the instance. It lets you easily view common hardware-specific performance metrics and a list of recently used queries (with metrics, code, and execution plans). You can sort all of the grids, and you can filter some of them. Out of the box, this is the place to begin if you need to do rudimentary troubleshooting and baselining.

To open the Activity Monitor window, In the **Object Explorer** pane, right-click the SQL Server instance, and then select **Activity Monitor**. The window opens in the **Object Explorer Details** pane.

Activity Monitor consists of six distinct parts:

- **Overview.** Displays a basic version of what you might already be familiar with viewing in the Task Manager window but with a SQL Server flair, with four distinct graphs

- **Processes.** Displays all non-system processes with open connections to the SQL Server instance

- **Resource Waits.** Displays the Wait Events of active, open connections

- **Data File I/O.** Displays a difference between two interval readings of the storage subsystem

- **Recent Expensive Queries.** Displays information about the most expensive queries from the past 30 seconds

- **Active Expensive Queries.** Displays a more detailed view of queries that are running at that moment

You can expand each of these parts to show more information, with the Overview section expanded by default. If you want to sort or filter the results, click the column header of any of the columns in each section.

Activity Monitor overview

Four graphs cover the most basic overview of the instance. The % Processor Time is an average combined value for all logical processors assigned to the instance (see the section "Carving up CPU cores using an affinity mask" in Chapter 3, "Designing and implementing an on-premises database infrastructure"). The other three graphs are Waiting Tasks (an instance-level value), Database I/O (all databases, measured in MB/sec) and Batch Requests/sec (all databases).

Each of the graphs display information in real time; however, you can configure the refresh interval by right-clicking any of the graphs. The default for each is 10 seconds; you can adjust this from as short as one second to as long as one hour. The graph settings are adjusted as a unified set, meaning that all four graphs use the same interval setting, so changing one interval changes them all. Likewise, selecting Pause on any of the graphs pauses the entire set.

Processes

The Processes section of Activity Monitor displays all non-system processes (also known as tasks) with open connections to the SQL Server instance, regardless of whether the process is actively running a query. Important metadata provided includes the following:

- **Session ID.** The session process identifier (SPID) of the current process

- **User Process.** Displays a 1 if this is a user process; 0 if it is a system process

- **Login.** The login name for the user running this process

- **Database.** The name of the database

- **Task State.** Populated from the list of possible tasks in the task_state column of the sys.dm_os_tasks dynamic management view

- **.** Populated from the list of command types in the command column of the sys.dm_exec_requests dynamic management view

- **Application.** The name of the application

- **Wait Time (ms).**   Amount of time that this task has been waiting, in milliseconds

- **Wait Type.**   The current wait type for this task

- **Wait Resource.**   The resource for which this task is waiting

- **Blocked By.**   If this task is being blocked by another process, this shows the SPID of the blocking process

- **Head Blocker.**   If there is a chain of blocking processes, this is the SPID of the process at the start of the blocking chain

- **Memory Use (KB).**   How much memory this process is using

- **Host Name.**   The host name of the machine that made this connection

- **Workload Group.**   The name of the Resource Governor workload group that this process belongs to (you can read more about the Resource Governor in Chapter 3)

Right-click any of the rows in the **Processes** pane to see the detailed T-SQL query being run (last T-SQL command batch), either to trace the process in SQL Profiler or to Kill the process.

Resource Waits

The Resource Waits section of the Activity Monitor tool displays the Wait Events of active, open connections, sorted by default by the Cumulative Wait Time in seconds. This can be very useful when you're trying to determine the root cause of a performance issue. Having a baseline for these counters when "things are good" is very useful later on when you're trying to gauge whether a problem being experienced is "new" or "normal." Understanding the meaning of certain wait times can help you to diagnose the root cause of slowness, be it storage, memory pressure, CPU, network latency, or a client struggling to receive and display a result set. Following are the wait statistics provided by this section:

- Wait Category

- Wait Time (ms/sec)

- Recent Wait Time (ms/sec)

- Average Waiter Count

- Cumulative Wait Time (sec)

➤ **You can read more about Resource Waits at**
 https://docs.microsoft.com/sql/relational-databases/system-dynamic-management-views/ sys-dm-os-wait-stats-transact-sql.

Data File I/O

The Data File I/O section of Activity Monitor displays the difference between two readings taken from the metadata stored in the `sys.dm_io_virtual_file_stats` dynamic management view. For this reason, when you first expand the section, you might not see results for a short while. The server needs to have at least two readings (so if your interval is 10 seconds, you'll wait 10 seconds before data appears). The information displayed shows each of the data files for all of the databases on the SQL Server, the file location and name, the megabytes per second read (MB/sec read), megabytes per second written (MB/sec written), and average response time in milliseconds (ms).

As a general rule, average response times of five milliseconds or less allow for acceptable performance, notwithstanding the occasional outlying peak.

Recent Expensive Queries

Activity Monitor's Recent Expensive Queries section displays information about the most expensive queries that have run on the SQL Server instance in the past 30 seconds. It includes both queries in flight and queries that finished. To see the full query text or to see the execution plan currently being used, right-click any of the queries listed. Here are the fields returned in this pane:

- Query

- Exections/min

- CPU (ms/sec)

- Physical Reads/sec

- Logical Writes/sec

- Logical Reads/sec

- Average Duration (ms)

- Plan Count

- Database

Active Expensive Queries

If you're trying to determine what is running at this precise moment that might be causing performance issues, Active Expensive Queries is the place to look. This section of Activity Monitor is more granular than the aggregated "past 30 seconds" view provided in the Recent Expensive Queries section. In addition, the list of queries here shows some very interesting details that are available at only a granular level:

CHAPTER 1

- Session ID

- Database

- Elapsed Time

- Row Count

- Memory Allocated

Again, you can see the full query text and the execution plan by right-clicking, but here you get an additional feature, Show Live Execution Plan, which might very well differ if a query is running long.

Inside OUT

Does Activity Monitor use resources?

Yes, it does. When you expand any of the detail areas in Activity Monitor, it must query the system metadata in real time to keep the columns and/or graphs populated on the screen. When you collapse the area, these queries stop.

After you have finished viewing a section, we recommend that you collapse that section, or close the Activity Monitor tab, to avoid any unnecessary "observer overhead."

SQL Server Agent

SQL Server Agent is a service on both Windows and Linux that you can use to schedule automated tasks, called Jobs, as illustrated in Figure 1-12. These Jobs are most commonly used to run routine maintenance (backups, index defragmentation, statistics updates, and integrity checks), but you can also use them to periodically run custom code.

NOTE
You can also filter SQL Server Agent nodes. This is described earlier in this chapter in the discussion on Object Explorer.

On Windows Server, there is built-in functionality for Job Notifications that makes it possible for a person or group to receive communications about the status of a job, using the Database Mail feature. The setup provides a few straightforward configuration options as to when notifications are sent: Success, Failure, and Completion.

➤ For more information on configuring Database Mail and configuring SQL Agent to use Database Mail, see Chapter 9, "Automating SQL Server administration."

SQL Server Agent's list of Jobs also includes any SQL Server Reporting Services subscriptions that have been created and scheduled on the server (see Figure 1-12).

```
⊟ 🖳 SQL Server Agent
  ⊟ ▦ Jobs
      ▣ collection_set_1_noncached_collect_and_upload
      ▣ collection_set_2_collection
      ▣ collection_set_2_upload
      ▣ collection_set_3_collection
      ▣ collection_set_3_upload
      ▣ mdw_purge_data
      ▣ syspolicy_purge_history
      ▣ sysutility_get_cache_tables_data_into_aggregate_tables_daily
      ▣ sysutility_get_cache_tables_data_into_aggregate_tables_hourly
      ▣ sysutility_get_views_data_into_cache_tables
    ♂ Job Activity Monitor
  ⊞ ▦ Alerts
  ⊞ ▦ Operators
  ⊞ ▦ Proxies
  ⊞ ▦ Error Logs
```

Figure 1-12   The SQL Server Agent tree view.

Job Activity Monitor

Job Activity Monitor gives a snapshot view of all jobs on a server. Using this feature, you can quickly see many attributes about the Jobs scheduled on a SQL Server instance. You can use many of these attributes to narrow the list of jobs being viewed. This can be especially handy if there are many hundreds of SQL Server Reporting Services reports scheduled, or the list of jobs is extensive. Table 1-3 lists the attributes.

TABLE 1-3   JOB ACTIVITY ATTRIBUTES

Job activity attribute	Values	Can use to filter?
Name		✓
Enabled	No Yes	✓
Status	Between Retries Executing	✓
Last Run Outcome	Idle Not Idle Performing Completed Action Suspended Waiting for Step to Finish Waiting for Worker Thread	

Last Run Date Time		✓
Next Scheduled Run Date Time		✓
Job Category		✓
Is The Job Runnable?	Yes No	✓
Is The Job Scheduled?	Yes No	✓
Job Category ID		

Notifying operators with alerts

You can configure alerts to notify you when a specific event occurs. Unlike jobs that run on a schedule, alert notifications can be sent as a reaction to a scenario that has been set off. Examples include emailing the DBA team when a data or log file experiences auto growth, or when Target Server Memory drops below a certain threshold on a virtual machine. SQL Server Agent's alerting feature gives an administrator the ability to create alerts of three different types:

- **Event alerts.**   Raised by SQL Server's Error and Severity mechanism. You can specify this for all databases or for a single database. You can use Error Number or Severity Level to set off an alert. Text within the System Message can be parsed to only alert in specific scenarios.

- **Performance condition alerts.**   These alerts use the entire library of SQL Server Performance Monitor counters. Any Counter Object can be chosen, the Sub Counter Object specified, the Counter Instance (if applicable), and a threshold (falls below, becomes equal to, rises above) at which an alert should fire. Figure 1-13 depicts setting up a Performance Condition Alert Definition to notify an administrator if Page Life Expectancy on an instance of SQL has dropped below five minutes.

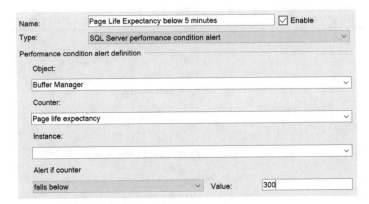

Figure 1-13   Creating a performance condition alert.

- **Windows Management Instrumentation (WMI) alerts.**   A WMI alert uses the Windows Management Instrumentation Event Provider to allow for more complicated actions upon event detection setting off an alert. One example is to use the alerting system to detect a deadlock and then save the XML deadlock graph information to a table for later analysis. Another use is to detect any DDL or system configuration changes that occur and to document them for review at a later time. Because the WMI Provider has access to many Server Event Classes and Properties, this feature is quite versatile. It does come with a couple of catches, however:

  - It requires that Service Broker is turned on in the msdb database of the instance.

  - If your code queries objects within a particular database on the server, Service Broker must be enabled on that database also.

  - It is not very GUI-friendly and requires a bit more programming know-how than the other alert options.

  - It is not supported on SQL Server on Linux or Docker containers.

  ➤ You can read more about creating WMI alerts in Chapter 8 as well as at *https://docs.microsoft.com/sql/ssms/agent/create-a-wmi-event-alert*.

A response to an alert can be to run a job, notify a list of operators, or both.

Operators

Operators are users or groups designated as points of contact to receive notifications from the SQL Server Agent. They are defined most commonly with email addresses, but there are additional delivery methods available.

Inside OUT

Does Azure SQL Database come with SQL Server Agent?

If you use SQL Server Management Studio to connect to an Azure SQL Database, you might notice the absence of SQL Server Agent.

Although at first this might seem puzzling, it makes perfect sense. SQL Server Agent is an OS service. Azure SQL Database is a database as a service (DBaaS), which is essentially a sole database (à la carte) minus the server and OS pieces of the platform.

The Azure environment comes with its own Azure Automation services and elastic jobs, which you can use to schedule routines similar to what DBAs are used to with SQL Server

Agent. But remember, with Azure SQL databases, point-in-time recovery is included automatically.

Another option is to use a managed instance, which is covered in Chapter 17, "Provisioning Azure SQL Database."

Azure Data Studio

Azure Data Studio is an exciting addition to the administration and development toolkit for the database platform, including SQL Server, Azure SQL Database, Azure Synapse Analytics (formerly Azure SQL Data Warehouse), and PostgreSQL.

Think of Azure Data Studio as more of a developer-focused tool as compared to SSMS. While Azure Data Studio performs many of the same tasks as SSMS, it is more focused on development as opposed to administration, and can run cross-platform on Windows, macOS and Linux.

➤ You can download the latest version of Azure Data Studio from *https://docs.microsoft.com/sql/azure-data-studio/download.*

Inside OUT

Is Azure Data Studio open source software?

Azure Data Studio is an open source software (OSS) project, based on the Electron shell and Node.js, a JavaScript runtime. It is free for use, and anyone can contribute to the project.

For more information about the project, and to contribute your own code, visit *https://github.com/microsoft/azuredatastudio.*

User interface

Azure Data Studio is based on the same shell as Visual Studio Code. Thus, it shares a similar development environment and is fully extensible. In other words, you can easily install third-party plugins and extensions to improve your workflow, or even write your own and contribute them back to the main product codebase. Many of the extensions for Visual Studio Code will run on Azure Data Studio.

The main interface for Azure Data Studio is made up of viewlets and tiles, similar in concept to the docked windows in SSMS. These elements present information to monitor and administer your database environment, which can be seen in Figure 1-14.

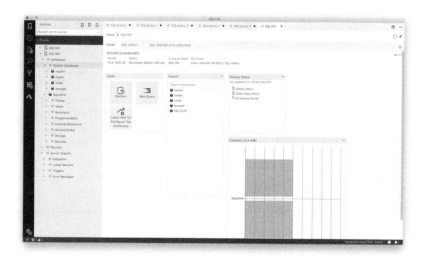

Figure 1-14   The Azure Data Studio user interface.

The interface is fully customizable, with a dashboard that shows:

- Insights, performance metrics and telemetry

- Recent connections

- An Object Explorer (similar to SSMS, see Figure 1-15)

- A query window for code

- A results grid which can be exported to CSV, Excel, JSON, and XML

The query window is mainly used for writing queries in Transact-SQL and targeting SQL Server and Azure SQL Database. However, the extensibility of Azure Data Studio allows a much richer coding experience, which means you might find yourself writing queries for other platforms (including PostgreSQL), PowerShell scripts, and notebooks.

➤ **See the next section for more information about notebooks.**

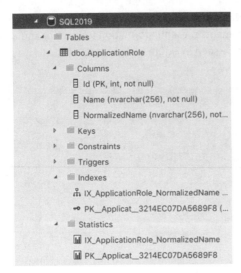

Figure 1-15   The object explorer view in Azure Data Studio.

NOTE

Whereas SSMS uses dialog windows that pop up in the center of the application interface, the Azure Data Studio dialogs, or flyouts, appear from the right of the user interface until the necessary action is performed. This takes some getting used to for people who are more familiar with the SSMS interface.

Highlighted features in Azure Data Studio

Azure Data Studio includes many of the same core features for administering and developing against SQL Server that you would expect to find in SSMS.

These include:

- Managing registered servers

- Viewing server and database reports

- Writing queries

- Managing security

- Generating scripts

- Viewing and analyzing query plans

- Performing tasks such as database consistency checks

- Index and statistics maintenance

- Running backups and restores

Certain dialog boxes in SSMS can be run from inside Azure Data Studio (and vice versa), as long as the latest versions of both applications are installed on the same Windows computer. This allows an integrated experience by using different features seamlessly across both applications from within the tool of your choice.

Extending the features of Azure Data Studio

Azure Data Studio allows for additional features that are not part of the base product, directly in the interface. To access the Extensions pane, you can click **View** > **Extensions** from the menu, or use keyboard the shortcut **Shift**+**Ctrl**+**X** in Windows and Linux, or **Shift**+**Cmd**+**X** in macOS.

Extensions recommended by Microsoft are identified by a white star on a green background on the top left of the extension item, as seen in Figure 1-16. To install an extension, click on the **Install** button. Once it is installed, you may be prompted to reload the application. Click the **Reload** button, and Azure Data Studio will reopen with the extension enabled.

> NOTE
>
> Some extensions may need to be installed manually, using the menu option File > Install Extension from VSIX Package. Take care when trusting third-party extensions installed in this manner.

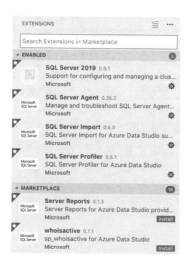

Figure 1-16   The Extensions Marketplace.

CHAPTER 1

Accessing the command line

One extremely useful feature in Azure Data Studio is the built-in command line interface, which allows interacting with the underlying OS from within the application. This improves productivity by not having to switch away from the Azure Data Studio interface to manipulate files or execute external scripts.

To access the Terminal (in Linux and macOS) or PowerShell (in Windows, as well as Linux and macOS if PowerShell Core is installed), use the menu to navigate to **View** > **Terminal**, or use the keyboard shortcut **Ctrl**+` (backtick) or **Cmd**+` on macOS.

Notebooks in Azure Data Studio

One of the fundamental ways in which Azure Data Studio is helpful to data professionals is with the concept of notebooks, based on Project Jupyter (pronounced "Jupiter").

Notebooks already support many languages including R, Python, and PowerShell, which makes them a natural addition to the data scientist's toolkit with SQL Server 2019.

Inside OUT

What is Project Jupyter?

Much like the book you are currently reading, technical documentation and code has traditionally been static. It appears in fixed type, sometimes with diagrams to assist with understanding a topic. Any code included in that documentation must usually be copied and pasted into an execution environment to be run.

On the other hand, web pages have made documentation and code easier to work with, especially with their interactive nature. Project Jupyter makes use of web technology to address the problem of static code, by presenting notebooks as interactive web applications. Code can now be executed from within the documentation, which itself is written in Markdown format.

➤ Find out more about Project Jupyter at *https://jupyter.org/*.

Notebooks as run books

One particularly interesting feature for data professionals is SQL Kernel support. This enables us to create powerful interactive and shareable notebooks with SQL Server and PostgreSQL as supported environments.

In this book, we refer to these notebooks as *SQL notebooks*.

Using the Markdown language, existing scripts and documentation can be converted into SQL notebooks. Since these documents are plain text files that render as web pages, they can be treated like source code, and checked into a source control system. This gives you a lot more control over versioning, especially around run books.

➤ See Chapter 10, "Developing, deploying, and managing data recovery" for a practical use case for a run book.

Inside OUT

What is Markdown?

Markdown (commonly written in lowercase as "markdown") is a plain-text markup language created by John Gruber and Aaron Swartz in 2004, originally designed to output HTML pages. It differs from other markup languages such as RTF, HTML and PDF formats, because its syntax makes the documents easier for humans to read.

The language has been adopted by many organizations including GitHub (a Microsoft subsidiary), and is the language in which Jupyter notebooks are written.

SQL Server Data Tools

SQL Server Data Tools (SSDT) provides a developer with a set of tools for working with SQL Server, as well as SQL Server Integration Services (SSIS), Reporting Services (SSRS), and Analysis Services (SSAS).

SQL Server Data Tools is installed as an optional component within Visual Studio 2019 or later, while the SSIS, SSRS, and SSAS project templates must be downloaded from within Visual Studio using the Extensions manager. You also need Visual Studio to work with database projects.

NOTE
Despite having similar names, Visual Studio is an entirely different product to Visual Studio Code. SSDT is not supported in Visual Studio Code.

SQL Server Integration Services

SQL Server Integration Services is a versatile platform for importing, transforming, and exporting data. Frequently used for Extract, Transform, and Load (ETL) processes, SQL Server Integration Services can integrate with many external systems using standard tasks, interfaces, and protocols.

SQL Server Integration Services manages these solutions using packages, which you create and modify via a graphical user interface.

SSISDB Upgrade Wizard

The SQL Server Integration Services Package Upgrade Wizard is a tool that you can use to upgrade SQL Server Integration Services packages that were created in versions earlier than SQL Server 2019. Although you most commonly access this tool from SQL Server Data Tools, you can also find and launch it from SSMS and also from the Windows command prompt. Part of the upgrade wizard in all of these scenarios involves the automated backup of the original packages.

From SQL Server Data Tools:

1. Open an **Integration Services Project**

2. Right-click **SSIS Packages**

3. Select **Upgrade**

From SSMS:

1. Connect to **Integration Services**

1. Expand **Stored Packages**

2. Right-click **MSDB (File System)**

3. Select **Upgrade**

From the Windows command prompt:

1. Navigate to the Microsoft SQL Server\150\DTS\Binn Folder

2. Locate and run the **SSISUpgrade.exe** file

The Import And Export Data Wizard

The SQL Server Import And Export Wizard is a tool that simplifies the copying of data from a source to a destination. It uses SQL Server Integration Services to copy data by creating a package in memory. You can choose to save the package the wizard creates for future reuse. The variety of source and destination platforms that you can use with the wizard is generous. In some cases, you might need to download and install additional drivers and providers from a vendor or from a Microsoft Feature Pack. Table 1-4 lists examples of compatible data sources.

Table 1-4   Data sources in the Import And Export Wizard

Type	Details
Enterprise databases	SQL Server, Oracle, DB2
Text files	CSV or any other delimiter
Excel/Access	May require Access Runtime
Azure	Azure Storage
Open source	PostgreSQL, MySQL
Others	ODBC, .Net Framework, OLEDB

Data Profiling Task and Viewer

You can use the Data Profiling Task within SQL Server Integration Services to clarify data patterns (normal versus abnormal) and identify data quality issues before they make their way to a destination (usually a data warehouse). The tool provides visibility around the data quality by calculating and documenting the metadata and statistical metrics shown in Table 1-5.

Table 1-5   Data profiling categories and details

Category	Details
Candidate keys	Key columns Key strength
Column length distribution	Minimum column length Maximum column length Detailed count by length Percentage distribution by length
Column null ratio	Null count by column Null percentage by column
Column statistics (numeric and date-based column data types only)	Minimum value by column Maximum value by column Mean value by column Standard deviation by column
Column value distribution	Number of distinct values by column Most frequent values by column

The Data Profiling Task creates an XML output file. You can view this file by using the Data Profile Viewer, which is a standalone application and does not require Visual Studio or SQL Server Integration Services to run.

Figure 1-17 presents an example of the Data Profile Viewer displaying the XML created by a Data Profile Tasks, pointed at Microsoft's WideWorldImporters sample database and analyzing the Sales.Customers table.

CHAPTER 1

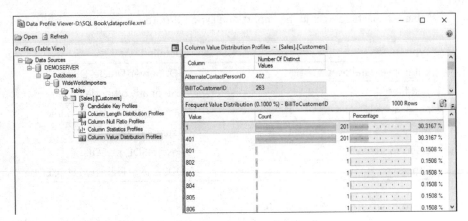

Figure 1-17   The Data Profile Viewer showing column distribution.

A note on discontinued and deprecated features

Every new version of SQL Server introduces some exciting new features, while deprecating or even discontinuing features from earlier versions of SQL Server. Deprecated features will be removed from a future version of the product, and you should not use them for new development. Discontinued features have already been removed and might block upgrades to the latest database compatibility level, or migrations to Azure SQL Database.

Reference is made in several chapters of this book about features that have been deprecated or discontinued over the years, but the easiest way to stay up to date is to check the Microsoft documentation. As of this writing, no features were deprecated between SQL Server 2017 and SQL Server 2019. For discontinued features, visit *https://docs.microsoft.com/sql/database-engine/discontinued-database-engine-functionality-in-sql-server.*

You can also access the list of deprecated features by using the T-SQL query that follows, which provides a list of more than 250 features that are deprecated, along with a count of the number of occurrences on your SQL Server instance. We leave as an exercise for you to identify and resolve specific occurrences.

```
SELECT object_name, counter_name, instance_name, cntr_value, cntr_type

FROM sys.dm_os_performance_counters

WHERE object_name = 'SQLServer:Deprecated Features';
```

#### CHAPTER 2

Introducing database server components

In this chapter, we cover the components that make up a typical database infrastructure. The chapters that follow provide more detail about designing, implementing, and provisioning databases.

SQL Server runs on Windows and Linux, as well as in Docker containers. Microsoft has crafted it to work the same way that it does on Windows. The saying "it's just SQL Server" applies, but here we highlight places where there are differences.

We first discuss hardware. No matter which configuration you end up using, there are four basic components in a database infrastructure:

- Memory

- Processor

- Permanent storage

- Network

We then introduce high availability (HA) offerings, including improvements to availability groups in SQL Server 2019. When considering strategies for SQL Server HA and disaster recovery (DR), you design according to the organization's requirements for business continuity in terms of a Recovery Point Objective (RPO) and Recovery Time Objective (RTO).

We next provide an overview of security, including Active Directory, Service Principle Names, federation and claims, Kerberos, and ways to access instances of SQL Server on-premises with Windows and Linux, and Microsoft Azure SQL Database. As data theft becomes more prevalent, you will need to consider the security of the database itself, the underlying OS and hardware (physical or virtual), the network, and the database backups.

Finally, we take a look at the similarities and differences between virtual machines (VMs) and containers, and why you would use them. Whether running on physical or virtual hardware, databases perform better when they can be cached in memory as much as possible and are backed by persistent storage that is redundant, with low latency and high random IOPS.

Memory

SQL Server is designed to use as much memory as it needs, and as much as you give it. By default, the upper limit of memory that SQL Server can access is limited only by the physical Random-Access Memory (RAM) available to the server, or the edition of SQL Server you're running, whichever is lower.

Understanding the working set

The physical memory made available to SQL Server by the operating system (OS), is called the working set. This working set is broken up into several sections by the SQL Server memory manager. The two largest and most important sections are the buffer pool and the procedure cache (also known as the plan cache).

In the strictest sense, "working set" applies only to physical memory. However, as you will soon see, the buffer pool extension blurs the lines because it uses non-volatile storage.

We look deeper into default memory settings in Chapter 3, "Designing and implementing an on-premises database infrastructure," in the "Configuration settings" section.

Caching data in the buffer pool

For best performance, SQL Server caches data in memory, because it is orders of magnitude faster to access data directly from memory than traditional storage.

The buffer pool is an in-memory cache of 8-KB data pages that are copies of pages in the database file. Initially the copy in the buffer pool is identical, but changes to data are applied to this buffer pool copy (and the transaction log) and then asynchronously applied to the data file.

When you run a query, the Database Engine requests the data page it needs from the buffer manager, as depicted in Figure 2-1. If the data is not already in the buffer pool, a page fault occurs (an OS feature that informs the application that the page isn't in memory). The buffer manager fetches the data from the storage subsystem and writes it to the buffer pool. When the data is in the buffer pool, the query continues.

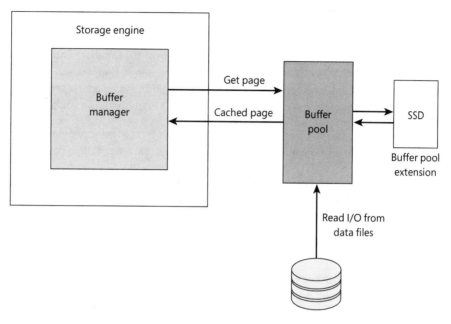

Figure 2-1   The buffer pool and the buffer pool extension.

The buffer pool is usually the largest consumer of the working set because that's where your data is. If the amount of data requested for a query exceeds the capacity of the buffer pool, the data pages will spill to a drive, using either the buffer pool extension or a portion of TempDB.

The buffer pool extension makes use of non-volatile storage to extend the size of the buffer pool. It effectively increases the database working set, forming a bridge between the storage layer where the data files are located and the buffer pool in physical memory.

For performance reasons, this non-volatile storage should be solid-state storage, directly attached to the server.

> ➤ To see how to turn on the buffer pool extension, read the section "Configuration settings" in Chapter 3. To learn more about TempDB, read the section "Physical database architecture" also in Chapter 3.

CHAPTER 2

Caching plans in the procedure cache

Generally speaking, the procedure cache is smaller than the buffer pool. When you run a query, the query optimizer compiles a query plan to explain to the Database Engine exactly how to run the query. To save time, it keeps a copy of that query plan so that it doesn't need to compile the plan each time the query runs. It is not quite as simple as this, of course (plans can be removed, and trivial plans are not cached, for instance), but it's enough to give you a basic understanding.

The procedure cache is split into various cache stores by the memory manager, and it's also here where you can see if there are single-use query plans that are polluting memory.

> ➤ For more information about cached execution plans, read Chapter 14, "Performance tuning SQL Server" or visit *https://blogs.msdn.microsoft.com/blogdoezequiel/2014/07/30/too-many-single-use-plans-now-what/*.

Lock pages in memory

Turning on the *Lock pages in memory* (LPIM) policy means that Windows will not be able to trim (reduce) SQL Server's working set.

Locking pages in memory ensures that Windows memory pressure cannot rob SQL Server of resources or shunt SQL Server memory into the Windows Server system page file, dramatically reducing performance. Windows doesn't "steal" memory from SQL Server flippantly; it is done in response to memory pressure on the Windows Server. Indeed, all applications can have their memory affected by pressure from Windows.

NOTE
The Linux kernel is far stricter with memory management and will forcibly terminate a process using too much memory. With SQL Server on Linux, there is a dedicated setting called `memory.memorylimitmb`**, which limits the amount of physical memory SQL Server can see (by default this is 80 percent of physical memory). This is covered in more detail in Chapter 5, "Installing and configuring SQL Server on Linux".**

On the other hand, without the ability to relieve pressure from other applications' memory demands or a virtual host's memory demands, LPIM means that Windows cannot deploy enough memory to remain stable. Because of this concern, LPIM cannot be the only method to use to protect SQL Server's memory allocation.

The controversy of the topic is stability versus performance, in which the latter was especially apparent on systems with limited memory resources and older operating systems. On larger servers with operating systems since Windows Server 2008, and especially virtualized systems, there is a lesser need for this policy to insulate SQL Server from memory pressure.

The prevailing wisdom is that the LPIM policy should be turned on by default for SQL Server 2019, provided the following:

- The server is physical, not virtual. See "Sharing more memory than you have (overcommit)" later in this chapter.

- Physical RAM exceeds 16 GB (the OS needs a working set of its own).

- Max Server Memory has been set appropriately (SQL Server can't use everything it sees).

- The **Memory\Available Mbytes** performance counter is monitored regularly (to keep some memory free).

If you would like to read more, Jonathan Kehayias explains this thinking in a Simple Talk article (*https://www.red-gate.com/simple-talk/sql/database-administration/ great-sql-server-debates-lock-pages-in-memory/*).

Editions and memory limits

Since SQL Server 2016 Service Pack 1, many Enterprise edition features have found their way into the lower editions. Ostensibly, this was done to allow software developers to have far more code that works across all editions of the product.

Although some features are still limited by edition (high availability, for instance), features such as columnstore and In-Memory OLTP are turned on in every edition, including Express. Enterprise edition can use all available physical RAM for these features, though other editions are artificially limited.

Inside OUT

What are some considerations for using In-Memory OLTP?

In-Memory OLTP requires an overhead of at least double the amount of data for a memory-optimized object. For example, if a memory-optimized table is 5 GB in size, you will need at least 10 GB of RAM available for the exclusive use of that table. Keep this in mind before turning on this feature in Standard edition.

Take care, too, when using memory-optimized table-valued functions (TVFs) in Standard edition, because each new object requires resources. Too many TVFs could starve the working set and cause SQL Server to crash.

You can learn more at Microsoft Docs: *https://docs.microsoft.com/sql/ relational-databases/in-memory-oltp/requirements-for-using-memory-optimized-tables*.

Central Processing Unit

The Central Processing Unit (CPU), often called the "brain" of a computer, is the most important part of a system. CPU speed is measured in hertz (Hz), or cycles per second. Current processor speed is measured in GHz, or billions of cycles per second.

Modern systems can have more than one CPU, and each CPU in turn can have more than one CPU core (which, in turn, might be split up into virtual cores).

For a typical SQL Server transactional workload, single-core speed matters. It is better to have fewer cores with higher clock speeds than more cores with lower speeds, so that queries requiring fewer resources will complete faster. This is useful on non-Enterprise editions, especially when considering licensing.

With systems that have more than one CPU, each CPU might be allocated its own set of memory, depending on the physical motherboard architecture.

Simultaneous multithreading

Some CPU manufacturers have split their physical cores into virtual cores to try to eke out even more performance (between 15 and 30 percent extra, depending on the type of SQL Server workload). They do this via a feature called simultaneous multithreading (SMT).

> ➤ **The Microsoft Support article KB 322385 has more information about the performance profile of SMT and SQL Server. Although it references SQL Server 2005, the information is still relevant: *https://support.microsoft.com/help/322385*.**

Intel calls this Hyper-Threading, so when you buy a single Intel® Xeon® CPU with 20 physical cores, the OS will see 40 virtual cores, because of SMT.

SMT becomes especially murky with virtualization because the guest OS might not have any insight into the physical versus logical core configuration.

> ### NOTE
> Think of symmetrical multithreading as an *increase* in overall CPU capacity, as opposed to a performance boost. Performance is dependent on the type of workload the CPU is processing, and in some cases SMT may be detrimental. Always test your workload against different hardware configurations.

Security vulnerabilities in modern CPUs

Over recent months and years, security vulnerabilities (known as *speculative execution* vulnerabilities; see the Inside OUT below) were discovered in Intel and other vendor CPUs. There are two Microsoft Knowledgebase articles which go into more detail:

- *https://support.microsoft.com/help/4073225/*

- *https://support.microsoft.com/help/4457951/*

For Intel CPUs, our advice is to disable SMT (Hyper-Threading) for both physical and virtual environments for all CPUs prior to the Whiskey Lake architecture, for both Windows and Linux. On AMD CPUs, we recommend disabling SMT for virtual environments. If any virtual machines are running untrusted code on the same host as your production servers, your risk increases.

➤ **For more information about allocating virtual CPUs, see "Understanding virtualization and containers" later in this chapter.**

Inside OUT

How do speculative execution vulnerabilities affect you?

Modern microprocessors (including CPUs) use a type of circuit called a *branch predictor*, which tries to guess the result of an instruction before it happens, improving overall performance in the execution pipeline if that result occurs. This is known as *speculative execution*.

When the instruction has a different result from the predicted outcome, the branch containing the incorrectly-predicted value may reveal private information to attackers observing the instructions as they occur before these results are discarded.

Because this is a hardware issue, affected CPU vendors have issued firmware patches to work around this class of vulnerability, but cannot completely defend against it without seriously affecting performance. For full protection, newer CPUs released since 2019 are required.

Unfortunately, it is not practical to replace every CPU manufactured before this date. In these cases, you must ensure that you have patched your operating system fully. Additionally, you must check that any firmware released for your CPUs has been applied (called microcode), even if it does impact performance. This is especially true for CPUs used in virtual machine hosts, where SMT should be disabled.

Ultimately, the type of threats you might expect to face in your environment will dictate whether you decide to disable SMT or patch against it.

Non-Uniform Memory Access

CPUs are the fastest component of a system, and they spend a lot of time waiting for data to come to them. In the past, all CPUs would share one bank of RAM on a motherboard, using a shared bus. This caused performance problems as more CPUs were added, because only one CPU could access the RAM at a time.

Multi-Channel Memory Architecture tries to resolve this by increasing the number of channels between CPUs and RAM to reduce contention during concurrent access.

A more practical solution is for each CPU to have its own local physical RAM, situated close to each CPU socket. This configuration is called Non-Uniform Memory Access (NUMA). The advantages are that each CPU can access its own RAM, making processing much faster. If a CPU needs more RAM than it has in its local set, however, it must request memory from one of the other CPUs in the system (called foreign memory access), which carries a performance penalty.

SQL Server is NUMA-aware. In other words, if the OS recognizes a NUMA configuration at the hardware layer, where more than one CPU is plugged in, and each CPU has its own set of physical RAM (see Figure 2-2), SQL Server will split its internal structures and service threads across each NUMA node.

Since the release of SQL Server 2014 Service Pack 2, the Database Engine automatically configures NUMA nodes at an instance level, using what it calls soft-NUMA. If more than eight CPU cores are detected (including SMT cores), soft-NUMA nodes are created automatically in memory.

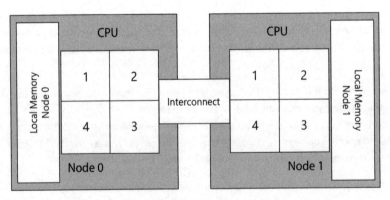

Figure 2-2   Two-socket NUMA configuration.

Inside OUT

What is the relationship between core counts and editions?

SQL Server Standard edition has an artificial limit of 4 sockets or 24 CPU physical cores that it can use, whichever is lower. For instance, if a system contains two 16-core CPUs, for a total of 32 cores, Standard edition will need to be licensed for all 32 cores, even though it won't use eight of them.

Additionally, the NUMA distribution will be unbalanced because SQL Server will use the first 16 cores on the first CPU, and eight from the second CPU, unless you configure the SQL Server CPU usage using the affinity settings (for more information on how to do this, see the section "Configuration settings" in Chapter 3).

Be careful when choosing the hardware and edition for your SQL Server installation. If you plan to install several VMs on one system, a better option would be Enterprise edition, licensed for all physical cores on the server. This would automatically cover all SQL Server VMs that you install on that hardware.

Disable power saving everywhere

Modern systems can use power saving settings to reduce the amount of electricity used by a server. Although this is good for the environment, it is bad for query performance because the CPU core speed might be reduced to save energy.

For all operating systems running SQL Server, turn on High Performance at the OS level, and double-check that High Performance is set at the BIOS level, as well. For dedicated VM hosts, this will require downtime to make the change at the BIOS level.

Storing your data

When data is not in memory, it is at rest, and must be persisted (saved) somewhere. Storage technology has evolved rapidly over the past few years, so we no longer think of storage as a mechanical hard drive containing one or more spinning metal disks with a magnetic surface.

NOTE

Old habits die hard, and colloquially you may still refer to a non-volatile storage subsystem as "the disk," even if it might take another form. We refer to it as a "drive."

Irrespective of the underlying mechanism, a SQL Server storage subsystem should have low latency, so that when the Database Engine accesses the drive to perform reads and writes, those reads and writes should complete as quickly as possible. In the following list, we present some commonly used terms with respect to storage devices.

- **Drive.** The physical storage device. This might be a mechanical drive, a solid-state drive with the same form-factor as a mechanical drive, or a card that plugs directly into the motherboard.

- **Volume.** A logical representation of storage, as viewed by the OS. This might be one drive, part of a drive, or a logical section of a storage array. On Microsoft Windows, a volume usually gets its own drive letter or mount point.

- **Latency.** Measured in milliseconds, latency is how long it takes for data to be read from a drive (seconds per read) and written to a drive (seconds per write).

- **IOPS.** Input/output operations per second, or IOPS, is the number of reads and writes per second. A storage device might have differing performance depending on whether the IOPS are sequential or random. IOPS are directly related to latency by means of the queue depth.

- **Queue depth.** The number of outstanding read and write requests in a storage device's request queue. The deeper the queue depth, the faster the drive.

SQL Server performance is directly related to storage performance. The move toward virtualization and shared storage arrays has placed more emphasis on random data access patterns. Low latency and high random IOPS will thus benefit the average SQL Server workload. In the next two chapters, we go into more detail about the preferred storage configuration for SQL Server.

Types of storage

Non-volatile storage can be split up into three main areas: mechanical, solid-state, and persistent memory.

Mechanical hard drives

Traditional spinning disks have a built-in latency, called seek time, due to their shape and physical nature. The read/write head is mounted on an arm that must scan the surface of the disk as it spins, seeking a particular area to perform the I/O operation. If the data on the spinning disk is fragmented, it can take longer to access because the head must skip around, finding data or free space.

The standard interfaces for mechanical drives are Serial ATA (SATA) and Serial Attached SCSI (SAS).

As spinning disks increase in capacity, the tracks between data become narrower, which causes performance to decrease, and increases the likelihood of mechanical failure or data corruption. The limits are pushed because of the rotational energy in the disk itself, so there is a physical speed limit to the motor.

In other words, mechanical disks grow bigger but slower and more prone to failure.

Solid-state drives

Solid-state technology, which makes use of flash memory, eliminates seek time entirely because the path to each cell where the data is stored is almost instantaneous. This is what makes solid-state storage so much faster than mechanical storage.

Solid-state storage devices can take many different forms. The most common in consumer devices is a 2.5-inch enclosure with a SATA interface, common with mechanical laptop drives. This accommodates a drop-in replacement of mechanical storage.

In server architecture, however, flash memory can take several forms. For local storage, they make use of the Peripheral Component Interconnect Express (PCIe) interface and plug directly into the motherboard. An example of this is Non-Volatile Memory Express (NVMe).

As the technology evolves, the performance will only improve as capacity grows. Solid-state storage is not perfect though; data can be written to a particular cell only a certain number of times before it fails. You might have experienced this yourself with thumb drives, which tend to fail after heavy usage. Algorithms to balance writes across cells, called wear-leveling, help to extend the lifespan of a solid-state device.

Another problem with flash memory is write-amplification. On a mechanical drive, if a file is overwritten, the previous file is marked for deletion but is not actually deleted from the disk surface. When the drive needs to write to that area again, it overwrites the location without removing what was there before.

Solid-state drives must erase the location in question before writing the new data, which has a performance impact. The size of the cells might also require a larger area to be erased than the file itself (if it is a small file), which compounds the performance impact. Various techniques exist to mitigate write amplification, but this reduces the lifespan of flash memory.

The performance problems with mechanical disks, and the lifespan problems with both mechanical and solid-state drives, can be mitigated by combining them into drive arrays, to reduce the risk of failure by balancing the load and increase performance.

Persistent memory

Persistent memory allows for data to remain in RAM without needing to be persisted to traditional storage. It is provided in the same form factor as RAM, which in turn is split evenly between traditional RAM and solid-state components, with a backup power requirement.

CHAPTER 2

Frequently-accessed data is retained in the RAM portion as usual. If there is a loss of main power, data in that RAM is immediately copied to the solid-state component while on backup power. When the main power supply returns, the contents of the solid-state component are copied back into RAM when it is safe to do so. This improves performance because SQL Server 2019 on both Windows Server and Linux is optimized to make use of this technology, which is covered in more detail in the next section under Persistent memory enlightenment.

➤ See more about persistent memory at *https://docs.pmem.io/*.

NOTE
Persistent memory is limited by the capacity of the motherboard, processor, and each memory module. At the time of this writing, persistent memory modules are available in sizes up to 512 GB.

Configuring the storage layer

Non-volatile storage can stand alone, in the form of Direct-Attached Storage, or be combined in many ways to provide redundancy or consolidation, perhaps even offering different levels of performance in order to better manage costs. For example, archive data might not need to be stored on the fastest available drive if it is infrequently accessed.

Direct-Attached Storage

Direct-Attached Storage (DAS) is plugged directly into the system that is accessing it. Also called local storage, it can comprise independent mechanical hard drives, solid-state drives, tape drives for backups, CD and DVD-ROM drives, or even enclosures containing storage arrays.

DAS has a lower latency than a Storage-Area Network or Network-Attached Storage (more on these later in the chapter) because there is no network to traverse between the system and the storage. DAS cannot be shared with other systems, however, unless the local file system is shared across the network using a protocol such as Server Message Block (SMB) 3.0.

For SQL Server, DAS comprising flash (solid-state) storage is preferred for TempDB, which is also supported and recommended in a Failover Cluster Instance. You can also use DAS for the buffer pool extension.

➤ To see how best to configure TempDB, see the section "Configuration settings" in Chapter 3.

Storage arrays and RAID

Combining drives in an enclosure with a controller to access each drive, without any thought to redundancy or performance, is called JBOD (colloquially, "just a bunch of disks"). These drives might be accessed individually or combined into a single volume.

When done correctly, combining drives into an array can increase overall performance and/or lower the risk of data loss should one or more of the drives in the array fail. This is called Redundant Array of Independent Disks (RAID).

RAID offers several levels of configuration, which trade redundancy for performance. More redundancy means less raw capacity for the array, but this can reduce data loss. Faster performance, on the other hand, can bring about data loss.

Striping without parity (RAID 0) uses multiple drives to improve raw read/write performance, but with zero redundancy. If one drive fails, there is significant chance of catastrophic data loss across the entire array. JBOD configurations that span across drives fall under this RAID level.

Mirroring (RAID 1) uses two drives that are written to simultaneously. Although there is a slight write penalty because both drives must save their data at the same time and one might take longer than the other, the read performance is nearly double that of a single drive because both drives can be read in parallel (with a small overhead caused by the RAID controller selecting the drive and fetching the data). Usable space is 50 percent of raw capacity, and only one drive in the array can be lost and still have all data recoverable.

Striping with parity (RAID 5) requires an odd number of three or more drives, and for every single write, one of the drives is randomly used for parity (a checksum validation). There is a larger write penalty because all drives must save their data and parity must be calculated and persisted. If a single drive is lost from the array, the other drives can rebuild the contents of the lost drive, based on the parity, but it can take some time to rebuild the array. Usable space is calculated as the number of drives minus one. If there are three drives in the array, the usable space is the sum of two of those drives, with the space from the third used for parity (which is evenly distributed over the array). Only one drive in the array can be lost and still have full data recovery.

Combinations of the base RAID configurations are used to provide more redundancy and performance, including RAID 1+0 (also known as RAID 10), RAID 0+1, and RAID 5+0 (also known as RAID 50):

In RAID 1+0, two drives are configured in a mirror (RAID 1) for redundancy, and then each mirror is striped together (RAID 0) for performance reasons.

In RAID 0+1, the drives are striped first (RAID 0), and then mirrored across the entire RAID 0 set (RAID 1). Usable space for RAID 0+1 and 1+0 is 50 percent of the raw capacity.

To ensure full recovery from failure in a RAID 1+0 or 0+1 configuration, an entire side of the mirror can be lost, or only one drive from each side of the mirror can be lost.

In RAID 5+0, a number of drives (three or more) is configured in a RAID 5 set, which is then striped (with no parity) with at least one other RAID 5 set of the same configuration. Usable space is $(x - 1) / y$, where x is the number of drives in each nested RAID 5 set, and y is the number of RAID 5 sets in this array. If there are nine drives, six of them are usable. Only one drive from each RAID 5 set can be lost with full recovery possible. If more than one drive in any of the RAID 5 sets is lost, the entire 5+0 array is lost.

SQL Server requires the best possible performance from a storage layer. When looking at RAID configurations, RAID 1+0 offers the best performance and redundancy.

NOTE

RAID is not an alternative to backups, because it does not protect 100 percent against data loss. A common backup medium is digital tape, due to its low cost and high capacity, but more organizations are making use of cloud storage options, such as Microsoft Azure Archive Storage and Amazon Glacier, for long-term, cost-effective backup storage solutions. Always make sure that you perform frequent SQL Server backups that are copied securely off-premises, and then tested regularly by restoring those database backups and running DBCC CHECKDB against them.

Centralized storage with a Storage-Area Network

A Storage-Area Network (SAN) is a network of storage arrays that can comprise tens, hundreds, or even thousands of drives (mechanical or solid-state) in a central location, with one or more RAID configurations, providing block-level access to storage. This reduces wasted space, and allows easier management across multiple systems, especially for virtualized environments.

Block-level means that the OS can read or write blocks of any size and any alignment. This offers the OS a lot of flexibility in making use of the storage.

You can carve the total storage capacity of the SAN into logical unit numbers (LUNs), and each LUN can be assigned to a physical or virtual server. You can move these LUNs around and resize them as required, which makes management much easier than attaching physical storage to a server.

The disadvantage of a SAN is that you might be at the mercy of misconfiguration or a slow network. For instance, the RAID might be set to a level that has poor write performance, or the blocks of the storage are not aligned appropriately.

Storage administrators might not understand specialized workloads like SQL Server and choose a performance model that satisfies the rest of the organization to reduce administration overhead but which penalizes you.

Inside OUT

What is the difference between Fibre Channel and iSCSI?

Storage arrays might use Fibre Channel (FC) or Internet Small Computer Systems Interface (iSCSI) to connect systems to their storage.

FC can support data transfer at a higher rate than iSCSI, which makes it better for systems that require lower latency, but it comes at a higher cost for specialized equipment.

iSCSI uses standard TCP/IP, which makes it potentially cheaper because it can run on existing network equipment. You can further improve iSCSI throughput by isolating the storage to its own dedicated network.

Network-Attached Storage

Network-Attached Storage (NAS), is usually a specialized hardware appliance connected to the network, typically containing an array of several drives, providing file-level access to storage.

Unlike the SAN's block-level support, NAS storage is configured on the appliance itself, and uses file sharing protocols such as SMB, Common Internet File System (CIFS) and Network File System (NFS) to share the storage over the network.

NAS appliances are fairly common because they provide access to shared storage at a much lower monetary cost than a SAN. You should keep in mind security considerations regarding file-sharing protocols.

Storage Spaces

Windows Server 2012 and later support Storage Spaces, which is a way to manage local storage in a more scalable and flexible way than RAID.

Instead of creating a RAID set at the storage layer, Windows Server can create a virtual drive at the OS level. It might use a combination of RAID levels, and you can decide to combine different physical drives to create performance tiers.

For example, a server might contain 16 drives. Eight of them are spinning disks, and eight are solid-state. You can use Storage Spaces to create a single volume with all 16 drives, and keep the active files on the solid-state portion, increasing performance dramatically.

CHAPTER 2

SMB 3.0 file share

SQL Server supports storage located on a network file share that uses the SMB 3.0 protocol or higher because it is now fast and stable enough to support the storage requirements of the Database Engine (performance and resilience). This means that you can build a Failover Cluster Instance (see the section on this later in the chapter) without shared storage such as a SAN.

Network performance is critically important, though, so we recommend a dedicated and isolated network for the SMB file share, using network interface cards that support Remote Direct Memory Access (RDMA). This allows the SMB Direct feature in Windows Server to create a low-latency, high-throughput connection using the SMB protocol.

SMB 3.0 might be a feasible option for smaller networks with limited storage capacity and a NAS, or in the case of a Failover Cluster Instance without shared storage. For more information, read Chapter 11, "Implementing high availability and disaster recovery."

Persistent memory enlightenment

Instead of having to go through the slower channels of the file system and underlying non-volatile storage layer, enlightenment refers to SQL Server 2019's ability to access more efficient persistent memory (PMEM) operations directly.

While this support has been available since SQL Server 2016 Service Pack 1 on Windows Server, Linux support is available for the first time in SQL Server 2019.

➤ **For more information about persistent memory support on Windows Server, visit** *https://blogs.msdn.microsoft.com/sqlserverstorageengine/2016/12/02/transaction-commit-latency-acceleration-using-storage-class-memory-in-windows-server-2016sql-server-2016-sp1/.*

➤ **For configuring DAX for SQL Server on Linux, visit** *https://docs.microsoft.com/sql/linux/sql-server-linux-configure-pmem.*

NOTE
The abbreviation for persistent memory Direct Access Mode is DAX, which should not be confused with Data Analysis Expressions in SQL Server Analysis Services.

The hybrid buffer pool

SQL Server 2019 on both Windows and Linux introduces the hybrid buffer pool, which leverages persistent memory enlightenment to automatically bypass RAM, and lets you access *clean* data pages directly from any database files stored on a PMEM device. Data files are automatically mapped on SQL Server startup; when a database is created, attached, or restored; or when the hybrid buffer pool is enabled. You enable this feature at the instance level, and if you don't need to use it on individual user databases you can disable it at the database level.

The PMEM device must be formatted with a file system that supports Direct Access Mode (DAX), namely XFS, ext4, or NTFS. Data file sizes should be in multiples of 2 MB, and if you are on Windows, a 2-MB allocation size is recommended for NTFS. You should also enable the Lock pages in memory (LPIM) option on Windows.

CAUTION

You should not use the hybrid buffer pool on an instance with less than 16 GB RAM.

This feature is considered hybrid, because dirty pages must be copied to the regular buffer pool in RAM, before making their way back to the PMEM device and marked clean during a regular checkpoint operation.

➤ For more information about hybrid buffer pools, visit Microsoft Docs at *https://docs.microsoft.com/sql/database-engine/configure-windows/hybrid-buffer-pool.*

Connecting to SQL Server over the network

We have covered a fair amount about networking discussing the storage layer, but there is far more to it. In this section, we look at what is involved when accessing the Database Engine over a network, and briefly discuss Virtual Local Area Networks.

Unless a SQL Server instance and the application accessing it is entirely self-contained, database access is performed over one or more network interfaces. This adds complexity with authentication, given that attackers might be scanning and modifying network packets in flight.

CAUTION

Ensure that all TCP/IP traffic to and from the SQL Server is encrypted. This isn't required when using the Shared Memory Protocol with applications located on the same server as the SQL Server instance.

SQL Server 2019 requires strict rules with respect to network security, which means that older versions of the connectors or protocols used by software developers might not work as expected.

Transport Security Layer and its forerunner Secure Sockets Layer (together known as TLS/SSL, or just SSL), are methods that allow network traffic between two points to be encrypted. Where possible, you should use newer libraries that support TLS encryption. If you cannot use TLS to encrypt application traffic, you should use IPSec, which is configured at the OS level.

➤ For more information about encryption in SQL Server, see Chapter 13, "Protecting data through encryption, privacy and auditing."

Protocols and ports

Connections to SQL Server are made over the Transport Control Protocol (TCP), with port 1433 as the default port for a default instance. Some of this is covered in Chapter 1, "Getting started with SQL Server tools", and again in Chapter 13. Any named instances are assigned random ports by the SQL Server Configuration Manager, and the SQL Browser service coordinates any connections to named instances. It is possible to assign static TCP ports to named instances by using the Configuration Manager.

There are ways to change the default port after SQL Server is installed, using SQL Server Configuration Manager. We do not recommend changing the port for security reasons, however, because it provides no security advantage to a port scanner, although some network administration policies require it.

Networking is also the foundation of cloud computing. Aside from the fact that the Azure cloud is accessed over the Internet (itself a network of networks), the entire Azure infrastructure, which underlies both infrastructure-as-a-service (virtual machines with Windows or Linux running SQL Server) and platform-as-a-service (Azure SQL Database) offerings, is a virtual fabric of innumerable components tied together with networking.

Added complexity with Virtual Local Area Networks

A Virtual Local Area Network (VLAN) gives network administrators the ability to logically group machines together even if they are not physically connected through the same network switch. It allows servers to share their resources with one another over the same physical LAN, without interacting with other devices on the same network.

VLANs work at a very low level (the data link layer, or OSI Layer 2), and are configured on a network switch. A port on the switch might be dedicated to a particular VLAN, and all traffic to and from that port is mapped to a particular VLAN by the switch.

High availability concepts

With each new version of Windows Server, terminology and definitions tend to change or adapt according to the new features available. With SQL Server on Linux, it is even more important to get our heads around what it means when we discuss high availability.

At its most basic, high availability (HA) means that a service offering of some kind (for example, SQL Server, a web server, an application, or a file share) will survive an outage of some kind, or at least fail predictably to a standby state, with minimal loss of data and minimal downtime.

Everything can fail. An outage might be caused by a failed hard drive, which could in turn be a result of excessive heat, excessive cold, excessive moisture, or a datacenter alarm that is so loud that its vibrational frequency damages the internal components and causes a head crash.

You should be aware of other things that can go wrong, as noted in the list that follows. The list is certainly not exhaustive, but it's incredibly important to never make assumptions about hardware, software, and network stability:

- A failed network interface card

- A failed RAID controller

- A power surge or brownout causing a failed power supply

- A broken or damaged network cable

- A broken or damaged power cable

- Moisture on the motherboard

- Dust on the motherboard

- Overheating caused by a failed fan

- A faulty keyboard that misinterprets keystrokes

- Failure due to bit rot

- Failure due to a bug in SQL Server

- Failure due to poorly written code in a file system driver that causes drive corruption

- Capacitors failing on the motherboard

- Insects or rodents electrocuting themselves on components (this smells really bad)

- Failure caused by a fire suppression system that uses water instead of gas

- Misconfiguration of a network router causing an entire geographical region to be inaccessible

- Failure due to an expired SSL or TLS certificate

- Human error, such as running a DELETE or UPDATE statement without a WHERE clause

Why redundancy matters

Armed with the knowledge that everything can fail, you should build in redundancy where possible. The sad reality is that these decisions are governed by budget constraints. The amount of money available is inversely proportional to the amount of acceptable data loss and length of downtime. For business-critical systems, however, uptime is paramount, and a highly available solution will be more cost effective than being down, considering the cost-per-minute to the organization.

It is nearly impossible to guarantee zero downtime with zero data loss. There is always a trade-off. The business needs define that trade-off, based on resources (equipment, people, money), and the technical solution is in turn developed around that trade-off. This strategy is driven by two values called the Recovery Point Objective and Recovery Time Objective, which are defined in a Service-Level Agreement (SLA).

Recovery Point Objective

A good way to think of Recovery Point Objective (RPO) is "How much data are you prepared to lose?" When a failure occurs, how much data will be lost between the last transaction log backup and the failure? This value is usually measured in seconds or minutes.

> NOTE
>
> **If your organization differentiates archive data from current data, this should form part of the discussion around RPO, specifically as it relates to the maximum allowed age of your data. You may not need to bring archived data online immediately after a disaster, as long as it is made available in some specified time in the future.**

Recovery Time Objective

The Recovery Time Objective (RTO) is defined as how much time is available to bring the environment up to a known and usable state after a failure. There might be different values for HA and disaster recovery scenarios. This value is usually measured in hours.

Disaster recovery

HA is not disaster recovery (DR). They are often grouped under the same heading (HA/DR), mainly because there are shared technology solutions for both concepts, but HA is about keeping the service running, whereas DR is what happens when the infrastructure fails entirely. DR is like insurance: you don't think you need it until it's too late. HA costs more money the shorter the RPO.

> NOTE
> **A disaster is any failure or event that causes an unplanned outage.**

Clustering

Clustering is the connecting of computers (nodes) in a set of two or more nodes, that work together and present themselves to the network as one computer.

In most cluster configurations, only one node can be *active* in a cluster. To ensure that this happens, a *quorum* instructs the cluster as to which node should be active. It also steps in if there is a communication failure between the nodes.

Each node has a *vote* in a quorum. However, if there is an even number of nodes, to ensure a simple majority an additional *witness* must be included in a quorum to allow for a majority vote to take place. You can see more about this process in the "Resolving cluster partitioning with quorum" section later in this chapter.

Inside OUT

What is Always On?

Always On is the name of a group of features, which is akin to a marketing term. It is not the name of a specific technology. There are two separate technologies that happen to fall under the Always On label, and these are addressed later in this chapter. The important thing to remember is that "Always On" does not mean "availability groups," and there is a space between "Always" and "On."

Windows Server Failover Clustering

"A failover cluster is a group of independent computers that work together to increase the availability and scalability of clustered roles. [...] If one or more of the cluster nodes fail, other nodes begin to provide service (a process known as failover). In addition, the clustered roles are proactively monitored to verify that they are working properly. If they are not working, they are restarted or moved to another node."
(https://docs.microsoft.com/windows-server/failover-clustering/failover-clustering-overview)

The terminology here matters. Windows Server Failover Clustering is the name of the technology that underpins a Failover Cluster Instance (FCI), where two or more Windows Server Failover Clustering nodes (computers) are connected together in a Windows Server Failover Clustering resource group and masquerade as a single machine behind a network endpoint called a Virtual Network Name (VNN). A SQL Server service that is installed on an FCI is cluster-aware.

Linux failover clustering with Pacemaker

Instead of relying on Windows Server Failover Clustering, SQL Server on a Linux cluster can make use of any cluster resource manager. When SQL Server 2017 was released, Microsoft recommended using Pacemaker because it ships with a number of Linux distributions, including Red Hat and Ubuntu. This advice still holds true for SQL Server 2019.

➤ You can read more about the Pacemaker recommendation in Microsoft Docs at *https://docs.microsoft.com/sql/linux/sql-server-linux-business-continuity-dr.*

Inside OUT

What happens when a Linux node fails?

If something goes wrong in a cluster, and a node is in an unknown state after a set time-out period, that node must be isolated from the cluster and restarted or reset. On Linux clusters, this is called node fencing, following the STONITH principle ("Shoot the Other Node in the Head"). If a node fails, STONITH will provide an effective, if drastic manner, of resetting or powering-off a failed Linux node.

Resolving cluster partitioning with quorum

Most clustering technologies make use of the quorum model to prevent a phenomenon called partitioning, or "split brain." If there is an even number of nodes, and half of these nodes go offline from the view of the other half of the cluster, and vice versa, you end up with two halves thinking that the cluster is still up and running, and each with a primary node (split brain).

Depending on connectivity to each half of the cluster, an application continues writing to one half of the cluster while another application writes to the other half. A best-case resolution to this scenario would require rolling back to a point in time before the event occurred, which would cause loss of any data written after the event.

To prevent this, each node in a cluster shares its health with the other nodes using a periodic heartbeat. If more than half do not respond in a timely fashion, the cluster is considered to have failed. Quorum works by having a simple majority vote on what constitutes "enough nodes."

In Windows Server Failover Clustering, there are four types of majority vote: Node, Node and File Share, Node and Disk, and Disk Only. In the latter three types, a separate witness is used, which does not participate in the cluster directly. This witness is given voting rights when there is an even number of nodes in a cluster, and therefore a simple majority (more than half) would not be possible.

Always On FCIs

You can think of a SQL Server FCI as two or more nodes with shared storage (usually a SAN because it is most likely to be accessed over the network).

On Windows Server, SQL Server can take advantage of Windows Server Failover Clustering to provide HA (the idea being minimal downtime) at the server-instance level, by creating an FCI of two or more nodes. From the network's perspective (application, end users, and so on), the FCI is presented as a single instance of SQL Server running on a single computer, and all connections point at the VNN.

When the FCI starts, one of the nodes assumes ownership and brings its SQL Server instance online. If a failure occurs on the first node (or there is a planned failover due to maintenance), there are at least a few seconds of downtime, during which the first node cleans up as best it can, and then the second node brings its SQL Server instance online. Client connections are redirected to the new node after the services are up and running.

Inside OUT

How long does the FCI failover take?

During a planned failover, any dirty pages in the buffer pool must be written to the drive; thus, the downtime could be longer than expected on a server with a large buffer pool. You can read more about checkpoints in Chapter 3 and Chapter 4, "Installing and configuring SQL Server instances and features."

On Linux, the principle is very similar. A cluster resource manager such as Pacemaker manages the cluster, and when a failover occurs, the same process is followed from SQL Server's perspective, in which the first node is brought down and the second node is brought up to take its place as the owner. The cluster has a virtual IP address, just as on Windows. You must add the virtual network name manually to the DNS server.

➤ You can read more about setting up a Linux cluster in Chapter 11, "Developing, deploying, and managing data recovery."

FCIs are supported on SQL Server Standard edition but are limited to two nodes.

The versatility of log shipping

SQL Server transaction log shipping is an extremely flexible technology to provide a relatively inexpensive and easily managed HA and DR solution.

The principle is as follows: a primary database is in either the full or bulk logged recovery model, with transaction log backups being taken regularly every few minutes. These transaction log backup files are transferred to a shared network location, where one or more secondary servers restore the transaction log backups to a standby database.

If you use the built-in Log Shipping Wizard in SQL Server Management Studio, on the **Restore** tab, click **Database State When Restoring Backups**, and then choose the **No Recovery Mode** or **Standby Mode** option (*https://docs.microsoft.com/sql/database-engine/ log-shipping/configure-log-shipping-sql-server*).

If you are building your own log shipping solution, remember to use the RESTORE feature with NORECOVERY, or RESTORE with STANDBY.

If a failover occurs, the tail of the log on the primary server is backed up in the same way (if available—this guarantees zero data loss of committed transactions), transferred to the shared location, and restored after the latest regular transaction logs. The database is then put into RECOVERY_PENDING state, which is where crash recovery takes place, rolling back incomplete transactions and rolling forward complete transactions.

> ➤ **You can read more about crash recovery in Chapter 3.**

As soon as the application is pointed to the new server, the environment is back up again with zero data loss (tail of the log was copied across) or minimal data loss (only the latest shipped transaction log was restored).

Log shipping is a feature that works on all editions of SQL Server, on Windows and Linux. Since Express edition does not include the SQL Server Agent, however, Express can only be a witness, and you must manage the process through a separate scheduling mechanism. You can even create your own solution for any edition of SQL Server, using Azure Storage and AzCopy.exe, for instance.

Always On availability groups

As mentioned previously, availability groups is generally what people mean when they incorrectly say "Always On." However, its official name is Always On availability groups. In shorthand, you can refer to these as availability groups (or AGs).

What is an availability group, anyway? In the past, SQL Server offered database mirroring and failover clustering as two distinct HA offerings. However, with database mirroring officially in maintenance mode since SQL Server 2012, coinciding with the introduction of availability groups, it is easier to think of availability groups as a consolidation of these two offerings as well as log shipping thrown in for good measure.

> ## Inside OUT
>
> *What was database mirroring?*
>
> Database mirroring worked at the database level by maintaining two copies of a single database across two separate SQL Server instances, keeping them synchronized with a steady stream of active transaction log records. It is a feature that is now in maintenance mode. Unlike a deprecated feature, it will not be removed from the product in a future version. However, it is no longer supported on Windows and it has not been made available for Linux.

Availability groups provide us with the ability to keep a discrete set of databases highly available across one or more nodes in a cluster. They work at the database level, as opposed to an entire server-instance level, like FCIs do.

Unlike the cluster-aware version of SQL Server when it is installed as part of an FCI, SQL Server on an availability group is installed as a standalone instance.

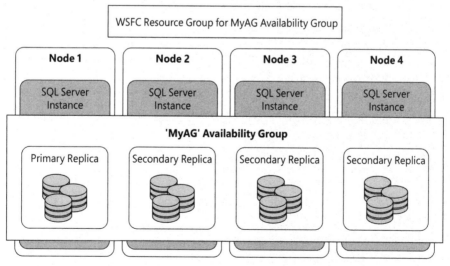

Figure 2-3 A Windows Server Failover Clustering cluster with four nodes.

CHAPTER 2

An availability group operates at the database level only, on Windows Server through Windows Server Failover Clustering, and on Linux through a cluster resource manager like Pacemaker. As depicted in Figure 2-3, it is a set of one or more databases in a group (an availability replica) that is replicated (using log shipping) from a primary replica. There can be only one primary replica, to a maximum of eight secondary replicas, using synchronous or asynchronous data synchronization. Let's take a closer look at each of these:

- **Synchronous data synchronization.**   The log is hardened (the transactions are committed to the transaction log) on every secondary replica before the transaction is committed on the primary replica. This guarantees zero data loss, with a potential performance impact on a highly transactional workload if network latency is high. You can have two synchronous-commit replicas per AG.

- **Asynchronous data synchronization.**   The transaction is considered committed as soon as it is hardened in the transaction log on the primary replica. If something were to happen before the logs are hardened on all of the secondary replicas, there is a chance of data loss, and the recovery point would be the most recently committed transaction that successfully made it to all of the secondary replicas. With delayed durability turned on, this can result in faster performance, but higher risk of data loss.

Inside OUT

What is delayed durability?

Delayed durability (also known as lazy commit) is a storage optimization feature that returns a successful commit before transaction logs are actually saved to the storage layer. Although this can improve performance, the risk of data loss is higher because the transaction logs are saved only when the logs are flushed to a drive asynchronously. There is even a risk of data loss when the SQL Server service is shut down.

To learn more, go to *https://docs.microsoft.com/sql/relational-databases/logs/control-transaction-durability*.

You can use read-only secondary replicas for running reports and other operations that reduce the load on the primary replica. This also includes backups and database consistency checks, but you must also perform these on the primary replica when there is a low-usage period or planned maintenance window.

If the primary replica fails, one of the secondary replicas is promoted to the primary, with a few seconds of downtime, while the databases run through crash recovery and minimal data loss.

Read-scale availability groups

SQL Server 2017 introduced a new architecture that allows for multiple read-only secondary replicas, but it does not offer HA. The major difference is that a read-scale availability group does not have a cluster resource manager.

What this allows is reduced contention on a business-critical workload by using read-only routing or connecting directly to a readable secondary replica, without relying on a clustering infrastructure on Windows or Linux.

> ➤ **For more information, go to Microsoft Docs at** *https://docs.microsoft.com/sql/ database-engine/availability-groups/windows/read-scale-availability-groups.*

Distributed availability groups

Instead of having an availability group on one cluster, a distributed availability group can span two separate availability groups, on two separate clusters (Windows Server Failover Clustering or Linux, where each cluster can run on a different OS) and is geographically separated. You can configure them in a distributed availability group, provided that these two availability groups can communicate with each other. This allows a more flexible DR scenario, plus it makes possible multi-site replicas in geographically diverse areas.

Each availability group in a distributed AG can contain the maximum number of replicas, and you can mix major versions of SQL Server in the same distributed AG.

The main difference from a normal availability group, is that the configuration is stored in SQL Server, not the underlying cluster. With a distributed availability group, only one availability group can perform data modification at any time, even though both availability groups have a primary replica. To allow another availability group to write to its primary replica database requires a manual failover, using FORCE_FAILOVER_ALLOW_DATA_LOSS, but note that this may result in the loss of data.

Basic availability groups

SQL Server Standard edition supports a single-database HA solution, with a limit of two replicas. The secondary replica does not allow backups or read access. Although these limits can be frustrating, they do make it possible to offer another kind of HA offering with the Standard edition.

> ➤ With SQL Server on Linux, you can have an additional configura-
> tion-only replica. Read more at *https://docs.microsoft.com/sql/linux/*
> *sql-server-linux-availability-group-overview#configuration-only-replica-and-quorum.*

NOTE

You cannot upgrade a basic availability group to a regular availability group.

> ➤ For more information, go to Microsoft Docs at
> *https://docs.microsoft.com/sql/database-engine/availability-groups/windows/*
> *basic-availability-groups-always-on-availability-groups.*

Securing SQL Server

Security is covered in more depth in Chapter 12, "Administering security and permissions," and
Chapter 13, so what follows is a basic overview of server access security, not a discussion about
permissions within SQL Server.

When connecting to SQL Server on Windows or Linux, or connecting to Azure SQL Database,
security is required to keep everyone out except the people who need access to the database.

Active Directory, using Integrated Authentication, is the primary method for connecting to SQL
Server on a Windows domain. When you sign in to an Active Directory domain, you are provided a token that contains your privileges and permissions.

This is different from SQL Server Authentication, however, which is managed directly on the SQL
Server instance and requires a user name and password to travel over the network.

Integrated authentication and Active Directory

Active Directory covers a number of different identity services, but the most important is Active
Directory Domain Services, which manages your network credentials (your user account) and
what you can do on the network (access rights). Having a network-wide directory of users and
permissions facilitates easier management of accounts, computers, servers, services, devices, file
sharing, and so on.

In this type of environment, SQL Server would be managed as just another service on the network, and the Active Directory Domain Service would control who has access to that SQL Server
instance. This is much easier than having to manage individual user access per server, which is
time consuming, difficult to troubleshoot, and prone to human error.

Inside OUT

Is Active Directory supported on Linux?

SQL Server 2019 on Linux supports integrated authentication using Active Directory. For more information, read the Microsoft Docs article titled "Active Directory Authentication with SQL Server on Linux," which is available at *https://docs.microsoft.com/sql/linux/sql-server-linux-active-directory-authentication.*

CHAPTER 2

Authenticating with Kerberos

Kerberos is the default authentication protocol used in a Windows Active Directory domain; it is the replacement of NT LAN Manager (NTLM).

Kerberos ensures that the authentication takes place in a secure manner, even if the network itself might not be secure, because passwords and weak hashes are not being transferred over the wire. Kerberos works by exchanging encrypted tickets verified by a Ticket Granting Server (TGS; usually the domain controller).

A service account that runs SQL Server on a particular server, under an Active Directory service account, must register its name with the TGS so that client computers are able to make a connection to that service over the network. This is called a Service Principal Name.

CAUTION

NTLM is the authentication protocol on standalone Windows systems and is used on older operating systems and older domains. You can also use NTLM as a fallback on Active Directory domains for backward compatibility.

The NTLM token created during the sign-in process consists of the domain name, the user name, and a one-way hash of the user's password. Unfortunately, this hash is considered cryptographically weak and can be cracked (decrypted) in a few seconds by modern cracking tools. It is incumbent on you to use Kerberos where possible.

Understanding the Service Principal Name

When a client logs into a Windows domain, it is issued a ticket by the TGS, as shown in Figure 2-4. This ticket is called a ticket-granting ticket (TGT), but it's easier to think of it as the client's credentials. When the client wants to communicate with another node on the network such as SQL Server, this node or "principal" must have a Service Principal Name (SPN) registered with the TGS.

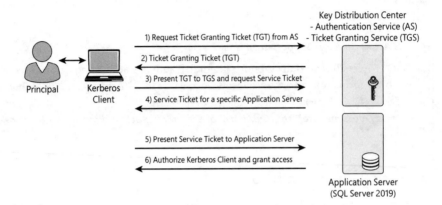

Figure 2-4   How Kerberos authentication works.

It is this SPN that the client uses to request access. After a verification step, a ticket and session key are sent from the TGS, to both the SQL Server and the client, respectively. When the client uses the ticket and session key on the SQL Server, the connection is authenticated by the SQL Server using its own copy of the session key.

For SQL Server to use Kerberos authentication instead of the older and insecure NTLM, the Windows domain account that runs the SQL Server service, must register the SPN with the domain controller. Otherwise, the authentication will fall back to NTLM, which is far less secure. The easiest way to achieve this is to grant the service account **Write ServicePrincipalName** permission in Active Directory Domain Service. To configure an SPN manually, you must use the Setspn.exe tool, which is built into Windows.

> **NOTE**
> Service Principal Names can also be managed using the dbatools PowerShell module, available from *https://dbatools.io*.

Accessing other servers and services with delegation

Kerberos delegation allows an application such as SQL Server to reuse end-user credentials to access a different server. This is intended to solve the so-called "double-hop issue," in which the TGS verifies only the first hop, namely the connection between the client and the registered server. In normal circumstances, any additional connections (the second hop) would require reauthentication.

Delegation impersonates the client by sending the client's TGT on the client's behalf. This in turn causes the TGS to send tickets and session keys to the original server and the new server, allowing authentication. Because the original connection is still authenticated using the same TGT, the client now has access to the second server.

For delegation to work, the service account for the first server must be trusted for delegation, and the second server must be in the same Active Directory forest or between forests with the appropriate trust relationship.

Azure Active Directory

Azure Active Directory (Azure AD) is concerned with identity management for Internet-based and on-premises services, which use HTTP and HTTPS to access websites and web services without the hierarchy associated with on-premises Active Directory.

You can use Azure AD for user and application authentication; for example, to connect to Azure SQL Database or Microsoft Office 365. There are no Organizational Units or Group Policy Objects. You cannot join a machine to an Azure AD domain, and there is no NTLM or Kerberos authentication. Instead, protocols like OAuth, OpenID Connect (based on OAuth 2.0), SAML, and WS-Federation are used.

You can authenticate (prove who you are), which then provides authorization (permission, or claims) to access certain services, and these services might not even be controlled by the service that authenticated you. Think back to network credentials. On an on-premises Active Directory, your user credentials know who you are (your authentication), and what you can do (your authorization).

Protocols like OpenID Connect blur these lines, by extending an authorization protocol (what you can do) into an authentication protocol (who you are), as well. Although this works in a similar manner to Kerberos, whereby an authorization server allows access to certain internet services and applications, permissions are granted with claims.

Asserting your identity with claims

Claims are a set of "assertions of information about the subject that has been authenticated" (*https://docs.microsoft.com/azure/active-directory/develop/ v1-authentication-scenarios#claims-in-azure-ad-security-tokens*).

Think of your user credentials as a security token that indicates who you are, based on how you were authenticated. This depends on the service you originally connected to (i.e., Facebook, LinkedIn, Google, Office 365, or Twitter).

Inside that user object is a series of properties, or attributes, usually in the form of key–value pairs. The specific attributes, or claims, are dependent on the authentication service used.

Authentication services like Azure AD might restrict the amount of information permissible in a user object, to provide the service or application just enough information about you to prove who you are, and give you access to the service you're requesting, without sharing too much about you or the originating authentication service.

Federation and single sign-on

Federation is a fancy word that means an independent collection of websites or services that can share information between them using claims. An authentication service allows you to sign in on one place (LinkedIn, GitHub, or Microsoft) and then use that identity for other services controlled by other entities.

This is what makes claims extremely useful. If you use a third-party authentication service, that third party will make certain information available in the form of claims (key–value pairs in your security token) that another service to which you're connecting can access, without needing to sign in again, and without that service having access into the third-party service.

For example, suppose that you use LinkedIn to sign in to a blogging service so that you can leave a comment on a post. The blogging service does not have any access to your LinkedIn profile, but the claims it provides might include a URL to your profile image, a string containing your full name, and a second URL back to your profile.

This way, the blogging service does not know anything about your LinkedIn account, including your employment history, because that information is not in the claims necessary to leave a blog post comment.

Logging in to Azure SQL Database

Azure SQL Database uses three levels of security to allow access to a database. First is the firewall, which is a set of rules based on origin IP address or ranges and allows connections to only TCP port 1433.

The second level is authentication (proving who you are). You can either connect by using SQL Authentication, with a user name and password (like connecting to a contained database on an on-premises SQL Server instance), or you can use Azure AD Authentication.

Microsoft recommends using Azure AD whenever possible, because it does the following (according to *https://docs.microsoft.com/azure/sql-database/sql-database-aad-authentication*):

- Centralizes user identities and offers password rotation in a single place

- Eliminates storing passwords by enabling integrated Windows authentication and other forms of authentication supported by Azure AD

- Offers token (claims-based) authentication for applications connecting to Azure SQL Database

The third level is authorization (what you can do). This is managed inside the Azure SQL database, using role memberships and object-level permissions, and works exactly the same way as it would with an on-premises SQL Server instance.

➤ You can read more about SQL Server security in Chapters 12 and 13.

Understanding virtualization and containers

Hardware abstraction has been around for many years, and, in fact, Windows NT was designed to be hardware independent. We can take this concept even further by abstracting through *virtualization* or *containers*.

- **Virtualization.**   Abstracts the entire *physical layer* behind what's called a hypervisor, or Virtual Machine Manager (VMM) so that physical hardware on a host system can be logically shared between different VMs, or guests, running their own operating systems.

- **Containers.**   Abstracts away not just the hardware, but the entire *operating system* as well. By not needing to include and maintain a separate OS, a container has a much smaller resource footprint, often dedicated to a single application or service with access to the subset of hardware it needs.

A *virtual consumer* (a guest OS or container) will access resources in the same way as a physical machine. As a rule, it has no knowledge that it is virtualized.

Inside OUT

What is the cloud?

Cloud technology can be thought of as a virtualized environment, but on a much larger scale. Millions of servers are sitting in datacenters all over the world, running tens or hundreds of virtual consumers (VMs and containers) on each server. The service fabric (the software that controls and manages the environment) is what differentiates each cloud vendor.

Going virtual

The move to virtualization and containers has come about because physical hardware in many organizations is not being used to its full potential, and systems might spend hundreds of hours per year sitting idle. By consolidating an infrastructure, you can share resources more easily, reducing the amount of waste and increasing the usefulness of hardware.

CHAPTER 2

Certain workloads and applications are not designed to share resources, and misconfiguration of the shared resources by system administrators might not take these specialized workloads into account. SQL Server is an excellent example of this, given that it is designed to make use of all the physical RAM in a server by default.

If the resources are allocated incorrectly from the host level, contention between the virtual consumers takes place. This phenomenon is known as the noisy neighbor, in which one consumer monopolizes resources on the host, and the other consumers are negatively affected. With some effort on the part of the network administrators, this problem can be alleviated.

The benefits far outweigh the downsides, of course. You can move consumers from one host to another in the case of resource contention or hardware failure, and some orchestrator software can do this without even shutting down that consumer.

It is also much easier to take snapshots of virtualized file systems than physical machines, which you can use to clone VMs, for instance. This reduces deployment costs and time when deploying new servers, by "spinning up" a VM template and configuring the OS and the application software that was already installed on that virtual hard drive. With containers, you can spin up a new container based on an image in much the same way.

NOTE
A Docker container is an *image* that is *composed* from a plain text configuration file called a *Dockerfile*.

Over time, the benefits become more apparent. New processors with low core counts are becoming more difficult to find. Virtualization makes it possible for you to move physical workloads to virtual consumers (now or later) that have the appropriate virtual core count, and gives you the freedom to use existing licenses, thereby reducing cost.

> ➤ David Klee writes more on this in the article "Point Counterpoint: Why Virtualize a SQL Server?" available at *http://www.davidklee.net/2017/07/12/point-counterpoint-why-virtualize-a-sql-server.*

While there are several OS-level virtualization technologies in use today (including Windows containers), we focus on Docker containers specifically. As for VM hypervisors, there are two main players in this space: Microsoft Hyper-V and VMware.

Resource provisioning for virtual consumers

Setting up VMs or containers requires understanding their anticipated workloads. Fortunately, as long as resources are allocated appropriately, a virtual consumer can run almost as fast as a physical server on the same hardware, but with all of the benefits that virtualization offers.

It makes sense, then, to overprovision resources for many general workloads.

Sharing more memory than you have (overcommit)

You might have 10 VMs running various tasks such as Active Directory Domain Controllers, DNS servers, file servers, and print servers (the plumbing of a Windows-based network, with a low RAM footprint), all running on a single host with 64 GB of physical RAM.

Each VM might require 16 GB of RAM to perform properly, but in practice, you have determined that 90 percent of the time, each VM can function with 4 to 8 GB RAM each, leaving 8 to 12 GB of RAM unused per VM. You could thus overcommit each VM with 16 GB of RAM (for a total of 160 GB), but still see acceptable performance without having a particular guest swapping memory to the drive as a result of low RAM, 90 percent of the time.

For the remaining 10 percent of the time, for which paging unavoidably takes place, you might decide that the performance impact is not sufficient to warrant increasing the physical RAM on the host. You are therefore able to run 10 virtualized servers on far less hardware than they would have required as physical servers.

> ### CAUTION
>
> **Because SQL Server makes use of all the memory it is configured to use (limited by edition), it is not good practice to overcommit memory for VMs that are running SQL Server. It is critical that the amount of RAM assigned to a SQL Server VM is available for exclusive use by the VM, and that the Max Server Memory setting is configured correctly (see Chapter 3).**

Provisioning virtual storage

In the same way that you can overcommit memory, so too can you overcommit storage. This is called thin provisioning, in which the consumer is configured to assume that there is a lot more space available than is physically on the host. When a VM begins writing to a drive, the actual space used is increased on the host, until it reaches the provisioned limit.

This practice is common with general workloads, for which the space requirements grow predictably. An OS like Windows Server might be installed on a guest with 127 GB of visible space, but there might be only 250 GB of actual space on the drive, shared across 10 VMs.

For specialized workloads like SQL Server, thin provisioning is not a good idea. Depending on the performance of the storage layer and the data access patterns of the workload, it is possible that the guest will be slow due to drive fragmentation (especially storage built on mechanical hard drives), or even run out of storage space. This can occur for any number of reasons, including long-running transactions, infrequent transaction log backups, or a growing TempDB.

It is therefore a better idea to use thick provisioning of storage for specialized workloads. That way the guest is guaranteed the storage it is promised by the hypervisor and is one less thing to worry about when SQL Server runs out of space at 3 AM on a Sunday morning.

> ### NOTE
>
> Most of the original use-cases around containers were web and application server workloads, so early implementations did not include options for persisting data across container restarts. This is why container storage was originally considered to be *ephemeral*.

➤ See Chapter 3, in the section on Kubernetes, to explore persistent storage options for Docker containers.

When processors are no longer processors

Virtualizing CPUs is challenging because the CPU works by having a certain number of clock cycles per second, which we looked at earlier in this chapter. For logical processors (the physical CPU core plus any logical cores if SMT is turned on), each core shares time slices, or time slots, with each VM. Every time the CPU clock ticks over, that time slot might be used by the hypervisor or any one of the guests.

Just as it is not recommended to overprovision RAM and storage for SQL Server, you should not overprovision CPU cores. If there are four quad-core CPUs in the host (four CPU sockets populated with a quad-core CPU in each socket), there are 16 cores available for use by the VMs, or 32 when accounting for SMT.

Inside OUT

How is CPU virtualization affected by SMT (Hyper-Threading)?

Even though it is possible to assign as many virtual CPUs as there are logical cores, we recommend that you limit the number of vCPUs to the number of physical cores available (in other words, excluding SMT) for two reasons.

First, the number of execution resources on the CPU itself is limited to the number of physical cores.

Second, keep in mind that CPUs manufactured before 2019 may be susceptible to security vulnerabilities discussed previously in the Security Vulnerabilities section, In this case you may want to disable SMT altogether, or just patch your OS and CPU microcode if the risks are acceptable.

Virtual CPU

A virtual CPU (vCPU) maps to a logical core, but in practice, the time slots are shared evenly over each core in the physical CPU. A vCPU will be more powerful than a single core because the load is parallelized across each core.

One of the risks of mixing different types of workloads on a single host is that a business-critical workload like SQL Server might require all the vCPUs to run a large parallelized query. If there are other guests that are using those vCPUs during that specific time slot and the CPU is over-committed, SQL Server's guest will need to wait.

There are certain algorithms in hypervisors that allow vCPUs to cut in line and take over a time slot, which results in a lag for the other guests, causing performance issues. Assume that a file server has two virtual processors assigned to it. Further assume that on the same host, a SQL Server has eight virtual processors assigned to it. It is possible for the VM with fewer virtual logical processors to "steal" time slots because it has a lower number allocated to it.

There are several ways to deal with this, but the easiest solution is to keep like with like. Any guests on the same host should have the same number of virtual processors assigned to them, running similar workloads. That way, the time slots are more evenly distributed, and it becomes easier to troubleshoot processor performance. It might also be practical to reduce the number of vCPUs allocated to a SQL Server instance so that the time slots are better distributed.

> **CAUTION**
>
> A VM running SQL Server might benefit from fewer vCPUs. If too many cores are allocated to the VM, it could cause performance issues due to foreign memory access because SQL Server might be unaware of the underlying NUMA configuration. Remember to size your VM CPU core allocation as a multiple of a NUMA node size.
>
> You can find more information on VMware's blog at *https://blogs.vmware.com/vsphere/2012/02/vspherenuma-loadbalancing.html*.

The network is virtual, too

Whereas before, certain hardware devices might be used to perform discrete tasks, such as network interface cards, routers, firewalls, and switches, these tasks can now be accomplished exclusively through a software layer, using virtual network devices.

Several VMs might share one or more physical NICs on a physical host, but because it's all virtualized, a VM might have several virtual NICs mapped to that one physical NIC.

This allows a number of things that previously might have been cumbersome and costly to implement. Software developers can now test against myriad configurations for their applications without having to build a physical lab environment using all of the different combinations.

With the general trend of consolidating VMs and containers, virtual networking facilitates combining and consolidating network devices and services into the same environment as these virtual consumers, lowering the cost of administration and reducing the need to purchase separate hardware. You can replace a virtualized network device almost immediately if something goes wrong, and downtime is vastly reduced.

CHAPTER 2

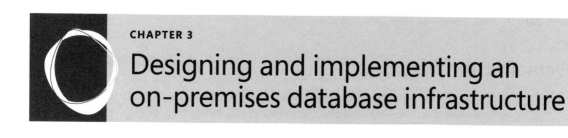

CHAPTER 3

Designing and implementing an on-premises database infrastructure

This chapter covers the architecture of an on-premises database infrastructure, including the differences between data and transaction log files, and how certain features work to ensure durability and consistency even during unexpected events.

We cover what certain important configuration settings mean, both from a performance and best practice perspective. We also go into detail about the different kinds of data compression and file system settings that are most appropriate for your environment.

Finally, we discuss how to deploy SQL Server using containers and Kubernetes.

The sample scripts in this chapter, and all scripts for this book, are available for download at *https://www.MicrosoftPressStore.com/SQLServer2019InsideOut/downloads*.

Introduction to SQL Server database architecture

The easiest way to observe the implementation of a SQL Server database is by its files. Every SQL Server database comprises at least two main kinds of file:

- **Data.** The data itself is stored in one or more filegroups. Each filegroup in turn comprises one or more physical data files.

- **Transaction Log.** This is where all data modifications are saved until committed or rolled back and then hardened to a data file. There is usually only one transaction log file per database.

NOTE

There are several other file types used by SQL Server, including logs, trace files, and memory-optimized filegroups, which we discuss later in this chapter.

Data files and filegroups

When you initially create a user database, SQL Server uses the *model* database as a template, which provides your new database with its default configuration, including ownership, compatibility level, file growth settings, recovery model (full, bulk-logged, simple), and physical file settings.

By default, each new database has one *transaction log file* and one data *filegroup*. This data filegroup is known as the *primary filegroup*, comprising a single data file by default. It is known as the primary data file, which has the file extension .mdf (see Figure 3-1).

NOTE
The file extensions used for SQL Server data and transaction log files are listed by convention only and are not required.

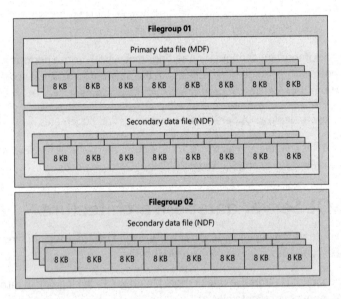

Figure 3-1   The data files as they make up one or more filegroups in a database.

You can have more than one file in a filegroup, which can provide better performance through parallel reads and writes (but please test this scenario before adding too many files). Secondary data files generally have the file extension .ndf.

The real benefit comes with adding new filegroups and splitting your logical data storage across those filegroups. This makes it possible for you to do things like piecemeal backups and online restore at a filegroup level in Enterprise edition.

NOTE

Offline filegroup restore is available in Standard edition.

Inside OUT

How do I manage partial recovery using filegroups?

When designing your database, we recommend that you avoid using the primary file-group for user data. For large databases (more than 100 GB), you can separate your data into multiple filegroups based on a business rule (one per year, for instance).

Should a disaster occur, you can restore your primary filegroup and most current data immediately (using partial restore), which brings the database online much quicker than having to restore everything from a single filegroup.

You can also age-out data into a filegroup that is set to read-only and store it on slower storage than the current data, to manage storage costs better.

If you use table partitioning (see the "Table partitioning" section later in the chapter), splitting partitions across filegroups makes even more sense.

Grouping data pages with extents

SQL Server data pages are 8 KB in size. Eight of these contiguous pages is called an extent, which is 64 KB in size.

There are two types of extents in a SQL Server data file:

- **Uniform Extent.**   All eight 8-KB pages per extent are assigned to a single object.

- **Mixed Extent.**   *(Rare)* Each page in the extent is assigned to its own separate object (one 8-KB page per object).

Mixed extents were originally created to reduce storage requirements for database objects, back when mechanical hard drives were much smaller and more expensive. As storage becomes faster and cheaper, and SQL Server more complex, this causes contention (a hotspot) at the beginning of a data file, especially if a lot of small objects are being created and deleted.

Mixed extents are turned off by default for TempDB and user databases, while they are turned on by default for system databases. If you want, you can configure mixed extents on a user database by using the following command:

```
ALTER DATABASE <dbname> SET MIXED_PAGE_ALLOCATION ON;
```

Contents and types of data pages

All data pages begin with a header of 96 bytes, followed by a body containing the data itself. At the end of the page is a slot array, which fills up in reverse order, beginning with the first row, as illustrated in Figure 3-2. It instructs the Database Engine where a particular row begins on that particular page. Note that the slot array does not need to be in any particular order after the first row.

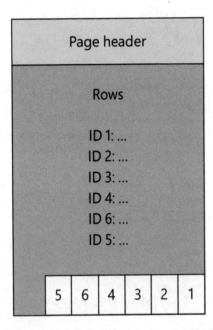

Figure 3-2   A typical 8-KB data page, showing the header, the data, and slot array.

At certain points in the data file, there are system-specific data pages (also 8 KB in size). These help SQL Server recognize and manage the different data within each file.

Several types of pages can be found in a data file:

- **Data.**   Regular data from a heap, or clustered index at the leaf level (the data itself; what you would see when querying a table).

- **Index.**   Nonclustered index data at the leaf and non-leaf level as well as clustered indexes at the non-leaf level.

- **Large object data types.**   These include text, ntext, image, nvarchar(max), varchar(max), varbinary(max), Common Language Runtime (CLR) data types, xml, and sql_variant where it exceeds 8 KB. Overflow data can also be stored here (data that has been moved "off-page" by the Database Engine), with a pointer from the original page.

- **Global Allocation Map (GAM).**   Keeps track of all free extents in a data file. There is one GAM page for every GAM interval (64,000 extents, or roughly 4 GB).

- **Shared Global Allocation Map (SGAM).**   Keeps track of all extents that can be mixed extents. It has the same interval as the GAM.

- **Page Free Space (PFS).**   Keeps track of free space inside heap and large object pages. There is one PFS page for every PFS interval (8,088 pages, or roughly 64 MB).

- **Index Allocation Map (IAM).**   Keeps track of which extents in a GAM interval belong to a particular allocation unit (an allocation unit is a bucket of pages that belong to a partition, which in turn belongs to a table). It has the same interval as the GAM. There is at least one IAM for every allocation unit. If more than one IAM belongs to an allocation unit, it forms an IAM chain.

- **Bulk Changed Map (BCM).**   Keeps track of extents that were modified by bulk-logged operations since the last full backup. It is used by transaction log backups in the bulk-logged recovery model to see which extents to back up.

- **Differential Changed Map (DCM).**   Sometimes called a *differential bitmap*. Keeps track of extents that were modified since the last full or differential backup that is used for differential backups.

- **Boot Page.**   Only one per database and contains information about the database.

- **File Header Page.**   One per data file and contains information about the file.

> To find out more about the internals of a data page, visit Microsoft Docs at *https://docs.microsoft.com/sql/relational-databases/pages-and-extents-architecture-guide*, and read Paul Randal's post, "Anatomy of a page," at *https://www.sqlskills.com/blogs/paul/inside-the-storage-engine-anatomy-of-a-page*.

CHAPTER 3

Inside OUT

What about memory-optimized objects?

Even memory-optimized objects rely on the storage subsystem (the transaction log must still be written to, though in a highly-efficient manner) and require significant IOPS (refer to Chapter 2, "Introducing database server components," to read more about storage).

Memory-optimized objects do not map to 8-KB data pages on disk the same way regular objects do. They use their own filegroup called the memory-optimized filegroup and they are implemented in a similar fashion as the FILESTREAM filegroup, in that all objects are stored in folders on the underlying file system.

All data files and delta file pairs for memory-optimized objects are stored in this memory-optimized filegroup. The file pairs record changes to the tables and are used during recovery (including when the SQL Server is restarted) to repopulate the objects in memory (if using the default SCHEMA_AND_DATA durability). You can remove the memory-optimized filegroup only by dropping a database.

You must provide four times the drive space that your memory-optimized tables require. We therefore recommend a minimum of four storage containers for this filegroup, spread across physical drives. To see more, go to *https://docs.microsoft.com/sql/ relational-databases/in-memory-oltp/the-memory-optimized-filegroup*.

Verifying data pages by using a checksum

By default, when a data page is read into the buffer pool, a checksum is automatically calculated over the entire 8-KB page and compared to the checksum stored in the page header on the drive. This is how SQL Server keeps track of page-level corruption. If the checksum stored on the drive does not match the checksum in memory, corruption has occurred. A record of this suspect page is stored in the msdb database and you will see an error message when that page is accessed.

The same checksum is performed when writing to a drive. If the checksum on the drive does not match the checksum in the data page in the buffer pool, page-level corruption has occurred.

Although the PAGE_VERIFY property on new databases is set to CHECKSUM by default, it might be necessary to check databases that have been upgraded from previous versions of SQL Server, especially those created prior to SQL Server 2005 (compatibility level 90).

You can look at the checksum verification status on all databases by using the following query:

```
SELECT name, page_verify_option_desc
```

```
FROM sys.databases;
```

You can reduce the likelihood of data page corruption by using Error-Correcting Code (ECC) memory. Data page corruption on the drive is detected by using DBCC CHECKDB and other operations.

➤ For information on how to proactively detect corruption, read the section "Database corruption" in Chapter 8, "Maintaining and monitoring SQL Server."

Recording changes in the transaction log

The transaction log is the most important component of a SQL Server database because it is where all units of work (transactions) performed on a database are recorded, before the data can be written (flushed) to the drive. The transaction log file usually has the file extension .ldf.

NOTE

Although it is possible to use more than one file to store the transaction logs for a database, we do not recommend this because there is no performance or maintenance benefit to using multiple files. To understand why and where it might be appropriate to have more than one, see the section "Inside the transaction log file with virtual log files" later in the chapter.

A successful transaction is said to be *committed*. An unsuccessful and completely reversed transaction is said to be *rolled back*.

In Chapter 2, we saw that when SQL Server needs an 8-KB data page from the data file, it usually copies it from the drive and stores a copy of this page in memory in an area called the *buffer pool* while that page is required. When a transaction needs to modify that page, it works directly on the copy of the page in the buffer pool. If the page is subsequently modified, a log record of the modification is created in the *log buffer* (also in memory), and that log record is then written to the drive.

By default, SQL Server uses a technique called Write-Ahead Logging (WAL), which ensures that no changes are written to the data file before the necessary log record is written to the drive in a permanent form (in this case, non-volatile storage).

However, you can use *delayed durability* (also known as *lazy commit*), that does not save every change to the transaction log as it happens. Instead, it waits until the log cache grows to a certain size (or sp_flushlog runs) before flushing it to the drive.

CAUTION

If you turn on delayed durability on your database, the performance benefit has a downside of potential data loss if the underlying storage layer experiences a failure before the log can be saved. Indeed, sp_flushlog should also be run before shutting down SQL Server for all databases with delayed durability enabled.

➤ You can read more about log persistence and how it affects durability of transactions in Chapter 14, "Performance tuning SQL Server", and at *https://docs.microsoft.com/sql/relational-databases/logs/control-transaction-durability*.

A transaction's outcome is unknown until a commit or rollback occurs. An error might occur during a transaction, or the operator might decide to roll back the transaction manually because the results were not as expected. In the case of a rollback, changes to the modified data pages must be undone. SQL Server will make use of the saved log records to undo the changes for an incomplete transaction.

Only when the transaction log file is written to can the modified 8-KB page be saved in the data file, though the page might be modified several times in the buffer pool before it is flushed to the drive, using a checkpoint operation.

Our guidance, therefore, is to use the fastest storage possible for the transaction log file(s), because of the low-latency requirements.

Flushing data to the storage subsystem with checkpoints

Recall from Chapter 2 that any changes to the data are written to the database file asynchronously, for performance reasons. This process is controlled by a *database checkpoint*. As its name implies, this is a database-level setting that can be changed under certain conditions by modifying the Recovery Interval or by running the CHECKPOINT command in the database context.

The checkpoint process takes all of the modified pages in the buffer pool, as well as transaction log information that is in memory, and writes that to the storage subsystem. This reduces the time it takes to recover a database because only the changes made after the latest checkpoint need to be rolled forward in the Redo phase (see the "Restarting with recovery" section later in the chapter).

Inside the transaction log file

A transaction log file is split into logical segments, called virtual log files (VLFs). These segments are dynamically allocated when the transaction log file is created and whenever the file grows. The size of each VLF is not fixed and is based on an internal algorithm, which depends on the version of SQL Server, the current file size, and file growth settings. Each VLF has a header containing a Minimum Log Sequence Number and whether it is active.

Every transaction is uniquely identified by a Log Sequence Number (LSN). Each LSN is ordered, so a later LSN will be greater than an earlier LSN. The LSN is also used by database backups and restores.

➤ **For more information see Chapter 8, and Chapter 10, "Developing, deploying, and managing data recovery."**

Figure 3-3 illustrates how the transaction log is circular. When a VLF is first allocated by creation or file growth, it is marked inactive in the VLF header. Transactions can be recorded only in active portions of the log file, so the SQL Server engine looks for inactive VLFs sequentially, and as it needs them, marks them as active to allow transactions to be recorded.

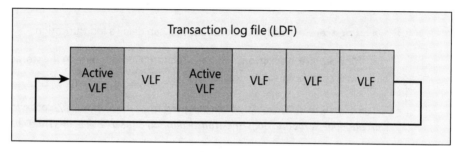

Figure 3-3   The transaction log file, showing active and inactive VLFs.

Marking a VLF inactive is called *log truncation*, but this operation does not affect the size of the physical transaction log file. It just means that an active VLF has been marked inactive and can be reused.

There are several reasons why log truncation can be delayed. After the transactions that make use of an active VLF are committed or rolled back, what happens next depends on a number of factors:

- The recovery model:

  - **Simple.**   An automatic checkpoint is queued after the recovery interval timeout is reached or if the log becomes 70 percent full.

  - **Full/bulk-logged.**   A transaction log backup must take place after a transaction is committed. A checkpoint is queued if the log backup is successful.

- Other processes that can delay log truncation:

  - **Active backup or restore.**   The transaction log cannot be truncated if it is being used by a backup or restore operation.

  - **Active transaction.**   If another transaction is using an active VLF, it cannot be truncated.

- **Database mirroring.** Mirrored changes must be synchronized before the log can be truncated. This occurs in high-performance mode or if the mirror is behind the principal database.

- **Replication.** Transactions that have not yet been delivered to the distribution database can delay log truncation.

- **Database snapshot creation.** This is usually brief, but creating snapshots (manually or through database consistency checks, for instance) can delay truncation.

- **Log scan.** Usually brief, but this, too, can delay a log truncation.

- **Checkpoint operation.** See the section "Flushing data to the storage subsystem with checkpoints" later in the chapter.

➤ To learn more, read **"Factors that can delay log truncation"** *at https://docs.microsoft.com/ sql/relational-databases/logs/the-transaction-log-sql-server#FactorsThatDelayTruncation.*

After the checkpoint is issued and the dependencies on the transaction log (as just listed) are removed, the log is truncated by marking those VLFs as inactive.

The log is accessed sequentially in this manner until it gets to the end of the file. At this point, the log wraps around to the beginning, and the Database Engine looks for an inactive VLF from the start of the file to mark active. If there are no inactive VLFs available, the log file must create new VLFs by growing in size according to the auto growth settings.

If the log file cannot grow, it will stop all operations on the database until VLFs can be reclaimed or created.

Inside OUT

What do I do if I run out of space in the transaction log file?

If a transaction log runs out of space because no inactive VLFs are available, you first must take a transaction log backup (if the database is in the full or bulk-logged recovery model). Failing that, you can grow the transaction log file. If there is insufficient space on the drive to grow the transaction log file, you can assign a second log file to the database on a different drive.

In many cases, a transaction log file runs out of space because the database is in the full or bulk-logged recovery model, and transaction log backups are not being taken regularly. We recommend that you allow transaction log files to grow automatically, with a fixed auto growth size, and to take regular transaction log backups.

If you find yourself running out of space on a regular basis due to long-running transactions, consider using shorter transactions and enabling Accelerated Database Recovery, which you can read about in "A faster recovery with Accelerated Database Recovery" section.

The Minimum Recovery LSN

When a checkpoint occurs, a log record is written to the transaction log stating that a checkpoint has commenced. After this, the Minimum Recovery LSN (MinLSN) must be recorded. This LSN is the minimum of either the LSN at the start of the checkpoint, the LSN of the oldest active transaction, or the LSN of the oldest replication transaction that hasn't been delivered to the transactional replication distribution database.

In other words, the MinLSN "...is the log sequence number of the oldest log record that is required for a successful database-wide rollback." (*https://docs.microsoft.com/sql/relational-databases/sql-server-transaction-log-architecture-and-management-guide*).

➤ To learn more about the distribution database, read the "Replication" section in Chapter 11, "Implementing high availability and disaster recovery."

This way, crash recovery knows to start recovery only at the MinLSN and can skip over any older LSNs in the transaction log if they exist.

The checkpoint also records the list of active transactions that have made changes to the database. If the database is in the simple recovery model, the unused portion of the transaction log before the MinLSN is marked for reuse. All dirty data pages and information about the transaction log are written to the storage subsystem, the end of the checkpoint is recorded in the log, and (importantly) the LSN from the start of the checkpoint is written to the boot page of the database.

NOTE

In the full and bulk-logged recovery models, a successful transaction log backup issues a checkpoint implicitly.

Types of database checkpoints

Checkpoints can be activated in a number of different scenarios. The most common is the automatic checkpoint, which is governed by the recovery interval setting (see the Inside OUT sidebar that follows to see how to modify this setting) and typically takes place approximately once every minute for active databases (those databases in which a change has occurred at all).

NOTE

Infrequently accessed databases with no transactions do not require a frequent check-point, because nothing has changed in the buffer pool.

Other checkpoint events include the following:

- Database backups (including transaction log backups)

- Database shutdowns

- Adding or removing files on a database

- SQL Server instance shutdown

- Minimally logged operations (for example, in a database in the simple or bulk-logged recovery model)

- Explicit use of the CHECKPOINT command

Inside OUT

How do you set the recovery interval?

The recovery interval "...defines an upper limit on the time recovering a database should take. The SQL Server Database Engine uses the value specified for this option to deter-mine approximately how often to issue automatic checkpoints on a given database." (*https://docs.microsoft.com/sql/database-engine/configure-windows/configure-the-recovery-interval-server-configuration-option*). You can also visit that page to learn how to configure this setting.

We recommend that you do not increase this value unless you have a very specific need. A longer recovery interval can increase database recovery time, which can affect your Recovery Time Objective (RTO).

Try to keep your transactions as short as possible, which will also improve recovery time if you have a crash and have to apply changes from the transaction log. Consider using Accelerated Database Recovery, which you can read about in the "A faster recovery with Accelerated Database Recovery" section.

You can read more about coding efficient transactions at *https://docs.microsoft.com/previous-versions/sql/sql-server-2008-r2/ms187484(v=sql.105)*.

There are four types of checkpoints that can occur:

- **Automatic.** Issued internally by the Database Engine to meet the value of the recovery interval setting at the instance level. On SQL Server 2016 and higher, the default is one minute.

- **Indirect.** Issued to meet a user-specified target recovery time at the database level, if the TARGET_RECOVERY_TIME has been set.

- **Manual.** Issued when the CHECKPOINT command is run.

- **Internal.** Issued internally by various features, such as backup and snapshot creation, to ensure consistency between the log and the drive image.

➤ **For more information about checkpoints, visit Microsoft Docs at**
https://docs.microsoft.com/sql/relational-databases/logs/database-checkpoints-sql-server.

Restarting with recovery

Whenever SQL Server starts, recovery (also referred to as crash recovery or restart recovery) takes place on every single database (on at least one thread per database, to ensure that it completes as quickly as possible) because SQL Server does not know for certain whether each database was shut down cleanly.

The transaction log is read from the latest checkpoint in the active portion of the log, or the LSN it gets from the boot page of the database (see the "The Minimum Recovery LSN" section earlier in the chapter), and scans all active VLFs looking for work to do.

All committed transactions are rolled forward (Redo portion) and then all uncommitted transactions are rolled back (Undo portion). The total number of rolled forward and rolled back transactions are recorded for each database with a respective entry in the ERRORLOG file.

SQL Server Enterprise edition brings the database online immediately after the Redo portion is complete. Other editions must wait for the Undo portion to complete before the database is brought online.

➤ **See Chapter 8 for more information about database corruption and recovery.**

The reason why we cover this in such depth in this introductory chapter is to help you to understand why drive performance is paramount when creating and allocating database files.

When a transaction log is first created or file growth occurs, the portion of the drive must be zeroed-out (the file system literally writes zeroes in every byte in that file segment).

Instant file initialization does not apply to transaction log files for this reason, so keep this in mind when growing or shrinking transaction log files. All activity in a database will stop until the file operation is complete.

As you can imagine, this can be time consuming for larger files, so you need to take care when setting file growth options, especially with transaction log files. You should measure the performance of the underlying storage layer and choose a fixed growth size that balances performance with reduced VLF count. Consider setting file growth for transaction log files in multiples of 8 GBs. At a sequential write speed of 200 MBps, this would take under a minute to grow the transaction log file.

MinLSN and the active log

As mentioned earlier, each VLF contains a header that includes an LSN and an indicator as to whether the VLF is active. The portion of the transaction log, from the VLF containing the MinLSN to the VLF containing the latest log record, is considered the active portion of the transaction log.

All records in the active log are required in order to perform a full recovery if something goes wrong. The active log must therefore include all log records for uncommitted transactions, too, which is why long-running transactions can be problematic. Replicated transactions that have not yet been delivered to the distribution database can also affect the MinLSN.

Any type of transaction that does not allow the MinLSN to increase during the normal course of events affects overall health and performance of the database environment, because the transaction log file might grow uncontrollably.

When VLFs cannot be made inactive until a long-running transaction is committed or rolled back, or if a VLF is in use by other processes (including database mirroring, availability groups, and transactional replication, for example), the log file is forced to grow. Any log backups that include these long-running transaction records will also be large. The recovery phase can also take longer because there is a much larger volume of active transactions to process.

> ➤ You can read more about transaction log file architecture at *https://docs.microsoft.com/sql/relational-databases/sql-server-transaction-log-architecture-and-management-guide*.

A faster recovery with Accelerated Database Recovery

In SQL Server 2019 and Azure SQL Database, you can enable Accelerated Database Recovery (ADR) at the database level. At a high level, ADR trades extra space in the data file for reduced space in the transaction log, and improved performance during manual transaction rollbacks and crash recovery, especially in environments where long-running transactions are common.

It introduces four components:

- **Persisted version store (PVS).**   This works in a similar way to Read Committed Snapshot Isolation (RCSI) by recording a previously committed version of a row until a transaction is committed. The main difference is that the PVS is stored in the user database and not in TempDB, which allows database-specific changes to be recorded in isolation from other instance-level operations.

- **Logical revert.**   If a long-running transaction is aborted, the versioned rows created by the PVS can be safely ignored by concurrent transactions. Additionally, upon rollback, the previous version of the row is immediately made available by releasing all locks.

- **Secondary log stream (sLog).**   The sLog is a low-volume in-memory log stream that records non-versioned operations (including lock acquisitions). It is persisted to the transaction log file during a checkpoint operation, and aggressively truncated when transactions are committed.

- **Cleaner.**   This asynchronous process periodically cleans page versions that are no longer required.

Where ADR shines is in the Redo and Undo phases of crash recovery. In the first part of the Redo phase, the sLog is processed first. Because it contains only uncommitted transactions since the last checkpoint, it is processed extremely quickly. The second part of the Redo phase begins from the last checkpoint in the transaction log, as opposed to the oldest committed transaction.

In the Undo phase, ADR is able to complete almost instantly by firstly undoing non-versioned operations recorded by the sLog, and then performing a logical revert on row-level versions in the PVS and releasing all locks.

Customers using this feature may notice faster rollbacks, a significant reduction in transaction log usage for long-running transactions, faster SQL Server startup times, and a small increase in the size of the data file for each database where this is enabled (on account of the storage required for the PVS). However, as with all features of SQL Server, we recommend that you do testing before enabling this on all production databases.

Table partitioning

SQL Server allows you to break up a table into logical units, or *partitions*, for easier management and maintenance while still treating it as a single table. All tables in SQL Server are already partitioned if you look deep enough into the internals. It just so happens that there is one logical partition per table by default.

➤ Chapter 7, "Understanding table features," goes into more detail about table partitioning.

CHAPTER 3

This concept is called *horizontal partitioning*. Suppose that a database table is growing extremely large, and adding new rows is time consuming. You might decide to split the table into groups of rows, based on a partitioning key (typically a date column), with each group in its own partition. In turn, you can store these in different filegroups to improve read and write performance.

Breaking up a table into logical partitions can also result in a query optimization called *partition elimination*, by which only the partition that contains the data you need is queried. However, it was not designed primarily as a performance feature. Partitioning tables will not automatically result in better query performance, and, in fact, performance might be worse due to other factors, specifically around statistics.

Even so, there are some major advantages to table partitioning, which benefit large datasets, specifically around rolling windows and moving data in and out of the table. This process is called *partition switching*, by which you can switch data into and out of a table almost instantly.

Assume that you need to load data into a table every month and then make it available for querying. With table partitioning, you put the data that you want to insert into a completely separate table in the same database, which has the same structure and clustered index as the main table. Then, a switch operation moves that data into the partitioned table almost instantly because no data movement is needed.

This makes it very easy to manage large groups of data or data that ages-out at regular intervals (sliding windows) because partitions can be switched out nearly immediately.

Inside OUT

Should you use partitioned tables or partitioned views?

Because table partitioning is available in all editions of SQL Server, you might find it an attractive option for smaller databases. However, it might be more prudent to use partitioned views instead.

Partitioned views make use of a database view that is a union query against a group of underlying tables. Instead of querying a partitioned table directly, you would query the view.

Using key constraints on the primary key for each base table still allows the query optimizer to use "partition" elimination (base table elimination). Performance-wise, moving data in and out of the partitioned view would be almost instantaneous because you need to update only the view itself to add or remove a particular base table.

Compressing data

SQL Server supports several types of data compression to reduce the amount of drive space required for data and backups, as a trade-off against higher CPU utilization.

➤ You can read more about data compression in Microsoft Docs at *https://docs.microsoft.com/sql/relational-databases/data-compression/data-compression*.

In general, the amount of CPU overhead required to perform compression and decompression depends on the type of data involved, and in the case of data compression, the type of queries running against the database, as well. Even though the higher CPU load might be offset by the savings in I/O, we always recommend testing before implementing this feature.

Table and index compression

SQL Server provides two main ways to reduce the amount of storage required for data in tables and indexes. We discuss compressing *rowstore* data in this section. You can read more about *columnstore* indexes in Chapter 15, "Understanding and designing indexes."

NOTE

SQL Server 2019 introduces a new collation type, UTF-8, which may improve storage of Latin-based strings. See Chapter 7 for more information.

Row compression

You turn on row compression at the table or index level. Each column in a row is evaluated according to the type of data and contents of that column, as follows:

- Numeric data types (such as integer, decimal, floating point, datetime, money, and their derived types) are stored as variable length at the physical layer.

- Fixed-length character data types are stored as variable length strings, where the blank trailing characters are not stored.

- Variable length data types, including large objects, are not affected by row compression.

- Bit columns actually take up more space due to associated metadata.

Row compression can be useful for tables with fixed-length character data types and where numeric types are overprovisioned (e.g., a `bigint` column that contains mostly `int` values). Unicode compression alone can save between 15 and 50 percent, depending on your locale and collation.

➤ You can read more about row compression in Microsoft Docs at *https://docs.microsoft.com/sql/relational-databases/data-compression/row-compression-implementation*.

Page compression

You turn on page compression at the table level, but it operates on all data pages associated with that table, including indexes, table partitions, and index partitions. Leaf-level pages (see Figure 3-4) are compressed using three steps:

1. Row compression
2. Prefix compression
3. Dictionary compression

Non-leaf-level pages are compressed using row compression only. This is for performance reasons.

Inside OUT

What is the difference between leaf-level and non-leaf-level pages?

Clustered and nonclustered indexes in SQL Server are stored in a structure known as a B+ tree. The tree has a root node, which fans out to child nodes, with the data itself at the leaf level.

Any nodes that appear between the root and leaf levels are called intermediate, or non-leaf-level nodes. Data in the leaf level is accessed (through a seek or a scan operation) by using page identifiers in the root and intermediate levels, which contain pointers to the respective starting key values in the leaf level. When the leaf level is reached, the slot array at the end of each page contains a pointer to the exact row.

Figure 3-4 presents an example of a clustered index.

➤ You can read more about indexes in Chapter 7 and Chapter 15. To learn more about index structures, visit *https://docs.microsoft.com/sql/relational-databases/sql-server-index-design-guide*.

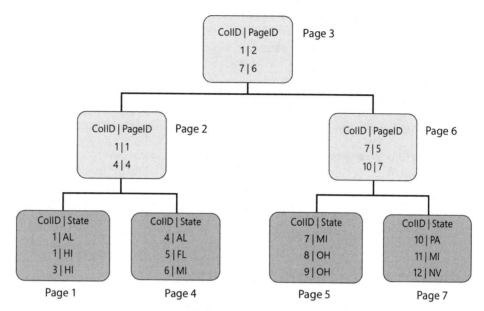

Figure 3-4   A small clustered index with leaf and non-leaf levels, clustered on ColID.

Prefix compression works per column, by searching for a common prefix in each column. A row is created just below the page header, called the compression information (CI) structure, containing a single row of each column with its own prefix.

If any of a column's rows on the page match the prefix, its value is replaced by a reference to that column's prefix.

Dictionary compression then searches across the entire page, looking for repeating values, irrespective of the column, and stores these in the CI structure. When a match is found, the column value in that row is replaced with a reference to the compressed value.

If a data page is not full, it will be compressed using only row compression. If the size of the compressed page along with the size of the CI structure is not significantly smaller than the uncompressed page, no page compression will be performed on that page.

Backup compression

Whereas page-level and row-level compression operate at the table level, backup compression applies to the backup file for the entire database.

Compressed backups are usually smaller than uncompressed backups, which means fewer drive I/O operations are involved, which in turn means a reduction in the time it takes to perform a backup or restore. For larger databases, this can have a dramatic effect on the time it takes to recover from a disaster.

Backup compression ratio is affected by the type of data involved, whether the database is encrypted, and whether the data is already compressed. In other words, a database making use of page and/or row compression might not gain any benefit from backup compression.

The CPU can be limited for backup compression in Resource Governor (you can read more about Resource Governor in the section "Configuration settings" later in the chapter, and in more detail in Chapter 8).

In most cases, we recommend turning on backup compression, keeping in mind that you might need to monitor CPU utilization.

Managing the temporary database

TempDB is the working area of every database on the instance, and there is only one TempDB per instance. SQL Server uses this temporary database for a number of things that are mostly invisible to you, including temporary tables, table variables, triggers, cursors, sorting, version data for snapshot isolation and read-committed snapshot isolation, index creation, user-defined functions, and many more.

Additionally, when performing queries with operations that don't fit in memory (the buffer pool and the buffer pool extension), these operations spill to the drive, requiring the use of TempDB.

Storage options for TempDB

Every time SQL Server restarts, TempDB is cleared out. If the files don't exist, they are recreated. If the files are configured at a size that is different from their last active size, they will automatically be resized. Like the database file structure described earlier, there is usually one TempDB transaction log file, and one or more data files in a single filegroup.

Performance is critical for TempDB, even more than with other databases, to the point that the current recommendation is to use your fastest storage for TempDB, before using it for user database transaction log files.

Where possible, use solid-state storage for TempDB. If you have a Failover Cluster Instance, have TempDB on local storage on each node.

Starting with SQL Server 2019, TempDB can store certain metadata in memory-optimized tables for increased performance.

Inside OUT

How does memory-optimized metadata make TempDB faster?

SQL Server 2019 introduces a feature where the system tables used for managing the metadata for temporary objects can be converted to in-memory tables, reducing contention on this metadata. This means that temporary objects can be created, modified and destroyed much faster due to better concurrency.

You can enable this feature at the instance level using the following command, and restarting SQL Server:

```
ALTER SERVER CONFIGURATION SET MEMORY_OPTIMIZED TEMPDB_METADATA = ON;
```

To read more about this feature, including the limitations around transactions and columnstore indexes, visit *https://docs.microsoft.com/sql/relational-databases/databases/tempdb-database?#memory-optimized-tempdb-metadata.*

Recommended number of files

As with every database, only one transaction log file should exist for TempDB.

For physical and virtual servers, the default number of TempDB data files recommended by SQL Server Setup should match the number of logical processor cores, up to a maximum of eight, keeping in mind that your logical core count includes symmetrical multithreading (for example, Hyper-Threading). Adding more TempDB data files than the number of logical processor cores rarely results in positive performance. Adding too many TempDB data files could in fact severely harm SQL Server performance.

> ➤ You can read more about processors in Chapter 2.

Increasing the number of files to eight (and other factors) reduces TempDB contention when allocating temporary objects. If the instance has more than eight logical processors allocated, you can test to see whether adding more files helps performance, and is very much dependent on the workload.

You can allocate the TempDB data files together on the same volume (see the "Types of storage" section in Chapter 2), provided that the underlying storage layer is able to meet the low-latency demands of TempDB on your instance. If you plan to share the storage with other database files, keep latency and IOPS in mind.

Inside OUT

Do you need Trace Flags 1118 and 1117 for TempDB?

On versions prior to SQL Server 2016, Trace Flag 1118 turned off mixed extents at the instance level, which reduced contention when creating and deleting many temporary objects. Trace Flag 1117 ensured that all files allocated to any database grew at the same rate.

Because trace flags are instance-wide, it meant that all databases were affected by these trace flags, even though they mainly benefited TempDB.

Since SQL Server 2016, these trace flags have no effect. Instead, uniform extents are turned on by default for TempDB (MIXED_PAGE_ALLOCATION was mentioned previously in this chapter), as is the setting to autogrow all files at the same time.

Configuration settings

SQL Server has scores of settings that you can tune to your particular workload. There are also best practices regarding the appropriate settings (such as file growth, memory settings, and parallelism). We cover some of these in this section.

> ➤ Chapter 4, "Provisioning databases," contains additional configuration settings for provisioning databases.

Managing system usage with Resource Governor

Using Resource Governor, you can specify limits on resource consumption at the application-session level. You can configure these in real time, which allows for flexibility in managing workloads without affecting other workloads on the system.

> ➤ You can find out more about Resource Governor in Chapter 8.

A resource pool represents the *physical resources* of an instance, which means that you can think of a resource pool itself as a mini SQL Server instance. To make the best use of Resource Governor, it is helpful to logically group similar workloads together into a *workload group* so that you can manage them under a specific resource pool.

This is done via *classification*, which looks at the incoming application session's characteristics. That incoming session will be categorized into a workload group based on your criteria. This facilitates fine-grained resource usage that reduces the impact of certain workloads on other, more critical workloads.

CAUTION

There is a lot of flexibility and control in classification because Resource Governor supports user-defined functions (UDFs), allowing you to use system functions and even tables to classify sessions. This means that a poorly written UDF can render the system unusable. Always test classifier functions and optimize them for performance. If you need to troubleshoot a classifier function, use the Dedicated Administrator Connection (DAC) because it is not subject to classification.

For example, a reporting application might have a negative impact on database performance due to resource contention at certain times of the day, so by classifying it into a specific workload group, you can limit the amount of memory or disk I/O that reporting application can use, reducing its effect on, say, a month-end process that needs to run at the same time.

Configuring the operating system page file

Operating systems use a portion of the storage subsystem for a page file (also known as a swap file, or swap partition on Linux) for virtual memory for all applications, including SQL Server, when available memory is not sufficient for the current working set. It does this by offloading (paging out) segments of RAM to the drive. Because storage is slower than memory (see Chapter 2), data that has been paged out is also slower when working from the system page file.

The page file also serves the role of capturing a system memory dump for crash forensic analysis, a factor that dictates its size on modern operating systems with large amounts of memory. This is why the general recommendation for the system page file is that it should be at least the same size as the server's amount of physical memory.

Another general recommendation is that the page file should be managed by the operating system. For Windows Server, this should be set to System Managed, and, since Windows Server 2012, that guideline has functioned well. However, in servers with large amounts of memory, this can result in a very large page file, so be aware of that if the page file is located on your operating system (OS) volume. This is also why the page file is often moved to its own volume, away from the OS volume.

On a dedicated SQL Server instance, you can set the page file to a fixed size, relative to the amount of Max Server Memory assigned to SQL Server. In principle, the database instance will use up as much RAM as you allow it, to that Max Server Memory limit, so Windows will preferably not need to page SQL Server out of RAM. On Linux, the swap partition can be left at the default size, or reduced to 80% of the physical RAM, whichever is lower.

NOTE

If the *Lock pages in memory* policy is on (recommended on a physical Windows-based server only), SQL Server will not be forced to page out of memory, and you can set the

CHAPTER 3

page file to a smaller size. This can free up valuable space on the OS drive, which can be beneficial to the OS.

➤ For more about *Lock pages in memory*, see the section by the same name later in this chapter.

Taking advantage of logical processors by using parallelism

SQL Server is designed to run on multiple logical processors (for more information, refer to the section "Central Processing Unit" in Chapter 2).

➤ You can find out more about parallel query plans in Chapter 14.

In SQL Server, parallelism makes it possible for portions of a query (or the entire query) to run on more than one logical processor at the same time. This has certain performance advantages for larger queries, because the workload can be split more evenly across resources. There is an implicit overhead with running queries in parallel, however, because a controller thread must manage the results from each logical processor and then combine them when each thread is completed.

The SQL Server query optimizer uses a *cost-based optimizer* when coming up with query plans. This means that it makes certain assumptions about the performance of the storage, CPU and memory, and how they relate to different query plan operators. Each operation has a cost associated with it.

SQL Server will consider creating parallel plan operations, governed by two parallelism settings: *Cost threshold for parallelism* and *Max degree of parallelism*. These two settings can make a world of difference to the performance of a SQL Server instance if it is using default settings.

Query plan costs are recorded in a *unitless* measure. In other words, the cost bears *no relation* to resources such as drive latency, IOPS, number of seconds, memory usage, or CPU power, which can make query tuning difficult without keeping this in mind. What matters is the *magnitude* of this measure.

Cost threshold for parallelism

This is the minimum cost a query plan can be before the optimizer will even consider parallel query plans. If the cost of a query plan exceeds this value, the query optimizer will take parallelism into account when coming up with a query plan. This does not necessarily mean that every plan with a higher cost is run across parallel processor cores, but the chances are increased.

The default setting for cost threshold for parallelism is 5. Any query plan with a cost of 5 or higher will be considered for parallelism. Given how much faster and more powerful modern server processors are than when this setting was first created, many queries will run just fine on a single core, again because of the overhead associated with parallel plans.

Inside OUT

Why doesn't Microsoft change the defaults?

Microsoft is reticent to change default values, because of its strong support of backward compatibility. There are many applications in use today that are no longer supported by their original creators that might depend on default settings in Microsoft products. Besides, if it is a best practice to change the default settings when setting up a new instance of SQL Server, it does not make much of a difference either way.

NOTE

Certain query operations can force some or all of a query plan to run serially, even if the plan cost exceeds the cost threshold for parallelism. Paul White's article "Forcing a Parallel Query Execution Plan" describes a few of these. You can read Paul's article at *https://www.sql.kiwi/2011/12/forcing-a-parallel-query-execution-plan.html*.

It might be possible to write a custom process to tune the cost threshold for parallelism setting automatically, using information from the Query Store. Because the Query Store works at the database level, it helps identify the average cost of queries per database and find an appropriate setting for the cost threshold relative to your specific workload.

> ➤ See more about the Query Store in the "Using the Query Store Feature" section in Chapter 14.

Until we get to an autotuning option, you can set the cost threshold for parallelism to 50 as a starting point for new instances, and then monitor the average execution plan costs, to adjust this value up or down (and you should adjust this value based on your own workload).

Cost threshold for parallelism is an advanced server setting; you can change it by using the command sp_configure 'cost threshold for parallelism'. You can also change it in SQL Server Management Studio by using the Cost Threshold For Parallelism setting, which can be found in the Advanced page of the Server Properties dialog.

Max degree of parallelism

SQL Server uses this value, also known as MAXDOP, to select the maximum number of logical processors to run a parallel query plan when the cost threshold for parallelism is reached.

The default setting for MAXDOP is 0, which instructs SQL Server to make use of all available logical processors to run a parallel query (taking processor affinity into account—see later in this chapter).

The problem with this default setting for most workloads is twofold:

- Parallel queries can consume all resources, preventing smaller queries from running or forcing them to run slowly while they find time in the CPU scheduler.

- If all logical processors are allocated to a plan, it can result in foreign memory access, which, as we explain in Chapter 2 in the "Non-Uniform Memory Access (NUMA)" section, carries a performance penalty.

Specialized workloads can have different requirements for the MAXDOP. For standard or Online Transaction Processing (OLTP) workloads, to make better use of modern server resources, the MAXDOP setting must take NUMA nodes into account:

- **Single NUMA node.**   With up to eight logical processors on a single node, the recommended value should be set to 0 or the number of cores. With more than eight logical processors, the recommended value should be set to 8.

- **Multiple NUMA nodes.**   With up to 16 logical processors on a single node, the recommended value should be set to 0 or the number of cores. With more than 16 logical processors, the recommended value should be set to 16.

➤ **For more recommendations about MAXDOP, visit Microsoft Support at** *https://support.microsoft.com/help/2806535.*

MAXDOP is an advanced server setting; you can change it by using the command `sp_configure 'max degree of parallelism'`. You can also change it in SQL Server Management Studio by using the Max Degree Of Parallelism setting, in the Advanced page of the Server Properties dialog.

SQL Server memory settings

Since SQL Server 2012, the artificial memory limits imposed by the license for lower editions (Standard, Web, and Express) apply to the buffer pool only (see *https://docs.microsoft.com/sql/ sql-server/editions-and-components-of-sql-server-version-15*).

This is not the same thing as the Max Server Memory, though. According to Microsoft Docs, the Max Server Memory setting controls all of SQL Server's memory allocation, which includes, but is not limited to the buffer pool, compile memory, caches, memory grants, and CLR (Common Language Runtime, or .NET) memory (*https://docs.microsoft.com/sql/ database-engine/configure-windows/server-memory-server-configuration-options*).

Additionally, limits to columnstore and memory-optimized object memory are over and above the buffer pool limit on non-Enterprise editions, which gives you a greater opportunity to make use of available physical memory.

This makes memory management for non-Enterprise editions more complicated, but certainly more flexible, especially taking columnstore and memory-optimized objects into account.

Max Server Memory

As noted in Chapter 2, SQL Server uses as much memory as you allow it. Therefore, you want to limit the amount of memory that each SQL Server instance can control on the server, ensuring that you leave enough system memory for the following:

- The OS itself (see the algorithm below).

- Other SQL Server instances installed on the server.

- Other SQL Server features installed on the server; for example, SQL Server Reporting Services, SQL Server Analysis Services, or SQL Server Integration Services.

- Remote desktop sessions and locally run administrative applications like SQL Server Management Studio (SSMS) and Azure Data Studio.

- Antimalware programs.

- System monitoring or remote management applications.

- Any additional applications that might be installed and running on the server (including web browsers).

CAUTION

If you connect to your SQL Server instance via a remote desktop session, make sure that you have a secure VPN connection in place.

The appropriate Max Server Memory setting will vary from server to server. A good starting point for the reduction from the total server memory is 10 percent less, or 4 GB less than the server's total memory capacity, whichever is the greater reduction (but see *OS reservation* later in this section for a more detailed recommendation). For a dedicated SQL Server instance and 16 GB of total memory, an initial value of 12 GB (or a value of 12288 in MB) for Max Server Memory is appropriate.

NOTE

SQL Server is supported on servers with as little as 4 GB of RAM, in which case a Max Server Memory value of 2,048 MB is recommended.

OS reservation

Jonathan Kehayias has published the following algorithm that can help with reserving the appropriate amount of RAM for the OS itself. Whatever remains can then be used for other processes, including SQL Server by means of Max Server Memory:

CHAPTER 3

- 1 GB of RAM for the OS

- Add 1 GB for each 4 GB of RAM installed, from 4 to 16 GB

- Add 1 GB for every 8 GB RAM installed, above 16 GB RAM

➤ **To learn more, read Kehayias, J and Kruger, T, *Troubleshooting SQL Server: A Guide for the Accidental DBA* (Redgate Books, 2011).**

Assuming that a server has 256 GB of available RAM, this requires a reservation of 35 GB for the OS. The remaining 221 GB can then be split between SQL Server and anything else that is running on the server.

Performance Monitor to the rescue

Ultimately, the best way to see if the correct value is assigned to Max Server Memory is to monitor the `Memory\Available MBytes` value in Performance Monitor. This way, you can ensure that Windows Server has enough working set of its own and adjust Max Server Memory downward if this value drops below 300 MB.

➤ **Performance Monitor is covered in more detail in Chapter 14.**

Max Server Memory is an advanced server setting; you can change it by using the command `sp_configure 'max server memory'`. You can also change it in SQL Server Management Studio by using the Max Server Memory setting, in the Server Properties section of the Memory node.

Max Worker Threads

Every process on SQL Server requires a *thread*, or time on a logical processor, including network access, database checkpoints, and user threads. Threads are managed internally by the SQL Server scheduler, one for each logical processor, and only one thread is processed at a time by each scheduler on its respective logical processor.

These threads consume memory, which is why it's generally a good idea to let SQL Server manage the maximum number of threads allowed automatically.

However, in certain special cases, changing this value from the default of 0 might help performance tuning. The default of 0 means that SQL Server will dynamically assign a value when starting, depending on the number of logical processors and other resources.

To check whether your server is currently under CPU pressure, run the following query, which returns one row per CPU core:

```
SELECT AVG(runnable_tasks_count)
```

```
FROM sys.dm_os_schedulers

WHERE status = 'VISIBLE ONLINE';
```

➤ Glenn Berry provides a history in one-minute increments using this same DMV at *https:// sqlserverperformance.wordpress.com/2010/04/20/a-dmv-a-day-%e2%80%93-day-21/*

If the number of tasks is consistently high (in the double digits), your server is under CPU pressure. You can mitigate this in a number of other ways that you should consider before increasing the number of Max Worker Threads.

In some scenarios, lowering the number of Max Worker Threads can improve performance.

➤ You can read more about setting Max Worker Threads on Microsoft Docs at *https:// docs.microsoft.com/sql/database-engine/configure-windows/configure-the-max-worker-threads-server-configuration-option.*

Lock pages in memory

The *Lock pages in memory* policy prevents Windows from taking memory away from applications such as SQL Server in low memory conditions, which can cause instability if you use it incorrectly. You can mitigate the danger of OS instability by carefully aligning Max Server Memory capacity for any installed SQL Server features (discussed earlier) and reducing the competition for memory resource from other applications.

When reducing memory pressure in virtualized systems, it is also important to avoid over-allocating memory to guests on the virtual host. Meanwhile, locking pages in memory can still prevent the paging of SQL Server memory to the drive due to memory pressure, which is a significant performance hit.

➤ For a more in-depth explanation of the Lock pages in memory policy, see Chapter 2.

Optimize for ad hoc workloads

Ad hoc queries are defined, in this context, as queries that are run only once. Applications and reports should be running the same queries many times, and SQL Server recognizes them and caches them over time.

By default, SQL Server caches the runtime plan for a query after the first time it runs, with the expectation of using it again and saving the compilation cost for future runs. For ad hoc queries though, these cached plans will never be reused yet will remain in cache.

When Optimize For Ad Hoc Workloads is set to True, a plan will not be cached until it is recognized to have been called twice (in other words, it will cache the full plan on the second execution). The third and all ensuing times it is run would then benefit from the cached runtime plan. Therefore, it is recommended that you set this option to True.

CHAPTER 3

For most workloads, the scenario in which plans might only ever run exactly twice is unrealistic, as is the scenario in which there is a high reuse of plans.

NOTE

Enabling Forced Parameterization at the database level can force query plans to be parameterized even if they are considered unique by the query optimizer, which then can reduce the number of unique plans. Provided you test this scenario, you can get better performance using this feature in combination with Optimize For Ad Hoc Workloads.

This is an advanced server setting; you can change it by using the command `sp_configure 'optimize for ad hoc workloads'`. You can also change it in SQL Server Management Studio by using the Optimize For Ad Hoc Workloads setting, in the Advanced page of the Server Properties dialog.

Allocating CPU cores with an affinity mask

It is possible to assign certain logical processors to SQL Server. This might be necessary on systems that are used for instance stacking (more than one SQL Server instance installed on the same OS) or when workloads are shared between SQL Server and other software.

SQL Server on Linux does not support instance stacking, and virtual consumers (virtual machines or containers) are probably a better way of allocating these resources, but there might be legitimate or legacy reasons for setting core affinity.

Suppose that you have a dual-socket NUMA server, with both CPUs populated by 16-core processors. Excluding simultaneous multithreading (SMT), this is a total of 32 cores, and SQL Server Standard edition is limited to 24 cores, or four sockets, whichever is lower.

When it starts, SQL Server will allocate all 16 cores from the first NUMA node, and eight from the second NUMA node. It will write an entry to the ERRORLOG stating this case, and that's where it ends. Unless you know about the core limit, you will be stuck with unbalanced CPU core and memory access, resulting in unpredictable performance.

One way to solve this without using a VM or container, is to limit 12 cores from each CPU to SQL Server, using an affinity mask (see Figure 3-5). This way, the cores are allocated evenly and combined with a reasonable MAXDOP setting of 8, foreign memory access is not a concern.

NOTE

I/O affinity allows you to assign specific CPU cores to I/O operations, which may be beneficial on enterprise-level hardware with more than 16 CPU cores. You can read more in Microsoft Support at *https://support.microsoft.com/help/298402*.

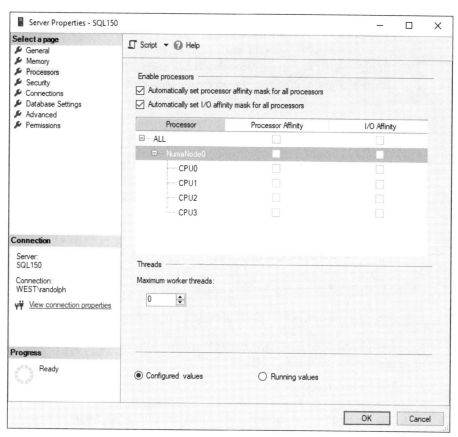

Figure 3-5   Setting the affinity mask in SQL Server Management Studio.

By setting an affinity mask, you are instructing SQL Server to use only specific cores. The remaining unused cores are marked as offline to SQL Server. When SQL Server starts, it will assign a scheduler to each online core.

> ## Inside OUT
>
> ### How do you balance schedulers across processors if you limit affinity?
>
> When no affinity is set, SQL Server doesn't assign schedulers to specific cores. With affinity set, it is possible that an external process (i.e., outside of SQL Server) is also bound to a particular core. This can result in queries being blocked by that external process.
>
> To avoid this unexpected behavior, you can use Trace Flag 8002, which lets SQL Server decide which core the scheduler will use to run your query.

For more information about this potential issue, you can read Klaus Aschenbrenner's article "Setting a Processor Affinity in SQL Server – the (unwanted) Side-Effects," which is available at *https://www.sqlpassion.at/archive/2017/10/02/ setting-a-processor-affinity-in-sql-server-the-unwanted-side-effects/*.

CAUTION

Affinity masking is not a legitimate way to circumvent licensing limitations with SQL Server Standard edition. If you have more cores than the maximum usable by a certain edition, all logical cores on that machine must be licensed.

Configuring affinity on Linux

For SQL Server on Linux, even when an instance is going to be using all of the logical processors, you should use the ALTER SERVER CONFIGURATION option to set the PROCESS AFFINITY value, which maintains efficient behavior between the Linux OS and the SQL Server Scheduler.

You can set the affinity by CPU or NUMA node, but the NUMA method is simpler.

Suppose that you have four NUMA nodes. You can use the configuration option to set the affinity to use all the NUMA nodes as follows:

```
ALTER SERVER CONFIGURATION SET PROCESS AFFINITY NUMANODE = 0 TO 3;
```

➤ You can read more about best practices for configuring SQL Server on Linux at *https://docs.microsoft.com/sql/linux/sql-server-linux-performance-best-practices*.

File system configuration

This section primarily deals with the default file system on Windows Server. Any references to other file systems, including Linux file systems are noted separately.

The NT File System (NTFS) was originally created for the first version of Windows NT, bringing with it more granular security than the older File Allocation Table (FAT)-based file system as well as a journaling file system (think of it as a transaction log for your file system). You can configure a number of settings that deal with NTFS in some way to improve your SQL Server implementation and performance.

Instant file initialization

As stated previously in this chapter, transaction log files need to be zeroed out at the file system in order for recovery to work properly. However, data files are different, and with their 8-KB page size and allocation rules, the underlying file might contain sections of unused space.

CHAPTER 3

With instant file initialization (IFI), a feature enabled by the Active Directory policy *Perform volume maintenance tasks*, data files can be instantly resized without zeroing-out the underlying file. This adds a major performance boost.

The trade-off is a tiny, perhaps insignificant security risk: data that was previously used in drive allocation currently dedicated to a database's data file now might not have been fully erased before use. Because you can examine the underlying bytes in data pages using built-in tools in SQL Server, individual pages of data that have not yet been overwritten inside the new allocation could be visible to a malicious administrator.

NOTE

It is important to control access to SQL Server's data files and backups. When a database is in use by SQL Server, only the SQL Server service account and the local administrator have access. However, if the database is detached or backed up, there is an opportunity to view that deleted data on the detached file or backup file that was created with instant file initialization turned on.

Because this is a possible security risk, the *Perform volume maintenance tasks* policy is not granted to the SQL Server service by default, and a summary of this warning is displayed during SQL Server setup.

Without IFI, you might find that the SQL Server wait type PREEMPTIVE_OS_WRITEFILEGATHER is prevalent during times of data-file growth. This wait type occurs when a file is being zero-initialized; thus, it can be a sign that your SQL Server is wasting time that could skipped with the benefit of IFI. Keep in mind that PREEMPTIVE_OS_WRITEFILEGATHER will also be generated by transaction log files, which do not benefit from IFI.

Note that SQL Server Setup takes a slightly different approach to granting this privilege than SQL Server administrators might take. SQL Server assigns Access Control Lists (ACLs) to automatically created security groups, not to the service accounts that you select on the Server Configuration Setup page. Instead of granting the privilege to the named SQL Server service account directly, SQL Server grants the privilege to the per-service security identifier (SID) for the SQL Server database service; for example, the NT SERVICE\MSSQLSERVER principal. This means that the SQL Server service will maintain the ability to use IFI even if its service account changes.

You can determine whether the SQL Server Database Engine service has been granted access to IFI by using the sys.dm_server_services dynamic management view via the following query:

```
SELECT servicename, instant_file_initialization_enabled

FROM sys.dm_server_services

WHERE filename LIKE '%sqlservr.exe%';
```

If IFI was not configured during SQL Server setup, and you want to do so later, go to the Windows Start menu, and then, in the Search box, type **Local Security Policy**. Next, in the pane on the left expand Local Policies (see Figure 3-6), and then click User Rights Assignment. Find the Perform Volume Maintenance Tasks policy, and then add the SQL Server service account to the list of objects with that privilege.

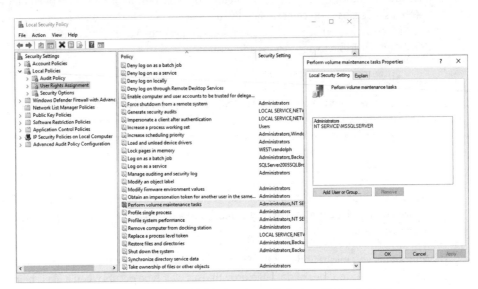

Figure 3-6   Turning on instant file initialization through the Local Security Policy setup page.

NTFS allocation unit size

SQL Server performs best with an allocation unit size of 64 KB.

Depending on the type of storage, the default allocation unit on NTFS might be 512 bytes, 4,096 bytes (also known as Advanced Format 4K sector size), or some other multiple of 512.

Because SQL Server deals with 64-KB extents (see the section "Mixed extents and uniform extents" earlier in the chapter), it makes sense to format a data volume with an allocation unit size of 64 KB, to align the extents with the allocation units. This applies to the Resilient File System (ReFS) on Windows Server, and XFS and ext4 file systems on Linux.

> NOTE
>
> **We cover aligned storage in more detail in Chapter 4.**

Container orchestration with Kubernetes

Kubernetes is a *container orchestration system* that was initially developed by Google. Processes like fault tolerance, workload schedule, and even networking, are all provided by the management layer of Kubernetes.

One of the reasons Kubernetes (also known as K8s, because there are eight letters between the *K* and the *s*) has become a staple in modern data centers is its flexibility in container orchestration and management. It provides enterprise-level infrastructure functionality to the container development process favored by most DevOps organizations, making it the "operating system for the data center" as coined by Google.

Let's use the analogy of an actual orchestra, comprising a conductor, instrument sections, musicians, their instruments, and their sheet music. While no analogy is perfect, this might help you picture things more easily. At the bottom are your musical instruments. Each instrument needs to be played by a musician, guided by their sheet music. Groups of musicians play together in a section. Finally, the conductor oversees the entire performance. In our analogy, Kubernetes is the conductor, and containers are the instruments. Clusters are the instrument families, like the string section or the brass section, and musicians are the pods with their sheet music.

➤ We introduced containers in the section on virtualization in Chapter 2.

CHAPTER 3

Inside OUT

What is the difference between a cluster, a node, and a pod?

Kubernetes clusters consist of two types of nodes: *masters* and *workers*. The master nodes run cluster operations and schedule work, while the worker nodes run the container workloads. While the lowest unit of deployment is a container, it is important to note that containers are always deployed into higher level pods. Pods provide location affinity within the cluster, meaning that dependent workloads are deployed together.

Kubernetes relies on a software-defined infrastructure (the sheet music in our analogy). When you deploy your containers, you use a YAML (a recursive acronym standing for "YAML Ain't Markup Language") file that defines:

- The container image you are using

- Any storage that you are persisting

- The container CPU and memory configuration of the pod

- The networking configuration

- Other metadata about the deployment

The deployment manifest is converted from YAML to JSON by `kubectl`, and then deployed to the Kubernetes API where it is parsed and then deployed into a key-value store (called `etcd`) that stores the cluster metadata. The objects in the manifest are deployed in their respective pods, services, and storage. The cluster controller (part of the *control plane*) ensures that the manifest is running and is in a healthy application state, and redeploys the manifest in the event of node failure or an unhealthy application state. The cluster will always attempt to maintain the desired state of the configuration, as defined in the deployed manifests.

Inside OUT

What is the Kubernetes control plane?

The Kubernetes control plane is a set of processes and pods that control cluster management. These services record all of the Kubernetes objects in the system and execute the desired state configuration for all objects within the cluster.

Kubernetes support for SQL Server

Microsoft introduced support for Kubernetes after the release of SQL Server 2017 (see Figure 3-7). Early releases of Kubernetes lacked support for persisted storage, which is an obvious problem for database containers. The implementation uses a Kubernetes service to act as a persisted front-end name and IP address for the container. In this scenario, if the pod fails, the service stays running, and a new copy of the pod is launched and then pointed at the persisted storage. This is nearly analogous to the architecture of a SQL Server Failover Cluster Instance (FCI).

➤ Refer to Chapter 2 for a more in-depth discussion on FCIs.

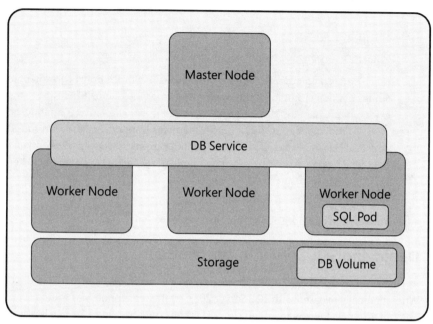

Figure 3-7   SQL Server on Kubernetes Architecture.

The SQL Server 2017 Kubernetes deployment provides for just a single container per SQL Server pod. SQL Server 2019 may include other services in the pod deployment. Services provide load balancing and persistent IP addressing, while *Persistent Volume Claims* ensure that storage is persisted across container failures or node movement. By defining a `PersistentVolumeClaim`, you are aligning a specific disk volume to your pod deployment to persist data files.

Recent releases of both Kubernetes and Windows Server allow for Kubernetes to support both Windows nodes and Windows containers, but SQL Server Big Data Clusters (BDC) currently only support containers on Linux. Kubernetes is also much more broadly used on Linux, so community support will be much more prevalent on that platform.

> ➤ You can learn more about Kubernetes from the following books: *The Kubernetes Book* (2019), by Nigel Poulton; and *Kubernetes: Up and Running* (2019), by Kelsey Hightower, Brendan Burns, *et al.*

BDC licensing offers some flexibility compared to traditional SQL Server core licensing. With Software Assurance on Enterprise edition, you can use those core licenses for your master instance node, and you will get eight BDC core node licenses for every master instance core.

> ➤ You can download the SQL Server 2019 licensing guide in PDF format directly from *https://aka.ms/sql2019licenseguide.*

Inside OUT

What is OpenShift?

Many organizations deploy open source software with a support agreement in place. Some common examples of this are Red Hat Enterprise Linux (RHEL) and Percona for MySQL databases. Red Hat has also introduced its own Kubernetes offering called OpenShift. While OpenShift is mainly core Kubernetes components, it also introduces some additional tooling into the space for licensed customers, specifically a project called Istio, which offers a service mesh management layer across Kubernetes clusters.

➤ You can find out more about RHEL in Chapter 5.

Deploying SQL Server in containers

As we mentioned previously, SQL Server runs on Windows, Linux, and in Docker containers. When originally released with SQL Server 2017, container support was touted for use in development. After all, there was limited support in the container world for persisted storage at the time, and SQL Server lacked support for an enterprise orchestration framework like Kubernetes. While database containers still make for a fantastic development environment, the future support in SQL Server for availability groups, Active Directory authentication (not yet available at the time of writing), and Big Data Clusters, means that container deployment is quickly becoming an option for production workloads as well.

➤ You can read more about availability groups in Chapter 11.

Getting started with SQL Server in a Docker container

One of the biggest attractions of running SQL Server in a container is that your choice of operating system does not matter. While the container images of SQL Server use Linux as their base, your host machine can run Windows, Linux, or macOS. First, you will need to install Docker Desktop on your workstation.

➤ Download Docker Desktop from *https://www.docker.com/products/docker-desktop*.

After you have Docker installed, you can deploy a SQL Server container with the following steps. The first thing you should do is *pull* a copy of the container image from the Microsoft Container Registry (MCR) to your local environment. You should run these commands from either a bash shell on Linux and macOS, or an elevated PowerShell prompt on Windows.

```
sudo docker pull mcr.microsoft.com/mssql/server:2019-latest
```

➤ **You can find out more about the bash shell in Chapter 5, and PowerShell in Chapter 9, "Automating SQL Server administration."**

After you have pulled down the image, you then need to deploy the container. The backslash in this command is a way to split a single bash command across multiple lines:

```
sudo docker run -e 'ACCEPT_EULA=Y' -e 'SA_PASSWORD=<YourStrong!Passw0rd>' \
   -p 1433:1433 --name sql2019 \
   -v /users/randolph/mssql:/mssql \
   -d mcr.microsoft.com/mssql/server:2019-latest
```

CAUTION

There is currently no secure way to obfuscate the SA password in a Docker deployment. Microsoft recommends that you change your SA password after you have deployed your container.

You may be curious what these parameters (also called *switches* in Linux) mean:

- The docker pull command downloads the container image to your local container repository.

- The docker run command is where the deployment takes place.

- The -e switch allows for an environmental variable to be passed into the deployment (we cover environment variables in Chapter 5). In this case, you are accepting the End-User License Agreement (EULA) for SQL Server, and providing a strong password for the SA account.

- The -p (or --publish, note the double-dash before the parameter) switch *publishes* the container's public and private port for your container. To run multiple SQL Server containers simultaneously, specify a TCP port other than 1433 for the subsequent containers that are deployed.

- The --name switch (note the double-dash before the parameter) specifies the name of your container (which is not required but will result in a system-generated name if not specified).

- The -v switch is probably the most important in terms of database use. It allows a persistent volume to be mounted from your local machine to your container. In this the case the local directory /users/randolph/mssql will appear in the container as /mssql. Use this directory to store database backups, or data files to be mounted to the container.

- The -d switch refers to the container image you are deploying. In this case you are a deploying a SQL Server 2019 container from the MCR.

NOTE

Docker on macOS does not support persistent volumes. Microsoft recommends that you use separate data container volumes to persist data files that are stored in /var/opt/mssql/data. You can read the background to this issue at *https://github.com/microsoft/mssql-docker/issues/12*, and you can learn more about data container volumes at *https://docs.docker.com/storage/volumes/*.

Inside OUT

Can you use containers in development?

Yes, development is one of the main uses for containers. Given the ease of deploying SQL Server in a container, you can envision a process where a software vendor builds an automated process to perform regression tests against every cumulative update (CU) of a release of SQL Server, or across multiple releases. This is just one excellent use case for databases in containers.

After the container has been deployed, you can execute the docker ps command (lists all of the running containers) to confirm that your container is running (in some environments you may need to run sudo docker ps). Also, you can connect to your container using SQL Server tools like SQL Server Management Studio (SSMS), Azure Data Studio, or sqlcmd, by connecting to localhost. This is possible because when you deployed the container, you configured it to run on TCP port 1433, which is the default SQL Server port.

```
randolph@charon        docker ps
CONTAINER ID    IMAGE                                         COMMAND
CREATED         STATUS              PORTS                     NAMES
24a2a3bda258    mcr.microsoft.com/mssql/server:2019-latest    "/opt/mssql/bin/perm…"
4 minutes ago   Up 4 minutes        0.0.0.0:1433→1433/tcp     sql2019
randolph@charon        sqlcmd -Usa -S localhost
Password:
1>
```

Figure 3-8   A screenshot of docker ps output and sqlcmd connection.

NOTE

If you use a custom TCP port (or deploy multiple SQL Server containers) you can connect to localhost followed by the port number, separated with a comma. For example, localhost,1455.

You can also connect into your container with an interactive shell and execute `sqlcmd`. The first command will launch the bash shell within your container:

```
sudo docker exec -it sql1 "/bin/bash"
```

After launching the interactive bash shell within your container, you will then call `sqlcmd` using the full path, since it is not in the path by default:

```
/opt/mssql-tools/bin/sqlcmd -S localhost -U SA -P '<YourNewStrong!Passw0rd>'
```

Once your SQL Server container is deployed, you can execute T-SQL just like it was any other SQL Server.

Getting started with SQL Server on Kubernetes

Although running SQL Server in a single Docker container is relatively easy, running SQL Server on a Kubernetes infrastructure is more challenging.

Kubernetes as part of Docker Desktop

You can install Kubernetes with Docker Desktop; however, as mentioned previously, persistent volumes are not supported on macOS. If you are using Docker on Windows and you are running Windows 10 Professional, you can configure Kubernetes after enabling Hyper-V.

> ➤ **You can find the instructions for deploying Docker with Kubernetes at**
> *https://docs.docker.com/docker-for-windows/kubernetes.*

Kubernetes using Minikube

Another commonly used option for development and testing of Kubernetes is Minikube, which runs across Windows, Linux, and macOS. Minikube is an open source project that allows for a deployment to your local workstation.

> ➤ **Configuring Minikube is part of the main Kubernetes documentation, available at**
> *https://kubernetes.io/docs/setup/learning-environment/minikube.*

Kubernetes using the Azure Kubernetes Service

The recommended way to fully simulate a production environment is to deploy using Azure Kubernetes Service (AKS). AKS is a managed service that allows you to quickly deploy a Kubernetes cluster of one node, up to 100 nodes.

> ➤ **Configuring AKS is part of the main Azure documentation, available at**
> *https://docs.microsoft.com/azure/aks/kubernetes-walkthrough.*

CHAPTER 3

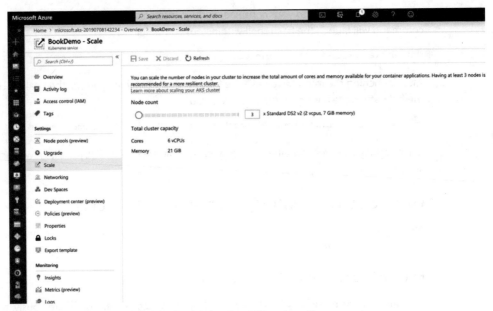

Figure 3-9   A screenshot of Azure Portal showing AKS scale options.

AKS offers the benefit of hosting a highly available control plane for the cluster in Azure, as well as deploying the latest release of Kubernetes without installing software, worrying about dependencies, or finding hardware to build on. The other benefit to AKS is that the service itself is free. You are only charged for the underlying VM compute costs. Storage in AKS is provided by either using Azure Managed Disks or the Azure File service that acts as a file share.

Deploying SQL Server on Kubernetes

Once you have a Kubernetes cluster or simulated cluster, you can get started with deploying SQL Server. First, you will need to create a secret in Kubernetes to store your SA password.

```
kubectl create secret generic mssql --from-literal=SA_PASSWORD="MyC0m9l&xP@ssw0rd"
```

If kubectl (the Kubernetes command line tool) is not installed on the machine where you are managing your cluster, you will need to install it in order to manage your deployment.

> ➤ **Instructions for installing** kubectl **are available at**
> *https://kubernetes.io/docs/tasks/tools/install-kubectl.*

Next, you will create a Persistent Volume Claim (PVC). As mentioned earlier, containers were originally designed to be ephemeral and not persist data across restarts or failures. A PVC will ask the cluster to provide a mapping to a Persistent Volume (PV). A PV can be statically or dynamically provisioned.

- A *statically-provisioned* PV is defined by the cluster administrator and a `PersistentVolumeClaim` will be matched to that PV based on size and access mode.

- A *dynamically-provisioned* PV will be provisioned from a cluster defined `StorageClass`. A PV asks the Storage Class to provision the volume from the underlying storage subsystem of the cluster. This can be a cloud provider's persistent volume such as Azure Disks, or even an on-premises SAN.

If you are using Azure Kubernetes Services, save the following code to a file called pvc.yaml.

```
kind: StorageClass

apiVersion: storage.k8s.io/v1beta1

metadata:

    name: azure-disk

provisioner: kubernetes.io/azure-disk

parameters:

  storageaccounttype: Standard_LRS

  kind: Managed

---

kind: PersistentVolumeClaim

apiVersion: v1

metadata:

  name: mssql-data

  annotations:

    volume.beta.kubernetes.io/storage-class: azure-disk

spec:

  accessModes:

  - ReadWriteOnce

  resources:

    requests:

      storage: 8Gi
```

This code defines the Azure storage class, and then defines an 8-GB volume. This code example uses Azure storage, which is how you would implement on AKS. You will use slightly different code if you are using storage local to your cluster, like you do when using Minikube or Docker.

CHAPTER 3

```
kind: PersistentVolumeClaim

apiVersion: v1

metadata:

  name: mssql-data-claim

spec:

  accessModes:

  - ReadWriteOnce

  resources:

   requests:

   storage: 8Gi
```

Just like in the Azure example, save this file to `pvc.yaml` and then deploy using the `kubectl apply` command shown next:

```
kubectl apply -f C:\scripts\pvc.yaml
```

CAUTION

ReadWriteOnce is one of three access modes available for persistent volumes. It is the only option that allows both writes and single-node mounting. You will corrupt your databases if a volume is mounted by multiple writers.

The next step is to deploy the SQL Server service and the pod itself. In the following code, you are specifying the load balancer service, as well as the container running SQL Server. Kubernetes can use extensive metadata to help describe and categorize your environment, as you will note from the metadata and label fields in the below YAML. Much like in the Docker script earlier, you are defining a port, passing in the SA password you defined in the secret, and accepting the EULA. Finally, in the last section, you are defining the load balancer, which will give you a persistent IP address for your SQL instance.

```
apiVersion: apps/v1beta1

kind: Deployment

metadata:

  name: mssql-deployment

spec:

  replicas: 1

  template:

   metadata:
```

```
      labels:

        app: mssql

    spec:

      terminationGracePeriodSeconds: 10

      containers:

      - name: mssql

        image: mcr.microsoft.com/mssql/server:2019-latest

        ports:

        - containerPort: 1433

        env:

        - name: MSSQL_PID

          value: "Developer"

        - name: ACCEPT_EULA

          value: "Y"

        - name: MSSQL_SA_PASSWORD

          valueFrom:

            secretKeyRef:

              name: mssql

              key: SA_PASSWORD

        volumeMounts:

        - name: mssqldb

          mountPath: /var/opt/mssql

      volumes:

      - name: mssqldb

        persistentVolumeClaim:

          claimName: mssql-data

---

apiVersion: v1

kind: Service

metadata:
```

CHAPTER 3

```
      name: mssql-deployment

spec:

  selector:

    app: mssql

  ports:

    - protocol: TCP

      port: 1433

      targetPort: 1433

  type: LoadBalancer
```

You can save this YAML as `sql.yaml`, and using the same `kubectl apply -f` command, you can deploy it from where you manage Kubernetes.

Congratulations! You now have SQL Server running on Kubernetes. You can run the `kubectl get pods` and `get services` commands as shown in Figure 3-10 to see your deployment.

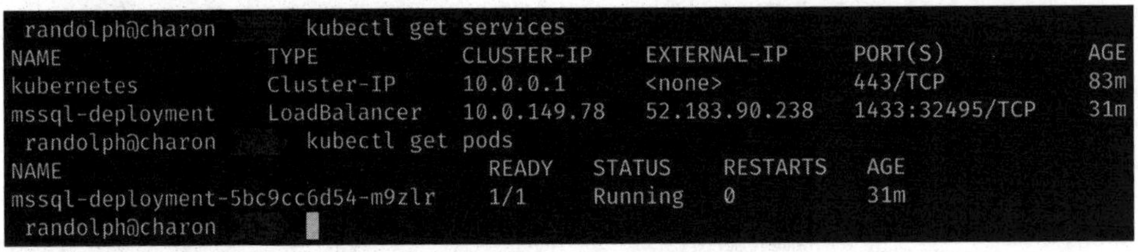

Figure 3-10   A screen shot showing the load balancer and SQL Server pod in a Kubernetes deployment.

If you review the output of the `kubectl get services` command, you will see the external IP address of your SQL Server service. You can now use any SQL Server client tool to connect to that address with the SA password you created in the secret.

CAUTION

This configuration exposes port 1433 to the Internet and should only be used for demonstration purposes. In order to secure your cluster for production usage, review AKS networking best practices at *https://docs.microsoft.com/azure/aks/best-practices*.

Reviewing cluster health

Kubernetes provides a built-in dashboard for monitoring the overall health of your cluster and its resource utilization. If you are using AKS, you can view this by running the `az aks browse` command with the resource group and cluster names. Depending on the configuration and version of your cluster, you may need to create a cluster role binding in order to view the dashboard as seen in Figure 3-11.

> ➤ **If you are not using AKS, you can find instructions on installing and configuring a dashboard for your cluster at**
> *https://kubernetes.io/docs/tasks/access-application-cluster/web-ui-dashboard.*

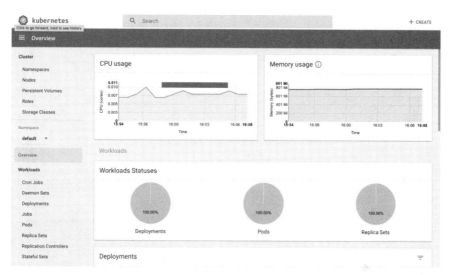

Figure 3-11   A screenshot of the Kubernetes web dashboard.

Kubernetes deployments move all of your infrastructure into scripts. For some automation-focused administrators, this may be the holy grail that they have been waiting for, but it is important to manage these scripts just as you would do with your application code. They should be version-controlled in a source control system like Azure DevOps or GitHub. If you are hosting your own repositories, you should ensure that they are backed up and highly available.

PART II

Deployment

Installing and configuring SQL Server instances and features

In this chapter, we review the process of installing and configuring a Microsoft SQL Server instance as well as the creation or migration of databases. We pay special attention to new features introduced in SQL Server 2019, and other recent features you may not have noticed in SQL Server 2017. We review a post-installation checklist for you to verify every time and, when necessary, direct you to where you can find other sources of information and details for critical steps elsewhere in this book.

The SQL Server Setup tool content of this chapter mainly applies to SQL Server installations on Windows operating systems. The installation or creation is vastly simplified for an Azure SQL Database, Azure SQL Database managed instance, SQL Server on Linux, SQL Server in Docker containers, or Azure VMs running SQL Server. Many recommended settings in this chapter still apply for server-based platforms of SQL Server, such as in Docker containers or SQL Server on Linux. They are, after all, still very much the same SQL Server product that has always existed on Windows.

In Chapter 6, "Provisioning and configuring SQL Server databases," we'll cover the initial creation and configuration of databases inside the SQL Server instance. This chapter, however, focuses on server-level setup and settings.

What to do before installing SQL Server

Before running the SQL Server installer on your Windows Server, there are a number of factors and settings to consider, some of which you *cannot* easily change after installation. For example, choosing between the default instance and a named instance, or choosing an instance collation, is not a choice you can easily reverse after installation. (More about the server level collation option later in this chapter, under the "Instance Collation" section.)

However, many mistakes made in installation can be resolved afterwards, likely with some tedium and outages. For example, skipping the initial default data and log directories may land all of your databases on the Operating System volume. They can be moved to the appropriate volumes later, but it's best to get it right the first time.

CAUTION

Do not install SQL Server on the same server as a domain controller. In some scenarios, it is not supported and can even cause Setup to fail. For more information on the risks and limitations, visit: *https://docs.microsoft.com/sql/sql-server/install/ hardware-and-software-requirements-for-installing-sql-server-ver15#DC_support.*

We recommend you acquire the contents of this list prior to beginning SQL Server Setup:

- Active Directory service accounts, for the SQL Server service, SQL Agent Service, and other features if needed

- The latest downloaded cumulative update to bring the instance up to the latest patch level

- A licensing decision around the number of processors and the edition to buy

- A secure enterprise digital location for various passwords you will be generating, backups of certificates, keys

- Whether to install the default or a named instance

- A plan for where SQL Server files will go, and each volume formatted to 64KB disk unit allocation size

Let's talk more about that last item now.

Deciding on volume usage

For many good reasons, various types of SQL Server files should be placed on separate volumes. Although you can move user and system database data and log files to other locations after installation, it's best to plan your volumes prior to installation.

The examples in this chapter assume that your Windows operating system installation is on the C volume of your server. You should have many other volumes for SQL Server files–we'll review a sample layout soon. One of the basic guiding principles for a SQL Server installation is that anywhere you see "C:\," change it to another volume. This helps minimize SQL Server's footprint on the operating system (OS) volume, especially if you install multiple SQL Server instances, and can have potential disaster recovery implications in terms of volume-level backup and restores.

Inside OUT

What if you are tight on space on the OS volume after installing SQL Server?

There are some easy ways and some tricky ways to minimize the footprint of a SQL Server installation on the OS volume of your server (typically the C volume, as it is for this example). In general, SQL Server Setup and cumulative updates will delete temporary files involved in their installation, but not log files or configuration files, which should have a minimal footprint. Outside of log files, we recommend that you do not delete any files installed by SQL Server Setup or cumulative updates. Instead, let's take a look at some proactive steps to move these files off of the C volume.

Some parts of SQL Server Setup will install on the OS volume (typically, and in this and future examples, the Windows C volume). These files, which are staging areas for SQL Server Setup, are created on the OS volume in a *C:\Program Files\Microsoft SQL Server\150\Setup Bootstrap* subfolder structure, where 150 is specific to the internal version number (15.0) of SQL 2019. This folder is used for future cumulative updates or feature changes.

If you're extremely tight on space before installing SQL Server, you will also find that the root binaries installation directory will be, by default, *C:\Program Files\Microsoft SQL Server*. When you're using the SQL Server Setup user interface, there is no option to change this. You will, however, find this installation directory folder path listed as the INSTANCEDIR parameter in the config file that is generated by SQL Server Setup. How to use the config file to install SQL Server is further covered in the "Automating SQL Server Setup by using configuration files" section later in this chapter.

If this is the first SQL Server instance you are installing on a server, you will have the opportunity to change the location of shared features files, the data root directory for the instance (which contains the system databases), default database locations for user database files, and their backups. If this is not the first SQL Server 2019 instance installation on this server, the shared features directory locations (for Program Files and Program Files x86) will already be set for you, and you cannot change it.

You should place as much of the installation as possible on other volumes, not the OS volume. Keep in mind that a full-featured installation of SQL Server 2019 can consume more than 14 GB.

Inside OUT

What can you do with the D: volume on an Azure VM?

For Microsoft Azure Windows virtual machines (VMs), do not set the installation directories for any settings on the D:\ "Temporary Storage" volume. In a Linux VM, the same applies to */dev/sdb1*.

The temporary storage volume in Azure VMs is a temporary disk that is locally present on the machine hosting your Azure VM, so it has better performance and lower latency than the default C: volume. The temporary storage volume contains only the Windows Page file by default and is wiped upon server restart, resize, or host migration!

The only possible long-term use for the temporary storage volume is for TempDB files, which can exist if certain other considerations are taken. For more about this, see Chapter 3: Designing and implementing an on-premises database infrastructure. Otherwise, do not store any non-temporary files in the temporary storage.

The following sample scenario is a good starting point for a volume layout for your SQL Server installation (the volume letters don't matter):

- **Volume C.**   OS, some SQL Server files must install here.

- **Volume E.**   SQL Server installation files, log files, SQL Server database data files.

- **Volume F.**   SQL Server database log files.

- **Volume G.**   SQL Server TempDB data files and log file. (Alternatively, use the D: Temporary Storage volume on Azure Windows VMs.)

- **Volume H.**   SQL Server backups (if written locally.)

And, here are some more advanced volume decisions:

- Use additional volumes for your largest data files (larger than 2 TB) for storage manageability:

  - For the most active databases

  - For FILESTREAM filegroups

  - For database replication snapshot files

  - For the Windows Page File, especially for servers with large amounts of memory

Inside OUT

Why separate SQL Server files onto different volumes?

There are good reasons to separate your SQL Server files onto various volumes, and not all of them are related to performance. You should still separate your files onto different volumes even if you exclusively use a Storage-Area Network (SAN).

More discrete storage I/O on a physical server with dedicated drives means better performance. But even in a SAN, separating files onto different volumes is also done for stability. Think of the volumes as bulkheads on a submarine. If a volume fills and has no available space, files cannot be allocated additional space. On the OS volume, running out of free space would result in Windows Server stability issues, user profile and remote desktop problems at least, and impact to other applications.

Important SQL Server volume settings

There are some settings to consider for volumes that host SQL Server data and log files, and this guidance applies specifically to these volumes. For other volumes—for example, those that contain the OS, application files, or backup files—the default Windows settings are acceptable unless otherwise specified.

When adding these volumes to Windows, there are four important volume configuration settings required to examine or discuss with your storage administrator.

- When creating new drives, opt for GUID Partition Table (GPT) over Master Boot Record (MBR) disk types for new SQL Server installations. GPT is a newer disk partitioning scheme than MBR, and GPT disk support files and volumes larger than 2 TB, whereas the older MBR disk type is capped at 2 TB.

- The appropriate file unit allocation size for SQL Server volumes is 64 KB, with few exceptions. Setting this to 64 KB for each volume can have a significant impact on storage efficiency and performance. The Windows default is 4 KB, which is not optimal for SQL Server data and log files.

  To check the file unit allocation size for an NT File System (NTFS) volume, run the following from the Administrator: Prompt, repeating for each volume:

  ```
  fsutil fsinfo ntfsinfo d:
  ```

  The file unit allocation size is returned with the Bytes Per Cluster; thus the desired 64 KB would be displayed as 65,536 (bytes). If formatted as the default, this will display 4096. Correcting the file unit allocation size requires formatting the drive, so it is important to check this setting prior to installation.

If you notice this on an existing SQL Server instance, your likely resolution steps are to create a new volume with the proper file unit allocation size and then move files to the new volume during an outage. Do *not* format or re-create the partition on volumes with existing data: you will of course lose the data.

- Modern storage devices are currently in a transition between disks that use a Bytes per Physical Sector size of 512 bytes (the old standard) and "4K Native" disks that have both a Bytes per Sector size and a Bytes per Physical Sector size of 4 KB. Usually a DBA will not notice or even be aware of this difference. When configuring Availability Groups or log shipping between servers on different storage systems with mixed Bytes per Physical Sector modes, however, this can result in very poor performance, with the transaction logs unable to truncate, and the error message "There have been *nnn* misaligned log IOs which required falling back to synchronous IO." You may encounter this with hybrid Availability Groups spanning on-premises and Azure VM-based SQL Server instances, for example.

  This cannot be resolved via a formatting decision, but can potentially be resolved via hardware-level storage or firmware settings. To avoid this, all storage that hosts the transaction log files of SQL Servers in an Availability Group or log shipping relationship should have the same Bytes per Physical Sector.

  A workaround is to apply Trace Flag 1800 as a startup flag on the SQL Server instances that use storage without having a Bytes per Physical Sector setting of 4K. TF1800 overrides disk default behavior and writes the transaction log in 4 KB sectors, resolving the issue. TF1800 must be enabled on the on-premises SQL Server instances, in the case of using the older on-premises and Azure VM Availability Group.

  Check the Bytes per Physical Sector setting of a volume by using the same Fsutil command noted in the previous code sample.

- There is a hardware-level concept related to file unit allocation size called "disk starting offset" that deals with how Windows, storage, disk controllers, and cache segments align their boundaries. Aligning disk starting offset was far more important prior to Windows Server 2008. Since then, the default partition offset of 1,024 KB has been sufficient to align with the underlying disk's stripe unit size, which is a vendor-determined value, and rarely a concern for DBA's. Still, it should be verified upon first use of a new storage system or the migration of disks to a new storage system. This can be verified in consultation with the drive vendor's information.

  To access the disk starting offset information, run the following from the Administrator: Prompt:

  ```
  wmic partition get BlockSize, StartingOffset, Name, Index
  ```

  A 1024 KB starting offset is a Windows default, which is displayed as 1048576 (bytes) for Disk #0 Partition #0.

Similar to the file unit allocation size, the only way to change a disk partition's starting offset is destructive—you must re-create the partition and reformat the volume to align with the vendor-supplied offset.

SQL Server editions

The following are brief descriptions for all of the editions in the SQL Server family, including past editions that you might recognize. It's important to use the appropriate licenses for SQL Server even in preproduction systems.

> **NOTE**
>
> **This book is not intended to be a reference for licensing or sales-related documentation; rather, editions are a key piece of knowledge for SQL administrators to understand what features may or may not be available.**

- **Enterprise edition.**   Appropriate for production environments. Not appropriate for preproduction environments such as User Acceptance Testing (UAT), Quality Assurance (QA), testing, development, or a sandbox. For these environments, instead use the free Developer edition. You'll have a far easier time in a licensing audit if your pre-production environment installations are Developer edition.

- **Developer edition.**   Appropriate for all preproduction environments, especially those under a production Enterprise edition. Not allowed for production environments. This edition supports the same features and capacity as Enterprise edition and is free.

- **Standard edition.**   Appropriate for production environments. Lacks the scale and compliance features of Enterprise edition that are required in some regulatory environments. Limited to the lesser of 4 sockets or 24 cores and also 128 GB of buffer pool memory, whereas Enterprise edition is limited only by the OS for compute and memory.

- **Web edition.**   Appropriate for production environments but limited to low-cost server environments for web applications.

- **Express edition.**   Not appropriate for most production environments or preproduction environments. Appropriate only for environments in which data size is small, is not expected to grow, and can be backed up with external tools or scripts (because Express edition has no SQL Server Agent to automate backups). The free Express edition is ideal for production proof-of-concepts, lightweight applications, or student projects. It lacks some critical features and is severely limited on compute (lesser of 1 socket or 4 cores), available buffer pool memory (1,410 MB), and individual database size (10 GB cap).

- **Express with Advanced Services.**   Similar to Express edition in all caveats and limitations, this edition includes some additional features including R integration, full-text search, and distributed replay.

- **Evaluation Edition.**   Functionally the same as Enterprise edition, and free with a 180-day shutdown timer, but it isn't supported. Can be upgraded to any edition but Express. Do not use it if you plan for a clustered installation, because an upgrade in that case is not supported.

- **It's worth noting that the hardware limitations of SQL Server editions have not changed since SQL Server 2016.**

NOTE

When you run the SQL Server 2019 installer, you are prompted to install a number of features outside of the core database features. Installing SQL Server features on multiple Windows servers requires multiple licenses per server, even if you intend to install each SQL Server instance's features only once.

There is an exception to this rule, and that is if you have licensed all physical cores on a virtual host server for SQL Server Enterprise edition, and purchased Software Assurance, you can install any number or combination of SQL Server instances and their standalone features on virtual guests.

Changing SQL Server editions and versions

Upgrading editions in-place is supported by a feature of the SQL Server 2019 installer. You can upgrade in the following order: Express, Web, Standard, and Enterprise.

It is important to note that you cannot downgrade a SQL Server version or licensed edition. This type of change requires a fresh installation and migration. For example, you cannot downgrade in-place from SQL Server 2019, from Enterprise edition to Standard edition.

In-place upgrades for major versions (from 2017 to 2019, for example) is supported but not recommended. Instead, we strongly recommend that you perform a fresh installation of the newer version and then migrate from old to new instances. This method offers major advantages in terms of duration of the planned outage, rollback capability, and robust testing in parallel.

Although in-place upgrades to SQL Server 2019 are not recommended, they are supported for versions as old as SQL Server 2012 on Windows Server 2016. SQL Server 2019 is the first SQL Server version that does not support Windows Server 2012 or 2012 R2.

A supported upgrade also assumes that the operating system and previous version of SQL Server are not 32-bit installations. Beginning with SQL Server 2016, SQL Server is available only for 64-bit platforms. For more information on upgrades to SQL Server 2019, visit *https://docs.microsoft.com/sql/database-engine/install-windows/supported-version-and-edition-upgrades-version-15*.

Beginning with SQL Server 2019, a SQL Server upgrade from SQL Server 2008 is no longer supported, though individual databases can still be migrated to SQL Server 2019. You can attach or restore its databases to SQL Server 2019, although they will be upgraded to compatibility level 100, the version level for SQL 2008.

Installing a new instance

In this section, you learn how to begin a new SQL Server 2019 instance installation, upgrade an existing installation, or add features to an existing instance.

The instructions in this chapter are the same for the first installation or any subsequent installations, whether it is for the default or any named instances of SQL Server 2019. As opposed to an exhaustive step-by-step instruction list for installations, we've opted to cover the important decision points and the information you need and highlight new features from SQL Server 2019.

It's important to note that even though you can change *almost* all of the decisions you make in SQL Server Setup after installation, those changes potentially require an outage or server restart. Making the proper decisions at installation time is the best way to ensure the least administrative effort. Some security and service account decisions should be changed only via the SQL Server Configuration Manager application, not through the Services console (services.msc). This guidance will be repeated elsewhere for emphasis.

We begin by going through the typical interactive installation. Later in this chapter, we go over some of the command-line installation methods that you can use to automate the installation of a SQL Server instance.

Planning for multiple SQL Server instances

You can install as many as 50 SQL Server instances on a Windows Server; obviously, we do not recommend this. In a Windows failover cluster, the maximum number of SQL Server instances is reduced by half if you're using shared cluster drives.

Only one of the SQL Server instances on a server can be the default instance. All, or all but one, of the SQL Server instances on a SQL Server will be named instances. The default instance is reachable by connecting to the name of the Windows Server, whereas named instances require an instance name, for example, *Servername\InstanceName*. The SQL Browser service is required to handle traffic for named instances on the SQL Server.

For example, you can reach the default instance of a SQL Server by connecting to *servername*. All named instances have a unique instance name, such as *servername\instancename*.

Creating an Azure VM running SQL Server

You should not need to install SQL Server on new Azure VMs, because provisioning new VMs with various versions and editions of Windows Server and SQL Server are available in the Azure Marketplace. For more information about bringing your existing SQL Server licensing to Azure VMs, visit *https://azure.microsoft.com/blog/easily-bring-your-sql-server-licenses-to-azure-vms/*.

When manually creating a new VM with SQL Server, however, there are still some configuration choices you can make in the browser. We will walk through some of those decision points in this section, although much of this is already handled for you.

Specifically in the *SQL Server settings* page of the *Create a virtual machine* wizard, you can choose to enable *Mixed Mode Authentication*. If you do, you must specify a username and password, but note that this probably isn't needed for you–administrators can and should use Azure Active Directory authentication when possible with your Azure VMs.

You can configure the Azure VM to be automatically powered down, which is very handy for rarely used VMs in your own sandbox. You can use Azure Automation to easily schedule VMs to run during pre-scheduled hours, thus lowering the monthly cost.

You can also enable Azure-specific integrations with Azure Key Vault, automatic patching, and automatic SQL backups for your new VM from the Azure Portal. Use Tags to organize your Azure infrastructure with information on environments, applications, locations, or other custom departmental metadata as desired, making it easy to monitor and manage objects in groups.

In the *Review + create* page, you can review the expected hourly spend and all of your Azure VM settings. Don't miss this detail, which is similar to SQL Server setup: there is a link to download a template for automation. An Azure VM template is a .json file that stores the options needed to create Azure resources, so that you can reference it within the Azure Portal, PowerShell, the Azure CLI (-Line Interface) and others to create Azure VMs with the same choices. Use the .json file to create a new Azure VM, for example, by choosing "Create a Resource" in Azure, then "Template deployment (deploy using custom templates)".

> ➤ You'll find much more on Azure infrastructure, including the differences between Azure VMs, Azure SQL Database, and Azure SQL Database Managed Instances in Chapter 16 "Designing and implementing hybrid and Azure database infrastructure."

Inside OUT

How does licensing work in Azure VMs?

This isn't an authoritative book on Azure or SQL Server licensing, but speaking broadly, there are two types of SQL Server licensing agreements for Azure VMs:

SQL Server VM images in the Azure Marketplace contain the SQL Server licensing costs as an all-in-one billing package.

Alternatively, if you'd like to leverage your existing Enterprise licensing agreement using the Azure Hybrid Benefit, there are three options:

- Bring-your-own-license (BYOL) VM images available for you to provision using the same process and then later associate your existing Enterprise license agreements. The image names you're looking for here are prefixed with BYOL.
- Manually upload an .iso to the VM and install SQL Server 2019 as you would on any other Windows Server.
- Upload an image of an on-premises VM to provision the new Azure VM.

It is important for you to keep in mind that you cannot change from the built-in licensing model to the BYOL licensing model after the VM has been provisioned. You need to make this decision prior to creating your Azure VM.

Installing SQL Server on Windows

The rest of this chapter is dedicated to installations of SQL Server not part of a pre-made Azure Marketplace VM and apply to installation of SQL Server on any Windows Server.

While logged in as a local Windows administrator, begin by mounting the installation .iso to the Windows server. These days, this rarely involves inserting a physical disc or USB flash drive; although you can use them if necessary.

Launching SQL Server Setup

You should not run Setup with the installation media mounted over a remote network connection, via a shared remote desktop drive, or any other high-latency connection. For a faster SQL Server Setup experience, unpack the contents of the .iso file to a physical file folder local to the server, instead of mounting a file or launching Setup from a location over the network.

Start setup.exe on the SQL Server Setup media, running the program as a Windows user with administrator privileges. If AutoPlay is not turned off (it usually is), Setup.exe will start when you first mount the media or double-click to open the .iso. Instead, as a best practice, right-click Setup.exe and then, on the shortcut menu that appears, click **Run As Administrator**.

We'll review here a few items (not all) in the SQL Server Installation Center worth noting before you begin an installation.

In the tab pane on the left, click **Planning** to open a long list of links to Microsoft documentation websites. Most helpful here might be a standalone version of the System Configuration Checker, which you run during SQL Server Setup later, but it could save you a few steps if you review it now. A link to download the Data Migration Assistant (DMA) is also present, which is a helpful Microsoft-provided tool when upgrading from prior versions of SQL Server.

On the *Maintenance* page, you will find the following:

- A link to launch the relatively painless Edition Upgrade Wizard. This is only for promoting your existing installation's edition as we discussed earlier.

- The Repair feature is not a commonly used feature. Its use is necessitated by a SQL Server with a corrupted installation. You might also need to repair an instance of SQL Server when the executables, .dll files, or Registry entries have become corrupted or damaged by disk corruption, antivirus, or malicious activity. A failed SQL Server in-place upgrade or cumulative update installation might also require a Repair, which could be better than starting from scratch.

- Note that whereas removing a node from an existing SQL Server failover cluster is an option in the *Maintenance* page, adding a node to an existing SQL Server failover cluster is an option in the *Installation* page.

- On the *Advanced* page, there is a link to perform an installation based on a configuration file. We will discuss how to easily generate and use a configuration file later in this chapter, in the section *Automating SQL Server Setup by* using configuration files. If you are tasked with installing multiple SQL Servers with mostly common settings, consider this time-saving method. There are also links to wizards for advanced failover cluster installations.

  ➤ We discuss Failover Cluster Instances (FCIs) in Chapter 11, "Implementing high availability and disaster recovery."

Windows Update in the SQL Server Setup

Since SQL Server 2012, the SQL Server installer has had the ability to patch itself while within the Setup wizard. The *Product Updates* page is presented after the *License Terms* page, and, after you accept it, it is downloaded from Windows Update (or Windows Server Update Services) and installed along with other SQL Server Setup files.

This is recommended, and so a SQL Server 2019 Setup with Internet connectivity is the easiest way to carry out the installation. This also could be described as a way to "slip-stream" updates, including hotfixes and cumulative updates, into the SQL Server installation process, eliminating these efforts post-installation.

For servers without Internet access, there are two Setup.exe parameters that support downloading these files to an accessible location and making them available to Setup. When starting Setup.exe from Windows PowerShell or the command line (you can read more about this in the next section), you should set the /UpdateEnabled parameter to FALSE to turn off the download from Windows Update. The /UpdateSource parameter can then be provided as an installation location of .exe files. Note that the /UpdateSource parameter is a folder location, not a file. You will find more on these two parameters later in the "Installing by using a configuration file" section.

Regardless, after installation is complete and before the SQL Server enters further use in your team, verify that the latest SQL Server patches have been applied. For SQL Server 2019, see the official build versions site:
https://support.microsoft.com/help/4518398/sql-server-2019-build-versions.

Installing SQL Server *stand-alone installation*

Although what follows in this chapter is not a step-by-step walk-through, we'll cover key new features and decision points of the *New SQL Server stand-alone installation* option of the SQL Server Installation Center.

Inside OUT

Where is SQL Server Management Studio and SQL Server Data Tools?

SQL Server Management Studio, SQL Server Data Tools (for Visual Studio 2015 and higher), and SQL Server Reporting Services are no longer installed with SQL Server's traditional setup media. These products are now updated regularly (as often as monthly) and available for download.

You should keep up-to-date versions of SQL Server Management Studio (SSMS) on administrator workstations and laptops.

Avoid installing SSMS locally on the SQL Server if possible. In fact, avoid needing to use Remote Desktop Connection to manage and administer the SQL Server altogether. For all SQL Server platforms, try to use SSMS, Azure Data Studio, PowerShell, and other tools to do as much of your work on SQL Server remotely as possible.

Granting Perform Volume Maintenance Tasks

On the same Server Configuration page on which service accounts are set, you will see a check box labeled *Grant Perform Volume Maintenance Task privilege to the SQL Server Database Engine Service*. This option was added to SQL Server Setup in SQL Server 2016.

This automates what used to be a standard post-installation checklist step for SQL DBAs since Windows Server 2003. The reason to grant this permission to use instant file initialization is to speed the allocation of large database data files, which could dramatically reduce the Recovery Time Objective (RTO) capacity for disaster recovery.

This can mean the difference between hours and minutes when restoring a very large database. It can also have a positive impact when creating databases with large initial sizes, or in large autogrowth events; for example, with multiple data files in the TempDB (more on this next). It is recommended that you allow SQL Server Setup to turn on this setting.

Inside OUT

How can you verify that Instant File Initialization is enabled?

IFI is granted to SQL Server service account via the *Perform Volume Maintenance Tasks* permission in Local Security Policy on the Windows server. But it's actually quite easy to verify whether or not IFI is in place for the SQL Server service via the sys.dm_server_services dynamic management view. The column instant_file_initialization_enabled was first added in a series of patches to supported SQL Servers: in SQL Server 2012 SP4, SQL Server 2014 SP2, SQL Server 2016 SP1.

```
SELECT servicename, instant_file_initialization_enabled
FROM sys.dm_server_services
WHERE filename LIKE '%sqlservr.exe%';
```

➤ For more information on instant file initialization, see Chapter 3.

Instance Collation

The Collation tab on the Server Configuration page allows you to choose a collation for the Database Engine. The collation determines how character data is stored, sorted and compared. For more information, see Chapter 7: "Understanding table features" in the section on Collation.

Initially the instance collation provided in SQL Setup is the default collation for the server's regionalization, but you may need to change this collation based on vendor or developer specifications.

While changing the collation of a database is easy, the instance collation is important to get right at the time of SQL Server installation, as changing the instance collation is quite difficult. To change the collation of the SQL Server instance, reference this lengthy and difficult Microsoft guide: *https://docs.microsoft.com/sql/relational-databases/collations/set-or-change-the-server-collation*. Note that in the case of Azure SQL managed instances, you cannot change the server-level collation after it is created. For more information, visit: *https://docs.microsoft.com/sql/relational-databases/collations/set-or-change-the-server-collation#setting-the-server-collation-in-managed-instance*.

The server collation you set here acts as the collation for all system databases as well as the default for any newly created user databases. In SQL Server 2019 and for new application development, you may choose to take advantage of the new support for UTF-8 collations as the server default. Pictured below is the new interface in SQL Server Setup for choosing a UTF-8 collation.

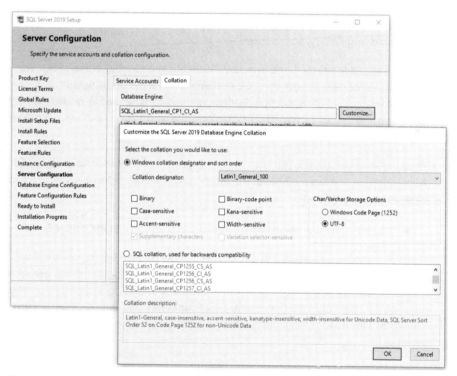

Figure 4-1   The options to set a server-level Windows collation using the new UTF-8 collation options now available in SQL Server 2019 Setup.

Mixed Mode authentication

SQL Server supports two modes of authentication: Windows and SQL Authentication. One is preferable to the other, and in multiple places in this book we will emphasize the preference for Windows Authentication over SQL Authentication.

> ➤ You can read more on this topic in Chapter 12, "Administering security and permissions," but it is important to note this decision point here.

Ideally, all authentication is made via Windows Authentication, through types of server principals called *logins*, that reference Windows accounts, which are ideally Active Directory domain accounts. These are created by your existing enterprise security team, which manages password policy, password resets, password expiration, and so on.

A redundant security model for connecting to SQL Server also exists within each instance: SQL Server Authenticated logins. Logins are maintained at the SQL Server level, are subject to local policy password complexity requirements, are reset/unlocked by SQL DBAs, have their own password change policy, and so forth.

Enabling Mixed Mode (SQL and Windows Authentication Mode) activates SQL Authenticated logins. It is important to note that SQL Authentication is not on by default, and isn't the recommended method of connection. By default, the recommended Windows Authentication is turned on and cannot be turned off. When possible, applications and users should use Windows Authentication.

Enabling Mixed Mode also activates the "sa" account, which is a special built-in SQL Server Authentication that is a member of the server sysadmin role. Setup will ask for a strong password to be provided at this time.

> ➤ You can learn more about the "sa" account and server roles in Chapter 7.

If you find you have an actual need to enable SQL Server Authentication, but didn't do this during SQL Server Setup, you can do this later on by connecting to the SQL Server instance via Object Explorer in SQL Server Management Studio. To do so, right-click the server name and then, on the shortcut menu that opens, click **Properties**, and then click the **Security** page, change to Mixed Mode. You must perform a SQL Server service restart to make this change effective.

Default settings for the TempDB database

Starting with SQL Server 2016, SQL Server Setup provides a more realistic default configuration for the number and size of TempDB data files. This has been a common to-do list for all post-installation checklists for DBAs since the early days of SQL Server.

The TempDB database page in SQL Server Setup provides not only the ability to specify the number and location of the TempDB's data and log files, but also their initial size and auto-growth rates. The best number of TempDB data files is almost certainly greater than one, and less than or equal to the number of logical processor cores, including hyperthreading for local machines. For example, with 16 logical processors, SQL Server Setup will default the installation to have 8 TempDB data files.

Adding too many TempDB data files can degrade SQL Server performance, perhaps severely if you add too many. For example, with 20 logical processors, SQL Server Setup will still default the installation to have 8 TempDB data files. If you add 20 TempDB data files, SQL Server may struggle to respond.

> ➤ **For more information on the best number of TempDB data files, see Chapter 3.**

Specifying TempDB's initial size to a larger, normal operating size is important and can improve performance after a SQL Server restart when the TempDB data files are reset to their initial size. Setup accommodates an individual TempDB data file initial size up to 256 GB. For data file initial sizes larger than 1 GB, you will be warned that SQL Server Setup can take a long time to complete if instant file initialization is not turned on.

Since SQL Server 2016, all TempDB files autogrow at the same time, keeping file sizes the same over time, which is critical to the way multiple TempDB data files are used. This is superior to the old way of ensuring TempDB data files stay the same size, using the server-level setting via server Trace Flag 1117, which applied the data file growth behavior to all databases. Trace Flag 1117 is no longer necessary.

Note also the new naming convention for the second TempDB data file and beyond: *tempdb_mssql_n.ndf*. A SQL Server uninstallation will automatically clean up TempDB data files with this naming convention—for this reason, we recommend that you follow this naming convention for TempDB data files.

> ➤ **TempDB is discussed in greater detail in Chapter 3.**

Default settings for MaxDOP

New in SQL Server 2019 are defaults for the configuration of the server-wide Maximum Degrees of Parallelism setting, included on the *Database Engine Configuration* page under the new *MaxDOP* tab.

Similar to how new TempDB defaults since SQL Server 2016 are dependent on the detected processors, a suggested default MaxDOP is also configured based on the number of logical processors. For many servers with 16 or fewer virtual processor cores, the default is the same as

CHAPTER 4

the number of the cores, effectively the same as *MaxDOP* setting = 0, which allows for unlimited parallelism.

For example, with 8 logical processors, SQL Server Setup will default the installation to use MaxDOP 8, as pictured in Figure 4-2. With over 16 logical processors, SQL Server Setup may default to half the number of logical processors—at most 16. For example, with 20 logical processors, SQL Server Setup will default the installation to use MaxDOP 10. For more recommendations about MAXDOP, visit Microsoft Support at *https://support.microsoft.com/ help/2806535*. See also the section on Max degree of parallelism in Chapter 3.

You can always reconfigure the MaxDOP after installation, without a restart, though not without potential disruption. While changing the server-wide (or database-level) MaxDOP setting takes effect immediately, it is definitely not advisable to do so during normal production operating hours, because it can lead to widespread plan recompilation and a heavy CPU spike. This server-wide MaxDOP setting can be overridden at the database, query, or Resource Governor group level.

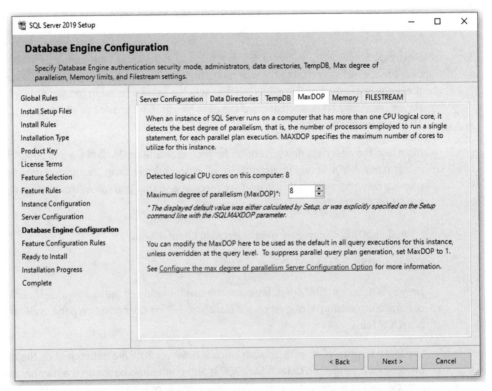

Figure 4-2   The new MaxDOP tab in the Database Engine Configuration tab in SQL Server 2019 Setup, which has recommended a MaxDOP of 8 for a server with 8 virtual cores. This is effectively the same as MaxDOP 0, but offers the administrator an option to potentially change MaxDOP at the time of installation.

NOTE

Some applications, including Microsoft SharePoint and other third-party vendor applications, recommend that parallelism be disabled on their databases. This can be accomplished at the server level now, or, can be configured and overridden at each database level after SQL Server Setup is complete. Consult your vendor's specifications and recommendations documentation.

➤ For much more information on performance tuning, parallelism, and the MaxDOP setting, see Chapter 14, "Performance tuning SQL Server."

Default settings for Maximum Server Memory

New in SQL Server 2019 are defaults for the configuration of the instance-level Maximum Server Memory option, a common post-installation checklist item, under the Memory tab of the Database Engine Configuration page. SQL Server Setup makes a guess based on total server memory for an appropriate option. In previous versions of SQL Server, it was important to remember to go and change the Max Server Memory setting after installation was complete, otherwise SQL Server memory would be uncapped, and have access to all memory on the server.

Now in SQL Server 2019, this max server memory option can be configured intelligently at the time of installation. It's important to note (and there's a checkbox to accept this guess) that SQL Server Setup is assuming this SQL Server instance will run alone on this server. If you expect to host other applications on this server, or memory-heavy features of SQL Server on the same server, such as SSAS or SSRS, you should reduce the maximum server memory for the SQL Server instance further.

➤ We discussed the Maximum Server Memory setting in Chapter 3, in the "Configuration Settings" section.

An example of the new max server memory recommendation configuring a Windows Server with one SQL Server instance and 16 GB of memory, SQL Server setup recommends a Max Server Memory setting of 12672 MB, as seen in Figure 4-3.

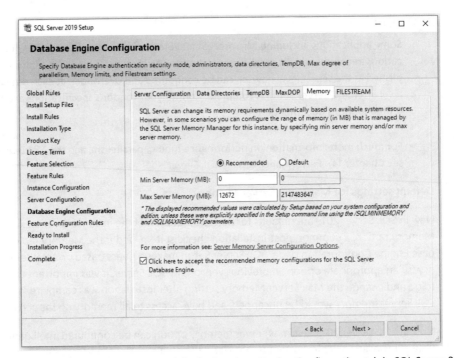

Figure 4-3   The new Memory tab in the Database Engine Configuration tab in SQL Server 2019 Setup.

Just above the *Maximum Server Memory* setting is the *Minimum Server Memory* setting, which establishes a floor for memory allocation. It is generally unnecessary to change this setting from the default of 0. You might find this setting useful for situations in which the total system memory is insufficient and many applications, including SQL Server instances, are present. The minimum server memory is not immediately allocated to the SQL Server instance upon startup; instead, it does not allow memory below this level to be freed for other applications.

After installation, server memory settings are accessible via SQL Server Management Studio, in Object Explorer, and on the Server Properties page.

You should assure that SQL Server leaves enough memory for the operating system and other applications. Keep in mind that SQL Server will slowly consume more memory over time, and may take hours or days, depending on your business cycle, for the SQL Server instance to consume the maximum amount of memory made available. Similarly, lowering this setting after installation and during operation does not return SQL Server memory back to the OS immediately; rather, it does so over time during SQL Server activity. Similarly, increasing this setting will not immediately show the effect of a change in memory utilization.

Installing common features

Aside from the SQL Server service itself, other features of the product might be common to your installations. SQL Server Analysis Services, SQL Server Integration Services, and SQL Server Reporting Services are part of the license and are provided at no additional cost. If you need them, this section covers installing these features using Setup. Later in this chapter, we cover the post-installation steps necessary to use them.

Installing SQL Server Analysis Services

Installing SQL Server Analysis Services (SSAS) requires you to make a decision at installation time regarding the mode in which it can be installed. Each instance of SQL Server Analysis Services can be in only one mode, which means that with a single license, you can run only Multidimensional mode, the newer Tabular mode (introduced in SQL 2012), or the Power Pivot mode.

Ask your business intelligence decision makers which platform you should use, though for most new development, Tabular mode is popular and recommended. Tabular mode databases can also run in Azure Analysis Services. The following are brief descriptions of each mode:

- **Multidimensional mode.** This is the SSAS setup that was first introduced in SQL 2000. This is also the only mode to support data mining and other features that existing SSAS data models predating SQL Server 2012 may be dependent on. The primary language for building and querying multidimensional models is MDX.

  - **Tabular mode.** This is the newer and recommended SQL Server Analysis Services setup that was first introduced in SQL 2012, using the in-memory VertiPaq processing engine. Since SQL Server 2017, this is the default installation mode selected on the Analysis Services Configuration page of Setup. The primary language for building and querying tabular models is DAX, which is similar to the Excel function language.

  - **Power Pivot mode.** This mode installs SQL Server Analysis Services in the Power Pivot for SharePoint mode. Power Pivot workbooks use both DAX and MAX. Note that Analysis Services Power Pivot for SharePoint support for Microsoft SharePoint 2019 has been discontinued.

For more on the differences between these SSAS installation options, visit *https://docs.microsoft. com/analysis-services/comparing-tabular-and-multidimensional-solutions-ssas*.

Inside OUT

What if you choose the wrong SQL Server Analysis Services mode?

If you choose one SQL Server Analysis Services mode at installation but your business intelligence developers want another mode, the supported option is to uninstall and

> reinstall the SQL Server Analysis Services feature. Changing the SQL Server Analysis Services mode from Multidimensional to Tabular, or vice versa, after installation is not supported, and administrators are specifically warned not to do this.
>
> Packages developed for each mode are not supported for the other. If no databases have been deployed to the SQL Server Analysis Services server instance, changing the *DeploymentMode* property in the MSMDSRV.ini file should make it possible to change an existing instance, but, again, this is not a supported change. The file is located in *%Programfiles%\Microsoft SQL Server\MSAS15.instancename\OLAP\Config*.

Installing SQL Server Integration Services

The SQL Server Integration Services instance for SQL Server 2019 is installed once per server per version, not once per instance, like other features. Starting in SQL Server 2017, however, a new Integration Services Scale Out Configuration is available. We discuss this new feature further in the next section.

A 64-bit version of SQL Server Integration Services is installed on 64-bit operating systems. If you worry about connecting to 32-bit servers, data sources, or applications installations (such as Microsoft Office), don't—those connections are not dependent on the 32-bit/64-bit installation and are handled at the package or connection-string level. Unlike other features, you can install SQL Server Integration Services on a 32-bit OS; however, we do not recommend this.

Installations of different versions of SQL Server Integration Services are installed side-by-side on a server; specifically, the service SQL Server Integration Services 15.0 is compatible with prior versions.

Outside of configuring the service account, you do not need any additional configuration when installing SQL Server Integration Services during SQL Server Setup. The default virtual service account is *NT Service\MsDtsServer150*.

Inside OUT

Should you install SQL Server Integration Services (SSIS) alone on a server?

A standalone installation of SQL Server Integration Services without a matching SQL Server Database Engine is possible but not recommended. For the modern Project Deployment model of SQL Server Integration Services, the storage and logging of packages will still be dependent on a SQL Server Database Engine, and the execution of packages on a schedule still requires a SQL Agent service. So isolation of the SQL Server Integration Services workload is not best isolated in this way. A dedicated installation including the SQL Server Database Engine and SQL Server Agent is a better configuration to isolate SQL Server Integration Services package runtime workloads from other database workloads. Both of these options would carry the same licensing cost.

Installing SQL Server Integration Services Scale Out configuration

Integration Services supports a Scale Out configuration by which you can run a package on the same or multiple SQL Server instances, a new feature that was first introduced in SQL Server 2017. This also allows for high availability of SQL Server Integration Services, and a similar architecture allows for integration and "lift and shift" code deployments from on-premises SQL Server Integration Servers to the Azure Integration Runtime.

The master node talks to worker nodes in a SQL Server Integration Services Scale Out, with the communication over a port (8391 by default) and secured via a new Secure Sockets Layer (SSL) certificate. The SQL Server installer can automatically create a 10-year self-signed certificate and endpoint for communication at the time the master node is set up.

When adding another SQL Server Integration Services installation as a Scale Out Worker, start the new SQL Server Integration Services Manage Scale Out window via SQL Server Management Studio. Right-click the Catalog you have created, and then click **Manage Scale Out**. At the bottom of the page, click the + button to add a new Scale Out Worker node. Provide the server name on which to connect. If using a named instance, provide only the server name of the node; do not include the instance name. A dialog box confirms the steps taken to add the Worker node, including copying and installing certificates between the Worker node and Master node, updating the endpoint and HttpsCertThumbprint of the worker, and restarting the Worker's Scale Out service. After the worker node is added, refresh the Worker Manager page, and then click the new Worker node entry, which will be red. You must turn on the Worker Node by clicking **Enable Worker**.

You also can copy and install the certificates manually between servers. You will find them in: *%program files%\Microsoft SQL Server\150\DTS\Binn*. For more information on certificates between servers, visit *https://docs.microsoft.com/sql/integration-services/ scale-out/deal-with-certificates-in-ssis-scale-out*. For a Microsoft-provided walkthrough of setting this up, visit *https://docs.microsoft.com/sql/integration-services/scale-out/ walkthrough-set-up-integration-services-scale-out*.

One major security difference with Scale Out is that even though the SQL Server Integration Services Service Account doesn't run packages or need permission to do very much, the Scale Out Master and Worker service accounts actually do run packages. The SQL Server Integration Services service account is different from the Scale Out Master and Scale Out Worker service accounts.

CHAPTER 4

The Worker and Master nodes do not appear in SQL Server Configuration Manager (as of SQL 2019) but do appear in Services.msc. By default, these services run under virtual accounts *NT Service\SSISScaleOutMaster150* and *NT Service\SSISScaleOutWorker150*, but you might want to change these to a Windows-authenticated Domain service account that will be used to run packages across the Scale Out.

Installing SQL Server Reporting Services

Starting with SQL Server 2017, SQL Server Reporting Services is no longer found in the SQL Server Setup media; it is instead available as a simplified, unified installer and a small download. SQL Server Reporting Services is now a 95+MB download named *SQLServerReportingServices. exe*, but still needs a SQL Server Database Engine instance as part of the license to host the two Report Server databases.

Note that SQL Server Reporting Services isn't free, and that the separate installer isn't a licensing change, though SQL Server Express with Advanced Services offers some limited SSRS support. For more information on the limitations of SSRS with SQL Server Express license, view *https://docs.microsoft.com/sql/reporting-services/ reporting-services-features-supported-by-the-editions-of-sql-server-2016*.

To install SSRS, you will need to provide a license key upon installation in a production environment. You can choose a free edition to install (Evaluation, Developer, or Express), though you should note that Developer edition is not allowed in a production environment.

The "native" mode of SQL Server Reporting Services is now the only mode, since SQL Server 2017. If you are familiar with Reporting Services Report Manager in the past, accessible via the URL *servername/Reports*, that is the "native mode" installation of Reporting Services.

You'll notice the Report Server Configuration Manager in a new location, in its own Program Files menu: *Microsoft SQL Server Reporting Services*. After installation, start the Report Server Configuration Manager (typically installed in a path like *\Program Files (x86)\Microsoft SQL Server\150\Tools\Binn\RSConfigTool.exe*). The Report Server Configuration Manager application itself is largely unchanged since SQL 2008.

The virtual service account *NT SERVICE\SQLServerReportingServices* is the default SQL Server Reporting Services service account. It is a second-best option, however: we recommend that you create a new domain service account to be used only for this service; for example, *Domain\ svc_ServerName_SSRS* or a similar naming convention. You will need to use a domain account if you choose to configure report server email with *Report server service account (NTLM)* authentication.

If you choose to change the SQL Server Reporting Services service account later, use only the Reporting Services Configuration Manager tool to make this change. Like other SQL Server services, never use the Services console (services.msc) to change service accounts.

After installation, you will need to follow-up on other changes and necessary administrative actions; for example, configuring the SQL Server Reporting Services Execution Account, email settings, or backing up the encryption key using Reporting Services Configuration Manager.

SQL Server 2019 Reporting Services also can integrate with Microsoft Power BI dashboards. A page in the Report Server Configuration Manager supports registering this installation of SQL Server Reporting Services with a Power BI account. You will be prompted to sign into Azure Active Directory. The account you provide must be a member of the Azure tenant where you intend to integrate with Power BI. The account should also be a member of the system administrator in SQL Server Reporting Services, via Report Manager, and a member of the sysadmin role in the SQL Server that hosts the Report Server database.

Inside OUT

Where is SQL Server Reporting Services SharePoint Integrated mode?

Starting with SQL Server 2017, there is no more SharePoint Integrated mode. The simplified "native" mode is the only installation available. This matches the moves that Microsoft has made in other areas that step away from the SharePoint on-premises product in favor of SharePoint Online features and development.

Instead, you can integrate SQL Server Reporting Services native mode with on-premises SharePoint sites via embedded SQL Server Reporting Services reports, including SQL Server Reporting Services reports stored in the Power BI Report Server.

Similarly, there is no future support for SQL Server Reporting Services integration with SharePoint Online.

Installing machine learning features

The Machine Learning Services (In-Database or the standalone Machine Learning Server) feature makes it possible for developers to integrate with the R language and/or Python language extensions using standard T-SQL statements.

Data scientists can take advantage of this feature to build advanced analytics, data forecasting, and algorithms for machine learning.

In SQL Server 2019, the Instance Feature Machine Learning Services (In-Database) is renamed to Machine Learning Services and Language Extensions, while the name for the standalone Shared Feature Machine Learning Server (Standalone) is the same.

Machine Learning Services and Language Extensions support Java code execution inside the Database Engine. By default it installs the Zulu Open JRE if you select the Java checkbox under "Machine Learning Services and Language Extensions" in the feature selection page. If you must use a different Java JRE because of an application dependency, such as the official Oracle JRE, you should add it via a home variable and the icacls Windows command, as detailed here: *https://docs.microsoft.com/sql/language-extensions/install/ install-sql-server-language-extensions-on-windows.*

➤ **For more on Installing and Leveraging Machine Learning Services, see Chapter 20, "Leveraging Big Data and Machine Learning."**

Installing PolyBase Query Service for External Data

The PolyBase connector is a much-marketed feature for allowing native connectors for external data sources, even non-Microsoft or non-relational database platforms like Oracle, Teradata, MongoDB, Cloudera, or Apache Hadoop.

Using PolyBase EXTERNAL tables, we can use SQL data types and T-SQL queries to seamless query data sources in-place, in what Microsoft calls "data virtualization." This eliminates the need for complex heterogeneous data movement, and reduces the need for developers to have knowledge of other external query languages. The PolyBase Query Engine feature is specifically designed for read and write queries against non-Microsoft database platforms like Oracle and DB2, but also for Hadoop nonrelational data or Azure Blob Storage files, MongoDB, and more. This is a superior alternative to linked servers to the same external data sources, because PolyBase allows "Push Down" computation for these external sources, reducing the amount of data transferred and increasing the performance of analytical-scale queries.

New to SQL Server 2019 is the ability to install the *Java connector for HDFS data sources* with SQL Server Setup. This 7GB+ option doesn't replace the requirement to install the Oracle JRE in order to install the PolyBase Query Service feature.

➤ **For more on the PolyBase Query Service feature, see Chapter 20.**

Logging SQL Server Setup

SQL Server Setup generates a large number of logging files for diagnostic and troubleshooting purposes. These logs should be the first place you go when you have an issue with Setup.

First, a System Configuration Check report .htm file is generated each time you run Setup, so you can view this report in SQL Server Setup near the start of the installation steps.

A new timestamp-named folder of log files is generated for each launch of SQL Server Setup. After you proceed past the *Ready To Install* page, and regardless of whether Setup was a complete success, it generates a number of log files in the following folder:

%programfiles%\Microsoft SQL Server\150\Setup Bootstrap\Log\YYYYMMDD_HHMMSS

However, when you run Setup using the /Q or /QS parameters for unattended installation, the log file is written to the Windows *%temp%* folder.

A log summary file of the installation is created that uses the following naming convention:

Summary_*instancename_YYYYMMDD_HHMMSS*.txt

Setup generates similar files for the Component and Global Rules portions of Setup as well as a file called Detail.txt in the same folder. These files might contain the detailed error messages you are looking for when troubleshooting a failed installation. The Windows Application Event log might also contain helpful information in that situation.

You'll also find the new SQL Server instance's first error log encoded at UTC time in this folder, showing the log from startup, similar to the normal SQL Server Error Log.

> ### NOTE
>
> **At the time of this writing, there is an outstanding installation issue with SQL Server 2019, installation media mounted on removeable media, and SQL Server Management Studio versions 18.0 through 18.3. The problem and solution are detailed here in a link provided by Microsoft: *https://techcommunity.microsoft.com/t5/SQL-Server-Support/ SQL-Server-2019-Installation-Error-An-error-occurred-for-a/ba-p/998033*. In short: copy the files locally, or, uninstall the SQL Server 2012 Native Client, then re-try installation of SQL Server 2019. You should always try to run the latest version of SSMS.**

Automating SQL Server Setup by using configuration files

Let's dig more into what you can do with setup.exe outside of the user interface. You can use configuration files to automate the selection process when installing SQL Server, which helps to create a consistent configuration.

Values provided in configuration files can prepopulate or override Setup settings. They also can configure Setup to run with the normal user interface, or silently without any interface.

Starting SQL Server Setup from the command line

You can start setup.exe from either Windows PowerShell or the command prompt, providing repeatability and standardization of parameter options. You also can use it to prefill sections of the Setup wizard or to change the default behavior of Setup.

For the purposes of the installer, ensure that you always use the Administrator level for these two shells. The title on each application window should be preceded by *Administrator:*, such as: *Administrator: Windows PowerShell*.

Sometimes, you also might find it necessary to start Setup from the command line or Windows PowerShell because of a workaround for a specific problem, or to automate and standardize future SQL Server installations. To start Windows PowerShell or command prompt as Administrator, in the Start menu, search for the desired application (see Figure 4-4), right-click it, and then, on the shortcut menu that opens, select **Run As Administrator**.

```
PS D:\> .\Setup.exe /ConfigurationFile=c:\install\SQL2019_basic.INI
Microsoft (R) SQL Server 2019 15.00.2000.05
Copyright (c) 2019 Microsoft.  All rights reserved.
```

Figure 4-4   Starting Setup.exe from PowerShell.

From the location of the SQL Server Setup installation files, for example the mounted .iso file, execute the following with PowerShell or the Windows Prompt:

```
.\Setup.exe /ConfigurationFile=c:\install\SQL2019_basic.INI
```

The previous sample script and all scripts for this book are available for download at *https://www.MicrosoftPressStore.com/SQLServer2019InsideOut/downloads*. The above code sample uses a configuration file to pre-select installation choices, for example, features to be installed. Let's talk more about configuration files.

Generating a configuration file

Writing a configuration file by hand is not necessary and can be tedious. Instead of going through that effort, you can let SQL Server Setup create a configuration file for you.

Work your way through the normal SQL Server Setup user interface, completing everything as you normally would, but pause when you get to the *Ready To Install* page. Near the bottom of this page is a path (see Figure 4-5). At that location, even before you hit the **Install** button, you'll find a generated configuration file, ready for future use and modification if needed.

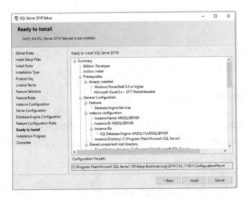

Figure 4-5   The Ready To Install page displays a summary of the installation steps as the Configuration File Path that has been prepared.

For example, the first modification you need to make to the .ini file is to accept the SQL Server license terms via the IACCEPTSQLSERVERLICENSETERMS parameter, which isn't automatically provided in the automatically generated .ini file. Unless you modify an .ini file to provide this, it isn't possible to run the installer without user interaction.

Installing by using a configuration file

Now that you have a configuration file generated by using a previous walk-through of Setup, you can take the next step to automating or standardizing your installation.

You can start Setup.exe from a Prompt with a configuration file by using the /CONFIGURATIONFILE parameter of Setup.exe. Or, you can launch SQL Server Setup with a configuration file by navigating to the Advanced page of the SQL Server Installation Center that starts with Setup.exe in Windows. Select the *Install Based On A Configuration File* check box. A message appears, asking you to browse to the .ini file. After you select the appropriate file, setup.exe will start with those options.

One thing to keep mind, however, is that configuration files generated by Setup.exe do not and should not store the passwords you provided for any service accounts. If you do want to configure service account credentials in your configuration file, for security reasons, do not store the service account passwords in plain text in a configuration file. You should instead store passwords separately and securely and provide them when you run setup.exe.

Each service's account parameters are available in a Setup.exe runtime parameter, which is listed in Table 4-1.

Table 4-1   Common Setup.exe parameters and their purposes

Service	Parameter name	Description
SQL Server Database Engine	/SQLSVCPASSWORD	Password for the SQL Server Database Engine Services service account. This is the service account for sqlservr.exe. It is required if a domain account is used for the service.
SQL Server Agent	/AGTSVCPASSWORD	Password for the SQL Server Agent service account. This is the service account for sqlagent.exe. It is required if a domain account is used for the service.
sa password	/SAPWD	Password for the sa account. It is required when /SECURITYMODE=SQL is used, which enables Mixed Mode authentication.
Integration Services	/ISSVCPASSWORD	Password for the Integration Services service. It is required if a domain account is used for the service.
Reporting Services (Native)	/RSSVCPASSWORD	Password for the Reporting Services service. It is required if a domain account is used for the service.

CHAPTER 4

Analysis Services	/ASSVCPASSWORD	Password for the Analysis Services service account. It is required if a domain account is used for the service.
PolyBase	/PBDMSSVCPASSWORD	Password for the PolyBase engine service account.
Full-Text filter launcher service	/FTSVCPASSWORD	Password for the Full-Text filter launcher service.

For example, in the snippet that follows, the PROD_ConfigurationFile_Install.INI has provided the account name of the of the SQL Server Database Engine service account, but the password is provided when Setup.exe runs in the command prompt or PowerShell:

```
Setup.exe /SQLSVCPASSWORD="securepwd" /ConfigurationFile="d:\SQL\PROD_Install.INI"
```

The previous sample script and all scripts for this book are available for download at *https://www.MicrosoftPressStore.com/SQLServer2019InsideOut/downloads*.

You can provide further parameters like passwords when you run Setup. Parameter settings provided will override any settings in the configuration file, just as the configuration file's settings will override any defaults in the Setup operation. Table 4-2 lists and describes the parameters.

By default the /UpdateEnabled parameter is enabled and doesn't need to be specified, and SQL Server will include updates found via Windows Update. If you choose to disable this behavior by provided /UpdateEnabled=False, you can also specify /UpdateSource the location of cumulative update or other SQL patch file executables to be included in the installation.

Table 4-2   Common Setup.exe parameters of which you should be aware

Parameter usage	Parameter	Description
Unattended installations	/Q	Specifies Quiet Mode with no user interface and user interactivity allowed.
Unattended installations	/QS	Specifies Quiet Mode with user interface but no user interactivity allowed. Will fail if all needed information or parameters are not provided.
Accept license terms	/IACCEPTSQLSERVERLICENSETERMS	Must provide in any Configuration File looking to avoid prompts for installation.
R open license terms	/IACCEPTROPENLICENSETERMS	Must provide this parameter for any unattended installation involving the R language option for Machine Learning Services.

Python open license terms	/IACCEPTPYTHONLICENSETERMS	Must provide this parameter for any unattended installation involving the Python language option for Machine Learning Services.
Instant file initialization	/SQLSVCINSTANTFILEINIT	Set to true to Grant Perform Volume Maintenance Task privilege to the SQL Server Database Engine Service (recommended).
Windows accounts to provision as members of the sysadmin role	/SQLSYSADMINACCOUNTS	Must provide groups or service accounts to specify as the initial members of the sysadmin role.
Provision the user running SQL Server Setup as a member of the sysadmin role	/ADDCURRENTUSERASSQLADMIN	If desired, also specify the current local Windows Server user running SQL Server Setup as an initial member of the sysadmin role. Not desired if using a personal named account, use a group instead.
TempDB data file count	/SQLTEMPDBFILECOUNT	Set to the number of desired TempDB data files to be installed initially.
Enable the TCP/IP Protocol	/TCPENABLED="1"	Disabled by default and used in many installations, enable the TCP/IP protocol here to save yourself a step in Configuration Manager later on.

Post-installation server configuration

After you install SQL Server, there are a number of changes to make or confirm on the Windows Server and in settings for SQL Server.

Post-installation checklist

You should run through the following checklist on your new SQL Server instance. The order of these items isn't necessarily specific, and many deal with SQL server and/or Windows configuration settings. Evaluate whether these are appropriate for your environment, but you should consider and apply them to most SQL Server installations.

1. Check your SQL Server patch level version, and apply patches if necessary.

2. Review Maximum server memory settings for other features.

3. Review Surface Area Configuration.

4. Set up SQL Agent.

5. Turn on TCP/IP if needed.

6. Verify power options for the server.

7. Configure antivirus exclusions for SQL Server processes and files.

8. Enable the server setting "optimize for ad hoc workloads."

9. Evaluate whether Lock pages in memory is necessary.

10. Review size and location of the Windows page file.

11. Set up scheduled backups, index maintenance, log retention maintenance, and integrity checks.

12. Backup service master and database master keys.

13. Increase SQL Agent and SQL Error log retention from the defaults.

14. Suppress successful backup messages.

Let's take a look at each of these in more detail in the subsections that follow.

Check your SQL Server version

After you install SQL Server, check the version number against the latest cumulative updates list, especially if you did not opt to or could not use Windows Update during SQL Server Setup. You can view the version number in SQL Server Management Studio's Object Explorer or via a T-SQL query on either the following built-in functions:

```
SELECT @@VERSION;
SELECT SERVERPROPERTY('ProductVersion');
SELECT SERVERPROPERTY('Edition');
```

While you're at it, doublecheck that you installed the right edition of SQL Server too!

NOTE

Take the opportunity before your SQL Server enters production to patch it. For information about the latest cumulative updates for SQL Server, search for KB321185 or visit *https://support.microsoft.com/help/321185/*.

Maximum server memory settings for other features

Other features of SQL Server have their own maximum server memory settings. As you will notice by their default settings, for servers on which both the SQL Server Database Engine and SQL Server Analysis Services and/or SQL Server Reporting Services are installed, competition for and exhaustion of memory is possible. It is recommended that you protect the Database Engine by lowering the potential memory impact of other applications.

Limiting SQL Server Analysis Services memory

SQL Server Analysis Services (SSAS) has not just one maximum server memory limit, but five, and you can enforce limits by hard values in bytes or by a percentage of total physical memory of the server.

You can change these memory settings via SSMS by connecting to the SSAS instance in Object Explorer. Right-click the server, and then, on the shortcut menu, click **Properties**. Some of the memory settings described here are identical for Multidimensional and Tabular installations, some are for Tabular mode only:

- **LowMemoryLimit.**   A value that serves as a floor for memory, but also the level at which SSAS begins to release memory for infrequently used or low-priority objects in its cache. Below this level no memory maintenance is performed by SSAS. The default value is 65, or 65 percent of total server physical memory (or the Virtual Address Space technically, but SSAS, among other features, is no longer supported on 32-bit systems, and so this is not a concern).

- **TotalMemoryLimit.**   A value that serves as a threshold for SSAS to begin to release memory for higher priority requests. It's important to note that this is not a hard limit. The default is 80 percent of total server memory.

- **HardMemoryLimit.**   This is a hard memory limit that will lead to more aggressive pruning of memory from cache and potentially to the rejection of new requests. By default, this is displayed as 0 and is effectively the midway point between the TotalMemoryLimit and the server physical memory. The TotalMemoryLimit must always be less than the HardMemoryLimit.

- **VertiPaqMemoryLimit.**   For SSAS installations in Tabular mode only, this limit has a default of 60, or 60 percent of server physical memory. Above this percentage, and only if VertiPaqPagingPolicy is turned on (it is by default), SSAS begins to page data to the hard drive using the OS page file. Paging to a drive can help prevent out-of-memory errors when the HardMemoryLimit is met.

- **QueryMemoryLimit.**   New to SQL Server 2019, this can limit the amount of memory used by individual DAX queries, preventing any one query from dominating memory. For any individual query, this setting can be overridden by a new XMLA property DbpropMsmdRequestMemoryLimit, specified for the query connection. This setting can be specified as a percentage (values <=100), or as a number of bytes greater than 100. The default setting of 0 implies no limit to the memory of individual queries.

Figure 4-6 shows the General page of the Analysis Server Properties dialog box, as started in Object Explorer in SSMS, and the locations of the preceding memory configuration properties with their defaults in SQL Server 2019 for a Tabular mode installation of SSAS. Note that the option to "Show Advanced (All) Properties" is checked.

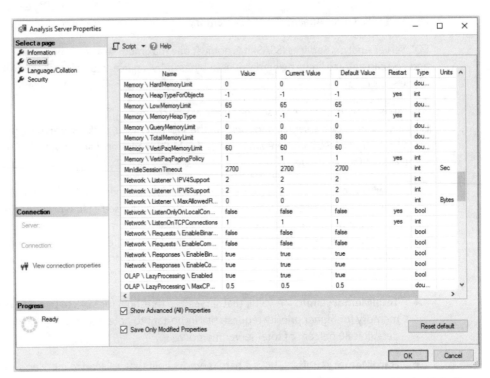

Figure 4-6 The General page in the Analysis Server Properties dialog box showing the default settings.

Limiting SQL Server Reporting Services memory

Four options are available for limiting SQL Server Reporting Services memory utilization, and all are based on numbers contained in tags within a .config file, so be sure to make a backup of it before editing. You can configure memory settings only in the RSReportServer.config file, which is a text file that is stored at *%ProgramFiles%\Microsoft SQL Server Reporting Services\SSRS\ ReportServer.*

> **NOTE**
>
> **This location has changed from previous versions, but the config file name has not.**

Two of the settings are in the .config file by default; two more are available to administrators to use in advanced scenarios.

Let's take a look at each one:

- **MemorySafetyMargin.** The percentage of WorkingSetMaximum that SQL Server Reporting Services will use before taking steps to reduce background task memory utilization and prioritize requests coming from the web service, attempting to protect user requests. User requests could still be denied.

- **MemoryThreshold.**   The percentage of `WorkSetMaximum` at which SQL Server Reporting Services will deny new requests, slow down existing requests, and page memory to a hard drive until memory conditions improve.

Two more settings are instead given values automatically upon service startup, but you can override them in the .config file. Two older memory settings from SQL Server 2005 with which SQL DBAs might be familiar, are `MemoryLimit` and `MaximumMemoryLimit`, but those two values have been ignored since SQL Server 2008.

- **WorkingSetMaximum.**   By default, this is the total server's physical memory. This setting does not appear by default in the .config file, but you can override it to reduce the amount of memory of which SQL Server Reporting Services will be aware. This value is expressed in kilobytes of memory.

- **WorkingSetMinimum.**   By default, this value is 60 percent of the `WorkingSetMaximum`. If SQL Server Reporting Services needs memory below this value, it will use memory and not release it due to memory pressure. This setting does not appear by default in the .config file, but you can override it to increase the variability of SQL Server Reporting Service's memory utilization.

These four settings can appear in the rsreportserver.config file. As demonstrated here, you could override the default settings to 4 GB maximum and 2 GB minimum (each expressed in KB):

```
<MemorySafetyMargin>80</MemorySafetyMargin>
<MemoryThreshold>90</MemoryThreshold>
<WorkingSetMaximum>4194304</WorkingSetMaximum>
<WorkingSetMinimum>2097152</WorkingSetMinimum>
```

Limiting Machine Learning Server memory

Similar to SSAS and SSRS, the Machine Learning Server has a .config file at *%ProgramFiles%\ Microsoft SQL Server\MSSQL15.instancename\MSSQL\Binn\rlauncher.config*.

By default, Machine Learning Server is similar to 20 percent of total server memory. You can override this by adding a tag to the .config file to provide a value for `MEMORY_LIMIT_PERCENT`. This value is not in the .config file by default.

Remember to make a backup of this config file before editing. The following is an example of the contents of the rlauncher.config file, with the default memory limit changed to 25 percent:

```
RHOME=C:\PROGRA~2\MICROS~1\MSSQL1~4.SQL\R_SERV~2
MPI_HOME=C:\Program Files\Microsoft MPI
INSTANCE_NAME=SQL2K19
```

```
TRACE_LEVEL=1
JOB_CLEANUP_ON_EXIT=1
USER_POOL_SIZE=0
WORKING_DIRECTORY=C:\Program Files\Microsoft SQL
Server\MSSQL15.SQL2K19\MSSQL\ExtensibilityData
PKG_MGMT_MODE=0
MEMORY_LIMIT_PERCENT=25
```

The previous sample script and all scripts for this book are available for download at
https://www.MicrosoftPressStore.com/SQLServer2019InsideOut/downloads.

Surface Area Configuration

If you are a veteran SQL Server DBA, you will remember when SQL Server Surface Area Configuration was a separate application. Surface Area Configuration is now considered a facet, accessed via the Facets dialog in SSMS starting with SQL Server 2008.

To view Surface Area Configuration in SSMS, in Object Explorer, connect to the *SQL Server*, right-click the server, and then, on the shortcut menu, click **Facets**. (Note that this window sometimes takes a moment to load.) In the dialog box that opens, change the value in the list box to **Surface Area Configuration**.

Keep in mind that most of these options should remain off unless needed because they present a specific potential for misuse by an administrator or unauthorized user. In typical installations of SQL Server 2019, however, you should consider enabling three of these options:

- Database Mail (more about this in Chapter 9: "Automating SQL Server administration"). This should be enabled on most instances, to allow SQL Server at the very least to send out a message in case of a high severity or job failure, and also to allow developers to send custom email message using the system procedure sp_send_dbmail. You also can turn this setting on or off via the Database Mail XPs option in sp_configure.

- Remote Dedicated Admin Connection (more on this in Chapter 13: "Protecting data through encryption, privacy and auditing"). This could be particularly useful for bypassing a malfunctioning login triggers or Resource Governor. You also can turn this setting on or off via the remote admin connections option in sp_configure.

- CLR Integration, which you will need to turn on if you need to use SQL Server Integration Services, or if you need to write CLR objects. You also can turn this setting on or off via the clr_enabled option in sp_configure.

You should turn on other options in Surface Area Configuration only if they are specifically required by an application and you are aware of the potential security concerns.

Setting up SQL Agent

There are several post-installation tasks to set up in SQL Agent before SQL Server can begin to help you automate, monitor, and back up your new instance.

➤ **Chapters 8 and 9 cover SQL Agent and monitoring topics in detail.**

You will likely want to do the following:

1. Change the SQL Agent service from Manual to Automatic startup.

2. To send email notifications for alerts or job status notifications, you must set up a Database Mail account and profile (see Chapter 9).

3. Set up an Operator for a distribution group of IT professionals in your organization who would respond to a SQL Server issue.

4. Configure SQL Server Agent to use Database Mail, including a fail-safe operator.

5. Set up SQL Server Alerts for desired errors and high severity (Severity 21+) errors.

At the very least, these steps are put in place so that SQL Server can send out a call for help. Even if you have centralized monitoring solutions in place, the most rare and severe of errors should be important enough to warrant an email.

You can choose to configure a large number of Windows Management Instrumentation (WMI) conditions, Perfmon counter conditions, and SQL Server Error messages by number or severity in SQL Server Alerts. However, do not overcommit your inboxes, and do not set an inbox rule to Mark As Read and file away emails from SQL Server. By careful selection of emails, you can assure yourself and your team that emails from SQL Server will be actionable concerns that rarely arrive.

➤ **For much more information on Managing and Monitoring SQL Server, see Chapter 13.**

Enabling the TCP/IP network protocol

The common network protocol TCP/IP is off by default, and the only protocol that is on is Shared Memory, which allows only local connections. You will likely not end up using Shared Memory alone to connect to the SQL Server for common business applications that use multiple servers for database, web, and application tiers.

> ### NOTE
>
> **It is possible to enable the TCP/IP protocol by default at the time of installation if using a configuration file for SQL Server Setup, but this option does not appear in the UI for SQL Server setup. It must be changed after installation is complete.**

When you connect to SQL Server using SSMS while local to the server, you connect to the Shared_Memory endpoint whenever you provide the name of the server, the server\instance, localhost, the dot character ("."), or (local), or .\instance, or (local)\instance.

TCP/IP, however, is ubiquitous in many SQL Server features and functionality. Many applications will need to use TCP/IP to connect to the SQL Server remotely. Many SQL Server features require TCP/IP to be enabled, including the Remote Dedicated Admin Connection (DAC), the Always On availability groups listener, and Kerberos authentication.

To configure the TCP/IP protocol, open the SQL Server Configuration Manager application locally on the server, in the left pane, click **SQL Server Network Configuration**. Browse to the protocols for your newly installed instance of SQL Server. The default instance of SQL Server, here and in many places, will appear as **MSSQLSERVER**.

You can also enable the TCP/IP protocol for a SQL Server instance with PowerShell:

```
Import-Module SqlServer
$wmi = new-object('Microsoft.SqlServer.Management.Smo.Wmi.ManagedComputer')
#Path to the local server
$path = "ManagedComputer[@Name='$env:COMPUTERNAME']/"
$path = $path+"ServerInstance[@Name='SQL2K19']/ServerProtocol[@Name='Tcp']"
#Enable the TCP protocol on the local server, on the named instance SQL2K19
$TCPIP = $wmi.GetSmoObject($path)
$TCPIP.IsEnabled = $true
$TCPIP.Alter()
$TCPIP.IsEnabled
#Restart SQL Server Database Engine service to apply the change
```

The previous sample script and all scripts for this book are available for download at *https://www.MicrosoftPressStore.com/SQLServer2019InsideOut/downloads*.

After turning on the TCP/IP protocol via any method, you need to restart the SQL Server Database Engine service for it to take effect.

NOTE

Turning on Named Pipes is not required or used unless an application specifically needs it.

Verifying server power options

The Windows Server Power Options setting should be set to High Performance for any server hosting a SQL Server instance.

In other power plans, Windows might not operate the processor at maximum frequency during normal or even busy periods of SQL Server activity. This applies to physical or virtual Windows servers.

Review this setting and ensure that the group policy will not change this setting back to Balanced or another setting. Also ensure that group preferences are configured for High Performance for new SQL Servers.

Configuring antivirus exclusions

Configure any antivirus software installed on the SQL Server to ignore scanning files with extensions used by your SQL Server data and log files. Typically, these will be .mdf, .ldf, and .ndf.

Also, configure any antivirus programs to ignore folders containing SQL Server files. This could include:

- Full-text catalog files

- Backup files

- Replication snapshot files

- SQL Server trace (.trc) files

- SQL Audit files

- Analysis Services database

- Log and backup files

- FILESTREAM and FileTable folders

- SQL Server Reporting Services temp files and log files

Processes might also be affected, so set antivirus programs to ignore the programs for all instances of the SQL Server Database Engine service, Reporting Services service, Analysis Services service, and R Server (RTerm.exe and BxlServer.exe).

In SQL Server Failover Cluter Instances (FCIs) and availability groups, also configure antivirus software to exclude the MSCS folder on the quorum drive if in use, the MSDTC directory on the MSDTC share, and the Windows\Cluster folder on each cluster node, if they exist.

Inside OUT

What if you suspect antivirus or antimalware software is interfering with SQL Server?

This is one of the more challenging troubleshooting exercises: a strange error message, DLL error, or file accessibility issue. It is critical to configure antivirus to exclude SQL Server files and folders from on-access scans, exclusive-lock scans, and more.

> If you notice, for example, random databases failing to recover upon SQL Server startup, or error messages regarding *File activation failure* or *Unable to open the physical file*, sqlservr.exe may not be able to gain exclusive access to the files because they are being scanned by another application. Use the Windows sysinternals Process Explorer application to search for handles including your SQL Server files, and potentially catch that other application accessing the file.
>
> Antivirus applications may also interfere with service packs and cumulative updates if those files, even if they are signed by Microsoft, have not been pre-approved for execution in the production environment. Communicate with the teams that control antivirus, anti-ransomware, or anti-malware solutions in your enterprise.

Enable Optimize For Ad Hoc Workloads

The server-level setting *Optimize For Ad Hoc Workloads* doesn't have the most intuitive name.

We are not optimizing ad hoc queries; we are optimizing SQL Server memory usage to prevent ad hoc queries from consuming unnecessary cache.

➤ For more about the *Optimize For Ad Hoc Workloads* setting, see Chapter 2: Introducing database server components.

For the unlikely scenario in which a large number of queries are executed only two times, setting this option to **True** would be a net negative for performance. However, like other design concepts in databases, we find that there are either one or many. There is no two.

➤ To read more about cached execution plans, see Chapter 14.

Lock Pages in Memory

You should consider using the *Lock Pages in Memory* setting for environments in which instances of SQL Server are expected to experience memory pressure due to other applications, server limitations, or overallocated virtualized systems. This is an in-depth topic to be carefully considered.

➤ For more about the *Lock Pages in Memory* setting, see Chapter 2.

➤ For more about the Windows page file, see Chapter 3.

Inside OUT

How can you tell if the permission to Lock Pages in Memory is in effect?

Starting with SQL Server 2016 SP1, you can check whether the *Lock Pages in Memory* **permission has been granted to the SQL Server Database Engine service:**

```
SELECT sql_memory_model_desc
FROM sys.dm_os_sys_info;
--CONVENTIONAL = Lock pages in memory privilege is not granted
--LOCK_PAGES = Lock pages in memory privilege is granted
--LARGE_PAGES = Lock pages in memory privilege is granted in Enterprise mode
--  with Trace Flag 834 ON
```

The previous sample script and all scripts for this book are available for download at *https://www.MicrosoftPressStore.com/SQLServer2019InsideOut/downloads.*

Backups, index maintenance, and integrity checks

Backups are a critical part of your disaster recovery, and they should begin as soon as possible after installation, and before the users or applications begin to use the SQL Server.

Begin taking database backups, at least of the master and msdb databases. You should also back up other SQL Server Setup-created databases, including ReportServer, ReportServer-TempDB, and SSISDB right away.

➤ For more information on backups, index maintenance, and monitoring, see Chapter 11.

As soon as your new SQL Server instance has databases in use, regularly perform selective index maintenance and integrity checks that take into account the current fragmentation levels of indexes, rather than performing index maintenance on entire databases.

➤ For more information on automating maintenance, see Chapter 13.

Backing up service master and database master keys

You should back up service master keys and any database master keys as they are created, securely storing their information.

➤ For more information on service master and database master keys, see Chapter 6.

To back up the instance service master key, use the following:

```
BACKUP SERVICE MASTER KEY TO FILE = 'localfilepath_or_UNC' ENCRYPTION BY PASSWORD =
'complexpassword'
```

CHAPTER 4

And as soon as database master keys come into existence in each user database, for example as you implement features like Transparent Data Encryption (TDE) or column data encryption, back up individual database master keys, as follows:

```
BACKUP MASTER KEY TO FILE = 'localfilepath_or_UNC' ENCRYPTION BY PASSWORD =
'complexpassword'
```

The previous sample script and all scripts for this book are available for download at *https://www.MicrosoftPressStore.com/SQLServer2019InsideOut/downloads*.

If you implement Transparent Data Encryption, Always Encrypted, native backup encryption, column encryption, or any other native or external solutions that generate certificates, keys and/or passwords, develop a secure storage and retrieval method inside your enterprise. Failure to back up master and database master keys could compromise future disaster recovery attempts!

Increasing default error and agent history retention

By default, SQL Server maintains the current SQL Server error log plus six more error logs of history. Logs are cycled each time the SQL Server service is started.

One eventful, fun weekend of server troubleshooting or maintenance where the SQL Server service is restarted many times could wipe out a significant amount of your error history. This could make the task of troubleshooting periodic or business-cycle related errors difficult or impossible. You need visibility into errors that occur only during a monthly processing, monthly patch day, or periodic reporting.

In SQL Server Management Studio, in Object Explorer, connect to the SQL Server instance. Expand the Management folder, right-click **SQL Server Logs**, and then, on the shortcut menu, click **Configure**. Select the *Limit The Number Of Error Logs Before They Are Recycled* check box and type a value larger than 6. You might find that a value between 25 and 50 will result in more useful log history contained for multiple business cycles.

On SQL Servers that generate a large amount of log "noise", consider other options to reduce the clutter of the SQL Error Log, including Trace Flag 3226 to suppress the logging of successful backup operations (much more on that in the next section).

You may also choose to configure a SQL Agent Job to manually cycle the SQL Error Log using sp_cycle_errorlog, so that no one log file contains too much data to be unwieldly for scan and analysis.

Similarly, you might find that the SQL Server Agent history is not sufficient to cover an adequate amount of job history, especially if you have frequent job runs.

To change the history settings for SQL Server Agent, in SSMS, in Object Explorer, connect to the SQL Server instance. Right-click **SQL Server Agent**, and then click **Properties**. Click the

History page. This page is not intuitive and can be confusing. The first option, *Limit Size Of The Job History Log*, is a rolling job history retention setting. Consider increasing the maximum log history size in rows from the default of 1,000 to 10,000 or more, and also increase the maximum job history per job in rows from the default of 100 to 2,000 or more. This data is stored in the msdb system database and will cause that database to grow larger over time. Consider pre-allocating now some additional file space to the msdb data file.

The second option, *Remove Agent History*, along with its companion *Older Than* text box is not a rolling job history retention setting; rather, it is an immediate and manual job history pruning. Select this second check box, and then click **OK** and return to this page; you will find the second check box is cleared. Behind the scenes, SQL Server Management Studio ran the msdb.dbo. sp_purge_jobhistory stored procedure to remove job history manually.

Suppress successful backup messages

By default, SQL Server writes an event to the error log upon a successful database backup, whether it be FULL, DIFFERENTIAL, or TRANSACTION LOG.

On instances with many databases and with many databases in FULL recovery model with regular transaction log backups, the amount of log activity generated by just their successful frequent log backups could flood the log with clutter, lowering log history retention.

> ### NOTE
> It is important to note that you can review successful backup history by querying the msdb system database, which has a series of tables dedicated to storing the backup history for all databases, including msdb.dbo.backupset and msdb.dbo. backupmediafamily. The built-in "Backup and Restore Events" report in SQL Server Management Studio provides access to this data, as well.

> ➤ For more on backups, see Chapter 10, "Developing, deploying, and managing data recovery."

SQL Server Trace Flag 3226 controls an option at the instance level to suppress successful backup notifications.

There are many trace flags available to administrators to alter default behavior—many more options than there are user interfaces to accommodate them in SQL Server Management Studio. Take care when turning them on and understand that many trace flags are intended only for temporary use when aiding troubleshooting.

As Trace Flag 3226 is intended to be a permanent setting, simply starting the trace by using DBCC TRACEON is not sufficient, given that the trace flag will no longer be active following a SQL Server service restart. Instead, add the trace flag as a startup parameter to the SQL Server Database Engine service by using SQL Server Configuration Manager. In the Properties of the SQL

CHAPTER 4

Server service, go to the Startup Parameters tab, and use the syntax -T*flagnumber*. This field is essentially adding parameters that are passed to the sqlserver.exe executable. For example, add "-T3226", then click Add. The change will not take effect until the SQL Server Database Engine service is restarted.

➤ For more information on SQL Server Configuration Manager, see Chapter 1.

Post-installation configuration of other features

SQL Server Database Engine installation is now complete, but three other features require post-installation configuration, including SQL Server Integration Services, SQL Server Reporting Services, and SQL Server Analysis Services. You will need to perform the steps detailed in this section before use if these features are installed.

SSISDB initial configuration and setup

Among the best features added by SQL Server 2012 were massive improvements to SQL Server Integration Services, specifically with a new server-integrated deployment, built-in performance data collector, environment variables, and more developer quality-of-life improvements. For these reasons, use the new Project Deployment Model and the built-in SSISDB for all new development.

When the Integration Services Catalog is created, a new user database called SSISDB is also created. You should back it up and treat it as an important production database.

You should create the SSISDB catalog soon after installation and before a SQL Server Integration Services development can take place. You will need to create the catalog only once. Because this will involve potential Surface Area Configuration changes and the creation of a new strong encryption password, a SQL DBA, not a SQL Server Integration Services developer, should perform this and store the password securely alongside others generated at the time of installation.

In Object Explorer, connect to your instance, right-click **Integration Services Catalog**, and then, on the shortcut menu, click **Create Catalog**. In this single-page setup, you must select the *Enable CLR Integration* check box, decide whether SQL Server Integration Services packages should be allowed to be run at SQL Server Startup (we recommend this due to the maintenance and cleanup performed then), and provide an encryption password for the SSISDB database.

The encryption password is for the SSISDB database master key. After you create it, you should then back up the SSISDB database master key.

➤ For more on database master keys, see Chapter 13.

The SSISDB database will contain SQL Server Integration Services packages, their connection strings, and more data about the packages. The encryption would not allow these sensitive contents to be decrypted by a malicious user who gains access to the database files or backups. This password would be required if the database were moved to another server, so you should store it in a secure location within your enterprise.

NOTE

If you receive an error when creating the SSSIDB catalog that reads "The catalog backup file 'C:\Program Files\Microsoft SQL Server\150\DTS\Binn\SSISDBBackup.bak' could not be accessed" or similar, it is likely because SQL Server Integration Services was not actually installed. It's likely that the 6MB template database backup was not copied from the SQL Server media, perhaps because the SSIS feature was not installed on this instance. You can run SQL Server Setup again or copy the SSISDBBackup.bak file from another SQL Server installation of the same version.

SQL Server Reporting Services initial configuration and setup

There are still tasks to perform upon first installation of a SQL Server Reporting Services native-mode installation from the downloaded installer file, SQLServerReportingServices.exe. At the end of the Microsoft SQL Server 2019 Reporting Services installer wizard, on the Setup Completed screen, click the **Configure report server** button to open the Reporting Services Configuration Manager application. Connect to the newly installed SQL Server Reporting Services instance, and then review the following options, from top to bottom:

- **Service Account.**   You can change the SQL Server Reporting Services service account here. Remember that you should use only the Reporting Services Configuration Manager tool to make this change.

- **Web Service URL.**   The web service URL is not for user interaction; rather, it is for the Report Manager and custom applications to programmatically connect to the SQL Server Reporting Services instance.

  By default, a web service on TCP Port 80 is created called ReportServer. For named instances, the web service will be called ReportServer_*instancename*. The URL for the webservice would then be:

  servername/ReportServer

  or:

  servername/ReportServer_*instancename*

  To accept defaults, at the bottom of the application window, click **Apply**.

  You can optionally configure an SSL certificate to a specific URL for the Web Portal in the Advanced section here. Choose an identity and an HTTPS certificate that's been loaded to the server, and the Reporting Services Configuration Manager will make the changes necessary. For more information on configuring SSL connections for the SSRS

Web Service and Web Portal, visit: *https://docs.microsoft.com/sql/reporting-services/security/configure-ssl-connections-on-a-native-mode-report-server.*

- **Database.**   Each instance of SSRS requires requires a pair of databases running on a SQL Server instance. Simply executing the SSRS installer alone does not configure the databases for SSRS, you need to configure them via the Reporting Services Configuration Manager. The database names by default are ReportServer and ReportServerTempDB, or, for a named instance, ReportServer$*InstanceName* and ReportServer$*InstanceName*TempDB. Both of these databases are important and you should create a backup schedule for each. The ReportServerTempDB is not a completely transient database like the SQL Server instance's TempDB system database.

    The databases for SSRS can be hosted on a on-premises SQL Server instance or Azure VM-hosted SQL Server instance or, new to SQL Server 2019, hosted on an Azure SQL Managed Instance.

    To set the databases for a new instance of SSRS, in the Database page of the Reporting Services Configuration Manager, click Change Database, and then follow the *Report Server Database Configuration Wizard*.

- **Web Portal URL.**   The web portal URL is the user-friendly website that hosts links to reports and provides for administrative features to the SQL Server Reporting Services instance. This is the link to share with users if you will be using the SQL Server Reporting Services portal.

    By default, the URL for the web portal is */Reports*

    servername/Reports for the default instance

    or:

    servername/Reports_*InstanceName* for named instances

    You can change the name from the default here if desired. To proceed, at the bottom of the application window, click **Apply**.

- **Email Settings.**   You use these email settings for sending reports to user subscribers via email. SQL Server Reporting Services uses its own Email Settings and does not inherit from the SQL Server instance's Database Mail settings. This setting is optional if you do not intend to send reports to subscribers via email.

    SQL Server Reporting Services can authenticate to an SMTP server using anonymous (No Authentication), Basic, or NT LAN Manager (NTLM) authentication, which will use the SQL Server Reporting Services service account to authenticate to the SMTP server.

    NOTE   Keep in mind that enterprise SMTP servers usually have an allow list of IP addresses, and you will need to add this server's IP to this list to relay email.

- **Execution Account.**   You can provide this domain account optionally to be used when reports are configured to run on a schedule, to run without credentials (select the Credentials Are Not Required Option), or to connect to remote servers for external images.

  The execution account should not be the same as the SQL Server Reporting Services service account.

  This account should have minimal read-only access to any data sources that will require it. You also can give it EXECUTE permissions for data sources that use stored procedures, but you should never give it any additional SQL Server permissions or let it be a member of any server roles, including sysadmin.

- **Encryption Keys.**   Immediately after installation and after the two SQL Server Reporting Services databases have been created, you should back up this instance's encryption keys. This key is used to encrypt sensitive information such as connection strings in the two databases. If the databases are restored to another server and this key is not available from the source server, credentials in connection strings will not be usable and you will need to provide them again for the reports to run successfully on a new server.

  If you can no longer locate the backup of a key, back it up again, or rotate the key by using the *Change* operation on this page to replace the key, and then back it up.

  To restore the original key to a new server to which the databases have been moved, use the Restore operation on this page.

- **Subscription Settings.**   Use this page to specify a credential to reach file shares to which report subscriptions can be written. Reports can be dropped in this file share location in PDF, Microsoft Excel, or other formats for consumption.

  Multiple subscriptions can use this file share credential, which can be used on this page in a central location.

  This account should be different from the SQL Server Reporting Services execution account to serve its purpose appropriately.

- **Scale-Out Deployment.**   Visit this page on multiple SQL Server Reporting Services instances to join them together. By using the same SQL Server Reporting Services databases for multiple SQL Server Reporting Services instances, multiple front ends can provide processing for heavy reporting workloads, including heavy subscription workloads. The server names can optionally be used in a network load balancer such as a Network Load Balancing Cluster, or you can distribute workload to each SSRS instance from different applications.

  Upon first installation, the Scale-Out Deployment page will show that the instance is "Joined" to a single server scale-out.

  Each scale-out instance of SQL Server Reporting Services must use the same settings on the Database page of the Reporting Services Configuration Manager. Connect to each instance in the scale-out and visit this page by opening it on each SQL Server Reporting Services instance to view the status, add servers to the scale-out, or remove servers.

For more detail on scale-out deployments of SSRS, visit:
*https://docs.microsoft.com/sql/reporting-services/
install-windows/configure-a-native-mode-report-server-scale-out-deployment*.

- **PowerBI Integration.**   Use this page to associate the SQL Server Reporting Services instance to a Microsoft Power BI account, specifically to an account in Azure Active Directory. The administrator joining the Power BI instance to the SQL Server Reporting Services instance must be:

  - A member of the Azure AD

  - A member of the system administrator role of the SQL Server Reporting Services instance

  - A sysadmin on the SQL Server instance that hosts the SQL Server Reporting Services databases.

➤ **For the latest information on Power BI/SQL Server Reporting Services integration and the latest Azure authentication features, visit** *https://docs.microsoft.com/sql/reporting-services/ install-windows/power-bi-report-server-integration-configuration-manager*.

SQL Server Analysis Services initial configuration and setup

No additional steps are required after setup to begin using a new SQL Server Analysis Services instance.

You can initiate manual backups of SQL Server Analysis Services databases in Object Explorer in SQL Server Management Studio as well as restore SQL Server Analysis Services databases. Because of the nature of SQL Server Analysis Services databases, their size, and how they are populated, typically they are not backed up on a schedule, but you can do so by passing an XMLA command via a SQL Server Agent job step: type **SQL Server Analysis Services** .

When installing SQL Server Analysis Services, a security group should have been chosen to grant permissions to SQL Server Analysis Services server administrators, granting a team full access to the server.

If you need to add a different group to the administrator role of the SQL Server Analysis Services instance, open SQL Server Management Studio, and then, in Object Explorer, connect to the *Analysis Services* instance. Right-click the server, and then, on the shortcut menu, click **Properties**. On the *Security* page, you can add additional windows-authenticated accounts or groups to the administrator role.

Installing and configuring SQL Server on Linux

Since SQL Server 2017, you can install SQL Server on multiple platforms: Windows, Linux, and in Docker containers. In Chapter 3, "Designing and implementing an on-premises database infra-structure," we discussed SQL Server on containers and in a Kubernetes environment. In Chapter 4, "Installing and configuring SQL Server instances and features," we covered setup and con-figuration on Windows Server.

This chapter covers Linux distributions, the basic differences between Windows and Linux, how to install SQL Server on the supported distributions of Linux, and the main differences in SQL Server on Windows and Linux. It is a shorter chapter because the differences are minimal.

What is Linux?

Linux, sometimes referred to as GNU/Linux, is an operating system (OS) including a *kernel*, *system libraries*, and a *package manager*. A Linux *distribution* (or "distro" for short) is a software collection comprising the Linux kernel, system libraries and tools, and numerous software pack-ages (the equivalent of installer files on Windows), maintained by commercial and non-com-mercial organizations from all over the world.

Inside OUT

Why is it sometimes called GNU/Linux?

As mentioned in Chapter 2, "Introducing database server components," a kernel is a low-level interface that manages computer hardware such as CPU, RAM, storage, and network devices. An operating system is software that provides an interface between the kernel and the applications that need to use it.

The Linux kernel was originally created by—and named after—a Finnish computer sci-ence student named Linus Torvalds, in 1991. When Torvalds made the kernel available for

> free online, it was then combined with an existing operating system called GNU (a recursive acronym that stands for "GNU's not Unix!") which was lacking its own kernel.
>
> Even though many GNU packages are still included in the myriad Linux distributions under active development today, the name "GNU/Linux" is not widely used. Many distribution maintainers and software vendors, even the authors of this book, usually just say "Linux" to refer to the kernel and operating system.

There are several hundred distributions in active development worldwide, with many of the same software packages available in each one, so it can be confusing trying to pick a distribution. Microsoft supports SQL Server on three distributions, which makes your decision easier.

Like Windows Server Core, Linux distributions may offer a server-only configuration with a smaller package footprint and a command-line user interface. You can also install a desktop user interface through a *window manager* package, which is similar to the Windows desktop. For the purposes of installing SQL Server on Linux, you can use whichever server or desktop configuration you prefer. However, the desktop environment uses more system resources.

Inside OUT

Why use Linux?

If you are familiar with Linux, you can now run SQL Server natively in your existing environment without needing to run Windows. On the other hand, if you're familiar with Windows, you can continue using SQL Server on Windows without concerning yourself with Linux.

You can use SQL Server in Docker containers for development and testing. Those Docker images are based on the Ubuntu distribution. Also, SQL Server big data clusters use Docker containers and Kubernetes. We cover Docker containers in Chapter 2, and Kubernetes in Chapter 3.

Differences between Windows and Linux

Windows is a *proprietary* OS created and maintained by Microsoft. Linux is an *open source* OS created and maintained by a loose collection of volunteers, as well as various commercial and non-commercial organizations.

The main difference between them is philosophical: because Linux is open source, if there is a feature you want to change or add, the end-user license lets you modify the source code yourself and recompile it. With a proprietary OS the license does not permit modification, so you must submit a feature request and hope that enough people think it is a worthwhile addition.

On a technical level, Linux has a different directory structure, file system, and user interface to Windows. Applications written for one OS do not run natively on the other without some form of code modification or recompilation. For example, you cannot simply copy the `sqlservr.exe` file from Windows to Linux and run it. We cover this in more detail in the section "Caveats of SQL Server on Linux" later in this chapter.

NOTE

Code written in certain languages with their own runtime engines (for example .NET Core, Python and Java) may run on both Windows and Linux, provided that they access resources that are common to each OS.

Active Directory authentication

Unlike with Windows, Active Directory (AD) is not built into Linux and must be installed separately. SQL Server can then use AD on both OSes, which is recommended for centralized security and management. This allows you to extend your current AD to access SQL Server instances on Linux as an extension of your Windows network. It is outside of the scope of this book, but you can follow the walkthrough for setting up Kerberos authentication on Linux (which Active Directory uses), available at *https://docs.microsoft.com/sql/linux/sql-server-linux-active-directory-authentication*.

File systems and directory structures

Windows Server supports NTFS and ReFS. Several file systems are supported on Linux and might differ between distribution and edition, but will usually be ext4. SQL Server is supported on both ext4 and XFS, because these two file systems provide similar features to NTFS, including journaling, large partitions, and fine-grained access control.

NOTE

A journaling file system keeps track of changes that are not yet committed. It helps prevent corruption in the case of a disaster (for example after a power failure or system crash).

On Windows, individual drives are addressed by a letter followed by a colon. For example, the default drive for a Windows OS is `C:` and all files beneath the root directory (`C:\`) are addressable through that drive letter. Files are stored logically in folders, and these folders and subfolders (also called directories and subdirectories) are located beneath the root directory on each drive and separated by a backslash (\).

On Linux, the directory structure is based off a root directory, called / (a single forward slash). While files are also stored in directories and subdirectories, everything including individual drives are addressed as subdirectories beneath the root directory, separated by a slash (/).

> ### NOTE
> On Linux, the forward slash character (/) is just referred to as a slash. This differentiates it from a backslash (\).

Package managers

Every Linux distribution comes with a package manager to install, manage, update, and delete packages using online repositories. For practical purposes, this is the major difference between distributions when installing software.

When a package manager installs an application (the package), it connects to a central repository controlled by the distribution maintainer. You can also register a third-party repository to install packages outside of that distribution, provided that the repository provides packages in the appropriate format.

Package managers use information from repositories to ensure that packages are compatible with one another, which makes it much easier to keep your system stable and up to date. This built-in dependency resolution means that you install only what you need. If a package is dependent on one or more other packages that are not installed, the package manager will automatically install those dependencies.

Inside OUT

How do you navigate around Linux?

On Windows, you typically use a combination of the mouse and keyboard to navigate around the OS using the Start menu and File Explorer, and in SQL Server with Configuration Manager and Management Studio. You can also use the Prompt, or the new Windows Terminal, to run commands from a command-line interface (CLI).

On Linux you will interact with the OS (and SQL Server) using the CLI. This is known as a shell, the most common of which is called bash (Bourne again shell). Other common shells are ksh (Korn shell) and zsh (Z shell). In this book, all script samples will run on bash.

NOTE

PowerShell runs on both Windows and Linux. You should familiarize yourself with PowerShell to give you an advantage managing SQL Server on both OSes. You can learn more about this in Chapter 9, "Automating SQL Server administration."

Running commands with elevated privileges

Many of the commands for installing, configuring, and administering Linux require administrative privileges, just like on Windows. The commands are preceded by the sudo keyword, which stands for "superuser do." This is less risky than logging in as the super user account (root). You will be prompted for the root password when you run sudo for the first time after a fixed period (usually 15 minutes).

NOTE

Some Linux distributions do not allow you to log in directly as the root account for added security. We recommend using the sudo command as a best practice.

Linux distributions supported by SQL Server

As noted previously, several hundred choices make it difficult to decide on which Linux distribution you should install. For SQL Server the choice is a lot easier because it is supported on the following three commercial distributions:

- **Red Hat Enterprise Linux (RHEL).**   Maintained by Red Hat, Inc., RHEL uses the RPM package manager through the command yum (which stands for Yellowdog Updater, Modified).

- **SUSE Linux Enterprise Server (SLES).**   Maintained by SUSE Group, SLES uses the ZYpp package manager through the command zypper (which stands for Zen / YaST Packages Patches Patterns Products).

- **Ubuntu Server (Ubuntu).**   Maintained by Canonical Ltd., Ubuntu uses the APT package manager through the command apt-get or aptitude (which stands for Advanced Package engine).

NOTE

Although Docker is frequently included in the list of supported Linux distributions, this is not technically correct. Docker is a virtualization engine that can run on many operating systems. You can read more about Docker containers in Chapter 2.

Having a vendor and support agreement behind an open source implementation can be comforting and beneficial to organizations that have limited experience with a new technology stack. This support is especially valuable for SQL Server administrators starting out with Linux, who are more familiar with Windows Server.

Considerations for installing SQL Server on Linux

As we discussed in previous chapters, SQL Server has a number of considerations for CPU, RAM, and storage. In the vast majority of cases you will apply the same principles as you would on Windows, with some minor caveats.

> ➤ **We cover CPU and RAM configuration in Chapters 2, 3, and 4. The next section adds Linux-specific configuration using** `mssql-conf`.

Configuring OS settings

Microsoft recommends the following OS settings for a dedicated SQL Server instance to run optimally on Linux.

CAUTION

Some configuration settings do not persist between reboots, so you will have to create an `init.d` **script, which runs at boot time. Refer to your distribution's documentation for details on how to configure the following options.**

Configuring high performance

Aside from the computer's BIOS where high performance should be enabled (in other words, power saving should be disabled), you can also modify CPU settings at the Linux kernel level.

- Set the CPU frequency governor to 100% using the `cpupower` command

- Use the *performance* option with the `x86_energy_perf_policy` command

- Set the `min_perf_pct` setting to 100%

- Set C-States to C1 only

These CPU settings are functionally equivalent to enabling High Performance on Windows.

> ➤ **You can read more about CPU C-States and power-saving modes at**
> *https://www.hardwaresecrets.com/*
> *everything-you-need-to-know-about-the-cpu-c-states-power-saving-modes.*

Configuring NUMA nodes

For computers with more than one NUMA node, use the `sysctl` command to disable auto-NUMA balancing by setting `kernel.numa_balancing` to 0, because SQL Server handles NUMA internally.

Configuring virtual address space

In Chapter 2 we discussed the working set, or memory provided by the OS for use by a process, which in this case is SQL Server. The working set resides in a virtual address space, which in turn is mapped to physical memory by internal OS structures. The default setting for the number of memory map areas in virtual memory might not be sufficient for SQL Server on Linux, so you should use the `sysctl` command to change `vm.max_map_count` to the upper limit of 262144 (262,144).

Configuring Transparent Huge Pages (THP)

Certain Linux distributions, including Red Hat, provide improved performance on systems by increasing the size of memory blocks transparently to the underlying process. This is beneficial for applications with contiguous memory access patterns and works to SQL Server's advantage. THP is already enabled on Linux by default, so you should leave this on for a dedicated SQL Server instance.

Setting up the file system

As mentioned in Chapter 3, SQL Server on Linux requires either the ext4 or XFS file system. If the file system supports it, use a 64-KB block size to match the size of an extent, otherwise the largest size that it supports (for example, ext4 may only support a block size of 4 KB). With newer storage subsystems and SANs, this block size is less important than it used to be.

By default, SQL Server places the data and log files in `/var/opt/mssql/data`. Notice that this path starts with a single forward slash, which is the root directory on a Linux system. This path starts in `/var`, which is a default directory created for the OS to write data during normal operation (var stands for "variable"). Then, opt stands for "optional," for optional packages that are not included in a default installation of Linux. The next directory is `mssql`, which stands for "Microsoft SQL."

> ### NOTE
> You can use *symbolic* or *hard links* to redirect the default data path to a different physical location (for instance, another drive), but we recommend using the `mssql-conf` tool to change the location instead, similar to how you would do this on Windows.

A good rule of thumb is to keep transaction log files and TempDB on your fastest available storage. Additionally, you should mount volumes using the `noatime` attribute, which prevents tracking the last accessed time for that volume, thereby improving performance. This is managed in the file system table configuration file, known as `fstab`. Refer to the `fstab` documentation for more information.

Recommended disk settings

For optimal settings at the physical disk level, you can do the following:

- Set the disk read-ahead to 4096 bytes using the `blockdev` command.

Additionally, there are several settings you can configure using the `sysctl` command:

- Set `kernel.sched_min_granularity_ns` to 10000000 (10,000,000)

- Set `kernel.sched_wakeup_granularity_ns` to 15000000 (15,000,000)

- Set `vm.dirty_ratio` to 40

- Set `vm.dirty_background_ratio` to 10

- Set `vm.swappiness` to 10

CAUTION

Some `sysctl` settings may be overridden by modules that load later in the boot process. You can read more about this at *https://linux.die.net/man/8/sysctl*.

Inside OUT

How do you edit files on Linux?

You will be editing files on Linux from the command line. While there are many text editors available, not all of them are installed by default.

The default file editor that will nearly always be available is *vi* (visual editor). It is extremely powerful, but that also means it is complex. Opening files is a matter of running vi from the command line, followed by the name of the file you wish to create or modify. To save and quit from a vi session however, you must type `:wq` and then press Enter. The colon instructs vi that you want to perform a command; the "w" writes (saves) the file; and "q" quits from the session.

If you're new to Linux, you might find that the vi editor is quite different to what you're used to, and you might want to replace it with *nano*, which you can install using your distribution's package manager.

> On Red Hat, you can install nano using the following command:
>
> ```
> yum install nano
> ```

Installing SQL Server on Linux

To integrate better with Linux, SQL Server leverages the package manager concept, meaning that you only install the components you need, starting with the Database Engine package. This can drastically reduce the amount of time it takes to install SQL Server compared to Windows. For instance, on an Internet-connected machine with a high-speed connection, you can download, install, and configure SQL Server 2019 in under five minutes.

Table 16-1 shows which packages are available for SQL Server on Linux. The command-line tools include SQLCMD and BCP, which work exactly the same way as their Windows counterparts.

Table 16-1 SQL Server packages for Linux

Component	Package name
SQL Server Database Engine	mssql-server
Full-text Search	mssql-server-fts
SQL Server Integration Services	mssql-server-is
PolyBase	mssql-server-polybase
SQL Server Agent (included in Database Engine)	mssql-server-agent
SQL Server command-line tools	mssql-tools
SQL Server 2019 Machine Learning Services	mssql-mlservices-mlm-py-* mssql-mlservices-mlm-r-*

NOTE

SQL Server Agent is installed with the Database Engine.

Inside OUT

Can you install named instances on SQL Server on Linux?

No, you can only install a single instance of SQL Server on Linux on a machine. Named instances are not supported. Installing more than one instance (known as "instance stacking") is also not supported on Linux.

If you find the need to install more than one SQL Server instance on the same machine, we recommend either creating individual virtual machines per SQL Server install, or consider using SQL Server in containers. It is worth keeping in mind that maintenance is much easier when SQL Server is installed on separate virtual consumers (VMs or containers), because that has a lower impact on other software.

You can find more information about virtual consumers in Chapter 2, and additional information about SQL Server in containers in Chapter 3.

Installation requirements

The minimum system requirements for SQL Server on Linux are as follows:

- CPU: 2 GHz (x64-compatible), with two physical cores

- Memory: 3.25 GB RAM

- Storage: 6 GB (formatted with either ext4 or XFS)

NOTE

While SQL Server Express edition is artificially limited to 1410 MB for the buffer pool, it can use additional memory for columnstore and memory-optimized objects. You can read more about edition scale limits at *https://docs.microsoft.com/sql/linux/sql-server-linux-editions-and-components-2019*.

Downloading and installing packages

You can install SQL Server on a computer that is connected to the Internet, or an offline computer. In the latter case you must download the packages you need and copy them to the machine that will be running SQL Server.

➤ A walkthrough for installing SQL Server on each distribution is available at *https://docs.microsoft.com/sql/linux/sql-server-linux-overview*.

Download the third-party repository configuration file

SQL Server packages must be downloaded from Microsoft directly, because they are not available from the official distribution repositories. You must add the Microsoft package repository to the list of approved repositories on your computer, depending on which version of the Linux distribution you have installed.

NOTE

When you add a third-party repository, you first need to import that repository's public keys to ensure that any files you are downloading are verified. You can read more about public key encryption in Chapter 13, "Protecting data through encryption, privacy and auditing."

The following sample bash command will load the package repository configuration for SQL Server 2019 for RHEL 7.x into the yum repository on your machine:

```
sudo curl -o /etc/yum.repos.d/mssql-server.repo \
https://packages.microsoft.com/config/rhel/7/mssql-server-2019.repo
```

Note in this example that the trailing space and backslash at the end of the first line is a bash convention to indicate that the command spans more than one line.

Downloading the package

Once the package manager is configured to accept packages from Microsoft and the list of available packages is refreshed, you can install SQL Server immediately or download the packages for offline installation on another computer. For RHEL, the following command will download the package locally (as well as any dependencies):

```
sudo yum localinstall mssql-server_2019.x86_64.rpm
```

Installing the package

Depending on the distribution and package manager, you will install the SQL Server Database Engine package using one of the following methods:

- **RHEL.**   `sudo yum install -y mssql-server`

- **SLES.**   `sudo zypper install -y mssql-server`

- **Ubuntu.**   `sudo apt-get install -y mssql-server`

Each `install` command has a -y switch, which forces any prompts to agree to the question in the affirmative. This is useful for agreeing to install dependencies without prompting for each one, for example in unattended installs (see the next section). If you wish to confirm every prompt manually, you can remove the -y switch.

Performing an unattended installation

You can also install SQL Server on Linux using a shell script, which is recommended for production deployments and deployments across multiple servers, to ensure a consistent experience.

The script should include all the steps you need to register the Microsoft package repository, download the requisite packages, and perform the post-installation configuration.

See the "Configuring SQL Server on Linux" section for more information about post-installation steps. You can also get a sample bash script from Microsoft Docs, depending on the distribution you have chosen, from the following locations:

- **RHEL.** *https://docs.microsoft.com/sql/linux/sample-unattended-install-redhat*

- **SLES.** *https://docs.microsoft.com/sql/linux/sample-unattended-install-suse*

- **Ubuntu.** *https://docs.microsoft.com/sql/linux/sample-unattended-install-ubuntu*

Updating packages

With the Microsoft SQL Server package repository as an approved third-party option, the distribution's package manager will update SQL Server components (including Cumulative Updates) at the same time as other OS updates. This is functionally equivalent to the Windows Update feature "Receive updates for other Microsoft products."

To update the packages on your Linux OS, including any updates of SQL Server components you have installed, you can use the following commands:

- **RHEL.**   `sudo yum update`

- **SLES.**   `sudo zypper update`

- **Ubuntu.**   `sudo apt-get update`

> **NOTE**
> On Red Hat Enterprise Linux, you must register your computer with the Red Hat Network (RHN) first using `subscription-manager`, before updates will work.

Configuring SQL Server for Linux

After you have installed the SQL Server Database Engine package, you need to configure SQL Server for the first time. This differs from the way SQL Server on Windows works (unless you perform an unattended install), because you can follow the SQL Server Setup and configure the settings as you go, whereas on Linux, you configure SQL Server after it is installed.

Inside OUT

How do you configure the Linux firewall to allow access to SQL Server?

With both Linux and Windows, you need to open TCP port 1433 (and TCP port 1434 for the Dedicated Admin Connection) to allow access to your SQL Server instance from other machines on your network.

Each Linux distribution might have a different firewall package installed as the default, but on RHEL, the `firewalld` package can be configured with the following commands:

```
sudo firewall-cmd --zone=public --add-port=1433/tcp --permanent

sudo firewall-cmd --zone=public --add-port=1434/tcp --permanent

sudo firewall-cmd -reload
```

Note that the firewall configuration must be reloaded after it has been modified in order to take effect.

➤ You can read more about TCP ports in Chapter 13.

Using mssql-conf to set up and configure SQL Server

Windows uses the SQL Server Configuration Manager to configure SQL Server at the OS level. Linux does not have its own registry, so SQL Server's configuration is stored in a plain text file and accessed when the SQL Server service starts up.

You will initially interact with SQL Server through the CLI, most likely the bash shell. To configure SQL Server after installing the Database Engine package, you must run `mssql-conf` from the command line.

Inside OUT

Is there another way to configure SQL Server on Linux?

`mssql-conf` is the preferred method for setting up SQL Server on Linux. However, you can also use environment variables for initial (first-run) setup and setting up a SQL Server Docker container, because Docker containers do not use `mssql-conf`. We cover the container scenario in Chapter 3.

For initial configuration, you can use the following variables.

- ACCEPT_EULA, required to use SQL Server, and can be set to any value.
- MSSQL_PID, the product ID, which can be one of Evaluation, Developer, Express, Web, Standard, Enterprise, or a product key.
- MSSQL_SA_PASSWORD, which must follow password complexity rules.
- MSSQL_TCP_PORT, which is usually TCP port 1433.

➤ You can view a complete list of these environment variables at *https://docs.microsoft.com/sql/linux/sql-server-linux-configure-environment-variables*.

NOTE

The `mssql-conf` tool is written in Python, as are several other command-line tools for working with SQL Server. When you install SQL Server on Linux, you may notice that one of the dependencies installed is the Python package.

Configuration settings

The executable package for mssql-conf is located in the /opt/mssql/bin path. You can see that /opt is a directory off the root directory where optional packages are stored, and `mssql` stands for Microsoft SQL. The `bin` directory stands for binaries, which are functionally the same as executable files on Windows.

NOTE

To execute a binary file on Linux and other Unix-like OSes, you must either provide the full path to the binary, or if you have navigated to the directory already, you must prefix the binary with `./` (a period and a slash).

`mssql-conf` makes use of a configuration file (called `mssql.conf`), which is a plain text file located at /var/opt/mssql/mssql.conf. Remember that /var is where files are written to, which is a convenient way to remember the difference between /opt and /var/opt.

The `mssql-conf` tool has two phases: first-run (initial) setup, and configuration, both of which we cover next.

NOTE

Once your SQL Server instance has been set up the first time, you can connect to it from any computer running SQL Server Management Studio, Azure Data Studio, sqlcmd, and mssql-conf, indeed any tool that can connect to SQL Server.

First-run setup

From bash, run the following command to enter the configuration tool to configure SQL Server 2019 on Linux:

```
sudo /opt/mssql/bin/mssql-conf setup
```

You are presented with a numbered list, and if you make an error, you can quit the tool and run it again.

Choosing the correct edition

SQL Server on Linux may not ask you to enter a license key. When you set up SQL Server for the first time, you are prompted for the edition you will be using. The following editions are available (this list is copied from the `mssql-conf setup` prompt):

1. Evaluation (free, no production use rights, 180-day limit)

2. Developer (free, no production use rights)

3. Express (free)

4. Web (PAID)

5. Standard (PAID)

6. Enterprise (PAID) - CPU Core utilization restricted to 20 physical/40 hyperthreaded

7. Enterprise Core (PAID) - CPU Core utilization up to Operating System Maximum

8. I bought a license through a retail sales channel and have a product key to enter.

Depending on the edition you want to install, you will make your selection and then move on to the next prompt. You are shown the path to the license agreement, and then prompted to agree to that agreement.

The Evaluation, Developer, and Express editions are free and do not require a paid license, but you will still be prompted to agree to the license terms. A good guideline for choosing a license is that if you plan to process production data under any circumstances (including if you want to test your database backups), you cannot use Evaluation or Developer edition and must purchase a paid license, or else you can use the artificially-limited Express edition.

Choosing the language

Now you are prompted to choose a default language for the SQL Server instance. You can choose between eleven different options: English, German, Spanish, French, Italian, Japanese, Korean, Portuguese, Russian, Simplified Chinese or Traditional Chinese.

Choosing a SQL Server system administrator password

Your system administrator (SA) password should be a strong password. Microsoft's guidance is to choose an alphanumeric password with a minimum length of 8 uppercase and lowercase characters, including letters, digits and symbols. If you plan to use Active Directory authentication, you can disable this account later.

> **NOTE**
>
> Our password recommendation is similar, but you should increase the minimum length to 15 characters. You can generate and save the password using a password manager, so there is no need to pick a memorable password. You should not use the SA account directly unless it is an emergency or setting up the instance.

Once you have chosen a password, you will be prompted to confirm it. Then the SQL Server service will restart, taking these settings into account.

Configuring the SQL Server instance

The configuration settings for SQL Server are managed using the same `mssql-conf` tool, replacing the SQL Server Configuration Manager on Windows.

> ## Inside OUT
>
> *How do you manage the SQL Server service on Linux?*
>
> Like Windows, Linux has services, called *daemons*. You can start, stop and restart the SQL Server service using the following commands.
>
> - Stop SQL Server: `systemctl stop mssql-server`
> - Start SQL Server: `systemctl start mssql-server`
> - Restart SQL Server: `systemctl restart mssql-server`
>
> Remember to restart the SQL Server service after you have made changes to the configuration.

There is a wide range of settings that you can use to customize your SQL Server instance. This is a brief overview of what is available (taken from *https://docs.microsoft.com/sql/linux/sql-server-linux-configure-mssql-conf*):

- **Agent.** Enables SQL Server Agent. Although SQL Server Agent is installed along with the Database Engine, you still need to enable it.

- **Collation.**   Sets a new collation for SQL Server on Linux.

- **Customer feedback.**   Chooses whether or not SQL Server sends feedback to Microsoft. This option cannot be disabled on free editions.

> You can read more about the collection of usage and diagnostic data at *https://docs. microsoft.com/sql/sql-server/usage-and-diagnostic-data-configuration-for-sql-server-tools*.

- **Database Mail Profile.**   Sets the default database mail profile for SQL Server on Linux.

- **Default data directory.**   Changes the default directory for new SQL Server database data files (.mdf). As noted in Chapter 3, we recommend moving this to a dedicated volume.

- **Default log directory.**   Changes the default directory for new SQL Server database log (.ldf) files. As noted in Chapter 3, we recommend moving this to a dedicated volume.

- **Default master database directory.**   Changes the default directory for the master database and log files. As noted in Chapter 3, we recommend moving this to a dedicated volume.

- **Default master database file name.**   Changes the name of master database files. We do not recommend changing this in the normal course of business, but this is useful in a disaster recovery scenario when restoring a master database.

- **Default dump directory.**   Changes the default directory for new memory dumps and other troubleshooting files. You can set the dump file type using the Dump type option (see below).

- **Default error log directory.**   Changes the default directory for new SQL Server ERRORLOG, Default Profiler Trace, System Health Session XE, and Hekaton (Memory-Optimized) Session XE files.

- **Default backup directory.**   Changes the default directory for new backup files. We recommend moving this to a dedicated volume separate from the data and log files, to ensure business continuity should a drive failure occur.

- **Dump type.**   In the case of a crash or exception in a SQL Server process, this sets the type of dump memory dump file to collect. Each size (*mini, miniplus, filtered* and *full*) provides a different level of detail in a memory dump for troubleshooting purposes. You can set the path for the dump directory using the Default dump directory option (see above).

- **High availability.**   Enable availability groups. Please refer to Chapter 11, "Implementing high availability and disaster recovery," for more information about availability groups on Linux.

CHAPTER 5

- **Local Audit directory.**   Sets a directory to add Local Audit files.

- **Locale.**   Sets the locale for SQL Server to use, in the form of a language identifier (LCID).

- **Memory limit.**   Set the memory limit for SQL Server. Take care to avoid going over the default of 80% of the maximum physical memory available on the server, because Linux will terminate the SQL Server instance without warning if it detects high resource utilization.

  ➤ You can read more about the aptly named out-of-memory (OOM) killer at *https://lwn.net/Articles/317814*.

- **TCP port.**   Change the port where SQL Server listens for connections. Change this only if you have a specific business case. We do not recommend changing it for security reasons, because a network sniffing tool will detect the new port almost instantly.

- **TLS.**   Configure Transport Level Security. This is used for enforcing encryption, as well as configuring the path to the certificate and private key. You can also set TLS versions here, but Microsoft recommends only using TLS 1.2 (and higher when available). We cover TLS in more depth in Chapter 13. If you use Kerberos authentication to connect your SQL Server instance to Active Directory, the Kerberos keytab file is also configured here.

- **Trace flags.**   Set the trace flags that the service is going to use. We recommend enabling at least trace flag 3226 here, which disables messages in the error log for successful database backups.

Caveats of SQL Server on Linux

SQL Server on Linux is implemented using a thin translation layer called the SQL Platform Abstraction Layer (SQLPAL), which maps Windows system calls to Linux system calls. This allows the exact same code for the Database Engine to be used on both OSes, meaning that the Linux version does not have internal awareness that it is running on a different platform. Generally speaking, as far as SQL Server is concerned, it is running inside Windows.

  ➤ You can read the introduction from the SQL Server team on how SQLPAL came about, at *https://cloudblogs.microsoft.com/sqlserver/2016/12/16/ sql-server-on-linux-how-introduction/*

This platform abstraction is both hugely powerful and limiting. It is powerful, because now SQL Server runs on Windows, Linux, in containers, and on ARM64 devices with Azure SQL Database Edge.

➤ You can find out more about Azure SQL Database Edge at
https://azure.microsoft.com/services/sql-database-edge.

It is also limiting, because only enough Windows system calls have been translated to the underlying OS to get these to work. Certain features are not available due to this limitation, including access to the Windows registry. Only a very small stub of the registry is included to support the required Windows system calls (including the Windows Data Protection API).

We have already covered the lack of the registry to explain why `mssql-conf` replaces SQL Server Configuration Manager in the previous section, but a number of other features of SQL Server, which are dependent on Windows features, have not been implemented

Missing SQL Server features on Linux

The list of features not available for SQL Server 2019 on Linux has shrunk since SQL Server 2017 was released. Microsoft has stated that new features will be enabled over time.

- **SQL Server Analysis Services (SSAS).**   If you need this feature, you must install it on SQL Server on Windows.

- **SQL Server Reporting Services (SSRS).**   If you need this feature, you must install it on Windows Server. However, the SSRS databases can be hosted on a Linux instance.

- **SQL Server Integration Services (SSIS).**   There is a component that lets you run SSIS packages, but the feature is quite limited otherwise. Another side-effect is that the designer for Maintenance Plans in SQL Server Management Studio does not work.

- **Master Data Services (MDS).**   If you need this feature, you must use SQL Server on Windows.

- **Data Quality Services (DQS).**   If you need this feature, you must use SQL Server on Windows.

- **SQL Server Browser Service.**   Linux does not allow more than one instance, so this is not a significant gap.

- **FILESTREAM and FileTable.**   Requires NTFS or ReFS. If you need this feature, you must use SQL Server on Windows.

- **Stretch DB.**   If you need this feature, you must use SQL Server on Windows.

- **Extended stored procedures.**   If you need this feature, you must use SQL Server on Windows.

- **VSS snapshots.** If you need this feature, you must use SQL Server on Windows.

- **Buffer Pool Extension.** If you need this feature, you must use SQL Server on Windows.

- **SQL Server Agent Alerts.** If you need this feature, you must use SQL Server on Windows.

- **Database mirroring.** Since this feature is in maintenance mode, we recommend that you use another high availability solution such as log shipping or availability groups.

Provisioning and configuring SQL Server databases

In this chapter, we review the various strategies for creating new databases or adding existing databases to a SQL Server. We'll cover considerations for database migrations, including important considerations to remember when moving databases from instance to instance and various strategies for moving databases. We'll review the creation of new user databases and run down important database properties to be aware of throughout the application development lifecycle.

Inside OUT

Which databases are system databases?

Just because a database is shipped and installed by Microsoft as part of a SQL Server feature doesn't mean it counts as a system database.

In SQL Server Management Studio (SSMS), and then in Object Explorer, you'll see at least four system databases, and perhaps additional databases for SQL Server Reporting Services and SQL Server Integration Services, if you have installed these features.

Only the four standard system databases placed in the system subfolder of Object Explorer are considered system databases in various features inside SQL Server. The Distribution database, for the replication feature, will also appear in the systems subfolder if present. The ReportServer, ReportServerTempDB, and SSISDB databases are Microsoft-installed user databases.

In Maintenance Plans, or in internal views such as sys.databases, you will see these SSRS and SSIS databases treated as user, not system databases. This is an important distinction for disaster recovery planning, configuration, and policy enforcement.

Adding databases to a SQL Server instance

We have discussed a number of database configurations in Chapter 3, "Designing and implementing an on-premises database infrastructure," including the physical configuration of files and storage.

Though many of the same database settings are available and should be considered for Azure SQL Databases, the remainder of this chapter refers to SQL Server databases on both Windows and Linux, as well as on Azure SQL Managed Instance. For information on Azure SQL Databases, refer to Chapter 17, "Provisioning Azure SQL Database."

> **NOTE**
>
> If you are tasked with moving or upgrading databases, you must understand how to create new databases. Later in this chapter we'll discuss tools to assist with upgrading database compatibility levels and other important considerations for database migrations.

Creating a database

Here, we review the basics of database settings and configuration. As a Database Administrator (DBA), you might not regularly create databases from scratch, but you should be familiar with all of the settings and design decisions that go into database creation, including the addition of database files and the required tools.

Managing default settings

It is important to understand the role of the model database when creating new databases, regardless of the method of creation. The model database and its entire contents and configuration options are copied to any new database, even TempDB upon service restart. For this reason, never store any data (even for testing) in the model database. Similarly, do not grow the model database from its default size, because this will require all future databases to be that size or larger.

However, the location of the model database's files is not used as a default for new databases. Instead, the default location for database files is stored at the server level. You can view these default storage locations, which should be changed and must be valid, in the *Server Properties* dialog box in SSMS, on the *Database Settings* page. There you will find the default locations for Data, Log, and Backup files, which are stored in the Registry.

On this the *Database Settings* page you'll also see the **recovery interval** setting, which is by default 0, meaning that SQL Server can manage the frequency of internal automatic CHECKPOINTs. This typically results in an internal checkpoint frequency of one minute. This setting is not the same as the TARGET_RECOVERY_TIME setting at the database level. We'll discuss TARGET_RECOVERY_TIME for individual databases later in this chapter under the section "Indirect checkpoints," but know that changing the instance-level **recovery interval** setting is not the same as changing the TARGET_RECOVERY TIME in each database.

Also on the *Database Settings* page of *Server Properties* you will find the default index fill factor and default backup compression setting. These are server-level defaults applied to each database, but you cannot configure them separately for each database. You can change fill factor with each index operation or choose a different backup compression option each time you perform a backup.

Inside OUT

Can default data and log file locations cause future cumulative updates to fail?

Portions of cumulative updates reference the default file locations. The patches will fail if these default database locations change to an invalid path, if the complete subfolder path does not exist, or if SQL Server loses permissions to access the locations. You might see errors such as "operating system error 3 (The system cannot find the path specified.)" in the detailed log of the cumulative update. You will need to restart the cumulative update after correcting the problem with the default locations.

The following settings are inherited by new databases from the model database unless they are overridden at the time of creation:

- Initial data and log file size

- Data and log file autogrowth setting

- Data and log file maximum size

- Recovery model

- Target Recovery Time (overrides the system default recovery interval)

- All Database-Scoped Configurations including the database-level settings for Legacy Cardinality Estimation, Max DOP, Parameter Sniffing, and Query Optimizer Fixes

- All Automatic settings, including auto close, auto shrink, and auto create/update statistics (discussed later in this chapter)

Inside OUT

Can your SSMS connections to the model database block CREATE DATABASE statements?

Close or disconnect any SSMS query windows that use the model database context. If you are configuring the model database by using Transact-SQL (T-SQL) commands, you might inadvertently leave SSMS query windows open. Create database statements need to reference the model database. User connections, including query windows in SSMS with the model database context, can block the creation of user databases.

You might see the error: "Could not obtain exclusive lock on database 'model'. Retry the operation later. CREATE DATABASE failed. Some file names listed could not be created. Check related errors. (Microsoft SQL Server, Error: 1807)."

For applications like SharePoint that create databases, this could lead to application errors.

Owning the databases you create

The login that runs the CREATE DATABASE statement will become the owner of any database you create, even if the account you are using is not a member of the sysadmin group. Any principal that can create a database becomes the owner of that database, even if, for example, they have only membership to the dbcreator built-in server role.

Ideally, databases are not owned by named individual accounts. You might decide to change each database to a service account specific to that database's dependent applications. You must do this after the database is created.

➤ For more information on the best practices with respect to database ownership and how to change the database owner, see Chapter 12, "Administering security and permissions."

Creating additional database files

Every SQL Server database needs at least one data file and one log file. You can use additional data files to maximize storage performance. (We discuss physical database architecture in detail in Chapter 3: Designing and implementing an on-premises database infrastructure.)

However, adding additional log files long term is not a wise decision. There is no performance advantage to be gained with more than one transaction log file for a database. SQL Server will not write to them randomly, but sequentially.

The only scenario in which a second transaction log file would be needed is if the first had filled up its volume. If no space can be created on the volume to allow for additional transaction log file data to be written, the database cannot accept new transactions and will refuse new application requests. In this scenario, one possible troubleshooting method is to temporarily add a second transaction log file on another volume to create the space to allow the database transactions to resume accepting transactions. The end resolution involves clearing the primary transaction log file, performing a one-time-only shrink to return it to its original size, and removing the second transaction log file.

Using SQL Server Management Studio to create a new database

You can create and configure database files, specifically their initial sizes, in SQL Server Management Studio (SSMS). In Object Explorer, right-click *Databases*, and then, on the shortcut menu, click **New Database** to open the *New Database* dialog box.

After you have configured the new database's settings, but before you click **OK**, you can script the T-SQL for the CREATE DATABASE statement.

Here are a few suggestions when creating a new database:

- Pre-grow your database and log file sizes to an expected size. This avoids autogrowth events as you initially populate your database. You can speed up this process greatly by using the Perform Volume Maintenance Task permission for the SQL Server service account so that instant file initialization is possible.

  ➤ **We covered instant file initialization in Chapter 4, "Installing and configuring SQL Server instances and features."**

- Consider the SIMPLE recovery model for your database until it enters production use. Then, the FULL or BULK_LOGGED recovery models might be more appropriate.

  ➤ **For more information on database backups and the appropriate recovery model, see Chapter 10, "Developing, deploying, and managing data recovery."**

- Review the logical and physical files names of your database and the locations. The default locations for the data and log files are a server-level setting, but you can override them here. You also can move the files later on (covered later in this chapter).

- As soon as the database is created, follow up with your backup strategy to ensure that it is covered as appropriate with its role. This may involve adding it to an existing maintenance plan, SQL Agent job, or third-party backup application.

Deploying a database via SQL Server Data Tools

You can also deploy developed databases to a SQL Server instance using a database project in SQL Server Data Tools. For databases for which objects will be developed by your team or another team within your enterprise, SQL Server Data Tools provides a professional and mature environment for teams to develop databases, check them into source control, generate change scripts for incremental deployments, and reduce object scripting errors.

SQL Server Data Tools can generate incremental change scripts, using the Data Compare feature, or deploy databases directly. It also has the option to drop or re-create databases for each deployment, though this is turned off by default.

You might find it easiest to create the new database by using SSMS and then deploy incremental changes to it with SQL Server Data Tools.

Moving existing databases

There are a number of strategies for moving or copying a SQL Server database from one instance to another. You should consider each as it relates to necessary changes to application connection strings, DNS, storage, and security environments. We'll review a number of options for migration in this section.

Restoring a database backup

Restoring a backup is an easily understandable way to copy data from one instance to another. You can also carry out this method in a way that minimizes an outage.

Let's compare two different simplified migration processes. The following is a sample, suboptimal migration checklist using only a FULL backup/restore:

> ➤ For more information on the types of database backups and database restores, see Chapter 10.

1. Begin application outage.

2. Perform a FULL backup of the database on the old instance.

3. Copy the database backup file to the new server.

4. Restore the FULL backup on the new instance.

5. Resolve any SQL-authenticated login issues or any other changes necessary before directing database queries to the new instance.

6. Change the connection strings in applications and/or DNS and/or aliases.

7. End application outage.

In the preceding scenario, the application outage must last the entire span of the backup, copy, and restore, which for large databases could be quite lengthy, even with native SQL Server backup compression reducing the file size.

Instead, consider the following strategy:

1. Perform a FULL backup of the database on the old instance.

2. Copy the database backup file to the new server.

3. Restore the FULL backup WITH NORECOVERY on the new instance.

4. Begin application outage.

5. Take a differential backup and then a log backup of the database on the old instance.

6. Copy the differential backup file and the log backup file to the new server.

7. Restore the differential backup file WITH NORECOVERY on the new instance.

8. Restore the transaction log backup WITH RECOVERY on the new instance.

9. Resolve any SQL-authenticated login issues or any other changes necessary before directing database queries to the new instance.

10. Change the connection strings in applications and/or DNS and/or aliases.

11. End application outage.

In this scenario, the application outage spans only the duration of the differential and transaction log's backup/copy/restore operation, which for large databases should be a tiny fraction of the overall size of the database. This scenario does require more preparation and scripting in advance, and it requires coordination with the usual backup system responsible for transaction log backups. By taking a manual transaction log backup, you can create a split transaction log backup chain for another system. You'll want to account for this in your planning.

Attaching detached database files

Detaching, copying, and attaching database files will also accomplish the goal of getting the database in place on a new instance. It is relatively straightforward to disassociate (detach) the files from the old SQL Server, copy the files to the new instance, and then attach the files to the new SQL Server. This is largely limited by the data transfer speed of copying the files. You might also consider moving the SAN drives to the new server to decrease the time spent waiting for files to copy.

Attaching copied database files can be faster than restoring a full database backup; however, it lacks the ability to minimize the outage by taking advantage of transaction log backups (see earlier).

Copying the full set of database files (remember that the database might contain many more files than just the .mdf and .ldf files, including secondary data files and FILESTREAM containers) is not faster than restoring a transaction log backup during the application outage, and it is not a true recovery method. Because database backup files can also be compressed natively by SQL Server, the data transfer duration between the Windows servers will be reduced by using the backup/restore strategy.

Moving data with BACPAC files

A BACPAC file is an open JSON-format file that contains the database schema and row data, allowing for the migration of databases, ideally, at the start of a development/migration phase and not for large databases. SSMS can both generate and import BACPAC files, and the Azure portal can import them when moving an on-premises SQL Server to an Azure SQL database.

Upgrading database compatibility levels

SQL Server databases upgraded from an older version to a new version will retain a prior compatibility mode. Compatibility mode is a database-level setting.

For example, restoring or attaching a database from SQL Server 2012 to SQL Server 2019 will result in the database assuming the SQL Server 2012 (110) compatibility mode. This is not necessarily a problem, but it does have consequences with respect to how you can use features or whether you can leverage improvements to performance. You will have to manually promote the database to SQL Server 2019 compatibility level 150.

Inside OUT

Are there any Microsoft-provided tools to assist with a database migration and/or upgrade?

In the summer of 2019, SQL Server 2008 and SQL Server 2008 R2 became unsupported, prompting a flood of migrations up and away from those older instances. Many other SQL Server workloads have been migrated to Azure SQL platforms (Azure SQL DB, Azure SQL MI, or Azure VMs running SQL Server). To assist these projects and aid consumption of their own new products, Microsoft has developed tools to assist with the evaluation and even the actual data migration.

The Data Migration Assistant (DMA) is important for legacy upgrades of databases off older versions. A clean assessment from DMA is actually needed and highly recommended for a Microsoft-supported upgrade of an old database. The DMA can help identify T-SQL code, features or option usage that is not supported in a newer version, and it can suggest the necessary remediation. The target of a DMA-supported migration can be any of the three Azure SQL platforms or an on-premises SQL Server installation.

The Azure Database Migration Service is a managed service to handle the upgrade and migrations of SQL Server databases to Azure. It relies on the DMA's assessment and recommendations, but then can help you take the next step of moving the data into an Azure platform, especially when a simple backup and restore is not possible, as with Azure SQL Database.

We'll discuss more about Azure Database Migration Service in Chapter 18, "Provisioning Azure SQL Database managed instance" and Chapter 19, "Migrating to SQL Server solutions in Azure."

You can view the compatibility level of a database in SSMS. To do so, in Object Explorer, right-click a database, click **Properties**, then on the Options page, the Compatibility Level list box displays the current setting. Use the ALTER DATABASE command to change the COMPATIBILITY_LEVEL setting. You can also view this setting for all databases in the system catalog via `sys.databases`; look for the `compatibility_level` column.

SQL Server provides database compatibility modes for backward compatibility to database-level features, including improvements to the query optimizer, additional fields in dynamic management objects, syntax improvements, and other database-level objects.

For the scenario in which a SQL Server 2019 (internal version 150) instance is hosting a database in SQL Server 2012 (internal version 110) compatibility mode, it is important to note that applications are still connecting to a SQL Server 2019 instance. Only database-level features and options are honored in the prior compatibility modes.

Inside OUT

Are there any new breaking code changes to SQL Server?

Since SQL 2005 and database compatibility level 90, there have been very few changes to allowed syntax that would cause working T-SQL code to break in a newer version of SQL Server. For example, the FASTFIRSTROW syntax stopped working in compatibility level 110. T-SQL code that works as far back as compatibility level 90 will almost certainly execute in SQL Server 2019 and compatibility level 150, though performance could vary.

As we mentioned earlier in this chapter, it is strongly recommended to use the Microsoft Data Migration Assistant (DMA) tool on SQL Server 2008 and later versions to assess a database.

For example, some recent syntax additions such as the new STRING_SPLIT() or OPENJSON functions, added in SQL Server 2016, will not work when run in the context of a database in a prior compatibility mode. Some syntax improvements, for example DATEFROMPARTS() and AT TIME ZONE, will work in any database in any database compatibility mode in SQL Server 2017 or later.

SQL Server 2019 supports compatibility levels down to SQL Server 2008 (internal version 100). Any database restored from a lower compatibility level will be upgraded to version 100.

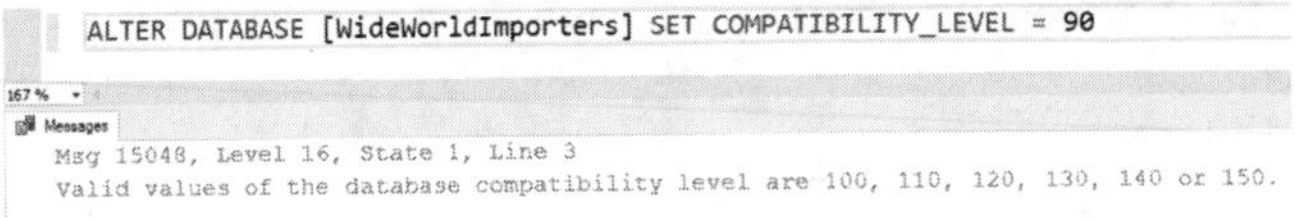

```
ALTER DATABASE [WideWorldImporters] SET COMPATIBILITY_LEVEL = 90
```

```
167 %   ▼   ◄
Messages
  Msg 15048, Level 16, State 1, Line 3
  Valid values of the database compatibility level are 100, 110, 120, 130, 140 or 150.
```

Figure 6-1 In SQL Server 2019, attempting to change a database compatibility level to a version older than SQL Server 2008 (version 100) will fail.

Changing the database compatibility level does not require a service restart to take place, but we strongly recommend that you do *not* perform this during normal operating hours. Promoting the database compatibility mode should be thoroughly tested in preproduction environments. Even though syntax errors are unlikely in the newer compatibility level, other changes to the query optimizer engine from version to version could result in performance changes to the application that must be evaluated prior to rollout to a production system. At the very least, the compatibility level change could cause widespread cached plan invalidation and an immediate CPU spike due to plan compilation.

➤ For more information on the differences between compatibility modes since SQL 2005, reference MSDN article bb510680 or visit *https://docs.microsoft.com/sql/t-sql/statements/ alter-database-transact-sql-compatibility-level*.

Inside OUT

When should you keep a database in a prior compatibility mode?

It is a common oversight to forget to promote the database compatibility level to the new SQL Server version level after a database upgrade. You are missing out on new database features, but there can be good, albeit temporary, reasons to keep a database in a prior compatibility mode. Changes from version to version in SQL Server are additive and rarely regressive.

The most common reason to run a database in prior compatibility mode is not technical at all; rather, the administrator might be handcuffed by vendor support or software certification.

One notable exception is one of the new features introduced in SQL Server 2014: improvements to the Cardinality Estimator resulted in the same or better performance for most situations, but poor query performance in rare situations. In the case of a query whose performance has regressed when executed in compatibility level 120 or higher, forcing the previous Cardinality Estimator back into use is the most realistic near-term solution. Changing the database's compatibility mode down to SQL Server 2012 (110) will accomplish this, but three less drastic options are now available.

1. Trace flag 9481 will force a database in SQL 2014 compatibility mode to use the legacy Cardinality Estimation model from SQL 2012 and earlier.

2. The LEGACY_CARDINALITY_ESTIMATION database scoped configuration option is also available starting with SQL Server 2016, to force the old Cardinality Estimation model into use only for that database. It has the same effect in the database at Trace Flag 9481.

3. You can also modify an individual query to use the legacy cardinality estimator with `OPTION (USE HINT ('FORCE_LEGACY_CARDINALITY_ESTIMATION'));`, which has been available since SQL Server 2016 SP1.

NOTE

You can upgrade the SSISDB database, which contains the SQL Server Integration Services Catalog, independently of other databases by using the SSISDB Database Upgrade Wizard. This makes it easier to move your SQL Server Integration Services packages and environments from server to server by restoring or attaching a database from a previous version to a SQL Server 2019 Server.

Other Considerations for migrating databases

As an administrator, you'll be faced with the need to move a database from one instance to another, perhaps for the purposes of refreshing a pre-production environment, moving to a new SQL Server instance, or promoting a database into production for the first time.

We just discussed database compatibility levels and SQL Server database version and compatibility modes. Additionally, when copying a database into a new environment, keep in mind the following:

- Database-scoped configurations

- Database settings (more on the differences between these two later in this section)

- SQL Server edition

- SQL logins

- Encryption

Let's look at each of these in more detail.

SQL Server edition

Generally speaking, databases progress upward in terms of cost and feature set, beginning with Express edition, Web, Standard, and finally Enterprise edition. (Developer edition is the same as Enterprise edition, except for the ability to use it in a production environment.) Moving a database up from Express, Web, or Standard edition expands the features available for use in the database.

The concern for DBAs is when databases need to move down from Enterprise, Standard, or Web edition. Many features that had historically been exclusive to Enterprise edition were included in Standard edition for the first time with SQL Server 2016 SP1, expanding what we can do with Standard edition as developers and administrators.

You will encounter errors related to higher-edition features when restoring or attaching to an instance that does not support those editions. For example, when attempting to restore a database containing compressed indexes (an Enterprise-edition feature) to an instance that does not support data compression, you will receive an error message similar to "cannot be started in this edition of SQL Server because part or all of object 'somecompressedindex' is enabled with data compression." In this case, you will need to manually remove data compression from the database in the source instance and then create a new backup or detach the database again before migrating to the lower-edition instance. You cannot turn off the use of higher-edition features on the lower-edition instance, you must disable the use of these features before restoring or attaching the database to a lower-edition instance.

You can foresee this problem by using a dynamic management view that lists all edition-specific features in use. Keep in mind that some features are supported in all editions but are limited. For example, memory-optimized databases are supported even in Express edition, but with only a small amount of allocated memory.

For example, to view all edition-specific features in use in a given database:

```
SELECT FEATURE_NAME
FROM SYS.DM_DB_PERSISTED_SKU_FEATURES;
```

This DMV may return no records if no edition-sensitive features are in use in the current database context. However, if you for example create a partitioning function, used for horizontal table partitioning, the DMV will immediately begin to return a row for the feature name "Partitioning". While table partitioning is supported in all editions of SQL Server, certain features of table partitioning are Enterprise edition only, for example, partitioned table parallelism and distributed partitioned views. Thus the performance of your partitioned tables may vary from edition to edition.

So `sys.dm_db_persisted_sku_features` can be a useful DMV for evaluating edition upgrades or compatibility. For more information on the data returned by this DMV, visit *https://docs.microsoft.com/sql/relational-databases/system-dynamic-management-views/sys-dm-db-persisted-sku-features-transact-sql*. For more information on features by edition, visit *https://docs.microsoft.com/sql/sql-server/editions-and-components-of-sql-server-version-15*.

SQL logins

SQL-authenticated logins and their associated database users are connected via security identifier (SID), not by name. When moving a database from one instance to another, the SIDs in the SQL logins on the old instance might be different from the SIDs in the SQL logins on the new instance, even if their names match. After migration to the new instance, SQL-authenticated logins will be unable to access databases where their database users have become "orphaned," and you must repair this. This does not affect Windows Authenticated logins for domain accounts.

This condition must be repaired before applications and end users will be able to access the database in its new location. Refer to the "Solving orphaned SIDs" section in Chapter 12.

The database owner should be included in the security objects that should be accounted for on the new server. Ensure that the owner of the database, listed either in the Database Properties dialog box or the `sys.databases  owner_sid` field, is still a valid principal on the new instance.

For databases with partial containment, contained logins for each type will be restored or attached along with the database, and this should not be a concern.

Database-scoped configurations

Database-scoped configurations were introduced in SQL Server 2016 (and also in Azure SQL Database v12) and represent a container for a set of options available to be configured at the database level. In earlier versions, these settings were available only at the server or individual query, such as Max Degree of Parallelism (MaxDOP).

> ➤ **For more information on Parallelism and MaxDOP, go to Chapter 14, "Performance tuning SQL Server."**

You should evaluate these options for each database after it is copied to a new instance to determine whether the settings are appropriate. The desired MaxDOP, for example, could change if the number of logical processors differs from the system default.

You can view each of these database-scoped configurations in SSMS. In Object Explorer, right-click a database, and then, on the shortcut menu, click **Properties**. In the pane on the left, click

Options. A heading just for database-scoped configurations appears at the top of the Other Options list. You can also view database-scoped configurations in the dynamic management view sys.database_scoped_configurations.

Database configuration settings

You should also review database-specific settings at the time of migration. You can review them with a quick glance of the sys.databases catalog view, or from the database properties window in SSMS.

The following is not a list of all database settings, but we will cover these and many more later in the chapter. You should pay attention to these when restoring, deploying, or attaching a database to a new instance.

- **Read Only.**   If the database was put in READ_ONLY mode before the migration to prevent data movement, be sure to change this setting back to READ_WRITE.

- **Recovery Model.**   Different servers might have different backup and recovery methods. In a typical environment, the full recovery model is appropriate for production environments when the data loss tolerance of the database is smaller than the frequency of full backups, or when point-in-time recovery is appropriate. If you are copying a database from a production environment to a development environment, it is likely you will want to change the recovery model from full to simple. If you are copying a database from a testing environment to a production environment for the first time, it is likely you will want to change the recovery model from simple to full.

NOTE

After changing a database recovery model from simple to full, immediately take a full backup of the database in order to start the transaction log recovery chain. Then, you can start taking transaction log backups on regular intervals.

➤ For more information about database backups and the appropriate recovery model, see Chapter 10.

- **Page Verify Option.**   For all databases, this setting should be CHECKSUM. The legacy TORN_PAGE_DETECTION option is a sign that this database has been moved over the years up from a pre-SQL 2005 version, but this setting has never changed. Since SQL 2005, CHECKSUM is the superior and default setting, but it requires an administrator to manually change. Always take a full database backup before changing this setting.

➤ Changing this setting alone unfortunately is not sufficient. For more information about the important Page Verify Option setting in each database, see the section "Setting the database's page verify option" in Chapter 8, "Maintaining and monitoring SQL Server."

- **Trustworthy.**   It is not recommended to ever turn on this setting unless it is made necessary because of an inflexible architecture requirement. It could allow for malicious activity on one database to affect other databases, even if specific permissions have not been granted. It is crucial to limit this setting and understand cross-database permission chains in a multitenant or web-hosted shared SQL Server environment.

NOTE

The Trustworthy setting if enabled is NOT remembered when restoring the database from one instance to another. If it was turned on for the previous system and was a requirement because of external assemblies, cross-database queries, and/or Service Broker, you will need to turn it on again. If your application security model is dependent on the Trustworthy setting, you must remember to enable it after restoring the database to another instance.

➤ For more on object ownership, see Chapter 12.

Transparent data encryption

Transparent data encryption (TDE) settings will follow the database as it is moved from one instance to another, but the certificate and the certificate's security method will not. For example, the server certificate created to encrypt the database key and the private key and its password are not backed up along with the database. This is, after all, the entire purpose of TDE—to prevent a database from being attached or restored to a server that lacks the proper certificate.

These objects must be moved to the new instance along with the database *prior to* any attempt to restore or attach the database. They must also be backed up and securely stored with the rest of your enterprise security credentials, certificates, and sensitive data.

NOTE

Restoring an unencrypted database over an encrypted database is allowed. When would you inadvertently do this? If you restore a backup from the database before it was encrypted, you will end up with an unencrypted database. You must then reapply transparent data encryption.

➤ For more information on Transparent Data Encryption (TDE), see Chapter 13, "Protecting data through encryption, privacy and auditing."

Database properties and options

In this section, we review some commonly changed and managed database settings. There are quite a few settings on the Options page in Database Properties, many involving rarely changed defaults or ANSI-standard deviations for legacy support.

You can view each of these settings in SSMS via Object Explorer. To do so, right-click a database, and then, on the shortcut menu, click **Properties**. In the Database Properties dialog box, in the pane on the left, click **Options**. You also can review database settings for all databases in the sys.databases catalog view.

The subsections that follow discuss the settings that you need to consider when creating and managing SQL Server databases.

Collation

Collations exist at three levels in a SQL Server instance: the database, the instance, and TempDB. The collation of the TempDB database by default matches the collation for the instance and should differ only in otherwise unavoidable circumstances. Ideally, the collations in all user databases match the collation at the instance level and for the TempDB, but there are scenarios in which and individual database might need to operate in a different collation.

Oftentimes databases differ from the server-level collation to enforce case sensitivity, but you can also enforce language usage differences (such as kana or accent sensitivity) and sort order differences at the database level.

The default collation for the server is decided at installation and is preselected for you based on the regionalization settings of the Windows Server. You can override this during installation. Some applications require a case-sensitive collation.

Although the server-level collation is very difficult to change (see Chapter 4: Installing and configuring SQL Server instances and features), databases can change collation. You should change a database's collation only before code is developed for the database, or only after extensive testing of existing code.

Be aware that unmatched collations in databases could cause issues when querying across those databases, so you should try to avoid collation differences between databases that will be shared by common applications.

For example, if you write a query that includes a table in a database that's set to the collation SQL_Latin1_General_CP1_CI_AS (which is **c**ase **i**nsensitive and **a**ccent **s**ensitive) and a join to a table in a database that's also set to SQL_Latin1_General_CP1_CS_AS, you will receive the following error:

```
Cannot resolve the collation conflict between "SQL_Latin1_General_CP1_CI_AS" and "SQL_
Latin1_General_CP1_CS_AS" in the equal to operation.
```

Short of changing either database to match the other, you will need to modify your code to use the COLLATE statement when referencing columns in each query. The following sample succeeds in joining two sample database tables together, despite the mismatched database collations:

```
SELECT * FROM CS_AS.sales.sales s1
INNER JOIN CI_AS.sales.sales s2
ON s1.[salestext] COLLATE SQL_Latin1_General_CP1_CI_AS = s2.[salestext];
```

The previous sample script and all scripts for this book are available for download at *https://www.MicrosoftPressStore.com/SQLServer2019InsideOut/downloads.*

NOTE

In contained databases, collation is defined at two different levels: the database and the catalog levels. You cannot change the catalog collation from Latin1_General_100_CI_ WS_KS_SC. Database metadata and variables are always in the catalog's collation. The COLLATE DATABASE_DEFAULT syntax can also be a very useful tool if you know the collation before execution.

Inside OUT

How do you take advantage of the new UTF-8 support?

New to SQL Server 2019 is support for UTF-8 collations, such as Latin1_General_100_CI_ AS_SC_UTF8. With SQL Server 2019, you can choose an instance-level UTF-8 collation, or, configure databases with UTF-8 collations.

UTF-8 is the most popular character encoding set for XML, HTML, and the World Wide Web. More than 90% of web pages are encoded with UTF-8. Until SQL Server 2019, nvarchar and nchar data types only supported UTF-16, while varchar and char support encoding via a code page, such as Windows Latin 1, Code Page 1252. You may be familiar with these options if you worked with flat files in SQL Server Integration Services (SSIS) development.

Choosing a UTF-8 collation allows for a wider variety of character values inside the varchar and char data types, at a fraction of the storage compared to UTF-16 in nvarchar or nchar.

➤ For more about UTF-8 in SQL Server 2019, see Chapter 7, "Understanding table features."

Recovery model

The full recovery model is appropriate for production environments when the data loss tolerance of the database is smaller than the frequency of full backups or when point-in-time recovery is appropriate. If you are copying a database from a production environment to a development environment, it is likely you will want to change the recovery model from full to simple. If you are copying a database from a testing environment to a production environment for the first time, it is likely that you will want to change the recovery model from simple to full.

> ► For more information on database backups and the appropriate recovery model, see Chapter 10.

Compatibility level

SQL Server provides database compatibility modes for backward compatibility to database-level features, including improvements to the query optimizer, additional fields in dynamic management objects, syntax improvements, and other database-level objects.

Compatibility mode is a database-level setting, and databases upgraded from an older version to a new version will retain a prior compatibility mode. You must manually promote a database's compatibility level when restoring up to a new version of SQL Server.

NOTE
Reverting the database's Compatibility Level to SQL Server 2012 (110) was a common tactic when databases were first upgraded to SQL Server 2014, because of changes to the SQL Server Cardinality Estimator. There are more nuanced and less drastic methods for dealing with the new Cardinality Estimator. See the section on "Upgrading database compatibility levels" earlier in this chapter for more information.

Containment type

Partially contained databases represent a fundamental change in the relationship between server and database. They are an architectural decision that you make when applications are intended to be portable between multiple SQL Server instances or when security should be entirely limited to the database context, not in the traditional server login/database user sense.

> ► For more information about the security implications of contained databases, see Chapter 12.

Azure SQL databases are themselves a type of contained database, able to move from host to host in the Azure platform-as-a-service (PaaS) environment, transparent to administrators and users. You can design databases that can be moved between SQL Server instances in a similar fashion, should the application architecture call for such capability.

Changing the Containment Type from None to Partial converts the database to a partially contained database and should not be taken lightly. We do not advise changing a database that has already been developed without the partial containment setting, because there are differences with how temporary objects behave and how collations are enforced. Some database features, including Change Data Capture, Change Tracking, replication, and some parts of Service Broker are not supported in partially contained databases. You should carefully review, while logged in as a member of the sysadmin server role or the db_owner database role, the system dynamic management view `sys.dm_db_uncontained_entities` for an inventory of objects that are not contained.

Autoclose

You should turn on this setting only in very specific and resource-exhausted environments. It activates the periodic closure of connections and the clearing of buffer allocations when user requests are not present. When active, it unravels the very purpose of application connection pooling; for example, rendering certain application architectures useless and increasing the number of login events. You should never turn on this setting as part of performance tuning or a troubleshooting exercise of a busy environment.

Auto Create statistics

When you turn on this setting, the query optimizer automatically creates statistics needed for runtime plans, even for read-only databases (statistics are stored in the TempDB for read-only databases). Some applications, such as SharePoint, handle the creation of statistics programmatically: due to the dynamic nature of its tables and queries, SharePoint handles statistics creation and updates by itself. Unless a sophisticated, complex application like SharePoint insists otherwise, you *should* turn on this setting. You can identify autocreated statistics in the database as they will use a naming convention similar to _WA_Sys_*<column_number>*_*<hexadecimal>*.

> ## Inside OUT
>
> ### What are statistics?
>
> SQL Server uses statistics to describe the distribution and nature of the data in tables. The query optimizer needs the Auto Create setting turned on so that it can create single-column statistics when compiling queries. These statistics help the query optimizer create optimal runtime plans. Without relevant and up-to-date statistics, the query optimizer may not choose the best way to execute queries. Unless an application has been specifically designed to replace the functionality of Auto Create and Auto Update statistics, such as SharePoint, these two settings should be turned on.

> ➤ For much more about statistics objects, see Chapter 15, "Understanding and designing indexes."

Autocreate incremental statistics

Introduced in SQL 2014, this setting allows for the creation of statistics that take advantage of table partitioning, reducing the overhead of statistics creation. This setting has no impact on nonpartitioned tables. Turn this setting on because it can reduce the cost of creating and updating statistics.

Once enabled, this setting will have an effect only on newly created statistics. To affect existing statistics objects on tables with partitions, you should update the statistics objects to include the INCREMENTAL = ON parameter, as shown here:

```
UPDATE STATISTICS [Purchasing].[SupplierTransactions]
[CX_Purchasing_SupplierTransactions] WITH RESAMPLE, INCREMENTAL = ON;
```

You should also, when applicable, update any manual scripts you have implemented to update statistics to use the ON PARTITIONS parameter. In the catalog view sys.stats, the is_incremental column will equal 1 if the statistics were created incrementally, as demonstrated here:

```
UPDATE STATISTICS  [Purchasing].[SupplierTransactions]
[CX_Purchasing_SupplierTransactions] WITH RESAMPLE ON PARTITIONS (1);
```

The previous sample script and all scripts for this book are available for download at *https://www.MicrosoftPressStore.com/SQLServer2019InsideOut/downloads*.

Autoshrink

You should *never* turn on this setting. It will automatically return any free space of more than 25 percent of the data file or transaction log. You should shrink a database only as a one-time operation to reduce file size after unplanned or unusual file growth. This setting could result in unnecessary fragmentation, overhead, and frequent rapid log autogrowth events.

Auto Update Statistics

When turned on, statistics will be updated periodically. Statistics are considered out of date by the query optimizer when a ratio of data modifications to rows in the table has been reached. The query optimizer checks for and updates the out-of-date statistic before running a query plan and therefore has some overhead, though the performance benefit of updated statistics usually outweighs this cost. This is especially true when the updated statistics result in a better optimization plan. Because the query optimizer updates the statistics first and then runs the plan, the update is described as synchronous.

> ### NOTE
> You must turn on Auto Update Statistics for Auto Update Statistics Asynchronously to have any effect. There is no warning or enforcement in SSMS for this, and though a Connect Item with this concern was raised in 2011, it was marked Closed as "Won't Fix."

Auto Update Statistics Asynchronously

This changes the behavior of the Auto Update Statistics by one important detail. Query runs will continue even if the query optimizer has identified an out-of-date statistics object. The statistics will be updated afterward.

Inside OUT

Should you turn on Auto Update Statistics and Auto Update Statistics Asynchronously in SQL Server 2019?

Yes! (Unless the application specifically recommends not to, such as SharePoint.)

Starting with database compatibility mode 130, the ratio of data modifications to rows in the table that helps identify out-of-date statistics has been aggressively lowered, causing statistics to be automatically updated more frequently. This is especially evident in large tables in which many rows were regularly updated. In SQL Server 2014 and earlier, this more aggressive behavior was not on by default, but could be turned on via Trace Flag 2371 starting with SQL 2008 R2 SP1.

It is more important starting with SQL Server 2016 than in previous versions to turn on Auto Update Statistics Asynchronously, which can reduce the overhead involved in automatic statistics maintenance, and provide for more consistent query performance.

Allow Snapshot Isolation

This setting allows for the use of Snapshot Isolation mode at the query level. When you turn this on, the row versioning process begins in TempDB, though this setting does little more than allow for this mechanism to be used in this database. To begin to use Snapshot Isolation mode in the database, you would need to change code; for example, to include SET TRANSACTION ISOLATION LEVEL SNAPSHOT.

➤ For much more on Snapshot Isolation, see Chapter 14.

Is Read Committed Snapshot On (RCSI)

Turning on this setting changes the default isolation mode of the database from READ COMMITTED to READ COMMITTED SNAPSHOT (RCSI). You should not turn this on during regular business hours; instead, do it during a maintenance window. Ideally, however, this setting is on and accounted for during development.

There will be an immediate impact to the utilization of TempDB as well as a rise in the IO_COMPLETION and WAIT_XTP_RECOVERY wait types, so you need to perform proper load testing. This setting, however, is potentially a major performance improvement and the core of enterprise-level concurrency.

➤ For much more about Read Committed Snapshot Isolation (RCSI), see Chapter 14.

Page Verify Option

For all databases, this setting should be CHECKSUM. The presence of the legacy TORN_PAGE_ DETECTION or NONE option is a sign that this database has been restored up from a pre-SQL 2005 version, but this setting has never changed. Since SQL 2005, CHECKSUM has the superior and default setting.

Always take a full database backup before changing this setting.

➤ Changing this setting alone unfortunately is not sufficient. For more information about the important Page Verify Option setting in each database, see the section "Setting the database's page verify option" in Chapter 8.

Trustworthy

It is not recommended to ever turn on this setting unless it is made necessary because of an inflexible architecture requirement.

Before turning on this setting, you should understand the implications of cross-database ownership chains in a multitenant or web-hosted shared SQL Server environment. Marking a database as Trustworthy could allow for malicious activity on one database to affect other databases, even if specific permissions have not been granted.

➤ For more on object ownership, see Chapter 12.

Database Read-Only

You can set an older database, or a database intended for nonchanging archival, to READ_ONLY mode to prevent changes. Any member of the server sysadmin role or the database db_owner role can revert this to READ_WRITE, so you should not consider this setting a security measure.

Database-Scoped Configurations

First introduced in SQL Server 2016 (and also in Azure SQL Database v12), Database-Scoped Configurations are a set of options previously available only at the server or individual query, such as Max Degree of Parallelism (MaxDOP). You can now change settings easily via database options that previously were available only via trace flags at the server level.

You can view each of these Database-Scoped Configurations in SSMS. In Object Explorer, right-click a database, and then, on the shortcut menu, click **Properties**. In the Database Properties dialog box, in the pane on the left, click **Options**. On the Options page, a heading just for Database-Scoped Configurations appears at the top of the Other Options list.

The current database context is important for determining which database's properties will be applied to a query that references objects in multiple databases. This means that the same query, run in two different database contexts, will have different execution plans, potentially because of differences in each database's MaxDOP setting, for example.

Among the new features of SQL Server 2019 are two new and related database scoped configurations you should know about:

- Lightweight Query Profiling is now enabled by default for all new or restored databases in SQL Server 2019, allowing the feature database-scoped configuration option (and which has existed since SQL Server 2014) to be leveraged without the need for trace flag 7412. A new database-scoped configuration option, LIGHTWEIGHT_QUERY_PROFILING, can be disabled, which is only recommended under continuous CPU-bound workloads. For older databases migrated to SQL Server 2019, is it recommended to enable this configuration if it is not already.

- A new database-scoped configuration option for LAST_QUERY_PLAN_STATS allows SQL Server to collect last known query plan statistics in the DMV sys.dm_exec_query_plan_stats and is disabled by default. When enabled, the lightweight query profiling mechanics are used to store last actual query plan xml for a given database object.

➤ **For more information about the retrieval of cached query plans, see Chapter 14.**

Query Store

Introduced in SQL Server 2016, the Query Store is a built-in reporting mechanism and data warehouse for measuring and tracking cached runtime plans. It is highly recommended, as it provides historical data for queries, not just for cached plans.

Though extremely useful, Query Store is not active by default, and you *should* turn it on as soon as possible if you intend to use it to aid performance tuning and troubleshooting cached runtime plans.

➤ **For more information on the Query Store, see Chapter 14.**

Inside OUT

How can you best use the Query Store to help with a database compatibility level upgrade?

Consider using the Query Tuning Advisor (QTA) tool, which is part of SSMS since 18.x. The QTA leverages the Query Store to evaluate workloads before and after a compatibility level change, and to identify regressed queries.

CHAPTER 6

> The QTA will also work hard to generate the best possible plan from various query opti-
> mizer models to generate the best plans. Unlike the Database Engine Tuning Advisor, the
> QTA does not and cannot generate workload, it only observes workload that you set up
> for it.

➤ For more information on using QTA, other tools, and strategies for migrating SQL Server
database to Azure, see Chapter 19.

Indirect checkpoints

If your database was created in SQL Server 2016 or later, your database is already configured to
use indirect checkpoint, which became the default for all new databases with SQL Server 2016,
even if you create the database in a previous compatibility level.

By default, in databases created in SQL Server 2016 or higher, this is 60 seconds. In databases
created in SQL Server 2012 or 2014, this option was available but set to 0, which indicates that
legacy automatic checkpoints are in use.

Databases created on prior versions of SQL Server, however, will continue to use the classic
automatic checkpoint, which has been in place since SQL Server 7.0 with only minor tweaks
since.

What is a checkpoint? This is the process by which SQL Server writes to the drive both data
and transaction log pages modified in memory, also known as "dirty" pages. Checkpoints can
be issued manually by using the CHECKPOINT command but are issued in the background for
you, so issuing CHECKPOINT is rarely necessary and is usually limited to troubleshooting.

What is a legacy or automatic checkpoint? Prior to SQL Server 2016 and since SQL Server 7.0,
all databases use automatic checkpoint by default. The rate with which dirty pages were committed to memory has increased with versions, as disk I/O and memory capacities of servers
have increased. The goal of automatic checkpoint was to ensure that all dirty pages were managed within a goal defined in the server configuration option Recovery Interval. By default, this
was 0, which meant that automatic checkpoints were in effect. The effective timing of a checkpoint tended to be around 60 seconds but was highly variable, and more or less unconcerned
with the number of pages dirtied by transactions between checkpoints.

What is an indirect checkpoint? This is a new strategy of taking care of "dirty pages" that is
far more scalable and can deliver a performance difference especially on modern systems with
a large amount of memory. Indirect checkpoints manage dirty pages in memory differently;
instead of scanning memory, indirect checkpoints proactively gather lists of dirty pages. Indirect
checkpoints then manage the list of dirty pages and continuously commit them from memory

to the drive, on a pace to not exceed an upper bound of recovery time. This upper bound is defined in the database configuration option TARGET_RECOVERY_TIME.

So, even though the recovery time goal hasn't really changed, the method by which it is achieved has. Indirect checkpoints are significantly faster than automatic checkpoints, especially as servers are configured with more and more memory. You might notice an improvement specifically in the performance of backups.

You can configure a database that was created on an older version of SQL Server to use indirect checkpoints instead of automatic checkpoints with a single command. The TARGET_RECOVERY_TIME will be 0 for databases still using automatic checkpoint. The master database will also have a TARGET_RECOVERY_TIME of 0 by default.

Consider setting the TARGET_RECOVERY_TIME database configuration to 60 seconds to match the default for all databases created in SQL Server 2016 or higher, as shown here:

```
ALTER DATABASE [database_name] SET TARGET_RECOVERY_TIME = 60 SECONDS;
```

You can check this setting for each database in the TARGET_RECOVERY_TIME_IN_SECONDS column of the system view `sys.databases`.

> **NOTE**
>
> There is a specific performance degradation involving nonyielding schedulers or excessive spinlocks that can arise because of the TARGET_RECOVERY_TIME setting being applied to the TempDB by default, as of SQL Server 2016. It is not common. It is identifiable and resolvable with analysis and a custom solution to disable indirect checkpoints on the TempDB, detailed in this blog post from the SQL Server Tiger Team: *https://docs.microsoft.com/archive/blogs/sql_server_team/ indirect-checkpoint-and-tempdb-the-good-the-bad-and-the-non-yielding-scheduler*.

For more on the differences between the different checkpoint types, and the interaction between the database TARGET_RECOVERY_TIME setting and the server's **recovery interval** setting, visit: *https://docs.microsoft.com/sql/relational-databases/logs/ database-checkpoints-sql-server*.

Accelerated Database Recovery (ADR)

New for SQL Server 2019, Accelerated Database Recovery (ADR) does not appear in the Database Properties page of SSMS as of this writing, nor is it enabled by default. There are tradeoffs to be aware of that we'll discuss later, but this is a powerful, much-desired, new feature of SQL Server 2019 that is available in both Enterprise and Standard editions.

ADR can be enabled with a T-SQL statement:

```
ALTER DATABASE whatever SET ACCELERATED_DATABASE_RECOVERY = ON;
```

Enabling this setting requires exclusive access to the database and could be blocked by other connections to the database, which could require closing other connections. You can then see the status of this setting in the system view `sys.databases`, in the new column `is_accelerated_database_recovery_on`.

ADR represents a significant overhaul of the SQL Server recovery process. It is a reworking of the machinery that the Database Engine uses to recover each database upon:

- SQL Server instance startup, especially after an unexpected shutdown

- Upon rollback of a long-running transaction

- Upon database mirroring or availability group failover

ADR results in much faster recovery times in these scenarios, including near-instant recovery for many operations.

ADR accomplishes this by a new progressive log management pattern inside the transaction log that eliminates the need for the transaction log to ever be scanned from the beginning of the oldest active transaction, and instead, can be processed at the recovery from only the last successful checkpoint.

The tradeoffs include an increase in storage requirements for each user database with ADR enabled. This could require a sudden increase of 10% or more space in the user database file, so administrators should be aware of this impact.

NOTE
The deprecated ancestor to availability groups, database mirroring, is not supported for databases with the new Accelerated Database Recovery option enabled.

Moving and removing databases

Earlier in this chapter, we discussed database migrations from older to newer servers, and the considerations involved. In this section, we review the steps and options to moving databases inside of a SQL Server instance, and the various methods and stages of removing databases from use.

Moving user and system databases

In this section, we discuss moving database files' physical locations, which becomes necessary either because of improper initial locations or the addition of new storage volumes to a server. Relocating system and user databases is similar to each other, with the master database being an exception. Let's look at each scenario.

Locating SQL Server files

As we discussed in our earlier checklist, you can review the location of all database files by querying the catalog view `sys.master_files`. If you did not specify the intended location for the data files while you were on the Data Directories page of the Database Engine Configuration step of SQL Server Setup, you will find your system database files on the OS volume at %programfiles%\Microsoft SQL Server*instance*\MSSQL\Data.

NOTE

In sys.master_files, the physical_name of each database file, the logical name of each database file (in the Name field of this view), and the name of the database do not need to match. It is possible, through restore operations, to accidentally create multiple databases with the same logical file names. Before moving database files around, consider storing the values in sys.master_files as reference, and be sure you understand the difference between the database names, logical file names, and physical file locations.

Ideally, there should be no data or log files on the OS volume, even system database files. You can, however, move these after SQL Server Setup is complete.

When you're planning to move your database data or log files, prepare their new file path location by granting FULL CONTROL permissions to the per-SID name for the SQL Server instance. (Note that this is not necessarily the SQL Server service account.) For the default instance, this will be NT SERVICE\MSSQLSERVER; for named instances, it will be NT SERVICE\ MSSQL$*instancename*.

> ## Inside OUT
>
> **Where does SQL Server keep track of the locations of database files?**
>
> When the SQL Server process is started, only three pieces of location information are provided to the service:
>
> - The location of the master database data file
> - The location of the master database log file
> - The location of the SQL Server error log
>
> You can find this information in the startup parameters of the SQL Server service in the SQL Server Configuration Manager application. All other database file locations are stored in the master database.

CHAPTER 6

Database actions: offline versus detach versus drop

Earlier in this chapter, we discussed strategies to move user database files by using the OFFLINE status. Let's discuss the differences between various ways to remove a database from a SQL Server instance.

The OFFLINE option is one way to quickly remove a database from usability.

```
ALTER DATABASE [database_name] SET OFFLINE;
```

Because this requires exclusive access to the database, you can use the ROLLBACK IMMEDIATE syntax to end all other user sessions:

```
ALTER DATABASE [database_name] SET OFFLINE WITH ROLLBACK IMMEDIATE;
```

It is also the most easily reversed:

```
ALTER DATABASE [database_name] SET ONLINE;
```

You should set maintenance activities to ignore databases that are offline because they cannot be accessed, maintained, or backed up. When a database offline, the data and log files remain in place in their location on the drive and can be moved. The database is still listed with its files in sys.master_files.

Taking a database offline is an excellent intermediate administrative step before you DETACH or DROP a database; for example, a database that is not believed to be used any more. Should a user report that she can no longer access the database, the administrator can simply bring the database back online—an immediate action.

You can separate a database's files from the SQL Server by using DETACH. The data and log files remain in place in their location on the drive and can be moved. But detaching a database removes it from sys.master_files.

To reattach the database, in SSMS, in Object Explorer, follow the Attach steps. It is not as immediate an action and requires more administrative intervention than taking the database offline.

When reattaching the database, you must locate at least the primary data file for the database. The Attach process will then attempt to reassociate all of the database files to SQL Server control, in their same locations. If their locations have changed, you must provide a list of all database files and their new locations.

NOTE

If you are detaching or restoring a database to attach or copy it to another server, do not forget to follow-up by also moving logins and then re-associating orphaned database users with their logins. For more information, review Chapter 12.

Inside OUT

When moving user database files, why should you use offline/online instead of detach/attach?

There are a number of reasons you need to take a user database offline instead of the strategy of detaching, moving, and reattaching the files.

While the database is offline, database information remains queryable in `sys.master_files` and other system catalog views. You can still reference the locations of database files after taking the database offline to ensure that everything is moved. Also, it is not possible to detach a database when the database is the source of a database snapshot or part of a replication publication. Taking a database offline is the only method possible in these scenarios.

Note that you cannot detach or take system databases offline to move them. A service restart is necessary to move system databases, including the master database.

Finally, a DROP DATABASE command, issued when you use the Delete feature of Object Explorer, removes the database from the SQL Server and deletes the database files on the drive. An exception to the delete files on drive behavior is if the destination database is offline. Deleting an offline database and detaching a database are therefore similar actions.

Dropping a database does not by default remove its backup and restore history from the msdb database, though there is a check box at the bottom of the Drop Database dialog box in SSMS that you can select for this action. The stored procedure `msdb.dbo.sp_delete_database_backuphistory` is run to remove this history. For databases with a long backup history that has not been maintained by a log history retention policy, the step to delete this history can take a long time and could cause SSMS to stop responding. Instead, delete old backup and restore history incrementally by using msdb.dbo.sp_delete_backuphistory and/or run multiple instances of the msdb.dbo.sp_delete_database_backuphistory procedure in separate SSMS query windows.

For more information on this and related stored procedures, visit:
https://docs.microsoft.com/sql/relational-databases/system-stored-procedures/sp-delete-database-backuphistory-transact-sql.

➤ For more information on backup and restore history, see Chapter 8.

Moving user database files

You can move user databases without a SQL Server instance restart and without disrupting other databases by taking the database offline, updating the files, moving them, and then bringing the database online again.

Use the following steps to move user database files:

1. Perform a manual full backup of the soon-to-be affected databases.

2. During a maintenance outage for the database and any applications that are dependent, begin by taking the user database offline and then running a T-SQL script to alter the location of each database file.

3. Here's an example of the T-SQL statements required:

```
ALTER DATABASE [database_name] SET OFFLINE WITH ROLLBACK IMMEDIATE

ALTER DATABASE [database_name] MODIFY FILE ( NAME = logical_data_file_name,

FILENAME = 'location\physical_data_file_name.mdf' );

ALTER DATABASE [database_name] MODIFY FILE ( NAME = logical_log_file_name,

FILENAME = 'location\physical_log_file_name.ldf' );

ALTER DATABASE [database_name] SET ONLINE;
```

4. While the database is offline, physically copy the database files to their new location. (You will delete the old copies when you've confirmed the new configuration.) When the file operation is complete, bring the database back online.

5. Verify that the data files have been moved by querying sys.master_files, which is a catalog view that returns all files for all databases. Look for the physical_name column to reflect the new location correctly.

6. After you have verified that SQL Server is recognizing the database files in their new locations, delete the files in the original location to reclaim the space.

7. After you have successfully moved the database files, you should perform a manual backup of the master database.

Moving system database files, except for master

You cannot move system database files while the SQL Server instance is online; thus, you must stop the SQL Server service.

NOTE

If you plan to move all of the system databases to a different volume, you also will need to move the SQL Server Agent Error Log, or SQL Server Agent will not be able to start.

You can do this in SSMS. In Object Explorer, connect to the SQL Server instance, and then expand the SQL Server Agent folder. Right-click **Error Logs**, and then, on the shortcut menu that opens, click **Configure**. Provide a new Error Log File location for the SQLAGENT.OUT file.

CHAPTER 6

Verify that the SQL Server Agent per-SID name for the SQL Server Agent service has FULL CONTROL permissions to the new folder. The per-service SID account will be NT Service\ SQLSERVERAGENT for default instances or NT Service\SQLAgent$*instancename* for named instances.

When you later restart the SQL Server service and the SQL Server Agent service, the Agent error log will be written to the new location.

1. Begin by performing a manual full backup of the soon-to-be affected databases.

2. For model, msdb, and TempDB, begin by running a T-SQL script (similar to the script for moving user databases). SQL Server will not use the new locations of the system databases until the next time the service is restarted. You cannot set the system databases to offline.

3. During a maintenance outage for the SQL Server instance, stop the SQL Server instance, and then copy the database files to their new location. (You will delete the old copies when you've confirmed the new configuration.) The only exception here is that the TempDB data and log files do not need to be moved—they will be re-created automatically by SQL Server upon service start.

4. When the file operation is complete, start the SQL Server service again.

5. Verify that the data files have been moved by querying `sys.master_files`. Look for the `physical_name` column to reflect the new location correctly.

6. After you have verified that SQL Server is recognizing the database files in their new locations, delete the files in the original location to reclaim the space.

7. After you have successfully moved the database files, perform a manual backup of the master database.

If you encounter problems starting SQL Server after moving system databases to another volume—for example if the SQL Server service account starts and then stops—check for the following:

1. Verify that the SQL Server service account and SQL Server Agent service account have permissions to the new file location. Review the following link for a list of File System Permissions Granted to SQL Server service accounts: ***https://docs.microsoft.com/sql/ database-engine/configure-windows/configure-windows-service-accounts-and- permissions#Reviewing_ACLs***

2. Check the Windows Application Event Log and System Event Log for errors.

3. If you cannot resolve the issue, and if necessary, start SQL Server with Trace Flag 3608, which does not start the SQL Server fully, only the master database. You then can move all

other database files, including the other system databases, back to their original location by using T-SQL commands issued through SSMS.

4. For more information on moving system database files, visit: ***https://docs.microsoft.com/ sql/relational-databases/databases/move-system-databases***.

Moving master database files

Moving the master database files is not difficult, but it is a more complicated process than for the other system databases. Instead of issuing an ALTER DATABASE ... ALTER FILE statement, you must edit the parameters passed to the SQL Server service in SQL Server Configuration Manager.

1. Open SQL Server Configuration Manager, select SQL Server Services on the left, right-click on SQL Server service, choose properties. On the Startup Parameters page, notice that there are three entries containing three files in their current paths. (If you have other startup parameters in this box, do *not* modify them now.)

   Edit the two parameters beginning with –d and –1 (lowercase "L"). The –e parameter is the location of the SQL Server Error Log; you might want to move that, as well.

   After editing the master database data file (-d) and the master database log file (-l) locations, click **OK**. Keep in mind that the SQL Server service will not look for the files in their new location until the service is restarted.

2. Stop the SQL Server service, and then copy the master database data and log files to their new location. (You will delete the old copies when you've confirmed the new configuration.)

3. When the file operation is complete, start the SQL Server service again.

4. Verify that the data files have been moved by querying sys.master_files, a dynamic management view that returns all files for all databases. Look for the physical_name column to correctly reflect the new location.

5. After you have verified that SQL Server is recognizing the database files in their new locations, delete the files in the original location to reclaim the space.

Single-user mode

By default, all databases are in MULTI_USER mode. Sometimes, it is necessary to gain exclusive access to a database with a single connection, typically in SQLCMD or in a SSMS query window.

For example, when performing a restore, the connection must have exclusive access to the database. By default, the restore will wait until it gains exclusive access. You could attempt to discontinue all connections, but there is a much easier way: setting a database to SINGLE_USER mode removes all other connections but your own.

Setting a database to SINGLE_USER mode also requires exclusive access. If other users are connected to the database, running the following statement will be unsuccessful:

```
ALTER DATABASE [database_name] SET SINGLE_USER;
```

It is then necessary to provide further syntax to decide how to treat other connections to the database.

- **WITH NO_WAIT.**   The ALTER DATABASE command will fail if it cannot gain exclusive access to the database. It is important to note that without this statement or other WITH commands below, the ALTER DATABASE command will wait indefinitely.

- **WITH ROLLBACK IMMEDIATE.**   Rollback all conflicting requests, killing other SSMS Query window connections, for example.

- **WITH ROLLBACK AFTER n SECONDS.**   Delays the effect of WITH ROLLBACK IMMEDIATE by *n* SECONDS, which is not particularly more graceful to competing user connections, just delayed.

For example:

```
ALTER DATABASE [database_name] SET SINGLE_USER WITH ROLLBACK IMMEDIATE;
```

Instead of issuing a WITH ROLLBACK, you might choose to identify other sessions connected to the destination database; for example, by using the following:

```
SELECT * FROM sys.dm_exec_sessions

WHERE db_name(database_id) = 'database_name';
```

And then evaluate the appropriate strategy for dealing with any requests coming from that session, including communication with that user and closing of unused connections to that database in dialog boxes, SSMS query windows, or user applications.

After you have completed the activities that required exclusive access, set the database back to MULTI_USER mode:

```
ALTER DATABASE [database_name] SET MULTI_USER;
```

You need to gain exclusive access to databases prior to a restore, or to take a database offline. This script to change the database to SINGLE_USER and back to MULTI_USER is a common step wrapped around a database restore.

➤ **For more information on database restores, see Chapter 10.**

CHAPTER 6

Understanding table features

This chapter discusses a fundamental concept in relational databases: tables. Tables are the database objects that store the data in the database. Thoroughly understanding the concepts in this chapter is a requirement for designing and maintaining an effective database. We first discuss table structure fundamentals, including data types, keys, and constraints. Next, we cover several specialized table types, such as temporal tables and graph tables. Then, we examine the specialized nature of storing binary large objects (BLOBs) in relational tables. Your understanding of table design would not be complete without including both vertical and horizontal partitioning, which we review before the chapter ends with an overview of change tracking methods.

A proper relational database design requires considerations beyond the SQL Server features included in this chapter. Mapping application requirements, normalization, and organization-specific requirements are not covered in this book. There are many texts available to learn about those elements of database design.

Reviewing table design

In this section, we review information that is relevant when creating tables. First, we look at system data types, emphasizing the data design decisions surrounding their use. Next, we briefly discuss primary and foreign key concepts. Then, we cover constraints, their impact on table design, and how they can help meet data integrity requirements. The section ends with user-defined data types and computed columns.

NOTE

Beyond coverage of primary keys and unique constraints, indexing is not covered in this chapter, although table design is not complete without considering it. For guidance on indexing, read Chapter 14, "Performance tuning SQL Server," and Chapter 15, "Understanding and designing indexes."

General purpose data types

Selecting the appropriate data type when designing relational databases is a crucial activity. Even though you can change the data types of columns, it might be an expensive operation. A poorly chosen data type can result in suboptimal performance or might allow for unexpected values to be stored in the column. The intent of this section is not to provide exhaustive coverage of each system data type available in SQL Server. Instead, the focus will be on providing the information and guidance necessary to make solid table design decisions.

Alphanumeric types

Alphanumeric types in SQL Server are commonly discussed in terms of fixed versus variable length, and with Unicode versus without Unicode support. The char data type is a fixed length type and varchar is variable length. With the release of SQL Server 2019, the Unicode support has become more nuanced than before. The nchar and nvarchar data types are fixed and variable length, respectively, and support Unicode, specifically UTF-16. When using one of the new SQL Server 2019 UTF-8 collations, char and varchar also support Unicode, though using the UTF-8 encoding. More information about these new collations and their purpose is included later in this section.

> **NOTE**
>
> **You might need Unicode support more often than you think. Increasingly, users expect to store emojis and other Unicode character data in columns. In addition, increasing internationalization of applications is also best supported by using Unicode string data types.**

As a database designer, you must understand that the *(n)* in a [var]char(n) column definition indicates the number of bytes allocated for the column, not the number of characters that can be stored. The same is true for n[var]char(n) columns, though the size indicates the number of byte-pairs that can be stored. This is important because:

- [var]char columns can store strings from double-byte character sets, and can use UTF-8 collations, which may require two or four bytes to store one character. Full coverage of UTF-8 collations is included in the following subsection.

- n[var]char columns can store characters in the Unicode supplementary character range, which may require four bytes.

> **CAUTION**
>
> **In SQL Server, *n* defines the column width in number of bytes. *n* never defines the number of characters that can be stored, though it is commonly but incorrectly thought of that way.**

Collation

With string data, collation becomes an important consideration. Among other things, collation determines how the high order bits in each character's byte(s) are interpreted. Collation supports internationalization by allowing different character representations for characters whose integer values is greater than 127 up to 255. This is determined using the code page, which is one element of the collation. Collation also determines how data is compared and sorted, such as whether casing and accented letters are considered different.

> **NOTE**
>
> If the full range of Unicode characters must be supported in a column, the collation should be set to a "supplementary characters" collation. These collations' names end in _SC and have been available since SQL Server 2012. The most frequently used characters have Unicode point values between 0x20 and 0xFFFF (point values below 0x20 are control characters). Thus, without using supplementary characters, 65,515 characters can be represented. Those include accented letters for most languages, many symbols, and characters for Asian and Cyrillic languages, and many more.

➤ The Microsoft Docs at *https://docs.microsoft.com/sql/relational-databases/collations/collation-and-unicode-support#Supplementary_Characters* have more information about Unicode supplementary characters.

SQL Server 2019 introduces a new family of collations which support UTF-8. These collations apply to the char and varchar data types only and store the string data using UTF-8 encoding. They effectively turn these two data types into Unicode data types, including support for supplementary characters. When you define a column or conversion to use a UTF-8 collation, the encoding is automatically updated.

The sidebar below discusses how using UTF-8 impacts the number of bytes needed to store a single character.

CHAPTER 7

Inside OUT

Should you expect space savings when using the UTF-8 collations?

Understanding the answer requires at least a cursory understanding of how character data is encoded in UTF-8. The number of bytes required to encode characters varies from one to four. The characters at the lowest code points (0-127) require only one byte, just like other collations. This is designed to maintain compatibility with ASCII. These 128 characters are the most common characters in Latin script, including uppercase and lowercase letters, digits, and many punctuation marks. However, code points 128-2,047 already require two bytes in UTF-8, while only requiring one byte in the non-UTF-8 collations. That code point range includes Latin accented characters, many additional punctuation marks (such as the semi-colon (;)) and symbols (such as currency symbols). UTF-8 requires more storage space than UTF-16 for characters in the code point range 2,048-65.535. An extra script file in the book's downloads illustrates some of these caveats.

Thus, whether or not you should expect space savings is quite nuanced and depends on how many characters in the average varchar column will require more than one byte to be encoded (when compared to varchar using collations other than UTF-8) or more than two bytes (when compared to nchar or nvarchar). For an internationalized application, this might be difficult to forecast.

We do not suggest switching collations to UTF-8 for the purpose of saving storage space. The UTF-8 collations are designed to support internationalization of existing applications and databases without incurring massive changes and associated test requirements. For new application or database development where internationalization is expected, the use of the UTF-16 encoding (using the nchar and nvarchar data types) is highly recommended.

➤ For complete details about collation and Unicode support, refer to Microsoft Docs at *https://docs.microsoft.com/sql/ relational-databases/collations/collation-and-unicode-support*.

CAUTION

If you decide that UTF-8 is the right encoding to use for an existing database, you will need to ensure that the column width in bytes can accommodate the potentially larger size of the existing column values once converted to UTF-8. During the collation conversion, SQL Server will silently truncate any values that do not fit.

Before converting, you can determine if any strings will require more bytes than the column width supports using a T-SQL statement like the one below, where val is a varchar(8) column in a table called CollationTest:

```
-- If COUNT > 0, then there are rows whose data size will be larger than the

-- current column width supports

SELECT COUNT(*)

FROM CollationTest

    /* This WHERE clause is used to determine which values will no longer fit

    * in the width of the column (8 bytes) after altering the column to use
```

```
* a collation from the UTF-8 family of collations, where a single character

* might take up four times as much space (8 * 4 = 32).

* Note: quadrupling the byte count of the source column isn't necessary:

* any value larger than the source column width will do.

* Two CASTs are required */
WHERE DATALENGTH(

CAST(CAST(val AS VARCHAR(32))

COLLATE Latin1_General_100_CS_AS_SC_UTF8 AS VARCHAR(32))) > 8;
```

Large value data

Finally, no discussion of alphanumeric types would be complete without investigating varchar(max) and nvarchar(max). By specifying max instead of a value between 1 and 8,000 bytes (for varchar) or between 1 and 4,000 byte-pairs (for nvarchar), the storage limit increases to 2 GB. If the column's value exceeds 8,000 bytes, the data is not stored in the table's storage structure. Large-value data is stored out-of-row, though for each such column, 24 bytes of overhead is stored in the row. Of those 24 bytes, the first 16 bytes are used to store metadata and the last eight bytes contain the pointer to the row in the row-overflow page.

NOTE

The details of storing large value data also apply to the varbinary(max) **and** xml **data types, both of which are discussed later in the chapter.**

SQL Server has a total row size limit of 8,060 bytes. Even if you do not use [n]varchar(max) columns, some data may be stored out of row. Any data that is stored off-row will incur some overhead when it is read. The flip side is that when a T-SQL statement does not reference a column whose data is stored off-row, there is a performance benefit. If your table's usage patterns indicate that large value type columns are not frequently included in statements, performance can be optimized by storing the data off-row, even if the size is less than 8,000 bytes. The T-SQL statement below will enable the large_value_types_out_of_row option for the PurchaseOrders table in the WideWorldImporters sample database:

```
DECLARE @TableName NVARCHAR(776) = N'Purchasing.PurchaseOrders';

-- Turn the option on

EXEC sp_tableoption @TableNamePattern = @TableName

    , @OptionName = 'large value types out of row'

    , @OptionValue = 1;

-- Verify the option setting
```

CHAPTER 7

```
SELECT [name], large_value_types_out_of_row

FROM sys.tables

WHERE object_id = OBJECT_ID(@TableName);
```

After running this statement, the values will not be migrated to out of row storage immediately. Rather, only when an existing data row is updated will the values be stored out of row. You could force such updates to happen by executing an UPDATE statement that sets the column value to itself, although this operation will be quite expensive on large tables. We don't recommend this unless you have determined that the immediate benefit of forcing those values to be stored off-row exceeds the cost of the update operation.

In the T-SQL CREATE statement (but not in an ALTER statement), you can opt to store the data for large value type columns in a separate filegroup. In the CREATE TABLE statement, use the TEXTIMAGE_ON clause to specify the name of the filegroup where large object (LOB) data should be stored.

> ➤ If you need to store more than 2 GB in a single column, consider the FILESTREAM feature, discussed in the "Storing BLOBs" section in this chapter.

Numeric types

When considering numeric types in computer systems, it is important to understand the nature of your data. One of the most important concepts to understand is the difference between exact and approximate numeric types. Approximate types store values using a floating-point structure. In SQL Server, the number of bits in the mantissa is limited to 24 or 53, resulting in a respective precision of seven or 15 digits. Due to the nature of the structure and the limited number of bits, these types cannot accurately store all numbers in the supported range. On the other hand, exact types store numbers without a loss of precision, but this comes at a loss of range. For approximate, floating point types, the range is very large and useful for scientific-like numbers and operations, where a small loss of precision might not matter. For exact types, the range is limited but sufficient for operations requiring precision, such as those involving monetary values.

SQL Server provides real and float as approximate data types, though their implementation is closely related. The real data type is lower precision than the float data type. It is possible to specify the number of bits for the mantissa when defining float, but SQL Server will always use either 24 bits or 53 bits—any other value you specify is rounded up to either 24 or 53. The real data type is the same as specifying float(24), or in effect any number of mantissa bits between 1 and 24.

NOTE

The sample scripts for this chapter include an extra file that illustrates important caveats when converting from approximate floating-point numbers to exact types.

Exact numeric types include `tinyint`, `smallint`, `int`, and `bigint`, which are all whole numbers of varying byte sizes and therefore range. SQL Server does not support unsigned integers.

There are exact numeric types that support decimal-point numbers. Foremost among those is the `decimal` data type. In SQL Server, another name for decimal is `numeric`. The `decimal` data type supports a precision of up to 38 digits, before or after the decimal point or a combination thereof. The number of digits determines the storage size. In addition, you can specify the scale, which determines the number of digits to the right of the decimal point.

Another category of exact numeric types that support decimal point numbers are `money` and `smallmoney`. These data types can store monetary data with a precision of up to four digits to the right of the decimal point, so the precision is to the ten-thousandth. Choosing between `decimal` and `money` or `smallmoney` is primarily determined by your need for range and precision. For monetary values, and if your multiplications and divisions will always return the desired result when using only four significant digits to the right of the decimal point, `smallmoney` and `money` are good choices because they are more efficient as it relates to storage space. For higher precision and larger scale, `decimal` is the right choice.

> ## Inside OUT
>
> ### When should you use a numeric data type instead of a character data type?
>
> You can store any numeric value, such as an amount or an identifier consisting only of digits, in an alphanumeric column or in a numeric data type column. Generally, you would choose a numeric data type if you use the values in some type of calculation or when magnitude matters. For example, you might need to calculate a discount on a monetary value. Another example for which numeric data types are used is in quantities because you might need to adjust the quantity by adding or subtracting additional units. On the other hand, a US Zip code is best stored as an alphanumeric value because leading zeroes must be preserved. The same can be true in an employee ID number.
>
> In addition to considering whether you need to use the value in calculations, there are also differences in how values are sorted. In a numeric column sorted in ascending order, the value "12" will come before "100". But in an alphanumeric column, 100 will come before 12. Either one can produce the desired answer based on your use case.

Date and time types

Date and time data types available in SQL Server 2019 include the venerable `datetime` and `smalldatetime` types. Although these are not technically deprecated, we strongly caution against using them for new development due to issues surrounding precision, available date range, and lack of control over the precision and storage size. Additionally, these data types are not aligned with the SQL standard, lowering portability of the data between platforms. Their immediate replacement is datetime2, which in no case consumes more than eight bytes of storage space (the same as datetime), but addresses precision, increases the date range, and can store dates in less than eight bytes in return for lower precision. As a matter of detail, specifying datetime2(6) provides the same precision as datetime, but does so while requiring two fewer bytes.

NOTE

All date and time data types discussed here are available in all currently supported versions of SQL Server. They are by no means new data types, but, unfortunately, are too frequently left unused for fear of backward-compatibility problems.

This does not mean, however, that all date or time of day values should be stored in datetime2. There are three additional data types that you should consider for storing date or time values:

- **date.** The date data type stores only a date and supports the same date range as datetime2. It stores the date in only three bytes, thereby being much more efficient than datetime (fixed at eight bytes) and datetime2 (minimally six bytes). If you need to store only a date without time or time zone information, this is your best choice. An example of such a case is a date of birth. A date of birth is commonly stored to calculate someone's age, and that is not generally dependent on the time zone or on the time. One of the authors was born at 11 PM Central European Summer Time. If he moved to southeast Asia, he would not celebrate his birthday a day later, even though the date in Southeast Asia was the next day. (We appreciate that some applications, such as one used in a neonatal facility, might need to store a more precise "time of birth," but in most cases, the aging logic above holds up.)

- **datetimeoffset.** The datetimeoffset data type provides the same precision and range as datetime2 but includes an offset value in hours and minutes used to indicate the difference from UTC. Even though a discussion of time zones and the impact of Daylight Saving Time (DST), also known as summer time, is beyond the scope of this book, we will note that this data type neither tracks or understands actual time zones nor DST. It would be up to the application to track the time zone where the value originated to allow the application or recent versions of SQL Server (see the note that follows) to perform correct date arithmetic.

NOTE

Prior to SQL Server 2016, SQL Server did not have any understanding of time zones or DST. SQL Server 2016 and Microsoft Azure SQL Database introduced the AT TIME ZONE function, which you can use to convert between time zones and apply or revert a DST offset. The rules SQL Server applies are based on the Windows functionality for time zones and DST. These rules are explained and illustrated with examples at *https://docs.microsoft.com/sql/t-sql/queries/at-time-zone-transact-sql*. **In SQL Server on**

Linux, this functionality is achieved through a shim, which provides for the same results as executing the function on a Windows host.

- **time.** The `time` data type stores only a time-of-day value consisting of hours, minutes, seconds, and fractional seconds, with a precision up to 100 nanoseconds. The exact fractional second precision and storage size is user defined by optionally specifying a precision between 0 and 7. The `time` data type is a good choice when storing only a time-of-day value that is not time-zone sensitive, such as for a reminder. A reminder set for 11 AM might need to be activated at 11 AM regardless of time zone and date.

NOTE

Due to its nature, the `time` data type is limited to storing no more than 23 hours, 59 minutes, 59 seconds, and 0.9999999 fractions of a second. This can make this data type unsuitable for storing elapsed time if there is a possibility that elapsed time might be 24 hours or more.

Inside OUT

How do you correctly retrieve the current system date and time?

In addition to continued use of the `datetime` data type despite the availability of the better `datetime2` type, we also observe the common use of the lower-precision functions CURRENT_TIMESTAMP, GETDATE(), and GETUTCDATE(). Although these functions continue to work, they return values of the `datetime` type.

There are replacement functions available in SYSDATETIME(), SYSDATETIMEOFFSET(), and SYSUTCDATETIME(). Despite that their names don't make it immediately clear, the SYSDATETIME() and SYSUTCDATETIME() functions return the improved `datetime2(7)` type. SYSDATETIMEOFFSET() returns a value of type `datetimeoffset(7)`. SYSDATETIME() and SYSUTCDATETIME() are functionally equivalent to GETDATE() and GETUTCDATE(), respectively. SYSDATETIMEOFFSET() did not have a functional equivalent and is thus the only option if you need to include the time zone offset on the server.

Even if you are unable to change the schema of your database to change all `datetime` columns to `datetime2` (or `datetimeoffset`), you might benefit in the long term from adopting the improved functions now. Even though the range of valid dates for `datetime` is much smaller on the lower end than for `datetime2` and `datetimeoffset`, the upper end is the same (December 31, 9999). Discarding the future possibility of time-travel to before the year 1753, none of the improved functions will return a `datetime2` or `datetimeoffset` value that cannot be cast to `datetime`.

CHAPTER 7

➤ For detailed technical comparisons between the available date and time data types, consult Microsoft Docs at *https://docs.microsoft.com/sql/t-sql/functions/date-and-time-data-types-and-functions-transact-sql*.

Binary types

Some data cannot be efficiently represented as an alphanumeric string. For example, data that has been encrypted by the application should be stored as a binary value. The same might also apply to storing contents of binary file formats, such as PDF files.

SQL Server provides the `binary` data type to store fixed-length binary values, and `varbinary` to store variable-length binary values. (The `image` data type is deprecated, and you should no longer use it.) For both data types, you specify the number of bytes that will be stored, up to 8,000. If you need to store more than 8,000 bytes, you can specify `varbinary(max)`. This will allow up to 2 GB to be stored, although if the value exceeds 8,000 bytes, those bytes are not stored in the data row. Like `[n]varchar`, `varbinary` values may be stored out of row if the total row size would exceed 8,000 bytes.

> ### NOTE
> When storing binary values that are on average larger than 1 MB, you should review whether using FILESTREAM is not a better choice. FILESTREAM is discussed in the "Understanding FILESTREAM" section later in this chapter.

➤ Refer to the section Large value data for details on how `varbinary(max)` data is stored and access can be optimized.

Specialized data types

In addition to the data types that are designed to store traditional numeric, alphanumeric, and date and time values, SQL Server provides more specialized data types. These data types are more specific to certain use cases than the general purpose data types.

Some specialized data types have SQL Common Language Runtime (CLR) functions that make working with them significantly easier. For example, the `hierarchyid` data type has a `ToString()` function that converts the stored binary value into a human-readable format. Such SQL CLR function names are case-sensitive, regardless of the case sensitivity of the instance or database.

Spatial data types: geometry and geography

The spatial data types provide a way to work with planar (flat) or ellipsoidal (round-earth) coordinates. The `geometry` data type is for a flat coordinate system, whereas the `geography` data type is for round-earth coordinates. In addition, both data types also support elevation, or Z, values. Both data types are CLR types that are available in every database, regardless of whether the SQL CLR feature is turned on.

SQL Server provides several methods to work with the values of these data types, including finding intersections, calculating surface area and distance, and many more. SQL Server supports methods defined by the Open Geospatial Consortium (OGC) as well as extended methods designed by Microsoft. The methods defined by the OGC are identified by their ST prefix.

Generally, you create a geometry or geography value by using the static STGeomFromText method. You can use this method to define points, lines, and polygons (closed shapes). The code example that follows creates two geometric points, one with coordinates (0, 0) and the second with coordinates (10, 10), and then the distance between both points is calculated and output:

```
-- Define the variables

DECLARE @point1 GEOMETRY, @point2 GEOMETRY, @distance FLOAT;

-- Initialize the geometric points

SET @point1 = geometry::STGeomFromText('POINT( 0  0)', 0);

SET @point2 = geometry::STGeomFromText('POINT(10 -10)', 0);

-- Calculate the distance

SET @distance = @point1.STDistance(@point2);

SELECT @distance;
```

The result in the output is approximately 14.14 (see Figure 7-1; note that no units are defined here). The second argument in the STGeomFromText method is the spatial reference ID (SRID), which is relevant only for the geography data type. Still, it is a required parameter for the function, and you should specify 0 for geometry data.

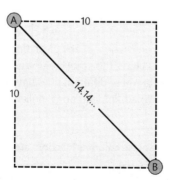

Figure 7-1   The geometry defined in the sample script.

Using spatial data types in a database is valuable when you use the Database Engine to perform spatial queries. You have probably experienced the results of spatial queries in many applications; for example, when searching for nearby pizza restaurants on Bing Maps. Application code can certainly also perform those spatial queries; however, that would require the database to return all pizza restaurants along with their coordinates. By performing the spatial query in the database, the data size that is returned to the application is significantly reduced. SQL Server supports indexing spatial data such that spatial queries can perform optimally.

➤ For a complete reference on the geometry and geography data types, the methods they support, and spatial reference identifiers, refer to Microsoft Docs at *https://docs.microsoft.com/sql/t-sql/spatial-geometry/spatial-types-geometry-transact-sql* and *https://docs.microsoft.com/sql/t-sql/spatial-geography/spatial-types-geography*.

NOTE

For an example of the geography data type, refer to the WideWorldImporters sample database. The Application.StateProvinces table includes a Border column of type geography. To visually see the geography data type at work, run a select statement on the table using SQL Server Management Studio (SSMS). In addition to the row results, SSMS will display a Spatial results tab on which a map will be drawn showing the US states, the District of Columbia, and Puerto Rico. An astute reader might remark that querying that table without a WHERE clause will return 53 rows, but only 52 territories are drawn. We'll leave it to our readers to determine why.

The XML data type

The xml data type is designed to store XML documents or snippets. Support for XML goes beyond just storing XML data. The XML data type can enforce XML Schema, in which case the column is referred to as *typed*. XML data can also be queried using XQuery syntax. SQL Server further supports XML by formatting relational data output as XML or retrieving XML data in a relational structure.

A relational database is generally used to store highly structured data, by which we mean data that has a known schema. And even though schemas can change, at any given time every row in a table will have the same columns. Yet, for some scenarios, this strict schema is not appropriate. It might be necessary to accommodate storing data where different rows have different attributes. Sometimes, you can meet this requirement by adding additional nullable sparse columns.

➤ You can read more about sparse columns in the "Sparse columns" section later in the chapter. For detailed guidance on the use of column sets, see *https://docs.microsoft.com/sql/relational-databases/tables/use-column-sets*.

Column sets are a feature by which you can manage a group of sparse columns as XML data. Column sets come with significant limitations. Defining many sparse columns becomes onerous because a substantial number of columns can introduce additional challenges in working with the table. There, the xml data type can alleviate the column sprawl. Additionally, if data is frequently used in XML format, it might be more efficient to store the data in that format in the database.

Although XML data could be stored in (n)varchar columns, using the specialized data type allows SQL Server to provide functionality for validating, querying, indexing, and modifying the XML data.

➤ Refer to the section Large value data for details on how xml data is stored and access can be optimized.

Inside OUT

How do you work with JSON in SQL Server?

SQL Server 2016 introduced support for JSON, though it is not a data type. JSON support includes parsing, querying, modifying, and transforming JSON stored in varchar columns using functions. The brief sample below illustrates how to check if a value is valid JSON, using the ISJSON() function, and extracting a scalar value, using the JSON_VALUE() function.

```
DECLARE @SomeJSON nvarchar(50) = '{ "test": "passed" }';

SELECT ISJSON(@SomeJSON) IsValid, JSON_VALUE(@SomeJSON, '$.test') [Status];
```

The output from this code will have two columns. The first column will have the value 1 because the variable holds valid JSON data, and the second column contains the value passed.

For an additional example, examine the columns CustomFields and OtherLanguages in the Application.People table in the WideWorldImporters sample database. OtherLanguages is a computed column, which extracts some JSON data from the CustomFields column using the JSON_QUERY() function.

➤ For complete information on handling JSON-formatted data in SQL Server and Azure SQL Database, refer to
https://docs.microsoft.com/sql/relational-databases/json/json-data-sql-server.

CHAPTER 7

Rowversion

This data type generates a database-wide unique binary value upon each modification of row data. This binary value increments with each insert or update statement that affects the row, even if no other row data is modified. A common use of this data type is as a row change indicator for use with applications that use optimistic concurrency or as a database-wide change indicator.

The name timestamp is the same as the SQL ISO standard timestamp, but it does not work according to the ISO standard. Contrary to what the timestamp name might imply, the data in a rowversion column does not map to a moment in time.

> ### NOTE
> The rowversion data type was previously known as timestamp. rowversion is the recommended name to use; timestamp is deprecated. Unfortunately, SSMS does not support the use of rowversion in the table designer or when scripting a table; it continues to use timestamp.

When designing tables with rowversion, keep the following restrictions in mind:

- A table can have only a single rowversion column. Considering the context of rowversion, this restriction is perfectly sensible and we've included it here only for completeness.

- You cannot specify a value for the rowversion column in INSERT or UPDATE statements. However, unlike with identity or computed columns, you must specify a column list in INSERT statements for tables with a rowversion column. We should note that specifying the column list is recommended anyway.

- Although the Database Engine will not generate duplicate rowversion values within a database, rowversion values are not unique across databases or across instances.

Duplicate rowversion values can exist in a single database if a new table is created by using the SELECT INTO syntax. The new table's rowversion values will be the same as those of the source table. This behavior might be desired, for example, when modifying a table's schema by creating a new table and copying all the data into it. In other instances, this behavior might not be desired. In those cases, do not include the rowversion column in the SELECT INTO statement. Then, alter the new table and add a rowversion column. This behavior and workaround are illustrated in an extra sample script file in the accompanying downloads for this book, which are available at https://www.*microsoftpressstore.com/SQLServer2019InsideOut/downloads*.

Implementing optimistic concurrency

A rowversion column in a table is an excellent way to implement a row change indicator to achieve *optimistic concurrency*. In optimistic concurrency, a client reads data with the intent of updating it. Unlike with *pessimistic concurrency*, however, a lock is not maintained. Instead, in the same transaction as the update statement, the client will verify that the rowversion was not changed by another process. If it hasn't, the update proceeds. But if the rowversion no longer matches what the client originally read, the update will fail. The client application then can retrieve the current values and present the user with a notification and suitable options, depending on the application needs. Many object-relational mappers (ORMs), including Entity Framework, support using a rowversion column type to implement optimistic concurrency.

Inside OUT

Can you implement optimistic concurrency without rowversion?

There are other ways to implement optimistic concurrency. A client application can track the value of each individual column in the row to be updated and verify that only the columns that will be updated by its own update statement have not been modified. Specifically, client A reads a row of data and intends to change only the Name column. Client B reads the same row of data and updates the Address column. When client A attempts to update the Name, it finds that the Name column's value is unchanged and will proceed with the update.

This approach is suitable in some scenarios, but it has some drawbacks. First, each client needs to maintain additional state, namely the original value of each column. In a web application, the amount of state to maintain can grow very large and consume a lot of memory. In a web farm scenario, maintaining such state might require shared state configuration because the web client might not communicate with the same web server on the POST that it did on the GET.

But, perhaps more importantly, the data row can be inconsistent after the second update. If each client updates a column in the same row, the row's data might not reflect a valid business scenario. Certainly, the row's values would not reflect what each client believes it would be.

The uniqueidentifier data type

The uniqueidentifier data type stores a 16-byte value known as a globally unique identifier (GUID). SQL Server can generate GUIDs using one of two functions: NEWID() and NEWSEQUEN-TIALID(). NEWSEQUENTIALID() generates a GUID that is greater than a previously generated GUID by this function *since the last restart of the server*. You can use NEWSEQUENTIALID() only in a default constraint for a column. It is more suitable to use as a clustered primary key than NEWID(). Unlike NEWID(), which generates random values, the increasing nature of the GUIDs generated by NEWSEQUENTIALID() means that data and index pages will fill completely. You might still experience fragmentation as a result of GUIDs having a smaller value than the previous one after a restart.

NOTE

Although we are not aware of a use for a SQL Server system without a network interface card (NIC), GUIDs generated on such a system might not be globally unique. A GUID is generated by incorporating MAC address values. On a system without a NIC, the generation algorithm will use random values, instead. The chance of collision is extremely low.

➤ The uniqueidentifier data type plays an important role in some replication techniques. For more information, see Chapter 11, "Implementing high availability and disaster recovery."

The hierarchyid data type

The hierarchyid data type provides a way for an application to store and query hierarchical data in a tree structure. A tree structure means that a row will have one parent and zero or more children. There is a single root element denoted by a single forward slash (/). Hierarchyid values are stored as a binary format but are commonly represented in their string format. Each element at the same level in the hierarchy (referred to as siblings) has a unique numeric value (which might include a decimal point). In the string representation of a hierarchyid value, each level is separated by a forward slash. The string representation always begins with a slash (to denote the root element) and ends with a slash.

For example, as illustrated in Figure 7-2, a hierarchyid whose string representation is /1/10/ is a descendant of the /1/ element, which itself is a descendant of the implicit root element /. It must be noted, however, that SQL Server does not enforce the existence of a row with the ancestor element. This means that it is possible to create an element /3/1/ without its ancestor /3/ being a value in a row. Implicitly, it is a child of /3/, even if no row with hierarchyid value /3/ exists. Similarly, the row with hierarchyid element /1/ can be deleted if another row has hierarchyid value /1/10/. If you don't want this, the application or database will need to include logic to enforce the existence of an ancestor when inserting and to prevent the deletion of an ancestor.

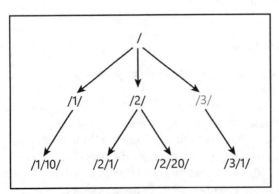

Figure 7-2   hierarchyid values – the value /3/ is in gray to indicate it is implicit.

Perhaps surprisingly, SQL Server does not enforce uniqueness of the hierarchyid values unless you define a unique index or constraint on the hierarchyid column. It is, therefore, possible that the element /3/1/ is defined twice. This is likely not the desired situation, so we recommend that you ensure uniqueness of the hierarchyid values.

Using the hierarchyid data type is an appropriate choice if the tree is most commonly queried to find descendants, such as children, children-of-children, and more. That is because the hierarchyid stores rows depth-first if it is indexed. You can create a breadth-first index by adding a computed column to the table, which uses the .GetLevel() method on the hierarchyid column, and then creating an index on the computed column followed by the hierarchyid column. You cannot, however, use a computed column in a clustered index, so this solution will still be less efficient compared to creating a clustered index on the hierarchyid value alone.

A hierarchyid method worth mentioning is .GetAncestor(). This method returns the hierarchyid value of the current node's parent. Conversely, .IsDescendantOf() determines if a node is a descendant, direct or otherwise, of the hierarchyid provided as the function's parameter.

> ➤ **For a complete overview of the hierarchyid data type, refer to**
> *https://docs.microsoft.com/sql/relational-databases/hierarchical-data-sql-server.*

The sql_variant data type

The sql_variant data type allows a single column to store data of diverse types. You can also use the type as a parameter or a variable. In addition to storing the actual value, each sql_variant instance also stores metadata about the value, which includes the system data type of the value, its maximum size, scale and precision, and collation. Using sql_variant can be indicative of a poor database design, and you should use it judiciously. Client libraries that do not know how to handle that data might convert it to nvarchar(4000), with potential consequences for data that doesn't convert well to character data.

In queries, you can retrieve the base type of the stored value and the base types' properties using the SQL_VARIANT_PROPERTY() function. For example, using SQL_VARIANT_PROPERTY(columnname, 'BaseType'), you can retrieve the sysname of the underlying type stored in columnname. Other values that can be provided as the property parameter value of the function are Precision, Scale, TotalBytes, Collation, and MaxLength. If a particular property doesn't apply to the underlying data type, such as Precision doesn't apply to varchar, the function returns NULL.

Data type precedence

When using a T-SQL operator that combines values that might be of different data types, how does the Database Engine handle the difference? The answer is that the data type with the lower precedence will be converted to the data type with the higher precedence, assuming the conversion is implicitly possible. If it's not, then an error is returned.

In the code sample below, the string variable @TheirString (a varchar) is first converted to datetime2 because datetime2 takes precedence over varchar. Then the comparison is executed.

```
DECLARE @MyDate datetime2(0) = '2019-12-22T20:05:00';

DECLARE @TheirString varchar(10) = '2019-12-20';

SELECT DATEDIFF(MINUTE, @TheirString, @MyDate);
```

➤ For the complete list of data types in precedence order, consult the Microsoft Docs at *https://docs.microsoft.com/sql/t-sql/data-types/data-type-precedence-transact-sql*.

Constraints

Constraints define rules to which your data must adhere, and those rules are enforced by the Database Engine. This makes constraints a very powerful mechanism for guaranteeing data integrity. In this section, we provide details on *primary* and *foreign keys*, which are used to establish relationships, and *unique*, *check*, and *default* constraints.

Primary keys, foreign keys, and relationships

Proper relational database design calls for a process called *normalization*. Normalization is not covered in this book; however, it leads to breaking logical entities into multiple related tables. Without intending to wax poetically, keys are like the nervous system of a relational database; they establish the relationships between the tables. A relational database system provides *primary* and *foreign keys*. In a single table, the primary key values must be unique because those values can be used as foreign key values in the related table. The foreign key values can also be unique in the related table, in which case the established relationship is a one-to-one relationship. This is referenced in the "Vertical partitioning" section later in the chapter.

> ### NOTE
> This chapter does not include any coverage of indexes, though a primary key and a unique constraint is always associated with an index. Frequently, foreign keys are also indexed as their values are often used to query the table. For information on indexing, see Chapter 15.

A table can have exactly one primary key. The primary key can consist of multiple columns, in which case it's referred to as a *compound primary key*. In no case can a nullable column be (part of) the primary key. If additional columns' values should be unique, you can apply a unique index or constraint. (See the next sections for coverage on additional constraint types.)

NOTE

In most cases, SQL Server does not require that tables have a primary key. Some features, such as using FILESTREAM or certain types of replication might require that tables have a primary key. In general, though, you should default to designing tables with primary keys unless there is an overriding reason to not do so.

Foreign keys are intended to establish *referential integrity*. Referential integrity enforces that the values found in the foreign key column(s) exist in either the primary key, unique constraint, or unique index column(s). By default, foreign keys in SQL Server have referential integrity enforced. It is possible to establish a foreign key without referential integrity enforced, or alter the foreign key to turn referential integrity off and on. This functionality is useful during import operations or certain types of database maintenance. However, during normal operations, foreign keys should have referential integrity turned on to protect the integrity of your data. Otherwise, establishing the relationship is of limited value, other than for documentary purposes.

NOTE

If a foreign key is a composite key in which one or more columns allow null, a row with a null value in just one of the foreign key columns will pass the integrity check, even if the other columns contain values that do not exist in the parent table. To provide referential integrity, we recommend not allowing null values in some columns of a composite foreign key and not in others. It's certainly acceptable to have null values in all columns of the composite foreign keys; this indicates that the relationship is optional. In that case, create a check constraint (covered later in this section) to ensure either all foreign key columns are NULL or none are.

One table can have multiple foreign keys.

When defining a foreign key, you can specify how to handle an operation in the parent row that would invalidate the relationship. Cascading specifically means that the same operation will be run on the child row(s) as was run on the parent. Thus, if the primary key value were updated, the foreign key values would be updated. If the parent row is deleted, the foreign key values will be deleted. Alternatively, on updates or deletes in the parent table, no action can be taken (the default, which would cause the update or delete statement to fail if referential integrity is enforced), the foreign-key value can be set to null (effectively creating an orphaned row), or the foreign-key value can be set to its default constraint's specification (effectively mapping the child row to another parent).

CHAPTER 7

Unique constraints

A unique constraint enforces unique values in one column or selected columns. Unlike a primary key, the unique constraint allows the column(s) to be nullable, though only one row can have a NULL.

> ➤ Refer to Chapter 15 for guidance on unique filtered indexes, which can be used to work around this limitation

The following sample adds a unique constraint to the column CountryName in the Application.Countries table in the WideWorldImporters sample database. Let's ignore the fact that such a unique constraint already exists; this is just for illustration.

```
ALTER TABLE [Application].Countries WITH CHECK

    ADD CONSTRAINT UC_CountryName UNIQUE (CountryName);
```

Check constraints

A check constraint enforces rules that can be expressed by using a Boolean expression. For example, in the Sales.Invoices table in the sample WideWorldImporters database, there is a check constraint defined that requires the ReturnedDeliveryData column to either be null or contain valid JSON. Check constraints can reference more than one column. A frequently encountered requirement is that when one column contains a specific value, another column cannot be null.

Using constraints with compound conditions also provides an opportunity to provide check constraints in the face of changing requirements. If a new business rule requires that a nullable column must now contain a value, but no suitable default can be provided for the existing rows, you should consider creating a check constraint that verifies whether an incrementing ID column or date column is larger than the value it held when the rule took effect. For example, consider the table Sales.Invoices in the previous sample, which has a nullable column Comments. If effective September 1, 2019, every new and modified invoice must have a value in the Comments column, the table could be altered using the following script:

```
ALTER TABLE Sales.Invoices WITH CHECK

    ADD CONSTRAINT CH_Comments CHECK (LastEditedWhen < '2019-09-01'

    OR Comments IS NOT NULL);
```

A problem that you cannot solve by using a constraint is when a column must contain unique values if a value is provided. In other words, the column should allow multiple rows with null, but otherwise should be unique. The solution then is to use a *filtered unique index*.

> ➤ Read about filtered unique indexes in Chapter 15.

Default constraints

The fourth and final constraint type is the *default constraint*. A default constraint specifies the value that will be used as the default value when an INSERT statement does not specify a value for the column.

Default constraints are useful in a number of scenarios, not the least of which is when adding a new non-nullable column to a table with existing data. This scenario is demonstrated in the next code sample, which adds a column PrimaryLanguage to the Application.People table in WideWorldImporters. We beg our international readers for forgiveness for the US-centric example default.

```
ALTER TABLE [Application].People

    ADD PrimaryLanguage nvarchar(50) NOT NULL

        CONSTRAINT DF_Application_People_PrimaryLanguage DEFAULT 'English';
```

Sequence objects

A sequence is a database object that generates a sequence of numeric values. How the sequence is generated is determined by its start value, increment value, and minimum and maximum values. A sequence can be ascending, which is the case when the increment value is positive. When the increment value is negative, the values provided by the sequence are descending. A sequence object has some similarities to a column with an identity specification, but there are important distinctions:

- You can define a sequence to cycle, meaning that when the numbers in the sequence are exhausted, the next use will return a previously generated number. Which number will be returned when the sequence cycles is determined by the increment: if it is an ascending sequence, the minimum value is returned; if it is a descending sequence, the maximum value is returned.

- A sequence is not bound to any table. You can use numbers generated by the sequence in any table in the database, or outside of a table.

- Sequence numbers can be generated without inserting a new row in a table.

- Values generated from a sequence can be updated or overridden without extra work.

Sequences are used when the application wants to have a numeric sequence generated at any time; for example, before inserting one or more rows. Consider the common case of a parent–child relationship. Even though most developer tools expect to work with identity columns, knowing the value of a new parent row's primary key value and using it as the foreign key value in the child rows can have benefits for the application.

A sequence is also useful when a single incrementing range is desired across multiple tables. More creative uses of a sequence include using a sequence with a small range—five, for example—to automatically place new rows in one of five buckets.

To create a sequence, use the CREATE SEQUENCE command. When creating the sequence, you specify the integer data type; the start, increment, minimum and maximum values; and whether the numbers should cycle when the minimum or maximum value is reached. However, all of these are optional. If no data type is specified, the type will be bigint. If no increment is specified, it will be 1. If no minimum or maximum value is specified, the minimum and maximum value of the underlying data type will be used. By default, a sequence does not cycle. The sample script that follows creates a sequence called MySequence of type int. The values start at 1001 and increment by 1 until 1003 is reached, after which 1001 will be generated again. The script demonstrates the cycling of the values using a WHILE loop.

```
-- Define the sequence
CREATE SEQUENCE dbo.MySequence AS int
    START WITH 1001
    INCREMENT BY 1
    MINVALUE 1001
    MAXVALUE 1003
    CYCLE;
-- Declare a loop counter
DECLARE @i int = 1;
-- Execute 4 times
WHILE (@i <= 4)
BEGIN
    -- Retrieve the next value from the sequence
    SELECT NEXT VALUE FOR dbo.MySequence AS NextValue;
    -- Increment the loop counter
    SET @i = @i + 1;
END;
```

The output of the script will be 1001, 1002, 1003, and 1001. The sequence is used by calling NEXT VALUE FOR. You can use NEXT VALUE FOR as a default constraint or as a function parameter, except if it's a table-valued function. There are quite a few more places where NEXT VALUE FOR cannot be used. Those include subqueries, views, user-defined functions, and conditional expressions.

➤ For a full listing of limitations, refer to Microsoft Docs at *https://docs.microsoft.com/sql/t-sql/functions/next-value-for-transact-sql#limitations-and-restrictions*.

NOTE

Sequences are cached by default. Caching might cause values to be skipped from the sequence on a server restart. You can turn off caching by specifying the NO CACHE clause in the CREATE or ALTER SEQUENCE statement. You can control the size of the cache by using the CACHE clause and specifying an integer constant.

CAUTION

Using NEXT VALUE FOR multiples times for the same sequence in the same statement will result in only one value per row being used. For example, in the following Transact-SQL (T-SQL) snippet, the first and the second column of the new row will have the same value:

```
INSERT INTO dbo.SomeTable VALUES (NEXT VALUE FOR dbo.MySequence,

    NEXT VALUE FOR dbo.MySequence, 'More data...');
```

This might not the desired scenario. One solution is to use two separate sequences, though there would not be a guarantee that they would return different numbers even if their start values are different. Another solution is to define the sequence object's increment to 2 and for one of the columns, add 1 to the sequence value, as in the snippet below:

```
INSERT INTO dbo.SomeTable VALUES (NEXT VALUE FOR dbo.MySequence,

    NEXT VALUE FOR dbo.MySequence + 1, 'More data...');
```

If you must guarantee that the values are different, you should place a CHECK CONSTRAINT on the table. However, we recommend evaluating the need for having two columns in the same table with autogenerated numeric values.

NEXT VALUE FOR generates and returns a single value at a time. If multiple values should be generated at once, the application can use the sp_sequence_get_range stored procedure. This procedure allocates as many numbers from the sequence as specified and returns metadata about the generated numbers. The actual values that have been generated are not returned. The sample script that follows uses the MySequence sequence to generate five numbers. The metadata is captured in variables and later output. You'll note that the data type of most output parameters is sql_variant. The underlying type of those parameters is the data type of the sequence.

```
-- Declare variables to hold the metadata

DECLARE @FirstVal sql_variant, @LastVal sql_variant,
```

CHAPTER 7

```
        @Increment sql_variant, @CycleCount int,

        @MinVal sql_variant, @MaxVal sql_variant;

-- Generate 5 numbers and capture all metadata

EXEC sp_sequence_get_range 'MySequence'

    , @range_size = 5

    , @range_first_value = @FirstVal OUTPUT

    , @range_last_value = @LastVal OUTPUT

    , @range_cycle_count = @CycleCount OUTPUT

    , @sequence_increment = @Increment OUTPUT

    , @sequence_min_value = @MinVal OUTPUT

    , @sequence_max_value = @MaxVal OUTPUT;

-- Output the values of the output parameters

SELECT @FirstVal AS FirstVal, @LastVal AS LastVal

    , @CycleCount AS CycleCount, @Increment AS Increment

    , @MinVal AS MinVal, @MaxVal AS MaxVal;
```

The output of this sample script will vary with each run. Because of the specific way in which the MySequence object was defined, however, every three cycles, the output will repeat.

NOTE

Although the only required output parameter is @range_first_value, if the application actually intends to use any value but the first, the application should consume all the metadata that is returned as part of the optional output parameters. Without it, the application cannot reliably infer the values that were generated. It is up to the application to calculate the actual numbers that were generated by using the first value, last value, increment, minimum and maximum value, and cycle count output parameters.

TROUBLESHOOTING

You might receive error 11732 when using sequences.

This error indicates that the maximum value of the sequence has been reached and the sequence does not cycle. If this error occurs when using the sp_sequence_get_range stored procedure, no values are returned. That is, the sequence is not affected at all.

User-defined data types and user-defined types

SQL Server supports creating new data types. Two variations exist: user-defined data types, which alias existing data types, and user-defined types, which are .NET Framework types.

A useful and common use for user-defined data types is creating table types. As the name implies, a table type defines a table structure as a type which can then be used as a function or stored procedure parameter. Such a parameter enables the easy passing of multiple values or rows to the function or procedure.

We should warn against the liberal use of either variant of custom data types. They can make a database schema significantly more difficult to understand and troubleshoot. Alias types add little value, because they do not create new behavior, though on the other hand, some architects find the "self-documenting" aspect attractive. SQL CLR user-defined types allow SQL Server to expose new behavior, but they might come with a significant security risk.

> ➤ **More details about the security of CLR user-defined types can be found in the Microsoft Docs at** *https://docs.microsoft.com/sql/relational-databases/clr-integration/ common-language-runtime-integration-overview*.

User-defined data types

Alias data types are merely a new name for an existing system data type, optionally augmented with length or precision and a default nullability specification. Specifying a default value or a validation rule for the alias is deprecated functionality.

For example, if you want to ensure that a customer name was always defined as an nvarchar column with a max length of 100 characters, you might use the CREATE TYPE statement, as shown here:

```
CREATE TYPE CustomerNameType FROM nvarchar(100);

GO
```

After creating this UDT, in any place where you would ordinarily specify nvarchar(100), you can use CustomerNameType, instead. This can be in a table's column definition, as the return type of a scalar function, or as a parameter to a stored procedure. The following abbreviated CREATE TABLE statement, which is based on the WideWorldImporters sample Customers table, illustrates how CustomerNameType replaces nvarchar(100):

```
CREATE TABLE Sales.Customers (

    CustomerID INT NOT NULL,

    CustomerName CustomerNameType, -- can override nullability of the type here

    ...
```

CLR user-defined types

You develop user-defined types in a .NET language such as C#, and you must compile them into a .NET assembly. This .NET assembly is then registered in the database where the type will be used. A database can use these types only if SQL CLR is turned on.

Sparse Columns

Sparse columns store null values in an optimized manner, reducing space requirements for storing null values at the expense of overhead to retrieve non-null values. As we discussed in the section on the XML data type, a potential workaround for saving storage space for tables with many columns that allow null and have many null values is using sparse columns. Microsoft suggests that a space savings of at least 20 percent should be achieved before the overhead is worth it.

▶ The Microsoft Docs at *https://docs.microsoft.com/sql/relational-databases/tables/use-sparse-columns* define the space savings by data type when using sparse columns.

NOTE
Not all data types can be defined as sparse columns. Specifically, you cannot define geography and geometry, image, text and ntext, rowversion, and user-defined data types as sparse columns.

Sparse columns are defined in CREATE or ALTER TABLE statements by using the SPARSE keyword. The sample script that follows creates a table, OrderDetails, with two sparse columns, ReturnedDate and ReturnedReason. Sparse columns are useful here because we might expect most products not to be returned, in addition to retrieving only the ReturnedDate and ReturnedReason columns occasionally.

```
CREATE TABLE dbo.OrderDetails (

    OrderId int NOT NULL,

    OrderDetailId int NOT NULL,

    ProductId int NOT NULL,

    Quantity int NOT NULL,

    ReturnedDate date SPARSE NULL,

    ReturnedReason varchar(50) SPARSE NULL);
```

NOTE
For brevity, the CREATE TABLE script in the preceding example does not define primary keys or foreign keys, or indeed columns that you might typically expect in an order details table.

Computed columns

Typically, columns store data that is original. Derived data—that is, data that is the result of a calculation—is not ordinarily stored. Instead, the application derives it every time it's needed. In some circumstances, storing derived data in the database can be beneficial. SQL Server supports creating derived data using computed columns and indexed views.

NOTE
Indexed views are beyond the scope of this chapter.

Computed columns are defined in a table as the result of an expression of other columns in the table, function calls, and perhaps constants. And although derived data can be stored in the database, by default a computed column is not persisted.

Using computed columns is always trade-off. By using a computed column, you decide that there is some benefit of having the database be aware of the derived data, which will require putting some business logic to compute that data in the database. You might find that beneficial because the database could be the central source of the computation instead of having to spread it out across multiple systems. Another trade-off is found when you persist computed columns; you are trading storage space for compute efficiency.

If the expression that calculates the computed column's value is deterministic, the computed column can be persisted and indexed. An expression is deterministic if that expression will always return the same result for the same inputs. An example of a deterministic expression is OrderQuantity + 1. Given the same value for OrderQuantity, the result will always be the same. An example of a nondeterministic expression is one that uses the SYSDATETIME() function; the expression returns a different result each time it is executed.

> ➤ **For a complete discussion of indexing computed columns, refer to Microsoft Docs at**
> *https://docs.microsoft.com/sql/relational-databases/indexes/*
> *indexes-on-computed-columns.*

In the WideWorldImporters sample database, you will find two computed columns in the Sales.Invoices table. One of those columns is ConfirmedDeliveryTime. It is derived by examining the contents of the JSON value stored in the ReturnedDeliveryData column and converting it to a datetime2 value. The datetime2 value is not persisted in this case. What this means is that each time the ConfirmedDeliveryTime is queried, the expression is evaluated. If the column was persisted, the expression would be evaluated only when the row is created or updated.

When you are defining a computed column, instead of specifying a data type, you specify the AS clause followed by an expression. Using the Sales.OrderLines table in the same sample database, you can create a computed column to calculate the order line's extended price. The following sample SQL statement illustrates how:

```
ALTER TABLE Sales.OrderLines

    ADD ExtendedPrice AS (Quantity * UnitPrice) PERSISTED;
```

This statement creates a new column in the table called `ExtendedPrice`. This column's value is computed by using the expression `Quantity * UnitPrice`. The column is persisted because we expect to be querying this value frequently. The type of the computed column is determined by SQL Server based on the result of the expression. In this case, the data type is set to `decimal(29,2)`. If the determined data type is not suitable for your needs, you can apply a cast in the expression to a more appropriate data type.

Special table types

As data storage needs have become more specialized, SQL Server has gained extended functionality to support these scenarios in the form of special table types. These table types support scenarios that would otherwise have required significant effort on behalf of the DBA to implement. This section discusses temporal tables, memory-optimized tables, external tables, and graph tables. We discuss another special table type, FileTable, in the next section.

> ➤ **External tables and PolyBase are discussed in Chapter 20, "Leveraging big data and machine learning."**

System-versioned temporal tables

System-versioned temporal tables, or "temporal tables" for short, are designed to keep not only current values of rows, but also historic values. In addition to the current table, there is a companion history table with the same schema structure. The history table stores the historic rows. SQL Server can create the history table at the time the current table is created, and you can opt to specify the history table's name or let SQL Server create an anonymous history table. Alternatively, you might use an existing table as the history table, in which case the Database Engine will validate that the schema matches that of the current table. Creating a history table by hand can be complex, but specifying a history table that was previously used and was disconnected for some reason is a valuable option.

When a table is designed to be a temporal table, it has two explicitly defined columns of type `datetime2` that are used to indicate the validity period of the row. You define the name of these columns and add the `GENERATED ALWAYS AS ROW START|END` clause. In addition to that clause, two more clauses are required: `PERIOD FOR SYSTEM_TIME (start_time_col, end_time_col)` and `WITH (SYSTEM_VERSIONING = ON)`.

NOTE

Temporal tables provide a solution that also might be addressed by change tracking or change data capture. Later sections in this chapter cover change tracking and change data capture and compare these features to temporal tables.

Creating a system-versioned temporal table

The simple CREATE TABLE statement below illustrates the use of these clauses to create a system-versioned temporal table with an anonymous history table:

```
CREATE TABLE dbo.Products (

    -- Clustered primary key is required

    ProductId int NOT NULL PRIMARY KEY CLUSTERED

, ProductName varchar(50) NOT NULL

, CategoryId int NOT NULL

, SalesPrice money NOT NULL

, SysStartTime datetime2 GENERATED ALWAYS AS ROW START NOT NULL

, SysEndTime datetime2 GENERATED ALWAYS AS ROW END NOT NULL

  -- PERIOD FOR SYSTEM_TIME to indicate columns storing validity start and end

, PERIOD FOR SYSTEM_TIME (SysStartTime, SysEndTime))
-- SYSTEM_VERSIONING clause without HISTORY_TABLE option creates

-- an anonymous history table, meaning the name will be auto-generated

WITH (SYSTEM_VERSIONING = ON);
```

> **NOTE**
>
> The row's start and end validity column values are managed by SQL Server. The values in those columns are in the UTC time zone. Neither validity period column will ever be NULL.

An existing table can also be altered to become a temporal table. This is a two-stage process, where you first alter the table to include the two required datetime2 columns and then alter the table to turn on system versioning while optionally specifying a history table name.

When creating a new table or altering an existing one, you can apply the optional HIDDEN property to the columns for the validity period. Using that property will exclude the columns from a standard SELECT statement. This might be useful to ensure backwards compatibility with existing applications that query the table.

Understanding data movement in temporal tables

The Database Engine manages the movement of data from the current table to the history table. The following list details the data movements that take place with each Data Manipulation Language (DML) operation:

- **INSERT and BULK INSERT.** A new row is added to the current table. The row's valid-ity start time is set to the transaction's start time. The validity end time is set to the datetime2 type's maximum value: December 31, 9999 at a fractional second, or whole second when using datetime2(0), before midnight. There is no change in the history table.

- **UPDATE.** A new row is added to the history table with the old values. The validity end time of the history row is set to the transaction's start time. In the current table, the row is updated with the new values and the validity start time is updated to the transaction's start time. Should the same row be updated multiple times in the same transaction, mul-tiple history rows with the same validity start and end time will be inserted. Those rows will not be retrieved using typical queries.

- **DELETE.** A new row is added to the history table containing the values from the current table. The validity end period of the history row is set to the transaction's start time. The row is removed from the current table.

Merge statements need no special consideration; a merge operation behaves as if separate insert, update, and delete statements are executed, as determined necessary by the MATCH clauses. Those statements will add rows to the history table, as just described.

Querying temporal tables

Querying a temporal table is no different from querying another table if your query only needs to return current data. This makes it possible to modify an existing database and alter tables into temporal tables without requiring application modifications. When using the HIDDEN property on the period columns, existing applications won't even be exposed to the additional columns in the table.

When designing queries that need to return historical data or even a mix of current and histori-cal data, you use the FOR SYSTEM_TIME clause in the FROM clause of the SELECT statement. There are five subclauses used with FOR SYSTEM_TIME that help you define the time frame for which you want to retrieve rows. The list that follows describes these subclauses as well as pro-vides a sample SQL statement of each one that you can run against the WideWorldImporters sample database to see the effects of the subclause.

> ### NOTE
> The IsCurrent column in the output indicates whether the row that is retrieved is the current row or a history row. This is accomplished by checking whether the ValidTo col-umn contains the maximum datetime2 value. Due to the nature of the WideWorldIm-porters sample data, you might need to scroll through several hundred rows before encountering a value of 0 for IsCurrent, which indicates that it is a history row.

- **ALL.** The result set is essentially the union between the current and the history tables. Multiple rows can be returned for the same primary key in the current table. This will be the case for any row that has one or more history entries, as shown here:

```
SELECT PersonID, FullName,
      CASE WHEN ValidTo = '9999-12-31 23:59:59.9999999' THEN 1
          ELSE 0 END AS IsCurrent
FROM Application.People FOR SYSTEM_TIME ALL
ORDER BY ValidFrom;
```

- **AS OF.** The AS OF clause returns rows that were valid at the single point in time in the UTC time zone. Rows that had been deleted from the current table or didn't exist yet will not be included:

```
/* AS OF sub-clause returns all rows that were valid at one point in time.
 * Recall the SYSTEM_TIME is UTC.
 * Showing an example here of how to convert a local time to UTC:
 * Local time is March 13, 2016 12:00 AM (midnight) US Pacific Time
 * (the start of the day).
 * March 13 is not in daylight saving time, so the offset is -8 hours.
 * Thus, records we're looking for were active on March 13, 2016 8 AM UTC.
 * Calling the AT TIME ZONE function twice gives the desired time in UTC.
 */
DECLARE @AsOfTime datetime2(7) = CONVERT(datetime2(7), '2016-03-13T00:00:00', 126)
    AT TIME ZONE 'Pacific Standard Time' AT TIME ZONE 'UTC';
SELECT PersonID, FullName
    , CASE WHEN ValidTo = '9999-12-31 23:59:59.9999999' THEN 1
          ELSE 0 END 'IsCurrent'
FROM [Application].People FOR SYSTEM_TIME AS OF @AsOfTime
ORDER BY ValidFrom;
```

- **FROM ... TO.** This subclause returns all rows that were active between the specified lower bound and upper bound. In other words, if the row's validity start time is before the upper bound or its validity end time is after the lower bound, the row will be included in the result set. Rows that became active exactly on the upper bound are not included.

Rows that closed exactly on the lower bound are not included. This clause might return multiple rows for the same primary key value:

```
SELECT PersonID, FullName,

    CASE WHEN ValidTo = '9999-12-31 23:59:59.9999999' THEN 1

        ELSE 0 END AS IsCurrent

FROM Application.People FOR SYSTEM_TIME FROM '2016-03-13' TO '2016-04-23'

ORDER BY ValidFrom;
```

- **BETWEEN ... AND.**   This is like FROM ... TO, but rows that opened exactly on the upper bound are included, as well:

```
SELECT PersonID, FullName,

    CASE WHEN ValidTo = '9999-12-31 23:59:59.9999999' THEN 1

        ELSE 0 END AS IsCurrent

FROM Application.People FOR SYSTEM_TIME BETWEEN '2016-03-13' AND '2016-04-23'

ORDER BY ValidFrom;
```

- **CONTAINED IN (,).**   This subclause returns rows that were active exclusively between the lower and the upper bound. If a row was valid earlier than the lower bound or valid past the upper bound, it is not included. A row that was opened exactly on the lower bound or closed exactly on the upper bound will be included. If the upper bound is earlier than the maximum value for datetime2, only history rows will be included:

```
DECLARE @now datetime2(7) = SYSDATETIMEUTC();

SELECT PersonID, FullName,

    CASE WHEN ValidTo = '9999-12-31 23:59:59.9999999' THEN 1

        ELSE 0 END AS IsCurrent

FROM Application.People FOR SYSTEM_TIME CONTAINED IN ('2016-03-13', @now)

ORDER BY ValidFrom;
```

NOTE

In the sample statement for the CONTAINED IN subclause, the variable @now is declared and initialized with the current UTC time. This is necessary because the FOR SYSTEM_ TIME clause does not support functions as arguments.

Managing temporal tables

Altering a temporal table will generally cause its associated history table to be altered in the same way. This applies when adding, altering, or removing columns. However, there are a few operations that require turning system versioning off. These include adding an identity, rowguidcol, or computed column; adding a sparse column in most cases; and adding a column set.

CAUTION

If you add a new column that does not allow NULL to a temporal table, the default value you're required to specify will be used to fill the new column in the current table, but also in the history table. While it's hard to imagine another solution that Microsoft could have implemented, one might argue that the history table doesn't reflect the truth at the time its records were active.

Dropping a temporal table requires turning off system versioning and then dropping both the current and history tables using two separate DROP TABLE statements.

Inside OUT

How do you design temporal tables to use the least amount of space?

Introduced in SQL Server 2017, you can use the HISTORY_RETENTION_PERIOD option with the SYSTEM_VERSIONING option when defining or altering system-versioned temporal tables. By default, the HISTORY_RETENTION_PERIOD is INFINITE, meaning that SQL Server will not automatically purge history data. By defining a finite period, such as 6 MONTHS, SQL Server will automatically purge history records with a valid end time older than the finite period. Two conditions must hold true: first, the temporal history retention flag must be turned on for the database (which it is by default), and second, the history table must have a clustered or columnstore index. For a rowstore clustered index, the first column in the index must be the column corresponding to the end of the validity period. If the conditions hold true, a background task is created to perform cleanup of the aged data.

In addition to using automatic retention, which controls the growth of the history table, you can also consider vertically partitioning the temporal table. Vertical partitioning is discussed in more detail in the "Vertical partitioning" section later in this chapter. By splitting the table vertically into two tables, and only making one table system versioned, you can achieve significant space savings because history will be kept only for the columns in the system-versioned table. This does come at the expense of potentially frequent JOINs between both tables. This approach is also not suitable if you are system-versioning tables for compliance requirements for which all row data must be available in exactly the form it was at any given point.

Besides reducing the history kept by setting a retention period and using vertical partitioning to avoid keeping history for columns that do not require it,

> you might also consider Stretch Database, horizontal partitioning, or a custom cleanup script to manage the history data. These options are described in detail at *https://docs.microsoft.com/sql/relational-databases/tables/manage-retention-of-historical-data-in-system-versioned-temporal-tables*.

Memory-optimized tables

A traditional disk-based table's data is loaded in memory as needed to efficiently run queries. The operations of loading data from durable storage to memory and removing the data from memory again is handled by the Database Engine. Many factors play a role in when data is loaded or released from memory. Data in memory-optimized tables is kept in memory all the time, using in-memory technology to avoid disk I/O operations . This data is durable by default by using the transaction log and saving to the drive (though the format of the data is different than that of disk-based tables). A "schema only" option is available, which does not retain data between service restarts and certain other operations.

The benefits of keeping all data from specific tables in memory is blazing-fast performance, which often can be improved by another order of magnitude by applying a columnstore index to the memory-optimized table. (Columnstore indexes are covered in Chapter 15.) This of course requires that the server has sufficient memory to hold the memory-optimized tables' data in memory while still leaving enough room for other operations. If the system runs out of memory (OOM), errors will occur, and you'll need to take specific steps to recover.

➤ To avoid OOM issues, monitor memory usage. The Microsoft Docs at *https://docs.microsoft.com/sql/relational-databases/in-memory-oltp/monitor-and-troubleshoot-memory-usage#bkmk_Monitoring* describe how to monitor and troubleshoot memory usage for memory-optimized tables.

➤ Guidance for resolving various OOM issues is available in the Microsoft Docs at *https://docs.microsoft.com/sql/relational-databases/in-memory-oltp/resolve-out-of-memory-issues*.

Memory-optimized tables are available in all editions of SQL Server and in Azure SQL Database's Premium and Business Critical tiers. However, memory limitations present in the Express and Standard editions of SQL Server do apply to memory-optimized tables.

NOTE

Over time, many limitations of memory-optimized tables that were present in earlier versions of SQL Server have been eliminated.

➤ This chapter discusses only the setup and configuration of memory-optimized tables along with caveats. You can find complete discussion of the purpose and the use of memory-optimized tables in Chapter 15.

Database preparation for memory-optimized tables

Before creating memory-optimized tables, you must first prepare the database. The database compatibility level must be at least 130. For SQL Server, you need to create a memory-optimized filegroup. There is no such requirement for Azure SQL Database; or, more accurately, the filegroup is intrinsically present.

Microsoft provides a T-SQL script to ensure that these settings are correct and that a memory-optimized filegroup is created. You can even run the script in Azure SQL Database to ensure that the database supports memory-optimized tables. Rather than reprinting this script here, we refer you to the GitHub content.

➤ See the GitHub user content page at *https://raw.githubusercontent.com/microsoft/sql-server-samples/master/samples/features/in-memory-database/in-memory-oltp/t-sql-scripts/enable-in-memory-oltp.sql.*

The script first checks to ensure that the instance or database supports memory-optimized tables, using the SERVERPROPERTY(N'IsXTPSupported') function. If you're running on SQL Server, the script will create a memory-optimized filegroup and container if none already exist. The script also checks and sets the database compatibility level.

After these actions are complete, you are ready to create one or more memory-optimized tables. The WITH (MEMORY_OPTIMIZED = ON) is the key clause that will create a memory-optimized table. Memory-optimized tables support indexing, but you must create and delete them using an ALTER TABLE … ADD/DROP INDEX statement instead of a CREATE/DROP INDEX statement.

Natively compiled stored procedures and user-defined functions

You can access memory-optimized tables via interpreted T-SQL statements and stored procedures. However, you can achieve significant additional performance gains if you use *natively compiled stored procedures*. These stored procedures are compiled to machine code the first time they are run rather than evaluated every time they run.

NOTE

Natively compiled stored procedures can access only memory-optimized tables. Traditional interpreted stored procedures and ad-hoc queries can reference both disk-based tables and memory-optimized tables in the same statement, for example to join a memory-optimized table with a disk-based table.

To create a natively compiled stored procedure, use the WITH NATIVE_COMPILATION clause of the CREATE PROCEDURE statement. This clause requires the use of the SCHEMABINDING option. In addition, the BEGIN ATOMIC statement is also required. It takes the place of BEGIN TRANSACTION for natively compiled procedures and functions. This statement either begins a new transaction or creates a savepoint in an existing transaction on the session. When creating a savepoint in an existing transaction, only the changes made by the stored procedure would be rolled back if the stored procedure fails or calls ROLLBACK.

The BEGIN ATOMIC statement has two required options:

- **TRANSACTION_ISOLATION.**   You must set this value to one of the three supported isolation levels: snapshot, repeatable read, or serializable.

- **LANGUAGE.**   This is a name value from the sys.syslanguages system compatibility view. For example, for United States English, it is us_english, and for Dutch it is Nederlands.

The BEGIN ATOMIC statement is also where delayed durability can be specified (DELAYED_DURABILITY = ON). Delayed durability means that the Database Engine will report to the client that the transaction committed before the log record has been committed to a drive. This creates a risk of data loss should the service or server shut down before the asynchronous log write is completed. You should take the same care to use delayed durability with BEGIN ATOMIC as with BEGIN TRANSACTION. Further, to use delayed durability, it must not be disallowed at the database level. Schema-only memory-optimized tables do not use transaction logging, so when modifying data in those tables, there is no benefit in specifying delayed durability.

➤ **For more information on delayed durability, see Chapter 14.**

The short sample script below creates a memory-optimized table and natively compiled stored procedure in a database that has been prepared previously.

```
CREATE TABLE dbo.UserDetails (

    UserId    int NOT NULL,

    DetailId  int NOT NULL,

    Detail    nvarchar(50) NOT NULL,

    CONSTRAINT PK_UserDetails PRIMARY KEY NONCLUSTERED (UserId, DetailId)

) WITH (MEMORY_OPTIMIZED = ON, DURABILITY = SCHEMA_AND_DATA);

GO

CREATE PROCEDURE dbo.GetUserName

    @userId int
```

```
WITH NATIVE_COMPILATION, SCHEMABINDING

AS

BEGIN ATOMIC

    WITH (TRANSACTION ISOLATION LEVEL = SNAPSHOT,

        LANGUAGE = N'us_english')

    SELECT Detail

    FROM dbo.UserDetails

    WHERE UserId = @userId

        -- Assume this refers to the name

        AND DetailId = 1;

END;

GO
```

NOTE

Several T-SQL statements and constructs are not supported combined with memory-optimized tables and natively compiled stored procedures. A full list of these unsupported constructs is available in Microsoft Docs at *https://docs.microsoft.com/sql/relational-databases/in-memory-oltp/ transact-sql-constructs-not-supported-by-in-memory-oltp*

Caveats to memory-optimized tables

To put it plainly, you should probably not convert all of your tables to memory-optimized tables. There are several caveats that must be considered before adopting memory-optimized tables and when deciding which tables to turn into memory-optimized tables. We discuss these caveats in this section.

Memory-optimized tables support only three transaction isolation levels: snapshot, repeatable read, and serializable. If your application has a need for other isolation levels, you will not be able to implement memory-optimized tables. Refer to Chapter 14 for complete details about transaction isolation levels.

CAUTION

Changing the database's read-commit snapshot property will cause schema-only memory-optimized tables to be truncated. Although database designers are aware that schema-only memory-optimized tables are not persisted and might load initial data into such tables when the SQL Server service starts, they might not know to re-load data after a database property change.

Due to all table data being kept in memory, you would expect additional memory requirements. When planning for memory size, however, you should consider that the memory requirement of a memory-optimized table can be more than twice that of the size of the data in the table. This is due to processing overhead requirements, including the row versions that are kept.

> ➤ To review specific guidance on planning for memory size, refer to Microsoft Docs at *https://docs.microsoft.com/sql/relational-databases/in-memory-oltp/ estimate-memory-requirements-for-memory-optimized-tables*.

When persisted memory-optimized tables are used, upon service start, the Database Engine will load all data from the drive to memory. The index(es) of memory-optimized tables are not persisted, and they are rebuilt upon service start. The service is not available while these operations take place. With large tables, this can lead to significantly longer service start times. Even though you might carefully plan your service or server restarts for a maintenance window, an unplanned failover on a failover cluster instance (FCI) will also take that amount of time. This might be detrimental to meeting your Service-Level Agreement (SLA), which might have been the entire reason to configure an FCI in the first place. If the performance of memory-optimized tables is needed in combination with a high-availability configuration, you might consider Always On availability groups, instead. Because the Database Engine service is running on the secondary, there is no delay caused by having to read the data from a drive and rebuilding indexes.

> ➤ Read about FCI and availability groups in Chapter 11.

One way to reduce database startup time due to memory-optimized tables is to ensure that checkpoints are taken frequently. That's because checkpoints cause the updated rows in the memory-optimized table to be committed to the data file. Any data that is not committed to the drive must be read from the transaction log. For large tables, this benefit is likely small.

Another contributor to delays, though after service start, is when natively compiled stored procedures are run for the first time; this can take about as long as running a traditional stored procedure. This is because the compiled version of the stored procedure is not saved. Any time a natively compiled stored procedure is run subsequently, the compiled version will be faster.

Memory-optimized tables use an optimistic concurrency model. Instead of locks, latches are used. This means that a client application might experience unexpected conflicts. You should design the application to handle those.

Not unlike when faster drive storage is used for SQL Server, when adopting memory-optimized tables, you might find that the CPU usage is much higher. This is because much less time is spent waiting for I/O operations to complete. The first consideration on this point is that this is exactly the reason why you implemented memory-optimized tables: the CPU utilization is higher because data is being processed faster! Another consideration could be that you might inadvertently reduce the number of concurrent requests that can be served, especially if one instance runs multiple databases. If this is a concern, you can consider using a Resource Governor to manage the relative CPU usage for each database.

Graph tables

Introduced in SQL Server 2017 and extended in SQL Server 2019, graph functionality provides schema extensions to store directed graph data—that is, nodes and edges—in the relational database. Fitting graph data in a relational database is challenging, and this feature attempts to resolve these challenges. The graph features in SQL Server solve common issues but are currently not a complete replacement for dedicated graph databases that support advanced scenarios.

Graph data is often associated with networks, such as social networks, and hierarchies. More generally, graphs are data structures that consist of nodes and edges. The nodes represent entities, and the edges represent the connections between those entities. Nodes are also referred to as vertices, and edges as relationships.

Some use cases lend themselves particularly well to be stored in a graph model. Examples of such use cases include the following:

- **Highly interconnected data.**   A commonly used example of highly interconnected data is that of social networks. Social network data expresses relationships among people, organizations, posts, pictures, events, and more. In such a data model, each entity can be connected to any other entity, creating lots of many-to-many relationships. In a relational database, this requires the creation of a table for each many-to-many relationship. Querying such relationships requires two or more JOIN clauses, which can quickly create lengthy SELECT statements. Such statements can be difficult to digest and are potentially error prone. Graph databases offer support for flexible definitions of relationships and query syntax that is less verbose.

- **Hierarchical data.**   SQL Server provides a specialized data type, hierarchyid (discussed earlier) that supports modeling simple tree hierarchies. One limitation of this data type is its inability to support multiple parents. A node in a graph is not limited like that, and a single node can have many parents in addition to many children. You may also find it conceptually easier to build even a simple tree, where a node has only one parent, using nodes and edges.

- **Many-to-many relationships that can be extended at any time during the data life cycle.**   Relational databases have strict requirements for the definition of tables and relationships. For a data model that is required to evolve quickly to support new relationships, this strict schema requirement can get in the way of meeting evolving requirements in a timely fashion.

You can effectively implement these use cases by employing a graph database, but it is important to note that SQL Server's graph features do not (yet) provide a solution that is on-par with dedicated graph databases. We discuss some of the limitations of the current implementation in the "Current graph table shortcomings" section later in the chapter.

Defining graph tables

In SQL Server, you store graph data in two table types: *node* and *edge* tables. These table types are still stored internally as relational structures, but the Database Engine has additional capabilities to manage and query the data that is stored within them. The T-SQL CREATE TABLE syntax has two clauses: AS NODE and AS EDGE. The following T-SQL script creates a People node table and a Relationships edge table, and you can run this script in any existing or new database; there are no specific requirements of the database:

```
CREATE TABLE dbo.People (

    PersonId int NOT NULL PRIMARY KEY CLUSTERED,

    FirstName nvarchar(50) NOT NULL,

    LastName nvarchar(50) NOT NULL

) AS NODE;

CREATE TABLE dbo.Relationships (

    RelationshipType nvarchar(50) NOT NULL,

    -- Two people can only be related once

    CONSTRAINT UX_Relationship UNIQUE ($from_id, $to_id),

    CONSTRAINT EC_Relationship CONNECTION (dbo.People TO dbo.People)

) AS EDGE;
```

In the sample script, both the node and the edge table contain user-defined columns. Edge tables are not required to have user-defined columns, but node tables must have at least one. In the case of edge tables, which model relationships, simply modeling the relationship without additional attributes can be desirable. In the case of node tables, which model entities, there is no value in a node without properties. Designing a node table is comparable to designing a relational table; you would still consider normalization and other concepts.

The sample script also defines an edge constraint, a feature introduced in SQL Server 2019. Edge constraints restrict which node types can be associated using a particular edge. In this case, a Relationships edge is defined to be between two nodes of type People.

The CONSTRAINT clause may be repeated multiple times in a single edge table definition, but the entries in the table must comply with all constraints. Alternatively, multiple edge constraint clauses may be defined, in which case any of the constraints must be satisfied. The next script defines a second node table, Animals, removes the existing edge constraint, and finally creates a new edge constraint with two clauses, allowing a relationship to exist between two People rows or between a People and Animals row.

```
CREATE TABLE dbo.Animals (

    AnimalId int NOT NULL PRIMARY KEY CLUSTERED,

    AnimalName nvarchar(50) NOT NULL

) AS NODE;

-- Drop and recreate the constraint, because an edge constraint cannot be altered

ALTER TABLE Relationships

    DROP CONSTRAINT EC_Relationship;

ALTER TABLE Relationships

    ADD CONSTRAINT EC_Relationship CONNECTION (dbo.People TO dbo.People,

        dbo.People TO dbo.Animals);
```

NOTE

Edge constraints not only enforce the type(s) of node that can be connected using the edge, they also enforce referential integrity between the nodes and the edge. SQL Server supports cascading deletes of edges when a node is deleted. Specify ON DELETE CASCADE in the CONSTRAINT clause to enable cascading the delete operation, or ON DELETE NO ACTION (the default) if deleting the node should fail.

In addition to user-defined columns, both table types also have one or more implicit columns. Node tables have one implicit (also called pseudo) column, $node_id, which uniquely identifies the node in the database. This pseudo-column is backed by two actual columns:

- **graph_id_<hex_string_1>.** This is a BIGINT column, which stores the internally generated graph ID for the row. This column is internal and cannot be explicitly queried.

- **$node_id_<hex_string_2>.** This column can be queried and returns a computed NVARCHAR value that includes the internally generated BIGINT value and schema information. You should avoid explicitly querying this column. Instead, you should query the $node_id implicit pseudo column.

In addition to optional user-defined columns, edge tables have three implicit columns:

- **$edge_id_<hex_string_3>.** This is a system-managed value, comparable to the $node_id column in a node table.

CHAPTER 7

- **$from_id_<hex_string_4>.**   This references a node ID from any node table in the graph that meets the edge constraints. This is the source node in the directed graph.

- **$to_id_<hex_string_5>.**   This references a node ID from any node table in the graph that meets the edge constraints. This is the target node in the directed graph.

Inside OUT

When should you choose graph tables over relational tables?

First, it's important to understand that there is nothing inherent to a graph database that makes it possible for you to solve a problem that you cannot also solve using a relational database. The relational database concept has been around for nearly five decades, and relational database management systems are as popular as ever.

The use cases described earlier, and queries described momentarily, are examples of data models and operations that might be better addressed by a graph structure. This is because the Database Engine has specific optimizations to address some of the particular types of queries that are often run against such models.

In addition, a graph table can still contain foreign keys referring to relational tables, and a relational table can contain a foreign key referring to a graph table.

Working with graph data

DML statements generally work the same in graph tables as they do in relational tables. Some operations are not supported. An edge table does not support updating either of the node values. Thus, to update a relationship, the existing edge row must be deleted and a new one inserted. User-defined columns of edge tables do support update operations.

When querying graph data, you can write your own table joins to join nodes to edges to nodes, though this approach offers none of the benefits of graph tables. Instead, we recommend using the MATCH comparison operator in the WHERE clause. The MATCH operator uses a style of expression referred to as *ASCII art* to indicate how nodes and edges should be traversed. You might be surprised to find that the node and edge tables are joined using old-style join syntax first. The MATCH subclause then performs the actual equi-joins necessary to traverse the graph.

The brief examples that follow are intended to provide an introduction only. They build on the creation of the People and Relationship tables shown in the previous example. First, a few rows of sample data are inserted. Then, the sample data is queried by using the MATCH subclause:

```
-- Insert a few sample people

-- $node_id is implicit and skipped
```

```
INSERT INTO dbo.People VALUES

    (1, 'Karina', 'Jakobsen'),

    (2, 'David', 'Hamilton'),

    (3, 'James', 'Hamilton'),

    (4, 'Stella', 'Rosenhain');
-- Insert a few sample relationships
-- The first sub-select retrieves the $node_id of the from_node
-- The second sub-select retrieves the $node_id of the to_node
INSERT INTO dbo.Relationships VALUES

    ((SELECT $node_id FROM People WHERE PersonId = 1),

    (SELECT $node_id FROM People WHERE PersonId = 2),

    'spouse'),

    ((SELECT $node_id FROM People WHERE PersonId = 2),

    (SELECT $node_id FROM People WHERE PersonId = 3),

    'father'),

    ((SELECT $node_id FROM People WHERE PersonId = 4),

    (SELECT $node_id FROM People WHERE PersonId = 2),

    'mother');
-- Simple graph query
SELECT P1.FirstName + ' is the ' + R.RelationshipType +

    ' of ' + P2.FirstName + '.'

FROM dbo.People P1, dbo.People P2, dbo.Relationships R

WHERE MATCH(P1-(R)->P2);
```

The arrow used in the MATCH subclause means that a node in the People table should be related to another node in the People table using the Relations edge. As with self-referencing many-to-many relationships, the People table needs to be present in the FROM clause twice to allow the second People node to be different from the first. Otherwise, the query would retrieve only edges in which people are related to themselves (there are no such relationships in our sample).

The true power of the MATCH subclause is evident when traversing the graph between three or more nodes. One such example would be finding restaurants your friends have liked in the city where your friends live and where you intend to travel.

CHAPTER 7

➤ **For a more comprehensive sample graph database, refer to Microsoft Docs at**
   https://docs.microsoft.com/sql/relational-databases/graphs/sql-graph-sample.

SQL Server 2019 introduced support for the shortest path algorithm. With this support, it is now possible for the MATCH clause to traverse an arbitrary number of nodes to find a related node. There are several T-SQL syntax elements that are required, including a SHORTEST_PATH function and FOR PATH and WITHIN GROUP (GRAPH PATH) clauses. The sample below retrieves all the direct descendants of one of the people in the same table:

```
-- Construct Stella Rosenhain's direct descendants' family tree

-- In our example data, two rows will be returned

SELECT P1.FirstName

    , STRING_AGG(' is ' + P2.FirstName + '''s ' + related_to1.RelationshipType, ' ->')
WITHIN GROUP (GRAPH PATH) AS [Descendants]

    , LAST_VALUE(P2.FirstName) WITHIN GROUP (GRAPH PATH) AS [Final relation]

    , COUNT(P2.PersonId) WITHIN GROUP (GRAPH PATH) AS [Level]

    , P1.FirstName + ' is ' + LAST_VALUE(P2.FirstName) WITHIN GROUP (GRAPH PATH)

        + '''s ' +

        CASE WHEN COUNT(P2.PersonId) WITHIN GROUP (GRAPH PATH) = 2 THEN 'grand'

            WHEN COUNT(P2.PersonId) WITHIN GROUP (GRAPH PATH) > 2 THEN 'great grand'

        END

FROM dbo.People P1

    , dbo.People FOR PATH P2

    , dbo.Relationships FOR PATH related_to1

WHERE (MATCH(SHORTEST_PATH(P1(-(related_to1)->P2)+)))

    -- Stella Rosenhain

    AND P1.PersonId = 4);
```

Graph table shortcomings

Since the first graph features were released with SQL Server 2017, additional investments have been made to overcome the limitations found in that release. Most notably, the SHORTEST_PATH function enables both the shortest path graph analytic function and transitive closures (the ability to recursively traverse edges). Still, some limitations compared to native graph databases remain. The following list contains the most notable graph limitations in SQL Server 2019 and a brief description of their significance for implementing a graph. Hopefully, this will provide the information you need to make an informed decision about using SQL Server for graph data.

- **Need to explicitly define edges as tables.**   Graphs model pairwise relations between entities (the nodes). Flexibility can be key in maximizing the benefits of graph models. Even though the nodes are often well understood, including their properties, new relationships can be modeled as new needs arise or additional possibilities emerge. The need to make schema modifications to support new types of edges reduces flexibility. Some of this can be addressed by defining one or few edge tables and storing the edge properties as XML or JSON. This approach, too, has drawbacks in terms of performance and ease of writing queries against the data.

- **No polymorphism.**   Polymorphism is the ability to find a node of any type connected to a specified starting node. In SQL Server, a workaround for graph models with few node and edge types is to query all known node and edge types and combine the result sets by using a UNION clause. For large graph models, this solution becomes impractical.

Storing BLOBs

Storing LOBs, and more specifically BLOBs, in the relational database has been known to cause debate. Prior to SQL Server offering the FILESTREAM feature as a specialized way for the Database Engine to manage BLOBs using the file system, database designers had two choices, neither of which may have met all your requirements:

- Store the BLOB, such as an image, video, or document file, in a `varbinary` column. Downsides of this approach include rapid growth of the data file, frequent page splits, and pollution of the buffer pool. Benefits include transactional integrity and integrated backup and recovery of the BLOB data.

- Have the application store the BLOB in the file system and use an NVARCHAR column to store a path to the file. Downsides of this approach include requiring the application to manage data integrity (avoiding orphaned or missing files) and lack of integrated security (the security mechanism to secure the BLOBs is an entirely different model than that for protecting the database). There are some benefits, though, primarily around performance and ease of programming for the client to work with the BLOBs (using traditional file I/O APIs provided by the OS).

The FILESTREAM feature is designed to provide a way to have the best of both alternatives. FILESTREAM is not a data type but an extension to `varbinary(MAX)` which changes how data is stored and provides additional capabilities. This section discusses FILESTREAM and FileTable. FileTable builds on FILESTREAM, so we first cover FILESTREAM and then FileTable.

CHAPTER 7

Understanding FILESTREAM

To take advantage of FILESTREAM, there are three requirements. First, the instance must be configured to allow at least one of several levels of FILESTREAM. Second, your database will need to have at least one FILESTREAM filegroup. Third, any table containing a FILESTREAM column requires a unique, non-null rowguid. A FILESTREAM filegroup refers to a location on an NT File System (NTFS) or Resilient File System (ReFS) volume that is under the control of the Database Engine. This location will be used by the Database Engine to store the binary data and log files for the binary data.

When a FILESTREAM filegroup is available in the database, FILESTREAM can be used as a modifier on varbinary(MAX) columns. When creating a table with a FILESTREAM column, you can specify on which filegroup the FILESTREAM data will be stored. When multiple FILESTREAM database files are added to a single filegroup, they will be used in round-robin fashion, as long as they don't exceed their maximum size.

In general, FILESTREAM's performance benefits kick in when the average BLOB size is 1 MB or larger. For smaller BLOB sizes, storing the BLOBs in the database file using a varbinary(MAX) column is better for performance. You might determine, however, that the ease of programming against file I/O APIs in the client application is an overriding factor and decide to use FILESTREAM even with smaller BLOBs.

Additionally, if any of your BLOBs exceed 2 GB in size, you will need to use FILESTREAM; varbinary(max) supports a maximum BLOB size of 2 GB. Another reason for choosing FILESTREAM is the ability to integrate the BLOBs with SQL Server Semantic Search. To be clear, varbinary(MAX) columns can also be integrated with Semantic Search, but BLOBs stored in traditional file systems files cannot. Semantic Search in SQL Server supports extracting and indexing statistically relevant key words or phrases, which in turn enables identifying similar or related documents. Among other uses, Semantic Search can be used to suggest tags for an article or identify resumes based on a job description.

> ➤ More information about Semantic Search is available online at
> *https://docs.microsoft.com/sql/relational-databases/search/semantic-search-sql-server.*

Inside OUT

How do you move data from a varbinary(MAX) column to FILESTREAM?

Unfortunately, moving from varbinary(MAX) columns to FILESTREAM is not as easy as modifying the column to add the FILESTREAM modifier. Attempting to modify the column in that way will result in an error. Instead, you should use the following three-step process, after creating a FILESTREAM file group:

1. Create a new `varbinary(MAX)` FILESTREAM column in the table or in another table if you want to use vertical partitioning.

2. Copy the data from the existing `varbinary(MAX)` column to the new FILESTREAM column. The amount of database activity that will be caused by this operation can be significant, depending on the number of rows and the size of the BLOBs.

3. Drop the `varbinary(MAX)` column. Optionally, you can then rename the FILESTREAM column to the name of the dropped column. Until you have (optionally) deployed a modified application that uses the I/O APIs with FILESTREAM to achieve better performance, the existing application's T-SQL statements will continue to work on the FILESTREAM column.

In addition to potentially causing significant database activity, you also need to ensure that sufficient storage space is available to hold both copies of the data. Perhaps you are using the opportunity to move the BLOBs to different storage hardware, in which case this might be less of a concern. After completing the process, you should consider whether shrinking the data file is appropriate.

Finally, while these operations take place, you should consider placing a lock on the table. Otherwise, transactions may modify the data in the `varbinary(MAX)` or add new rows. In step 3, that data could be lost.

Even though FILESTREAM BLOBs are stored in the file system, they are managed by the Database Engine. That includes transactional consistency and point-in-time restores. Thus, when a BLOB is deleted, the file on the drive backing that BLOB is not immediately deleted. Similarly, when a BLOB is updated, an entirely new file is written and the previous version is kept on the drive. When the deleted file or previous file version is no longer needed, the Database Engine will eventually delete the file using a garbage collection process. You are already aware of the importance of taking transaction log backups with databases in the full recovery model. That way, the transaction log can be truncated and stop growing. When using FILESTREAM, this mantra applies double: the number of files will keep growing until they are deleted by the garbage collector.

CAUTION

You should never modify the FILESTREAM folder's (a "data container") contents manually. Doing so can lead to FILESTREAM data corruption.

FileTable

FileTable makes it possible to access BLOBs managed by the Database Engine using traditional file share semantics. Applications that can read and write from a file share can access the BLOBs managed by the SQL Server engine as if it were a regular Server Message Block (SMB) file share. Although clients can use file I/O APIs to work with FILESTREAM, obtaining a handle to the BLOB requires using specific client libraries and application modifications. There might be applications that cannot be modified to work with FILESTREAM but for which having the BLOBs managed by the relational engine would have significant advantages. To that end, FileTable, which is a special table type, was developed.

NOTE

FileTable is not currently available on SQL Server on Linux.

A FileTable has a fixed schema. This means that you can neither add user-defined columns nor can you remove columns. The only control provided is the ability to define indexes on some FileTable columns. The fixed schema has a FILESTREAM column that stores the actual file data in addition to many metadata columns and the non-null unique rowguid column required of any table containing FILESTREAM data. FileTable can organize data hierarchically, meaning folders and subfolders are supported concepts.

➤ **For a detailed discussion of the FileTable schema, refer to Microsoft Docs at** *https://docs.microsoft.com/sql/relational-databases/blob/filetable-schema.*

Table partitioning

Table partitioning occurs when you design a table that stores data from a single logical entity in physically separate structures. In other words, rather than storing all the entity's data in a single physical data structure, it is split into multiple physical data structures. They continue to be treated by the user as a single unit. Table partitioning has multiple purposes, most of which relate to performance, either when querying or when loading data. We discuss this later in detail. We first distinguish between horizontal and vertical partitioning, as illustrated in Figure 7-3, and then discuss each separately with its common use cases and recommendations.

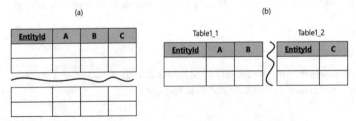

Figure 7-3   (A) Horizontal partitioning splits a table's data rows. (B) Vertical partitioning splits a table's columns.

As Figure 7-3 illustrates, horizontal and vertical partitioning are distinctly different. Horizontal partitioning splits the data rows, and each partition has the same schema. Vertical partitioning splits the entity's columns across multiple tables. The diagram shows a table partitioned in only two partitions. However, you can partition tables into many partitions. You can also mix horizontal and vertical partitioning.

> **NOTE**
>
> In SQL Server, "partitioning" usually refers to horizontal partitioning only because it is the name of a feature. In this book, we discuss both horizontal and vertical partitioning, and, as such, we always explicitly define which partitioning type is being discussed.

Horizontally partitioned tables and indexes

In a large-scale database, in which a single table can grow to hundreds of gigabytes and more, some operations become more difficult. For example, adding new rows can take an excessive amount of time and might also cause SELECT queries against the table to fail due to lock escalation. Similar concerns exist with respect to removing data and index maintenance.

Horizontal partitioning can address these concerns, but it is also important to understand that it is not a silver bullet that will make all performance problems in large tables disappear. On the contrary, when applied incorrectly, horizontal partitioning can have a negative effect on your database workload. This section builds on the brief discussion of partitioning found in Chapter 3, "Designing and implementing an on-premises database infrastructure."

> **NOTE**
>
> Support for horizontal partitioning was limited to the Enterprise edition of SQL Server until the release of SQL Server 2016 Service Pack 1. Since then, all editions support horizontal table and index partitioning.

About horizontal partitioning

SQL Server's partitioning feature supports horizontal partitioning through the use of a partition function, which determines in which partition of the table a given row will be stored. Each partition may be stored in its own filegroup in the same database.

Thus, when partitioning a table, the rows of the table are not all stored in the same physical place. When designing partitions, you decide on a partition key, which is the column that will be used to assign a row to exactly one partition. From a logical viewpoint, however, all rows belong to the same table. A query without a WHERE clause returns all rows, regardless of which partition they are stored in. This means that the Database Engine must do more work to retrieve rows from different partitions. Your goal when partitioning for query performance should be to write queries that eliminate partitions. You can accomplish this by including the partition key in the WHERE clause.

Additional benefits of horizontal partitioning include the ability to set specific filegroups to read-only. By mapping partitions containing older data to read-only filegroups, you can be assured that this data is unchangeable without affecting your ability to insert new rows. In addition, you could exclude the read-only filegroups from regular backups. Finally, during a restore, filegroups containing the most recent data could be restored first, allowing new transactions to be recorded faster than if the entire database would need to be restored.

NOTE

Restoring selected files or filegroups while keeping the database available is called an *online restore*, which is still supported only in the Enterprise edition.

Index partitioning

In addition to horizontal table partitioning, SQL Server also supports *index partitioning*. A partitioned index is said to be aligned with the table if the table and the index are partitioned in the same number of partitions using the same column and boundary values. When a partitioned index is aligned, you can direct index maintenance operations to a specific partition. This can significantly speed up the maintenance operation because you can rebuild or reorganize a partition rather than the entire index. On the other hand, if the entire index needs to be rebuilt, SQL Server will attempt to do so in a parallel fashion. Rebuilding multiple indexes simultaneously will create memory pressure. Because of this concern, we recommend that you do not use partitioning on a system with less than 16 GB of RAM.

NOTE

Most commonly, achieving an aligned index is done by using the same partition function and scheme as the table. However, it is not strictly necessary to create an aligned partitioned index. If you choose to use a different function or scheme, you will need to remember to modify the function for the index simultaneously with the table's partition function. Therefore, we recommend that you use one partition function for both database objects.

You might benefit from creating a partitioned index without partitioning the table. You can still use this nonaligned index to improve query efficiency if only one or a few of the index partitions need to be used. In this case, you will also use the index's partition key in the WHERE clause to gain the performance benefit of eliminating partitions.

Defining partitions and partitioning a table

We now demonstrate how to create a horizontally partitioned table. Three database objects are involved in defining partitions and partitioning a table:

- A partition function, which defines the number of partitions and the boundary values

- A partition scheme, which defines on which filegroup each partition is placed

- The table to be partitioned

> **NOTE**
>
> For brevity, the following script does not show the creation of the database with the file-groups and files necessary to support the partition scheme. The sample script included with the book downloads does include the CREATE DATABASE statement, as well as a CREATE TABLE statement followed by an INSERT statement and SELECT statements from DMVs to review the table's partition statistics.

```
-- Create a partition function for February 1, 2019 through January 1, 2020
CREATE PARTITION FUNCTION MonthPartitioningFx (datetime2)
    -- Store the boundary values in the right partition
    AS RANGE RIGHT
    -- Each month is defined by its first day (the boundary value)
    FOR VALUES ('20190201', '20190301', '20190401',
        '20190501', '20190601', '20190701', '20190801',
        '20190901', '20191001', '20191101', '20191201', '20200101');
-- Create a partition scheme using the partition function
-- Place each trimester on its own partition
-- The most recent of the 13 months goes in the latest partition
CREATE PARTITION SCHEME MonthPartitioningScheme
    AS PARTITION MonthPartitioningFx
    TO (FILEGROUP2, FILEGROUP2, FILEGROUP2, FILEGROUP2,
        FILEGROUP3, FILEGROUP3, FILEGROUP3, FILEGROUP3,
        FILEGROUP4, FILEGROUP4, FILEGROUP4, FILEGROUP4, FILEGROUP4);
```

If you visualize the table data as being sorted by the partition key in ascending order, the left partition is the partition that is on top. When defining a partition function, you indicate whether

the boundary value—in our example, the first day of each month—will be stored in the partition on the left (which is the default), or the partition on the right (as specified in the sample).

Figure 7-4 shows the relationship between the partition function and the partition scheme. The
partition function created 13 partitions using 12 boundary values. The partition scheme directed
these 13 partitions to three filegroups by specifying each filegroup four times, and the last filegroup five times because it will hold the last partition.

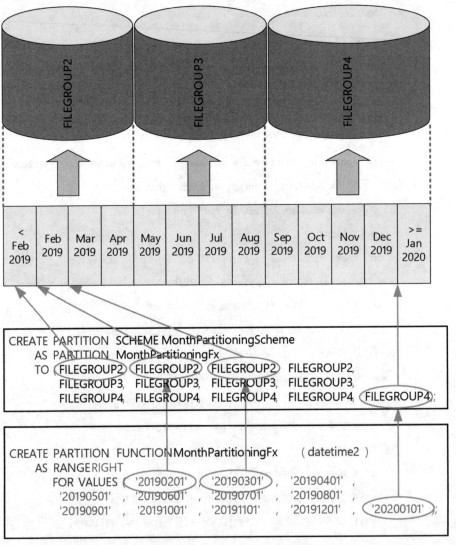

Figure 7-4   The relationship between the partition function, the partition scheme, and the filegroups
on which the partitions will be stored.

Horizontal partition design guidelines

When designing horizontal partitions, keep the following guidelines in mind, though also keep in mind that your mileage may vary:

- The number of parallel operations that can be run depends on the number of processor cores in the system. Using more partitions than processor cores will limit the number of partitions that will be processed in parallel. So, even though SQL Server now supports up to 15,000 partitions, on a system with 12 processor cores, at most 12 partitions will be processed in parallel. You may choose to use fewer partitions than the number of available processor cores to set aside capacity for other queries.

- Choose the partition key based on the column's values growing. This could be a date value or an incrementing identity column. The goal is to always have new rows added to the right-most partition.

- The selected partition key should be immutable, meaning that there should be no business reason for this key value to change. If the value of a partition key changes, SQL Server will execute the UPDATE statement as a DELETE and INSERT statement; there is no provision to "move" a row to another filegroup. You'll find that this approach is similar to when the value of a clustered index changes.

- For the partition key, a narrow data type is preferable over a wide data type.

- To achieve most benefits of partitioning, specifically those related to performance, you will need to put each partition into its own filegroup. This is not a requirement, and some or all partitions can share a single filegroup. For example, the next section discusses a sliding window partition strategy, in which partitioning is beneficial even if all are on the same filegroup.

- Consider the storage that is backing the filegroups. For example, your storage system might not provide higher performance if all filegroups have been placed on the same physical drives.

- Tables that are good candidates for partitioning are tables with many—as in millions or billions—rows for which data is mostly added as opposed to updated, and against which queries are frequently run that would return data from one or a few partitions.

Implementing a sliding window partition strategy

Horizontal partitioning is often applied to relational data warehouses. A common data warehouse operation is loading a significant amount of data to a fact table while simultaneously purging old data. The sliding window partition strategy is particularly well suited for tables for which data is regularly added and removed. For example, data in a fact table can be purged after 13 months. Perhaps each time data is loaded into the data warehouse, rows older than 13 months are removed while new rows are added. This is a sliding window in so much as the fact table always contains the most recent 13 months of data.

To set up a sliding window, you'll need a partition function and scheme as well as the fact table. You should also set up a stored procedure that modifies the partition function to accommodate the new boundary values. You will also need a staging table with the same columns and clustered index as the partitioned table.

NOTE

For the next example, we assume that data is loaded in the data warehouse only once every month. This is not particularly realistic, but the example still works when data is loaded more frequently, even in real time. It's only the first load operation for a new month that will need to modify the partition function.

Figure 7-5 illustrates what happens on March 1, 2020, when data is loaded for the month of February 2020. The fact table is partitioned into 13 partitions, one for each month. An automated process, which is not depicted here, takes care of modifying the partition function to accommodate the new date range by splitting the rightmost partition, holding the most recent data, in two. Then, the partition holding the oldest month's data is switched out to a staging table and the new data is switched in from a staging table. Finally, the leftmost partition, which held the oldest data but is now empty, is merged with the second left-most partition.

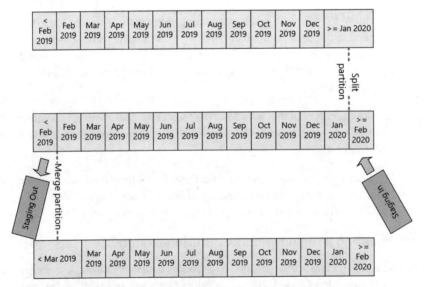

Figure 7-5 An overview of the sliding window partition strategy.

NOTE

Implementing a sliding window partition strategy is not without pitfalls. To fully auto-mate it, job auditing is required to ensure that the process that modifies the partition function operates successfully. Additional complexity is introduced if the switched out, old data is to be archived rather than purged.

You can optimize switching the old partition out and the new partition in by using a memory-optimized table as the staging table.

NOTE

Now that you have read in detail about horizontal partitioning, we encourage you to refer to the earlier section about temporal tables and consider that temporal tables are a specialized case of the horizontal partitioning concept. In addition, you can use the SQL Server partition feature for the history table, as described in Microsoft Docs at *https://docs.microsoft.com/sql/relational-databases/tables/manage-retention-of-historical-data-in-system-versioned-temporal-tables#using-table-partitioning-approach*.

Vertical partitioning

Vertical partitioning makes sense when a single table would ordinarily contain a large number of columns, some of which might contain large values that are infrequently queried. You can improve performance by storing the infrequently accessed columns in another table. Another problem that you can solve by vertical partitioning is when you run into a maximum row size limit or maximum column count limit.

NOTE

We would encourage you to first review your database design to ensure that one logical entity really needs such wide columns or that many attributes. If that's the case, splitting the entity vertically into two or more tables can be a workaround.

An entity that is vertically partitioned into multiple tables can usually be identified by the fact that the tables have a common name prefix or suffix and share the same primary key values. A conceptual one-to-one relationship exists between the tables, which you can enforce by using a foreign key constraint.

Unlike horizontal partitioning, SQL Server does not have a feature that directly supports vertical partitioning. As the database designer, you will need to create the necessary schema to verti-cally partition tables yourself.

Be careful not to abuse vertical partitioning as a strategy. Every time data from two tables is needed in a single result set, a join operation will be required. These joins could be expensive operations or are at least more expensive than reading data from a single page and might nullify other performance benefits if you run them frequently.

There are a few special cases for using vertical partitioning. One relates to FileTable. FileTables, as described previously in this chapter, have a fixed schema. You might, however, need to store additional metadata about the files. Because you are unable to extend the schema, you will need to create a new table which uses the same primary key as the FileTable. Using insert and delete triggers, you can guarantee data integrity by ensuring that for every row in the FileTable, there is a matching row in your extended metadata table.

A second special case is related to temporal tables. Also discussed earlier in this chapter, if there is no requirement to capture the history of all columns in the temporal table, splitting the logical entity into two vertical partitions (or perhaps more if additional considerations apply) can reduce the amount of space consumed by unneeded historical data.

Capturing modifications to data

SQL Server supports several methods for capturing row data that has been modified. Temporal tables have been discussed earlier in this chapter. In this section, we discuss *change tracking* and *change data capture*. Although these features allow applications to detect when data has changed, they operate very differently and serve different purposes. This section first discusses change tracking, then change data capture, and then finally provides recommendations on their use.

NOTE

The SQL Server auditing feature is not covered in this section. Auditing may also meet your needs, especially if you need to track the execution of SELECT and DDL statements or include the principal that executed the statements.

➤ Auditing is a security feature and is discussed in Chapter 13, "Protecting data through encryption, privacy, and auditing."

Inside OUT

How do application developers make best use of change tracking and change data capture?

There are two important considerations to effectively use these SQL Server features in client applications.

First, an application should identify itself by using a source ID when synchronizing data. By providing a source ID, the client can avoid obtaining the same data again. A client specifies its own source ID by using the `WITH CHANGE_TRACKING_CONTEXT` clause at the start of statements.

Second, an application should perform the request for changed data in a snapshot isolation–level transaction. This will avoid another application updating data between the check for updated data and sending data updates. The snapshot isolation level needs to be turned on at the database level, which was demonstrated in the previous section.

Using change tracking

Change tracking only tracks that a row has changed. If you need to also track the data that has changed, refer to the the next section, Change data capture. Change tracking is mostly useful for synchronizing copies of data with occasionally offline clients or for Extract, Transform, and Load (ETL) operations. For example, an application that facilitates offline editing of data will need to perform a two-way synchronization when reconnected. One approach to implementing this requirement is to copy (a subset of) the data to the client. When the client goes offline, the application reads and updates data using the offline copy. When the client re-establishes connectivity to the server, changes can be merged efficiently. The application is responsible for detecting and managing conflicting changes.

Configuring change tracking is a two-step process: first, change tracking must be turned on for the database. Then, change tracking must be turned on for the table(s) that you want to track.

NOTE
Change tracking and memory-optimized tables are mutually exclusive. A database cannot have both at the same time.

Before performing these steps, we recommend setting up snapshot isolation for the database. Snapshot isolation is not required for proper operation of change tracking, but it is very helpful for accurately querying the changes. Because data can change as you are querying it, using the snapshot isolation level and an explicit transaction, you will see consistent results until you commit the transaction. This is described in the detail in the "Working with change tracking" article referenced at *https://docs.microsoft.com/sql/relational-databases/track-changes/work-with-change-tracking-sql-server.*

The sample script that follows turns on snapshot isolation on the WideWorldImporters sample database. Then, change tracking on the WideWorldImporters sample database and on two tables, Sales.Orders and Sales.OrderLines, is turned on. Only on the Sales.Orders table is column tracking activated, so change tracking will include which columns were included in

CHAPTER 7

UPDATE statements (whether or not the values were actually changed). Next, change tracking is turned off for `Sales.OrderLines`. Finally, the `sys.change_tracking_tables` catalog view is queried to retrieve a list of tables with change tracking turned on.

```
USE master;
GO
-- Enable snapshot isolation for the database, if desired
ALTER DATABASE WideWorldImporters
    SET ALLOW_SNAPSHOT_ISOLATION ON;
-- Enable change tracking for the database
ALTER DATABASE WideWorldImporters
    SET CHANGE_TRACKING = ON
    (CHANGE_RETENTION = 5 DAYS, AUTO_CLEANUP = ON);
USE WideWorldImporters;
GO
-- Enable change tracking for Orders
ALTER TABLE Sales.Orders
    ENABLE CHANGE_TRACKING
    -- and track which columns were included in the statements
WITH (TRACK_COLUMNS_UPDATED = ON);
-- Enable change tracking for OrderLines
ALTER TABLE Sales.OrderLines
    ENABLE CHANGE_TRACKING;
-- Disable change tracking for OrderLines
ALTER TABLE Sales.OrderLines
    DISABLE CHANGE_TRACKING;
-- Query the current state of change tracking in the database
SELECT *
FROM sys.change_tracking_tables;
```

➤ For an end-to-end example of how an application can use change tracking to accomplish two-way data synchronization with an occasionally offline data

store, see *https://docs.microsoft.com/sql/relational-databases/track-changes/*
work-with-change-tracking-sql-server.

A major benefit of change tracking compared to implementing a custom solution is that change tracking does not make any schema changes to the user tables that are tracked, like triggers or additional user tables to store the captured changes. In addition, change tracking is available in all editions of SQL Server and in Azure SQL Database. Autocleanup ensures that the database does not grow unchecked.

NOTE

We recommend turning on autocleanup and setting a retention period sufficiently long to ensure that data synchronization has taken place. Applications can check whether they have waited too long to synchronize; that is, applications can find out whether cleanup has already removed tracking information since the application last synchronized.

Although change tracking can track which rows have changed, and optionally which columns were included in an UPDATE statement's SET clause, it is not able to indicate what the old values were or how often the row has been changed. If your use case does not require this, change tracking provides a light-weight option for tracking. If your use case does require one or both, consider change data capture. We discuss change data capture in the next section.

Using change data capture

Change data capture varies in some important ways from change tracking. Foremost, change data capture captures the historical values of the data. This requires a significantly higher amount of storage than change tracking. Unlike change tracking, change data capture uses an asynchronous process for writing the change data. This means that the client does not need to wait for the change data to be committed before the database returns the result of the DML operation.

NOTE

Because change data capture relies on the SQL Server Agent, it is not available in Azure SQL Database, though it is available in managed instance. Starting with SQL Server 2016 Service Pack 1, change data capture is available in the Standard edition.

NOTE

Since SQL Server 2017 CU 15, change data capture and memory-optimized tables can be used in the same database. Previously, a database could not have both at the same time.

The following script turns on change data capture on a database using the
`sys.sp_cdc_enable_db` stored procedure. Then, the script turns on change data capture for

the Sales.Invoices table. The script assumes that a user-defined database role cdc_reader has been created. Members of this role will be able to query the captured data changes.

```
USE WideWorldImporters;

GO

EXEC sys.sp_cdc_enable_db;

EXEC sys.sp_cdc_enable_table
    @source_schema = 'Sales',
    @source_name = 'Invoices',
    @role_name = 'cdc_reader';
```

After executing these statements, data changes to the Sales.Invoices table will be tracked, complete with before and after data.

Additional optional settings for change data capture include which columns to track and on which filegroup to store the change table. These are discussed in the Microsoft Docs at *https://docs.microsoft.com/sql/relational-databases/track-changes/enable-and-disable-change-data-capture-sql-server*.

Querying change tracking and change data capture

Once change tracking or change data capture are enabled, SQL Server offers functions for querying the tracking and capture information. These functions are demonstrated here using the WideWorldImporters sample as modified in the preceding two sections.

Querying change tracking

The code sample below updates a row in the Sales.Orders table, which has change tracking enabled. The next statement in the sample then demonstrates how to query the information gathered by change tracking and change data capture.

```
-- Modify a row in the Orders table,
-- which has change tracking enabled
UPDATE Sales.Orders
    SET Comments = 'I am a new comment!'
    WHERE OrderID = 1;
DECLARE @OrderCommentsColumnId int =
    COLUMNPROPERTY(OBJECT_ID('Sales.Orders'), N'Comments', 'ColumnId'),
    @DeliveryInstructionsColumnId int =
```

```
        COLUMNPROPERTY(OBJECT_ID('Sales.Orders'), N'DeliveryInstructions', 'ColumnId');

-- Query all changes to Sales.Orders

SELECT *

    -- Determine if the Comments column was included in the UPDATE

    , CHANGE_TRACKING_IS_COLUMN_IN_MASK(@OrderCommentsColumnId,

        CT.SYS_CHANGE_COLUMNS) CommentsChanged

    -- Determine if the DeliveryInstructions column was included

    , CHANGE_TRACKING_IS_COLUMN_IN_MASK(@DeliveryInstructionsColumnId,

        CT.SYS_CHANGE_COLUMNS) DeliveryInstructionsChanged

FROM CHANGETABLE(CHANGES Sales.Orders, 0) as CT

ORDER BY SYS_CHANGE_VERSION;
```

The output includes the values of the primary key, in this case the values of the single column OrderID, and a SYS_CHANGE_OPERATION column indicating that an UPDATE statement was executed using the value 'U'. Because you enabled column tracking for the Orders table, there is a non-null value for the SYS_CHANGE_COLUMNS column in the output.

For each column for which you'd like to determine if it was included in the UPDATE statement, use the CHANGE_TRACKING_IS_COLUMN_IN_MASK function. In the sample, two output columns are added that determine if the Comments and DeliveryInstructions columns were included in the UPDATE statement. A value of 1 indicates yes, 0 indicates no.

Querying change data capture

The code sample below updates a row in the Sales.Invoices table which has change data capture enabled. Then the change data capture table is queried with the option all update old, which will cause the single update statement to have two rows in the output: one row contains the old image and the second row contains the updated data.

```
-- Modify a row in the Invoices table,

-- which has change data capture enabled

UPDATE Sales.Invoices

    SET Comments = 'I am a new invoice comment again'

    WHERE InvoiceID = 1;

DECLARE @from_lsn binary(10) = sys.fn_cdc_get_min_lsn('Sales_Invoices'),

    @to_lsn binary(10) = sys.fn_cdc_get_max_lsn();

-- Each capture instance will have unique function names
```

```
-- By default, the capture instance name is schema_table

-- Note: there may be a slight delay before output is returned

SELECT *

FROM cdc.fn_cdc_get_all_changes_Sales_Invoices(@from_lsn, @to_lsn,

    N'all update old');
```

> ## NOTE
>
> There are many more change data capture functions and stored procedures available. These are respectively covered in the Microsoft Docs at *https://docs.microsoft.com/sql/ relational-databases/system-functions/change-data-capture-functions-transact-sql* and at *https://docs.microsoft.com/sql/relational-databases/system-stored-procedures/ change-data-capture-stored-procedures-transact-sql*.

Comparing change tracking, change data capture, and temporal tables

In this section, we present a comparison between three features that have common use cases. Table 7-1 should prove helpful when you're deciding which change tracking feature is appropriate for your needs.

Table 7-1   A comparison of features and uses of change tracking, change data capture, and temporal tables.

	Change tracking	Change data capture	Temporal tables
Requires user schema modification	No	No	Yes
Available in Azure SQL Database	Yes	No	Yes
Edition support	Any	Enterprise only	Any
Provides historical data	No	Yes	Yes
Tracks DML type	Yes	Yes	No
Has autocleanup	Yes	Yes	Yes
Time of change indicator	LSN	LSN	datetime2

PART III

SQL Server management

Maintaining and monitoring SQL Server

The previous chapter covered the importance and logistics of database backups, but what else do you need to do on a regular basis to maintain a healthy SQL Server?

In this chapter, we lay the foundation for the what and why of Microsoft SQL Server monitoring, based on dynamic management objects (DMOs), DBCC commands, extended events (the replacement for profiler/trace), and other tools Microsoft has provided.

More than just how to set up these tools, we will review what to look for on SQL Server instances on Windows and Linux, as well as SQL monitoring solutions in the Azure Portal.

There is a lot for a DBA to be concerned with to monitor your databases. Corruption of data files, indexes and stats not being used, keeping your data files properly sized, getting proper performance metrics, just to start. We will cover these topics and more in this chapter.

All sample scripts in this book are available for download at *https://MicrosoftPressStore.com/SQLServer2019InsideOut/downloads*.

Detecting, preventing, and responding to database corruption

After database backups, the second most important task concerning database page integrity is the proper configuration to prevent—and the monitoring to mitigate—database corruption.

A very large part of this is a proactive schedule of detection for rare cases when corruption occurs despite your best efforts. This isn't a complicated topic and mostly revolves around one setting and one command run regularly.

Setting the database's page verify option

For all databases the Page Verify Option setting should be CHECKSUM. Since SQL Server 2005, CHECKSUM is the superior and default setting, but it requires a manual change after a database is restored up to a new SQL Server version.

If you still have databases with a page verify option that is not CHECKSUM, you should change this setting immediately. The legacy NONE or TORN_PAGE_DETECTION options for this setting are a clear sign that this database has been moved over the years, from a pre–SQL Server 2005 version. This setting must be changed after restoring the database up to a new version of SQL Server.

Inside OUT

Is enabling the CHECKSUM Page Verify Option as easy as changing the setting in the database?

Unfortunately, no. Changing the page verify option to CHECKSUM is a quick change, but the checksums are not immediately created and so does not begin to protect the data pages immediately.

A checksum must be generated and stored for each page, so in order to truly verify that no corruption exists, it is recommended that you rebuild every index on every table after changing the page verify option to CHECKSUM. This obviously can be time consuming, and could create a lot of transaction log activity, but it is necessary.

If corruption is found with the newly-enabled CHECKSUM setting, the database can drop into SUSPECT state and be inaccessible. It is entirely possible that changing a database from NONE or TORN_PAGE_DETECTION to CHECKSUM could result in the discovery of existing, even long-present database corruption. It is paramount that good backups are taken regularly, including directly before making the change to the CHECKSUM Page Verify Option.

Using DBCC CHECKDB

You should periodically run CHECKDB on all databases. This is a time-consuming but crucial process. You should run DBCC CHECKDB at least as often as your backup retention plan, and consider DBCC CHECKDB nearly as important as regular database backups. It's worth noting that the only reliable solution to database corruption is restoring from a known good backup.

For example, if you keep local backups around for one month, you should ensure that you perform a successful DBCC CHECKDB no less than once per month, but more often is recommended.

This ensures that you will at least have a recovery point for uncorrupted, unchanged data, and a starting point for corrupted data fixes. On large databases, DBCC CHECKDB can take hours and block other user queries.

The DBCC CHECKDB command actually covers other more-granular database integrity check tasks, including DBCC CHECKALLOC, DBCC CHECKTABLE, or DBCC CHECKCATALOG, all of which are important, and in only rare cases need to be run separately to split up the workload.

Running DBCC CHECKDB with no other parameters or syntax, performs an integrity test on the current database context. Without specifying a database, however, no other additional options can be provided.

Keep in mind that DBCC CHECKDB may take hours to complete and tie up CPU resources, so it should be considered only outside of business hours. To mitigate this, consider the specifying the MAXDOP option (more below). You can evaluate the progress of a DBCC CHECKDB operation (as well as backup and restore operations) by referencing the value in sys.dm_exec_requests. percent_complete for the executing session.

Here are some parameters worth noting:

- **NOINDEX.** This can reduce the duration of the integrity check by skipping checks on nonclustered rowstore and columnstore indexes. It is not recommended.

  Example usage:

  ```
  DBCC CHECKDB (databasename, NOINDEX);
  ```

- **REPAIR_REBUILD.** You should run this only after considering other options, including a backup restore, because although it might have some success, it is unlikely to result in a complete repair. It can also be very time consuming, involving the rebuilding of indexes based on attempted repair data. We suggest that you review the DBCC CHECKDB documentation for a number of caveats at *https://docs.microsoft.com/sql/t-sql/ database-console-commands/dbcc-checkdb-transact-sql*.

  Example usage:

  ```
  DBCC CHECKDB (databasename) WITH REPAIR_REBUILD;
  ```

- **REPAIR_ALLOW_DATA_LOSS.** You should run this only as a last resort to achieve a partial database recovery because it can force a database to resolve errors by simply deallocating pages, potentially creating gaps in rows or columns. You must run this in SINGLE_USER mode, and you should run it in EMERGENCY mode. Review the DBCC CHECKDB documentation for a number of caveats and do not execute this command casually.

- Example usage: (last resort only, not recommended!)

  ```
  ALTER DATABASE WorldWideImporters SET EMERGENCY, SINGLE_USER;
  ```

CHAPTER 8

```
DBCC CHECKDB('WideWorldImporters', REPAIR_ALLOW_DATA_LOSS);

ALTER DATABASE WorldWideImporters SET MULTI_USER;
```

NOTE

A complete review of how EMERGENCY mode and REPAIR_ALLOW_
DATA_LOSS is detailed in this blog post by Microsoft's original DBCC
CHECKDB developer Paul Randal: *https://sqlskills.com/blogs/paul/
checkdb-from-every-angle-emergency-mode-repair-the-very-very-last-resort/.*

- **WITH NO_INFOMSGS.**   This suppresses informational status messages and returns only errors.

  Example usage:

  ```
  DBCC CHECKDB (databasename) WITH NO_INFOMSGS;
  ```

- **WITH ESTIMATEONLY.**   This does not provide an estimate of the duration of a CHECKDB (without other parameters), only an amount of space required in TempDB.

  Example usage:

  ```
  DBCC CHECKDB (databasename) WITH ESTIMATEONLY;
  ```

- **WITH MAXDOP = n.**   Similar to limiting the Maximum Degrees of Parallelism in other areas of SQL Server, this option limits the CHECKDB operation's parallelism, potentially extending duration but dramatically reducing the CPU utilization. SQL Server Enterprise edition supports parallel execution of the DBCC CHECKDB command, up to the server's MAXDOP setting. Therefore, in Enterprise edition, consider MAXDOP = 1 to run the command single-threaded, or, overriding the other limitations on max degree of parallelism with MAXDOP = 0, allowing the CHECKDB unlimited parallelism to potentially finish sooner. Outside of Enterprise and Developer edition of SQL Server, objects are not checked in parallel.

  Example usage, combined with the earlier NO_INFOMSGS to show multiple parameters:

  ```
  DBCC CHECKDB (databasename) WITH NO_INFOMSGS, MAXDOP = 0;
  ```

These scripts are all available in the accompanying downloads for this book at
https://www.MicrosoftPressStore.com/SQLServer2019InsideOut/downloads.

➤ **For more information on automating DBCC CHECKDB, see Chapter 9, "Automating SQL Server administration."**

Inside OUT

How do you tell when a DBCC CHECKDB was last run on a database?

SQL Server writes each execution of DBCC CHECKDB to the SQL Server Error Log, but also records it internally.

You can retrieve the latest good known execution date of DBCC CHECKDB from the undocumented but well-known command DBCC DBINFO. One of the fields returned by this query is 'dbi_dbccLastKnownGood'. This date value defaults to 1900-01-01 if no CHECKDB has ever been run. It should be noted that a piecemeal integrity checks strategy of executing DBCC CHECKALLOC, DBCC CHECKCATALOG, and DBCC CHECKTABLE separately does not update dbccLastKnownGood.

Sample:

```
DBCC DBINFO ([databasename]) WITH TABLERESULTS;
```

Or, use this snippet to review all databases in a SQL instance, leveraging another undocumented stored procedure, sp_msforeachdb, which cursors through each database, substituting the database name for the '?' character:

```
EXEC sp_MSforeachdb '

--Table variable to capture the DBCC DBINFO output,
look for the field we want in each database output

DECLARE @DBCC_DBINFO TABLE (ParentObject VARCHAR(255) NOT NULL, [Object]
VARCHAR(255)  NOT NULL, [Field] VARCHAR(255) NOT NULL INDEX idx_dbinfo_field
CLUSTERED, [Value] VARCHAR(255));

INSERT INTO @DBCC_DBINFO EXECUTE ("DBCC DBINFO ([?]) WITH TABLERESULTS");

SELECT "?", [Value] FROM @DBCC_DBINFO WHERE Field = "dbi_dbccLastKnownGood";

';
```

Repairing database data file corruption

Of course, the only real remedy to data corruption after it has happened is by restoring from a backup that predates the corruption. The well-documented DBCC CHECKDB option for REPAIR_ALLOW_DATA_LOSS, as discussed above, should be a last resort.

It is possible to repair missing pages in clustered indexes by piecing together missing columns in nonclustered indexes. In reality, this is an academic solution because data corruption rarely happens in such a tidy and convenient way.

It's also potentially possible to recover from data corruption, admittedly a lucky endeavor that this author has benefited from, by identifying the objects reported by DBCC CHECKDB and performing index rebuild operations on them.

Availability groups also provide a built-in data corruption detection and automatic repair capability by using uncorrupted data on one replica to replace inaccessible data on another.

➤ For more information on this feature of availability groups, see Chapter 11, "Implementing high availability and disaster recovery."

Recovering from database transaction log file corruption

In addition to the previous chapter's guidance on the importance of backups, you can reconstitute a corrupted or lost database transaction log file by using the example that follows. A lost transaction log file will result in the loss of uncommitted data (or in the case of delayed durability tables, the loss of data that hasn't been made durable in the log yet), but in the event of a disaster recovery involving the loss of the .ldf file with an intact .mdf file, this could be a valuable step.

It is possible to rebuild a blank transaction log file in a new file location for a database by using the following command:

```
ALTER DATABASE WorldWideImporters SET EMERGENCY, SINGLE_USER;

ALTER DATABASE WorldWideImporters REBUILD LOG

ON (NAME=WWI_Log, FILENAME='F:\DATA\WideWorldImporters_new.ldf');

ALTER DATABASE WorldWideImporters SET MULTI_USER;
```

These scripts are all available in the accompanying downloads for this book at *https://MicrosoftPressStore.com/SQLServer2019InsideOut/downloads*.

NOTE

Rebuilding a blank transaction log file using ALTER DATABASE ... REBUILD LOG is not supported for databases containing a MEMORY_OPTIMIZED_DATA filegroup.

Database corruption in databases in Azure SQL Database

Like many other administrative concerns with a Platform as a Service (PaaS) database, integrity checks for Azure SQL DB is automated. Microsoft takes data integrity in its platform-as-a-service (PaaS) database offering very seriously and provides strong assurances of assistance and recovery for its product. Albeit rare, Azure engineering teams respond 24x7 globally to data corruption reports. The Azure SQL Database engineering team details its response promises at *https://azure.microsoft.com/blog/data-integrity-in-azure-sql-database/.*

> ### NOTE
>
> While Azure SQL managed instance has many PaaS-like qualities, automated integrity checks is not one of them. You should setup maintenance plans to execute DBCC CHECKDB, index maintenance, and other maintenance topics in this chapter for Azure SQL managed instance.

> ➤ We discuss Azure SQL Managed Instances in detail in Chapter 18, "Provisioning Azure SQL Database managed instance."

Maintaining indexes and statistics

Maintaining index fragmentation is about proper organization of rowstore data within the file that SQL Server maintains. Removing fragmentation is really about minimizing the number of pages that must be involved when queries read or write those data pages. Reducing fragmentation in database objects is vastly different from reducing fragmentation at the drive level and has little in common with the Disk Defragmenter application of Windows. Although this doesn't translate to page locations on disk, and this has even less relevance on Storage-Area Networks, it does translate to the activity of I/O systems when retrieving data.

In performance terms, the higher the amount of fragmentation (easily measurable in dynamic management views as discussed later), the more activity is required for the same amount of data.

The causes of index fragmentation are writes. Our data would stay nice and tidy if applications would stop writing to it! There will inevitably be a significant effect that updates and deletes have on clustered and nonclustered index fragmentation, plus the effect that inserts can have on fragmentation because of clustered index design.

> ### NOTE
>
> A heap (a table without a clustered index) doesn't suffer from fragmentation (how can pages be out of order?); rather, it suffers from wasted space within the heap structure. This is due to the use of Forwarding Pointers, a mechanism for keeping data associated, but is realistically far worse for performance than fragmentation. Forwarding Pointers are followed from pointer to pointer as the table is scanned, until finally arriving at the page where the data is now stored. Deletes and updates leave wasted space in a heap that cannot be reclaimed even with an Index Rebuild operation. To reclaim wasted space within a heap, you must drop and recreate the table, or ironically, create a clustered index on the table, and then, to make it a heap again, drop the clustered index. The latter

process can be very costly if you have nonclustered indexes on the table, as they will all be rebuilt twice in the process.

The information in this section is largely unchanged from previous versions of SQL Server and applies to SQL Server instances, databases in Azure SQL Database, Azure SQL Managed Instances, and even Azure SQL Data Warehouse. (All tables in Azure SQL Data Warehouse have a clustered columnstore index by default.)

Changing the Fill Factor property when beneficial

Each rowstore index on disk-based objects has a numeric property called a Fill Factor that specifies the percentage of space to be filled with rowstore data in each leaf-level data page of the index when it is created or rebuilt. The instance-wide default Fill Factor is 100%, which is represented by the setting value 0, and means that each leaf-level data page will be filled. A Fill Factor setting of 80 means that 20% of leaf-level data pages will be intentionally left empty when data is inserted. We can adjust this Fill Factor percentage for each index to manage the efficiency of data pages.

A non-default Fill Factor may help reduce the number page splits, which occur when the Database Engine attempts to add a new row of data or update an existing row with more data to a page that is already full. In this case, the Database Engine will clear out space for the new row by moving a proportion of the old rows to a new page. A page split can be a time-consuming and resource-consuming operation, with many page splits possible during writes, and will lead to index fragmentation.

However, setting a non-default Fill Factor will also increase the number of pages needed to store the same data and increase the number of reads needed for query operations. For example, a Fill Factor of 50 will roughly double the space on the drive that it initially takes to store and therefore access the data, when compared to the default Fill Factor of 0.

In most instances, data is read far more often that it is written and inserted, updated, and deleted upon occasion. Indexes will therefore benefit from a high or default Fill Factor, almost always more than 80, because it is almost always more important to keep the number of reads to a manageable level than minimizing the resources needed to perform a page split. You can deal with the index fragmentation by using the REBUILD or REORGANIZE commands, as discussed in the next section.

If the key value for an index is constantly increasing, such as an autoincrementing IDENTITY or SEQUENCE-populated field as the first key of a clustered index, the data is added to the end of a data page and any gaps would not need to be filled. In the case of a table for which data is always inserted sequentially and never updated, setting a Fill Factor other than the default may have no benefits. Even after fine tuning a Fill Factor, the benefit of reducing page splits may not have any noticeable benefit to write performance.

You can set a Fill Factor when an index is first created, or you can change it by using the ALTER INDEX ... REBUILD syntax, as discussed in the next section.

> **NOTE**
>
> The new OPTIMIZE_FOR_SEQUENTIAL_KEY feature, introduced in SQL Server 2019, can further benefit IDENTITY and SEQUENCE-populated columns. For more on this recommended new feature, see Chapter 15, "Understanding and designing indexes."

Tracking page splits

If you intend to fine tune the Fill Factor for important tables to maximize the performance/storage space ratio, you can measure page splits in two ways, here with a query against a DMV, and next with an Extended Event session.

You can use the performance counter DMV to measure page splits in aggregate on Windows server, as shown here:

```
SELECT * FROM sys.dm_os_performance_counters WHERE counter_name ='Page Splits/sec';
```

The `cntr_value` will increment whenever a page split is detected. This is a bit misleading because to calculate the page splits per second, you must sample the incrementing value twice, and divide by the time difference between the samples. When viewing this metric in Performance Monitor, the math is done for you.

You can also track `page_split` events alongside statement execution by adding the `page_split` event to sessions such as the Transact-SQL (T-SQL) template in the extended events wizard. We'll provide a sample of this later in this chapter, in the section "Using extended events to detect page splits."

We will review extended events and the `sys.dm_os_performance_counters` DMV later in this chapter in the section "Querying performance metrics by using DMVs," including a sample session script to track `page_split` events.

Monitoring index fragmentation

You can find the extent to which an index is fragmented by interrogating the `sys.dm_db_index_physical_stats` dynamic management function (DMF).

Be aware that unlike most DMVs, this function can have a significant impact on server performance because it can tax I/O. Granting permission to query `sys.dm_db_index_physical_stats` should be carefully considered given this potential impact to performance.

To query this DMF, you must be a member of the sysadmin server role, or the db_ddladmin or db_owner database roles. Alternatively, you can grant the VIEW DATABASE STATE or VIEW

SERVER STATE permissions. The `sys.dm_db_index_physical_stats` DMF is often joined to catalog views like sys.indexes or sys.objects, which require the user to have some permissions to the tables in addition to VIEW DATABASE STATE or VIEW SERVER STATE. For more information, refer to *https://docs.microsoft.com/sql/relational-databases/system-dynamic-management-views/sys-dm-db-index-physical-stats-transact-sql#permissions* and *https://docs.microsoft.com//sql/relational-databases/security/metadata-visibility-configuration*.

Keep this in mind when scripting this operation for automated index maintenance. We discuss more about automating index maintenance in Chapter 9.

For example, to find the fragmentation level of all indexes on the `Sales.Orders` table in the WideWorldImporters sample database, you can use a query such as the following:

```
SELECT

DB = db_name(s.database_id)

, [schema_name] = sc.name

, [table_name] = o.name

, index_name = i.name

, s.index_type_desc

, s.partition_number -- if the object is partitioned

, avg_fragmentation_pct = s.avg_fragmentation_in_percent

, s.page_count -- pages in object partition

FROM sys.indexes AS i

CROSS APPLY sys.dm_db_index_physical_stats

(DB_ID(),i.object_id,i.index_id, NULL, NULL) AS s

INNER JOIN sys.objects AS o ON o.object_id = s.object_id

INNER JOIN sys.schemas AS sc ON o.schema_id = sc.schema_id

WHERE i.is_disabled = 0

AND o.object_id = OBJECT_ID('Sales.Orders');
```

The `sys.dm_db_index_physical_stats` DMF accepts five parameters: `database_id`, `object_id`, `index_id`, `partition_id`, and `mode`. The mode parameter defaults to `LIMITED`, the fastest method, but you can set it to `Sampled` and `Detailed`. These additional modes are rarely necessary, but they provide more data and more precise data. Some result set columns will be `NULL` in LIMITED mode. For the purposes of determining fragmentation, the default mode of `LIMITED` (used when the parameter value of `NULL` is provided) suffices.

The five parameters of the sys.dm_db_index_physical_stats DMF are all nullable. For example, if you run the following you will see fragmentation statistics for all databases, all objects, all indexes, and all partitions. We recommend that you do not execute this in a production environment during operational hours; again, because this can have a significant impact on server resources, resulting in a noticeable drop in performance.

```
SELECT * FROM sys.dm_db_index_physical_stats(NULL,NULL,NULL,NULL,NULL);
```

The previous sample script and all scripts for this book are available for download at *https://MicrosoftPressStore.com/SQLServer2019InsideOut/downloads*.

Maintaining Indexes

Once your automated script has identified the objects most in need of maintenance with the aid of sys.dm_db_index_physical_stats, it should proceed with steps to remove fragmentation in a timely fashion during a maintenance window. The commands to remove fragmentation are rebuild or reorganize, we'll explain the differences later but in short: a rebuild is more thorough and potentially disruptive, a reorganize is less thorough, not disruptive, but often sufficient.

Note that you must implement index maintenance for both rowstore and columnstore indexes, and we cover strategies for both in this section.

Ideally, your automated index maintenance script runs as often as possible during regularly scheduled maintenance windows, and for a limited amount of time. For example, if your business environment allows for a maintenance window each night between 1am and 4am, try to run your index maintenance each night in that window. If possible, modify your script to avoid starting new work after 4am, or, to use the RESUMABLE PAUSE feature at 4am. (More on the latter strategy soon, in section "Rebuilding Indexes.") In databases with very large tables, your index maintenance may require more time that you have to work with in a single maintenance window. Try to use the limited amount of time given each maintenance window to maintain fragmented indexes each opportunity. Given ample time, this approach tends to work best to reduce fragmentation, as opposed to a single very long maintenance period during a weekend, for example.

➤ For more on Maintenance Plans and automation of index maintenance, including the typical "Care and Feeding" of a SQL Server, see Chapter 9.

Inside OUT

Can you cancel an index maintenance operation?

When index maintenance runs long and begins to disrupt other activity, be careful when stopping/killing the process and forcing a rollback. Killing the session or cancelling the request of a long-running index rebuild is no quick remedy but a painful rollback can be avoided in two ways:

1. If you started the index maintenance operation with the RESUMABLE option, introduced in SQL Server 2017, issue a PAUSE command. More on the RESUMABLE option later in this chapter.

2. SQL Server 2019's new Accelerated Database Recovery (ADR) feature can prevent a lengthy rollback after the operation is killed.

Without ADR, the rollback of a large, long-running index REBUILD step could take a very long time and continue blocking, even after a SQL Server service restart. Even when an ONLINE index REBUILD operation is killed, its rollback is not an ONLINE operation!

Instead, consider the following measures to prevent this scenario from happening:

1. In your index maintenance loop that performs index maintenance, perform index as granularly as possible. Avoid using the ALL keyword to process all indexes on a table. Perform index maintenance on individual index partitions if possible.

2. In your index maintenance script, write code to check the time. If your index maintenance is outside of an allowed time window, don't begin a new index maintenance operation, or use the PAUSE option explained next.

3. Specify ONLINE = ON, RESUMABLE = ON when beginning the REBUILD operation. We cover the RESUMABLE syntax in the coming pages. If an index maintenance step has overrun a maintenance window, you can issue a PAUSE, saving you the time of a lengthy and disruptive rollback. You could also specify a MAX_DURATION option when starting index rebuild, and it will automatically pause itself if it exceeds the duration. The rebuild can then be resumed later on. More on the RESUMABLE option later in this chapter, in section "Rebuilding Indexes."

4. In SQL Server 2019, be sure to enable the new Accelerated Database Recovery (ADR) option in each database.

➤ For more on enabling the new Accelerated Database Recovery database option, see Chapter 6, "Provisioning and configuration SQL Server databases."

Rebuilding indexes

Performing an INDEX REBUILD operation on a rowstore index (clustered or nonclustered) will physically re-create the index B-tree leaf level. The goal of moving the pages is to make storage more efficient and to match the logical order provided by the index key. A rebuild operation is both destructive to the index object and will block other queries attempting to access the pages unless you provide the ONLINE option. Because the rebuild operation destroys and re-creates the index, it must update the index statistics afterward, eliminating the need to perform a subsequent UPDATE STATISTICS operation as part of regular maintenance.

Long-term table locks are held during the rebuild operation. One of the major advantages of SQL Server Enterprise edition remains the ability to specify the ONLINE option, which allows for rebuild operations to be significantly less disruptive to other queries, though not completely. This makes index maintenance feasible on SQL Servers with round-the-clock activity.

You should consider using ONLINE with index rebuild operations whenever short maintenance windows are insufficient for rebuilding fragmented indexes offline. An ONLINE index rebuild, however, might take longer than an offline rebuild. There are also scenarios for which an ONLINE rebuild is not possible, including deprecated data types image, text and ntext, or the xml data type. Since SQL Server 2012, it is possible to perform ONLINE index rebuilds on the MAX lengths of the data types varchar, nvarchar, and varbinary.

For the syntax to rebuild the FK_Sales_Orders_CustomerID nonclustered index on the Sales.Orders table with the ONLINE functionality in Enterprise edition, see the following code sample:

```
ALTER INDEX FK_Sales_Orders_CustomerID

ON Sales.Orders

REBUILD WITH (ONLINE=ON);
```

It's important to note that if you perform any kind of index maintenance on the clustered index of a rowstore table, it does not affect the nonclustered indexes. Nonclustered index fragmentation will not change if you rebuild the clustered index.

Instead of rebuilding each index on a table individually, you can rebuild all indexes on a table by replacing the name of the index with the keyword ALL. This is usually overkill and inefficient, because not all indexes may have the same level of fragmentation and need for maintenance. For example, to rebuild all indexes on the Sales.OrderLines table, do the following:

```
ALTER INDEX ALL ON [Sales].[OrderLines] REBUILD;
```

> ## NOTE
>
> For memory-optimized tables, we recommend a manual routine maintenance step using the ALTER TABLE ... ALTER INDEX ... REBUILD syntax. This is not to reduce fragmentation in the in-memory data; rather, it is to examine the number of buckets in a memory-optimized table's hash index(es). For more information on rebuilding hash indexes and bucket counts, see Chapter 15.

CHAPTER 8

> **NOTE**
>
> You can change the data compression option for indexes by using the rebuild operation using the DATA_COMPRESSION option. For more detail on Data Compression, see Chapter 3: "Designing and implementing an on-premises database infrastructure."

Aside from ONLINE, there are other options that you might want to consider for INDEX REBUILD operations. Let's take a look at them:

- **SORT_IN_TEMPDB.** Use this when you want to create or rebuild an index using TempDB for sorting the index data, potentially increasing performance by distributing the I/O activity across multiple drives. This also means that these sorting work tables are written to the TempDB database transaction log instead of the user database transaction log, potentially reducing the impact on the user database log file, and allowing for the user database transaction log to be backed up during the operation.

- **MAXDOP.** You can use this to mitigate some of the impact of index maintenance by preventing the operation from using parallel processors. This can cause the index maintenance operation to run longer, but to have less impact on performance.

- **WAIT_AT_LOW_PRIORITY.** First introduced in SQL Server 2014, this is the first of a set of parameters that you can use to instruct the ONLINE index maintenance operation to try not to block other operations, and how. This feature is known as Managed Lock Priority, and this syntax is not usable outside of online index operations and partition switching operations. Here is the full syntax:

```
ALTER INDEX PK_Sales_OrderLines on [Sales].[OrderLines]

REBUILD WITH (ONLINE=ON (WAIT_AT_LOW_PRIORITY (MAX_DURATION = 0 MINUTES,

ABORT_AFTER_WAIT = SELF)));
```

The parameters for MAX_DURATION and ABORT_AFTER_WAIT instruct the statement how to proceed if it begins to be blocked by another operation. The online index operation will wait, allowing other operations to proceed.

The MAX_DURATION parameter can be 0 (wait indefinitely) or a measure of time in minutes (no other unit of measure is supported).

The ABORT_AFTER_WAIT parameter provides an action at the end of the MAX_DURATION wait:

- SELF instructs the statement to terminate its own process, ending the online rebuild step.

- BLOCKERS instructs the statement to terminate the other process that is being blocked, terminating what is potentially a user transactions. Use with caution.

- NONE instructs the statement to continue to wait, and when combined with MAX_DURATION = 0, essentially the same behavior as not specifying WAIT_AT_LOW_PRIORITY.

- **RESUMABLE.**   Introduced in SQL Server 2017, the RESUMABLE feature makes it possible to initiate ONLINE index create or rebuild that can be paused and resumed later, even after a server shutdown. You can also specify a MAX_DURATION in minutes when starting an index rebuild operation, which will PAUSE the operation if it exceeds the specified duration. You cannot specify the ALL keyword for a resumable operation. The SORT_IN_TEMPDB=ON option is not compatible with the RESUMEABLE option.

NOTE
Starting with SQL 2019, the RESUMEABLE syntax can also be used when creating an index. An ALTER INDEX and CREATE INDEX statement can be similarly paused and resumed.

A sample scenario of a paused/resumed index maintenance operation on a large table in the sample WideWorldImporters database:

```
ALTER INDEX PK_Sales_OrderLines on [Sales].[OrderLines]
REBUILD WITH (ONLINE = ON, RESUMABLE = ON);
```

From another session, show that the index rebuild is RUNNING with the RESUMABLE option:

```
SELECT object_name = object_name (object_id), *
FROM sys.index_resumable_operations;
```

From another session, run the below to pause the operation:

```
ALTER INDEX PK_Sales_OrderLines on [Sales].[OrderLines] PAUSE;
```

Show that the index rebuild is PAUSED:

```
SELECT object_name = object_name (object_id), *
FROM sys.index_resumable_operations;
```

This will result in a disconnection of the session of the original index maintenance, and a severe error message. In the SQL Server Error Log, the event is not a severe error message, but an informative note that "An ALTER INDEX 'PAUSE' was executed for…".

To resume the index maintenance operation, two options:

1. Reissue the same index maintenance operation, which will warn you it'll just resume instead.

```
ALTER INDEX PK_Sales_OrderLines on [Sales].[OrderLines]
REBUILD WITH (ONLINE = ON, RESUMABLE = ON);
```

2. Or, issue a RESUME to the same index.

```
ALTER INDEX PK_Sales_OrderLines on [Sales].[OrderLines] RESUME;
```

> ## Inside OUT
>
> ### Are all CREATE and ALTER INDEX operations resumable now?
>
> Not by default, but only with those operations that were started with the syntax RESUMABLE = ON. The default of this parameter is RESUMABLE=OFF, so index operations are not resumable by default.
>
> Be aware of this beneficial new feature for both index CREATE and ALTER operations, and prep to take advantage of it from now on. For very large tables, you should consider using the RESUMABLE feature to pause index maintenance during normal utilization.

Let's discuss more about how to leverage resumable index maintenance operations. You can see a list of resumable and paused index operations in a new DMV, sys.index_resumable_operations, where the state_desc field will reflect RUNNING (and pausable) or PAUSED (and resumable).

NOTE

It is possible for a RESUMABLE rebuild operation to be blocked by uncommitted transactions and to be unpausable. In this case, you will see the ALTER INDEX ... PAUSE statement is blocked by the ALTER INDEX ... REBUILD statement. Long-running transactions can be a problem for many reasons, with this among them.

The RESUMABLE syntax also supports a MAX_DURATION syntax, which has a different meaning than the MAX_DURATION syntax used in the ABORT_AFTER_WAIT. The MAX_ DURATION option could be very useful to you, by automatically pausing an ONLINE index operation after a specified amount of time. For example, this allows for the index operation to be resumed during the next maintenance window. The MAX_DURATION=0 option allows for operation to run indefinitely, and is not a required parameter for RESUMABLE=ON. Here's an example:

```
ALTER INDEX PK_Sales_OrderLines on [Sales].[OrderLines]

REBUILD WITH (ONLINE=ON, RESUMABLE=ON, MAX_DURATION = 60 MINUTES);
```

Reorganizing indexes

Performing a REORGANIZE operation on an index uses far less system resources and is much less disruptive than performing a full REBUILD while still accomplishing the goal of reducing fragmentation. It physically reorders the leaf-level pages of the index to match the logical order. It also compacts the pages based on the existing fill factor, though it does not allow the fill factor to be changed. This operation is always performed online, so long-term table locks (except for schema locks) are not held and queries or modifications to the underlying table will not be blocked during the REORGANIZE transaction.

Because the REORGANIZE operation is not destructive, it does not automatically update the statistics for the index afterward, as a rebuild operation does. Thus, you should always follow a REORGANIZE step with an UPDATE STATISTICS step.

> ➤ **For more on statistics objects and their impact on performance, see Chapter 15.**

The following example presents the syntax to reorganize the PK_Sales_OrderLines index on the Sales.OrderLines table:

```
ALTER INDEX PK_Sales_OrderLines on [Sales].[OrderLines] REORGANIZE;
```

None of the options available to REBUILD that we covered in the previous section are available to the REORGANIZE command. The only additional option that is specific to REORGANIZE is the LOB_COMPACTION option, which affects only large object (LOB) data types: image, text, ntext, varchar(max), nvarchar(max), varbinary(max), and xml. By default, this option is turned on, but you can turn it off for non-heap tables to potentially skip some activity, though we do not recommend it. For heap tables, LOB data is always compacted.

Updating index statistics

SQL Server uses statistics to describe the distribution and nature of the data in tables. The query optimizer needs the Auto Create setting turned on so that it can create single-column statistics when compiling queries. These statistics help the query optimizer create optimal query plans at runtime. Auto Update Statistics prompts statistics to be updated automatically when accessed by a T-SQL query. This only occurs when the table is discovered to have passed a threshold of rows changed. Without relevant and up-to-date statistics, the query optimizer might not choose the best way to run queries.

An update of index statistics should accompany INDEX REORGANIZE steps, but not INDEX REBUILD steps. Remember that the INDEX REBUILD command also updates the index statistics.

The basic syntax to update the statistics for an individual table is simple:

```
UPDATE STATISTICS [Sales].[Invoices];
```

The only command option to be aware of concerns the depth to which the statistics are scanned before being recalculated. By default, SQL Server samples a statistically significant number of rows in the table. This sampling is done with a parallel process starting with database compatibility level 130. This is fast and adequate for most workloads. You can optionally choose to scan the entire table by specifying the FULLSCAN option, or a sample of the table based on a percentage of rows or a fixed number of rows using the SAMPLE option, but we generally do not recommend these options.

You can manually verify that indexes are being kept up to date by the query optimizer when `auto_create_stats` is turned on. The `sys.dm_db_stats_properties` DMF accepts an `object_id` and `stats_id`, which is functionally the same as the `index_id`, if the statistics object corresponds to an index. The `sys.dm_db_stats_properties` DMF returns information such as `modification_counter` of rows changed since the last statistics update, and the `last_updated` date, which is NULL if the statistics object has never been updated since it was created.

Not all statistics are associated with an index, such as statistics that are automatically created. There will generally be more stats objects than index objects. This function works in SQL Server and Azure SQL Database. You can easily tell if a statistics object is automatically created by its naming convention, WA_Sys_<column_name>_<object_id_hex>.

➤ For more on statistics objects and their impact on performance, see Chapter 15.

Inside OUT

Do you need to update statistics regularly even if `auto_create_stats` is turned on for the database?

Yes, you should still maintain the health of Update Statistics regularly.

Updating statistics regularly, if your maintenance window time allows, will definitely not hurt, and will likely help by reducing the number of statistics updates that happen automatically during regular business hours.

When `auto_update_stats` is on, statistics are updated periodically based on (and during) actual usage. Statistics are considered out of date by the query optimizer when a ratio of data modifications to rows in the table has been reached. The query optimizer will check for and update the out-of-date statistic before running a query plan. Therefore, the `auto_update_stats` option has some small runtime overhead, though the performance benefit of updated statistics usually outweighs this cost. We also highly recommend turning on the `auto_update_stats_async` option because it helps minimize this runtime overhead by updating the statistics after running the query, instead of before.

We also recommend that you turn on the `auto_update_stats` and `auto_update_stats_async` options, as discussed in Chapter 4, "Installing and configuring SQL Server instances and features" and Chapter 14, "Performance tuning SQL Server" on all user databases, unless the application specifically requests that it be turned off, such as with Microsoft SharePoint.

Reorganizing columnstore indexes

Columnstore indexes need to also be maintained, but they use different internal objects to measure the fragmentation of the internal columnstore structure. Columnstore indexes need only the REORGANIZE operation. For more on designing columnstore indexes, see Chapter 15.

You can review the current structure of the groups of columnstore indexes by using the DMV `sys.dm_db_column_store_row_group_physical_stats`. This returns one row per row group of the columnstore structure. The state of a rowgroup, and the current count of rowgroup by their states, provides some insight into the health of the columnstore index. The vast majority of row group states should be COMPRESSED. Row groups in the OPEN and CLOSED states are part of the delta store and are awaiting compression. These delta store row groups are served up alongside compressed data seamlessly when queries use columnstore data.

The number of deleted rows in a rowgroup is also an indication that the index needs maintenance. As the ratio of `deleted_rows` to total rows in a row group that is in the COMPRESSED state increases, the performance of the columnstore index will be reduced. If the `delete_rows` is larger than or greater than the total rows in a rowgroup, a REORGANIZE step will be beneficial.

Performing a REBUILD operation on a columnstore index is essentially the same as a drop/re-create and is not necessary. However, if you want to force the rebuild process, starting with SQL Server 2019 using the WITH (ONLINE = ON) syntax is supported for rebuilding (and creating) columnstore indexes. A REORGANIZE step for a columnstore index, just as for a nonclustered index, is an ONLINE operation that has minimal impact to concurrent queries.

You can also use the option to REORGANIZE WITH (COMPRESS_ALL_ROW_GROUPS=ON) to force all delta store row groups to be compressed into a COMPRESSED row group. This can be useful when you observe a large number of COMPRESSED row groups with fewer than 100,000 rows.

Without COMPRESS_ALL_ROW_GROUPS, only COMPRESSED row groups will be compressed and combined. Typically, COMPRESSED row groups should contain up to one million rows each, but SQL might align rows in COMPRESSED row groups that align with how the rows were inserted, especially if they were inserted in bulk operations.

➤ We discuss more about automating index maintenance in Chapter 9.

CHAPTER 8

Managing database file sizes

It is important to understand the distinction between the size of a database data or log files, which act simply as reservations for SQL Server to work in, and the data within those reservations. Note that this section does not apply to Azure SQL Database, because this level of file management is not available and is automatically managed.

In SQL Server Management Studio (SSMS), you can right-click a database, click Reports, and then view the Disk Usage report for a database, which will contain information about how much data is actually in the database's files.

Alternatively, the following query uses the FILEPROPERTY function to reveal how much data there actually is inside a file reservation. We again use the undocumented but well-understood sp_msforeachdb sproc to iterate through each of the databases, accessing the sys.database_files catalog view.

```
DECLARE @FILEPROPERTY TABLE

( DatabaseName sysname

,DatabaseFileName nvarchar(500)

,FileLocation nvarchar(500)

,FileId int

,[type_desc] varchar(50)

,FileSizeMB decimal(19,2)

,SpaceUsedMB decimal(19,2)

,AvailableMB decimal(19,2)

,FreePercent decimal(19,2) );

INSERT INTO @FILEPROPERTY

exec sp_MSforeachdb  'USE [?];

SELECT

  Database_Name              = d.name

, Database_Logical_File_Name = df.name

, File_Location              = df.physical_name

, df.File_ID

, df.type_desc

, FileSize_MB = CAST(size/128.0 as Decimal(19,2))
```

```
, SpaceUsed_MB = CAST(CAST(FILEPROPERTY(df.name, "SpaceUsed")
AS int)/128.0 AS decimal(19,2))

, Available_MB = CAST(size/128.0 - CAST(FILEPROPERTY(df.name, "SpaceUsed")
AS int)/128.0 AS decimal(19,2))

, FreePercent = CAST(((((size/128.0) - (CAST(FILEPROPERTY(df.name, "SpaceUsed")
AS int)*8/1024.0)) / (size*8/1024.0) ) * 100. AS decimal(19,2))

 FROM sys.database_files as df

 CROSS APPLY sys.databases as d

 WHERE d.database_id = DB_ID();'

SELECT * FROM @FILEPROPERTY

WHERE SpaceUsedMB is not null

ORDER BY FreePercent asc; --Find files with least amount of free space at top
```

The previous sample script and all scripts for this book are available for download at *https://MicrosoftPressStore.com/SQLServer2019InsideOut/downloads*.

Run this on a database in your environment to see how much data there is within database files. You might find that some data or log files are near full, whereas others have a large amount of space. Why would this be?

Files that have a large amount of free space might have grown in the past but have since been emptied out. If a transaction log in the full recovery model has grown for a long time without having a transaction log backup, the .ldf file will have grown unchecked. Later, when a transaction log backup is taken, causing the log to truncate, it will been nearly empty, but the size of the .ldf file itself will not have changed. It isn't until a shrink operation has taken place that the .ldf file will give its unused space back to the operating system. We never recommend shrinking a file flippantly or on a schedule.

You should manually grow your database and log file sizes to a size that is well ahead of the database's growth pattern. You might fret over the best autogrowth rate, but ideally, autogrowth events are best avoided altogether by proactive file management.

Autogrowth events can be disruptive to user activity, causing all transactions to wait while the database file asks the operating system (OS) for more space and grows. Depending on the performance of the I/O system, this could take seconds, during which activity on the database must wait. Depending on the autogrowth setting and the size of the write transactions, multiple autogrowth events could be suffered sequentially.

> ➤ **Growth of database data files will also be greatly sped up by instant file initialization. See Chapter 4.**

Understanding and finding autogrowth events

You should change autogrowth rates for database data and log files from the initial (and far too small) default settings, but, more important, you should maintain enough free space in your data and log files so that autogrowth events do not occur. As a proactive DBA, you should monitor the space in database files and grow the files ahead of time, manually and outside of peak business hours.

You can view recent autogrowth events in a database via a report in SSMS or via a T-SQL script (see the code example that follows). In SSMS, in Object Explorer, right-click the database name. On the shortcut menu that opens, select Reports, select Standard Reports, and then click Disk Usage. An expandable/collapsible region of the report contains Data/Log Files Autogrow/Autoshrink Events.

The autogrowth report in SSMS reads data from the SQL Server instance's default trace, which captures autogrowth events. This data is not captured by default Extended Events session called `system_health`, but you could capture autogrowth events with the `sqlserver.database_file_size_change` event in an Extended Event session.

To view and analyze autogrowth events faster, and for all databases simultaneously, you can query the SQL Server instance's default trace yourself. The default trace files are limited to 20 MB, and there are at most five rollover files, yielding 100 MB of history. The amount of time this covers depends on server activity. The following sample code query uses the `fn_trace_gettable()` function to open the default trace file in its current location:

```
SELECT

DB = g.DatabaseName

, Logical_File_Name = mf.name

, Physical_File_Loc = mf.physical_name

, mf.type

-- The size in MB (converted from the number of 8KB pages) the file increased.

, EventGrowth_MB = convert(decimal(19,2),g.IntegerData*8/1024.)

, g.StartTime --Time of the autogrowth event

-- Length of time (in seconds) necessary to extend the file.

, EventDuration_s = convert(decimal(19,2),g.Duration/1000./1000.)

, Current_Auto_Growth_Set = CASE

WHEN mf.is_percent_growth = 1

    THEN CONVERT(char(2), mf.growth) + '%'
```

```
    ELSE CONVERT(varchar(30), mf.growth*8./1024.) + 'MB'
END
, Current_File_Size_MB = CONVERT(decimal(19,2),mf.size*8./1024.)
, d.recovery_model_desc
FROM fn_trace_gettable(
(select substring((SELECT path
FROM sys.traces WHERE is_default =1), 0, charindex('\log_',
(SELECT path FROM sys.traces WHERE is_default =1),0)+4)
+ '.trc'), default) g
INNER JOIN sys.master_files mf
ON mf.database_id = g.DatabaseID
AND g.FileName = mf.name
INNER JOIN sys.databases d
ON d.database_id = g.DatabaseID
ORDER BY StartTime desc;
```

Understanding autogrowth events helps explain what happens to database files when they don't have enough space. They have to grow, or transactions cannot be accepted. What about the opposite scenario, where a database file has "too much" space?

Shrinking database files

We need to be as clear as possible about this: shrinking database files is not something that you should do regularly or casually. If you find yourself every morning shrinking a database file that grows overnight, stop. Think. Isn't it just going to grow again tonight?

One of the main concerns with shrinking a file is that it indiscriminately returns free pages to the operating system, helping to create fragmentation. Aside from potentially ensuring autogrowth events in the future, shrinking a file creates the need for further index maintenance to alleviate the fragmentation. A shrink step can be time consuming, can block other user activity, and is not part of a healthy complete maintenance plan.

Database data and logs under normal circumstances—and in the case of the full recovery model with regular transaction log backups—grow to the size they need to be because of actual usage. And frequent autogrowth events and shrink operations are bad for performance and create fragmentation.

Try to proactively grow database files to avoid autogrowth events altogether. You should shrink a file only as one-time events to solve one of two problems:

- A drive volume is out of space, and in an emergency break-fix scenario, you reclaim unused space from a database data or log file.

- A database transaction log grew to a much larger size than is normally needed because of an adverse condition and should be reduced back to its normal operating size. An adverse condition could be transaction log backups that stopped working for a timespan, or a large uncommitted transaction, or replication or high availability (HA) issues which prevented the transaction log from truncating.

For the case of a database data file, there is rarely any good reason to shrink the file, except for the emergency scenario of a volume being out of space. For the rare situation in which a database had a large amount of data deleted from the file, an amount of data that is unlikely ever to exist in the database again, a one-shrink file operation might be appropriate.

For the case in which a transaction log file should be reduced in size, the best way to reclaim the space and recreate the file with optimal virtual log file (VLF) alignment is to first take a transaction log backup to truncate the log file as much as possible. If transaction log backups have not been happening on a schedule recently, it may be necessary to take another transaction log backup in order to fully clear out the log file. Once empty, shrink the log file to reclaim all unused space, then immediately grow the log file back to its expected size in increments of no more than 8,000 MB at a time. This allows SQL Server to create the underlying VLF structures in the most efficient way possible.

> ➤ **For more information on VLFs in your database log files, see Chapter 3.**

A following sample script of this process assumes a preceding transaction log backup has been taken to truncate the database transaction log, and that the database log file is mostly empty. It also grows the transaction log file backup to an example size of 9 GB (9,216 MB or 9,437,184 KB). Note the intermediate step of growing the file first to 8000MB, then to its intended size.

```
USE [WideWorldImporters];

--TRUNCATEONLY returns all free space to the OS

DBCC SHRINKFILE (N'WWI_Log' , 0, TRUNCATEONLY);

GO

USE [master];

ALTER DATABASE [WideWorldImporters]

MODIFY FILE ( NAME = N'WWI_Log', SIZE = 8192000KB );

ALTER DATABASE [WideWorldImporters]
```

```
MODIFY FILE ( NAME = N'WWI_Log', SIZE = 9437184KB );

GO
```

> **CAUTION**
>
> You should never turn on the autoshrink database setting. It will automatically return any free space of more than 25% of the data file or transaction log. You should shrink a database only as a one-time operation to reduce file size after unplanned or unusual file growth. This setting could result in unnecessary fragmentation, overhead, and frequent rapid log autogrowth events. This setting was originally intended for, and might only be appropriate for, tiny local and/or embedded databases.

Monitoring activity by using DMOs

SQL Server provides a suite of internal dynamic management objects (DBO's), which come in the form of views (DMVs) and functions (DMFs). It is important for you as a DBA to have a working knowledge of these objects because they unlock the analysis of SQL Server outside of built-in reporting capabilities and third-party tools. In fact, third-party tools that monitor SQL Server almost certainly must use these same dynamic management objects. DMO queries are discussed in several other places in this book:

- For more on understanding index usage statistics and missing index statistics, see Chapter 15.

- For more information on reviewing, aggregating, and analyzing cached execution plan statistics, including the Query Store feature introduced in SQL Server 2016, see Chapter 14.

- For more information on monitoring availability groups performance, health, and automatic seeding, see Chapter 11.

- For more information on automatic reporting from DMOs and querying performance monitor metrics from inside SQL Server DMOs, see Chapter 14.

- To read about using a DMF to query index fragmentation refer to the section "Monitoring index fragmentation" earlier in this chapter.

The previous sample script and all scripts for this book are available for download at *https://MicrosoftPressStore.com/SQLServer2019InsideOut/downloads*.

Observing sessions and requests

Any connection to a SQL Server instance is a session and is reported live in the DMV `sys.dm_exec_sessions`. Any actively running query on a SQL Server instance is a request and is reported live in the DMV `sys.dm_exec_requests`. Together, these two DMVs provide a thorough and far more detailed replacement to the sp_who or sp_who2 system stored procedures, as well as the deprecated `sys.sysprocesses` system view, with which long-time DBAs might be more familiar. With DMVs, you can do so much more than replace sp_who.

By adding a handful of other DMVs or DMFs, we can turn this query into a wealth of live information, including:

- Complete connection source information

- The actual runtime statement currently being run (similar to DBCC INPUTBUFFER)

- The actual plan XML (provided with a blue hyperlink in the SSMS results grid)

- Request duration

- Cumulative resource consumption

- The current and most recent wait types experienced

- And more

Sure, it might not be as easy to type in as "sp_who2," but it provides much more data, which you can easily query and filter. Save this as a go-to script in your personal DBA toolbelt. If you are unfamiliar with any of the data being returned, take some time to dive into the result set and explore the information it provides; it will be an excellent hands-on learning resource. You might choose to add more filters to the WHERE clause specific to your environment. Let's take a look:

```
SELECT
    when_observed = sysdatetime()
, s.session_id, r.request_id
, session_status = s.[status] -- running, sleeping, dormant, preconnect
, request_status = r.[status] -- running, runnable, suspended, sleeping, background
, blocked_by = r.blocking_session_id
, database_name = db_name(r.database_id)
, s.login_time, r.start_time
, query_text = CASE
    WHEN r.statement_start_offset = 0
    and r.statement_end_offset= 0 THEN left(est.text, 4000)
    ELSE SUBSTRING (est.[text], r.statement_start_offset/2 + 1,
```

```
    CASE WHEN r.statement_end_offset = -1

        THEN LEN (CONVERT(nvarchar(max), est.[text]))

        ELSE r.statement_end_offset/2 - r.statement_start_offset/2 + 1

    END

) END --the actual query text is stored as nvarchar,

--so we must divide by 2 for the character offsets

, qp.query_plan

, cacheobjtype = LEFT (p.cacheobjtype + ' (' + p.objtype + ')', 35)

, est.objectid

, s.login_name, s.client_interface_name

, endpoint_name = e.name, protocol = e.protocol_desc

, s.host_name, s.program_name

, cpu_time_s = r.cpu_time, tot_time_s = r.total_elapsed_time

, wait_time_s = r.wait_time, r.wait_type, r.wait_resource, r.last_wait_type

, r.reads, r.writes, r.logical_reads --accumulated request statistics

FROM sys.dm_exec_sessions as s

LEFT OUTER JOIN sys.dm_exec_requests as r on r.session_id = s.session_id

LEFT OUTER JOIN sys.endpoints as e ON e.endpoint_id = s.endpoint_id

LEFT OUTER JOIN sys.dm_exec_cached_plans as p ON p.plan_handle = r.plan_handle

OUTER APPLY sys.dm_exec_query_plan (r.plan_handle) as qp

OUTER APPLY sys.dm_exec_sql_text (r.sql_handle) as est

LEFT OUTER JOIN sys.dm_exec_query_stats as stat on stat.plan_handle = r.plan_handle

AND r.statement_start_offset = stat.statement_start_offset

AND r.statement_end_offset = stat.statement_end_offset

WHERE 1=1 --Veteran trick that makes for easier commenting of filters

AND s.session_id >= 50 --retrieve only user spids

AND s.session_id <> @@SPID --ignore this session

ORDER BY r.blocking_session_id desc, s.session_id asc;
```

One of the things returned in the above script was wait_type and last_wait_type. Let's dive into these important performance signals now.

CHAPTER 8

Understanding wait types and wait statistics

Wait statistics in SQL Server are an important source of information and can be a key resource to finding bottlenecks in performance, both at the aggregate level and at the individual query level. A wait is a signal recorded by SQL Server indicating what SQL Server is waiting on when attempting to finish processing a query. This section attempts to provide insights into this broad and important topic, but entire books, training sessions, and software packages have been developed to address wait type analysis; thus, this section is not exhaustive.

Wait statistics can be queried and provide value to SQL Server instances as well as databases in Azure SQL Database, though there are some waits specific to the Azure SQL Database platform (which we'll review). Like many DMOs, membership in the sysadmin server role is not required, only the permission VIEW SERVER STATE, or in the case of Azure SQL Database, VIEW DATABASE STATE.

We saw in the query in the previous section the ability to see the current and most recent wait type for a session. Let's dive into how to observe wait types in the aggregate, accumulated at the server level or at the session level. Waits are accumulated in many different ways in SQL Server but typically occur when a request is in the runnable or suspended states. The request is not accumulating *waits* statistics, only *durations* statistics, when in the runnable state. We saw the ability to see the request state in the previous section's sample query.

SQL Server can track and accumulate many different wait types for a single query, many of which are of negligible duration or are benign in nature. There are quite a few waits that can be ignored or that indicate idle activity, as opposed to waits that indicate resource constraints and blocking. There are more than 1,000 distinct wait types in SQL Server 2019 and even more in Azure SQL Database. Some are better documented and understood than others. We review some that you should know about later in this section.

Monitoring wait type aggregates

To view accumulated waits for a session, which live only until the close or reset of the session, use the DMV sys.dm_exec_session_wait_stats. In sys.dm_exec_sessions you can see the current wait type and most recent wait type, but this isn't always that interesting or informative. Potentially more interesting would be to see all of the accumulated wait stats for an ongoing session. This code sample shows how the DMV returns one row per session, per wait type experienced, for user sessions:

```
SELECT * FROM sys.dm_exec_session_wait_stats AS wt;
```

There is a distinction between the two time measurements in this query and others. The value from signal_wait_time_ms indicates the amount of time the thread waited on CPU activity, correlated with time spent in the runnable state. The wait_time_ms value indicates the accumulated time for the wait type including the signal_wait_time_ms, and so includes time the request spent in the runnable and suspended states. Typically, wait_time_ms is the wait measurement that we aggregate. The waiting_tasks_count will also be informative, indicating the number of times this wait_type was encountered. By dividing `wait_time_ms` by `waiting_tasks_count`, you can get an average number of ms each task encountered this wait.

We can view aggregate wait types at the instance level with the `sys.dm_os_wait_stats` DMV. This is the same as `sys.dm_exec_session_wait_stats`, but without the `session_id`, which includes all activity in the SQL Server instance, without any granularity to database, query, time-frame, and so on. This can be useful for getting the "big picture," but it is limited over long spans of time because the `wait_time_ms` counter accumulates, as illustrated here:

```
SELECT TOP (25)

  wait_type

, wait_time_s = wait_time_ms / 1000.

, Pct = 100. * wait_time_ms/nullif(sum(wait_time_ms) OVER(),0)

, avg_ms_per_wait = wait_time_ms / nullif(waiting_tasks_count,0)

FROM sys.dm_os_wait_stats as wt ORDER BY Pct desc;
```

Over time, the `wait_time_ms` numbers will be so large for certain wait types, that trends or changes in wait type accumulations rates will be mathematically difficult to see. You want to use the wait stats to keep a close eye on server performance as it trends and changes over time, so you need to capture these accumulated wait statistics in chunks of time, such as one day or one week.

```
--Script to setup capturing these statistics over time

CREATE TABLE dbo.sys_dm_os_wait_stats

(     id int NOT NULL IDENTITY(1,1)

,     datecapture datetimeoffset(0) NOT NULL

,     wait_type nvarchar(512) NOT NULL

,     wait_time_s decimal(19,1) NOT NULL

,     Pct decimal(9,1) NOT NULL

,     avg_ms_per_wait decimal(19,1) NOT NULL

,     CONSTRAINT PK_sys_dm_os_wait_stats PRIMARY KEY CLUSTERED (id)

);

--This part of the script should be in a SQL Agent job, run regularly

INSERT INTO

dbo.sys_dm_os_wait_stats
```

```
(datecapture, wait_type, wait_time_s, Pct, avg_ms_per_wait)

SELECT

datecapture = SYSDATETIMEOFFSET()

, wait_type

, wait_time_s = convert(decimal(19,1), round( wait_time_ms / 1000.0,1))

, Pct = wait_time_ms/ nullif(sum(wait_time_ms) OVER(),0)

, avg_ms_per_wait = wait_time_ms / nullif(waiting_tasks_count,0)

FROM sys.dm_os_wait_stats wt

WHERE wait_time_ms > 0

ORDER BY wait_time_s;
```

Using the metrics returned above, you can calculate the difference between always-ascending wait times and counts to determine the counts between intervals. You can customize the schedule for this data to be captured in tables, building your own internal wait stats reporting table.

The sys.dm_os_wait_stats DMV is reset and all accumulated metrics are lost upon restart of the SQL Server service, but you can also clear them manually if you desire. Understandably, this would clear the statistics for the SQL instance. Here is a sample script of how you can capture wait statistics at any interval:

```
DBCC SQLPERF ('sys.dm_os_wait_stats', CLEAR);
```

You can also view statistics for a query currently running in the DMV sys.dm_os_waiting_tasks, which contains more data than simply the wait_type; it also shows the blocking resource address in the resource_description field. This data is also available in sys.dm_exec_requests. A complete breakdown of the information that can be contained in the resource_description field and is detailed in the documentation at *https://docs.microsoft.com/sql/relational-databases/system-dynamic-management-views/ sys-dm-os-waiting-tasks-transact-sql.*

➤ **For more information on monitoring wait types with Availability Groups, see Chapter 11.**

Understanding wait resources

What if you observe a query wait occurring live, and want to figure out what data the query is actually waiting on?

SQL Server 2019 delivers some new tools exploring the archaeology involved with identifying the data that is causing wait retention. While an exhaustive look at the different wait resource types—some more cryptic than others—is best documented in Microsoft's online resources, let's review the new tools provided by SQL Server 2019.

The undocumented DBCC PAGE command (and its accompanying trace flag 3604) were used for years to review the information contained in a page, based upon a specific page number. Whether trying to see the data at the source of waits or trying to peek at corrupted pages reported by DBCC CHECKDB, the DBCC PAGE command didn't return any visible data without first enabling trace flag 3604. Now, for some cases, we have the pair of new functions `sys.dm_db_page_info` and `sys.fn_PageResCracker`. Both can be used only when the `sys.dm_exec_requests.wait_resource` value begins with PAGE. So the new tools leave out other common `wait_resource` types like KEY.

The new tools in SQL Server 2019 are preferable to using DBCC PAGE because they are fully documented and supported. They can be combined with `sys.dm_exec_requests`—the hub DMV for all things active in SQL Server—to return potentially useful information about the object in contention when PAGE blocking is present:

```
SELECT r.request_id, pi.database_id, pi.file_id, pi.page_id, pi.object_id,
pi.page_type_desc, pi.index_id, pi.page_level, rows_in_page = pi.slot_count

FROM sys.dm_exec_requests AS r

CROSS APPLY sys.fn_PageResCracker (r.page_resource) AS  prc

CROSS APPLY sys.dm_db_page_info(r.database_id, prc.file_id, prc.page_id, 'DETAILED')
AS pi;
```

At the time of this writing, you may have to resort to the old undocumented, and sometimes unstable, DBCC PAGE command to see the user data in those pages.

Wait types that you can mostly ignore

The following is a starter list of wait types that you can mostly ignore when querying the `sys.dm_os_wait_stats` DMV for aggregate wait statistics. You can append the following sample list WHERE clause.

Through your own research into your workload and in future versions of SQL Server as more wait types are added, you can grow this list so that important and actionable wait types rise to the top of your queries. A prevalence of these wait types shouldn't be a concern, they're unlikely to be generated by or negatively affect user requests.

```
WHERE

    wt.wait_type NOT LIKE '%SLEEP%' --can be safely ignored, sleeping

AND wt.wait_type NOT LIKE 'BROKER%' -- internal process

AND wt.wait_type NOT LIKE '%XTP_WAIT%' -- for memory-optimized tables
```

```
        AND wt.wait_type NOT LIKE '%SQLTRACE%' -- internal process

        AND wt.wait_type NOT LIKE 'QDS%' -- asynchronous Query Store data

        AND wt.wait_type NOT IN ( -- common benign wait types

        'CHECKPOINT_QUEUE'

        ,'CLR_AUTO_EVENT','CLR_MANUAL_EVENT' ,'CLR_SEMAPHORE'

        ,'DBMIRROR_DBM_MUTEX','DBMIRROR_EVENTS_QUEUE','DBMIRRORING_CMD'

        ,'DIRTY_PAGE_POLL'

        ,'DISPATCHER_QUEUE_SEMAPHORE'

        ,'FT_IFTS_SCHEDULER_IDLE_WAIT','FT_IFTSHC_MUTEX'

        ,'HADR_FILESTREAM_IOMGR_IOCOMPLETION'

        ,'KSOURCE_WAKEUP'

        ,'LOGMGR_QUEUE'

        ,'ONDEMAND_TASK_QUEUE'

        ,'REQUEST_FOR_DEADLOCK_SEARCH'

        ,'XE_DISPATCHER_WAIT','XE_TIMER_EVENT'

        --Ignorable HADR waits

        , 'HADR_WORK_QUEUE'

        ,'HADR_TIMER_TASK'

        ,'HADR_CLUSAPI_CALL');
```

The previous sample script and all scripts for this book are available for download at
https://MicrosoftPressStore.com/SQLServer2019InsideOut/downloads.

Wait types to be aware of

This section shouldn't be the start and end of your understanding or research into wait types.
Many of them have multiple avenues to explore in your SQL Server instance, or at the very least,
names that are misleading to the DBA considering their origin. Here are some, or groups of
some, that you should understand because they will be indicative of a condition worth investigating. Many wait types will always be present in all applications, but become problematic
when they appear in large frequency and/or with large cumulative waits. "Large" here is of
course relative to your workload and your server.

Different instance workloads will have a different profile of wait types, and just because a wait
type is at the top of the aggregate sys.dm_os_wait_stats list doesn't mean that is the main or
only performance problem with a SQL Server instance. It is likely that all SQL Server instances,

even those finely tuned, will show these wait types near the top of the aggregate waits list. You should track and trend these wait stats, perhaps using the script example in the previous section.

More important waits include the following provided in alphabetical order:

- **ASYNC_NETWORK_IO.**   This wait type is associated with the retrieval of data to a client, and the wait while the remote client receives and finally acknowledges the data received. This wait almost certainly has very little to do with network speed, network interfaces, switches, or firewalls. Any client, including your workstation or even SSMS running locally to the server, can incur small amounts of ASYNC_NETWORK_IO as data is retrieved to be processed. Transactional and snapshot replication distribution will incur ASYNC_NETWORK_IO. You will see a large amount of ASYNC_NETWORK_IO generated by reporting applications such as Tableau, SSRS, SQL Server Profiler, and Microsoft Office products. The next time a rudimentary Access database application tries to load the entire contents of the Sales.OrderLines table, you'll likely see ASYNC_NETWORK_IO.

    Reducing ASYNC_NETWORK_IO, like many of the waits we discuss in this chapter, has little to do with hardware purchases or upgrades; rather, it's more to do with poorly designed queries and applications. The solution therefore would be an application change. Try suggesting to the developers or client applications incurring large amounts of ASYNC_NETWORK_IO that they eliminate redundant queries, use server-side filtering as opposed to client-side filtering, use server-side data paging as opposed to client-side data paging, or to use client-side caching.

- **CXPACKET.**   A common and often-overreacted-to wait type, CXPACKET is a parallelism wait. In a vacuum, execution plans that are created with parallelism run faster. But at scale, with many execution plans running in parallel, the server's resources might take longer to process the requests. This wait is measured in part as CXPACKET waits.

    When the CXPACKET wait is the predominant wait type experienced over time by your SQL Server, both Maximum Degree of Parallelism (MAXDOP) and Cost Threshold for Parallelism (CTFP) settings are dials to consider turning when performance tuning. Make these changes in small, measured gestures, and don't overreact to performance problems with a small number of queries. Use the Query Store to benchmark and trend the performance of high-value and high-cost queries as you change configuration settings.

    If large queries are already a problem for performance and multiple large queries regularly run simultaneously, raising the CTFP might not solve the problem. In addition to the obvious solutions of query tuning and index changes, including the creation of column-store indexes, use MAXDOP as well to limit parallelization for very large queries.

    Until SQL Server 2016, MAXDOP was either a setting at the server-level, a setting enforced at the query level, or a setting enforced to sessions selectively via Resource Governor (more on this towards the end of this chapter in the section "Protecting important workloads by using Resource Governor"). Since SQL Server 2016, the MAXDOP setting is now available as a Database-Scoped Configuration. You can also use the MAXDOP query hint in any statement to override the database or server level MAXDOP setting.

Inside OUT

What about the new CXCONSUMER wait type?

First introduced in SQL Server 2017 CU3 (and included in SQL Server 2016 SP2), the CXCONSUMER wait type eats into the previous activity that would incur CXPACKET waits. So since 2017 CU3, and including SQL Server 2019, you'll see a mix of both of these wait types.

Before the introduction of CXCONSUMER, CXPACKET would be incurred by both threads that consume and produce data as part of an execution plan. However, the producer threads were most problematic, were most impacted by the Max Degree of Parallelism (MAXDOP) and Cost Threshold for Parallelism (CTFP), and were most affected by out-of-date statistics. So you have more control over the problematic producer threads. These are still reported by CXPACKET. The consumer threads are now reported by CXCONSUMER.

On the other hand, the consumer threads in parallelism aren't easily influenceable by query tuners, so reporting these as CXCONSUMER waits helps you focus on the more correctable waits reported by CXPACKET.

- **IO_COMPLETION.** Associated with synchronous read and write operations that are not related to row data pages, such as reading log blocks or virtual log file (VLF) information from the transaction log, or reading or writing merge join operator results, spools, and buffers to disk. It is difficult to associate this wait type with a single activity or event, but a spike in IO_COMPLETION could be an indication that these same events are now waiting on the I/O system to complete.

- **LCK_M_*.** Lock waits have to do with blocking and concurrency (or lack thereof). (Chapter 14 looks at isolation levels and concurrency.) When a request is writing and another request in READ COMMITTED or higher isolation is trying to lock that same row data, one of the 60+ different LCK_M_* wait types will be the reported wait type of the blocked request. For example, LCK_M_IS means that the thread wants to acquire an Intent Shared lock, but some other thread has it locked in an incompatible manner.

- In the aggregate, this doesn't mean you should reduce the isolation level of your transactions. Whereas READ UNCOMMITTED is not a good solution, read-committed snapshot isolation (RCSI) and snapshot isolation are good solutions; see Chapter 14 for more details.

Rather, you should optimize execution plans for efficient access, for example, by reducing scans as well as avoiding long-running multistep transactions. Also, avoid index rebuild operations without the `ONLINE` option (see earlier in this chapter for more information about "Rebuilding Indexes").

The `wait_resource` provided in `sys.dm_exec_requests`, or `resource_description` in `sys.dm_os_waiting_tasks`, each provide a map to the exact location of the lock contention inside the database. A complete breakdown of the information that can be contained in the `resource_description` field is detailed in the documentation at *https://docs.microsoft.com/sql/relational-databases/system-dynamic-management-views/ sys-dm-os-waiting-tasks-transact-sql*.

- **MEMORYCLERK_XE.**   The `MEMORYCLERK_XE` wait type could spike if you have allowed extended events session targets to consume too much memory. We discuss extended events in the next section, but you should watch out for the maximum buffer size allowed to the `ring_buffer` session target, among other in-memory targets.

- **OLEDB.**   This self-explanatory wait type describes waits associated with long-running external communication via the OLE DB provider, which is commonly used by SQL Server Integration Services (SSIS) packages, Microsoft Office applications (including querying Excel files), linked servers using the OLE DB provider, and third party tools. It could also be generated by internal commands like DBCC CHECKDB.

Inside OUT

What design changes could avoid OLEDB wait types?

For the most part, reducing OLEDB wait types is done by reducing execution time for queries executing via the OLE DB provider, or by better integrating data flows by avoiding flat files, data manipulation via Access or Excel, or the use of linked servers. For connections to non-SQL database platforms, instead of flat file extract/imports to send data, consider PolyBase to connect directly and write T-SQL queries on Oracle data sources, for example.

- **PAGELATCH_*** and **PAGEIOLATCH_*.**   These two wait types are presented together here not because they are similar in nature—they are not—but because they are often confused. To be clear, `PAGELATCH` has to do with contention over pages in memory, whereas `PAGEIOLATCH` has to do with contention over pages in the I/O system (on the drive).

CHAPTER 8

PAGELATCH_* contention deals with pages in memory, which can rise because of overuse of temporary objects in memory, potentially with rapid access to the same temporary objects. This can also be experienced when reading in data from an index in memory, or reading from a heap in memory.

A rise in PAGEIOLATCH_ could be due to performance of the storage system, remembering that the performance of drive systems does not always respond linearly to increases in activity. Aside from throwing (a lot of!) money at faster drives, a more economical solution is to modify queries and/or indexes and reduce the footprint of memory-intensive operations, especially operations involving index and table scans.

PAGEIOLATCH_* contention deals with a far more limiting and troubling performance condition: the overuse of reading from the slowest subsystem of all, the physical drives. PAGEIOLATCH_SH deals with reading data from a drive into memory so that the data can be accessed. Keep in mind that this doesn't necessarily translate to a request's rowcount, especially if index or table scans are required in the execution plan. PAGEIOLATCH_EX and _UP are waits associated with reading data from a drive into memory so that the data can be written to.

Inside OUT

How can SQL Server 2019 help alleviate high durations for the PAGELATCH_* category of wait types?

If long PAGELATCH waits are encountered in TempDB system tables, a new feature of SQL Server 2019 may improve performance. The new Memory-Optimized TempDB Metadata server option moves system tables containing tempdb metadata into non-durable memory-optimized tables, eliminating latches on tables that become "hot spots" because of rapid inserts and updates. For more on this topic, see Chapter 3.

Also new in SQL Server 2019 is an index option to specific address one of the common causes of PAGELATCH_EX waits. These can be related to inserts that are happening rapidly and/or page splits related to inserts. The index option OPTIMIZE_FOR_ SEQUENTIAL_KEY specifically for tables with clustered keys on IDENTITY or SEQUENCE that have high write volumes, creating "hot spots" for sequential inserts. If you observe high amounts of PAGELATCH_EX, it may be because of contention for individual pages in memory due to sequential inserts. This new index option in SQL Server 2019 improves performance for tables that have a sequential key.

- **RESOURCE_SEMAPHORE.** This wait type is accumulated when a request is waiting on memory to be allocated before it can start. Although this could be an indication of memory pressure caused by insufficient memory available to the SQL Server instance, it is more likely caused by poor query design and poor indexing, resulting in inefficient execution plans. Aside from throwing money at more system memory, a more economical solution is to tune queries and reduce the footprint of memory-intensive operations.

- **SOS_SCHEDULER_YIELD.**   Another flavor of CPU pressure, and in some ways the opposite of the CXPACKET wait type, is the SOS_SCHEDULER_YIELD wait type. The SOS_SCHEDULER_YIELD is an indicator of CPU pressure, indicating that SQL Server had to share time or "yield" to other CPU tasks, which can be normal and expected on busy servers. Whereas CXPACKET is the SQL Server complaining about too many threads in parallel, the SOS_SCHEDULER_YIELD is the acknowledgement that there were more runnable tasks for the available threads. In either case, first take a strategy of reducing CPU-intensive queries and rescheduling or optimizing CPU-intense maintenance operations. This is more economical than simply adding CPU capacity.

- **WAIT_XTP_RECOVERY.**   This wait type can occur when a database with memory-optimized tables is in recovery at startup and is expected. As with all wait_types on performance-sensitive production SQL Server instances, baseline and measure it, but be aware this is not usually a sign of any problem.

- **WRITELOG.**   The WRITELOG wait type is likely to appear on any SQL Server instance, including availability group primary and secondary replicas, when there is heavy write activity. The WRITELOG wait is time spent flushing the transaction log to a drive and is due to physical I/O subsystem performance. On systems with heavy writes, this wait type is expected.

  You could consider re-creating the heavy-write tables as memory optimized tables to increase the performance of writes. Memory-optimized tables optionally allow for delayed durability, which would resolving a bottleneck writing to the transaction log by using a memory buffer. For more information, see Chapter 14.

- **XE_FILE_TARGET_TVF** and **XE_LIVE_TARGET_TVF.**   These waits are associated with writing extended events sessions to their targets. A sudden spike in these waits would indicate that too much is being captured by an extended events session. Usually these aren't a problem, because the asynchronous nature of extended events has a much lower impact than traces.

Monitoring with the SQL Assessment API

The SQL Assessment API is a code-delivered method for programmatically evaluating SQL instance and database configuration. First introduced to SQL Server Management Objects (SMO) and the SqlServer PowerShell module in July 2019, the calls to the API can be used to initially evaluate alignment with best practices and then scheduled to regular monitor for variance.

You can use this new API to assess SQL Servers starting with version 11.0 (SQL Server 2012), for SQL Server on Windows and Linux.

The assessment is performed by comparing SQL Server configuration to rules, stored as JSON files, and a standard array of rules has been provided by Microsoft. Review the default JSON configuration file here: *https://github.com/microsoft/sql-server-samples/blob/master/samples/ manage/sql-assessment-api/config.json*.

Use this standard JSON file as a template to assess your own best practices if you like. The assessment configuration files are organized into **probes** and **checks**.

- Probes usually contain a TSQL query, for example, to return data from dynamic management objects (DMOs) that have been reviewed earlier in this chapter. You can also write probes against your own user tables, to query for code-driven states, or statuses that can be provided by applications, ETL packages, or custom error-handling.

- Checks are comparisons for evaluating desired values against the values returned by probes. They include logical conditions and thresholds. Here, like with any SQL Server monitoring tool, you may want to change numeric thresholds to suit your SQL environment.

Getting Started with the SQL Assessment API

In order to begin evaluating default or custom rules against your SQL Server, you must verify the presence of .NET Framework 4.0, and the latest versions of SMO and the SqlServer Power-Shell module.

First off, if you want to try this out on a server with an installation of SQL Server 2019 and the latest PowerShell SqlServer module, this will work:

```
Get-SqlInstance -ServerInstance .  |  Invoke-SqlAssessment  |  Out-GridView
```

If it doesn't work, or if you want to use a remote machine to run the SqlAssessment, follow the next steps.

Inside OUT

What do you need to know about SMO?

SMO is a framework for developers of third-party applications to interface with SQL Server programmatically, bypassing T-SQL or PowerShell commands. SMO is necessary for third-party enterprise backup software to talk to SQL Server instances and issue commands to write backups to virtual file locations, for example. While custom development of SMO applications is far out of scope for this book, the use of SMO for the purposes

> of interacting with the new SQL Assessment API is relatively easy and should not require assistance from developers.
>
> SMO used to be installed via the SQL Feature Pack, in the SharedManagementObjects. msi file. Starting with SQL Server 2017, the NuGet package is how the binaries are distributed. More details below.

1. For servers with installations of SQL Server 2019, SMO should already be present on the Windows Server. For your local administration machine or a centralized server from which you'll monitor your SQL Server environment, you'll need to install SMO and the latest PowerShell SqlServer module.

    While a developer might use Visual Studio's Package Manager, you do not need to install Visual Studio in order to install the SMO NuGet package. Instead, you can use the cross-platform nuget.exe command-line utility. You can also install and use the command line interface tool dotnet.exe if desired, there is more information about the options here: *https://docs.microsoft.com/nuget/install-nuget-client-tools*.

    After downloading nuget.exe, open a Prompt with Administrator permissions and navigate to the folder you saved the nuget.exe. The command to download and install SMO via nuget.exe is simple and should take just seconds to complete:

    ```
    nuget install Microsoft.SqlServer.SqlManagementObjects
    ```

    You can optionally specify an installation location for the installation:

    ```
    nuget install Microsoft.SqlServer.SqlManagementObjects -OutputDirectory
    "c:\nuget\packages"
    ```

    SMO is maintained and distributed via a NuGet package here: *https://nuget.org/packages/Microsoft.SqlServer.SqlManagementObjects*.

    In the installation directory, you'll find two new folders. These version numbers are the latest at the time of writing and will likely be higher for you in the future.

    - System.Data.SqlClient.4.6.0

    - Microsoft.SqlServer.SqlManagementObjects.150.18147.0

2. With SMO in place, the second step to using the SQL Assessment API is to install the SqlServer PowerShell module. If you don't already have the latest SqlServer PowerShell module installed, launch a PowerShell console as an Administrator, launch Visual Studio Code as an administrator, or use your favorite PowerShell scripting environment. The following command will download and install the latest version, even if you have a previous version installed:

    ```
    Install-Module -Name SqlServer -AllowClobber -Force
    ```

CHAPTER 8

The `AllowClobber` parameter instructs `Install-Module` to overwrite cmdlet aliases already in place. Without `AllowClobber`, the installation will fail if it finds that the new module contains commands with the same name as existing commands.

➤ **For more information on installing and using the SqlServer PowerShell module, including how to install without Internet connectivity, see Chapter 9.**

3. With SMO and the SqlServer PowerShell module installed, you can then assess SQL Server health against the default rule set with a PowerShell command, for example as we demonstrated at the start of this section:

```
Get-SqlInstance -ServerInstance . | Invoke-SqlAssessment | Out-GridView
```

Here, the period is shorthand for localhost, so this command would execute an assessment against the API of the local default instance of SQL Server. To run the assessment against a remote SQL Server instance using Windows Authentication:

```
Get-SqlInstance -ServerInstance servername | Invoke-SqlAssessment | `
Out-GridView
```

Or, for a named instance:

```
Get-SqlInstance -ServerInstance servername\instancename | `
Invoke-SqlAssessment | Out-GridView
```

The common Out-GridView cmdlet will pop open a new window to make reviewing multiple findings easier than reading what could be many pages of findings in a PowerShell console. You can output the data any way you like, using common PowerShell cmdlets.

NOTE

For more sample syntax on assessing SQL Server instances via the Invoke-SqlAssessment cmdlet, visit *https://docs.microsoft.com/powershell/module/sqlserver/invoke-sqlassessm ent?view=sqlserver-ps*.

The output of the `Invoke-SqlAssessment` includes a helpful link to Microsoft documentation on any finding, severity, the name of the check that resulted in a finding, an id for the check for more granular review, and a helpful message. Again, all of this is pre-provided by Microsoft's default ruleset, from which you can base your own custom checks and probes, with custom severity and messages.

Review the default JSON configuration file here: *https://github.com/microsoft/sql-server-samples/blob/master/samples/manage/sql-assessment-api/config.json*. To use your own customized configuration file, use the -`Configuration` parameter:

```
Get-SqlInstance -ServerInstance servername | Invoke-SqlAssessment `
-Configuration "C:\toolbox\sqlassessment_api_config.json" | Out-GridView
```

Utilizing extended events

Extended events are the best way to "look live" at SQL Server activity, replacing deprecated traces. Even though the default extended event sessions are not yet complete replacements for the default system trace (we give an example a bit later), consider extended events for all new activity related to troubleshooting and diagnostic data collection. We understand that the messaging around extended events has been the replacement for traces for nearly a decade. The Xevent UI in SSMS is easier than ever to use, so if you haven't switched to using extended events to do what you used to use traces for, the time is now!

We'll assume that you've not had a lot of experience with creating your own extended events sessions. Let's become familiar with some of the most basic terminology for extended events:

- **Sessions.** A set of data collection that can be started and stopped; the new equivalent of a "trace."

- **Events.** Selected from an event library, events are what you remember "tracing" with SQL Server Profiler. These are predetermined, detectable operations during runtime. Events you'll most commonly want to look for include `sql_statement_completed` and `sql_batch_completed`, for example, for catching an application's T-SQL code.

  Examples: `sql_batch_starting`, `sql_statement_completed`, `login`, `error_reported`, `sort_warning`, `table_scan`

- **Actions.** These are the headers of the columns of data you'll see in the extended events data describing an event, such as when the event happened, who and what called the event, its duration, the number of writes and reads, CPU time, and so on. So, in this way, actions are additional data captured when an event is recorded. In SSMS, Global Fields is the name for actions, which allow additional information to be captured for any event, for example, database_name or database_id.

  Examples: `sql_text`, `batch_text`, `timestamp`, `session_id`, `client_hostname`

- **Predicates.** These are filter conditions created on actions so that you can limit the data you capture. You can filter on any action or field that is returned by an event you have added to the session.

  Examples: `database_id > 4`, `database_name = 'WideWorldImporters'`, `is_system = 0`

CHAPTER 8

- **Targets.**   This is where the data should be sent. You can always watch detailed and "live" extended events data captured asynchronously in memory for any session. A session, however, can also have multiple targets, such as a ring_buffer (an in-memory buffer), an event_file (a .xel file on the server), or a histogram (an in-memory counter with grouping by actions). A session can have only one of each target. We dive into the different targets in the "Understanding the variety of extended events targets" section later in this chapter.

SQL Server installs with three extended events sessions ready to view: two that start by default, system_health and telemetry_xevents, and another that starts when needed, AlwaysOn_ Health. These sessions provide a basic coverage for system health, though they are not an exact replacement for the system default trace. Do not stop or delete these sessions, which should start automatically.

NOTE

Should the system_health, telemetry_xevents, and/or AlwaysOn_Health sessions be accidentally dropped from the server, you can find the scripts to re-create them for your instance in this file: *instancepath*\MSSQL\Install\u_tables.sql. For example: E:\Program Files\Microsoft SQL Server\MSSQL15.SQL2K19\MSSQL\Install\u_tables.sql.

You'll see the well-documented definitions of the two Xevent sessions toward the bottom of the file. If you'd just like to see the script that created the definitions for the built-in extended events sessions, you can script them via SSMS by right-clicking the session, and then, on the shortcut menu, point to Script Session As, and then click Create To and a destination for the script.

NOTE

Used to using SQL Server Profiler? The Xevent Profiler delivers an improved "tracing" experience that mimics the legacy SQL Profiler trace templates. Extended events sessions provide a modern, asynchronous, and far more versatile replacement for SQL Server traces, which are, in fact, deprecated. For troubleshooting, debugging, performance tuning, and event gathering, extended events provides a faster and more configurable solution than traces.

Viewing extended events data

The Xevent Profiler in SSMS is the perfect place to start viewing extended events data. Since SQL Server Management Studio 17.3, the Xevent Profiler tool is built in. You'll find the Xevent Profiler in the SSMS Object Explorer window, beneath the SQL Server Agent menu.

See Figure 8-1 for an example of the TSQL quick session.

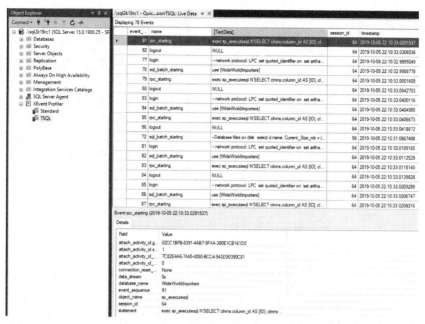

Figure 8-1   The Xevent Profiler T-SQL live events display in SQL Server Management Studio, similar to the deprecated Profiler T-SQL trace template.

➤ For more information on the Xevent Profiler QuickSessions, see Chapter 1.

NOTE

Though not a full replacement for SSMS, Azure Data Studio also has capabilities for managing Extended Event sessions, via the SQL Server Profiler extension that can be quickly downloaded and added. Search for the "SQL Server Profiler" extension or add the "Admin Pack for SQL Server" extension via the Extensions Marketplace in Azure Data Studio.

An Extended Events session can generate simultaneous output to multiple destinations, only one of which closely resembles the .trc files of old.

You can create other targets for a session on the Data Storage page of the New Session dialog box in SSMS. To view data collected by the target, expand the session, right-click the package, and then, on the shortcut menu, click View Target Data, as demonstrated in Figure 8-2.

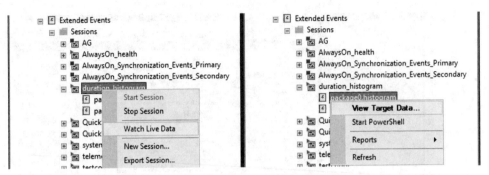

Figure 8-2   A side-by-side look at the difference between Watch Live Data on an extended events session and View Target Data on an extended events session target.

When viewing target data, you can right-click to re-sort, copy the data to clipboard, and export most of the target data to .csv files for analysis in other software.

Unlike Watch Live Data, View Target Data does not refresh automatically, though for some targets you can configure SSMS to poll the target automatically, by right-clicking the View Target Data window and then clicking Refresh Interval in the context menu and choosing one of a few refresh intervals between 5 seconds and 1 hour.

> ### NOTE
> Currently, there is no built-in way in SQL Server Management Studio to write extended events session data directly to a SQL Server table, but the Watch Live Data interface provides easy point-and-click analysis, grouping, and filtering of live session data. We'll review the target types next. Take some time to explore the other available target types; they can easily and quickly reproduce your analysis of trace data written to SQL Server tables.

The section that follows presents a breakdown of the possible targets, many of which do some of the serious heavy lifting that you might have done previously by writing or exporting SQL trace data to a table and then performing your own aggregations, counts, or data analysis. Remember that you don't need to pick just one target type to collect data for your session.

Understanding the variety of extended events targets

As we said earlier, you can always watch detailed and "live" extended events data captured asynchronously in memory for any session through SSMS by right-clicking a session and then selecting Watch Live Data. You'll see asynchronously delivered detailed data, and you can customize the columns you see, apply filters on the data, and even create groups and on-the-fly aggregations, all by right-clicking inside the Live Data window.

The Live Data window, however, isn't a target. The data isn't saved anywhere outside of the SSMS window, and you can't look back at data you missed before launching Watch Live Data. You can create a session without a target, and Watch Live Data is all you'll get, but often that is all you need for a quick observation.

Here is a summary of the extended event targets available to be created. Remember you can create more than one target per Session.

- **Event File target** (.xel), which writes the event data to a physical file on a drive asynchronously. You can then open and analyze it later, much like deprecated trace files, or merge it with other .xel files to assist analysis (in SSMS, click the File menu, click Open, and then click Merge Extended Events Files).

  When you view the event file data in SSMS by right-clicking the event file and selecting View Target Data, the data does not refresh live. Data continues to be written to the file behind the scenes while the session is running, so to view the latest data, close the .xel file and open it again.

  By default, .xel files are written to the *instancepath*/MSSQL/Log folder.

- **Histogram target,** which counts the number of times an event has occurred and bucketizes an action, storing the data in memory. For example, you can capture a histogram of the `sql_statement_completed` broken down by the number of observed events by client-hostname action, or by the duration field.

  When configuring the histogram type target, you will be required to choose a number of buckets (or slots, in the T-SQL syntax) that is greater than the number of unique values you expect for the action or field. If you're bucketizing by a numeric value such as duration, be sure to provide a number of buckets larger than the largest duration you could capture over time. If the histogram runs out of buckets for new values for your action or field, it will not capture data for them.

  Note that you can provide any number of histogram buckets, but the histogram target will round the number up to the nearest power of 2. Thus, if you provide a value of 10 buckets, you'll see 16 buckets.

- **Pair matching or Pairing target**, which is used to match events, such as the start and end of a SQL Server batch execution, and find occasions when an event in a pair occurs without the other, such as `sql_statement_starting` and `sql_statement_completed`. Select a start and an end from the list of actions you've selected.

- **Ring_buffer** target provides a fast, in-memory First-In, First-Out (FIFO) asynchronous memory buffer to collect rapidly occurring events. Stored in a memory buffer, the data is never written to a drive, allowing for robust data collection without performance overhead. The customizable dataset is provided in XML format and must be queried. Because this data is in-memory, you should be careful how high you configure the Maximum Buffer Memory size, and never set the size to 0 (unlimited).

- Finally, you can use the **Service Broker** target to send messages to a target service of a customizable message type.

Although all of the aforementioned targets are high-performing asynchronous targets, there are two synchronous targets: ETW and event counter. Be aware when using synchronous targets that the resource demand of synchronous targets might be more noticeable. Following is a brief description of each asynchronous target:

- **ETW (Event Tracing for Windows) target** is used to gather SQL Server data for later combination to Windows event log data for troubleshooting and debugging Windows applications.

- **Event counter target** simply counts the number of events in an extended events session. You use this to provide data for trending and later aggregate analysis. The resulting dataset has one row per event with a count. This data is stored in memory, so although it's synchronous, you shouldn't expect any noticeable performance impact.

Further, there are two session options that can affect the performance impact of an Extended Event session. The defaults are fairly safe and are unlikely to result in noticeable performance overhead, and so don't typically need to be changed. You may want to change them if the event you're trying to observe is rare, temporary, and outweighs your performance overhead concerns.

- **EVENT_RETENTION_MODE** by determines whether, under pressure, the Extended Event session can miss a captured event. By default, the ALLOW_SINGLE_EVENT_LOSS option here can let target(s) miss a single event when memory buffers used to stream the data to the target(s) are full. You may choose to specify ALLOW_MULTIPLE_EVENT_LOSS, which would further minimize the potential for performance impact on the monitored server, by allowing more events to be missed.

  Or, you can specify NO_EVENT_LOSS, which does not allow events to be missed, even if memory buffers are full. All events are retained and presented to the target. While not the same as using a synchronous target, it can result in the same effect: performance of the SQL Server could suffer under the weight of the Extended Event session. Using this option is not recommended.

- **MAX_DISPATCH_LATENCY** determines the upper limit to when events are sent from the memory buffer to the target. By default, events are buffered in memory for up to 30 seconds before being sent to the targets. You could change this value to 1 to force data out of memory buffers faster, reducing the benefit of the memory buffers. A value of INFINITE or 0 would allow for events to be retained until memory buffers are full or until the session closes.

Let's look at querying extended events session data in T-SQL with a couple of practical common examples.

Using extended events to capture deadlocks

We've talked about viewing data in SSMS, so let's review querying extended events data via T-SQL. Let's query one of the default extended events sessions, system_health, for deadlocks. Back in the dark ages, before SQL Server 2008, it was not possible to see a deadlock. You had to see it coming—to turn on a trace flag prior to the deadlock.

With the system_health extended events session, a recent history of event data is captured, included deadlock graphs. This data is captured to both a ring_buffer target with a rolling 4-MB buffer and also to an .xel file with a total of 20 MB in rollover files. Either target will contain the most recent occurrences of the xml_deadlock_report event, and though the ring_buffer is faster to read from, the .xel file by default contains more history. Further, the .xel file isn't subject to the limitations of the 4-MB ring_buffer target, or the same potential for missed rows. The T-SQL code sample that follows demonstrates the retrieval of the .xel file target as XML:

```
DECLARE @XELFile nvarchar(256), @XELFiles nvarchar(256)

        , @XELPath nvarchar(256);

--Get the folder path where the system_health .xel files are

SELECT        @XELFile =        CAST(t.target_data as XML)

              .value('EventFileTarget[1]/File[1]/@name', 'NVARCHAR(256)')
FROM sys.dm_xe_session_targets t

     INNER JOIN sys.dm_xe_sessions s

     ON s.address = t.event_session_address
WHERE s.name = 'system_health' AND t.target_name = 'event_file';

--Provide wildcard path search for all currently retained .xel files

SELECT @XELPath =

     LEFT(@XELFile, Len(@XELFile)-CHARINDEX('\',REVERSE(@XELFile)))

SELECT @XELFiles = @XELPath + '\system_health_*.xel';

--Query the .xel files for deadlock reports

SELECT DeadlockGraph = CAST(event_data AS XML)
```

```
, DeadlockID = Row_Number() OVER(ORDER BY file_name, file_offset)
FROM sys.fn_xe_file_target_read_file(@XELFiles, null, null, null) AS F
WHERE event_data like '<event name="xml_deadlock_report%';
```

Inside OUT

How can you test your deadlock capture strategy?

Here's a quick, two connection script to produce a deadlock. Open two query connections in SSMS to a testing database. You should then be able to use the default system_health Extended Events session to view the details of the deadlock. Run this script in connection 1:

```
CREATE TABLE dbo.dead (col1 INT);

INSERT INTO dbo.dead SELECT 1;

CREATE TABLE dbo.lock (col1 INT);

INSERT INTO dbo.lock SELECT 1;

BEGIN TRAN t1;

UPDATE dbo.dead WITH (TABLOCK) SET col1 = 2;
```

Run this script in connection 2:

```
BEGIN TRAN t2;

UPDATE dbo.lock WITH (TABLOCK) SET col1 = 3;

UPDATE dbo.dead WITH (TABLOCK) SET col1 = 3;

COMMIT TRAN t2;
```

Now, back in connection 1:

```
UPDATE dbo.lock WITH (TABLOCK) SET col1 = 4;

COMMIT TRAN t1;
```

Within a moment, the session in connection 2 is closed as the victim of a deadlock.

This example returns one row per captured xml_deadlock_report event and includes an XML document, which in SSMS Grid results will appear to be a blue hyperlink. Click the hyperlink to open the XML document, which will contain the complete detail of all elements of the deadlock. If you'd like to see a Deadlock Graph, save this file as an .xdl file, and then open it in SSMS.

You can download the previous script and other accompanying sample scripts for this book from *https://MicrosoftPressStore.com/SQLServer2019InsideOut/downloads*.

Using extended events to detect autogrowth events

The SQL Server default trace captures historical database data and log file autogrowth events, but the default extended events sessions shipped with SQL Server do not. The extended events that capture autogrowth events are database_file_size_change and databases_log_file_size_changed. Both events capture autogrowths and manual file growths run by ALTER DATABASE ... MODIFY FILE statements, and include an event field called is_automatic to differentiate. Additionally, you can identify the query statement sql_text that prompted the autogrowth event.

The following is a sample T-SQL script to create a startup session that captures autogrowth events to an .xel event file and also a histogram target that counts the number of autogrowth instances per database:

```
CREATE EVENT SESSION [autogrowths] ON SERVER

ADD EVENT sqlserver.database_file_size_change(

    ACTION(package0.collect_system_time,sqlserver.database_id

,sqlserver.database_name,sqlserver.sql_text)),

ADD EVENT sqlserver.databases_log_file_size_changed(

    ACTION(package0.collect_system_time,sqlserver.database_id

,sqlserver.database_name,sqlserver.sql_text))

ADD TARGET package0.event_file(

--.xel file target

SET filename=N'F:\DATA\autogrowths.xel'),

ADD TARGET package0.histogram(

--Histogram target, counting events per database_name

SET filtering_event_name=N'sqlserver.database_file_size_change'
```

```
,source=N'database_name',source_type=(0))

--Start session at server startup

WITH (STARTUP_STATE=ON);

GO

--Start the session now

ALTER EVENT SESSION [autogrowths]

ON SERVER STATE = START;
```

See information earlier in this chapter in the section "Understanding and finding autogrowth events" for more information and how to prevent autogrowth events.

Using extended events to detect page splits

As we discussed earlier in this chapter, detecting page splits can be useful. You might choose to monitor page_splits when load testing a table design with its intended workload or when finding insert statements that cause the most fragmentation.

The following sample T-SQL script creates a startup session that captures autogrowth events to an .xel event file and also a histogram target that counts the number of page_splits per database:

```
CREATE EVENT SESSION [page_splits] ON SERVER

ADD EVENT sqlserver.page_split(

    ACTION(sqlserver.database_name,sqlserver.sql_text))

ADD TARGET package0.event_file(

SET filename=N'page_splits',max_file_size=(100)),

ADD TARGET package0.histogram(

SET filtering_event_name=N'sqlserver.page_split'

,source=N'database_id',source_type=(0))

--Start session at server startup

WITH (STARTUP_STATE=ON);

GO

--Start the session now

    ALTER EVENT SESSION [page_splits]ON SERVER STATE = START;
```

See information earlier in this chapter in the section "Tracking Page Splits" for more information and how to prevent page splits.

Securing extended events

Consider extended events not only an administrative tool, but a diagnostic tool for developers as well. Given knowledge of your own data classification and regulatory requirements, you should consider granting the necessary permissions to developers, even if temporarily.

There are certain sensitive events that you cannot capture with a trace or extended event session; for example, the T-SQL statement CREATE LOGIN for a SQL-authenticated login.

To access extended events in SQL Server, a developer needs the ALTER ANY EVENT SESSION permission. This grants that person access to create extended events sessions by using T-SQL commands, but it will not grant access to view server metadata in the New Extended Events Session Wizard in SSMS. For that, the person needs one further commonly granted developer permission, VIEW SERVER STATE.

In Azure SQL Database, extended events have the same capability, but for developers to view extended events sessions, you must grant them an ownership-level permission CONTROL DATABASE. However, we do not recommend this for developers or non-administrators in production environments.

➤ For more about object permissions, see Chapter 12: "Administering security and permissions."

Capturing performance metrics with DMOs and Data Collectors

The Windows Performance Monitor (perfmon.exe) application has been used for years by server administrators to visually track and collect performance of server resources, application memory usage, disk response times, and so on. In addition to the live Performance Monitor graph, you can also configure Data Collector Sets in Performance Monitor to gather the same metrics over time.

SQL Server has a large number of metrics made visible through DMV's as well. Although we have neither the scope nor space to investigate and explain every performance metric available to you, or even every one that is useful. In this section we will review the tools and cover a sampling important performance metrics.

These metrics exist at the operating system or instance level, so for the scope of this chapter we are not reviewing granular data for individual databases, workloads, or queries; however, identifying performance with isolated workloads in near-production systems is possible. Like aggregate wait statistics, there is significant value in trending these Performance Monitor metrics on server workloads, monitoring peak behavior metrics, and for immediate troubleshooting and problem diagnosis.

Querying performance metrics by using DMVs

Beyond the Windows Performance Monitor or Linux metrics, we've already seen in this chapter a DMV that exposes most of the performance metrics within SQL Server, `sys.dm_os_performance_counters`. It behaves the same in Windows and Linux thanks to the magic of the SQL Platform Abstraction Layer (SQLPAL), which helps SQL Server look and act much the same way on both Windows and Linux.

There are some advantages to this DMV in that you can combine it with other DMVs that report on system resource activity (check out `sys.dm_os_sys_info`, for example), and you can fine-tune the query for ease of monitoring and custom data collecting. However, `sys.dm_os_ performance_counters` does not currently have access to metrics outside of the SQL Server instance categories, even the most basic operating system metrics such as "% Processor Time."

> **NOTE**
> The dynamic management view `sys.dm_os_performance_counters` behaves the same and delivers identical output on Windows and Linux.

This following code sample uses `sys.dm_os_performance_counters` to return the server total memory, the instance's current target server memory, total server memory, and page life expectancy:

```
SELECT Time_Observed = SYSDATETIMEOFFSET()

, OS_Memory_GB = MAX(convert(decimal(19,3), os.physical_memory_kb/1024./1024.))

, OS_Available_Memory_GB = max(convert(decimal(19,3),
sm.available_physical_memory_kb/1024./1024.))

, SQL_Target_Server_Mem_GB = max(CASE counter_name

WHEN 'Target Server Memory (KB)' THEN convert(decimal(19,3), cntr_value/1024./1024.)

END)

, SQL_Total_Server_Mem_GB = max(CASE counter_name

WHEN 'Total Server Memory (KB)' THEN convert(decimal(19,3), cntr_value/1024./1024.)

END)

, PLE_s = MAX(CASE counter_name WHEN 'Page life expectancy' THEN cntr_value END)

FROM sys.dm_os_performance_counters as pc
```

```
CROSS APPLY sys.dm_os_sys_info as os

CROSS APPLY sys.dm_os_sys_memory as sm;
```

NOTE

In servers with multiple SQL Server instances, `sys.dm_os_performance_counters` displays only metrics for the instance on which it is run. You cannot access performance metrics for other instances on the same server via this DMV.

Some queries against `sys.dm_os_performance_counters` are not as straightforward. As an example, although Performance Monitor returns Buffer Cache Hit Ratio as a single value, querying this same memory metric via the DMV requires creating the ratio from two metrics. This code sample divides two metrics to provide the Buffer Cache Hit Ratio:

```
SELECT Time_Observed = SYSDATETIMEOFFSET(),

Buffer_Cache_Hit_Ratio = convert(int, 100 *

(SELECT cntr_value = convert(decimal (9,1), cntr_value)

FROM sys.dm_os_performance_counters as pc

WHERE pc.COUNTER_NAME = 'Buffer cache hit ratio'

AND pc.OBJECT_NAME like '%:Buffer Manager%')

/

(SELECT cntr_value = convert(decimal (9,1), cntr_value)

FROM sys.dm_os_performance_counters as pc

WHERE pc.COUNTER_NAME = 'Buffer cache hit ratio base'

AND pc.OBJECT_NAME like '%:Buffer Manager%'));
```

Finally, some counters returned by `sys.dm_os_performance_counters` are continually incrementing integers. Let's return to our earlier example of finding page splits where we demonstrated how to find the accumulating value. The `counter_name` "Page Splits/sec" is misleading when accessed via the DMV, because it is an incrementing number. To calculate the rate of page splits per second, we need two samples. This strategy is appropriate only for single-value counters for the entire server or instance. For counters that return one value per database, you would need a temporary table in order to calculate the rate for each database between the two samples. You could also capture these values to a table at regular intervals to enable reporting over time.

```
DECLARE @page_splits_Start_ms bigint, @page_splits_Start bigint

, @page_splits_End_ms bigint, @page_splits_End bigint;

SELECT @page_splits_Start_ms = ms_ticks
```

```
, @page_splits_Start = cntr_value

FROM sys.dm_os_sys_info CROSS APPLY

sys.dm_os_performance_counters

WHERE counter_name ='Page Splits/sec'

AND object_name LIKE '%SQL%Access Methods%'; --Find the object that contains page splits

WAITFOR DELAY '00:00:05'; --Duration between samples 5s

SELECT @page_splits_End_ms = MAX(ms_ticks),

@page_splits_End = MAX(cntr_value)

FROM sys.dm_os_sys_info CROSS APPLY

sys.dm_os_performance_counters

WHERE counter_name ='Page Splits/sec'

AND object_name LIKE '%SQL%Access Methods%'; --Find the object that contains page splits

SELECT Time_Observed = SYSDATETIMEOFFSET(),

Page_Splits_per_s = convert(decimal(19,3),

(@page_splits_End - @page_splits_Start)*1.

/ NULLIF(@page_splits_End_ms - @page_splits_Start_ms,0));
```

You can gain access to some OS metrics via the DMV `sys.dm_os_ring_buffers`, including metrics on CPU utilization and memory. This DMV returns thousands of XML documents, generated every second, loaded with information on SQL exceptions, memory, schedulers, connectivity, and more. It is worth noting that the `sys.dm_os_ring_buffers` DMV is one of several Operating System-level views that are documented but not supported. More information here: *https://docs.microsoft.com/sql/relational-databases/system-dynamic-management-views/ sql-server-operating-system-related-dynamic-management-views-transact-sql*.

In the code sample that follows, we pull the SQL Server instance's CPU utilization and the server idle CPU percentage for the past few hours. The remaining CPU percentage can be chalked up to other applications or services running on the server, including other SQL Server instances

```
SELECT  [Event_Time] = DATEADD(ms, -1 * (si.cpu_ticks / (si.cpu_ticks/si.ms_ticks) –

x.[timestamp]), SYSDATETIMEOFFSET())

, CPU_SQL_pct = bufferxml.value('(./Record/SchedulerMonitorEvent

/SystemHealth/ProcessUtilization)[1]', 'int')

, CPU_Idle_pct = bufferxml.value('(./Record/SchedulerMonitorEvent

/SystemHealth/SystemIdle)[1]', 'int')
```

```
FROM (SELECT timestamp, CONVERT(xml, record) AS bufferxml

    FROM sys.dm_os_ring_buffers

    WHERE ring_buffer_type = N'RING_BUFFER_SCHEDULER_MONITOR') AS x

CROSS APPLY sys.dm_os_sys_info AS si

ORDER BY [Event_Time] desc;
```

Now you should have a grasp on using the most DMV's for gathering performance metrics to capture various types of data streams coming out of SQL Server.

Inside OUT

Does the ring buffer incur overhead with all this data it is capturing to memory?

There is some background overhead for `ring_buffer` data collection, but compared to other data collection methods, it is far more efficient. SQL Server instances always have this diagnostic activity present, constantly and by design, so the `ring_buffer` won't be at fault for sudden or even gradual performance degradation.

Only appropriate on resource-limited servers and/or instances with extremely high frequency transaction activity, it's possible that you could turn off the `ring_buffer` by using trace flags. This can result in a small performance gain, but you should test and measure it against the loss of diagnostic data on which your own administrative queries or third-party products rely. For more information on using trace flags to turn off ring buffer data collection, visit *https://support.microsoft.com/help/920093/ tuning-options-for-sql-server-when-running-in-high-performance-workloa.*

Capturing performance metrics by using Performance Monitor

To get a complete and graphical picture of server resource utilization, using a server resource tool is necessary. Performance Monitor is more than just a pretty graph, it is a suite of data collection tools that can persist outside of your user profile.

You can configure the live Performance Monitor graph, available in the Monitoring Tools folder, to show a live picture of server performance. To do so, right-click the (mostly empty) grid to access properties, add counters, clear the graph, and so on. In the Properties dialog box, under General, you can configure the sample rate and duration of the graph. You can display up to 1,000 sample points on the graph live. This can be 1,000 one-second sample points for a total of 16 minutes and 40 seconds, or more time if you continue to decrease the sample frequency. For example, you can display 5,000 five-second sample points for more than 83 minutes of duration in the graph.

Data Collectors operate a little differently from the Performance Monitor main graphical window, and don't require you to keep a Windows session open on the Windows Server to capture data. To view data collected by Data Collectors, stop the data collector and restart it. In the Reports folder, in the User Defined folder, you'll see a new report that contains the graph that the Data Collector created. Figure 8-3 shows that more than 15 days of data performance was collected in the Data Collector, which we're viewing in the Memory folder, selecting the most recent report that was generated when we stopped the Memory Data Collector Set.

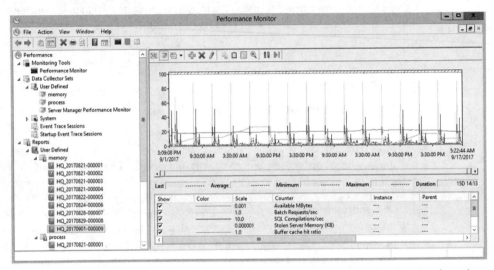

Figure 8-3   The Windows Performance Monitor Application. Instead of showing live data from the Monitoring Tools-Performance Monitor screen, we're showing 15 days' worth of data recorded by a User Defined Data Collector Set, which generated a User Defined Report.

Monitoring key performance metrics

Here are some Performance Monitor metrics to take a look at when gauging the health and performance of your SQL Server. Although we don't have the space in this book to provide a deep dive into each metric, its causes, and indicators, you should take time to investigate and research metrics that appear out of line with the guidelines provided here.

We don't provide many hard numbers in this section; for example, "Metric X should always be lower than Y." You should trend, measure metrics at peak activity, and investigate how metrics respond to server, query, or configuration changes. What might be normal for an instance with a read-heavy workload might be problematic for an instance with a high-volume write workload, and vice versa.

Let's review common performance monitoring metrics, including where to find them in Windows Performance Monitor and in SQL Server dynamic management objects if available. When listed below via the DMV, the metrics are available in Window and Linux. When not available via DMV's, you can find these same Operating System-level metrics in Linux using tools detailed in the next section, "Monitoring key performance metrics in Linux".

Average Disk seconds per Read or Write

Performance Monitor: PhysicalDisk:Avg. Disk sec/Read and PhysicalDisk:Avg. Disk sec/Write

DMV: Not Available

View this metric on each volume. The "_Total" metric doesn't have any value here; you should look at individual volumes in which SQL Server files are present. This metric has the clearest guidance of any with respect to what is acceptable or not for a server. Try to measure this value during your busiest workload and also during backups. You want to see the average disk seconds per read and write operation (considering that a single query could have thousands or millions of operations) below 20 ms, or .02 seconds. Below 10 ms is optimal and very achievable with modern storage systems. (This is the rare case for which we actually have hard and fast numbers specified by Microsoft to rely on. For more information, visit: *https://social.technet.microsoft.com/wiki/contents/articles/3214.monitoring-disk-usage.aspx.*)

Seeing this value spike to very high values (such as .1 second or 100 ms) isn't a major cause for concern, but if you see these metrics sustaining an average higher than .02 seconds during peak activity, this is a fairly clear indication that the physical I/O subsystem is being stressed beyond its capacity to keep up. Low, healthy measurements for this number don't provide any insight into the quality of or efficiency of queries and execution plans, only the response from the disk subsystem. The Avg. Disk sec/Transfer counter is simply a combination of both read and write activity, unrelated to Avg. Disk Transfers/sec.

Page Life Expectancy (PLE)

Performance Monitor: MSSQL$InstanceName:Buffer Manager/Page Life Expectancy (s)

```
DMV: sys.dm_os_performance_counters
WHERE object_name like '%Buffer Manager%'
AND counter_name = 'Page life expectancy'
```

PLE is a measure of time (in seconds) that indicates the age of data in memory. PLE is one of the most direct indicators of memory pressure, though it doesn't provide a complete picture of memory utilization in SQL Server. In general, you want pages of data in memory to grow to a ripe old age—it means that there is ample memory available to SQL Server to store data to serve reads without going back to the storage layer. A dated, oft-quoted metric of 300 seconds isn't applicable to many SQL Server instances. 300 seconds might be appropriate for a server with 4 GB of memory, but far too low for a server with 64 GB of memory. Instead, you should monitor this value over time. Does PLE bottom out and stay there during certain operations or scheduled tasks? If so, your SQL Server performance may benefit from more memory during those operations. Does PLE grow steadily throughout production hours? The data in memory is likely be sufficient for the observed workload.

Page Reads

Performance Monitor: MSSQL$InstanceName:Buffer Manager/Page reads/sec

```
DMV: sys.dm_os_performance_counters
WHERE object_name like '%Buffer Manager%'
AND counter_name = 'Page reads/sec'
```

This is an average of the number of Page Read operations completed recently. The title is a bit misleading—these aren't page reads out of the buffer; rather, they are out of physical pages on the drive, which is slower than data pages coming out of memory. You should make the effort to lower this number by optimizing queries and indexing, efficiency of cache storage, and, of course, as a last resort, increasing the amount of server memory. Although every workload is different, a value less than 90 is a broad, over-simple guideline. High numbers indicate inefficient query and index design in read-write workloads, or memory constraints in read-heavy workloads.

Memory Pages

Performance Monitor: Memory:Pages/sec

```
DMV: Not available
```

Similar to Buffer Manager\Page Reads/sec, this is a way to measure data coming from a drive as opposed to coming out of memory. This metric is a recent average of the number of pages pulled from a drive into memory, which will be high after SQL Server startup. Although every workload is different, a value less than 50 is a broad guideline. Sustained high or climbing levels during typical production usage indicate inefficient query and index design in read-write workloads, or memory constraints in read-heavy workloads. Spikes during database backup and restore operations, bulk copies, and data extracts are expected.

Batch Requests

Performance Monitor: MSSQL$InstanceName:SQL Statistics\Batch Requests/sec

```
DMV: sys.dm_os_performance_counters
WHERE object_name like '%SQL Statistics%'
AND counter_name = 'Batch Requests/sec'
```

A measure of aggregate SQL Server user activity, indicating the recent average of the number of batch requests. Any command issued to the SQL Server from within or within contains at least one batch request. Higher sustained numbers are good; they mean your SQL instance is sustaining more traffic. Should this number trend downward during peak business hours, your SQL Server instance is being outstripped by increasing user activity.

Page Faults

Performance Monitor: Memory\Page Faults/sec

DMV: `Not Available`

A memory page fault occurs when an application seeks a data page in memory, only to find it isn't there because of memory churn. A soft page fault indicates the page was moved or otherwise unavailable; a hard page fault indicates the data page was not in memory and must be retrieved from the drive. The Page Faults/sec metric captures both. Page faults are a symptom, the cause being memory churn, so you might see an accompanying drop in the Page Life Expectancy. Spikes in Page Faults, or an upward trend, indicate the amount of server memory was insufficient to serve requests from all applications, not just SQL Server.

Available Memory

Performance Monitor: Memory\Available Bytes or Memory\Available KBytes or Memory\Available MBytes

DMV: `select available_physical_memory_kb`
`FROM sys.dm_os_sys_memory`

Available Memory is operating system memory currently unallocated to any application. Server memory above and beyond what the SQL Server instance(s) total MAX_SERVER_MEMORY setting, minus memory in use by other SQL Server features and services or other applications, are available. This will roughly match what shows as available memory in the Windows Task Manager.

Total Server Memory

Performance Monitor: MSSQL$InstanceName:Memory Manager\Total Server Memory (KB)

DMV: `sys.dm_os_performance_counters`
`WHERE object_name like '%Memory Manager%'`
`AND counter_name = 'Total Server Memory (KB)'`

This is the actual amount of memory that SQL Server is using. It is often contrasted with the next metric (Target Server Memory). This number might be far larger than what Windows Task Manager shows allocated to the SQL Server Windows NT – 64 Bit background application, which shows only a portion of the memory that sqlserver.exe controls. The Total Server Memory metric is correct.

Target Server Memory

Performance Monitor: MSSQL$InstanceName:Memory Manager\Target Server Memory (KB)

DMV: `sys.dm_os_performance_counters`
`WHERE object_name like '%Memory Manager%'`
`AND counter_name = 'Target Server Memory (KB)'`

This is the amount of memory to which SQL Server *wants* to have access and is currently working toward consuming. If the difference between Target Server Memory and Total Server Memory is larger than the value for Available Memory, SQL Server wants more memory than the

Windows Server can currently acquire. SQL Server will eventually consume all memory available to it under the Max Server Memory setting, but it might take time.

Monitoring key performance metrics in Linux

While monitoring SQL Server on Linux is identical to SQL Server on Windows in most ways, there are some exceptions, especially when the monitoring source is coming from outside of the SQL Platform Abstraction Layer (SQLPAL). As stated earlier, you'll find the dynamic management objects to perform the same for SQL Server instances on Windows and in Linux. It's the operating system layer where the differences in metrics available, and especially the tools used to collect them, are stark. In this section, we'll review a sampling of some of the tools you can use for Linux-specific operating system monitoring, keeping in mind that there is a wealth of monitoring solutions on various Linux distributions.

> ➤ **For more about SQL Server on Linux, see Chapter 5, "Installing and configuring SQL Server on Linux."**

Viewing Performance counters in Linux

The dynamic management view `sys.dm_os_performance_counters` behaves the same and delivers identical output on Windows and Linux. For example, the Performance Monitor metrics in the previous section listed as available in the DMV are available in SQL Server on Linux.

The `top` command, built-in to Linux and with near-identical output on all distributions, launches a live full-console display of CPU and memory utilization and process metrics, not dissimilar from Windows Task Manager. The screen is data rich and starkly black and white, so consider the more graphical command `htop`. Though not present by default on all Linux distributions, it can be quickly downloaded and easily installed. The command `htop` shows much of the same commonly useful data with a more pleasant format and with color highlights, as seen in Figure 8-4.

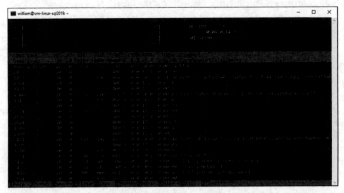

Figure 8-4 The htop command's live, updating look at Linux server's CPU, memory, and process utilization.

Another built-in Linux tool, vmstat includes extended information on process memory, including runnable/sleeping processes, memory availability, swap memory use, memory I/O activity, system interrupts, and CPU utilization percentages. While vmstat returns a snapshot of the data, the syntax vmstat n appends fresh data to the console, once every n seconds.

For querying items in SQL Server on Linux not available in sys.dm_os_performance_counters, such as Avg Disk s/read and Avg Disk s/write for each volume, different Linux tools are needed.

The tool iostat, available to install via the syststat performance monitoring tools. Source code for iostat is available at *https://github.com/sysstat/sysstat*.

For example:

```
user@instance:~$ iostat -x
```

Using the -x parameter to return extended statistics, returns basic host information, a current CPU activity utilization breakdown, and a variety of live measurements for devices, including logical disk volumes. The measures r_await and w_await are the average durations in milliseconds for read and write requests.

Other alternative packages include dtrace and nmon, the latter of which includes a simple GUI based in bash.

Querying DMOs with bash

Microsoft has released an open source tool called dbfs for querying SQL Server from within bash, available at *https://github.com/Microsoft/dbfs*.

You use dbfs to create virtual file system objects tied to SQL Server queries, often just local .sql files with custom scripts. You can then leverage sys.dm_os_performance_counters and other dynamic management objects for query reference in bash.

Monitoring key performance metrics in Azure Data Portal

The Azure Portal provides a significant amount of intelligence to cloud-based SQL operations with built-in dashboarding. This book won't go too deep into those continuously improving standard features, however, we can spend a little time talking about the sophisticated custom dashboarding and monitoring via Kusto and Azure Log Analytics.

Viewing Data in Azure Monitor

Any Azure SQL Database created has several basic key performance and usage metrics automatically tracked by Azure Monitor–the platforms built-in metrics platform accessible via the Azure Portal.

Querying this data is easy via Monitor's Metrics blade, wherein simply drilling down to an Azure resource and choosing a specified metric is enough to generate visualizations. Azure Monitor supports pinning generated visualizations to Azure Portal dashboards, allowing you to create and monitor key database metrics at a glance.

When using Metrics for an Azure SQL Database, for example, you can add metrics for DTU usage, or for percentages of the measures that make up a DTU. In the example in Figure 8-5, the Azure Monitor Metrics blade is displaying both DTU used and the average Log IO percentage on the same graph.

More complicated charting via Monitor can be done by adding more metrics, which can allow for visualization of multiple dimensions of inter-related data simultaneously, such as service request count per hour versus database CPU or DTU utilization.

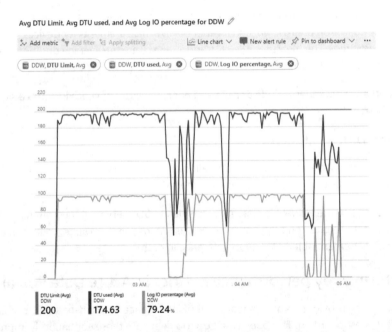

Figure 8-5 The Azure Monitor Metrics blade for an Azure SQL Database. In this image, metrics for DTU Limit, DTU used and Log IO percentage have been displayed simultaneously on the same graph.

Use filtering or splitting to further break down metrics with more than one value, for example, disk metrics. You can either Filter on specific LUNs when viewing Data Disk Read Bytes/sec, for example, or, you can split the data into different graph series, one for each LUN. If this sounds familiar, Filtering and Splitting is not dissimilar from in Windows Performance Monitor. For example this is similar to the selection of instances of each object in Windows Performance Monitor, such as the selection of volumes when adding the Physical Disk/Avg. Disk sec/Read counter.

Leveraging Azure Monitor logs

Azure Monitor is built upon the Azure Log Analytics platform, using the same data storage and query mechanisms. Azure Log Analytics is itself a separate platform built to aggregate and query big data of varying schemas in near-real time. The Azure Monitor log data is stored in a Log Analytics workspace, but is distinctly under the Azure Monitor product name, which also includes Application Insights.

Many Microsoft Azure resource types natively support syncing varying diagnostic and metric information to Azure Log Analytics. Azure SQL Database natively supports export of information to Log Analytics via the Diagnostic settings blade for the respective database in the Azure Portal. Diagnostic settings support streaming basic metrics, as well as varying types of logs to log analytics.

Contrary to Azure Monitor, Log Analytics supports ingesting information from on premises servers as well via the Azure Log Analytics agent. You may be familiar with the System Center Operations Manager (SCOM) monitoring tool, the Microsoft Monitoring Agent (MMA). The Azure Log Analytics agent is the evolution and replacement of the MMA and allows you to attach to an Azure Monitor or send data to a Log Analytics workspace.

Once your Log Analytics workspace is receiving data, you can query the workspace via the Logs blade in the Log Analytics workspace resource using the Kusto Query Language.

The following sample query will gather all DTU consumption metrics for Azure SQL Databases sending their logs to the Log Analytics workspace. It will display the 80th percentile of DTU consumption per time grain—in this case every 60 minutes. The intent is to normalize spikes of DTU usage and help to visualize sustained increase in DTU percentage that may be indicative of inefficient queries or a degradation between deployments.

As with Azure Monitor, results of Log Analytics queries can be pinned to a Microsoft Azure Portal dashboard by using the Pin to Dashboard button in the header bar. The results of this query below are visualized in Figure 8-6. This query will work with any Log Analytics workspaces that have SQL databases sending log data.

```
AzureMetrics

| where MetricName == 'dtu_consumption_percent'

| summarize percentile(Average, 80) by bin(TimeGenerated, 1h)

| render timechart
```

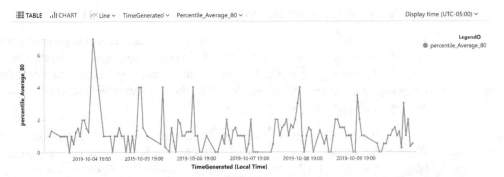

Figure 8-6 A Log Analytics query using Kusto and its charted result of average DTU utilization over time.

The query above extrapolates the 80th percentile of average DTU usage as a percent of quota, denoted by 'dtu_consumption_percent', in one hour increments. While useful, variances in usage patterns of the databases can lead to numerous peaks and valleys in the data rendered. This can make it hard to visually spot when the analyzed data is indicating a regression in performance, that is, a spike in DTU consumption.

As an alternative, the following query visualized in Figure 8-7 applies a finite impulse response to produce a 12 hour moving average of the analyzed data. This type of function is often used in signal processing, which log stream resembles. For more about the Kusto query language, visit: *https://docs.microsoft.com/azure/kusto/query/*. For more on series_fir(), see: *https://docs.microsoft.com/azure/kusto/query/series-firfunction*.

This second example is a minor demonstration of the power and ease of drawing meaningful metrics out of the log data stream coming from Azure SQL resources, a more sophisticated look that should be more useful and readable at larger time scales.

```
AzureMetrics
| where MetricName == 'dtu_consumption_percent'
| make-series 80thPercentile=percentile(Average, 80)
    on TimeGenerated in range(ago(7d), now(), 60m)
| extend 80thPercentile=series_fir(80thPercentile, repeat(1, 12), true, true)
| mv-expand 80thPercentile, TimeGenerated
| project todouble(80thPercentile), todatetime(TimeGenerated)
| render timechart with (xcolumn=TimeGenerated)
```

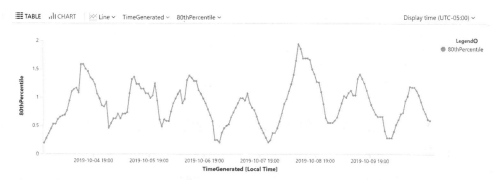

Figure 8-7 A Log Analytics query graph shows the output of the Kusto query language query displayed near the top. The Log Analytics query shows the 12-hour moving average of the 80th percentile of DTU utilization over time.

The previous sample script and all scripts for this book are available for download at *https://MicrosoftPressStore.com/SQLServer2019InsideOut/downloads*.

Creating Microsoft Log Analytics Solutions

Perhaps the most important takeaway from Log Analytics is the ability to add or create Solution packages, that can encapsulate queries, dashboards, and drill down reports of information.

Added via the Azure Marketplace, the Azure SQL Analytics solution and SQL Health Check solution attach to a Log Analytics workspace and can provide near immediate feedback across your environment, scaling to the hundreds of thousands of databases if necessary.

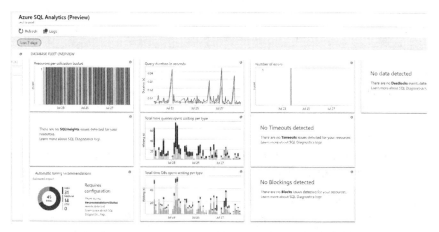

Figure 8-8 Output from the Azure SQL Analytics Solution available from the Microsoft Azure marketplace. Each of these graphs/queries provides the ability to click-through to more detailed information. This allows you to navigate from a fleet-wide view to a drilled down introspection of a problem with ease.

Figure 8-8 is a sample live display from a production Azure SQL Analytics solution (still in Preview at the time of this writing) backed by a Log Analytics workspace, showing at-a-glance information from production Azure SQL databases regarding database tuning recommendations, resource utilization, wait types and duration, as well as health check outcomes for metrics like timeouts and deadlocks.

Protecting important workloads by using Resource Governor

Resource Governor is an Enterprise edition feature, and is the only feature that you can use to identify connections as they connect and limit the resources they can consume.

You can identify connections from virtually any connection property, including the login name, hostname, application name, and so on. Anything you can get from a system function, including the login name (SUSER_SNAME() or ORIGINAL_LOGIN()), host name (HOST_NAME()), application_name (APP_NAME()), time functions (SYSDATETIME()), etc. After you've identified the connection properties and classified them, you can limit properties at the individual session level or limit the resources of a Resource Pool. You can override the MAXDOP setting for these sessions; or lower their priority; or cap the CPU, memory, or drive I/O that individual sessions can consume.

For example, you can limit all read-heavy queries coming from a SQL Server Reporting Services server, or long-running reports coming from a third-party reporting application, or dashboard/search queries based on their application name or login. Then, you can limit these queries as a set, capping them to 25% of the process, disk I/O, or SQL Server memory. SQL Server will enforce these limitations and potentially slow down the identified queries, but meanwhile, the important read-write workloads continue to operate with the remaining 75% of the server's resources.

Be aware that using Resource Governor to limit long-running SELECT statements, for example, does not alleviate concurrency issues caused by locking. In fact, limiting long-running queries could alleviate memory or CPU contention but exacerbate existing locking problems.

> ➤ See Chapter 14 for strategies to overcome concurrency issues, and keep in mind that using the READ UNCOMMITTED isolation level is a risky, clumsy strategy to solving concurrency issues in your applications.

When turned on, Resource Governor is transparent to connecting applications. No code changes are required in the queries to implement Resource Governor, only a working knowledge of the connection properties you will use to identify queries, such as those returned by the APP_NAME(), HOST_NAME(), or SUSER_SNAME().

NOTE

Keep in mind that the value returned by APP_NAME(), or that appears in `sys.dm_exec_`
`sessions.program_name` column, are specified in the application connection string.
Filtering by these values should not be used as a security method, as connection strings
can be changed to specify any string. If you're a paranoid DBA, it may also be something
to watch for, if savvy users or tricky developers realize they can change their application
connection strings and get more resources for their queries!

By default, sessions are split between Workload Group = 1 named "internal" for system queries
internal to the Database Engine, and Workload Group = 2 named "default," for all user other
user queries. You can find the current groups in the DMV `sys.resource_governor_workload_`
`groups`. While these groups still appear in SQL Server editions other than Enterprise (or
Developer or Evaluation), Resource Governor is an Enterprise-only feature.

Configuring the Resource Governor classifier function

Before configuring Resource Governor to classify workloads arriving at your SQL Server, you
must create a classifier function in the master database that operates at the creation of every
new session.

You can write the classifier function however you like, but keep in mind that it will be run for
each new connection, and so it should be as efficient and simple as possible.

The classifier function must return a `sysname` datatype value. (The sysname built-in user-defined
data type is equivalent to `nvarchar(128) NOT NULL`.) The classifier function return value
must be the name of a Resource Governor Workload Group to which a new connection is to be
assigned. Though sysname defaults to a NOT NULL datatype, the function can return a NULL
value, meaning that the session is assigned to the default group.

A Workload Group is simply a container of sessions. Remember, when configuring Resource
Governor defensively (as is most common), it is the default Workload Group that you want to
protect; it contains "all other" sessions including high business-value connections that perform
application-critical functions, writes, and so on.

The sample code that follows defines a classifier function that returns GovGroupReports for all
queries coming from two known-fictional reporting servers. You can see in the comments other
sample connection identifying functions, with many more options possible.

```
CREATE FUNCTION dbo.fnCLASSIFIER() RETURNS sysname

WITH SCHEMABINDING AS

BEGIN
```

```
-- Note that any request that you do not assign a @grp_name value for returns NULL,
and is classified into the 'default' group.

DECLARE @grp_name sysname

IF (

--Use built-in functions for connection string properties

    HOST_NAME() IN ('reportserver1','reportserver2')

--OR APP_NAME() IN ('some application') --further samples you can use

--AND SUSER_SNAME() IN ('whateveruser') --further samples you can use

)

    BEGIN

        SET @grp_name = 'GovGroupReports';

    END

RETURN @grp_name

END;
```

The previous sample script and all scripts for this book are available for download at
https://MicrosoftPressStore.com/SQLServer2019InsideOut/downloads.

Be mindful in querying other user resources such as tables in a user database, because this can
cause a noticeable delay in connection creation. If you must have the classifier function query a
table, store the table in the master database, and keep the table small and the query efficient.

After creating the function, which can have any name, you must register it as the classifier
function for this instance's Resource Governor feature. The function is still not active yet for new
logins; you must set up Workload Groups and Resource Pools first, then enable your changes.

Configuring Resource Governor pools and groups

Configuring Resource Pools (limitations that many sessions share) and Workload Groups
(limitations for individual sessions) is the next step. You should take an iterative, gradual
approach to configuring the Governor, and avoid making large changes or large initial
limitations to the affected groups.

If you have a preproduction environment to test the impact of Resource Governor on workloads
with realistic production scale, you should consider performance load testing to make sure that
the chosen settings will not cause application issues due to throttling resources.

The sample code that follows can be an instructional template to creating an initial Pool
and Group. If you seek to divide your sessions up further, multiple groups can belong to the

same pool, and multiple pools can be limited differently. Commented-out examples of other common uses for Resource Governor are included.

In this example, we create a pool that limits all covered sessions to 50% of the instance's memory, and a group that limits any single query to 30% of the instance's memory, and forces the sessions into MAXDOP = 1, overriding any server, database, or query-level setting:

```
CREATE RESOURCE POOL GovPoolMAXDOP1;

CREATE WORKLOAD GROUP GovGroupReports;

GO

ALTER RESOURCE POOL GovPoolMAXDOP1

WITH (-- MIN_CPU_PERCENT = value

    --,MAX_CPU_PERCENT = value

    --,MIN_MEMORY_PERCENT = value

    MAX_MEMORY_PERCENT = 50

);

GO

ALTER WORKLOAD GROUP GovGroupReports

WITH (

    --IMPORTANCE = { LOW | MEDIUM | HIGH }

    --,REQUEST_MAX_CPU_TIME_SEC = value

    --,REQUEST_MEMORY_GRANT_TIMEOUT_SEC = value

    --,GROUP_MAX_REQUESTS = value

    REQUEST_MAX_MEMORY_GRANT_PERCENT = 30

    , MAX_DOP = 1

)

USING GovPoolMAXDOP1;
```

For complete documentation of the possible ways to limit groups and pools, go to *https://docs.microsoft.com/sql/t-sql/statements/alter-workload-group-transact-sql* and *https://docs.microsoft.com/sql/t-sql/statements/alter-resource-pool-transact-sql*.

With the Workload Groups and Resource Pools in place, you are ready to tell Resource Governor to start using your changes.

```
-- Register the classifier function with Resource Governor
```

```
ALTER RESOURCE GOVERNOR WITH (CLASSIFIER_FUNCTION= dbo.fnCLASSIFIER);
```

After you have configured the classifier function, groups, and pools, you can turn on Resource Governor by using the query that follows, placing its functionality into memory. New sessions will begin being sorted by the classifier function and new sessions will appear in their groups. You should also issue the reconfigure command to apply changes made:

```
-- Start or Reconfigure Resource Governor

ALTER RESOURCE GOVERNOR RECONFIGURE;
```

If anything goes awry, you can disable resource governor with the following command, and re-enable with with the same command as above.

```
--Disable Resource Governor

ALTER RESOURCE GOVERNOR DISABLE;
```

After you disable Resource Governor, existing sessions will continue to operate under the rules of Resource Governor, but new queries will not be sorted into your Workload Groups, only into the default. Sessions will behave with the default settings when disabled.

After you configure it and turn it on, you can query the status of Resource Governor and the name of the classifier function by using the following sample script:

```
SELECT rgc.is_enabled, o.name

FROM sys.resource_governor_configuration AS rgc

LEFT OUTER JOIN master.sys.objects AS o

ON rgc.classifier_function_id = o.object_id

        INNER JOIN master.sys.schemas AS s

          ON o.schema_id = s.schema_id;
```

The previous sample script and all scripts for this book are available for download at *https://MicrosoftPressStore.com/SQLServer2019InsideOut/downloads*.

Monitoring Resource Pools and Workload Groups

The `group_id` columns in both `sys.dm_exec_requests` and `sys.dm_exec_sessions` define to which Resource Governor Group the request or session is a part. Groups are members of pools.

You can query the groups and pools via the DMVs `sys.resource_governor_workload_groups` and `sys.resource_governor_resource_pools`. Use the following sample query to observe the number of sessions that have been sorted into groups, noting that `group_id = 1` is the internal group, `group_id = 2` is the default group, and other groups defined by you, the administrator:

```
SELECT

    rgg.group_id, rgp.pool_id

, Pool_Name = rgp.name, Group_Name = rgg.name

, session_count= ISNULL(count(s.session_id) ,0)

FROM sys.dm_resource_governor_workload_groups AS rgg

LEFT OUTER JOIN sys.dm_resource_governor_resource_pools AS rgp

ON rgg.pool_id = rgp.pool_id

LEFT OUTER JOIN sys.dm_exec_sessions AS s

ON s.group_id = rgg.group_id

GROUP BY rgg.group_id, rgp.pool_id, rgg.name, rgp.name

ORDER BY rgg.name, rgp.name;
```

> ➤ You can reference a (dated) Resource Governor troubleshooting guide for a list of
> error numbers and their meanings that might be raised by Resource Governor at
> *https://docs.microsoft.com/previous-versions/sql/sql-server-2008-r2/cc627395(v=sql.105)*.
> Unfortunately, there does not appear to be a more up to date version of this reference
> material.

Understanding the new servicing model

Database administrators and CIOs alike must adjust their normal comfort levels with new SQL
Server editions. No longer can IT leadership say, "Wait until the first service pack," before moving because as of SQL Server 2017, there are no more service packs, only Cumulative Updates!

In this section, we will outline the current processes for SQL Server on premises versions. Note
that Azure SQL Database and Managed Instances keep your server up to date very soon after
new versions are deployed.

Inside OUT

How do you patch SQL Server Reporting Services (SSRS)?

Starting with SQL Server 2017, SSRS is no longer patched with SQL Server CUs. Instead,
you upgrade SSRS by downloading and running the same SSRS installer again.

Note that your patching procedures for SQL Server need to include this second and
separate step to keep all related SQL Server software up to date.

Updated servicing model

Microsoft has adopted a new model for its product life cycles. In the past, this servicing model included Service Packs (SPs), Cumulative Updates (CUs), and General Distribution Releases (GDRs).

Beginning with SQL Server 2017 and continuing with SQL Server 2019, the following changes are in effect:

- SPs will no longer be released.

- CUs will be released every month for the first twelve months of general release, and then bi-monthly for the remaining four years of the five-year duration of the Mainstream Support period. In October 2018, this cadence was increased from quarterly to bi-monthly for SQL Server 2017 and all future releases.

- CUs might now include localized content and will be delivered on a standardized schedule: as of this writing, this is the week of the third Tuesday of the month.

- Unlike in the past, critical updates via GDR patches (which contain critical security-only fixes) will not have their own path for updates between CUs.

- Slipstream media will not be provided any more for SQL Server (after SQL 2017 CU11), for those who still used slipstream media for new instance installs. Instead, Microsoft recommends leveraging the existing SQL Server Setup provides automatic download and installation of the latest CUs or downloading CUs manually for offline installations.

➤ **For more information on offline installations of SQL Server on Windows Servers, see Chapter 4.**

Microsoft has maintained in recent years that there is no need to wait for an SP, because the General Availability (GA) release has been extensively tested by both internal Microsoft QA and external preview customers. For those dealing with clients or leadership who are stubborn or reactionary, a possible alternative under the new model could be to target an arbitrary CU, such as CU2.

Inside OUT

Do you need to patch SQL Server on Linux and container images after creation?

No, Linux mssql-server packages and "latest" tagged images are always updated and install with the latest CU baked in. This is the default behavior. You can optionally install a non-current version.

You can review past SQL Server on Linux versions here: *https://docs.microsoft.com/sql/linux/sql-server-linux-release-notes*.

You can review the docker images available here: *https://hub.docker.com/_/microsoft-mssql-server*. (Note the underscore in the URL.)

Planning for the product support life cycle

As we saw during the writing process for this book, SQL Server 2008 and 2008 R2 reached their end of support. Unless paying a hefty ransom for continuing support of these products is an option for you, databases on these old versions must be migrated as soon as possible. Similarly, Windows Server 2008 and 2008 R2 are reaching their end of support dates in January 2020, soon after this book is published. No more security patches, even critical, will be released publicly, putting their use in violation of any sensible policy for secure software policy and a red flag on any security audit.

In you're planning for long-term use of a particular version of SQL Server, you should keep in mind the following life cycle:

- 0 to 5 Years: Mainstream Support Period

  Security and functional issues are addressed through CUs. Security issues only might also be addressed through GDRs.

- 6 to 10 Years: Extended Support

  Only critical functional issues will be addressed. Security issues might still be addressed through GDRs

- 11 to 16 Years: Premium Assurance

  The Extended Support level can be lengthened with optional payments.

Automating SQL Server administration

As you've made your way through the book, covering the many things you need to keep your SQL Server healthy might feel overwhelming, given the prospect of doing everything manually. However, what separates a novice DBA from a seasoned one is the ability to automate many common administration tasks.

This chapter reviews the common ways of automating Microsoft SQL Server instance administration, starting with an exploration of the tools that enable them:

- Tools including Database Mail and SQL Server Agent

- Basic "care and feeding" maintenance, including Maintenance Plans built into SQL Server Management Studio (SSMS)

- Strategies for administering multiple SQL Servers, including Master/Target Agent servers (MSX/TSX)

- Event forwarding and Policy-Based Management (PBM)

- An introduction to PowerShell with realistic sample code

This chapter varies little for SQL Server instances on Windows or Linux except in the case of PowerShell. In some cases, you might have to run these commands from a Windows server. Where there are exceptions for Linux, we point them out.

Little in this chapter applies to Microsoft Azure SQL Database because many of the administration tasks are already automated, including most performance tuning and backups. No initial configuration is needed. If you need more control, many of the features available in Azure SQL Database are being released through managed instances. As the Azure SQL Database platform-as-a-service (PaaS) offering has matured, it has become a powerful cloud-based and complementary platform to SQL Server, neither fully replacing nor overlapping with the feature set or purpose of on-premises SQL Server instances.

➤ See Chapter 17, "Provisioning Azure SQL Database", and Chapter 18, "Provisioning Azure SQL Database managed instance," for more information about automation.

Sample scripts in this chapter, and all scripts for this book, are all available for download at *https://www.MicrosoftPressStore.com/SQLServer2019InsideOut/downloads.*

Components of SQL Server automated administration

Since automation implies a mostly hands-off approach to repeatable tasks, DBAs need to understand two foundational tools of automation**:**

- **Database Mail.**   Allows SQL Server to send emails to notify you of the outcome of SQL Server Agent Jobs, server performance and error alerts, or custom notifications with Transact-SQL (T-SQL) calls to the dbo.sp_send_dbmail stored procedure (located in the msdb database).

- **SQL Server Agent.**   The automation engine available in all editions of SQL Server except for Express, which can be used to automate most maintenance tasks in SQL Server.

Let's review these two key features, both of which are fully supported on Windows and Linux.

Database Mail

Database Mail uses Simple Mail Transfer Protocol (SMTP) to send email. Email is handled asynchronously outside of the SQL Server process, isolating both the process and any potential performance impact to the SQL Server instance. By design, this process is run outside of SQL Server using a separate executable DatabaseMail.exe, which is started asynchronously using Service Broker.

Setting up Database Mail

To begin sending automated emails, you need to configure Database Mail and then configure SQL Server Agent to use the Database Mail profile you create. First, in SQL Server Management Studio (SSMS), use the Database Mail Configuration Wizard, which you will find in the **Management** folder of the server node you are configuring, and clicking on **Configure Database Mail**. You'll need to set up a profile and then an associated account.

The wizard will turn on the Database Mail feature in the Surface Area facet of the SQL Server instance. You need to do this only once. Database Mail is among a select few Surface Area facets that you should turn on for most SQL Server instances.

➤ For more information on Surface Area facets in each SQL instance, see Chapter 4, "Installing and configuring SQL Server instances and features."

A Database Mail Profile can be public or private. In the case of private, only specific associated server principals are given access (users or roles in databases). A public profile allows any principal that is a member of the built-in database role DatabaseMailUsersRole in the msdb database.

Ideally, all Database Mail profiles are private, and only those credentials that will be used to send emails will be given access. This is crucial in a multitenant environment, or an environment that allows access to external developers or vendors, but even in internal environments this could provide protection against malicious use to send emails.

You can configure a Database Mail Profile to use almost any SMTP configuration, including nonstandard ports and Secure Sockets Layer (SSL); see Chapter 13, "Protecting data through encryption, privacy and auditing" for more on SSL and TLS. You also can configure it with Windows Authentication (common for SMTP servers in the same domain), basic authentication (common for web authentication), or no authentication (common for anonymous relay in the local network, usually with an IP allow list).

You can configure Database Mail to use any SMTP server that it can reach, including web-based SMTP servers. You can even use Outlook web mail or another web-based email account if you're configuring for testing purposes or have no other viable internal SMTP options. An internal SMTP server with Windows authentication using a service account is preferred though, because you have more control over your own environment.

NOTE

For Azure infrastructure-as-a-service (IaaS) environments without an internal SMTP presence, Twilio SendGrid is a common and supported SMTP solution. For more information, visit *https://docs.microsoft.com/azure/sendgrid-dotnet-how-to-send-email.*

After configuring your account's SMTP settings (you'll need to test them later), the Database Mail account has a number of options that you can adjust:

- **Account Retry Attempts.**   Defaults to 1, which you should probably leave as-is to avoid excessive retries that could lock out an account or trigger spam detection.

- **Account Retry Delay (seconds).**   Defaults to 60. Again, you should leave this for the same reasons as for Account Retry Attempts.

- **Maximum File Size (Bytes).**   Defaults to roughly 1 MB. You should change this only if necessary.

- **Prohibited Attachment File Extensions.**   Specifies which file extensions cannot be sent, commonly set if third-party or multitenant development occurs on the SQL instance. This is a comma-delimited list that by default is "exe,dll,vbs,js."

- **Database Mail Executable Minimum Lifetime (seconds).**   Defaults to 600 seconds (10 minutes), which is a counter that starts after an email message is sent. If no other

CHAPTER 9

messages are sent in that time frame, the Database Mail executable stops. If stopped, the Database Mail process is started again any time a new email is sent. You'll see messages indicating "Database Mail process is started" and "Database Mail process is shutting down" in the Database Mail Log when this happens.

- **Logging Level.**   Defaults to Extended, which includes basic start/stop and error messages that should be kept in the Database Mail log. Change to Verbose if you are troubleshooting Database Mail and need more information, or Normal to suppress informational messages and see errors only.

After you've set up a Database Mail profile and account, you can send a test email via SSMS. Right-click Database Mail, and then, on the shortcut menu that opens, click Send Test E-Mail. Or, you can send a plain-and-simple test email via T-SQL by using the following code:

```
exec msdb.dbo.sp_send_dbmail

@recipients ='yournamehere@domain.com',

@subject ='test';
```

This code does not specify a `@profile` parameter, so the command will use the default profile for the current user, the default private if it exists, or the global (default public) profile.

This is all that is necessary for developers and applications to send emails using Database Mail.

➤ Don't forget to read the "Troubleshooting Database Mail" section later in this chapter.

To allow SQL Server Agent to send emails based on job outcomes and alerts, you will need to create an Operator in SQL Server Agent, and then configure SQL Server Agent's Alert System to use a Database Mail profile. We look at SQL Server Agent and its initial configuration in depth later in this chapter.

Inside OUT

What about Database Mail on Linux?

SQL Server on Linux requires the Database Mail Profile to be set using `mssql-conf` or an environment variable. We recommend using `mssql-conf` with the following command (where "default" is the name of the profile you created):

```
sudo /opt/mssql/bin/mssql-conf set sqlagent.databasemailprofile
default
```

You can visit *https://docs.microsoft.com/sql/linux/sql-server-linux-db-mail-sql-agent* for step-by-step instructions.

Allow anonymous relay for anonymous authentication

If you're using anonymous authentication internally with Microsoft Exchange, verify that the internal SMTP anonymous relay has a dedicated Receive connector that allows for anonymous relay. By design, a Receive connector just for anonymous relay should allow only a small list of internal hosts, your SQL Server instance(s) among them.

Authentication with the SMTP server is likely the problem if you observe errors in the Database Mail log after attempting to send email, such as:

```
Cannot send mails to mail server. (Mailbox unavailable. The server response
was: 5.7.1 Unable to relay...
```

or:

```
Cannot send mails to mail server. (Mailbox unavailable. The server response
was: 5.7.1 Service unavailable...
```

Maintaining email history in the msdb database

The email messages sent by Database Mail are recorded and queued in a table in the msdb database named dbo.sysmail_mailitems. As you might suspect, data in the msdb tables for Database Mail will grow, potentially to an unmanageable size. This can cause queries to the msdb's Database Mail tables to run for a long time. There is no automated process in place to maintain a retention policy for these tables, though there is a stored procedure to delete older messages as well as a lengthy reference article in place to guide you through creating a set of archive tables and a SQL Server Agent job to maintain data over time. You can find both of these at ***https://docs.microsoft.com/sql/relational-databases/database-mail/create-a-sql-server-agent-job-to-archive-database-mail-messages-and-event-logs***.

Troubleshooting Database Mail

We've already mentioned the Database Mail log, now let's go over the other diagnostics available for Database Mail.

> ➤ You can find out more about reading the Database Mail log from Microsoft Docs at *https://docs.microsoft.com/sql/relational-databases/database-mail/database-mail-log-and-audits*.

Reading email logs in the msdb database

If the SMTP Server or the Database Mail process becomes unavailable, the messages are queued in a table in the msdb database named dbo.sysmail_mailitems.

The msdb database contains metadata tables for the Database Mail feature, including dbo.sysmail_allitems, which tracks all outbound email activity. Look for items for which the sent_status doesn't equal sent for signs of messages that weren't successfully sent; for example:

```
--Find recent unsent emails

SELECT m.send_request_date, m.recipients, m.copy_recipients, m.blind_copy_recipients

, m.[subject], m.send_request_user, m.sent_status

FROM msdb.dbo.sysmail_allitems m

WHERE

-- Only show recent day(s)

m.send_request_date > dateadd(day, -3, sysdatetime())

-- Possible values are sent (successful), unsent (in process),

-- retrying (failed but retrying), failed (no longer retrying)

AND m.sent_status<>'sent' ORDER BY m.send_request_date DESC;
```

There is also a view provided in msdb, dbo.sysmail_unsentitems, that filters on (sent_status = 'unsent' OR sent_status = 'retrying'). There are four possible values for sent_status in sysmail_allitems: sent, unsent, retrying, and failed.

➤ You can find more information about these and other sysmail views, including failed items and sent items, at *https://docs.microsoft.com/sql/relational-databases/system-catalog-views/sysmail-allitems-transact-sql.*

Inside OUT

How do you monitor SQL Server Reporting Services report subscription emails?

SQL Server Reporting Services uses an entirely different process, SMTP configuration, and authentication to send report subscriptions via email. If you wish to monitor these, look for SQL Server Reporting Services log messages in the log files in the following subfolder:

```
%programfiles%\Microsoft SQL Server Reporting Services\SSRS\LogFiles\
```

Enabling Service Broker on the msdb database

After restoring the msdb database or setting up Database Mail for the first time, the Service Broker feature might not be turned on for the msdb database. You can check the is_broker_enabled field in the system catalog view sys.databases; if it is 0, this is the case, and you must remedy this. If you try to send email and the Service Broker is disabled, you will receive the following self-explanatory error message:

```
Msg 14650, Level 16, State 1, Procedure msdb.dbo.sp_send_dbmail, Line 73 [Batch Start
Line 18] Service Broker message delivery is not enabled in this database. Use the ALTER
DATABASE statement to enable Service Broker message delivery.
```

To turn on Service Broker on the msdb database, you must stop the SQL Server Agent service and close any connections active to the msdb database prior to running the following code:

```
ALTER DATABASE msdb SET ENABLE_BROKER;
```

SQL Server Agent

The SQL Server Agent is the native automation platform for internal task automation, maintenance, log and file retention, even backups. SQL Server Agent is similar to the Windows Task Scheduler (and cron on Linux), but it has a number of advantages for automating SQL Server tasks, including integration with SQL Server security, authentication, logging, and native T-SQL programming.

On Windows, SQL Server Agent can accomplish many of the same tasks as Windows Task Scheduler, including running operating system (CmdExec) and PowerShell commands (though CmdExec and PowerShell tasks are not available on Linux). Metadata, configuration, and history data for the SQL Server Agent are kept in the msdb database.

> ### Inside OUT
>
> **How do you enable the SQL Server Agent?**
>
> On Windows Server, SQL Server Agent is a service that is managed through SQL Server Configuration Manager.
>
> On Linux, SQL Server Agent is managed using the `mssql-conf` command line utility. You can read more in Chapter 5, "Installing and configuring SQL Server on Linux."

Configuring SQL Server Agent jobs

A job contains a series of steps. Each job step is of a type that allows for different actions to take place, such as the aforementioned T-SQL, CmdExec, or PowerShell tasks.

A job can be automatically started based on a number of conditions, including:

- predefined schedule or schedules

CHAPTER 9

- in response to an alert

- as a result of running the dbo.sp_start_job stored procedure in the msdb database

- when SQL Server Agent starts

- when the host computer is idle

You can script jobs in their entirety through SSMS, providing a script-level recoverability, migration to other servers, and source control possibility for SQL Server Agent jobs. Jobs are backed up and restored via the msdb database, or scripted for backup and migration.

In SSMS, in Object Explorer, expand **SQL Server Agent**, then the **Jobs** folder. Right-click on any job and click **Properties**. Navigate to the **Steps** page. Here you will see that job steps do not necessarily need to run linearly. You can set a job to default to start at any job step, and additionally, when starting a job, you can manually change the start step for the job. Each job step reports back whether it succeeded or failed, and you can configure it to move to another step or fail based on the job step outcome. These step completion actions are defined on the Advanced page of the Job Step Properties dialog box. However, for ease of management in the future, we recommend that you create job steps that run as linearly as possible.

You can assign jobs to categories; in fact, many system-generated jobs (such as replication) are assigned to categories. You can create your own categories in SSMS by right-clicking the Jobs folder under SQL Server Agent, and then, on the shortcut menu, clicking **Manage Categories**.

In T-SQL, you can run this script to add a new category:

```
EXEC msdb.dbo.sp_add_category @class=N'JOB', @type=N'LOCAL', @name=N'Database
Maintenance';
```

This should aid your efforts to report on, maintain, redeploy, and migrate jobs in the future.

Understanding job step security

Although creating SQL Server Agent jobs themselves is easy to do through SSMS, a critical step that many developers and administrators skip is the use of Credentials and Proxies in SQL Server Agent job steps. SQL Server Agent jobs, by default, run steps in the security context of the SQL Agent service account. This may be acceptable for some local usage such as indexing, but using a proxy to run a job step instead of the SQL Server Agent service account or another named user is the most secure way to run jobs. Proxies make it possible for administrators to set job steps to run under a specific credential, rather than giving the SQL Server Agent service account access to everything that each job needs.

Proxies are used for all job step types but one. It is not possible to run a T-SQL script job step using a proxy. A T-SQL step will run in the security context of the owner of the job if the owner is not a sysadmin. If the owner of the job is a member of the sysadmin server role, the job will run as the SQL Server Agent service account.

For all other job step types, there is a proxy. On the Job Step Properties page, you can select the job step to "Run as" a proxy. SQL Server Agent checks for access to the subsystem each time the job step is run to verify that the security has not changed.

A subsystem can be one of the following items:

- Operating System (CmdExec)

- Replication Agent (Snapshot, Log Reader, Distribution, Merge, or Queue Reader)

- Analysis Services Query or

- SSIS package execution

- PowerShell Script

- Microsoft ActiveX Script (deprecated; do not use)

You can associate each proxy with one or more subsystems, though to reduce your attack surface, you should create many proxies for different job step security requirements and subsystems.

Without a proxy specified, jobs must be owned by a member of the sysadmin role to run job steps other than the T-SQL step type. These job steps will then run as the SQL Server Agent service account. This isn't ideal, for two reasons:

- The SQL Server Agent service account should not have local administrator privileges on the server. This reduces the risk to the operating system (OS) from potential misuse for SQL Server Agent jobs. Service accounts are discussed in Chapter 4 and Chapter 12, "Administering security and permissions."

- The SQL Server Agent service account must be a member of the sysadmin server role, so it might have far too many privileges inside SQL Server than necessary to safely run SQL Agent jobs.

Further, the owner of the job must also have permissions to use any proxy subsystem that the job's steps use. It is also important because job steps often need to access other servers, and proxies give you the ability to assign pinpoint rights to the other resources. You will not be able to create or modify a job step for a subsystem if the job owner is not listed as a principal who has access to the proxy. Sysadmins automatically have access to all proxies.

Proxies map to credentials on the SQL Server; you'll find a subfolder for credentials in the Security folder on the Server level in Object Explorer in SSMS. Each proxy is linked to a credential in

SQL Server. The credential stores the account's username and password, which means that if it changes, the proxy and SQL Server Agent job steps that depend on it will not be able to authenticate and will fail. Therefore, you should use service accounts, not individuals' named accounts, in credentials that will be used by proxies. Credential account passwords shouldn't be widely known, and the accounts shouldn't be used interactively regularly by administrators, so that they cannot accidentally become locked out.

NOTE

You should keep a script for recovering locked service accounts in a safe place.

You can create a credential for a local Windows account or a domain account. You also can create credentials for accounts on Enterprise Key Management (EKM) modules, including the Azure Key Vault service. The Windows account of the credential must have "Log on as a batch job" permission on the server. As a local administrator, you can grant this permission in the Local Security Policy dialog box.

➤ **You can read more about Azure Key Vault and EKM modules in Chapter 13.**

Securing permissions to interact with jobs

Your login must be a member of the sysadmin server role or one of the SQL Server Agent database roles in the msdb database, to set up a SQL Server Agent job in SSMS.

The SQLAgentOperatorRole, SQLAgentReaderRole, and SQLAgentUserRole each have permission to create jobs, start jobs, view job history, view, and edit properties of jobs, though mostly only for jobs they own. For granular details on the limitations and overlapping of each role, visit *https://docs.microsoft.com/sql/ssms/agent/sql-server-agent-fixed-database-roles*.

The SQLAgentUserRole is the least privileged of the three roles, but the other two roles are members of the SQLAgentUserRole. Typically, membership to these roles is limited to service accounts and third-party developers. Grant permission on proxies to custom database roles, individuals or service accounts. Do not grant permissions directly to the SQLAgentUserRole database role, including the ability to use proxies

Scheduling and monitoring jobs

A job is run based on one or more schedules assigned to it. You give schedules a name upon creation and can assign them to multiple jobs, which can be especially useful for uncommon or esoteric job schedules, or to centralized management of jobs that should run simultaneously. To view and select schedules from other jobs, in the Job Properties dialog box, on the Schedules tab, click the Pick button. You will see only the job schedules to which you have access.

There are four schedule types:

- Start automatically when SQL Server Agent starts

- Start whenever the CPUs become idle

- Recurring

- One time (for running a schedule manually, for instance during testing, or a one-off index rebuild)

Jobs run asynchronously when they are started manually or by SQL Server Agent. A dialog box with a spinning progress icon appears, but you can close this, and the job will continue to run until completion. You can monitor the progress of jobs in SSMS by viewing the Job Activity Monitor, or you can observe the job's current request in sys.dm_exec_requests.

NOTE
Using the SQL Server Agent extension, you can view and manage SQL Agent jobs in Azure Data Studio as well. For more information, visit
https://docs.microsoft.com/sql/azure-data-studio/sql-server-agent-extension.

You can also use T-SQL to query the status of jobs with the undocumented stored procedure master.dbo.xp_sqlagent_enum_jobs, which you can join to msdb.dbo.sysjobs, as shown here:

```
--jobs still running

declare @xp_sqlagent_enum_jobs table (

id int not null IDENTITY(1,1) PRIMARY KEY,

Job_ID uniqueidentifier not null,

Last_Run_Date int not null,

Last_Run_Time int not null,

Next_Run_Date int not null,

Next_Run_Time int not null,

Next_Run_Schedule_ID int not null,

Requested_To_Run int not null,

Request_Source int not null,

Request_Source_ID varchar(100) null,

Running int not null,

Current_Step int not null,

Current_Retry_Attempt int not null,

[State] int not null);
```

```
INSERT INTO @xp_sqlagent_enum_jobs

EXEC master.dbo.xp_sqlagent_enum_jobs 1,'';

SELECT j.name

, state_desc = CASE ej.state

WHEN 0 THEN 'not idle or suspended'

WHEN 1 THEN 'Executing'

WHEN 2 THEN 'Waiting for thread'

WHEN 3 THEN 'Between retries'

WHEN 4 THEN 'Idle'

WHEN 5 THEN 'Suspended'

WHEN 7 THEN 'Performing completion actions'

END

, *

    FROM msdb.dbo.sysjobs j

    LEFT OUTER JOIN @xp_sqlagent_enum_jobs ej

    ON j.job_id = ej.Job_ID

ORDER BY j.name;
```

Configuring and viewing job history

Every time a job is run, a record is maintained in the msdb database in the dbo.sysjobhistory table. To review the job's history, in SSMS, right-click it, and then, on the shortcut menu, select Job History. History is stored for each job step. You can expand a given job to view the output for each step, including any errors.

With jobs that run frequently (for example, transaction log backup jobs), a large amount of job history will be created and stored in msdb. It is initially defaulted to two very low and likely unrealistic row caps: 1,000 rows of history for all jobs, and 100 rows of history at most for one job. If a job runs once per hour, it loses visibility into history after just four days—a likely unrealistic window for troubleshooting and diagnostic information.

In SSMS, in Object Explorer, right-click **SQL Server Agent**, and then click **Properties**. Click the **History** page. As Figure 9-1 demonstrates, this page is not intuitive and can be confusing. The first option, *Limit size of job history log*, is a rolling job history retention setting. You might find it a good start to simply add a 0 to each value, increasing the maximum log history size in rows from the default of 1,000 to 10,000 or more, and also increase the maximum job history per job in rows from the default of 100 to 1,000 or more. These settings would store just more than 41 days of history for a job that runs hourly if this were the only job on the server. You might find these numbers also insufficient on a SQL Server instance with many frequently running jobs, and you should increase until you have a comfortable retention of job run history.

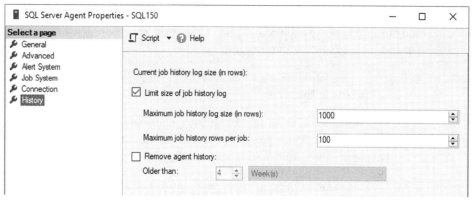

Figure 9-1   The two options to retain SQL Agent job history.

The job history log can be useful, but there are two limitations of which you should be aware:

- The message text in this Job History viewer is truncated after 1,024 characters. If you need to view the full results of the output, you need to query the dbo.sysjobhistory table. The message column in that table is considerably larger at 8,000 characters.

- The history of SQL Server Integration Services package execution in the SQL Server Agent job history is extremely limited, reduced to details around the fact that the package started, completed, and/or errored, without detail. More verbose detail will appear in the thorough history available in the SSISDB. To access and view that history, in SSMS, use the Integration Services Catalogs menu and then go to the project and packages that failed.

Inside OUT

Where should you deploy SQL Server Integration Services packages?

Using the Project Deployment model for your SQL Server Integration Services packages provides superior built-in logging and trending when running a package.

The Project Deployment model and the SSISDB database, both originally released in SQL Server 2012, combined with further integration with SQL Server Agent, make for a far superior option for SQL Server Integration Services development than the old Package Deployment model.

You can still deploy legacy Package Deployment model packages to msdb, but we do not recommend this for new development.

You can also configure additional logging for each job step in order to capture the full step output and, more commonly, the error text.

Going back to the job editor, the following options are available on the Advanced page of the Job Step Properties dialog box:

- The output history to an output text file option, and additionally to append history to that log file. Be careful of keeping the Append Output To Existing File option turned on long term—the output file can grow to a significant size in a short amount of time.

- The Log To Table option, which writes to the dbo.sysjobstepslogs table in the msdb database. That table has an nvarchar(max) data type for the Log field, allowing for more output data to be captured per step if needed. Be careful of this option, as well—the table can grow to a significant size in a short amount of time. You should schedule the stored procedure sp_delete_jobsteplog to remove old records from the table over time.

- Finally, there is the Include Step Output In History option, which adds a row to the job history log to include the output of the job step. This should contain valuable information, and, unlike the other two options, job history is automatically maintained over time by SQL Server Agent.

Administering SQL Server Agent operators

Operators are aliases in SQL Server Agent, allowing you to set up a name and email address for sending messages to. Note that the pager email name is deprecated, along with the on-duty schedule, so don't use these. Alerting using Net Send is deprecated and has been removed from the user interface.

Operators usually should not be pointed at individuals (even though you can create a semi-colon-delimited list of email address), but instead to a distribution group (even if that group initially contains only one person). In most situations, you will create an operator to notify SQL Server first responders in your environment. You should maintain your environment's list of DBA personnel in distribution lists, and not inside the Operator lists of each SQL Server instance.

To set up an operator, in SSMS, in Object Explorer, expand the **SQL Server Agent** folder, right-click **Operator**, and then, on the shortcut menu, click **New Operator**.

NOTE

If you have a big team and an on-call rotation, set up a scheduled process in a SQL Server Agent job that updates an "on call rotation" operator's email address to resource(s) currently "on call." Use the `sp_update_operator` stored procedure to update the email address for an operator on a schedule.

Configuring alerts

Alerts are created to set conditions and, when met, prompt email notifications or the kickoff of SQL Server Agent jobs in response. Alerts are versatile and can look for SQL Server events in the error log, or performance conditions that you would view in the Performance Monitor application or even by Windows Management Instrumentation (WMI) queries.

As recommended in Chapter 4, you should set up alerts for high-severity SQL Server errors. However, do not overcommit your personal inbox with alerts, and do not set an inbox rule to Mark As Read and file away emails from SQL Server. By careful selection of emails, you can assure yourself and your team that emails from SQL Server will be actionable concerns that rarely arrive.

With a large number of SQL instances under your purview, email alerts for even severe issues can become too numerous. We then recommend a way to gather and queue actionable errors in a system that provides for aggregation, dashboarding, and team assignment. There are several third-party *log collection* or *log management* software applications that perform the task of log aggregation and centralized alerting.

You might also configure the Delay Between Responses in each alert, to prevent an unchecked flooding of emails arriving from a repeating error. Consider a delay of up to five minutes between responses, as your environment deems appropriate.

You can specify only a single error message or severity per alert, so we recommend scripting the mass creation of a standard batch of alerts, to be created consistently on all your SQL Server instances. See the script CH09_SQL_add_standard_error_alerts.sql in the accompanying downloads for this book for an example that includes the alerts we examine in just a moment.

Next, we review the three types of Alerts that you can set up: SQL Server event, performance conditions, and WMI event alerts. On Linux you can only set up a SQL Server event alert, but as we'll show, it is possible to query performance counters using a dynamic management view.

SQL Server event

You should set up alerts on actual error messages that are important enough for you to receive emails. SQL Server generates a lot of informational-only events, such as successful backup messages, for which you would not want to receive messages.

CHAPTER 9

You can set up alerts based on the actual error number (samples follow shortly) or any error of a certain severity (1 to 25). You can optionally filter the alert to a single database, or for a specific message text.

It is common practice to set up alerts for severity 16 through 19 and 21 through 25, because these tend to be actionable errors. Severities 21 and above are severe and unrecoverable errors.

The most common Severity 20 errors are nuisance authentication-related and transient (the user tried, experienced an error, tried again, and succeeded). An alert for Severity 20 might send out a large number of unactionable alerts to the SQL Server DBA team. You will still see Severity 20 issues in the SQL Server Error Log and should make note of them as they appear, especially if they appear in large numbers, given that this can be a sign of greater authentication or domain issues, or malicious intrusion attempts. The goal of alerts is to send out actionable errors or performance conditions worth investigating.

NOTE

Every SQL Server error message includes a severity, but that doesn't mean you want to be alerted to them. For example, basic syntax errors that you might make while writing queries in SQL Server Management Studio or Azure Data Studio will surface as Severity 15 or 16 errors, which aren't worth alerting.

You might also want to configure alerts to send out error messages for these SQL Server error numbers that are not already covered in the severities 16 through 19 and 21 through 25. These following errors are rare, but immediately actionable:

- **825 (Severity 10).** A dreaded "read-retry" error, after the read of a file succeeded after failing x number of times. This is often a harbinger of potential database integrity failure that should prompt immediate action.

- **854, 855, 856 (Severity 10).** This is an uncorrectable hardware memory corruption detected via the operating system's memory diagnostics that indicates a potentially immediate stability thread to the system due to memory.

- **3624 (Severity 20).** This is an internal SQL Server error called an "assertion failure" that is typically a software bug, though it could indicate internal data corruption. This is oftentimes addressed via a SQL Server Cumulative Update or patch.

Performance conditions

On Windows, you can set up performance condition alerts for any performance counter in the SQLServer category, the same set of alerts you would see in the Windows Performance Monitor application with the prefix "SQLServer" or "MSSQL$*instancename*." For Linux, see the Inside OUT box below.

For example, if you want to receive an email when the SQL Server's Page Life Expectancy (PLE) drops below a certain value, you would select PLE in the same way that you would find it in Performance Monitor. Choose the object Buffer Manager, the counter Page Life Expectancy, and the comparison operator Falls Below and comparison value. In the case of PLE, this is measured in seconds.

Inside OUT

How do you query performance counters using DMVs?

On both Windows and Linux you can query most performance counters from SQLServer: or MSSQL$*instancename*: objects via the dynamic management view (DMV) `sys.dm_os_performance_counters`. There is one caveat: in some cases the calculation is not as straightforward.

For example, consider the Buffer Cache Hit Ratio (BCHR) metric, one piece of the puzzle of looking at memory utilization. Calculating the actual BCHR as it appears in Performance Monitor requires division of two simultaneous counter values:

```
DECLARE @object_name SYSNAME = CASE
    WHEN CHARINDEX('\', @@SERVERNAME) = 0
    THEN 'SQLServer'
    ELSE 'MSSQL$' + SUBSTRING(@@SERVERNAME, CHARINDEX('\', @@
SERVERNAME) + 1, 100)
    END + ':Buffer Manager'
SELECT [BufferCacheHitRatio] = (bchr * 1.0 / bchrb) * 100.0
FROM (
    SELECT bchr = cntr_value
    FROM sys.dm_os_performance_counters
    WHERE counter_name = 'Buffer cache hit ratio'
    AND object_name = @object_name
    ) AS r
CROSS APPLY (
    SELECT bchrb = cntr_value
    FROM sys.dm_os_performance_counters
    WHERE counter_name = 'Buffer cache hit ratio base'
    AND object_name = @object_name
    ) AS rb;
```

NOTE

SQL Server samples the data periodically, so there might be a few seconds' delay between when you receive the alert and when the threshold was reached.

WMI event alert conditions

The third option for SQL Server Agent alerts allows for custom WMI queries to be run (for SQL Server on Windows only). WMI queries can gather alerts on a variety of Data Definition Language (DDL) events in SQL Server, such as CREATE, ALTER and DROP, and while WMI queries follow the basic syntax of T-SQL queries, the FROM of the WMI query will be a WMI object, not an object in a SQL Server database.

➤ You can see an example of a WMI event alert at
https://docs.microsoft.com/sql/relational-databases/wmi-provider-server-events/sample-creating-a-sql-server-agent-alert-with-the-wmi-provider.

➤ You can reference the WMI provider classes and properties at
https://docs.microsoft.com/sql/relational-databases/wmi-provider-server-events/wmi-provider-for-server-events-classes-and-properties.

This type of alert is not as straightforward as the other types. In general, you might find better results, more flexibility, and less complexity by using extended events, SQL Server Agent jobs, SQL Server Audit, and/or third-party monitoring tools than by using WMI alert queries.

Setting up an email recipient for a WMI event alert does not send over any useful or actionable information in the email aside from the alert's name. This does little more than let you know that a WMI event occurred (observed asynchronously, so there might be some delay).

To view the information regarding the event—for example, the T-SQL command associated with the event—you must turn on Token Replacement in the SQL Server Agent Properties dialog box. On the Alert System page, at the bottom, select the Token Replacement check box. This allows for the tokenization (replacement at runtime) of WMI commands in a T-SQL job step.

➤ For more on the tokens that you can use in a T-SQL job step, visit
https://docs.microsoft.com/sql/ssms/agent/use-tokens-in-job-steps.

We have prepared a sample WMI event alert to capture the CREATE DATABASE DDL event. For a simple but lengthy working example of the creation of a sample table, SQL Server Agent job, and alert, see the script CH09_SQL_wmi_alert_data_capture.sql in the accompanying downloads for this book.

SQL Server Agent job considerations when using availability groups

If you are running SQL Server Agent jobs in an availability group environment, you will still need to configure your maintenance plans on each SQL Server instance, some of which will cover databases not included in availability groups and the system databases master and msdb, for example. You should ensure that your maintenance plans, regardless of platform, are consistently updated on all replicas and also are aware of their local replica role, so that maintenance plans do not need to be turned on, turned off, or reconfigured when a failover occurs.

The SQL Server Agent must be enabled, and your SQL Server Agent jobs must exist on all replicas of the availability group and be replica-aware (the script should know if it is running on the primary replica for a database). You will need multiple versions of any custom maintenance task in order to separate scripts for databases in each availability group and one more for databases not in an availability group (including any system databases that you intend to maintain with custom scripts).

To avoid having SQL Server Agent jobs error when their local replica is not the primary replica for a database, you can add a T-SQL step to the start of the job to detect and raise a failure. The goal of the first step is to prevent subsequent job steps from running and failing against secondary replica databases, which will not be not writeable. Name the first step "Am I Primary?" or something similar, and then add the following script:

```
--add as step 1 on every AG-aware job

IF NOT EXISTS (

SELECT @@SERVERNAME, *

    FROM sys.dm_hadr_availability_replica_states rs

    inner join sys.availability_databases_cluster dc

    on rs.group_id = dc.group_id

    WHERE is_local = 1

    and role_desc = 'PRIMARY'

--Any databases in the same Availability Group

    and dc.database_name in (N'databasename1', N'databasename2'))

BEGIN

    print 'local SQL instance is not primary, skipping';

    throw 50000, 'Do not continue', 1;

END;
```

This code causes Step 1 to fail when it is not run on a primary replica for the specified database(s). In the Advanced settings of the "Am I Primary?" job step, the On Success Action should be Go To The Next Step, as usual, but the On Failure Action should be Quit The Job Reporting Success, which would not register as a job failure. Instead of a green check mark or a red "X" next to the job, SQL Server Job History displays a yellow triangle. This prevents subsequent job steps from running and failing against secondary replica databases, which will not be writeable.

> ### NOTE
> The previous script is not appropriate for Maintenance Plans jobs. Any change to the Maintenance Plan will re-create the job and overwrite the new "Am I Primary?" task you added. Instead, take advantage of the availability group–aware backup priority settings in the Back Up Database Task. We look at this in more detail in the next section.

> ➤ For more about availability groups, see Chapter 11, "Implementing high availability and disaster recovery."

Maintaining SQL Server

In this section, we review what you should be doing as a day-to-day database administrator of a SQL Server instance, how to accomplish these tasks, and the built-in tools that SQL Server provides. SQL Server editions above Express edition (because Express has no Agent) ship fully featured and ready for you to configure to perform basic maintenance.

> ### NOTE
> This section provides ways to accomplish all major maintenance objectives using tools built into SQL Server. However, that doesn't mean you shouldn't use third-party tools.

For the most part, the tasks in this section are built into Azure SQL Database. In some cases, the maintenance tasks are completely automated, especially in the case of disaster recovery, or partially automated, in the case of index maintenance. We'll be focusing on SQL Server instances in this section because the fast evolution of Azure SQL Database reduces the hands-on maintenance required by DBAs on the PaaS platform, and even managed instance to a lesser extent.

> ➤ For more information on Azure SQL databases and Managed Instances, see Chapter 17 and Chapter 18.

Basic "care and feeding" of SQL Server

You can carry out the regular proactive maintenance of a SQL Server instance by using one or more of the following strategies:

- SQL Server Maintenance Plans, including the option to use a Maintenance Plan Wizard

- Custom scripting using DMVs and T-SQL or PowerShell commands

- Third-party tools

Each has advantages and disadvantages, and each makes different compromises between ease of setup and customizability.

You can run these strategies via SQL Server Agent jobs, except for some third-party software packages that would utilize an external scheduling apparatus. You can configure each to provide customized activity logging, retention, and the ability to view history in different ways.

Regardless of the strategy or strategies adopted, whether with built-in or third-party tools, you should accomplish the following as a **bare minimum** on a regular schedule, tailored to meet your Service-Level Agreement and recovery objectives agreed with your organization:

1. Backup system and user databases.

    a. Full backups for all databases.

    b. Transaction log backups for databases not in the simple recovery model.

    c. To save space and reduce time to recover using transaction log restores, differential backups between less frequent full backups.

2. Implement a retention policy for database backups, if backups are stored locally, by deleting backups after a business-approved amount of time. In the case of tape backups, have a rotation policy instead.

3. Implement a retention policy for maintenance plan log files, backup and restore history records in msdb, old Database Mail row entries.

    a. SQL Server Error Log files are already maintained by SQL Server to a configurable number of log files. (The default is 6 which should likely be increased.)

    b. SQL Server Agent job history is also maintained automatically by settings in the SQL Server Agent properties.

    c. Backup history is kept in the msdb database and should be pruned over time.

4. Maintain index and heap health in SQL Server.

    a. There are different strategies to reduce fragmentation in clustered and nonclustered indexes.

    b. Columnstore indexes also require maintenance via REORGANIZE steps, especially if there is update or delete activity in the table, and fragmentation is measured differently.

    c. Monitor heap structures (tables without a clustered index) for excessive forwarding pointers.

5. Update statistics.

    a. This should accompany INDEX REORGANIZE steps, but not INDEX REBUILD steps. Remember that the INDEX REBUILD command also updates index statistics.

CHAPTER 9

6. Check database integrity via DBCC CHECKDB.

7. Maintain copies of backed up data in secure off-premises facilities.

   a. Storage-Area Network (SAN) replication or another file-level backup system can accomplish this, as can integration with Azure Storage for easy cloud-based backup.

   b. Remember that your data loss tolerance isn't defined by how often you take backups, but by how often those backups get securely off-premises and tested!

What will vary is how often these tasks need to run on each server and database and even what type of backups you need. This section of the chapter walks you through the process of creating tools to manage the previous tasks, by writing T-SQL Scripts scheduled using SQL Server Agent; using the Maintenance Plan designer and the Maintenance Plan Wizard.

Even though we won't make any recommendations regarding third-party tools, we should note that many third-party tools do not provide an end-to-end solution for maintaining secure off-site backups (item 7 in the previous list), which typically involves coordination with the storage administrators and/or cloud hosting such as Azure Storage. SQL Server Managed Backup to Azure is a full-featured SQL Server backup solution (though not free, it is relatively inexpensive). It is the Microsoft-recommended backup solution for SQL Server instances running on Azure virtual machines (VMs).

If you want to maintain direct control of backing up off-premises, you can use BACKUP ... TO URL statements to write backups directly to Azure Storage, often to complement local backup storage. (Scripting that yourself is free of course, but Azure Storage is not). To meet your Recovery Time Objective (RTO) goals, or in the event of external network failure, you should also maintain local backups within your network for a time. Remember to take regulatory data retention guidelines into account.

➤ For more details about backups, schedules, T-SQL command parameters, and backup strategy, refer to Chapter 10, "Developing, deploying, and managing data recovery."

Using SQL Server Maintenance Plans

SQL Server Maintenance Plans are a free, low-cost, low-complexity, visually built option to implement SQL Server maintenance and disaster recovery. The drag-and-drop tasks built in to Maintenance Plans' design surface have some distinct shortcomings that we'll review. You will see differences when creating Maintenance Plans in SSMS from version to version of SQL Server.

NOTE

As of this writing, Maintenance Plans are not supported for SQL Server on Linux, but that doesn't prevent you from targeting a Linux instance from SQL Server on Windows.

The Maintenance Plan Wizard is a step-by-step tour through most of the steps necessary for SQL Server. The Maintenance Plan Wizard guides you through an easy process of creating a Maintenance Plan with most of the basics, which you'll then be able to review with the Maintenance Plan design surface in SSMS. To begin with a fresh slate, click **New Maintenance Plan**. This prepopulates objects for you in the designer, with which we recommend you become familiar.

The maintenance plan designer has three main sections: the subplans list, the design surface, and the Maintenance Plan tasks toolbox. When you open a maintenance plan, the first two will be obvious, but the toolbox might not be docked. To display the toolbox and pin it to the side of SSMS, press Ctrl+Alt+X, or, on the View menu, click Toolbox. If you have any experience with SQL Server Integration Services (SSIS), the interface will feel very familiar. Behind the scenes, Maintenance Plans create and store SSIS packages internally.

The tasks in a Maintenance Plan and the choices in the Maintenance Plan Wizard translate directly to the options you're already familiar with in SQL Server Agent jobs or the options for backups and index maintenance T-SQL commands. For example, the Run As option on the first screen of the wizard or in the Subplan properties of the designer, provides a list of proxies just as a SQL Server Agent job step does. Instead of using the SQL Server Agent service account, ideally you should choose a proxy that has access to the SQL Server Integration Services Package Execution subsystem.

> ### NOTE
> You may see an explanation screen as the first screen of many wizards in SSMS, and you can choose not to show these explanations in the future.

Covering databases with the Maintenance Plan

When you select the maintenance tasks that you want the wizard to configure, you'll be able to select the databases you want to run the tasks against. The options are:

- all databases
- system databases
- all user databases
- specify a list of databases

You also have the option to ignore databases for which the status is not online, which we also recommend.

To isolate the configuration, maintenance, and logging from one another, it is a common to create two Maintenance Plans: one for system databases (master, model, and msdb) and at least one for all user databases, depending on business requirements. The system plan just handles system database backups, the user plan handles everything else. This ensures that if there are any issues with ongoing changes to the User Maintenance Plan, the crucial system database backups are unaffected.

Inside OUT

Will a SQL Server Maintenance Plan automatically detect a new database created on SQL Server?

Yes, a Maintenance Plan can accomplish this if you configure it correctly, which could be invaluable to you when applications are configured to procedurally create new databases, such as SharePoint.

You should try to configure Maintenance Plan tasks to use either the All Databases, or All User Databases (assuming that you have another task that covers system databases). When you select either of these, new databases are automatically included in the maintenance plan. This makes your job as an administrator easier. If you choose a specific fixed list of databases using the These Databases option and list, new databases will be ignored, and you will need to remember to add the databases to the Maintenance Plan.

If you have databases that are no longer in use that you no longer want to cover with Maintenance Plans, consider taking the database offline, and then using the option in many Maintenance Plan tasks to ignore databases where the status is not online.

There is one caveat regarding transaction log backups tasks using either of the two All options for databases. After you create a new database in the full recovery model, the backup task that takes transaction log backups in the Maintenance Plan will attempt to take a transaction log backup, and will fail. This is because a database must first have a full database backup taken before a transaction log backup will succeed. When you create a new database, take a manual full backup, or your Maintenance Plan will show errors until a full backup is performed. Other database's transaction log backups will continue to run as usual, even if one or more databases fail.

Maintenance plan tasks

On the first page of the Maintenance Plan Wizard, you have the option to run each task with separate schedules or with a single schedule for the entire plan. We recommend that you choose the Separate Schedules For Each Task option here, or if you're building the maintenance plan in the designer, break activities into multiple subplans, each with its own schedules.

This is because some tasks such as index maintenance or database integrity checks can take a long time to run, and you do not want your backups in serial with those, and then delayed and inconsistently occurring. To work the maintenance plan into your after-hours windows, you will want more scheduling flexibility than a single start time for all tasks to run serially.

On the Select Maintenance Tasks page of the Maintenance Plan Wizard, there is a list of all of the built-in maintenance tasks. In the graphical designer, you have one additional tool to run custom T-SQL scripts titled Execute T-SQL Statement Task. You can use this to run your custom maintenance scripting or other administrative scripts. We review that later in this section.

NOTE

The Maintenance Plan Wizard can create only one copy of each available task. To create two different tasks of the types we'll be looking at in a moment—for example, one for system databases and one for user databases—you will need to use the Maintenance Plan designer in SQL Server Management Studio.

The following sections present the available tasks that you can select from, along with descriptions of what they do.

Check Database Integrity task

The Check Database Integrity task runs DBCC CHECKDB to check for database corruption, a necessary task that you should run periodically. You should run DBCC CHECKDB at least as often as your backup retention plan. For example, if you keep local backups around for one month, you should make sure that you perform a successful DBCC CHECKDB no less than once per month. More often, if possible, is recommended. On large databases, this task could take hours.

> ➤ For more about data corruption and checking database integrity, see Chapter 8, "Maintaining and monitoring SQL Server."

The options available in the Maintenance Plan task match the common parameters you would use in the DBCC CHECKDB command. The Physical Only check box uses the PHYSICAL_ONLY parameter of DBCC CHECKDB, which limits DBCC CHECKDB to checking physical structures, torn pages, checksum failures, and common hardware failures. It is less comprehensive as a result. However, using PHYSICAL_ONLY can take significantly less time to complete while still detecting the signs of common storage hardware failure.

NOTE

A common practice when using the PHYSICAL_ONLY option of DBCC CHECKDB or the Check Database Integrity Maintenance Plan task is to maintain a system in which production databases are restored on a matching nonproduction system, and running a time-consuming full integrity check (without the PHYSICAL_ONLY parameter) to catch any corruption issues. However, there is no substitute for running a full DBCC CHECKDB on your production system.

Shrink Database task

There is no sound reason to ever perform a Shrink Database task on a schedule. A Shrink Database step removes free space from a file and returns it to the OS, causing the file to experience an autogrowth event the next time data it is written to it. Do not ever include the Shrink Database task in the Maintenance Plan.

Inside OUT

When should you shrink your database?

If you have deleted a significant portion of data from your database, you can perform a one-off shrink of the database to reclaim drive space, provided that the immediate next step is to rebuild all indexes in that database. A shrink database (or shrink file) task heavily fragments the database, and rebuilding the indexes will remove this fragmentation.

Reorganize Index task

A reorganize task runs an ALTER INDEX ... REORGANIZE statement, which reduces index fragmentation but does not update statistics. On large databases, this could take hours, but will have less overhead, less query disruption, and finish faster than a Rebuild Index.

Because Reorganize Index is an online operation and reads only one 8-KB data page at a time, it will not take long-term table locks and might block other user queries for only a very short period of time. Online index operations will consume server resources and generate large amounts of logged transactions.

If you use this task in your Maintenance Plan, remember to add an Update Statistics task to run immediately after it.

> ➤ In the "Rebuild Index task" section, we cover a method to maintain indexes that are above a certain fragmentation percentage.

Rebuild Index task

More thorough than a Reorganize step at removing index fragmentation, this task runs an ALTER INDEX ... REBUILD statement and does update statistics. The options available in the Rebuild Index dialog box correspond to the options for the ALTER INDEX ... REBUILD syntax.

NOTE

At the time of this writing, Maintenance Plans currently do not support RESUMABLE index rebuilds, which might be a necessity for you on very large tables. See Chapter 8 for more information on ALTER INDEX ... REORGANIZE and REBUILD.

With Enterprise edition, you can perform a Rebuild step as an online operation, which is not likely to block other user queries like an offline rebuild does. Not all indexes and data types can have an online rebuild performed, so the Maintenance Plan dialog box for the Rebuild Index task will ask you what you want to happen.

Rebuilding indexes without the ONLINE option will block other user queries attempting to use that index, and will consume server resources. On large tables, this could take hours to finish, and even more without the ONLINE option due to the overhead of managing blocking.

Inside OUT

Do you need to maintain memory-optimized table indexes?

Memory-optimized table indexes do not accumulate fragmentation on-disk and do not need regular maintenance for fragmentation. However, you should routinely monitor the number of distinct values in hash index keys, and adjust the number of buckets in a hash index over time with the ALTER TABLE ... ALTER INDEX ... REBUILD syntax.

Memory-optimized tables are ignored by Maintenance Plans in SSMS.

Maintaining indexes above a certain fragmentation percentage

You can intelligently limit index maintenance to certain thresholds, starting with the options to select between Fast (LIMITED), Sampled, and Detailed. This corresponds the parameters provided to the structural statistics dynamic management function (DMF), sys. dm_db_index_physical_stats.

NOTE

This task does not operate on columnstore indexes. See Chapter 8 for more information on maintaining columnstore indexes.

You can configure the Reorganize and Rebuild tasks to maintain only indexes filtered by percentage of fragmentation and page count, both from sys.dm_db_index_physical_stats, and/or actual index usage (based on the sys.dm_db_index_usage_stats DMF). The fragmentation threshold is 15% by default in the Reorganize task, 30% in the Rebuild task, as illustrated in Figure 9-2.

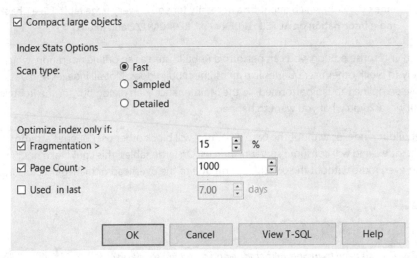

Figure 9-2   The options to maintain indexes available in the Maintenance Plan Index Reorganize and Index Rebuild tasks.

Other options added to the Reorganize and Rebuild tasks match the options for the ALTER INDEX ... REORGANIZE, and REBUILD T-SQL commands, which we covered in detail in Chapter 8.

Update Statistics task

The Update Statistics task runs an UPDATE STATISTICS statement, rebuilding index statistics, which we review in Chapter 15, "Understanding and designing indexes". Do not follow an Index Rebuild task with an Update Statistics task for the same objects, because this is redundant work. Updating statistics is an online operation, so it will not block other user queries, but it will consume server resources. This task should finish faster than either a REORGANIZE or REBUILD step. On larger databases, or databases with flash storage, this task can replace more frequent Index Rebuild or Index Reorganize tasks.

Inside OUT

How does `auto_create_stats` *affect the Update Statistics task in a Maintenance Plan?*

You should maintain the health of Update Statistics with regularity, even if not in a Maintenance Plan. When `auto_update_stats` is turned on, statistics are updated periodically based on usage. Statistics are considered out of date by the query optimizer when a ratio of data modifications to rows in the table has been reached. The query optimizer checks for and updates the out-of-date statistic before running a query plan. Therefore, `auto_update_stats` has some small runtime overhead, though the performance benefit of updated statistics usually outweighs this cost. We also recommend turning on `auto_update_stats_async` option, which helps minimize this runtime overhead by updating the statistics after the query is run, instead of before.

Turn these on for all user databases unless the application specifically requests that it be turned off, such as is the case with Microsoft SharePoint.

You can also manually identify the date on which any statistics object was last updated by using the `sys.dm_db_stats_properties` DMF. In your databases, you might see that there are statistics that are quite old. This means that they might not have been accessed in a way that prompts the `auto_update_stats` update and have not had an `INDEX REBUILD`, which would also update the statistics.

Updating both column and index statistics for a database regularly, if your maintenance window time allows, will almost certainly help. By updating statistics regularly, you can reduce the number of statistics updates that happen automatically during transactions in regular business hours.

History Cleanup task

This task deletes older rows in msdb tables that contain database backup and restore history, prunes the SQL Server Agent log file, and also removes older Maintenance Plan log records. These are accomplished by running three stored procedures in the msdb database: `dbo.sp_delete_backuphistory`, `dbo.sp_purge_jobhistory`, and `dbo.sp_maintplan_delete_log` respectively. You should run this task to prevent excessively old data from being retained, according to your environmental data retention requirements. This will save space and prevent large table sizes from degrading the performance of maintenance tasks. This step should finish quickly and would not disrupt user queries. This step does not delete backup files or Maintenance Plan log files; that is the job of the Maintenance Cleanup task.

Maintenance Cleanup task

The Maintenance Cleanup task deletes files from folders and is commonly used to delete old database backup files, using the system stored procedure `master.dbo.xp_delete_file`. You also can use it to clean up the .txt files that Maintenance Plans write their history to in the SQL Server instance's Log folder. You can configure the task to look for and delete any extension and by folder directory, and then specify that subdirectories be included. The date filter uses the Date Modified file attribute (not the Date Created attribute). Combined with the option to create a subdirectory for each database, this means that you can create and remove backups files in the folder structure for each database.

NOTE

In the case of Maintenance Plans, by default logs are kept in a table, `msdb.dbo.sys-maintplan_log`, as well as in text files in the SQL Server instance default Log folder. Deleting one does not delete the other. You should maintain a retention policy on both sources of Maintenance Plan run history.

The Maintenance Cleanup task deletes files only from folders, and thus isn't an option to enforce a retention policy for backups to URL in Azure Storage. And currently, Maintenance Plans in SSMS are not supported at all on SQL Server on Linux, although this capability might be added in the near future.

Inside OUT

How do you delete old backups in Azure Storage?

You should use the stored procedure `sp_delete_backup` to clean up file-snapshot based backups taken in Azure Storage, which are continuous chains of backup starting from a single full database backup.

To clean up old backups taken to Blob storage using the BACKUP ... TO URL syntax, you should not try to delete the base blob of the backup using Microsoft Azure Storage Explorer or the Azure Storage viewer in SQL Server Management Studio for example. Aside from the files, there are pointers to the file-snapshots in a file-snapshot backup set that must be deleted as well.

Note also that SQL Server Managed Backup to Azure has its own retention plan, which is currently limited to a maximum of 30 days.

Execute SQL Server Agent Job task

Using this task, you can orchestrate the asynchronous start of another SQL Server Agent job during the Maintenance Plan, perhaps to start another middle-of-the-night process as soon as possible after maintenance is complete.

Back Up Database (Full, Differential, Transaction Log) task

With this task, you can take a backup of any kind of the specified databases. The options in the Maintenance Plan dialog box for the backup are similar to the SSMS Database Backup dialog box, plus some minor extra options, including an option to ignore replica priority in an availability group database.

NOTE

The standard extensions for backup files are .bak (full), .dif (differential), and .trn (log), but these are just conventions. You can provide any file extension (or none at all) for your backup types, as long as you are consistent across your entire SQL Server environment with backup file extensions.

The Back Up Database task affords you multiple strategies for backups, including backing up to disk or to Azure Storage via URL as well as to the deprecated tape backup support.

Backing up to URL writes files directly to Azure Storage natively, without the need to install any software or network connections. This was a fairly limited feature prior to SQL Server 2016 but now can be accomplished via a shared access signature credential for secure access to Azure Blob storage.

➤ A step-by-step walkthrough is available at *https://docs.microsoft.com/sql/ relational-databases/tutorial-use-azure-blob-storage-service-with-sql-server-2016*.

You can configure disk backups to append multiple database backups multiple times to the same file or files, or create a backup file and a subdirectory for each database per backup. For backups to disk, we recommend that each database has a subdirectory in the folder location you select, to separate the backup files of databases with potentially different retention plans or recovery strategies. The Maintenance Plan backup will automatically create subdirectories for new databases, and when performing backups, append a time stamp and a unique string to backup names in the following format: *databasename_backup_yyyy_mm_dd_hhmmss_uniquenumber.bak|dif|trn*.

We recommend that you select the options for Verify Backup Integrity, CHECKSUM, and Compress Backup for all database types, for all databases.

NOTE

If you are backing up your databases to a compressed location, you may want to disable database backup compression.

This is supported even for backups to URL. Keep in mind that the Verify Backup step performs a RESTORE VERIFYONLY statement to examine the backup file and verify that it was valid, complete, and should be restorable. "Should be" is key, because the only way to truly test whether the backup was valid is to test a restore. The RESTORE VERIFYONLY does not actually restore the database backup, but could give you an early heads-up on a potential drive or backup issue, and is always recommended when time permits. The verify step could significantly increase the duration of the backup, scaling with the size of the database backup, but is time well worth spending in your regular maintenance window.

CHAPTER 9

Execute T-SQL Statement task (not available in the wizard)

This task can run T-SQL statements against any SQL Server connection, with a configurable time-out. A simple text box accepts T-SQL statements, and because of its simplicity, we recommend that instead of pasting lengthy commands, you instead reference a stored procedure. This would be easier to maintain and potentially keep in source control by developing the stored procedure in other tools. You may find it useful to keep this and other stored procedures in a database specifically dedicated to database administration tasks.

Maintenance Plan report options

By default, Maintenance Plans create a report in two places to record the history for each time a subplan runs. Logs are kept in a table, `msdb.dbo.sysmaintplan_log`, as well as in .txt files in the SQL Server instance default Log folder. You can also choose the Email Report option in the Maintenance Plan Wizard, which adds a Notify Operator Task.

Building Maintenance Plans using the designer in SSMS

Owing to the nature of wizards, there are some inherent issues with configuring a robust maintenance solution that covers all the needs of your databases. The Maintenance Plan designer in SSMS gives you the ability to set up your task run order and precedence constraints as well as to maintain multiple subplan schedules within a maintenance plan (see Figure 9-3).

Figure 9-3 displays a sample Maintenance Plan.

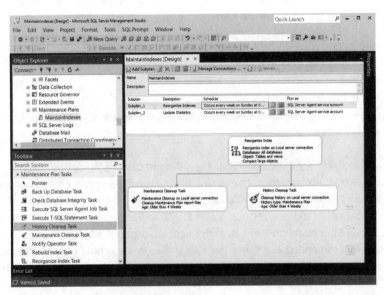

Figure 9-3 A sample maintenance plan for User databases has been created, with multiple subplans, each running on a different schedule.

When you save the maintenance plan, each of the subplans in the maintenance plan will become a SQL Server Agent job with a naming convention *maintenance plan name.subplan name*.

NOTE

When you save a Maintenance Plan, the job(s) it creates might be owned by your personal login to the SQL Server. Be aware that if your account becomes disabled or locked out, this will prevent the SQL Server Agent job from running.

At the top of the Maintenance Plan window is where the subplans are listed; initially, there will be just one plan called Subplan_1. You should break down the tasks that will be accomplished in the subplan by the schedules they will follow, and name them accordingly. You can add subplans and manage their schedules in the Maintenance Plan window. Note that you should not make changes to the SQL Server Agent jobs after they've been created—the next time you edit the Maintenance Plan, your changes will most likely be overwritten.

The large gray area beneath the subplan list is the design surface for Maintenance Plans, a graphical, drag-and-drop interface. To add tasks to a subplan, you can drag a task from the toolbox to the design surface. To serialize the running of multiple tasks, click one, and then click the green arrow beneath the box, dragging it to the task that should follow. You can create a long string of sequential activities or a wide set of parallel-running activities, similar to designing SQL Server Integration Services (SSIS) packages.

NOTE

When in the Database Maintenance Plan Designer task, there is a View T-SQL button that shows you the exact T-SQL that will be run to perform the maintenance tasks. You can use this to learn the commands for maintenance tasks so that you can make your own customized plans, which we talk about in the next section.

When not to use SQL Server Maintenance Plans

Personal preference, of course, is a fine enough reason not to use built-in Maintenance Plans. You can write your own, as long as your library of scripts or third-party tools accomplishes the necessary maintenance tasks with consistency, configurability, and good logging for review.

For SQL Server instances with manageable maintenance windows, Maintenance Plans will meet your needs if the schedules are set up appropriately. You can create a variety of Maintenance Plans to cover databases with various levels of importance or availability based on business requirements (with the caveat of not being able to detect new databases). For very large databases or databases with 24x7 availability requirements, more granularity for maintenance operations will likely be necessary.

Not every business has the luxury of having all night and/or all weekend to perform maintenance outside of business hours. When you become familiar with the T-SQL commands and
their various options, you can be creative to overcome tight scheduling, crowded maintenance
windows, very large databases, or other Maintenance Plan complications.

After reviewing the capabilities of the Backup Up task and Rebuild Index task, you should consider Maintenance Plans more full-featured and capable of handling the bulk of maintenance,
even on larger databases with tight schedules. Ultimately, the success of Maintenance Plans or
custom scripts will depend on your understanding of the various options available for the seven
core maintenance tasks listed earlier in this chapter and elsewhere in this book.

Backing up availability groups using a secondary replica

This section may look out of place here, but rest assured it makes sense. We have been looking
at single-instance SQL Server maintenance tasks up to now, but automation applies to availability groups as well.

> ➤ You can read more about availability groups in Chapter 2, "Introducing database server
> components" and Chapter 11.

One of the many useful features in availability groups is the ability to utilize read-only secondary replicas for remote backups. Performing backups on a secondary replica, including a geographically separated replica, introduces complexity but has a big advantage. Backups do not
take locks and will never block a user query, but they will incur significant CPU, memory, and
I/O overhead. Backups can slow database response, so on servers with large databases and/or
busy 24x7 utilization, it might be helpful, and in some cases necessary, to find alternative strategies to backups. Taking database backups on secondary replicas is one of the alternatives and
moves the resource expense of backups off the primary replica.

Understanding backup priority values

In SSMS, in Object Explorer, expand the **Always On High Availability** node for the instance
of the primary replica, and then the **Availability Groups** node. Right-click on the availability
group you wish to view, click **Properties**, and take a look at the Backup Preferences page. It's
important to understand the priority values and how they interact with various backup tasks.

The default option is to Prefer Secondary, which specifies that backups occur on the secondary
replica first or, if it is not available, on the primary replica. You then can provide priority values (0
to 100, where 100 is highest) to decide which of multiple secondary replicas should be the preferred backup location. The values apply to both full and transaction log backups.

Other self-explanatory options include Primary, Secondary Only, or Any Replica, which uses the
priority values to decide which replica is preferred for the backups. When failing over to another
replica, you will need to review and script the changes to the backup priority. Your planned
failover scripts should include the reassignment of backup priority values.

It's also important to note that this Backup Preferences page affects only backup systems or scripts that are aware of the backup preferences. For example, in SSMS, in Object Explorer, right-click a database, and then, on the shortcut menu, click Tasks, and then Backup. The dialog box that opens takes a backup of a database but does not include any availability groups–aware settings. On the other hand, the Back Up Database task in SQL Server Maintenance Plans is aware of availability group backup priority value settings.

You are limited to taking full copy-only database backups and transaction log backups on readable secondary replica databases. When including databases in an availability group, the Maintenance Plan Back Up Database task will warn you if you are attempting to configure a full database backup without a copy-only check or differential backup, or if you select the "For availability databases, ignore replica priority for backup and backup on primary settings" check box. If this is misconfigured, it is possible to create a Maintenance Plan that will run but not take backups of databases in an availability group.

➤ For more information on using replica backup priorities, visit *https://docs. microsoft.com/sql/database-engine/availability-groups/windows/active-secondaries-backup-on-secondary-replicas-always-on-availability-groups* and *https://docs.microsoft.com/sql/database-engine/availability-groups/ windows/configure-backup-on-availability-replicas-sql-server*.

Use replica backup priority in your backup schedules

If you attempt to configure a full database backup without copy-only or a differential backup, you will see the warning in the Back Up Database task "This backup type is not supported on a secondary replica and this task will fail if the task runs on a secondary replica." If you select the Ignore Replica Priority check box, the warning will read "Note: Ignoring the backup priority and availability group settings may result in simultaneous parallel backups if the maintenance plan is cloned on all replicas."

Maintenance Plans should run on a schedule on all availability group replicas. The priority values for backups can cause a backup not to be taken on a primary or nonpreferred secondary replica, but the Maintenance Plan backup task will start and complete as usual. The Maintenance Plans will use the backup priority values and do not need to be configured when different replicas in the availability group become primary.

You can still take a manual backup of any type of the databases and bypass the availability group backup preferences, and, in fact, your backup strategy might include intentionally taking full backups in more than one node of a geographically dispersed availability group.

If you are not using SQL Server Maintenance Plans or scripting to take backups, be aware that not all third-party backup solutions are aware of availability group backup preferences or even availability groups in general. Maintenance Plans in SSMS are aware of the backup preferences, as can be your custom scripting via the function `master.`

`sys.fn_hadr_backup_is_preferred_replica`. It returns a 0 or 1, based on whether the current SQL Server instance is operating as the preferred backup.

> ## Inside OUT
>
> ### How do you prevent a broken chain when taking backups on secondary replicas?
>
> Taking backups of the same database on multiple servers could lead to some parts of a backup recovery chain being stored on different servers. The solution to this is rather obvious: you should always ensure that backups are copied securely off-premises to the same location, from one datacenter or secured site to another, which is likely where your availability group replicas are.
>
> Just as you would copy your backups of a standalone SQL Server instance to another location, you must copy your backups of availability group databases off-premises, ideally to each other. You can accomplish this with two strategies.
>
> Copy the backups taken on the secondary node to the primary regularly, and make sure you maintain a chain of transaction log backups together with their root full and/or differential backups, regardless of where the backups were taken. You should keep a complete chain intact in multiple locations.

Strategies for administering multiple SQL Servers

There are some options for creating orchestration in SQL Server, to allow for a multiplication and standardization of SQL Server DBA effort across multiple servers. The potential to set up SQL Server Agent jobs that are run simultaneously on multiple servers is powerful, especially for custom-developed scripts to gather and report information back to a central SQL Server.

> ➤ You should be aware of the Registered Servers and Central Management Server features of SSMS that we reviewed in Chapter 1.

Master and Target servers for SQL Agent jobs

The Master and Target servers (known as the MSX/TSX) feature is built in to SQL Server Agent to aid DBAs who want to manage identical jobs across multiple SQL Server instances. This feature has been in the product since SQL Server 7.0, but many DBAs are unaware of the convenience that it can deliver. There is no doubt that the feature is useful and works seamlessly with technologies it could not have foreseen, including availability groups (more on that later).

You can designate one SQL Server as a Master server (MSX) and set up multiserver jobs on that server, and configure each instance to have its SQL Server Agent jobs remotely managed into a

Target server (TSX). The MSX cannot be a TSX of itself, so using a separate production server to orchestrate multiserver administration of SQL Server Agent jobs is necessary. The MSX server should be a production environment server that does not host performance-sensitive production workloads.

Other considerations for the MSX server include the following:

- Of the servers you have available, choose the most recent version of SQL Server for the MSX server. You can communicate with up to two previous versions for TSX servers.

- Each TSX can have only one MSX.

- Before changing the name of a TSX, first defect it from the MSX and then reenlist it. However, we recommend modifying a TSX name using DNS instead.

- Do not use a built-in account for the SQL Server Agent service account on all servers; instead, use a domain service account, as recommended earlier in this chapter in the "Understanding job step security" section.

Creating MSX and TSX Servers by using SSMS

In SSMS, in Object Explorer, right-click SQL Server Agent, select Multi Server Administration, and then click **Make This A Master**.

The Master Server Wizard launches and first sets up a special operator just for running multi-server jobs, called MSXOperator. You can specify only one operator to run multiserver jobs, so think carefully about who should be notified about these jobs. Specify the email address. As always with operators, it's best not to use an individual's email addresses, but to use an email distribution group, instead.

Next, the wizard presents locally registered and central-management registered servers so that you can select them as targets for the MSX. Select the target servers from the list or, at the bottom, click Add Connection and add servers not registered in your list.

When you are finished with the wizard, the labels in Object Explorer will be different for both Master and Target SQL Server Agents. Similarly, on the MSX, under SQL Server Agent in Object Explorer, you will see two new subfolders under Jobs: Local Jobs and Multi-Server Jobs.

By default, SSL encryption is used between the servers, but you can change that through a registry setting. You should not need to change this, because encrypted communication between the servers is recommended, even on your internal networks. An SSL certificate will need to be installed on the server before using it through the wizard.

> ➤ If you cannot use SSL but need to secure the connection between TSX and MSX servers, see *https://docs.microsoft.com/sql/ssms/agent/set-encryption-options-on-target-servers* for the exact entries.

Though we do not recommend it, you can turn off the encryption of Master-Target servers by changing the registry set to not use encryption. The registry key `HKEY_LOCAL_MACHINE\SOFTWARE\Microsoft\Microsoft SQL Server\isntance\SQLServerAgent\MSxEncryptChannelOptions` is by default 2, which means all communication is encrypted. Changing this to 0 on all servers removes encryption.

> ➤ **For more information, visit** *https://docs.microsoft.com/sql/ssms/agent/set-encryption-options-on-target-servers.*

Managing multiserver (MSX/TSX) administration

To manage SQL Server Agent jobs in a multiserver environment, set up the job in the same way you would for any other job on the MSX server. Then, navigate to the Targets page on the job, which outside of a multiserver environment has no use. From there, select Target Multiple Servers and then select the servers on which the job should run. In the background, code is run to send the jobs to the TSX servers.

Any jobs with steps that use proxies will need the proxy accounts to have access to the TSX, and a proxy by that same name on the TSX, otherwise the job will not find a proxy on the TSX. By default, matching proxy names from MSX to TSX isn't allowed, because of the potential for malicious action. This must be turned on via the registry on the TSX.

> ➤ **For more information, visit** *https://docs.microsoft.com/sql/ssms/agent/troubleshoot-multiserver-jobs-that-use-proxies.*

On Target servers, jobs will appear in the SQL Server Agent, in the Jobs folder, but you can't edit them.

Sometimes, the synchronizing of job definitions to the TSX will not be queued up and not post to a server. In this case, issue the following the command, but be aware that this cancels any running jobs on the TSX:

```
EXEC msdb.dbo.sp_resync_targetserver '<Target Server Name>';
```

Most other issues with multiserver jobs are solved by defecting the TSX and then adding it again.

Managing multiserver administration in availability groups

The MSX/TSX feature works with availability groups and can be quite useful for ensuring that jobs stay synchronized across servers. The MSX/TSX data is stored in system tables in the msdb database, which cannot be part of an availability group.

You should not have the MSX on a SQL Server instance in the availability group, because this would limit your ability to failover and use SQL Server Agent Multi Server Administration. You would lose your ability to orchestrate jobs across the Target servers if one of the nodes in your availability group was unreachable, compromising your failover state. Instead, consider other high availability solutions for the server that functions at the master.

Note that using MSX/TSX for availability group SQL Server Agents doesn't change the need to set up the "Am I Primary?" logic in step 1 of any job that should run only on a SQL Server instance that currently hosts the primary replica.

> ➤ For a code sample, refer to the section "SQL Agent Job considerations when using availability groups" earlier in this chapter.

SQL Server Agent event forwarding

Event forwarding refers to having one central Windows server to receive the SQL Server events of many. The server that is the destination of many servers' forwarded events might handle a heavy workload, especially network traffic. The destination server should be a production-environment server that does not host performance-sensitive production workloads. You can refer to this server as the alerts management server.

Event forwarding allows for the Windows Event Viewer to be a single pane view of events on many instances of SQL Server. Further, it allows for alerts on the alerts management server to prompt a response to the originating server, via SQL Server Agent alerts. Forwarded errors arrive in the Windows Application Event log, not the SQL Server Error Log, and because of this, the SQL Server Agent service account needs to be a local Windows administrator.

Typically, this setup is the same server as your Multi Server Administration (MSX/TSX) server; in fact, the features work together. If your MSX server and alerts management server are on separate SQL Server instances, you will lose the ability to run jobs when events happen.

Setting up event forwarding

You configure event forwarding in the SQL Server Agent Properties dialog box. In SSMS, open the SQL Server Agent Properties dialog box, and then go to the Advanced page. In the SQL Server Event Forwarding section, select the Forward Events To A Different Server check box. In the text box, type the name of the alerts management server. Be aware that the alerts management server that receives forwarded events must be the SQL Server default instance of a server.

You can also choose whether to send all events or only unhandled alerts that have not been handled by local alerts on each SQL Server instance. You can then specify a minimum error severity to be forwarded. We recommend that you select errors of Severity 16 and above, keeping in mind the caveat of nuisance Severity errors.

> ➤ For information about alerts and error severity, see the section "Components of SQL Server automated administration" earlier in this chapter.

Policy-Based Management

Policy-Based Management (PBM) is a powerful tool for enforcing rules for configuration settings, options for databases and servers, security principals, table design, even database object naming conventions. As of this writing, this feature does not yet apply to Azure SQL Database.

PBM is structured around policies. Policies contain a single condition, which is a Boolean expression. The condition expression is evaluated against properties and setting of destination objects, such as the server itself, a database, a table, or an index.

For example, you might set up a condition around the AdHocRemoteQueries server-level setting. SQL Server has a large list of facet properties built into it, such as AdHocRemoveQueriesEnabled in the Surface Area Configuration facet. (As we covered in Chapter 4, the Surface Area Configuration facet contains a number of security-sensitive features, many of which—but not all—we recommend that you turn off unless needed.) To check that this Surface Area Configuration option is always turned off, create an expression that checks whether AdHocRemoveQueriesEnabled can be evaluated to Enabled = False.

Policies can contain only one condition, but you can configure many different expressions, any one of which could initiate the expression. You can, for example, create a PBM policy called "Configuration Settings," a PBM condition called "Settings That Should be Disabled," and a list of expressions, each of which evaluates a different Surface Area Configuration option.

In fact, in the View Facets dialog box of SSMS, you can click Export Current State As Policy to ease the implementation of many configuration options into policy. You can apply the resulting settings to the local server as a policy right away, or export them as .xml, which then can be imported as a new policy. To export or import a policy, in SSMS, in Object Explorer, in the Policy Management folder, right-click a policy.

Evaluating policies and gathering compliance data

After you create a policy, you have multiple options for when to evaluate it: on demand (manually); on a schedule; and continuously, which either logs or blocks policy violations.

PBM is built in to SSMS, accessible via the Policy Management subfolder within the Management folder. SQL Server maintains history of all policy evaluations in a Policy History log, which is available within SSMS. To access it, expand the **Management** folder for the instance, right-click **Policy Management**, and then, on the shortcut menu, click **View History**. In the System Policies subfolder, you'll find 14 prebuilt policies for checking the health of availability groups, and two more for the SQL Server Managed Backup feature, first introduced in SQL Server 2014.

For example, after creating a policy, we can configure it with On Demand Evaluation Mode (see the code examples at the end of this section), and then test it by turning on the AdHocRemote-Queries setting in the Surface Area Configuration facet. You can also enable it using T-SQL with the command:

```
EXEC sp_configure 'Ad Hoc Distributed Queries', 1;
GO
RECONFIGURE;
GO
```

A message will immediately appear in the SQL Server Error Log stating: "Policy 'Keep AdHocRemoteQueries Disabled' has been violated by target 'SQLSERVER:\SQL*servername*\ *instancename*'", accompanied by a Severity 16 error 34053 message.

The on-demand Evaluate Mode gives the administrator an immediate report of all policy compliance. From the Evaluate Policies window, which you access by expanding **Policy Management**, right-clicking on **Policies**, and choosing **Evaluate**, you can view any number of policies. Should any expressions fail, the policy will display a red "X" beside it. In this example, evaluating the policy with the AdHocRemoteQueries facet turned on displays an error message and provides you with the ability to apply the change to bring the servers in line with policy.

In the Target Details pane of the Evaluate Policies window, you can click Details to start an analysis of all expression evaluations in the condition.

The scheduled Evaluate Mode generates only SQL Server Error log activity.

This option makes it possible for you to create a policy that will prevent developers or other administrations from making DDL changes that violate condition expressions. Note, however, that not all facet expressions allow for the On Change: Prevent Evaluation Mode.

This is accomplished by rolling back the transaction that contains the violating action. As with all rollbacks, this transaction could contain other statements and could cause a database change deployment to fail in a manner that could complicate your change process. This is a heavy-handed way to enforce policy, especially reversible activity such as naming conventions or table designs. Administrators and database developers should be aware of the potential impact to database deployments. You should limit the use of the On Change: Prevent Evaluation Mode to security-related or stability-related properties in both production and QA environments, such as the following:

- Server Security: @CrossDBOwnershipChainingEnabled

Enforce that this evaluates to False, unless this is part application security design

- Server Security: @PublicServerRoleIsGrantedPermissions

Enforce that this evaluates to False, in any circumstance

- Login: @PasswordPolicyEnforced

Enforce that this evaluates to True for all logins

- Certificate: @ExpirationDate

CHAPTER 9

Enforce that this date is not within a certain time frame in the future (6 months), in every database (sample code to follow)

- Database: @AutoShrink

Enforce that this evaluates to False, in all databases

- Database: @AutoClose

Enforce that this evaluates to False, in all databases

Samples

You can script policies to T-SQL for application to multiple servers, though be wary of applying policies for production systems to development systems, and vice versa. You can use a T-SQL script to create the two aforementioned samples. This script is available in the CH09_SQL_policy_based_management.sql file in the accompanying downloads for this book.

The first part of the script creates a sample policy to keep the Surface Area Configuration option AdHocRemoteQueries turned off (it will be evaluated on demand). The result sets returned by these queries contain only the integer IDs of new policy objects that have been created.

The second part of the script verifies whether any non-system certificates have an expiration in the next three months and fail the policy if so. It ignores any certificates with "##" in the name because these are built into SQL Server and are for internal use only, and are generated when SQL Server is installed and cannot be modified. Keep in mind also that certificates used for TDE will continue to work just fine after expiration, so there's no cause for concern if they show up in this list.

The result sets returned by these queries contain only the integer IDs of new policy objects that have been created.

Using PowerShell to automate SQL Server administration

SQL Server has supported close integration with PowerShell for over a decade. PowerShell is a robust scripting shell language which you can use to script many administrative tasks. It was first released in 2006, has integrated with SQL Server since 2008, and was made open source and cross-platform in 2016.

The goal of this section is not to list every possible interaction of PowerShell with SQL Server, Azure, or availability groups, but to provide instructional, realistic samples that will help you to learn the PowerShell language and add it to your DBA toolbox. All the scripts in this section are available in the accompanying downloads for this book.

> ➤ We review a number of useful PowerShell scripts for Azure SQL Database interaction in Chapter 17.

IT professionals in all walks of life are learning PowerShell to ease their administrative tasks with various technologies, not just SQL Server on Windows and Linux, but Active Directory, Machine Learning, Azure, Office 365, SharePoint, Exchange, even Office products like Microsoft Excel. There is very little in the Microsoft stack for which PowerShell cannot help. Developers have created third-party downloadable modules, available for download in the PowerShell Gallery (*https://powershellgallery.com*), to further enhance PowerShell's ability to interact even with non-Microsoft platforms such as Amazon Web Services, Slack, Internet of Things (IoT) devices, Linux, and more.

Inside OUT

How do you make better use of PowerShell?

If you'd like to adopt more PowerShell for administration in your database, you'll need more than the samples in this chapter, though we selected these because we feel them to be good learning examples.

Consider adding the open source suite of PowerShell cmdlets: dbatools, which is available to download from the PowerShell Gallery or directly from *https://dbatools.io*.

Though we won't be looking at any of its highly regarded cmdlets here, this suite has furthered the development of helpful PowerShell cmdlets for automating high availability, security migrations, backups, and more. You can read more in LeMaire, C and Sewell R, *Learn dbatools in a Month of Lunches* (Manning Publications, 2020).

There are even scenarios for which PowerShell fills feature gaps in configuration panels and UI, necessitating some basic literacy for PowerShell on the part of the modern system administrator, DBA, or developer. PowerShell is especially useful when building code to automate the failover of Windows Server Failover Clusters or for interacting with DNS. You also can use PowerShell remoting to manage multiple Windows servers and SQL Server instances from a single command prompt.

PowerShell is a full-featured shell, more powerful than the Prompt, where you can still manage the file system and launch applications you're familiar with as a Windows or Linux user; for example, `ping`, `ipconfig`, `ifconfig`, `telnet`, `net start`, `regedit`, `notepad`, `sqlcmd`, and even `shutdown`.

NOTE

You should get into the habit of using the PowerShell console window directly, as well as in Visual Studio Code or Azure Data Studio with PowerShell extensions.

You can also start a PowerShell console from within SSMS. Right-click most folders, and then, on the shortcut menu, select **Launch PowerShell**.

➤ Follow the instructions in the "Installing the PowerShell SQLServer module" section before using this feature.

You might find the Visual Studio Code or Azure Data Studio environments more conducive to authoring multiline PowerShell scripts, especially if you have any prior familiarity with Visual Studio or Visual Studio Code.

PowerShell basics

Cmdlets for PowerShell follow a pattern of *Verb-Noun*. This helps provide ease and consistency when trying to find cmdlets to run your desired task.

For database administration tasks, we will become familiar with cmdlets and using SQL Server Management Objects (SMO). Starting with the release of SSMS 17.0, PowerShell for SQL Server is installed separately from SQL Server Setup or the SSMS installation and can be installed from the PowerShell Gallery. We will demonstrate how to install and check the current version of the SQLServer module.

For each cmdlet, there is a built-in way to receive a description of the cmdlet and see all of the parameters along with descriptions and examples (if provided by the author) of the cmdlet. Let's try it on Invoke-Sqlcmd, a cmdlet that runs a T-SQL query using statements supported by the sqlcmd command. At the time of this writing, Invoke-SqlCmd is not available in PowerShell 6.

First, run the cmdlet Update-Help. This command updates the extensive and helpful local help files for PowerShell and installed modules.

NOTE

The Visual Studio Code shortcuts for running scripts are different from SSMS, and you need to be aware of the following:

- In SSMS, pressing F5 runs the entire script if no text is highlighted, or just the highlighted text if any is selected. Pressing Ctrl+E has the same behavior by default.
- In Visual Studio Code, pressing F5 saves then runs the entire script file, regardless of whether any code is highlighted. Pressing F8 runs only highlighted code.

To access the help information for any cmdlet, use the Get-Help cmdlet. Here are some examples:

```
#Basic Reference

Get-Help Invoke-SqlCmd

#See actual examples of code use

Get-Help Invoke-SqlCmd -Examples

#All cmdlets that match a wildcard search

Get-Help -Name "*Backup*database*"
```

Note that the # character begins a single-line comment in PowerShell code. Alternatively, you can use <# and #> to enclose and declare a multiline comment block.

Installing the PowerShell SQLServer module

You must be running at least Windows PowerShell 5.0 on Windows to download modules from the PowerShell Gallery. On Linux you need PowerShell Core, but note that PowerShell Core also runs on Windows and macOS. To determine the version of PowerShell on your system, run the following code in the PowerShell window:

```
$PSVersionTable
```

The PSVersion value contains the current installed version of PowerShell.

Inside OUT

How do you install Windows PowerShell and PowerShell Core?

As of this writing, the latest version of Windows PowerShell, version 5.1, ships in every supported version of Windows. Windows 10 and Windows Server 2016 or higher already have PowerShell 5.0 or 5.1 installed. To upgrade your version of PowerShell to 5.1, you should install the latest version of Windows Management Framework 5.1, which includes PowerShell.

https://docs.microsoft.com/powershell/scripting/install/installing-windows-powershell provides links to the current download by OS to upgrade your Windows PowerShell. Note that installing this package will require that you reboot your server or workstation.

To install the newer PowerShell Core for Windows, Linux and macOS, visit *https://docs.microsoft.com/powershell*. While the SQLServer PowerShell module will install correctly on PowerShell Core on macOS and Linux, some of the cmdlets may not work as expected due to underlying OS dependencies.

To install the latest version of the SQLServer module, use the following code on an Internet-connected device, running the PowerShell console or Visual Studio Code in administrator mode:

```
Install-Module -Name SQLServer -Force -AllowClobber
```

In the preceding script, we used a few handy parameters. Let's review them:

- **-Name.**   Specify the unique name of the module we want.

- **-Force.**   Avoid having to answer Yes to confirm that you want to download.

- **-AllowClobber.**   Allows this module to overwrite cmdlet aliases already in place. Without AllowClobber, the installation will fail if it finds that the new module contains commands with the same name as existing commands.

To find the current installed versions of the SQLServer PowerShell module as well as other SQL modules including SQLPS, use the following:

```
Get-Module -ListAvailable -Name '*sql*' | Select-Object Name, Version, RootModule
```

Offline installation

To install the module on a server or workstation that is not Internet-connected or cannot reach the PowerShell Gallery, go to a workstation that can reach the PowerShell Gallery and has at least Windows PowerShell 5.0 or PowerShell Core. Then, use the following command to download the module (be aware that it's over 100 MB in size uncompressed):

```
Save-Module -Name SQLServer -LiteralPath "c:\temp\"
```

Then, copy the entire C:*Temp*\SqlServer\ folder to the machine that cannot reach the PowerShell Gallery. Copy the folder to a path that is in the list of PSModule paths. The potential paths for modules list is stored in an PSModulePath environment variable, which you can view in Windows System Properties, or mode easily with this PowerShell script:

```
$env:PSModulePath.replace(";","'n")
```

The default folder for the module downloaded from the gallery would likely be "C:\Program Files\WindowsPowerShell\Modules" on Windows, or "/usr/local/share/powershell/Modules" on Linux. Verify that this path is available or choose another PSModule folder, and then copy the downloaded SQLServer folder there. The following script adds the SQLServer module, and then shows a list of all available modules on your workstation:

```
Import-Module SQLServer
```

```
Get-Module
```

NOTE

When writing code for readability, we recommend that you use the actual cmdlet names. With PowerShell, there are a large number of shorthand and shortcuts possible, but you should try to write easy-to-read code that is approachable and maintainable for the next administrator.

Using PowerShell with SQL Server

PowerShell can interact with SQL Server instances all the way back to SQL Server 2000 (with some limitations in earlier versions). This book is not a good medium to demonstrate the full capability that PowerShell can bring to your regular DBA tasks, nor should it try to detail all the possibilities. Nonetheless, here are some selected, representative, but simple examples.

Backup-SqlDatabase

Let's learn about some more basics and syntax of PowerShell via the Backup-SQLDatabase cmdlet. With this PowerShell cmdlet, you have access to the same parameters as the T-SQL command BACKUP DATABASE.

Again, use PowerShell's built-in help files to see full syntax and examples, many of which will be familiar to you if you have a good understanding of the BACKUP DATABASE options.

```
Get-Help Backup-SQLDatabase -Examples
```

Here is an example of how to back up all databases on a local SQL Server instance, providing the backup path, and including a subfolder with the database's name. The script also adds the current date and time to the name of the backup file:

```
#Backup all databases (except for TempDB)

$instanceName = "localhost" #set instance to back up
$path = "F:\Backup"
Get-SqlDatabase -ServerInstance $instanceName | `
   Where-Object { $_.Name -ne 'tempdb' } | `
   ForEach-Object {
    Backup-SqlDatabase -DatabaseObject $_ `
    -BackupAction "Database" `
    -CompressionOption On `
    -BackupFile "$($path)\$($_.Name)\$($_.Name)_$(`
    Get-Date -Format "yyyyMMdd")_$(`
    Get-Date -Format "HHmmss_FFFF").bak" `
    -Script #The -Script generates TSQL, but does not execute
   }
```

Here are the learning notes about this script:

- Adding the -Script parameter to this and many other cmdlets outputs only the T-SQL code, split by GO batch separators; it does not actually perform the operation.

- The back tick, or grave accent (`) symbol (below the tilde on most standard keyboards), is a line extension operator. Adding the ` character to the end of a line gives you the ability to display long commands, such as in the previous example, over multiple lines.

- The pipe character (|) is an important concept in PowerShell to grasp. It passes the output of one cmdlet to the next. In the previous script, the list of databases is passed as an array from Get-SQLDatabase to Where-Object, which filters the array and passes to ForEach-Object, which loops through each value in the array.

This script is available in the CH09_PS_backup_database.ps1 file in the accompanying downloads for this book.

Remove-Item

Let's learn some more about common PowerShell syntax parameters. You can use the Remove-Item cmdlet to write your own retention policy to delete old files, including backup files, stored locally. Remember to coordinate the removal of old local backups with your off-premises strategy that keeps backups safely in a different location.

In this script, we use the Get-ChildItem cmdlet to Recurse through a subfolder, ignore folders, and select only files that are more than $RetentionDays old and have a file extension in a list we provide:

```
$path = "F:\Backup\"

$RetentionDays = -1

$BackupFileExtensions = ".bak", ".trn", ".dif"

Get-ChildItem -path $path -Recurse | `

    Where-Object { !$_.PSIsContainer `

        -and $_.CreationTime -lt (get-date).AddDays($RetentionDays) `

        -and ($_.Extension -In $BackupFileExtensions) `

        } | Remove-Item -WhatIf
```

Here are the learning notes about this script:

- The $RetentionDays parameter is a negative value, because the AddDays() method requires a negative integer to subtract the number of retention days from the current date (specified with get-date).

- The `Get-ChildItem` cmdlet gathers a list of objects from the provided path, including files and folders. The `-Recurse` parameter of `Get-ChildItem` causes the cmdlet to include subfolders.

- The `$_` syntax is used to accept the data from the object prior to the previous pipe character (|). In this example, the objects discovered by `Get-ChildItem` are passed to the `Where-Object`, which filters the objects and passes that data to `Remove-Item`.

- Adding the `-WhatIf` parameter to this and many other cmdlets does not actually perform the operation, but provides a verbose summary of the action, instead. For example, rather than deleting old backup files, this PowerShell script returns something similar to the following sample:

```
What if: Performing the operation "Remove File" on target "F:\
Backup\backup_test_201902010200.bak".
```

This script is available in the CH09_PS_backup_file_retention.ps1 file in the accompanying downloads for this book.

Invoke-Sqlcmd

The `Invoke-Sqlcmd` cmdlet can run T-SQL commands, including on remote SQL Server instances and Azure SQL databases. `Invoke-Sqlcmd` can run batch file scripts that used to be run by `sqlcmd`. Use `Invoke-Sqlcmd` when there doesn't exist a cmdlet to return the same data for which you're already looking. In this script, we connect to a database in Azure SQL Database and run a query to see current sessions:

```
$instanceName = "localhost"

Invoke-Sqlcmd -Database master -ServerInstance $instanceName `

-Query "select * from sys.dm_exec_sessions" | `

Format-Table | Out-File -FilePath "C:\Temp\Sessions.txt" -Append
```

> **NOTE**
>
> If you see the error message "Could not load file or assembly 'Microsoft. SqlServer.BatchParser'", you can visit *https://social.technet.microsoft.com/wiki/contents/ articles/35832.sql-server-troubleshooting-could-not-load-file-or-assembly-microsoft- sqlserver-batchparser.aspx* for step-by-step instructions on how to resolve it.

Here are the learning notes about this script:

- As you might be familiar with in SSMS and other connection strings, the "." character is a shorthand substitute for "localhost."

CHAPTER 9

- The `Invoke-SqlCmd` cmdlet uses Windows Authentication by default. Notice that we passed no authentication information at all. You can also provide the `UserName` and `Password` parameters to the `Invoke-SqlCmd` to connect via SQL Authentication to SQL Server instances and Azure SQL databases, though this is not recommended unless you are on a secure connection.

- The `| Format-Table` cmdlet has a big impact on readability of the script output. Without `Format-Table`, the script returns a long list of column names and row values. The `Format-Table` output does not include all columns by default, but returns a wide line of column headers and row values, similar to how SSMS returns results in Text mode.

- The `| Out-File` cmdlet dumps the output to a text file instead of to the PowerShell console, creating the script if needed. The -Append parameter adds the text to the bottom of an existing file.

- The `Out-File` can be handy for archival purposes, but for viewing live rowsets, especially SQL Server command results, try using the `Out-GridView` cmdlet instead (Windows-only), which provides a full-featured grid dialog box with re-sortable and filterable columns, and so on. `Out-GridView` is used instead in the following sample:

```
$instanceName = "localhost"

Invoke-Sqlcmd -Database master -ServerInstance $instanceName `

-Query "select * from sys.dm_exec_sessions" | `

Out-GridView
```

These scripts are available in the CH09_PS_invoke_sql.ps1 file in the accompanying downloads for this book.

Inside OUT

What happened to my cursor in Visual Studio Code when running PowerShell?

Unlike SQL Server Management Studio, running a script in PowerShell by default moves the cursor to the PowerShell terminal pane (which is actually not a Results window, but a live terminal window). This means that you need to move your cursor back up to the script pane after each run to continue to edit your PowerShell code.

You can change this behavior in Visual Studio Code. Type Ctrl+, (comma) to access the Visual Studio Code User Settings, or start Settings by clicking the File Menu, and then choosing Preferences, and then Settings. On the right side, provide the following code to override the Default Setting:

```
"powershell.integratedConsole.focusConsoleOnExecute": false
```

No restart is necessary. Now the cursor will remain in the scripting pane after running a PowerShell command.

Using PowerShell with availability groups

You can script the creation and administration of availability groups and automate them with PowerShell instead of using SSMS commands or wizards. If you work in an environment in which creating, managing, or failing over availability groups is a repeated process, you should invest time in automating and standardizing these activities with PowerShell.

Following are some samples of code that can help you along the way, starting with the very beginning—a new group of servers has been created for availability groups, and you need to add the Failover Clustering feature to each server. This could be time consuming and click-heavy in a remote desktop session to each server. Instead, consider the following script in which we deploy the Failover Clustering feature and tools on four servers, quickly (you can parameterize the computer names as you require):

```
Invoke- -script {Install-WindowsFeature -Name "Failover-Clustering" } `
    -ComputerName SQLDEV11, SQLDEV12, SQLDEV14, SQLDEV15
Invoke- -script {Install-WindowsFeature -Name "RSAT-Clustering-Mgmt" } `
    -ComputerName SQLDEV11, SQLDEV12, SQLDEV14, SQLDEV15
Invoke- -script {Install-WindowsFeature -Name "RSAT-Clustering-PowerShell" } `
    -ComputerName SQLDEV11, SQLDEV12, SQLDEV14, SQLDEV15
```

➤ For more about turning on and configuring availability groups, see Chapter 11.

Inside OUT

Why is Invoke- *not working correctly across remote machines?*

You should verify that the same module and versions are installed on any machines to which you will be issuing commands remotely. You can also install the modules via Invoke-, **as well:**

```
#Local server
    Install-Module -Name SQLServer -Force -AllowClobber
    Import-Module -Name SQLServer
#Remove Server
Invoke- -script {
```

```
Install-Module -Name SQLServer -Force -AllowClobber
Import-Module -Name SQLServer
} -ComputerName "SQLSERVER-1"
```

Let's fast forward to an in-place availability group, with two replicas set to asynchronous synchronization. A planned failover is coming up, and you need to automate the script as much as possible. Start with the sample script that follows, which accomplishes these goals:

- Sets asynchronous replicas to synchronous and waits so that we can perform a planned failover with no data loss

- Performs availability group failover

- Sets replicas back to asynchronous

You can adapt the script CH09_PS_availability_groups.ps1 file, found in the accompanying downloads for this book, for your own purposes and environment.

Here are a few learning notes about the script:

- We need to do some character trickery to pass in a named instance in the SMO Path for the availability group, providing %5C for the backslash (\) in the replica name, SQLSERVER-0\SQL2019. The need here is rare albeit frustrating.

- We see another control structure, Do ... Until. In this case, we're waiting until the availability group RollupSynchronizationState has changed from Synchronizing to Synchronized, indicating that the synchronization has changed from asynchronous to synchronous.

- After the replica is set to synchronous, the failover can occur without data loss, without being Forced. In an emergency, in which the primary server SQLSERVER-0 is offline, we could skip the steps where we change the synchronization and proceed straight to the most important cmdlet in the script: Switch-SqlAvailabilityGroup. Except in a Forced failover, for which data loss is possible, we must specify the -AllowDataLoss and -Force parameters.

- You must run this entire script from the primary node, as it is currently written. A hint of how you could rewrite the script to be run from anywhere lies in Invoke-, where we connect to the original secondary replica (now the primary replica) and set the synchronization from asynchronous back to synchronous.

Developing, deploying, and managing data recovery

The first and foremost responsibility of a production DBA is to ensure that a database can be recovered in the event of a disaster. In this chapter, we first outline fundamentals of data recovery and SQL Server recovery models. Then, we move to a review of available backup devices in SQL Server, before discussing the different type of available backups. Next, we show you how to create and verify database backups, and how to restore databases from those backups. Finally, we end with a discussion defining a recovery strategy based on a fictitious scenario.

NOTE

As discussed in Chapter 2, "Introducing database server components," a disaster is any unplanned event caused by, but not limited to, natural disaster, hardware or software failure, malicious activity, or human error. Quite a few adverse events and disasters are caused by human error.

This chapter does not provide any guidance on fixing a corrupt database. Microsoft recommends restoring from a last known good database backup if you experience corruption. As you've read in the preceding paragraph, this chapter focuses on database backups and restores. The next chapter, Chapter 11, "Implementing high availability and disaster recovery," covers how to achieve high availability and use SQL Server disaster recovery features to keep your environment running even in the face of disaster. By the end of this and the next chapter, you will understand how to achieve close to zero data loss with minimal downtime.

➤ You can read more about data corruption in Chapter 8, "Maintaining and monitoring SQL Server."

You don't design a *backup strategy*, you design a *recovery strategy*. You need to allow for potential downtime and loss of data, within acceptable limits. These are defined by the business requirements for getting an environment back up and running after a disaster.

Technical solutions such as high availability (HA) and disaster recovery (DR) are available in Microsoft SQL Server to support these organizational requirements. In other words, business requirements define the approach that you will take in your organization to plan for and survive a disaster. We should also point out that this is only a small but important part of a larger business continuity plan (BCP). A BCP is designed to enable ongoing business operations while a disaster recovery plan is being executed. A BCP defines the critical business functions and processes that might be supported by your SQL Server environment, and how these functions will continue after disaster strikes.

> ➤ The US federal government provides guidance and tools for developing a business continuity plan at *https://www.ready.gov/business-continuity-plan.*

NOTE

This chapter makes several references to Chapter 3, "Designing and implementing an on-premises database infrastructure," particularly transaction log files, virtual log files (VLFs), and Log Sequence Numbers (LSNs). If you have not yet read that chapter, we highly recommend that you do so before reading any further here.

This chapter includes recovery strategies for hybrid and cloud environments, but the sections on backup devices, types of backups, and creating and restoring backups apply to on-premises environments. Preparing Azure SQL Database for disaster recovery is covered in Chapter 17, "Provisioning Azure SQL Database."

Preparing for data recovery

It is incredibly expensive and almost impossible to design a recovery strategy that achieves zero data loss with zero downtime. Recovery is a balance between budget, acceptable downtime, and acceptable data loss. Also, emotions run high when systems are down, so it is incumbent on all organizations to define possible outcomes at the outset and how to deal with them.

The governance of these requirements is outlined in a *Service-Level Agreement* (SLA). An SLA is a business document that specifies measurable commitments you make to the business related to availability and recovery objectives in case of a failure. Included in the SLA is the *Recovery Point Objective* (RPO) and *Recovery Time Objective* (RTO). The RPO expresses the amount of work that may be lost, in units of time such as minutes, when the service is returned to normal operation. The RTO expresses the amount of time that the service may be unavailable in case of a failure or disaster. The SLA might also include the consequences and penalties (financial or otherwise) if you do not meet the timelines. Although you will use technical solutions to satisfy these requirements, it is important to keep in mind that your recovery strategy should be the best fit for the organization's business needs.

> ➤ For more information about achieving HA, read Chapter 11, "Implementing high availability and disaster recovery."

A disaster recovery scenario

Let's paint a picture of a beautiful, sunny Friday afternoon, at 4:57 PM. This scenario spirals out of control pretty fast, so buckle up.

Disaster strikes in your office, just as you are about to head home for the weekend. The electricity goes out for the entire city block, and the uninterruptible power supply (UPS) in the server room has been removed for repairs.

You haven't rehearsed this scenario, because no one ever thought the UPS would be removed for maintenance for an extended period.

Your transaction log backups run every 15 minutes because that's what the RPO stipulates, and you have a batch script in the Windows Task Scheduler that copies your files remotely, so your logs should have been copied safely offsite. Well...that is, you're pretty sure the log backups were copied correctly, right?

Except that you get a sinking feeling in the pit of your stomach as you remember a warning you saw among your email this morning, while a colleague was on the phone to you, and your finger had slipped on the mouse and accidentally deleted the notification instead of moving it. Plus, you have that annoying muscle-memory habit of emptying deleted items whenever you see them.

Your phone squawks because it has 2% battery remaining. Your laptop has some charge, but not much because you were planning on charging it when you arrived home. You crack open your laptop to check whether you can somehow undelete your mail. Oh, right, your Internet is down.

Your smartphone rings. It's the vice president of marketing, who is away this week at a conference and wants to check the sales figures for a report the board is putting together for an important meeting this evening. The pressure is on!

And then your phone dies while the VP, who coincidentally doesn't care about power failures because the company spent thousands of dollars on that UPS, is asking you when the reports will be available again and wants you to just get it done.

You could charge the phone off the laptop and use the tethered cellular connection to log into the disaster recovery (DR) site. But the signal in this area is weak, so you need to move to the window on the other side of the office. As you stand up, the laptop decides that it's time to install operating system updates because it's now after 5 PM.

After an agonizing few minutes, your phone finally starts. Meanwhile your laptop has cancelled the updates because there's no Internet access. You connect to your offsite datacenter through a Remote Desktop Protocol (RDP) session. It takes three attempts because you had forgotten that RDP to this server works only with the administrator user account.

The SQL Server instance has its own service account, so you need to download and use psexec to run SQL Server Management Studio as the service account in interactive mode, after changing a registry entry to allow that user to use interactive login. You check the backup folder, and thankfully the latest log file is from 4:30 PM. Great. That means the 4:45 PM backup didn't copy over. Oh, it's because the drive is full. That must have been what the email warning was about.

After clearing out some files that another colleague had put on the drive temporarily, you need to write the script you've been meaning to write to restore the database because you didn't have time to set up log shipping.

You export the backup directory listing to a text file and begin looking for the latest full backup, differential backup, and transaction log backup files. But now you've seen that the last differential backup doesn't make sense, because the size is all wrong.

You remember that one of your developers had made a full backup of the production database this week on Monday evening, didn't use the COPY_ONLY option, and you don't have access to that file. The latest differential file is useless. You need to start from Sunday's full backup file and then use Monday afternoon's differential backup and all transaction log files since then. That's more than 400 files to restore.

Eventually, with a bit of luck and text manipulation, you begin running the restore script. One particular log file takes a very long time, and in your panicked state you wonder whether it has somehow become stuck. After a minute or two of clicking around, you realize SQL Server had to grow the transaction log of the restored database because it was replaying that annoying index rebuild script that failed on Tuesday morning and needed to roll back.

Finally, at 6:33 PM, your offsite database is up and running with the latest database backups up to and including the one from 4:30 PM. Just then, the lights come on in the office, because the power failure that affected the downtown area where your office is has been resolved. Now you need to do a full DBCC CHECKDB of the production server as soon as it starts, which always takes forever because the server is five years old and was installed with ECC RAM (which is useful but causes longer bootup times), which will push you out of the two-hour RTO that you and your boss agreed to, so you stick with the failover plan.

You update the connection settings in the application to point to the offsite datacenter just as your phone dies once more, but at least the office again has power to charge everything. You send the VP an email to say the reports should be working. The cellular data bill is coming out of his next trip, you tell yourself as you pack up to go home.

As you walk to the bus stop, it occurs to you that the files you cleared out to free up drive space probably included the full database backup taken by the developer from Monday night, and that you might have saved some time by checking them first.

Defining acceptable data loss: RPO

When disaster strikes, you might lose a single byte in a single row in a single 8-KB data page due to memory or drive corruption. How do you recover from that corruption? What happens if you lose an entire volume or drive, the storage array, or even the entire building?

The RPO should answer the question: "How much data are you prepared to lose?" You need to consider whether your backups are being done correctly, regularly, and copied offsite securely and in a timely manner. The RPO is usually measured in seconds or minutes. Your job is to deliver a technical implementation that meets this object, perhaps by ensuring there is less time between the last known good backup and the moment of the point of failure.

In this hellish scenario that we just laid out, the organization decided that losing 15 minutes' worth of data was acceptable, but ultimately any data changes over 27 minutes was lost. This is because the drive on the server at the disaster recovery site was full, and the most recent backup did not copy over.

To satisfy a 15-minute window, the transaction log backups would need to be taken more frequently, as would the offsite copy.

If the organization requires "zero data loss," the budget will need to significantly increase to ensure that whatever unplanned event happens, SQL Server's memory and transaction log remains online and that all backups are working and being securely copied offsite as soon as possible.

CHAPTER 10

Inside OUT

Why is the RPO measured in time, and not drive usage?

Transactions vary in size, but time is constant.

In Chapter 3, we looked at how every transaction is assigned an LSN to keep track of things in the active portion of the transaction log. Each new LSN is greater than the previous one (this is where the word "sequence" in Log Sequence Number comes from).

The RPO refers to the most recent point in time in the transaction log history to which you will restore the database, based on the most recently committed LSN at that specific moment in time, or the latest LSN in the log backup, whichever satisfies the organization's RPO.

Defining acceptable downtime: RTO

Time is money. Every minute that an organization is unable to work has a cost, and lost productivity adds up quickly. The RTO is the amount of time you need to get everything up and running again after a disaster. This might be orchestrating a failover to your disaster recovery site in another building, or a manual failover using log shipping. The RTO is usually measured in hours.

In our disaster scenario, the RTO was two hours. Our intrepid but woefully unprepared and accident-prone DBA barely made it. A few factors acted against the plan (if it could be called a plan).

For an organization to require zero downtime, the budget is exponentially increased. This is where a combination of HA and DR technologies combine to support the requirements.

It may be worth pointing out that different types of adverse events may have different RPOs and RTOs defined. A failure of a single drive in the enterprise SAN shouldn't come with any data loss or downtime. A power failure in a branch office might result in downtime, but no data loss. The loss of an entire facility due to a surprise natural disaster may require the organization accepting both data loss and downtime.

Establishing and using a run book

When panic sets in, you need a clear set of instructions to follow, just like our deer-in-the-headlights DBA in our fictional scenario. This set of instructions is called a run book.

The run book is one of many documents that make up a disaster recovery plan. It is part of the BCP. It covers the steps necessary for someone (including your future self) to bring the databases and supporting services back online after a disaster. In an eventuality in which you or your team members become incapacitated, the document should be accessible and understandable to another DBA who has appropriate access, but doesn't have intimate knowledge of the environment.

From our example scenario, issues like the Remote Desktop Protocol (RDP) user account not being able to log in to SQL Server Management Studio, downloading the requisite tools, knowing to skip an out-of-band differential backup, and so on would not be immediately obvious to many people. Even the most experienced DBA in a panic will struggle with thinking clearly.

The level of detail in a run book is defined by the complexity of the systems that need recovery and the time available to bring them back again. Your organization might be satisfied with a simple Microsoft Excel spreadsheet containing configurations for a few business-critical systems. Or, it might be something more in-depth, complete with screenshots, links to vendor documentation and downloads, and expected outcomes at each step. In either case, the run book should be updated as the system changes, and stored in a version control system (which itself should be backed up properly).

The rest of this chapter describes how SQL Server provides backup and restore features to help you come up with a recovery strategy that is most appropriate to your environment, so that when your organization wants to produce business continuity documentation, you have sufficient knowledge to guide an appropriate and achievable technical response.

Most important, you need to be able to rehearse a DR plan. The run book won't be perfect, and rehearsing scenarios will help you to produce better documentation so that when disaster strikes, even the most panicked individual will be able to figure things out.

Understanding different types of backups

SQL Server offers three different types of backup: full, differential, and transaction log. A key part of understanding backups and their ability to restore is understanding recovery models. After these introductory paragraphs, we discuss recovery models first. The backup types, along with partial database backups and backup options, are covered afterward.

Regardless of the type of backup, the backup will always include the active portion of the transaction log, including relevant LSNs, which ensures full transactional consistency when the backup is restored.

In Enterprise edition, you can take file-level and filegroup-level backups (known as partial backups) to allow a more controlled procedure when restoring. This is especially useful for very large databases (VLDBs).

➤ You can read more about the files that make up a SQL Server database in Chapter 3.

> ## Inside OUT
>
> *How large is a VLDB?*
>
> Opinions differ as to what constitutes a VLDB, based on individual experience and available hardware resources (such as memory and drive space).
>
> For the purposes of this chapter, any database that exceeds 100 GB is considered very large. Although modern solid-state storage arrays do mitigate many of the challenges facing databases of this size, they are not cost-effective for all environments.
>
> You can read more about solid-state storage, and storage arrays, in Chapter 2.

CHAPTER 10

CAUTION

A database snapshot is a read-only static view of a database at the point in the time the snapshot was created. You can use database snapshots to ease administration when testing new functionality to reduce the time required to restore to a point in time, but they are at the same risk as regular database files. Snapshots are not guaranteed backups, and you should not use them to replace native SQL Server backups. To learn more about database snapshots, go to *https://docs.microsoft.com/sql/relational-databases/databases/database-snapshots-sql-server.*

Every backup contains a header and a payload. The header describes the backup device, what type of backup it is, backup start and stop information (including LSN information), and information about the database files. The payload is the content of the data or transaction log files in that backup. If Transparent Data Encryption (TDE) or Backup Encryption was turned on, the payload is encrypted.

➤ **You can read more about TDE in Chapter 13, "Protecting data through encryption, privacy, and auditing."**

An overview of SQL Server recovery models

In SQL Server, a database's recovery model determines how the transaction log is maintained. This affects your options for backups and restores. SQL Server supports three recovery models: full, bulk-logged, and simple. These models provide a high level of control over the types of backups, and thus restore options, available to your databases. Let's take a brief look at each one before discussing each in more detail.

- **Full recovery model.** In this model, transactions are logged and kept at least until the transaction log has been backed up. This model allows a full point-in-time recovery. Full, differential, and transaction log backups can be taken. The transaction log must be backed up to avoid continuous growth. All database changes are fully logged and can be replayed.

- **Bulk-logged recovery model.** This model reduces the amount of transaction log used for certain bulk operations. SQL Server only logs what the Database Engine needs to undo the bulk operation, but the bulk operation cannot be replayed. Non-bulk operations are logged and maintained as in the full recovery model. This model can allow a point-in-time recovery only if no bulk-logged operations are in that portion of the transaction log backup. Full, differential, and transaction log backups can be taken. Here too, the transaction log must be backed up to avoid continuous growth.

- **Simple recovery model.** Transactions are logged only until they are committed to the data file(s) on disk. Only full and differential backups can be taken.

NOTE

These are called *recovery models*. If you see the term "recovery mode," it is incorrect.

You can change the recovery model of a database in SQL Server Management Studio in Object Explorer, or by using the following Transact-SQL (T-SQL) statement (and choosing the appropriate option in the square brackets):

```
ALTER DATABASE <dbname> SET RECOVERY [ FULL | BULK_LOGGED | SIMPLE ];
```

Full recovery model

For databases that require point-in-time recovery, which is the case for most business-critical systems, we recommend the full recovery model. The recovery model for new databases is based on the recovery model for the model database. By default, the model database is in the full recovery model.

In this recovery model, after the first full backup takes place, the virtual log files in the transaction log remain active and are not cleared until a transaction log backup writes these log records to a log backup. Only then will the log be truncated (cleared).

Assuming that you implement a process to ensure that these backups are securely copied offsite as soon as the backups are completed, and that you regularly test these backups, you can restore your database in the event of a disaster. Provided the right circumstances are in play, you might even be able to take a tail-log backup to achieve zero data loss, if that data has been committed and made durable.

> ➤ Tail-log backups are defined in the "Transaction log backups" section below.

> ➤ You can read more about durability, including delayed durability, in Chapter 2.

Bulk-logged recovery model

Under the bulk-logged recovery model, typical commands are logged like in the full recovery model, but bulk operations are minimally logged. This reduces the size of the transaction log records and subsequent log backups. The downside is that this model eliminates the option of replaying these operations from a transaction log backup. These operations include BULK INSERT, INSERT … SELECT, SELECT … INTO (all using the TABLOCK hint), and bcp operations. Certain indexing operations are also minimally logged.

> ➤ For more details, see the Microsoft Docs at *https://docs.microsoft.com/sql/ relational-databases/logs/the-transaction-log-sql-server#MinimallyLogged*.

This affects the ability to restore a database to a point in time if that time is included in a transaction log backup that includes bulk logged operations. There is a way to get mostly-point-in-time recovery. This allows a more flexible recovery strategy than the simple recovery model (more on this in the next section), without generating large transaction logs for bulk operations.

Suppose that you want to use the bulk-logged recovery model to perform minimally logged operations, without breaking the log backup chain. Your database must be in the full recovery model before the bulk-logged operation is performed.

- First, take a transaction log backup.

- Then switch to the bulk-logged recovery model and perform the bulk-logged operations.

- Immediately switch the database back to the full recovery model.

- Finally, back up the log again.

This ensures that the backup chain remains unbroken and allows point-in-time recovery to any point before or after the bulk-logged operation. The Microsoft Docs note that the bulk-logged recovery model is intended specifically for this scenario to temporarily replace the full recovery model during bulk operations.

Simple recovery model

Databases in the simple recovery model can only be restored to the point in time when the backups were completed. Point-in-time recovery cannot be used. After a transaction in the simple recovery model is committed or rolled back, a checkpoint is implicitly issued, which truncates (clears) the log.

Databases in the simple recovery model can make use of full and differential backups. This recovery model is better suited to development databases, databases that change infrequently, and databases that can be rebuilt from other sources.

Backup types

To recover a database, you'll need at least a full database backup. Differential backups are optional. They only include the data pages that have changed since the last full backup. Differential backups can reduce the amount of time required to restore a database. Transaction log backups are incremental backups that enable point-in-time restores.

Full backups

A full database backup is a transactionally consistent copy of the entire database. The payload of this type of backup includes every 8-KB data page in every database file in all the filegroups, FILESTREAM and memory-optimized files,. and the portion of the transaction log that is necessary to roll forward or roll back transactions that overlapped with the backup window.

➤ You can read more about the active portion of the transaction log in Chapter 3.

You can perform full backups on databases in all recovery models, and you can compress them. Since SQL Server 2016, you can also compress databases that were encrypted with TDE.

You can perform a full backup to a backup disk target with a minimal amount of T-SQL code. For example, a WideWorldImporters database on a default instance with a machine called SERVER can be backed up to local disk by using the following code:

```
BACKUP DATABASE WideWorldImporters

TO DISK = N'C:\SQLData\Backup\SERVER_WWI_FULL_20191218_210912.BAK';

GO
```

Transaction log backups

Transaction log backups are incremental backups of a database. In the full recovery model, all transactions are fully logged. This means that you can bring back a database to the exact state it was when that transaction log backup was taken, provided that the restore is successful. These backups allow for a recovery to any moment in time in the sequence (the backup chain).

In this type of backup, the active portion of the transaction log is backed up. Transaction log backups apply only to databases in the full and bulk-logged recovery models. Databases in the full recovery model can be restored to a point in time, and databases in the bulk-logged recovery model can be restored to a point in time if the transaction log does not contain bulk-logged operations. The transaction log does not contain the information necessary to replay bulk operations in the bulk-logged recovery model.

Inside OUT

What is a tail-log backup?

A tail-log (or tail-of-the-log) backup, is fundamentally the same thing as an ordinary transaction log backup. The difference is in the circumstances in which you would perform this kind of log backup. You might also need to use the NO_TRUNCATE clause on the BACKUP statement if the database is damaged. The NO_TRUNCATE clause allows the transaction log to be backed up even if only the transaction log file is accessible and undamaged. Thus, even if the database is inaccessible or damaged, the committed transactions can be backed up.

In a disaster scenario, the automation for performing transaction log backups might be offline, or your backup drive might not be available. Any time you need to manually perform a transaction log backup to ensure that the remaining transactions in the log are safely stored somewhere after a failure occurred, this is a tail-log backup. Performing a

> tail-log backup that you can restore properly later is how you can achieve zero data loss following some adverse events.
>
> You can read more about tail-log backups at *https://docs. microsoft.com/sql/relational-databases/backup-restore/ back-up-the-transaction-log-when-the-database-is-damaged-sql-server.*

Differential backups

Differential backups, which are based on a full database backup, are a convenience feature to reduce the number of transaction log backups (and time) required to restore a database to a point in time. They contain all changed extents, FILESTREAM files, and memory-optimized data files since the last full backup. They cannot be restored on their own. To restore a database using a differential backup, you need that differential backup's base full backup.

In many cases, a differential backup is much smaller than a full backup, which allows for a more flexible backup schedule. You can run a full backup less frequently, and have differential backups running more regularly, taking up less space than the full backup would have taken.

Think back to Chapter 3 in which we looked at extents. As a reminder, an extent is a 64-KB segment in the data file, comprising a group of eight physically contiguous 8-KB data pages. After a default full backup completes (without the copy-only option, which we cover later), the differential bitmap is cleared. All subsequent changes in the database, at the extent level, are recorded in the differential bitmap. When the differential backup runs, it looks at the differential bitmap and backs up only the extents that have been modified since the full backup, along with the active portion of the transaction log.

This is quite different to a transaction log backup, which records every change in the database even if it's to the same rows in the same tables repeatedly. Thus, a differential backup is not the same thing as an incremental backup.

Even though you cannot restore a database to a point in time (or LSN) that occurs within the differential backup itself, it can vastly reduce the number of transaction log files required to effect those same changes.

Differential backups apply to databases in the full, bulk-logged, and simple recovery models.

CAUTION

If a full backup is taken out-of-band without the COPY_ONLY option, this will affect subsequent differential backups. In that case, you will be restricted to using transaction log backups exclusively to restore the backup chain. If you want to take a full backup of a database without affecting the differential backup schedule, always use the COPY_ONLY option. The copy-only backup mechanism is covered in a later section.

Inside OUT

What do you do if my differential backup is larger than my full backup?

Differential backups will grow larger as the number of changed extents in the database increases. It is feasible that the differential backup can end up being larger than a full backup over time.

This is possible for situations in which every extent is modified in some way (for instance if all the indexes in the database are rebuilt), which makes the differential backup the same size as a full backup. When it adds the active portion of the log, you end up with a differential backup that is the same size than a full backup.

SQL Server 2017 and later provide a column called modified_extent_page_count in the DMV sys.dm_db_file_space_usage to let you know how large a differential backup will be. A good rule of thumb is to take a full backup if the differential backup approaches 80% of the size of a full backup.

➤ You can read more about differential backups at *https://docs.microsoft.com/sql/ relational-databases/backup-restore/differential-backups-sql-server.*

The backup chain

A backup chain starts with a full backup, followed by differential and/or transaction log backups that you can combine into a recovery sequence to restore a database to a particular point in time after the full backup or to the time of the latest backup, whichever is required.

Databases in the full recovery model can be restored to a point in time because transactions are fully logged in that recovery model.

NOTE

You can also restore a database in the bulk-logged recovery model to a point in time, provided that the transaction log backup does not contain bulk-logged operations up to that point in time.

Figure 10-1 illustrates a backup chain that starts with a full backup, which contains the most recent LSN of the active portion of the transaction log at the time that backup finished, and then multiple transaction log backups and differential backups based on that full backup.

You can use a combination of the most recent differential backup (which must be based on that same full backup) and any additional transaction log backups to produce a point-in-time recovery. If you do not have a differential backup or the point in time you want to restore to is before the end of the differential backup, you must use transaction log backups. Either option will work provided the LSNs required in the sequence are contained in each of those backups.

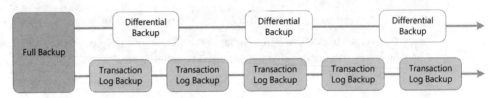

Figure 10-1 A backup chain

Until you run the very first full backup on a database using the full or bulk-logged recovery model, the database is "pseudo-simple," behaving as though it is in the simple recovery model. Active portions of the log are cleared whenever a database checkpoint is issued, and the transaction log remains at a reasonably stable size, unless a large transaction causes it to grow. This may seem unexpected, but there's no need in keeping a transaction log that couldn't be restored. Always remember that a database restore begins with a full backup. Until there is a full backup, there's no need for historic transactions to be kept.

Conversely, once the first full backup is taken, less-experienced DBAs can be taken by surprise by the sudden and seemingly uncontrolled growth of the transaction log.

We recommend that you configure appropriate maintenance plans (including transaction log backups and monitoring) at the time you create a new database. Also, it is a good idea to continue taking log backups even while a full backup is in progress. These log backups will ensure the backup chain is preserved even if the full backup fails or is canceled.

> **NOTE**
> Backup chains can survive database migrations and upgrades, as long as LSNs remain intact. This is what makes certain HA features possible in SQL Server.

Inside OUT

How long can the backup chain be?

Provided that you have an unbroken backup chain for which the LSNs are all intact, you can potentially have many thousands of log backups stretching back over months or even years. You can apply these backups, along with the full backup on which they are based (and assuming the files are intact), to restore the database to a current point in time, even if the database was moved or upgraded during that time.

However, this can be extremely time consuming and will negatively affect the RTO, especially if the backups need to be retrieved from slow storage (including tape). Legend has it that some organizations were forced to close down as a result of missing the RTO.

It is far better practice to perform regular full backups (and differential database backups if they are useful) along with transaction log backups so that the dependency chain is shorter.

➤ You can read more about designing an appropriate backup schedule in the "Creating and verifying backups" section later in this chapter. For more on maintenance plans, read Chapter 9, "Automating SQL Server administration."

Fixing a broken backup chain by using differential backups

A backup chain is broken when a database is switched from the full recovery model to the bulk-logged or simple recovery model for any reason (such as shrinking the transaction log file during an emergency). A backup chain can also be broken if a full database backup is taken "out-of-band" and is then discarded or becomes unavailable when a restore is required.

After you switch back to the full recovery model, you can restart the log backup chain without having to perform a full database backup by taking a differential backup. As long as you make use of this or a more recent differential backup in a later recovery, along with the accompanying transaction log backups, the backup chain has been repaired.

If you keep the database in the bulk-logged recovery model, you can restore the backup chain by taking a differential backup after bulk logged operations. Combined with the transaction log backups taken after the differential, you can restore the database back to a point in time after the bulk-logged operation, or to a point in time before the transaction log backup containing a bulk-logged operation.

File and filegroup backups

You can take a more granular approach by backing up individual data files and filegroups, which make use of the full or differential options, as well. These options are available in the SQL Server Management Studio user interface, or you can use the official documentation to create appropriate T-SQL statements.

CAUTION

If a single file in a filegroup is offline (for instance during a restore), the entire filegroup is offline, as well, which affects backups.

CHAPTER 10

Partial backups

Because read-only filegroups do not change, it does not make sense to include them in ongoing backup processes. Primarily used for VLDBs that contain read-only filegroups, partial backups will exclude those read-only filegroups, as required.

Partial backups contain the primary filegroup, any read-write filegroups, and one or more optional read-only filegroups. Partial backups can also contain a single file from a filegroup, but be aware that a filegroup cannot be brought online until all the files are available.

> ➤ To read more about partial backups, go to *https://docs.microsoft.com/sql/relational-databases/backup-restore/partial-backups-sql-server.*

File backups

You can use file backups to restore individual files if they become corrupt. This makes restoring easier, because for VLDBs it would take much less time to restore a single file than the entire database

Unfortunately, file backups increase the complexity due to increased administration of the additional file backups over and above the full, differential, and transaction log backups. This overhead extends to recovery script maintenance.

> ➤ To read more about file backups, visit *https://docs.microsoft.com/sql/relational-databases/backup-restore/full-file-backups-sql-server.*

Additional backup options and considerations

This section includes several options and special considerations for backup in SQL Server.

Backup encryption

Since SQL Server 2014, it is possible to encrypt database backups using an asymmetric key pair. This is not the same as the encryption provided for backups with TDE turned on. The key difference between both is that to restore an encrypted backup, you'll need the asymmetric key, and not the database master key or the certificate encrypted by the database master key.

Like any asymmetric encryption process, you will require a cipher (the encryption algorithm) and an asymmetric key or certificate. Supported ciphers are Advanced Encryption Standard (AES; you can use key sizes of 128, 192, and 256 bits), and 3DES (also known as Triple DES). As discussed in depth in Chapter 13, AES is a safer and faster cipher than 3DES. You must back up and store the key or certificate in a secure location.

As noted in Chapter 3, you can also compress backups, which is recommended unless the database makes compression, in which case you should first evaluate if your case will benefit from backup compression. SQL Server 2016 provided support for backup compression of databases encrypted with TDE.

CAUTION

Initial releases of SQL Server 2016 contained flaws that could have corrupted your backups when compressing backups of databases encrypted with TDE. These flaws were fixed in cumulative updates. We recommend that you follow Microsoft's guidance and evaluate and apply cumulative updates as they are released for just this reason. This is also a cautionary tale for testing your backups to ensure that they can be restored successfully.

NOTE

The MAXTRANSFERSIZE data transfer option with the BACKUP statement specifies, in bytes, the largest possible size of transfers between SQL Server and the backup media. Backup compression for a database encrypted with TDE does not kick in unless the BACKUP statement contains a MAXTRANSFERSIZE value greater than 65,536. If MAXTRANSFERSIZE is not specified or is set to its minimum value of 65,536 bytes (64 KB), the backup will not be compressed. Valid values for MAXTRANSFERSIZE are multiples of 64 KB up to 4 MB.

➤ To learn more about security and encryption, read Chapter 13.

Backup checksums

SQL Server can perform optional checksum verifications on database backups. By default, backups do not perform a checksum. You can change this behavior either by a trace flag (TF3023), in the SQL Server Management Studio properties of a backup, or in any T-SQL script you create to perform backups. We recommend that you turn on backup checksum where possible, ideally using the trace flag so it is default behavior.

Without backup checksum turned on, no validation is performed on data pages or log blocks. This means that any logical corruption will also be backed up without showing any of the errors you might see with a DBCC CHECKDB operation. This is to allow for scenarios in which you can back up a corrupt database before attempting to fix the corruption. Alternatively, you can take the backup with the checksum option enabled, but add the CONTINUE_AFTER_ERROR option.

➤ To read more about recovering from corruption, see Chapter 8.

With backup checksum turned on, a checksum is calculated over the entire backup file. Additionally, the page checksum on every 8-KB data page (for both page verification types of checksum or torn-page detection), and log block checksum from the active portion of the log, will be validated.

CAUTION

Physical corruption, in which the data cannot be read from the drive, including corruption in memory-optimized filegroups, will cause the backup to fail.

The backup checksum can significantly increase the time for a backup to run, but adds some peace of mind, short of running a recommended DBCC CHECKDB on a restored database.

Copy-only backup

When a full backup runs with the default settings, a reserved data page known as the *differential bitmap* is cleared. Any differential backups that are taken on the database after that will be based off that full backup. You can change the default behavior by using the COPY_ONLY option, which does not clear the differential bitmap. Copy-only backups are useful for taking out-of-band backups without affecting the differential backup schedule.

In other words, only differential backups are affected by the lack of the COPY_ONLY option. Transaction log backups, and thus the backup chain, are not affected.

Memory-optimized tables

Standard backups include memory-optimized tables. During the backup process, a checksum is performed on the data and delta file pairs to check for corruption. Any corruption detected in a memory-optimized filegroup will cause a backup to fail, and you will be required to restore from the last known good backup.

Remember that the storage requirements for a memory-optimized table can be much larger than its usage in memory, which will affect the size of your backups.

> ➤ To learn more about how to back up memory-optimized files,
> go to *https://docs.microsoft.com/sql/relational-databases/
> in-memory-oltp/backing-up-a-database-with-memory-optimized-tables.*

System database backups

The SQL Server system databases contain important information about your system and some of these should be backed up as well. A system database that does not need to be backed up is tempdb. This database is recreated every time your SQL Server instance restarts anyway. It is noteworthy that the tempdb database cannot be backed up or restored.

The master system database holds all the instance-level information and should be backed up on regular intervals. You should also take a full backup of the master database immediately before and after any significant changes, such as installation of a cumulative update.

Another system database that should be backed up is msdb. This system database is used by the SQL Server Agent for job control. This database also contains the backup and restore history tables.

In addition to these four system databases (master, msdb, model, and tempdb) that are present on every SQL Server instance, you might also have a distribution system database. This database exists if you have configured replication. This database should also be backed up regularly, generally on the same schedule as the full backups for the replicated databases.

> ➤ Microsoft provides additional guidance for backing up replicated databases in the Microsoft Docs at *https://docs.microsoft.com/sql/relational-databases/replication/administration/back-up-and-restore-replicated-databases.*

Backing up non-database items

Successfully restoring data may require more than just the backup files. For example, restoring a database with TDE enabled will require the original certificate used to setup encryption. If you're restoring to a different server, you'll need to restore the certificate, including its private key, before attempting to restore the database.

Items you should consider backing up in addition to the database:

- Certificates

- Logins

- Agent jobs (in the msdb system database)

Availability and security of backup media

Your backups must be appropriately safeguarded from corruption or deletion and from the disasters that you're trying to defend against. Usually, this means that backup files should be available in multiple locations, including both on-premises and offsite. It's not wise to keep backups only on-premises because a disaster might affect your entire site. However, it's advisable to keep one backup copy local because that copy is easier and quicker to access.

The devices that store your backups must be secured with appropriate access controls, physical and virtual. Authorized individuals, and only those, must be able to access the backups to implement the data recovery plan. The backups contain the same sensitive information as your databases. Unauthorized access may lead to a security breach (and, unfortunately, hackers know organizations sometimes neglect to protect backups as well as the data stores). However, you must also plan for the eventuality that the disaster rendered your identity and access management (IAM) infrastructure unavailable.

Similar considerations apply for backups to Azure Storage. You must verify that access to the storage account is limited to authorized individuals. Azure provides mechanisms for securing storage accounts, which are outside the scope of this text.

> ➤ Information on the many options for securing Azure Storage accounts is available from the Microsoft Docs at *https://docs.microsoft.com/azure/storage/blobs/ security-recommendations*. Additional best practices for using shared access signatures is covered at *https://docs.microsoft.com/azure/storage/common/ storage-sas-overview#best-practices-when-using-sas*.

Understanding backup devices

SQL Server writes database backups to physical backup devices. These storage media might be virtualized, but for the purposes of this section, they are considered physical. They include disk, tape, and URL. Tape backup is now deprecated and we will not cover it in detail.

CAUTION

The option to back up SQL Server databases to tape will be removed from a future version of SQL Server. When creating a recovery strategy, use disk or URL. You should change any existing recovery strategies that involve tape to use another media type.

Backup to disk

The most common form of SQL Server backup is stored directly on a local drive or network path, referred to as the *backup disk*. A backup disk contains one or more backup files, and each file contains one or more database backups.

A database backup might also be split across multiple files. For backing up VLDBs in less time, striping the backup across multiple files can be a valuable strategy. Be careful however, you must have all files in the set to successfully restore.

Backup to URL

Since SQL Server 2012 (Service Pack 1 with Cumulative Update 2), you can back up your SQL Server database directly to Azure Blob storage. This is made possible by using an Azure Storage account URL as a destination.

SQL Server 2016 added the ability to back up to Azure block blobs. This is now the preferred blob type when backing up to Azure Storage. By enabling striping a backup over up to 64 blobs, block blobs support much larger backups and enable higher throughput than page blobs.

NOTE

Backup to URL is especially useful for hybrid scenarios or for Azure SQL Database managed instance.

To backup a database to a block blob, you will need to provide a token for a Shared Access Signature (SAS) for a standard Azure Storage account (premium storage accounts are not supported). A SAS can be created using the Azure Portal, PowerShell, or other means. Before creating the SAS, you should define a matching *Stored Access Policy* for the blob container that will store the backup files. This policy allows for making changes to or revoking the SAS.

A SAS token represents the SAS and is a query string that contains several elements referring to the SAS. When creating a SAS token, you must specify the permissions that will be allowed using the SAS token. Minimally, read, write, delete, and list permissions are required. The SAS token you obtain will begin with a question mark (?), but that question mark must be removed before SQL Server can successfully use the SAS token. (Readers versed in web technologies will understand that the question mark is the beginning of a URL query string and not part of the content.)

NOTE

A Shared Access Signature must have an expiration date. Make sure that the expiration date is sufficiently far in the future so that your backups don't start failing unexpectedly. Regardless of the expiration date of the SAS token, it's a good idea to rotate the secret on an established schedule.

The SAS token must be used to create a credential. The credential's name is the URL to the Azure Storage container. After the credential is created, backing up the database to Azure Storage only requires specifying the TO URL clause, as illustrated in the sample below.

The sample statements create a credential using a SAS token and backup the SSIO2019 database to the SSIO2019 Azure Storage account. The sample uses the WITH FORMAT option to overwrite an existing backup at the same URL. Your use case may require you to keep historic backups, in which case you should probably generate the backup file name by including the date and time of the backup. If you keep historic backups, you'll need to create a scheme to remove outdated backup files; the RETAINDAYS and EXPIREDATE options are not supported with the TO URL clause.

```
CREATE CREDENTIAL [https://ssio2019.blob.core.windows.net/onprembackup]

    WITH IDENTITY = 'SHARED ACCESS SIGNATURE',

    -- Remember to remove the leading ? from the token

    SECRET = 'sv=2018-03-28&ss=…';

BACKUP DATABASE SamplesTest
```

CHAPTER 10

```
TO URL = 'https://ssio2019.blob.core.windows.net/onprembackup/db.bak'

-- WITH FORMAT to overwrite the existing file

WITH FORMAT;
```

> ➤ Extensive guidance on backup to URL is available in the Microsoft Docs at *https://docs. microsoft.com/sql/relational-databases/backup-restore/sql-server-backup-to-url.*

For security, the container holding your SQL Server database backups should be configured as Private. We recommend that you configure the storage account to require secure transfer, meaning only HTTPS connections are allowed. Secure transfer is required by default of all new Azure Storage accounts. You may further secure the SAS token by restricting the IP addresses that can connect to the Storage service using the token. If you choose to do so, you'll need to remember to obtain a new token and update the database credential when your organization's outbound IP addresses change.

NOTE

Did you know that SSMS 18 and later support connecting to Azure Storage? While Azure Storage Explorer is a great tool for managing Azure Storage accounts, the option to connect to an Azure Storage account used for SQL Server backups directly from within SSMS can be a time saver. You can access this functionality from the Back Up Database dialog.

Backup and media sets

As noted previously, SQL Server backups are written to media types (devices), namely tape, disk (which include solid-state drives and UNC network paths), and Azure Blob Storage. Each of these types have specific properties, including format and block size.

Media set

This is an ordered collection of a fixed type and number of devices (see Figure 10-2). For example, if you are using a backup disk, your media set will comprise a fixed number of one or more files.

A backup will always be comprised of at least one media set. With tape backup now deprecated, media sets with multiple devices are less common. When backing up to a disk or URL, we recommend limiting backup operations to one file at a time, except in these situations related to VLDBs:

- **Backup window.** The backup window might be too short to enable the backup to finish unless it's striped across multiple files or URLs.

- **Backup to URL.** The recommended block blobs in Azure Storage can hold at most 200 GB per blob. If your backup is larger than 200 GB, you'll need to use multiple block blobs. Better backup performance may also be achieved using multiple block blobs, assuming your Internet upload speed is sufficient. We should note that concerns surrounding the integrity of striped backups are less acute in Azure Storage because you can, and should, configure the storage account with redundancy.

The Enterprise edition supports mirroring media sets. A mirrored media set contains another copy of the backup. This feature provides you with a redundant copy of your backup on the same type of media. When the mirrored media sets are appropriately segmented on different storage hardware, this redundant copy increases the reliability of the backup, because an error in one backup set might not have affected the mirrored copy.

➤ **To read more about mirrored backup media sets, go to** *https://docs.microsoft.com/sql/ relational-databases/backup-restore/mirrored-backup-media-sets-sql-server.*

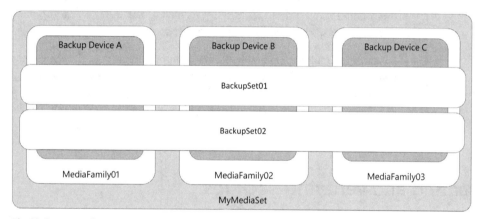

Fig 10-2   A media set, containing three media families spread over three devices.

Media family

In each media set, all backup devices used in that media set make up the media family. The number of devices in that set is the number of media families. If a media set uses three backup devices that are not mirrored, there are three media families in that media set.

Backup set

A successful backup added to a media set is called a backup set. Information about the successful backups is stored in the header of the backup set.

You can reuse an existing backup set by adding new backups for a database to the end of that media. This grows the media by appending the backup to the end of it. However, we do not recommend this practice, because the integrity of previous backups relies on the consistency of that media. An errant INIT option in the backup command could even accidentally overwrite existing backups in the backup set.

Inside OUT

What media set, media family, and backup set should you use?

For typical SQL Server instances, we recommend that you back up your databases to strongly named, self-contained files, where only the backup in question is stored in each file. If you are using a third-party solution (free or paid), make sure that they follow a strong naming convention, as well.

In other words, the file name itself should contain the server and instance name, the database name, the type of backup (full, differential, or log), as well as the date and time of the backup. This makes locating, managing, and restoring backups much easier because every file is a separate backup set, media family, and media set.

For example, a full backup of the WideWorldImporters database on the default instance of a SQL Server called SERVER, taken on February 9th, 2020 at 10:53:44 PM might have the following filename: SERVER_WideWorldImporters_FULL_20200209_225344. BAK. To avoid issues with filenames during Daylight Saving Time (DST) changeover, we recommend specifying the time in UTC.

Creating and verifying backups

You should completely automate backups when possible, whether you make use of the built-in Maintenance Plan Wizard in SQL Server Management Studio or a third-party solution (free or paid). Always ensure that backups are successful by observing that the backup files exist, and the backup task does not error out. Additionally, you must test those backups regularly by restoring them, which you can also do with an automated process.

➤ You can read more about maintenance plans in Chapter 9.

SQL Server Agent is an excellent resource for automating backups, and many third-party solutions make use of it too (as does the Maintenance Plan Wizard).

Creating backups

You can design a backup solution to satisfy a recovery strategy by using all or a combination of the available backup types. The backup types and code samples have already been covered above.

Inside OUT

How frequently should you run backups?

Business requirements and database size will dictate how long your maintenance window is and what needs to be backed up in that window. You might have a critical database small enough that it can be fully backed up daily and has no need for differential backups. Larger databases might require a weekly schedule, augmented by daily differential backups.

A database in the full recovery model should have transaction log backups occurring as a factor of the RPO. Transaction logs should be backed up and securely copied offsite at a more frequent interval than your RPO. Assuming that your RPO is five minutes, backup your transaction log so that it takes less than five minutes to backup and copy offsite. For example, you can backup the log every three minutes, which gives you two minutes of time to get the backup offsite.. This is to accommodate the implicit delay between when a backup ends and when the backup has been copied offsite. In the case of a disaster, there is a higher chance that the files are copied offsite with a smaller copy interval. A backup is realistically not available to meet the RPO until it is copied offsite.

Databases that can be rebuilt using existing processes might not need to be backed up at all. Such databases should use the simple recovery model.

The buffer pool (see Chapter 2) is not used for database backups. The *backup buffer* is a portion of memory outside of the buffer pool, big enough to read pages from the data file and write those pages to the backup file. The backup buffer is usually between 16 MB and 32 MB in size. Be aware that memory pressure can reduce the backup and restore buffer sizes, causing backups and restores to take longer.

CAUTION

It is possible to increase the number of backup buffers (using the BUFFERCOUNT option) as well as the transfer size of each block to the backup media (using the MAXTRANSFERSIZE option) to improve throughput, but we recommend this cautiously and on only in circumstances where the defaults calculated by SQL Server prove problematic. Allocating too many buffers or increasing the transfer size too high might cause out-of-memory exceptions during the backup operation, which will cause the backup to fail. While this is not a situation which would require a server restart, it diminishes the automation you set up for backups. You can read more about this possible issue at *https://blogs.msdn.microsoft.com/sqlserverfaq/2010/05/06/incorrect-buffercount-data-transfer-option-can-lead-to-oom-condition/*.

Verifying backups

After you create a backup, we highly recommend that you immediately verify that the backup was successful. Although rare, corruption is always a possibility. Most of the time it is caused by the storage layer (including as a result of device drivers, network drivers, and filter drivers), but it can also occur in non-ECC RAM or as the result of a bug in SQL Server itself.

NOTE

A filter driver is software that intercepts all drive reads and writes. This class of software includes defragmentation tools and security products like antivirus. This is a good opportunity to remind you to exclude SQL Server files (data, log, and backups) from antivirus scanners, and to note that defragmenting solid-state storage is a bad idea because it will dramatically reduce the lifespan of the drive.

There are two ways to verify a backup, and you can probably guess that the most complete way is to restore it and perform a full consistency check on the restored database by using DBCC CHECKDB.

The other, quicker method is to use RESTORE VERIFYONLY. If you backed up your database using the checksum option (which is on by default on compressed backups), the restore will verify the backup checksum as well as the data page and log block checksums as it reads through the backup media.

The convenience with RESTORE VERIFYONLY is that you do not need to allocate drive space to restore the data and log files, because the restore will read directly from the backup itself.

Inside OUT

Why should you perform a DBCC CHECKDB if you have backup checksums turned on?

Although backup checksums are verified by RESTORE VERIFYONLY, it is possible for corruption to occur after a page was verified as it is being written to the drive or while it is copied offsite. A successful RESTORE VERIFYONLY is not a clean bill of health for the backup.

You can build an automated process on another server with a lot of cheaper drive space to restore all databases after they have been backed up and perform a DBCC CHECKDB on them. This also gives you an excellent idea of whether you can meet your RTO as databases grow.

A DBCC CHECKDB is the only way to know that a database is free of corruption.

Restoring a database

To restore a database, you will generally start with a full backup (piecemeal restore is covered in a later section).

If you plan to make use of differential and/or transaction log backups, you must use the NORECOVERY keyword for all but the last of the backup files you will restore.

You restore a database in the simple recovery model by using a full backup to begin, plus the most recent differential backup based on the full backup.

You can restore a database in the bulk-logged recovery model by using a full backup, along with the most recent differential backup based on that full backup if available. Should you want to restore to a specific point in time for a bulk-logged database, this might be possible if no bulk-logged operations exist in the transaction log backups you use.

You can restore a database in the full recovery model to a point in time using a full backup, plus any transaction log backups that form part of the backup chain. You can use a more recent differential backup (based off that full backup) to bypass a number of those transaction log backups, where appropriate.

CAUTION

Differential and transaction log backups rely on a corresponding full backup. If the full backup is not available, the differential and transaction log backups are useless. All transaction log backups must be available at least to the point in time you're trying to restore.

Each transaction log backup is replayed against the database being recovered, using the NORECOVERY option, as though those transactions are happening in real time. Each file is restored in sequential order up to the required point in time or until the last transaction log backup is reached, whichever comes first.

NOTE

When restoring a chain of transaction log backups, especially the first one in the sequence after a full or differential backup, it can happen that the LSN of the transaction log backup is earlier than the latest LSN of the full or differential backup that was restored. In most cases, you can ignore the error message that is displayed because the next transaction log file in the restore sequence will usually contain the required LSN.

After the entire chain has been restored (indicated by the WITH RECOVERY option), only then does the recovery kick in (which was covered in some detail in Chapter 3). All transactions that are committed will be rolled forward, and any in-flight transactions will be rolled back.

CHAPTER 10

Some examples of restoring a database are included in the section that follows.

Restoring a database using a full backup

You can perform a database restore through SQL Server Management Studio or by using a T-SQL statement. In this example, only a full backup file is available to restore a database. The full backup comes from a different server, where the path of the original database is different, so the files need to be relocated (moved) on the new server with the MOVE option.

To see the progress of the restore, you can set the statistics to display to the output window with the STATS option. The default is to write progress for every 5% complete. No statistics will be output until the files have been created on the file system.

```
RESTORE DATABASE WideWorldImporters

FROM DISK = N'C:\SQLData\Backup\SERVER_WideWorldImporters_FULL_20190918_210912.BAK'

WITH

MOVE N'WideWorldImporters' TO N'C:\SQLData\WWI.mdf',

MOVE N'WideWorldImporters_log' TO N'C:\SQLData\WWI.ldf',

STATS = 5,

RECOVERY;

GO
```

The RECOVERY option (the default) at the end brings the database online immediately after the full backup has been restored. This prevents any further backups from being applied. If you want to restore a differential backup after this full backup, you will need to use the NORECOVERY option and bring the database online only after restoring the differential backup. This is covered in the next section.

Restoring a database with differential and log backups

Restoring using full, differential, and transaction log backups is more complicated, but you can still perform it through SQL Server Management Studio or by using a series of T-SQL statements.

For this scenario, we recommend creating your own automated scripts. For example, after every transaction log backup, you can use the information in the msdb database to build a script to restore the entire database to that point in time and then save the script in the same folder as the backup file(s).

➤ **To see an example by Steve Stedman, go to** *https://stevestedman.com/2017/10/ building-sql-restore-script-backup-runs/.*

NOTE

When restoring a database using more than one backup type (full, plus differential and/ or transaction log), each RESTORE **statement that will be followed by another restore file must include a** WITH NORECOVERY **option. This prevents recovery from running until needed. You can either use the** WITH RECOVERY **option on the final file to run recovery and bring the database online or you can add an extra line to the end of the script as in the following example.**

You restore a database by using the RESTORE command. Full and differential restores use the RESTORE DATABASE option by convention. You can also restore transaction logs by using the RESTORE DATABASE option, but you might prefer to use RESTORE LOG, instead, for clarity:

```
-- First, restore the full backup

RESTORE DATABASE WideWorldImporters

FROM DISK = N'C:\SQLData\Backup\SERVER_WideWorldImporters_FULL_20190918_210912.BAK'

WITH

MOVE N'WideWorldImporters' TO N'C:\SQLData\WWI.mdf',

MOVE N'WideWorldImporters_log' TO N'C:\SQLData\WWI.ldf',

NORECOVERY;

GO

-- Second, restore the most recent differential backup

RESTORE DATABASE WideWorldImporters

FROM DISK = N'C:\SQLData\Backup\SERVER_WideWorldImporters_DIFF_20190926_120100.BAK'

WITH NORECOVERY;

GO

-- Finally, restore all transaction log backups after the differential

RESTORE LOG WideWorldImporters

FROM DISK = N'C:\SQLData\Backup\SERVER_WideWorldImporters_LOG_20190926_121500.BAK'

WITH NORECOVERY;

GO

RESTORE LOG WideWorldImporters

FROM DISK = N'C:\SQLData\Backup\SERVER_WideWorldImporters_LOG_20190926_123000.BAK'

WITH NORECOVERY;
```

```
GO

-- Bring the database online

RESTORE LOG WideWorldImporters WITH RECOVERY;

GO
```

Remember that you can use the WITH RECOVERY option in the final transaction log file restore and exclude the final statement in the previous example.

The RECOVERY option instructs SQL Server to run recovery on the database, which might include an upgrade step if the new instance has a newer version of SQL Server on it. When recovery is complete, the database is brought online.

Restoring a database to a point in time

If configured properly, it is possible to restore a database to the exact moment in time (or more precisely, to the exact LSN) before any disaster occurs. A point-in-time restore requires an LSN or timestamp (meaning any specific date and time value) to let the RESTORE command know when to stop restoring. You can even restore to a specific mark in the transaction log backup, which you specify at transaction creation time by explicitly naming a transaction. This is requires knowing in advance that this transaction might be the cause for a point-in-time restore, which is rarely the case in a disaster scenario.

NOTE

Some scenarios where you might suspect in advance that a point-in-time recovery is required include performing a schema upgrade, perhaps as part of an application release. You should also consider using database snapshots.

➤ To see more about marking transactions, go to *https://docs.microsoft.com/sql/t-sql/ statements/restore-statements-transact-sql*.

CAUTION

The timestamp used for a point-in-time restore comes from the transaction log itself and refers to the local date and time on the SQL Server instance when the transaction started. Remember to take time zones and daylight saving into consideration when restoring a database to a point in time.

Depending on the cause of the disaster, you might want to investigate the current state of the database to determine the best recovery approach. You might need to close connections to the database and set the database to single user mode. In single user mode, you have time to find out what happened (without making modifications), take a tail-log backup when possible and necessary, and recover the database to the moment the disaster struck. In some cases, you may opt to leave the database active, but restore it to a new database and reload changes from the restored version. The feasibility of this depends on the database schema, the number of changes that have been made since the adverse event, and the RTO.

A point-in-time restore works only when restoring transaction log backups, not full or differential backups. The point in time must be after the full backup from which you begin the restore process. This fact may make it valuable to keep several full backups prior to the most recent one. Some errors, perhaps human error or database corruption, may not always be detected before a new full backup is taken.

Inside OUT

How can you tell when the unplanned event took place?

To find out when a disaster occurred that isn't immediately apparent, you can query the active portion of the transaction log if it is available, making use of an undocumented system function that reads from the active VLF(s), as demonstrated here:

```
SELECT * FROM sys.fn_dblog(NULL, NULL);
```

This displays all transactions that have not yet been flushed as a result of a checkpoint operation. The NULL parameters are the start and end LSN, but of course, if you knew those, you wouldn't be searching the log in the first place.

Using a standard WHERE clause, you can trace back to the point immediately before the event took place. For example, if you know that a user deleted a row from a table, you would write a query looking for all delete operations:

```
SELECT * FROM sys.fn_dblog(NULL, NULL)

WHERE Operation LIKE '%delete%';
```

To get this to work, SQL Server should still be running, and the transaction log should still be available (although this technique does work on offline transaction log files using `sys.fn_dump_dblog`).

To see more from Paul Randal about reading from the transaction log, go to *https://www.sqlskills.com/blogs/paul/using-fn_dblog-fn_dump_dblog-and-restoring-with-stopbeforemark-to-an-lsn/*.

The process is the same as in the previous example, except for the final transaction log file, for which the point in time is specified by using the STOPAT or STOPBEFOREMARK options. Let's look at each option:

- **STOPAT.**   A timestamp. You will need to know this value from the time an unexpected event occurred. If it's unclear when the event occurred, exploring the transaction log might be required.

- **STOPBEFOREMARK** (also **STOPATMARK**).   A log sequence number or transaction name. You will need to know the LSN value from exploring the active portion of the transaction log (see the Inside OUT above).

Assuming that you have followed the same sequence as shown in the previous example, the final transaction log restore might look like this:

```
-- Restore point in time using timestamp

RESTORE LOG WideWorldImporters

FROM DISK = N'C:\SQLData\Backup\SERVER_WideWorldImporters_LOG_20170926_123000.BAK'

WITH STOPAT = 'Sep 26, 2017 12:28 AM',

RECOVERY;

GO

-- Or restore point in time using LSN

-- Assume that this LSN is where the bad thing happened

RESTORE LOG WideWorldImporters

FROM DISK = N'C:\SQLData\Backup\SERVER_WideWorldImporters_LOG_20170926_123000.BAK'

WITH STOPBEFOREMARK = 'lsn:0x0000029f:00300212:0002',

RECOVERY;

GO
```

➤ To read more about database recovery, including syntax and examples, visit *https://docs.microsoft.com/sql/t-sql/statements/restore-statements-transact-sql*.

Restoring a database piecemeal

Partial database backups deal with file and filegroup backups in order to ease the manageability of your VLDB. This is an advanced topic, so this section is a very high-level overview, which does not cover all the intricacies involved.

Partial recovery is useful for bringing a database online as quickly as possible to allow the organization to continue working. You can then restore any secondary filegroups later, during a planned maintenance window.

Piecemeal restores begin with what is known as the partial-restore sequence. In this sequence, the primary filegroup is restored and recovered first. If the database is under the simple recovery model, all read/write filegroups are then restored.

➤ **To learn more about the SQL Server recovery process, read Chapter 3.**

While this is taking place, the database is offline until restore and recovery is complete. Any unrestored files or filegroups remain offline, but you can bring them online later by restoring them.

Regardless of the database's recovery model, the RESTORE command must include the PARTIAL option when doing a piecemeal restore, but only at the beginning of the sequence. Because transactions might span more than just the recovered filegroups, these transactions can become deferred, meaning that any transaction that needs to roll back cannot do so while a filegroup is offline. The transactions are deferred until the filegroup can be brought online again, and any data involved in that deferred transaction is locked in the meantime.

Restoring a database piecemeal under the simple recovery model

To initialize a partial recovery of a database under the simple recovery model, you must begin with a full database or a partial backup. The restore will bring the primary filegroup and all read/write secondary filegroups online. You can then bring the database online. Finally, if any read-only filegroups were damaged or corrupted and you need to restore them, you will do those last.

Restoring a database piecemeal under the full recovery model

As with the simple recovery model that we just looked at, you must begin with a full database or partial backup (which must include the primary filegroup). When possible, you should also have a tail-log backup to help restore the database to the most recent point in time.

It is possible to restore and recover only the most important read-write filegroups first, then restore additional read-write filegroups, before finally restoring any read-only filegroups. Depending on the design of the database and applications, the organization may resume critical operations sooner than if the entire database needed to be restored.

Point-in-time restore is provided under the following conditions:

● The first RESTORE DATABASE command must include the PARTIAL option.

● For a point-in-time restore against read-write filegroups, you need an unbroken log backup chain, and you must specify the time in the restore statement.

➤ **To see more about piecemeal restores, including code examples, visit *https://docs.microsoft. com/sql/relational-databases/backup-restore/piecemeal-restores-sql-server.***

CHAPTER 10

> **NOTE**
> If you skip a FILESTREAM filegroup during partial recovery, you can never again recover it unless the entire database is restored in full.

Defining a recovery strategy

Consider our scenario from the beginning of the chapter, in which anything and everything that could go wrong did go wrong. We will highlight certain issues that could be addressed by an appropriate recovery plan. This recovery plan can then be implemented, step-by-step, using your run book.

The word "strategy" means that there is a long-term goal. Your recovery strategy will need to adapt to your environmental changes. A run book is a living document; it requires incremental improvements as you test it.

We also discuss recovery strategies around hybrid environments, and briefly discuss Azure SQL Database.

A sample recovery strategy for our DR scenario

Several avoidable problems occurred in the DR scenario at the beginning of the chapter:

- There was no redundant backup for the UPS.

- The Internet connection did not have a redundant backup.

- There was no run book to guide the accident-prone DBA.

- The security on the DR server does not follow recommended best practices.

- The offsite backups were failing.

In the next subsections, we'll discuss some key considerations for your recovery strategy beyond taking backups.

Keeping the lights on

In your run book, ensure that your UPS collection and backup generators can run all necessary equipment for long enough to keep emergency lights on, laptops charging, network equipment live, and the servers running, so that your DBA can log in to the SQL Server instance long enough to run a tail-log backup if necessary. If the RTO allows it, you may have the option of pro-actively shutting down gracefully rather than attempting to keep less critical systems running with limited power.

It might sound like a small detail, but you should even have a list of diesel suppliers in your run book, especially if your generators need to keep running for several hours.

Clean power is also important. Generators cause power fluctuations, which can damage sensitive electronic equipment. A power conditioner should be installed with your generator, so you need to make sure that it works correctly.

In our scenario, the backup power was inappropriate. There was no sufficient way to ensure that electricity would continue to flow after the building lost power, which had a number of knock-on effects including the inability to charge laptops and cellphone batteries.

Redundant Internet connection

If your backups are being copied securely offsite or you have a hybrid environment in which systems are connected across datacenters using Virtual Private Networks (VPNs), make sure that these routes can stay connected if one of the links goes down.

In our scenario, the DBA had no option but to use a low-quality cellular connection. While cellular modems can be a part of your recovery strategy, they can be fickle. It's also difficult to connect servers that way.

Know where the run book is

The run book itself should be printed out and stored in a secure but easily accessible location (for example, a fireproof safe or lock box). Don't forget to have an electronic copy available, as well, stored with a cloud provider of your choice and kept up to date.

Make sure your offsite backups are secure and tamper-proof

Security of the offsite location for backups is critical, and no one should have access to that unless they are required to do a recovery.

In our example scenario, our DBA accidentally deleted an email alert indicating that the offsite storage for backups was almost full. This alert is a good one to have, but it was not acted on appropriately. Also, the cause of the alert was an avoidable situation because the colleague who used up the free space should not have been able to use critical organization resources.

Check your backups regularly and test them regularly

Automate your backups. Use maintenance plans (see Chapter 9), or make use of established third-party backup tools such as Ola Hallengren's Maintenance Solution (available from *https://ola.hallengren.com*) or MinionWare Backup (available from *https://www.minionware.net/*).

Verify that you have a process to check that your backups are taking place. Test that process often. For example, if SQL Server Agent is crashing, none of your notifications might ever fire. Test the backups, as well, by having a machine that restores backups continuously and running

DBCC CHECKDB where possible. If you can afford it, have log shipping configured so that all back-ups are restored as soon as they come into offsite storage. Ensure that the backup files are being securely copied offsite as soon as they can.

If you're unable to continuously restore databases, run random spot-checks of your backups by picking a date and time in the backup history and restoring the backup. Aside from testing the databases themselves, this is a good rehearsal for when something goes wrong. Use the run book for these exercises to ensure it is and remains up-to-date. Remember to run DBCC CHECKDB on any database you restore.

You might find as databases grow that the SLA becomes out of date and that the RTO is no longer achievable. Running these tests will alert you to this situation long before it becomes a problem and will allow you to tweak how you perform backups in the future.

For example, you might discover that it is much quicker to spin up an Azure virtual machine with SQL Server and restore the business-critical databases that are stored in Azure Blob Stor-age, than having to struggle with VPN connections and failed hardware on-premises.

Our DBA assumed that the backups were taking place every 15 minutes and being copied off-site immediately afterward. This was not the case, and instead of losing 15 minutes of data, the organization lost as much as 27 minutes' worth.

Check the security of your disaster recovery site

Your DR site might have outdated security access controls, whether physical or virtual. Be sure that you stay up to date, especially when people leave the company. You don't want to be in the position of having to call someone who left your organization two years ago to ask for a firewall password—especially not at 3 AM on a Sunday. If you must use a remote desktop connection to access a server, protect it by using a VPN.

Prepare tools and credentials

Check that you have already downloaded additional tools and documented how to use them. Unless they pose a security risk, have them available on the recovery systems in advance.

Keep all passwords and keys (symmetric and asymmetric) in a password manager as well as printed and stored in a secure location with the run book where practical. Make sure that all digital certificates are backed up securely.

Automate restore scripts

In the case of an msdb database being inaccessible and you are unable to generate a restore script from a database backup history, make sure that you have a tool that generates a restore script based on files in a folder in your offsite storage. Many tools exist to do this, including the `Restore-DbaDatabase` command in the free dbatools (available from *https://dbatools.io*).

Practice your disaster recovery plan

In concert with your HA strategy, which involves automated and manual failovers (see Chapter 11 for more on this), you should perform regular drills to test your run book. You can also have people in your organization who are unfamiliar with the environment look through the run book. They can provide valuable information with regard to assumptions you might have made.

The cadence is up to your organization, but a full DR scenario should be tested at least once a year. Any changes you need to make to the run book should be made immediately. If the recovery fails, add notes of how it failed and what you did to resolve the failure. All of this information is extremely valuable.

Recovery strategies for hybrid and cloud environments

Many organizations are making use of a combination of on-premises infrastructure and services in remote locations, including Azure services, third-party datacenters, and other cloud vendors.

Recovering data in hybrid and cloud environments

The strategy for recovering data in a hybrid environment is very similar to an on-premises strategy, except that you must take network connection, latency, and bandwidth into account. When designing a recovery strategy for a hybrid environment, pick a DR site that is central, but geo-replicated.

It can be prudent to make use of virtualization technologies that allow for virtual machine snapshots and file system snapshots to ensure that your virtual servers are backed up regularly. These VM backups can be spun up in case of a disaster quicker than rebuilding physical servers. You can augment these with appropriate native SQL Server backups that are tested properly.

If you are already making use of Azure Storage for your backups, this reduces the network bandwidth and latency issues if you can restore your organization's databases to Azure virtual machines or databases in Azure SQL Database.

Remember that after failing over to a DR site, you will need to fail back to your on-premises site when it is up and running again. Based on the magnitude of the disaster, you may need to keep the DR site as the new primary, in which case you'll need to set up a new DR site.

Recovering a database in Azure SQL Database

Chapter 17 offers an in-depth look at managing Azure SQL Database, including preparing for disaster recovery. There are three options to consider when restoring a point-in-time backup, which plays into your run book:

- **Database replacement.** You can replace an existing database using a database backup. This requires that you verify the service tier and performance level of the restored database. To replace your existing database, rename the old existing and restore to the old name.

- **Data recovery.**   If you need to recover data from a previous point in time, you can restore the database to a new database. Azure SQL DB lets you specify the point in time within the backup retention period to which you wish to restore.

- **Deleted database.**   If you deleted a database and you are still within the recovery window, you can restore that deleted database to the time just before it was deleted.

The geo-restore feature can restore a full backup to any server in any Azure region from a geo-redundant backup. Databases on the basic performance tier can take up to 12 hours to geo-restore. This Estimated Recovery Time should be a consideration in your RTO. With Azure SQL Database, you're also giving up control over the RPO. When properly implemented, as discussed in Chapter 17, Azure SQL Database supports an RPO of as little as five seconds.

➤ To read more about recovering a database in Azure SQL Database, including associated costs, refer to Chapter 17, or visit *https://docs.microsoft.com/azure/sql-database/sql-database-recovery-using-backups*.

Implementing high availability and disaster recovery

No server is (intended to be) an island. Application downtime is costly. Loss of data can be fatal to an organization. In this chapter, we detail the Microsoft SQL Server technologies designed to provide high availability and disaster recovery, adding to the discussion of backups in Chapter 10, "Developing, deploying, and managing data recovery." What's beyond taking backups?

First, we take an overview of the available technologies, including log shipping, replication, failover clustering, and availability groups. Then, we look at configuration of failover clusters and availability groups on Windows and Linux. SQL Server 2019 support for Linux extends to Always On availability groups as well as replication, and we provide a guide to your first availability group on Red Hat Linux. Finally, we cover the administration of availability groups, such as monitoring, performance analysis, and alerting.

➤ This chapter deals with SQL Server instances. Disaster recovery technologies provided in Microsoft Azure SQL Database are covered in Chapter 17, "Provisioning Azure SQL Database." And while some concepts for availability groups also apply to Azure SQL Managed Instances, we discuss more about Azure MI high availability in Chapter 18, "Provisioning Azure SQL Database managed instance."

Overview of high availability and disaster recovery technologies in SQL Server

As an enterprise-grade data platform, SQL Server provides features to ensure high availability (HA) and prepare for disaster recovery (DR). This requires some effort and extra investment. You must configure these technologies correctly to provide the desired benefits. The level of effort and investment required in ensuring HA should never exceed the value of the data to the organization.

In other words, not every database on every server must be configured for HA and geo-replicated for DR. Depending on the value of the data and any Service-Level Agreements (SLAs), having backups available off-premises might be sufficient to prepare for disaster. (As always, you should copy your backups off-premises as soon as possible after they are taken, and you should test them regularly.)

For cases in which additional investment is warranted, there are many technologies available. Some are suitable for HA and others for DR, and a few are suitable for both uses. In this first section, we cover the variety of technologies available in SQL Server to build a highly available environment and to prepare for DR.

Inside OUT

What's the difference between HA and DR anyway?

Before covering the different technologies, we should clarify the difference between HA and DR.

HA means that your databases remain available, automatically, in the face of hardware or software failures. HA requires redundant hardware and platforms, and the automation and planning for how secondary systems can assume the role of the primary system. This book and chapter talks about the High Availability of the SQL Server layer, though you should also consider the high availability of other layers necessary for running applications for end users, such as the network, storage, and application layers.

DR means that your data is not lost after a substantial incident (a "disaster"), such as human error introducing bad data, a storage failure, or a ransomware attack, though data might be temporarily unavailable until you run your DR plan. A proper DR plan involves redundant storage of backup files, accomplished by copying backups offsite. As discussed more in the preceding chapter, a backup shouldn't be considered taken until it is copied offsite.

Comparing HA and DR technologies

Table 11-1 compares the four major technologies for HA and DR using a variety of attributes. We do not intend for this table to provide a complete comparison; rather, it gathers the details relevant for HA and DR.

Table 11-1   Comparison of four HA and DR technologies in SQL Server 2019

	Log shipping	SQL Replication	Failover clustering	Availability groups	Basic availability groups
Capable of Automatic failover	No	N/A	Yes	Yes	Yes
Instance versions	Should match exactly*	Up to two major versions apart	Match exactly**	Match exactly**	Match exactly**
Edition	Web, Standard, Enterprise	Standard, Enterprise‡	Standard, Enterprise	Enterprise	Standard
Readable secondary	Yes, but interrupted by log restores	Yes	No	Yes	No
Different indexing on readable secondary	No	Yes	No	No	No
Schema changes required to tables	No	Yes (except snapshot)	No	No	No
Schema changes replicated	Yes	Yes	N/A	Yes	Yes
Primary purpose	DR	Custom sync, DR	HA	HA/DR/ Readable secondary	HA/DR
Level	Database	Articles	Instance	Databases	Databases
FILESTREAM and FileTable	Yes and Yes	Yes and No	Yes with shared disk, Yes	Yes and Partially‡‡	Yes and Partially‡‡

* In theory, log shipping to a higher version of SQL Server is possible, in which case there is no path to return to the primary copy after recovering from a disaster.

** Temporarily, these environments can be different versions while applying cumulative updates in a rolling fashion.

‡ All editions, including Azure SQL Database, can be subscribers. Only Standard and Enterprise Edition instances can be publishers.

‡‡ FILESTREAM is fully supported. FileTables are supported on the primary replica, but FileTables are not readable on a secondary replica, regardless of replica settings.

CHAPTER 11

Understanding log shipping

The log shipping feature in SQL Server makes it possible for you to create a copy of a database on a secondary instance by automatically restoring transaction log backups from the database on a primary instance to one or more secondary instances. You need to set up log shipping for each individual database. Therefore, if your application uses multiple databases, you will need to independently configure each database for log shipping.

> **NOTE**
>
> **You can perform transaction log backups only if the database uses the full or bulk-logged recovery model. You cannot configure log shipping on a database in the simple recovery model. For more information on database recovery models, refer to Chapter 10.**

The real role of log shipping isn't to provide HA—unlike other features available to you, there is no way to failover to the secondary copy of the database, something resembling failover would involve manual intervention and connection string redirection outside of SQL Server. You can configure the log shipping job to set the secondary database to Standby mode, allowing for read-only access. In that case, users concurrently accessing the database will block the next transaction log restore in the chain. You can configure the transaction log restore to kick users out of the secondary database in time for the restore.

All of the logs are stored to the log shipping secondary database and restored WITH NORECOVERY, meaning that the database will remain "In Recovery..." status without any way for you to access them. In the event of a disaster, you can restore the last good transaction log backup from the source, or if no more are available, simply bring the destination database online.

In the most common log shipping use case, it serves simply as a way to stream backups to an off-premises DR SQL Server. You can recover the secondary database, take a new backup of the secondary database, and restore it to the primary after a disaster that claims the primary database. Another common use of log shipping is to provide a "rewind" copy of the database, given that the restoration of the transaction log backups on the secondary instance can be delayed, and provide an uncorrupted backup of the database in the event of a data-related disaster, perhaps caused by an application fault or human error.

You cannot currently configure log shipping with a database in Azure SQL Database or Azure SQL Database managed instance as the destination.

Although log shipping is a straightforward and effective way to set up secondary databases, it does have a few shortcomings. First, you can take no other transaction log backups than those used for log shipping. This means that you must find a balance between the replication frequency for DR and the frequency of taking transaction log backups for point-in-time restores, for example, to recover from user error. Second, you can take log-shipped backups quite frequently, even every minute, but you must plan appropriately for the overhead of taking the transaction log backups and having the files copied over the network to the file share.

Overall, log shipping is considered a rudimentary form of DR (indeed, it was first introduced in SQL Server 7.0) that does what it can and does it well, capable of continuously shipping a chain of transaction logs to a remote database for months or even years. Let's take a quick look at setting up and configuring log shipping.

Understanding up log shipping

Log shipping relies on a network share for the folder where the transaction log backups will be stored. This folder and share require specific permissions which depend on a few factors. Log shipping uses the SQL Server Agent to run scheduled jobs.

Be sure that the SQL Server Agent service is scheduled to start automatically. We recommend using domain proxy accounts for the SQL Server Agent jobs. The account for the transaction log backup job (which runs on the primary server) must have read and write access to the folder (if the folder is located on the primary server) or the network share (if the folder is not located on the primary server). The proxy account for the backup copy job, which runs on the secondary server, must have read access to the file share.

If you are using SQL Server Management Studio (SSMS) to configure log shipping, it will restore a full backup of the database on the secondary server from the network share, using your credentials. If you are using Transact-SQL (T-SQL) scripts, to create the log shipping you will need to copy and restore this backup manually.

CAUTION

If you let SQL Server create the secondary database(s) during the configuration steps, the data and log files for the secondary database will be placed on the same volume as the data and log file for the destination instance's master database by default. You can use the Restore Options button in the Initialize Secondary Database to change the destination data and log file directories on the secondary server.

On the primary SQL Server instance, log shipping creates a SQL Server Agent job called LSBackup_*dbname* to back up the transaction logs to the network share. You will need to schedule the log shipping log backup job to occur at a schedule that meets your needs for DR, while taking into the account the overhead and duration of creating, transferring, and restoring the backups.

Log shipping also creates a SQL Server Agent job called LSAlert_*primaryinstancename* that will fail if no backup is detected in the desired window. You monitor the job for failure and monitor the SQL Server Error Log for the Severity 16 errors that may be thrown related to Log Shipping not performing or restoring a backup log operation, error numbers 14420 and 14421.

> ➤ To configure SQL alerts in Chapter 9, "Automating SQL Server administration."

On the secondary SQL Server instance, log shipping creates three SQL Server Agent jobs:

- LSCopy_*primaryinstancename* to copy the backup files from the file share to the secondary server.

- LSRestore_*primaryinstancename* to restore the transaction log backups continually.

- LSAlert_*secondaryinstancename* to raise an error if no log backup is detected after a certain time.

When using SSMS, these steps are mostly automated. Otherwise, you will need to manually schedule and turn on these jobs. Following are a couple of recommendations for configuring log shipping optimally:

- You should configure the file share on a server other than the primary database server. That way, the log files need to be copied from the primary server only once. If you configure the file share on the primary server, each secondary will initiate a copy of the backup files. If you have more than one secondary, this will increase the network traffic to your primary server.

- You can monitor log shipping activity using the report available in SSMS and configure alerts.

Understanding types of replication

Replication provides several approaches to copy schema and data from one database to another. Because this chapter focuses on HA and DR technologies, we discuss replication in this context. Other uses for replication include support for occasionally offline clients, integrating heterogeneous data stores, offloading processing and reporting workloads, and partial and filtered table synchronization.

There are three main types of replication: *transactional*, *merge*, and *snapshot*. Each of these types has specific benefits and drawbacks that makes them more or less suitable for HA or DR purposes.

Transactional and merge replication can optionally support two-way replication. These are powerful, complex, albeit veteran features of the product, in place for over a decade, but the databases must be designed to support the fact that updates will take place in more than one place. The application also might need to be aware of such operations, and table changes may be needed for implementation on existing databases. Both transactional and merge replication use snapshot replication–which is straightforward bulk sending of data–as part of their initial setup.

Peer-to-peer replication supports multimaster or bidirectional replication, and, like merge replication, it can be the core foundation of an application architecture. In addition to scale-out functionality, peer-to-peer replication can provide HA if the application is designed to attempt to connect to another instance in case of failed connection attempts to its preferred instance.

All types of replication employ a concept of a publisher and one or more subscribers. The *publisher* is the SQL Server instance that holds the original database. A *subscriber* is the SQL Server instance holding a destination database for replication.

In addition, the *distributor* is the component responsible for obtaining data from the publisher and directing it to the subscribers. The distributor is, in effect, the middle man: the publisher and the subscriber do not directly interact. Note that the distributor component can be located on the same SQL Server instance as the publisher, but for performance purposes, it is best to configure a different SQL Server instance to serve as the distributor.

When the publishing instance serves as its own distributor, this is called a *push subscription*. This is the only model in which it is possible to replicate to a database in Azure SQL Database. When another instance serves as the distributor, it is called a *pull subscription*.

All types of replication deal with *articles*. An article can be a one table, stored procedure, or view, synchronizing both data and most schema changes. With views, the underlying data tables are also required to be added as articles to the same replication publication. You can filter articles, and they do not need to include all the columns or rows of a table.

CHAPTER 11

Inside OUT

What are some of the limitations on schema changes in SQL Server replication?

Table schema changes on publication databases can be made only by using T-SQL or SQL Server Management Objects (SMO). SSMS attempts to drop and re-create tables, as opposed to running ALTER TABLE statements. Dropping replication articles is not allowed, and the schema change will fail when performed within SSMS. Similarly, schema changes dependent on objects that are not replicated may succeed on the publisher but fail on the subscriber.

You should consider explicitly naming all constraints and not allowing system-generated names for default constraints, primary keys, foreign keys. Replication may fail upon synchronization to the subscriber if the system-generated names for objects are different.

You can create different indexes on the publisher and subscriber. Though a CREATE INDEX statement will not be immediately replicated, it will be applied to the subscriber upon resynchronization via the snapshot agent.

> **NOTE**
>
> For more information on replicated schema change details and exceptions, reference the documentation here: *https://docs.microsoft.com/sql/relational-databases/replication/administration/frequently-asked-questions-for-replication-administrators.*

The components of replication are:

- **Publisher.**   The SQL Server instance that publishes the database for replication.

- **Subscriber.**   The SQL Server instance that receives the replicated data.

- **Distributor.**   The SQL Server instance that distributes the replicated data from the publisher to the subscriber. Think of the distributor as the middle man. This can be the same SQL Server instance as the publisher or subscriber.

- **Article.**   The database object that is replicated. In addition to replicating the schema and data for tables, you can also replicate the running of stored procedures. Articles can have row and column filters to limit the data that is replicated.

- **Log Reader Agent.**   The Log Reader Agent, which runs at the distributor, reads the publication database's transaction log and extracts commands to be replicated. These commands are added to the distribution database, which will hold these commands until all subscribers have received them or until the retention period has been reached.

- **Distribution Agent.**   The Distribution Agent moves transactions from the distribution database to the subscriber(s). The distribution agent can run on the distributor, which is a push subscription, or at the subscriber, which is a pull subscription. Optionally, the Distribution Agent can validate that data between the publisher and the subscriber match.

- **Distribution database.**   The distribution database is hosted on the distributor. For all types of replication, it stores metadata and history data. For transactional replication, it also contains the transactions that have not yet been moved to the subscriber(s).

- **Snapshot Agent.** Performs bulk data movement to synchronize a subscriber database to the publication, including an initial synchronization. Can optionally be used alone to regularly push data to a subscriber, or started manually to resynchronize a subscriber.

Snapshot replication

We first cover snapshot replication because it serves a role in the initial distribution of schema and data for transactional and merge replication, via bulk insert operations. Even though there are other ways to get an initial copy of the database to a subscriber, snapshot replication integrates with merge and transactional replication to seed the subscribers.

Snapshot replication is described very well by its name: this replication method takes a snapshot of the database state at a point in time and can then replicate that state to another SQL Server instance. Unlike merge and transactional replication, it's not usually scheduled and repeated to the same subscriber. Data and schema changes are not monitored: if you need additional replication, you take a new snapshot of the entire database and replicate it to all subscribers.

This type of replication can be beneficial if data changes are infrequent, but for those that do occur, they are substantial. Conceptually, it's very similar to taking and restoring a database backup; however, unlike with a backup, you can select individual database objects to include in the snapshot. You can even filter the tables with standard WHERE clauses on the articles.

A trade-off to consider when using snapshot replication is that there is no continuous overhead for tracking incremental changes, but there is a significant resource requirement when generating and delivering a new snapshot.

When using snapshot replication to create the initial snapshot for transactional or merge replication, you should keep the default synchronization method of concurrent snapshot processing. Otherwise, the creation of the snapshot will place and hold locks on the tables that are selected for replication. Depending on several factors, including the data size and the available resources on the publisher, the snapshot creation can take long enough for update operations to fail due to the locks. With concurrent snapshot processing, locks are not held for the entire snapshot creation operation.

You can also execute custom scripts to apply to the subscriber databases before or after a snapshot is completed, for customizing the state of the subscriber database after synchronization. Use the SSMS to view the Publication Properties, then the Snapshot page. Use the text boxes for "Before/After applying the snapshot, execute this script", and paste the path to a custom SQL Server script that will run under the context of the Distribution Agent service account. The path to the pre- or post-snapshot scripts should be to a UNC or to an identically-named folder on each subscriber.

Another important option to be aware of is the location of the snapshot files. For large publication databases, the snapshot files may become quite large. You can change the location of the Snapshot files by specifying a different folder in the Default Snapshot Folder of the Publisher Properties page in SSMS. For a new location, be sure to grant the Distribution Agent or Merge Agent read permissions, as well as granting the Snapshot agent read/write permissions on the folder location. If a pull subscription setup is being used, the snapshot folder should be a UNC path.

> ➤ **For descriptions of the roles played by each component in snapshot replication, refer to Microsoft Docs at**
> *https://docs.microsoft.com/sql/relational-databases/replication/snapshot-replication.*

Merge replication

Merge replication is not commonly used for HA or DR. It is well-suited for two-way synchronization between copies of a database on multiple SQL Server instances. At a high level, merge replication operates by tracking schema and data changes using triggers.

Every table that is published requires a column of type `uniqueidentifier` with the `ROWGUIDCOL` property set. If no such column exists, one will be created with the name `rowguid`. If such a column exists, its name does not matter. Merge replication can also be the basis of application architecture, used to synchronize changes in articles to and from instances.

> ➤ For more information on merge replication, refer to Microsoft Docs at
> *https://docs.microsoft.com/sql/relational-databases/replication/merge/merge-replication*.

Transactional replication

Transactional replication is the best suited of the three approaches for DR purposes. It works well with high-volume transactions, provides low latency, and guarantees transactional consistency.

Beyond DR, transactional replication can even be the foundation of data warehousing projects, moving only needed tables, columns, and rows; however, you might find that custom-developed SQL Server Integration Services packages provide better performance, customizability, and maintainability.

> NOTE
> Transactional replication supports updatable subscriptions, peer-to-peer replication, and bidirectional replication. These publication types each have benefits and drawbacks as it relates to handling changes that originated at subscribers. Because a peer-to-peer topology is designed to increase read-scale and move data between instances but is not designed for HA, it is not covered in this chapter.

> ➤ For details on the different publication types, refer to Microsoft Docs at
> *https://docs.microsoft.com/sql/relational-databases/replication/transactional/publication-types-for-transactional-replication*.

Understanding the capabilities of failover clustering

Failover clustering's purpose is to provide a fully automated HA solution that protects against server failures due to hardware or software. Failover cluster instances (FCIs) build on the Windows Server Failover Cluster (WSFC) technology to implement this. In SQL Server on Linux instances, Pacemaker can be used as the cluster manager. Conceptually, when the server hardware or software of an active cluster node fails, the cluster manager detects this and starts the SQL Server instance on another node.

NOTE

"Always On" is a marketing term to cover two HA technologies: Failover Cluster Instances (FCI) and availability groups (AG). Though these two technologies are completely different and accomplish different tasks in different ways, they can also be combined.

This is beneficial because the failover is automated, and also because it often just takes mere seconds for the failover of the SQL Server instance from one server to another. And even though clients will experience connection disruption in the event of a failover and the SQL Server experiences a restart, no special configuration on the client is required and reconnection is usually prompt. After a failover, the active instance will have the same DNS name and IP address as before. Clients simply open a new connection using the same connection string and continue operating.

Failover clustering does not require any form of replication or data duplication. Instead, the SQL Server data and logs are stored on shared storage. Each cluster node has access to the shared storage; which node is actively connected to shared storage is determined by WSFC. WSFC ensures that only one node can write to the shared storage at a time. Cluster disks appear only on the server that "owns" them.

NOTE

We refer to any form of storage that all nodes in the cluster can access as shared storage. Versions of SQL Server prior to 2012 required this to be storage that was connected to all cluster nodes. Since SQL Server 2012, shared storage can include file shares, as well. Since SQL Server 2016 and Windows Server 2016, shared storage can also include Storage Spaces Direct (S2D) and Cluster Shared Volumes (CSV). Although all of these options can make selecting the appropriate one a little more difficult, they bring SQL failover clusters within reach for a much broader set of deployments.

Whichever option you select for storage, make sure that it does not become a single point of failure. The entire path from the cluster nodes to the storage should be redundant. With traditional shared storage, this will likely involve configuring Multipath I/O (MPIO) to avoid a single shared drive from being discovered multiple times by each node. Many storage vendors provide the necessary device-specific module (DSM), a software driver that works with the Windows MPIO feature. For Fibre Channel SANs and iSCSI SANs, you can also use the generic Microsoft DSM if your vendor does not provide one.

Using WSFC poses additional requirements on the hardware and software configuration of each node as well as on shared storage. As to the hardware, WSFC requires that the hardware on each node is the same, including driver versions. The software on each node must also be the same, including operating system (OS) patches. WSFC provides a validation configuration wizard or the Test-Cluster PowerShell cmdlet that will provide detailed analysis and reports about the suitability of the selected servers to become cluster nodes.

➤ For details on the OS and SQL Server configuration necessary to create a Failover Cluster Instance, see the "Configuring Failover Cluster Instances" section later in the chapter.

> ## Inside OUT
>
> ### Are SQL Server Integration Services (SSIS) and SQL Server Reporting Services (SSRS) part of the FCI?
>
> SSIS and SSRS are not part of the FCI and are not cluster aware services, so they will not follow SQL Server from one server to another during a failover. There are methods for making those services highly available.
>
> In general, SSRS should be configured on a separate Windows Server, using the FCI as its database only, or configured on each Windows Server in the WSFC, in scale-out. Similarly, SSIS should also be installed on each server in the WSFC. It can be manually made into a cluster-aware service, but there are other options. Review the options at *https://docs.microsoft.com/sql/integration-services/service/ integration-services-ssis-in-a-cluster*.

Configuring Failover Cluster Instances for DR

SQL Server failover clusters can provide DR options in case a stretch cluster is configured. In a stretch cluster, some of the nodes are geographically located at a distance from one another, in different data centers. This would provide the ability to failover to another data center in the event of a disaster at the primary data center. The cluster will be configured to work across a Wide-Area Network (WAN) and the outlying nodes will not have access to the same shared storage. This requires that replication is configured from the cluster nodes in the primary site to the cluster nodes in the remote site(s).

➤ For information on multi-subnet clustering with SQL Server, including considerations for the IP address cluster resource, refer to Microsoft Docs at *https://docs.microsoft.com/sql/ sql-server/failover-clusters/windows/sql-server-multi-subnet-clustering-sql-server*. To read more about multi-subnet cluster configuration for availability groups, see the "Configuring RegisterAllProvidersIP and MultiSubNetFailover correctly" section later in the chapter.

NOTE

Instead of configuring a single stretch cluster to provide DR, you should configure two independent clusters, one at each site. To replicate data between sites, set up availability groups.

Understanding the capabilities of availability groups

Availability groups provide both HA and DR capabilities in a single feature. An availability group consists of one or more databases, the *availability databases*, that failover together.

Failover can be automatic or manual, and a manual failover can either be planned or forced. Of these three failover methods, when fully synchronized, only forced failover can cause data loss. The secondary replica(s) can optionally be readable in Enterprise Edition, allowing some read-only access to be offloaded from the primary read-write databases.

As discussed in previous chapters, availability groups are the successor and replacement to the deprecated database mirroring feature. Availability groups provide true disaster recovery and read-only secondary database utility that database mirroring did not. In fact, availability groups have totally encompassed database mirroring—see the "Basic availability groups" section later in the chapter.

Compared to mirroring or replication, availability groups provide a superior set of dynamic management views for monitoring and user interface dialog boxes in SSMS (and other tools). Availability groups offer a formidable and capable feature set of which all DBAs should be aware.

> ### NOTE
>
> Many administrators are familiar with the Microsoft Exchange term "database availability group" and its acronym "DAG." This is not an acronym used to describe Always On availability groups; "DAG" is incorrect, and the technologies are very different, though perhaps appear similar at a high level. To prevent miscommunication, you should not use the DAG to describe availability groups, or to describe Distributed Availability Groups, wherein multiple availability groups can be configured to synchronize with each other.

Remembering the availability groups feature set

The early code name for the availability groups project internally at Microsoft was *HADRON*. But, this wasn't just a cool name that had contemporary science relevance: you have probably heard of the Large Hadron Collider (LHC) beneath the France–Switzerland border, which first collided beams of high-energy particles in 2010 while HADRON was being developed for its initial release in SQL Server Denali CTP1 in December 2010.

In SQL Server, the acronym HADRON also spells out the three big features of availability groups:

- **HA: High Availability.**   The automatic failover to one or more synchronous secondary replicas, or manual failover to asynchronous secondary replicas.

- **DR: Disaster Recovery.** The ability to take valid backups directly on secondary replicas, including integrated backup tools that use customizable replica backup priority.

- **ON: ONline.** The secondary replicas could be read-only, and allow for the offloading of heavy-duty report workloads, using snapshot isolation to prevent blocking of transactions arriving from the primary replica.

Additionally, availability groups include automatic data corruption correction to repair damaged pages with data from other replicas, and database health detection that can initiate failover in response to database status.

NOTE

According to Microsoft Docs, failovers will not be initiated by a database becoming suspect due to factors such as transaction log corruption, data file loss, or database deletion. For more, read *https://docs.microsoft.com/sql/database-engine/ availability-groups/windows/always-on-availability-groups-sql-server.*

You should keep all the features of availability groups in mind when developing an architecture to meet your environment's requirements for Recovery Point Objective (RPO; or data loss tolerance) and Recovery Time Objective (RTO; or how long before the systems are back online after a disaster).

Differentiating availability groups from other HA solutions

Availability groups operate by transmitting segments of transaction log data from a primary replica to one or more secondary nodes.

Like transactional replication, availability groups use the transaction log data itself. Blocks of transaction logs are sent to the replicas, which is a scalable approach.

Superior to the deprecated database mirroring feature, availability groups begin to send blocks of log data as soon as the data is ready to be flushed to a drive, not afterward, resulting in transaction log data being sent to the secondary availability replica(s) sooner, tightening the gap between replicas.

Finally, unlike a SQL Server instance running on a Failover Cluster Instance (FCI), availability groups require minimally two copies of the data—no shared storage in use here—and minimally two active instances of SQL Server to accomplish HA. Unlike with FCI, both servers can be of use to the enterprise: one as the primary read/write replica, and one as a secondary read-only replica.

The availability group listener provides redirection to the primary node at all times, but additionally can also provide redirection to readable nodes. The Listener is an object that works via DNS to maintain the single name for the AG regardless of which instance is primary.

The Listener has its own IP address, and has an IP address in each subnet where AG instances exist. Applications can use the same connection string and instead provide a new parameter, `ApplicationIntent`, to declare whether the transactions in the connection will be read-write or read-only. You can route read-write connections to the primary replica, and read-only connections to one of the possible secondary replicas, thus splitting the workloads, even across a WAN. For detailed configuration information, refer to Microsoft Docs at *https://docs.microsoft.com/sql/database-engine/availability-groups/ windows/configure-read-only-access-on-an-availability-replica-sql-server*.

Configuring failover cluster instances

The WSFC is a Windows Server feature. Each server that will act as a cluster node must have this feature (not a role, but a feature) installed. Cluster nodes can join or leave a cluster at any time. However, simply adding a node to a cluster is not all that is required to run the SQL Server instance(s). We first cover (briefly) some key concepts of the WSFC and then move into configuring SQL Server Failover Cluster Instances.

When creating your cluster initially, Windows sets up an Active Directory computer account for the cluster's Virtual Network Name (VNN). By default, this VNN is created in the same Active Directory Organizational Unit (OU) as the cluster node. We recommend creating an OU for each cluster you create because permissions to create additional computer objects are then more easily delegated. Additional computer objects are created for each cluster resource, including each SQL Server instance. The cluster's VNN computer object should be given permission to create new computer objects in the OU. Alternatively, you could pre-stage the computer objects for the new virtual network names in the OU. The IP address associated with any VNN should be a static address instead of a dynamically assigned address.

Understanding FCI quorum

Creating and operating a WSFC requires an understanding of *quorum*. Similar to rules in a governmental meeting, quorum establishes that a majority of voting parties are present. The quorum of the cluster determines which nodes in the cluster are operating and how many failed nodes the cluster can sustain. This is tracked in a file called the quorum log, by default stored by default in the \MSCS\quolog.log file on the quorum resource and continuously accessed by the Cluster service.

> NOTE
> Also refer to this information below for Always On availability groups. In common Windows-based configurations, Always On availability groups (covered later in the "Configuring availability groups" section) use the WSFC as a cluster manager.
>
> In Windows, this is the "Windows Server Failover Clustering" cluster type option. When using WSFC for availability groups, the same guidance for quorum in this section applies.

CHAPTER 11

In Linux, there is an external cluster manager, or the EXTERNAL cluster type option. A clusterless configuration that does not require a cluster manager is also available with the cluster type option NONE. For more information on these two types, see the section later in this chapter, "Comparing different cluster types."

Correctly selecting a quorum configuration is important to avoid a *split-brain* scenario, which would occur when two instances of the cluster are running, unaware that each other is running. You can choose from five quorum configurations, each of which accomplish the basic goal of allowing for a majority of the nodes to maintain quorum, often by the use of an extra vote called a "witness" to increase an even number of votes into an odd number:

- **Node majority.** This is the recommended configuration choice for clusters that have an odd number of nodes. To determine whether the cluster will function, and if so, which nodes will be active cluster members, a majority of nodes must "vote." The number of failures that can be sustained for the cluster to remain operational is $(n / 2) - 1$, where n is the number of cluster nodes, and the result of the division is rounded up. Thus, in a five-node cluster, you can sustain at most two failed nodes, or two nodes that have lost communication with the other nodes, and so on, because $(5 / 2) - 1 = 3 - 1 = 2$.

- **Node and disk majority.** This is a recommended configuration choice for clusters with an even number of nodes. Each node gets a vote, and the presence of a shared witness disk, designated as the quorum disk, adds a vote to whichever node owns it. In the case of a four-node cluster, two nodes can fail if the shared disk is online or can be brought online on one of the remaining two nodes. If the shared disk cannot be brought online, the number of nodes that can fail is half minus one, $(n / 2) - 1$. In the case of a four-node cluster with the witness disk unavailable, only one node can fail for the cluster to remain available.

- **Node and file share majority.** In this configuration, which is used for clusters with an even number of nodes but without shared drives. The file share witness adds the extra vote only when the number of nodes is even. The witness file share isn't owned by any particular node, but the nodes that aren't able to reach the file share (due to whatever problem prompted them to no longer be able to communicate with their peers) will not be active.

- **Node and cloud witness.** Cloud witness, pointing to an Azure Blob Storage as a type of file share witness, is available only in Windows Server 2016 and later. In this configuration, which is very similar to node and file share majority, the witness is a cloud service; specifically, an Azure storage account. To configure this option, you need to provide the name of the storage account and one of its access keys.

- **Disk only.** In the disk-only quorum configuration, node count is never considered. Only the shared witness disk's availability to nodes matters. This means that the (single) shared disk becomes a single point of failure: even if all nodes can communicate but the disk is unavailable, the cluster will not be operational. This mode is largely available for legacy purposes, but it can make it possible for you to start the cluster in case of a significant disaster when there is no other way to achieve quorum.

Because of the intricacies of quorum configuration, we recommend that you use node majority (for a cluster with an odd number of nodes) or node and disk majority as the configuration (for a cluster with an even number of nodes) if shared storage is available. If shared storage is not available, configure node and file share majority for a cluster with an even number of nodes. You should not use the disk-only quorum configuration to operate the cluster; its value lies in recovering a severely broken cluster using only a single node.

Inside OUT

Should you use dynamic quorum management for your availability group?

Yes. In Windows Server 2012 R2 and later, dynamic quorum management can remove nodes that drop from a cluster. Dynamic quorum is turned on by default in Windows Server 2012 R2 and 2016.

Consider a five-node cluster. With dynamic quorum, when three nodes are shut down in a planned manner, their votes are removed leaving only two votes remaining, allowing the cluster to maintain quorum and stay functioning because those two votes are available on the two remaining nodes.

But, this can be dangerous in the event of a total site failure. Should a site in a cluster that spans two physical locations be left with no way to achieve Node Majority, no automatic failover would be possible without manually "rigging" the node weights to force a failover. Forcing quorum and manually performing a failover is a temporary measure and will require the reestablishment of proper node weights after DR.

As an example, if you have only two nodes at two physical sites, the third vote (a fileshare witness, for example) should be located at the primary site and moved upon planned failover. This ensures the best chance for the current primary replica for remain online even if there is a network loss between the two sites. If you have three nodes, you should still create a quorum witness, though with dynamic quorum management, it will not be assigned a vote unless needed to make the total quorum vote count an odd number.

NOTE

In a multi-instance clustered scenario, there is no requirement that every SQL Server instance must be installed on every cluster node. In two-node deployments, it is naturally required to achieve HA. For larger clusters, this is not necessary. For example, on a four-node cluster, each instance could be installed on only three nodes. Three nodes provide HA, even when faced with the failure of a single node. There isn't really an additional benefit in deploying each instance to a fourth node, but there are additional maintenance requirements: you must patch and test each instance on each node. We will explain a potential process for patching in the next section.

Configuring a SQL Server FCI

When configuring SQL Server as a cluster resource, you should configure the cluster resources for a single instance in a single cluster resource group. A cluster resource group is the level at which a failover happens, that is, all the resources on a single cluster node that will move together from one node to another during a failover. Cluster resources in a cluster resource group can include the IP address, the SQL Server instance's network name, the shared disks (if any; there aren't any shared disks with CSV and S2D), the SQL Server service itself, the SQL Server Agent, SQL Server Analysis Services, the Machine Learning Services Launchpad service, and the FILESTREAM file share. If multiple SQL Server instances are configured on a single cluster, each will need a resource group.

If you would like to have multiple servers running active instances of SQL Server simultaneously, you can install additional instances on each FCI. Each SQL Server instance can be active on only one server at a time, but when using multiple instances, each instance can run independently of another. We recommend always keeping a passive cluster node, that is, a node that has no active responsibilities. Otherwise, in case of a failover, one server will need to run at least one additional instance, increasing the load on the server. If you run each instance on separate hardware, you'll need $n + 1$ cluster nodes, where n is the number of SQL Server instances.

Keep in mind that any cluster configuration of more than two nodes requires SQL Server Enterprise edition.

Inside OUT

How should you configure service accounts for SQL Server in a Windows Server Failover Cluster?

With a standalone installation, SQL Server will default to virtual service accounts for all services during setup. With a cluster installation, you should specify a domain account for the clustered services: Database Engine, SQL Server Agent, and SQL Server Analysis Services. Shared services, such as SQL Server Reporting Services, can continue to use a virtual service account.

The domain accounts require no special privileges or rights in advance, so use a domain user account for each SQL Server service that will run on the cluster. SQL Server Setup will grant the necessary permissions to each service account, such as access to the data and log folders. The account that is running the installer will need permissions to make these changes.

You can choose to create a group managed service account (gMSA) for each service. It reduces management overhead because the password for these service accounts is managed by Active Directory and regularly changed. In addition, the security configuration is enhanced because there is no one who actually knows the password.

With SQL Server 2016 (and later) and Windows Server 2016, you can create WSFCs with certificates instead of using Active Directory service accounts, which is known as a Workgroup Cluster. This is based on a Windows Server 2012 R2 concept called Active Directory-Detached Cluster, that still required a domain. You can create a domain-independent availability group on a workgroup cluster, for any mixture of Windows Server nodes that are not joined to the same domain or any domain. For more information, visit *https://docs.microsoft.com/sql/database-engine/availability-groups/ windows/domain-independent-availability-groups*.

Just like the hardware and the operating system patch levels should be identical on every cluster node, so should the SQL Server configuration. The best way to guarantee initial exact configuration is to use configuration scripts to first prepare each cluster node, and then complete the cluster installation with another script. The scripts are valuable because they ensure consistent installation of the SQL Server binaries. Additionally, they also serve as DR preparation because they document the configuration of each instance, and you can use them to set up a new cluster in case of a disaster.

You can create these scripts by hand; however, that is a tedious and error-prone process. Instead, we recommend starting SQL Server Setup and initiating the Advanced Cluster Preparation setup. On the Ready To Install step of the installation wizard, the path to the configuration file will be displayed. Open the configuration file and save it somewhere. A network share is ideal because then it can be referenced from all cluster nodes that will run the SQL Server instance.

If you prefer to have a completely automated configuration file, you will need to modify the script as outlined in the example that follows. You start Setup from the command line by using the /ConfigurationFile=path parameter and specify the full path to the configuration file:

```
; Add this line

IACCEPTSQLSERVERLICENSETERMS="True"

; Modify the next lines

; Change to True to enable unattended installation to progress
```

```
IACCEPTPYTHONLICENSETERMS="True"

; Quiet simple means you'll see the UI auto-progress.

QUIETSIMPLE="True"

; Or, leave QUIETSIMPLE="False" and modify this line for no UI

QUIET="True"

; Delete, or comment out, this line

UIMODE="Normal"
```

This sample and all samples for this book are available for download at
https://www.MicrosoftPressStore.com/SQLServer2019InsideOut/downloads.

> ➤ For more about installing SQL Server from the command line in Chapter 4, "Installing and
> configuring SQL Server instances and features."

To complete the cluster installation, in SQL Setup run the Advanced Cluster Completion setup
option. There again, you can choose to save the script for later. The cluster completion phase is
where you will do the following (in no particular order):

- Select or create the cluster resource group

- Set the virtual network name and IP address for the SQL Server instance—how your clients will connect

- Select the shared storage for the database files

NOTE

**Azure VMs hosting SQL Server FCI used to be limited to one SQL Server instance per
cluster. This was a unique limitation to Azure VMs, but since in recent years Azure VMs
were updated to allow for multiple frontend Virtual IPs on internal load balancers. You
can now have multiple SQL Server failover cluster instances per cluster, just like in an on-
prem Windows Server cluster.**

Patching A Failover Cluster

Near-zero downtime is the objective when configuring FCIs. Some events are unexpected, but
some regular maintenance tasks such as patching the OS and SQL Server instance are regular
activities. You can perform these maintenance tasks with near-zero downtime by using *rolling
upgrades*.

To conduct a rolling upgrade, you should have a passive node; that is, a node that under normal
circumstances does not run any workload. You upgrade the passive node first and, if necessary,

reboot it. This reboot does not cause any downtime because this node is not running a work-load. When the reboot is completed and the upgrade is validated, the roles from any active node should be failed over to the passive node.

As we indicated earlier, a brief amount of downtime is incurred while this takes place (on the order of seconds). The newly passive node is then upgraded, and so on, until all nodes in the cluster are at the same software version. Although you can choose to return the original passive node to its passive state when all nodes have finished upgrading, this would incur one more interruption and will likely not provide any benefits other than consistency.

First introduced in Windows Server 2012, Cluster-Aware Updating (CAU) automates this process, and you can even schedule it. In addition to rolling upgrades and updates for Windows patches and SQL Server updates, Windows Server 2012 R2 and later also supports rolling upgrades for operating systems. Even though this is not automated, it will be a significant benefit with the frequent updates available for modern Windows Server operating systems.

Designing availability groups solutions

This section contains information about designing, configuring, troubleshooting and the features of Always On availability groups, a core feature of SQL Server's high availability capabilities. Much of the content applies to SQL Server instances on-prem on Windows, in Azure VMs, in Azure MI, and in SQL Server on Linux. Later in this chapter, we talk in detail about configuring an availability group in Red Hat Enterprise Linux (RHEL).

> ➤ For considerations for high availability options in containers, see Chapter 3, "Designing and implementing an on-premises database infrastructure."

You can create availability groups within the Availability Groups Wizard in SSMS, via T-SQL, or PowerShell. If this is your first time creating an availability group, we recommend using the Availability Groups Wizard and scripting out the steps and objects it creates with T-SQL to further your understanding.

Creating a copy of a database on a secondary replica SQL Server can be fairly wizard-driven in SSMS, including the ability for SSMS to automate the process of taking a full and transaction log backup of the database, copying the data to a file share, and restoring the database to any secondary replica(s). You can script these tasks at the end of the wizard and deploy them to future availability groups via T-SQL or PowerShell.

As in many places in this book, although we won't provide a step-by-step, click-by-click walk-through, the following are pointers and key decisions to make when creating availability groups. We also provide a more in-depth walk-through of availability groups in SQL Server in Linux later in this chapter.

Inside OUT

What server principal owns an availability group replica?

The server security principal used to create the availability group will own the availability group replica object by default, creating an immediate follow-up action item for administrators after setup. Each replica object has an owner, listed in the dynamic management view (DMV) `sys.availability_replicas`, where the owner_sid is a server-level security principal.

It isn't fully documented what the `owner_sid` is used for, but because it could be used as the authority to make changes to availability groups, it should not be an administrator's personal named account. You should either create the availability group (and create future replicas) under the security context of a service account that does not expire, or immediately change the owner of the availability group replica to a service account.

A similar problem occurs when you create an availability group with a login that doesn't have an explicit server principal or SQL Server login, but rather has access via a security group. In that case, an availability group will be created with the built-in public server role as the `owner_id`. In general, ownership or additional permissions should not be granted to the public role, so you should change this.

Changing the owner of the availability group replica to the instance's sa login, on instances with mixed mode authentication turned on, is also an acceptable and common practice; for example:

```
ALTER AUTHORIZATION ON AVAILABILITY GROUP::[AG1] to [domain\serviceaccount];
```

The previous sample script and all scripts for this book are available for download at *https://www.MicrosoftPressStore.com/SQLServer2019InsideOut/downloads.*

Comparing different cluster types

While most enterprise implementations of availability groups involve Enterprise edition SQL Servers and a Windows Server Failover Cluster (WSFC), the instance does not necessarily need to reside on a Windows Server that is a member of a WSFC. You can turn on the HA feature and create clusterless availability groups starting with SQL Server 2017. The only cluster types available when creating an availability group without the presence of a Windows Server Failover Cluster are External and None. Those cluster types created for non-Windows cluster managers and clusterless availability groups, respectively.

Let's compare the three cluster type options that are possible, WSFC, EXTERNAL, NONE, and other possible cluster architectures.

Windows Server failover cluster (WSFC)

This is the original supported architecture that relies on the underlying cluster quorum for failover, which was discussed earlier in this chapter in the previous section. Even though SQL Server creates the objects necessary inside the WSFC and managed settings such as preferred/possible resource ownership, and also runs any user-initiated failovers, the WSFC quorum is used to detect node outage and trigger automatic failover.

Just because failover isn't automatically prompted by SQL, doesn't mean you can't have HA. There are production enterprise environments with availability groups configured for manual failover, but with the failover automated along with other server assets (such web or app servers) so that the automation isn't piecemeal. PowerShell is a common automation tool for this task, and we provide a sample of such a failover script in Chapter 9.

External

This type of cluster uses an external cluster manager, not the WSFC. SQL Server on Linux supports the use of external cluster managers, preferably Pacemaker. Red Hat Enterprise Linux, Ubuntu, and SUSE Linux Enterprise Server are all supported platforms. Availability groups on Linux clusters require at least *two* synchronous replicas to guarantee HA, but at least *three* replicas for automatic recovery, so we recommend that you set up your availability group on at least three nodes.

SQL Server on Linux is not cluster-aware, and availability groups on Linux are not tightly bound to the clustering resource manager as they are on Windows. This means that you cannot control failovers from within SQL Server. To manually perform a failover, for example, you must use the pcs command line to manage the Pacemaker cluster manager.

> ➤ To learn more about setting up availability groups in Linux, see the "Configuring an availability group on Red Hat Linux" section later in this chapter.

None

You can implement clusterless availability groups that, like the deprecated database mirroring feature, do not require a failover cluster network. Introduced in SQL Server 2017 and available in Standard and Enterprise editions, this was initially referred to as a "read-scale availability group" in documentation. Now, Microsoft is staring to refer to this availability groups option as "clusterless". The None option provides a subset of features of availability groups features.

The biggest feature gap currently is the complete lack of automatic failover, though a new feature of SQL Server 2019 helps mitigate the feature gap: automatic traffic redirection provides for routing of read/write traffic back to the primary node and does not require a Listener. More on this later in the section "Improvements to availability groups recently."

Similar to database mirroring, all of the machinery of synchronization and failover is within the SQL Server instances. The None setting supports availability groups on SQL Servers on Windows and/or Linux replicas.

One of the biggest sources of complexity and problems (especially during failover) with availability groups based on WSFC was not the SQL Server configuration or behavior, but the configuration or behavior of quorum and the various forms of quorum witnesses, which we discussed earlier in this chapter in the section "Understanding FCI quorum". Since 2012, the cause of availability group issues are more likely to have been because of misconfigurations of Windows Server, cluster networks, DNS, or cluster quorum settings, than because of SQL Server–based issues.

Although automatic failover is not possible with a "read-scale" availability group, manual planned and forced failover is still possible as well as the usual availability groups features to which you're accustomed, including both synchronous and asynchronous synchronization modes, readable secondary nodes, and secondary replica backups. (More on these options later in this chapter.) Availability groups without a WSFC cluster can still provide readable secondary nodes, read-only routing, and load balancing. It is also worth noting that failover can be automated with external tools and often is, so that the database, application and web layers of a multi-tier application fail over from one datacenter to another, together.

You must turn on the availability groups feature in SQL Server Configuration Manager, as always, in the properties of the SQL Server Database Engine service. The Properties page of the SQL Server instance service contains a tab labeled "Always On Availability Groups" (Figure 11-1).

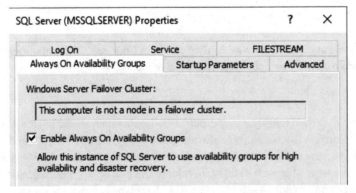

Figure 11-1 In Configuration Manager, you can turn on availability groups even if the Windows Server is not a member of a WSFC, to use with clusterless, read-scale availability groups. This behavior is only possible in SQL Server 2017 and above.

Other possible architectures

Consider also the following alternate architectures, which might be more appropriate for your environment if you are not running Enterprise edition, or if you have geographically separated environment HA requirements.

Basic availability groups

Basic availability groups are a limited version of the real thing and are supported only on SQL Server Standard edition. This feature wholly replaces the deprecated database mirroring feature but with the modern SSMS dialog box options and monitoring tools.

As with database mirroring, the single secondary replica cannot be readable or backed up. Although each basic availability group can support only two replicas, you can create more than one basic availability group per server. Basic availability groups are supported only on SQL Server 2016 and above and are mostly there to match the features of database mirroring. Otherwise basic availability groups allow for many of the same features of availability groups including synchronous or asynchronous replication, manual or automatic failovers, plus the management DMV's and commands that are superior to those with database mirroring.

Distributed availability groups

This allows an availability group to treat another availability group, typically over a WAN, to act as a secondary replica. The read-only secondary replicas can be globally dispersed, offloading workloads to regional read-only secondary replicas. The two availability groups, each with their own listener, do not need to be in same network or WSFC. This allows for local hardware and geographically remote HA and DR across multisite deployments. With distributed availability groups, you do not need to span a WSFC across the WAN or subnet. There is no risk of accidental failover of the WSFC over the WAN; in fact, there is no automatic failover supported at all between the primary availability group and the secondary availability group. The availability group that is not primary can only serve read-only queries, but does have a "primary" replica itself. The "primary" replica in the secondary availability group is charged with replicating transactions to the other secondary replicas in the secondary availability group. Otherwise, distributed availability groups operate in much the same way of a traditional availability group.

This architecture could be especially useful for OS and future SQL Server version upgrades of instances in an availability group because you can have different versions of Windows Server (2012 minimum) and SQL Server (2016 minimum) and perform a fast migration with minimal downtime.

Although each partner availability group in a distributed scenario has its own listener, the distributed availability group as a whole does not. Applications, perhaps with the aid of DNS aliases, will connect to each availability group directly after a failover to take advantage of readable secondary replicas.

You can also use distributed availability groups to migrate Windows-based availability groups to Linux-based availability groups, though this is not a permanent, stable, or recommended configuration.

FCIs + availability groups

SQL Server FCIs can themselves be members of availability groups, though without the possibility for automatic failover of the availability group. The FCI is still capable of automatic failover of the instance, allowing for local HA and hardware availability, but not remote HA.

We do not recommend creating a WSFC that spans a WAN, even if the subnet spans the network. Instead, you should consider availability groups without FCIs, or distributed availability groups if you require local hardware HA.

Creating WSFC for use with availability groups

We covered WSFCs earlier in this chapter, and a failover cluster can be the underlying technology for both FCI's and AG's. If you choose to set up an availability group that uses the underlying structure of a WSFC, the first big decision is the same for setting up any WSFC. Quorum votes and, specifically, where quorum votes will reside, is key to understanding how the servers will eventually failover.

So these recommendations remain the same: you should use the Node Majority quorum mode when you have an odd number of voting nodes; use the Node and File Share Majority quorum mode when you have an even number of voting nodes. See the section earlier in this chapter "Understanding FCI quorum" for more information.

Your quorum strategy might also be different based on two factors. First, do you intend to mostly run out of one datacenter, with the other datacenter to be used in disaster operations only? Second, do you intend to have manual failover only, without any automatic failover? If you answered yes to both, having a quorum vote maintaining uptime in the primary node, including placing a file share witness in the primary node datacenter, makes sense. If you answered no to either, you should follow best practices for WSFC quorum alignment, including an odd number of quorum votes, with one of the quorum votes in a third location. This can include an Azure Storage Account Cloud Witness, which is a relatively inexpensive and very reliable witness, a feature introduced with Windows Server 2016.

When validating your cluster, you do not need to run validation checks on your storage, and do not select the Add All Eligible Storage check box for the cluster. The storage validation is time consuming and not needed. The WSFC for your availability group won't have any storage, unless you choose to use a shared storage witness as your "odd" vote. Add that separately. You can view the current quorum votes per member roles in the `sys.dm_hadr_cluster_members` DMV.

During the cluster validation and after the WSFC is online, you might see warnings in the Windows Server Failover Cluster Manager that storage is not configured. Because storage is not clustered in availability groups, you can ignore these warnings and, in the future, use the Failover Cluster Manager only to view the overall health state of the cluster or to manage quorum.

Do not initiate failovers from the Failover Cluster Manager unless you are forcing quorum. All failovers for the availability group should be initiated through SQL Server; for example, via SSMS, T-SQL statements, or PowerShell commands. See the section on availability group failovers later in this section.

Inside OUT

What permissions are needed to create the availability group objects?

When creating the WSFC without domain administrator permissions, you might encounter errors when creating a Cluster Name Object (CNO) or the listener objects in Active Directory. The listener object is created by the CNO, so the CNO must have access to read all properties and Create Computer Objects in the cluster's OU. The user creating the cluster must have rights to grant the CNO these permissions, as well, or grant these permissions to the CNO after it is created. The listener object can also be pre-created by a domain administrator instead of giving the CNO these rights.

Understanding the database mirroring endpoint

The endpoint for availability group communication, which exists on each SQL Server instance in the availability group, is also called the database mirroring endpoint. It shares a name, functionality, and port with the endpoint created by the deprecated database mirroring feature. The endpoint name `Hadr_endpoint` is given by default to the endpoint. It is used by SQL Server to communicate between instances, not user connections, and is created only for the purposes of availability groups (or the deprecated database mirroring feature.)

By default, the endpoint communicates on TCP port 5022 and does not need to change unless it is already in use by another availability group. You can view information about the endpoint in the system reference tables `sys.database_mirroring_endpoints` (including its current status, role, and encryption settings) and `sys.tcp_endpoints` (including its port number, IP settings, and Listener IP).

If you're creating the availability group database_mirroring endpoint manually, you can use T-SQL, using the CREATE ENDPOINT command, or PowerShell, using the New-SqlHadrEndpoint cmdlet.

Network connectivity to the endpoint is a common source of initial Availability Group problems. For more information on troubleshooting initial configuration, visit: *https://docs.microsoft.com/sql/database-engine/availability-groups/windows/troubleshoot-always-on-availability-groups-configuration-sql-server*.

Improvements to availability groups recently

Always On availability groups were first released in SQL Server 2012 and have seen dramatic improvements since. If you are still the administrator of an availability group running on SQL Server 2012, you should consider the advantages of these feature improvements.

Replica read-write traffic redirection

New to SQL Server 2019 is the optional ability to redirect read/write connections from a secondary replica back to the primary replica.

This behavior is not coordinated by the listener and ensures quick reconnection after a failover for availability groups that do not have a listener. Do not use the WSFC cluster manager (for example, as with SQL Server on Linux), or use the clusterless availability group setup where cluster_type = NONE.

Not set by default, the new READ_WRITE_ROUTING_URL parameter for the primary replica is required for this behavior in SQL Server 2019. It is also required that secondary replicas allow all connections, so they must have the ALLOW CONNECTIONS = ALL parameter set, which is also not a default.

When PRIMARY_ROLE(READ_WRITE_ROUTING_URL=...) is provided on each replica, the behavior is similar to how read-only traffic can be routed to secondary replicas when connections with Application_Intent=ReadOnly arrive at the primary replica via the Listener, via the SECONDARY_ROLE(READ_ONLY_ROUTING_URL=...) on each replica. The new feature of routing of read/write traffic back to the primary does not require a Listener.

When a connection with Application_Intent=ReadWrite arrives at an online secondary replica with ALLOW CONNECTIONS = ALL, the connection is routed to the primary replica automatically.

Prior to SQL Server 2019, a connection with Application_Intent=ReadWrite that arrives at a secondary replica with ALLOW CONNECTIONS = ALL would communicate with the secondary replica, but a transaction would fail if it attempted to write to the secondary replica, which is all scenarios remains read-only. For more information on the various scenarios of connecting to a secondary replica before and after this new feature of SQL Server 2019, see *https://docs.microsoft.com/sql/database-engine/availability-groups/windows/secondary-replica-connection-redirection-always-on-availability-groups*.

To take advantage of this feature in SQL Server 2019, you should:

- Set a READ_WRITE_ROUTING_URL on all replicas. This is not set by default.

- Make a habit of declaring Application_Intent in all connection strings, including read-write connections.

- Set the secondary replica to allow ALL connections.

Cluster types

Improvements introduced in SQL Server 2017 include structural expansion to the very foundation of availability groups, including support for replicas to SQL Server on Linux instances and the possibility of cross-platform availability groups using an external cluster manager. Obviously, Linux servers cannot be part of a WSFC, so this means that the architecture of availability groups must be expanded to operate without a WSFC.

As a result, clusterless availability groups, referred to as "read-scale availability groups" in documentation, are possible since SQL Server 2017. We discussed the "NONE" cluster type, and its potential advantages for Windows-based SQL Servers without failover clusters, earlier in this chapter.

Distributed availability groups, where individual clusters treat another cluster as a replica, are also possible beginning with SQL Server 2016. We discussed possible cluster architectures earlier in this chapter.

Replica limits

In SQL Server 2019, the cap on synchronous replicas has increased to five total, meaning that there is one primary replica plus up to four synchronous secondary replicas. This was capped at 1+2 in SQL Server 2017.

Originally in SQL Server 2012, the total number of secondary replicas was capped at four, this is now eight.

Prior to SQL Server 2016, you could only specify two automatic failover replicas, primary plus only one secondary. But since SQL Server 2016, you can specify three, the primary plus up to two secondary replicas.

Distributed transaction support

The Microsoft Distributed Transaction Coordinator (DTC) is now fully supported for SQL Server availability groups on Windows.

Initially, availability groups in SQL Server 2012 did not support distributed transactions using the Microsoft Distribution Transaction Coordinator (DTC), which communicates on port TCP 135. This was a dealbreaker for migrating some legacy applications to take advantage of Always On availability groups.

Since SQL Server 2017 (and including SQL Server 2016 SP2), cross-database transactions using the DTC are fully supported on the same or different instances. The DTC_SUPPORT setup parameter when creating or altering an availability group is provided to enable (DTC_SUPPORT = PER_DB) or disable (DTC_SUPPORT = NONE) distributed transactions.

The DTC is supported under Linux starting with SQL Server 2019 (and including SQL 2017 CU16) but is not yet supported for availability groups for SQL Server on Linux.

> **NOTE**
> Prior to SQL Server 2016 SP2, it was not possible to modify the DTC_Support setting of an availability group; it must be recreated.

Configuring the minimum synchronized required nodes

The REQUIRED_SYNCHRONIZED_SECONDARIES_TO_COMMIT setting establishes a minimum number of synchronized replicas, which you can set to an integer value between 0 and the number of replicas minus 1.

By default, this setting is 0, which mimics the behavior prior to this feature's introduction in SQL Server 2017. In that case, a synchronous replica that stops responding does not stop the primary replica from committing transactions. Instead, that problematic synchronous replica's state is set to NOT SYNCHRONIZED until it is reachable again and catches up, at which point its state is set back to SYNCHRONIZED. (You can see each replica state in the DMV sys.dm_hadr_database_replica_states on the primary replica or in the Availability Group dashboard on the primary replica in SSMS.)

When more than zero, this setting creates guarantees that transactions commit to that number of secondary replicas. At least as many secondary replicas as the value of the setting must be SYNCHRONIZED, or transactions on the primary replica will not be allowed to commit!

This guarantees that the primary database replica cannot introduce new data while there are insufficient secondary synchronous replicas, and therefore automatic failover targets. You should carefully consider the impact of transaction rollbacks on client applications and your data-loss tolerance requirements before changing this setting from the default.

Choosing the correct secondary replica availability mode

The most important consideration of choosing between asynchronous-commit availability mode and synchronous-commit availability mode for each secondary replica is the requirement for automatic or manual failover.

Three overall considerations guide this decision:

- If your HA goals require automatic failover, you must choose synchronous.

- If your databases are geographically separated, even if in the same subnet, you should consider choosing asynchronous-commit availability mode because the performance impact discussed in the section that follows will be significant.

- Replicas in asynchronous-commit availability mode will not place as much of a performance burden on the primary replica and are more appropriate for high-latency network environments than synchronous mode, especially over geographically separated datacenters. Performance of the primary replica with only asynchronous-commit availability mode replicas will also be noticeably improved during index maintenance and other bulk data operations. We will discuss the performance impact of secondary replicas in the next section.

- If your databases are in the same physical network area, you should consider whether your performance requirements allow for synchronous commit mode.

In this section, we discuss how synchronous-commit availability mode replicas work and how the commit mode affects their behavior and that of the primary replica.

Choosing synchronous-commit availability mode is not without a performance impact on the primary replica. The performance impact has two causes: the actual delay of the commit due to the time it takes to receive the acknowledgements from the secondary replica(s), and the potential for concurrency issues due to the longer lock periods. The commit delay can be measured by using performance counters (if you want to measure the delay for a specific duration) or by querying wait statistics.

> ➤ Methods for measuring the commit delay are detailed in the Microsoft blog post at *https://blogs.msdn.microsoft.com/saponsqlserver/2013/04/24/ sql-server-2012-alwayson-part-12-performance-aspects-and-performance-monitoring-ii/.*

Inside OUT

Does SQL Server compress the transaction log data sent to secondary replicas?

By default, asynchronous-commit availability mode will compress the transaction log transport over the network, reducing network bandwidth but increasing CPU load and potentially increasing the amount of time it takes to commit. You can disable this log stream compression with global trace flag 1462. This is not generally needed because of the benefits of the log stream compression over a WAN, but asynchronous replicas within the same datacenter may not benefit from the compression.

The log transport of synchronous commit availability mode is not compressed, in order to speed the commit to the secondary replica as fast as possible. You can choose to enable log stream compression with global trace flag 9592 if you believe network bandwidth to be a bottleneck to the performance of secondary replica synchronization.

Keep in mind that in either case, enabling or disabling compression via the global trace flag will affect all availability groups on the instance.

Understanding the impact of secondary replicas on performance

If you exceed the amount of replica data that your secondary replica hardware can process in a timely fashion, the log redo queue on the secondary replica(s) and the log send queue on the primary replica will begin to grow, as it is unable to truncate committed transactional data. These log queues will grow under heavy load and will need to process before the secondary replica can come online. Synchronous commit mode delays commits on the primary replica. In asynchronous commit mode, there are still transaction delay repercussions if the secondary replica(s) cannot match the performance of the primary replica.

A redo backlog on a secondary replica will cause the following problematic conditions:

- Delay automatic failover by preventing a failover without data loss, forcing any failover to be a manual failover.

- Delaying database recovery at startup after a crash or reboot.

- The data on the secondary replica will be stale, which might reveal itself in queries against read-only secondary nodes.

- The delay of data being backed up when using the secondary replica for database or log backups.

- Transactions in the primary replica's transaction log will be delayed, truncating only during transaction log backups, due to transactions being unable to be applied to secondary replicas.

For these reasons, to protect the performance of the primary replica, a secondary synchronous replica might switch to asynchronous because of time-outs when communicating with the primary node.

This switch to asynchronous happens automatically and temporarily, and would logically block the possibility for automatic failover. Due to this favoring of the performance of the primary, synchronous replicas are not guaranteed to provide zero data loss in all workloads and are best described as *potential* automatic failover partners.

If a synchronous commit secondary replica does not send confirmation before a time-out period, the primary replica will mark the secondary replica status as DISCONNECTED, essentially removing it from the availability group. The time-out period is 10 seconds by default, but you can change this via the SESSION_TIMEOUT property of the secondary replica. This prevents the primary replica from suffering transaction hardening delays. You can detect when this happens by setting a SQL Agent alert for error numbers like 41416 and 41418, or monitoring databases for the policy "Availability replica is disconnected".

> ➤ **For more information on SQL Agent alerts and Policy-Based Management (PBM) see Chapter 9.**

A secondary replica that has become DISCONNECTED will need to be added back to the availability group by an administrator and, depending on how far behind it is, might need to be reseeded with a new full backup.

You should consider switching the availability group's secondary replicas from synchronous to asynchronous if you anticipate a period of heavy, performance-sensitive writes to the system; for example, when performing index maintenance, modifying or moving large tables, or running bulk operations. Afterward, change the replicas back to synchronous. You'll be able to observe their state change from SYNCHRONIZING to SYNCHRONIZED as soon as the secondary replicas have caught up.

Similarly, you could also consider switching your asynchronous secondary replicas to synchronous mode, temporarily, in order to perform a manual failover without data loss, and without having to use the FORCE parameter. After the failover, you can switch the replicas back to asynchronous mode. You'll be able to observe their state change from SYNCHRONIZED to SYNCHRONIZING as soon as the secondary replicas have switched to asynchronous.

In SQL Server on Windows, manual failovers of an availability group should always be initiated via SQL Server, not by the failover cluster manager. In SQL Server on Linux, all manual or automatic failover actions are initiated by the external cluster manager.

Inside OUT

How many potential synchronous automatic failover partners can a replica have?

Prior to SQL Server 2016, only one secondary replica could be a potential automatic failover partner with the primary replica. Starting with SQL Server 2016, you can set up to two synchronous commit secondary replicas in an automatic failover set using the WSFC cluster type, for a total of three (including the current primary) replicas that you can set to be a part of automatic failover. For more information on failover sets, see: *https://docs.microsoft.com/sql/database-engine/availability-groups/windows/ failover-and-failover-modes-always-on-availability-groups#failover-sets*.

The preferred owner properties of the availability group object in the WSFC determine which of the two secondary replicas is the target of an automatic failover.

SQL Server automatically manages the potential and preferred owners list of availability group resources in the WSFC, and there is no method in SQL Server to control this. If you change these settings in the WSFC, they will be overwritten the next time SQL Server performs a failover, and thus we do not recommend doing so.

You can view the current possible and preferred owners in the Windows Failover Cluster Manager. On the Roles page of the Failover Cluster Manager, double-click the availability group object to open its Properties dialog box. On the General tab, you'll find the Preferred Owners list. Then, back in Failover Cluster Manager, under Other Resources, double-click the availability group object. On the Advanced Policies tab, you'll find the Possible Owners list.

Understanding failovers in availability groups

When an availability group fails over, a secondary replica becomes the new primary, and the primary replica (if available) becomes a secondary replica. The properties of replicas after they become primary or secondary should be reviewed and reconfigured after a failover, especially after an unplanned and/or forced failover. It might not be appropriate given the loss of one or more nodes to support automatic failover, readable secondary nodes, or backup priority settings.

Automatic failover

Automatic failovers provide HA and rely on properly configured listener and WSFC objects for their success. Only a synchronous-commit availability mode replica can be the destination of an automatic failover. You can configure the conditions that prompt an automatic failover on a scale of 1 to 5, where 1 indicates that only a total outage of the SQL Server service on the primary replica would initiate a failover, and 5 indicates any of a number of critical to less-severe SQL Server errors.

The default is 3, which prompts an automatic failure in the case of an outage or unresponsive primary replica, but also for some critical server conditions. These "flexible failover policy" conditions are detailed at *https://docs.microsoft.com/sql/database-engine/availability-groups/windows/flexible-automatic-failover-policy-availability-group#FClevel.*

Automatic failovers will not occur unless they meet the same conditions as a planned failover, which we look at next. Specifically, automatic failovers cannot occur with the possibility of data loss.

Planned failover

A planned failover can occur only if there is no possibility for data loss. Specifically, this means the failover occurs without using the FORCE parameter to acknowledge warnings in code or in the SSMS dialog boxes.

It is therefore only possible to have a planned failover to a secondary replica in synchronous-commit availability mode, but that doesn't mean that asynchronous is out of the question. You can move an asynchronous-commit availability mode replica to synchronous, wait for the SYNCHRONIZED state, and then issue a planned failover without data loss.

You should not attempt a planned failover from within the Windows Server Failover Cluster Manager. Instead, you should always use SQL Server commands via SSMS, T-SQL, or PowerShell.

> ➤ **For PowerShell code examples of scripted failover, see Chapter 9.**

Forced failover

You should attempt a manually-initiated, forced failover only in response to adverse cluster conditions such as the loss of the primary node. You should not attempt to force failover from within the Windows Server Failover Cluster Manager unless adverse cluster conditions have made it impossible to force failover from SQL Server commands via SSMS wizards, T-SQL commands, or PowerShell.

Force failover if WSFC quorum is down

You will not be able to force a failover for availability groups based on a WSFC if the WSFC has no quorum. You will first have to force quorum in the Configuration Manager by "rigging" the vote and modifying node weights. You should consider this step only in emergencies, such as when a disaster has disrupted a majority of cluster nodes.

You can accomplish this with a relatively straightforward PowerShell script, to force an online node to assume the primary role without a majority of votes.

```
Import-Module FailoverClusters

$node = "desired_primary_servername"

Stop-ClusterNode -Name $node

Start-ClusterNode -Name $node -FixQuorum

#FixQuorum forces the cluster to start

# without a valid quorum, which we're about to fix

(Get-ClusterNode $node).NodeWeight = 1

$nodes = Get-ClusterNode -Cluster $node

#Force this node's weight in the quorum
```

After execution of this temporary fix above, you will then address issues with the cluster and nodes to repair long-term stability and/or restore what a partial disaster has wrought. Subsequent nodes or witnesses coming back online could change the vote and cause a quorum failover or failure.

Force failover in other scenarios

First off, if you initiate a forced failover to a synchronous, synchronized secondary replica, the behavior is the same as if you had performed a planned manual failover, as detailed in the previous section. In this way, the behavior of a planned failover in healthy circumstances is no different for the FORCE syntax. But what if the availability group isn't healthy, or is in asynchronous commit mode, and a failover must be forced regardless of the risk?

The T-SQL command to issue a forced failover, allowing for data loss, for execution on the primary replica of the availability group named AG1:

```
ALTER AVAILABILITY GROUP [AG1] FORCE_FAILOVER_ALLOW_DATA_LOSS;
```

Again, you should only consider the above step if efforts to get the target secondary replica into a synchronized state in synchronous commit mode. However, just because you're forcing a failover doesn't mean you have to tolerate data loss. (Also, this is the only option for a manual failover for availability groups with cluster_type = NONE.) Use the following steps to try and ensure no data loss:

1.   Before any failover, try to get the intended failover target secondary replica into Synchronous commit mode. Wait for the synchronization state to indicate "Synchronized", not "Synchronizing," as is indicated in the availability groups dashboard or the sys.dm_hadr_database_replica_states DMV. This is the sample T-SQL code for execution on the primary replica:

```
ALTER AVAILABILITY GROUP [AG1]

    MODIFY REPLICA ON N'secondary_replica_name'

    WITH (AVAILABILITY_MODE = SYNCHRONOUS_COMMIT);
```

2. Use the REQUIRED_SYNCHRONIZED_SECONDARIES_TO_COMMIT setting to require a secondary replica to commit any transaction before committing to the primary replica. This is a safety measure to ensure no transactions will be lost in failover. By default, this is 0. Execute this on the primary replica:

```
ALTER AVAILABILITY GROUP [AG1]
SET REQUIRED_SYNCHRONIZED_SECONDARIES_TO_COMMIT = 1;
```

3. Demote the primary replica to a secondary replica, and ensure that it is configured as a readable secondary replica, meaning that briefly, the availability group will have no writeable replica. This is also a safety measure to ensure no transactions will be lost in failover. Execute this on the primary replica:

```
ALTER AVAILABILITY GROUP [AG1] SET (ROLE = SECONDARY);
```

4. Force the failover, now with no chance of data loss, by executing this on the primary replica:

```
ALTER AVAILABILITY GROUP [AG1] FORCE_FAILOVER_ALLOW_DATA_LOSS;
```

5. Your job, however, is not done. After a forced failover, you may need to execute the following on all secondary replicas to resume data movement after the interruption.

```
ALTER DATABASE [WideWorldImportersDW]
SET HADR RESUME;
```

6. And, because it is a high-safety measure that could impact performance, don't forget to revert the REQUIRED_SYNCHRONIZED_SECONDARIES_TO_COMMIT setting back to its original state for your environment. By default, this is 0. Execute this on the primary replica:

```
ALTER AVAILABILITY GROUP [AG1]
SET REQUIRED_SYNCHRONIZED_SECONDARIES_TO_COMMIT = 1;
```

The previous sample script and all scripts for this book are available for download at *https://www.MicrosoftPressStore.com/SQLServer2019InsideOut/downloads*.

CHAPTER 11

> **NOTE**
>
> You should always use SQL Server commands via the SSMS Availability Group dashboard, T-SQL, or PowerShell to initiate failovers, not via the Windows Server Failover Cluster Manager interface or directly to the WSFC. An exception to this rule is with availability groups for which the cluster_type = EXTERNAL. This would be the case for instances on SQL Server on Linux, using a Linux-based cluster manager such as Pacemaker. In this case, you must use the external cluster manager to initiate all failovers.

Seeding options when adding replicas

Copying the data to the secondary replica to begin synchronization is a prerequisite step for adding a database to an availability group. There are a few different ways this can occur, some more automatic than others.

Next are your options when using the Add Database To Availability Group page of the Availability Groups Wizard in SSMS, and an explanation of when you should use each. Each of the four options has a different strategy for moving the data across the network to the secondary replica: Automatic Seeding, Full, Join Only, and Skip.

Automatic seeding

First introduced in SQL Server 2016, automatic seeding handles the data copy, performing a backup using the endpoint as a virtual backup device. This is a clever way to automate the backup/restore without using network file shares or requiring administrator backup/copy/restore effort. This works seamlessly for most cases, given the following caveats:

- In general, you should use the same data and log file paths for all replicas on the same OS (Windows or Linux), but starting with SQL Server 2017 this is no longer a requirement for automatic seeding. Keep in mind that the default path to the instance data and log folders includes the named instance names, which could be different from instance to instance; for example, the path on my named instance on Windows:

  ```
  F:\Program Files\Microsoft SQL Server\MSSQL15.InstanceA\MSSQL\DATA
  ```

  This will not match the path on another server with a different instance name:

  ```
  F:\Program Files\Microsoft SQL Server\MSSQL15.InstanceB\MSSQL\DATA
  ```

- The only manual intervention required by the administrator is to grant the availability group object permissions to create databases on the secondary replicas. This is slightly different from a typical GRANT statement for permissions:

  ```
  ALTER AVAILABILITY GROUP [AG_WWI] GRANT CREATE ANY DATABASE;
  ```

- After automatic seeding, the AUTHORIZATION (also known as owner) of the database on the secondary replica might be different from the AUTHORIZATION of the database on the primary. You should check to ensure that they are the same, and alter the database if needed:

```
ALTER AUTHORIZATION ON DATABASE::WideWorldImporters TO [serverprincipal];
```

➤ For more about database authorization, see Chapter 12, "Administering security and permissions."

- Compression of the log stream sent over the network for the automatic seeding backup transfer is turned off by default. You may choose to enable log stream compression if you suspect that network bandwidth is a bottleneck to the automatic seeding transfer. We do not recommend that you perform automatic seeding during regular production usage anyway, so turning on compression to speed the transfer at the cost of CPU overhead might be worthwhile. You cannot currently turn on compression via SSMS dialog boxes; instead, you enable compression via global trace flag 9567. Keep in mind that turning on automatic seeding compression via the global trace flag will affect all availability groups on the instance.

- The automatic seeding backup can take longer than a normal backup, especially if it is over a WAN network connection or a distributed availability group. During automatic seeding, the source database's transaction log cannot truncate. If automatic seeding takes too long, you can stop it for databases that have yet to complete by using the following code, which changes the replica synchronization preference to MANUAL or Join Only. Use the following T-SQL example on the primary replica:

```
--Stop automatic seeding

ALTER AVAILABILITY GROUP [AG_WWI] --availability group name

    MODIFY REPLICA ON 'SQLSERVER-1\SQL2K19' --Replica name

    WITH (SEEDING_MODE = MANUAL); --"Join Only" in SSMS

GO
```

You can view the progress of automatic seeding (on all replicas) in the system DMV sys.dm_hadr_physical_seeding_stats, which includes a column that estimates the completion of the automatic seeding, estimate_time_complete_utc. Even though data is displayed for sys.dm_hadr_physical_seeding_stats on both the primary and secondary replica, an estimate might be available only on the primary node. The role_desc field will indicate which end of the automatic seeding the local SQL instance is: source or destination.

You can review the history of automatic seeding activity in the DMV sys.dm_hadr_automatic_seeding, on both the primary and the target secondary replica. The current_state field will equal 'SEEDING' for in-progress automatic seeding sessions, as shown in the following T-SQL examples:

```
--Monitor automatic seeding
```

```
SELECT s.* FROM sys.dm_hadr_physical_seeding_stats s

ORDER BY start_time_utc desc;

--Automatic seeding history

SELECT TOP 10 ag.name, dc.database_name, s.start_time, s.completion_time,

    s.current_state, s.performed_seeding, s.failure_state_desc, s.error_code,

  s.number_of_attempts

FROM sys.dm_hadr_automatic_seeding s

INNER JOIN sys.availability_databases_cluster dc ON s.ag_db_id = dc.group_database_id

INNER JOIN sys.availability_groups ag ON s.ag_id = ag.group_id

ORDER BY start_time desc;
```

Troubleshooting automatic seeding

In addition to the above guidance, here is a checklist of troubleshooting steps for unsuccessful automatic seeding attempts:

- Remember that you must grant permissions to the availability group object to create databases on each secondary replica. For example:

  ```
  ALTER AVAILABILITY GROUP [AG_WWI] GRANT CREATE ANY DATABASE;
  ```

- Check the primary and secondary replica's SQL Server Error Log, which will contain error messages related to the attempted automatic seeding backup and restore events.

- Make sure that the secondary replica's SQL Server service account has permissions to create and have full control over the path where the restore is attempting to place the seeded files. On each replica, you can use different paths, but we do not recommend doing this, because it would increase complexity and could be the source of errors in future reconfigurations or restores.

- Check also that the same features, including FILESTREAM if applicable, are turned on for the secondary instance prior to automatic seeding.

- During a lengthy automatic seeding, turn off transaction log backups to the database on the primary replica. Transaction log backups could cause automatic seeding to fail, with the message "The remote copy of database '*databasename*' has not been rolled forward to a point in time that is encompassed in the local copy of the database log."

If automatic seeding fails, remember to drop the unsuccessfully-seeded database on the secondary replica, including the database data and log files in the file path. After you have resolved the errors and want to retry automatic seeding, you can do so by using the following example T-SQL statement. Run this code sample on the primary replica to retry automatic seeding:

```
ALTER AVAILABILITY GROUP [AG_WWI] --availability group name

    MODIFY REPLICA ON 'SQLSERVER-1\SQL2K19' --Replica name

    WITH (SEEDING_MODE = AUTOMATIC); --Automatic Seeding
```

Inside OUT

Can you use automatic seeding to add a database with Transparent Data Encryption (TDE) turned on?

Databases that already have TDE turned on are supported in availability groups but are problematic with automatic seeding. You cannot have a database with TDE turned on for one replica but not turned on for another replica. If you're setting up a new database, seed it to all secondary replicas first, and then turn on TDE. If adding an existing database with TDE turned on to a new replica, do not use automatic seeding at this time. This might be improved in a future version of SQL Server.

Turning on TDE on a database that is already a member of an availability group is supported in the SSMS wizards starting with SQL Server 2016 with other seeding modes. (This feature was required to place the SQL Server Integration Services database into an availability group.)

Full

This option performs an automatic background backup of the database and log, copies them via a network share (Windows or Linux) that you must set up beforehand, and restores the databases. Configuring the network share and its permissions successfully is the trickiest part of this strategy. The SQL Server service account of the primary replica instance must have read and write permissions to the network share. The SQL Server service account of the secondary replica instance(s) must have read permissions to the network share.

Make sure that the secondary replica's SQL Server service account has permissions to create and have full control over the path where the restore is attempting to restore the copied backup files. Because you cannot specify REPLACE, the databases and database files should not already exist in place on the secondary replicas. Check also that the same features, including FILESTREAM if applicable, are turned on for the secondary instance prior to adding the database to the secondary replica.

Join Only (Manual Backup/Copy/Restore)

As a fallback to more automated options, when creating an availability group outside of the SSMS dialog boxes, with T-SQL or PowerShell, "Join only" is the default and least complicated option.

Consider this strategy also when the Full option above would take too long, consider moving the data prior to the creation of the availability group, or is otherwise not feasible. "Join only" requires the administrator to do the following manually, in this order: take full and log backups of each database (or use recently taken backups), copy them to the secondary replica(s), restore the full backup WITH NORECOVERY, and restore one or more log backups WITH NORECOVERY. The closer the log chain is to live, the sooner the database will catch up after it is joined to the availability group. After the transaction log backup is restored, the database is ready to be joined to the availability group on that replica, via SSMS or code.

Skip

Using this option, you can complete setup of the rest of the availability group without synchronizing any databases. Choose this if you want to synchronize the replica databases later.

Additional actions after creating an availability group

Availability groups replicate database-level data, but not server-level, such as logins. As the DBA, your job is to prepare the secondary instances for failover by creating the necessary server-level settings and objects to support normal operations during a failover. We recommend creating these by using a script, which can easily be run on multiple secondaries, including new secondaries which might be added later on, or after a disaster affects the primary or secondary server(s). Using scripts will ensure that the server-level configuration is consistently and efficiently applied.

Although database-level settings are moved, including users, user permissions, and database roles, there are server-level objects that the SQL DBA needs to move after creating the availability group during a failover.

Prior to adding a SQL Server instance as a secondary replica of an availability group, you should move the server-level objects from the primary replica to the new secondary replica SQL Server instances. Consider the following checklist for all of the server-level objects that should exist on all SQL Server replica instances:

- Server-level security, including logins and server roles, can be used to access the replicated databases, plus any explicit server-level permissions or role memberships for logins and roles. The SID's and passwords of any SQL authenticated logins must match on all replicas.

- The owner_sid of the database owner should also exist in the new secondary replica instance.

- Server-level certificates, endpoints, Transport Layer Security (TLS) settings, including certificates used by TDE for databases in the availability group, SQL Server Audit configurations.

- SQL Server Agent jobs, operators, alerts, retention policies enforced for backup files, log files, various msdb history, policy-based management (PBM).

- Server-level configuration options and surface area configuration options.

- Backup devices and a backup plan.

- Resource Governor configuration, classifier functions, groups, and pools.

- Custom extended events sessions for monitoring.

- User-defined messages.

- Server-level triggers including logon triggers.

- Azure Network load balancer backend pools (if applicable).

- Corporate network firewall settings.

After the availability group is set up, perform also the following:

- Review all settings and document the current configuration. Document the planned settings for each replica in all failover scenarios. When any replica is primary, which should be synchronous/asynchronous, automatic/manual failover, and readable?

- Perform a planned failover to each replica (with replicas in synchronous mode, even if temporarily). Confirm application network connectivity where each replica is primary. A regular failover exercise is recommended.

- Confirm that the cluster network RegisterAllProvidersIP setting is configured correctly to work with application connection strings (see the next section). If turned on, confirm that the listener has IPs in each subnet. Confirm that application connection strings are using the proper value for MultiSubnetFailover.

- Confirm that application connection strings are using appropriate values for ApplicationIntent.

- Configure the read-only secondary replica endpoints and routing URLs for all replicas.

- Confirm that all SQL Server Agent jobs are aware of the replica status of necessary databases, if necessary.

- Confirm the backup strategy for databases in availability groups. If the method for backups is aware of backup priority values, verify that the availability group's Backup Preferences are appropriate.

Reading secondary database copies

In this section, we provide an overview of how the synchronization of secondary replicas works and then move into using the secondary replicas to offload heavy read-only workloads from the primary replica. This is the *ONline* portion of the original HADRON code name acronym for availability groups, and it can be integral to the architecture of an enterprise transactional system.

One of the biggest advantages of availability groups over the legacy database mirroring feature is the ability to get some value out of the secondary database, a live, remote copy of the data. Read-only replicas can be part of your enterprise architecture, providing an easy way to offload heavy workloads to another server, including business intelligence (BI); Extract, Transform, and Load (ETL); and integration workloads. Secondary replica databases are not set to read-only using the database settings using the READ_ONLY option; rather, they are written to by the availability group mechanism, and available to be read by transactions.

How synchronizing secondary replicas works

In synchronous commit mode, transactions must write to the primary server, send to secondary replica(s), commit to secondary replica(s), and then receive an acknowledgement from each secondary replica before it can commit on the primary server.

Log data is written to the drive (also known as being "flushed") to the primary replica log file, and that data is received by the secondary replicas and applied to the secondary replicas' data files. The log data is then written to the drive to the secondary replica(s) log file(s). The amount of data waiting to be flushed on the secondary replica is known as the log redo queue.

In asynchronous commit mode, transactions must write to the primary server and commit, then transactions are sent to secondary replica(s), commit to secondary replica(s), and the primary replica receives an acknowledgement from each secondary replica.

As a result, asynchronous replicas will never display SYNCHRONIZED with the primary replica, but they can be "caught up" to reflect the same state of all row data. You should expect asynchronous replicas to be SYNCHRONIZING during normal operation. You cannot trust an asynchronous replica to be completely caught up with all transactions from the primary, but the replica will rarely be behind by more than a few seconds for most workloads. You can measure the backlog of transactions waiting to be committed to an asynchronous replica by using the `sys.dm_hadr_database_replica_states` DMV. For a sample of such a query, see the section "Monitoring availability group health and status" later in this chapter.

To avoid blocking transactions that are arriving from the primary replica, secondary replicas use snapshot isolation to return queries using row versioning, stored in the secondary replica's TempDB database. Queries against secondary replicas use the snapshot isolation level, overriding any transaction isolation level settings or table hints.

Readable secondary databases automatically append a 14-byte overhead to each data row to facilitate the row versioning, just as a 14-byte overhead is added to row data on the primary database if snapshot isolation or Read-Committed Snapshot Isolation (RCSI) are used. The TempDB database also is used to store temporary statistics for indexes in secondary replica databases.

> ➤ **For more information about snapshot isolation and RCSI, see Chapter 14, "Performance tuning SQL Server."**

Using the listener for traffic redirection

The availability groups listener not only forwards traffic to the current primary replica and handles redirection automatically during failover, but the listener can also redirect traffic that identifies itself as read-only to readable secondary replicas. This is especially effective for long-running SELECT statements coming from reports or other BI systems.

Each replica, when primary, provides a list of endpoints to the listener. You can configure this routing list on each listener in advance; however, in certain failover scenarios, your desired routing list might change. Updating the read-only routing lists for each replica should be part of your failover scripting if necessary.

Each replica should have a Read-Only Routing URL regardless of whether it is currently serving as a secondary replica. You should also set this in advance but use it only when the replica is serving as a readable secondary replica.

The options to set the READ_ONLY_ROUTING_URL property and Routing List for each replica are available for the first time in the Availability Group Properties (see Figure 11-2) of SSMS as of version 17.3.

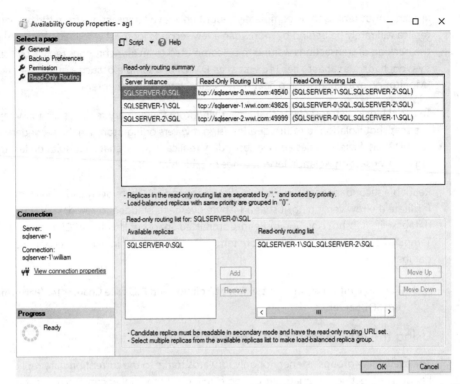

Figure 11-2   The Read-Only Routing page of the Availability Group Properties dialog box in SSMS.

You can configure the Read-Only Routing URLs and Routing Lists for each replica. Note that each routing list is wrapped in parenthesis, indicating that the secondary readable replicas will be load balanced. Without the parentheses, traffic is only directly to the first replica in the list that was online.

The read-only routing URL is not used for application connection strings. You should always use the listener name for connection strings.

To be routed to a secondary readable replica by the listener, a connection string must specify the ApplicationIntent = ReadOnly. The listener does not otherwise have a way to determine whether the user connection will run only read-only statements. However, a new SQL Server 2019 feature mentioned before, Replica Traffic Redirection, can prevent errors when accidentally trying to write to a secondary replica via the use of READ_WRITE_ROUTING_URL, when ApplicationIntent = ReadWrite is specified.

Each replica has a property indicating what types of connections it can receive when it is a secondary replica. Here are the three options for the ALLOW_CONNECTIONS parameter for replicas:

- **No.**   No user connections are allowed to the secondary replica.

- **Read-intent only.**   Only user connections that use the `ApplicationIntent = ReadOnly` parameter in their connection string are allowed, and only read-only statements can be run.

- **Yes.**   Any user connections are allowed, though only read-only statements can be run.

NOTE

Be aware that if application connection strings do not provide a value for Application-Intent, specifying SECONDARY_ROLE (ALLOW_CONNECTIONS = NO) **or** SECONDARY_ROLE (ALLOW_CONNECTIONS = READ_ONLY) **makes the databases on a secondary replica inaccessible and blocks access to your normal query connections, even in SSMS. This will hide databases on secondary replicas from DMV's and your monitoring tools.**

Each replica also has a property indicating the types of connections it can receive when it is a primary replica. Here are the two options:

- **Allow all connections.**   This is the default, allows connections to a secondary replica even if they declare `ApplicationIntent=ReadWrite`. In SQL Server 2019, they will be automatically redirected to the primary replica.

- **Allow read/write connections.**   Use this when your application connections strings use `ApplicationIntent`. This setting blocks any user connection that specifies `ApplicationIntent = ReadOnly`. This could be useful if you have report connection strings that use instance names instead of the listener name (not recommended). If you have no secondary replicas set up for read-only access, connections to the replica database via the listener with `ReadOnly` intent will fail.

When connecting to availability groups, we recommend that you provide both the `ApplicationIntent` and `MultiSubnetFailover` parameters and appropriate values for each connection string. The default value for `ApplicationIntent` is ReadWrite if not otherwise provided, which will always be directed to the primary replica of the availability group. `MultiSubnetFailover`, as explained in the next section, is critical for basic connectivity.

Connections directly to a secondary readable database without using a listener are possible. However, we do not recommend designing connection strings for reporting systems that use a secondary readable SQL Server instance. In future failover scenarios, you would not be able to separate read-write traffic from read-only traffic without reconfiguration. Consider hardcoding a readable secondary replica name only if you're using a connection string that cannot use the `ApplicationIntent` parameter or if using a listener for some reason is not possible.

Configuring RegisterAllProvidersIP and MultiSubNetFailover correctly

In a multi-subnet cluster, you should have the `RegisterAllProvidersIP` setting turned on (1) if your application connection strings will be using the listener using

`MultiSubNetFailover` = Yes. When `RegisterAllProvidersIP` is turned on in the cluster, the listener has IPs in each subnet.

You can verify that `RegisterAllProvidersIP` is turned on in your cluster and that the listener has an IP in each subnet by using the following command-line command, in this example with Listener1 as the name of the availability group listener:

```
nslookup Listener1
```

You should see two IP addresses listed, one per subnet, if `RegisterAllProvidersIP` is turned on.

Optimally, you both turn on the `RegisterAllProvidersIP` setting and specify `MultiSubNetFailover` = Yes when in a multi-subnet cluster. The `MultiSubNetFailover` connection string parameter allows both IPs for the listener to be registered at all times and modern connection strings to use a parallel connection attempt to each IP address. The result is a quick connection to the active IP address during normal operation and immediately after failover.

Misconfiguration of the `RegisterAllProvidersIP` and `MultiSubNetFailover` options will be noticeable in the following circumstances:

- If you turn on `RegisterAllProvidersIP` without your connection strings using `MultiSubNetFailover` = No, or not specifying `MultiSubNetFailover`, your application could have very high latency connection times because connection strings attempt to connect to IPs in a non-determinant sequence, based on the DNS query results. As a result, your application may experience network timeouts upon connection to the listener.

- If you turn off `RegisterAllProvidersIP`, then `MultiSubNetFailover` = Yes will have no effect, and your applications will not reconnect promptly after availability group failovers. Instead, they will need to wait for DNS to resolve the new primary subnet IP address for the listener. (By default, the TTL is 20 minutes!)

If you are using any non-Microsoft connection strings that do not support `MultiSubNetFailover` or do not have the ability to turn on that connection string parameter, the `RegisterAllProvidersIP` setting in the cluster should be turned off (0), which is the default.

Inside OUT

Can you use OLEDB to connect to a multi-subnet availability group?

There is some confusion about preferred modern data providers due to the temporary deprecation of the popular OLEDB standard.

The older OLEDB-based SQL Native Client (SNAC), appearing as SQLNCLI*, is no longer advised for new development, and especially not for connecting to a multi-subnet availability group because it cannot specify the needed parameter `MultiSubNetFailover=True`. This could cause long periods of timeouts, as explained in the previous section.

Older applications should be able to transition with no code changes to using the newer SQL Native Client (SNAC) provider, appearing as SQLNCLI11, however, this is no longer maintained by Microsoft. Instead, consider the new MSOLEDBSQL provider, released in 2018 when OLEDB was un-deprecated. It is highly recommended you recommend that developers convert connection strings from the old SQLNCLI* or SQLOLEDB providers to MSOLEDBSQL. For more information on the new MSOLEDBSQL provider, visit *https://blogs.msdn.microsoft.com/sqlnativeclient/2017/10/06/announcing-the-new-release-of-ole-db-driver-for-sql-server/*

To change the `RegisterAllProvidersIP` setting in the cluster network, you can use the following PowerShell script:

```
Import-Module FailoverClusters

# Get cluster network name

Get-ClusterResource -Cluster "CLUSTER1"

Get-ClusterResource "AG1_Network" -Cluster "CLUSTER1" | `

   Get-ClusterParameter RegisterAllProvidersIP -Cluster "CLUSTER1"

# 1 to enable, 0 to disable

Get-ClusterResource "AG1_Network" -Cluster "CLUSTER1" | `

    Set-ClusterParameter RegisterAllProvidersIP 1 -Cluster "CLUSTER1"

# All changes will take effect once AG1 is taken offline and brought online again.

Stop-ClusterResource "AG1_Network" -Cluster "CLUSTER1"

Start-ClusterResource "AG1_Network" -Cluster "CLUSTER1"

# Must bring the AAG Back online

Start-ClusterResource "AG1" -Cluster "CLUSTER1"

# Should see the appropriate number of IPs listed now, one in each subnet.

nslookup Listener1
```

CHAPTER 11

NOTE

The `FailoverPartner` **connection keyword used with database mirroring does not apply to availability groups or the listener. If you're upgrading from database mirroring to availability groups, be sure to remove the** `FailoverPartner` **keyword from connection strings. A connection string will fail if both the** `MultiSubetFailover` **and** `FailoverPartner` **keywords are present.**

Configuring availability groups load balanced read-only routing

First introduced in SQL Server 2016, you can load-balance connections that use `ApplicationIntent = ReadOnly` across multiple read-only replicas in the availability group. You can implement this easily by changing the read-only routing list to use parenthesis to create load-balanced groups.

For example, the ALTER statement that follows provides a read-only routing list for a three-node availability group that is not load balanced. All read-only queries will be sent to the secondary node SQLSERVER-1, and if it is unavailable, to SQLSERVER-2, and if that is also unavailable, to SQLSERVER-0. This is the behavior prior to SQL Server 2016.

Here is a sample script to configure a read-only routing list for the availability group wwi.

```
ALTER AVAILABILITY GROUP [wwi]

MODIFY REPLICA ON 'SQLSERVER-0'

WITH (PRIMARY_ROLE(READ_ONLY_ROUTING_LIST =

('SQLSERVER-1','SQLSERVER-2', 'SQLSERVER-0')));
```

This ALTER statement provides a read-only routing list that is load balanced. Note the extra set of parentheses.

With the configuration in the following sample, read-only traffic will be routed to a load-balance group of SQLSERVER-1 and SQLSERVER-0, but failing those connections, to SQLSERVER-0:

```
ALTER AVAILABILITY GROUP [wwi]

MODIFY REPLICA ON 'SQLSERVER-0'

WITH (PRIMARY_ROLE(READ_ONLY_ROUTING_LIST =

(('SQLSERVER-1','SQLSERVER-2'), 'SQLSERVER-0')));
```

To add load-balanced replica groups, in SSMS, in the Availability Group Properties dialog box, go to the Read-Only Routing page, and then, in the Availability Replicas window, press the Ctrl key while clicking to select multiple nodes. Then, click Add to add them simultaneously as a load-balanced group.

Although it is possible to add the primary replica itself to its own read-only routing list, this might be a self-defeating strategy of offloading read-only workloads from the primary replica.

Implementing a hybrid availability group topology

You can include Azure virtual machines (VMs) running SQL Server instances in an availability group alongside on-premises SQL Server instances. Azure VMs in multiple regions can be part of the same availability group, as well. In terms of SQL Server functionality, the availability groups feature operates the same, but there are differences in the network setup. Communication is accomplished via a prerequisite site-to-site VPN with Azure to your on-premises subnet.

The member Azure VMs of the availability group should also be in the same availability set per region. (Note that you cannot move a VM from one availability set to another after they are created in an availability set.)

The Add Replica dialog box in SSMS provides an easy method to add Azure Replicas, and the Add Azure Replicas button appears on the Specify Replicas page of the Add Replica Wizard when the prerequisites have been met.

The Add Azure Replica button does significantly more work than the Add Replica button to the new secondary replica, including creating the Azure VM. You are given an opportunity to select the Azure VM tenant, the image for the VM, and to specify the domain. The Availability Group Wizard handles creating the VM based off the image, configuring the VMs administrator user, and joining the VM to your domain.

> ### NOTE
> An important licensing change was introduced in October 2019, allowing for customers with Software Assurance as part of the SQL Server licensing to run free Azure VMs as replicas in their availability groups. This will dramatically lower the cost to moving a replica of your existing availability group into Azure. For more information, talk to your licensing reseller and read the announcement blog here: *https://cloudblogs.microsoft.com/sqlserver/2019/10/30/new-high-availability-and-disaster-recovery-benefits-for-sql-server/*.

Availability group listeners using Azure VMs use an internal Azure load balancer; one per region. You must create the load balancer before you create the listener, so skip this step in your initial availability group setup and/or wizard. When creating the load balancer, add all Azure SQL Server VMs in that region to the Backend pool. You can then configure the availability group listener configured to use the Load Balancer IP.

With Azure VMs, creating an availability group listener requires an internal load balancer. The load balancer's IP address becomes the listener's IP address. For a Microsoft-provided walkthrough on configuring Azure VM-specific objects such as an internal load balancer, visit: *https://docs.microsoft.com/azure/virtual-machines/windows/sql/virtual-machines-windows-portal-sql-availability-group-tutorial*.

A detailed walkthrough on creating and configuring a new listener between Azure VMs is provided here: *https://docs.microsoft.com/azure/virtual-machines/windows/sql/virtual-machines-windows-portal-sql-ps-alwayson-int-listener*.

> ### CAUTION
> It is possible that a hybrid on-prem and Azure VM availability group will experience a mismatch of the Bytes per Cluster disk setting, resulting in poor performance on the Azure VM, transaction logs unable to truncate, and the error message "There have been *nnn* misaligned log IOs which required falling back to synchronous IO." See the section "Important SQL Server volume settings" in Chapter 4 for a workaround involving trace flag 1800.

> ➤ For more on Azure VMs, see Chapter 16, "Designing and implementing hybrid and Azure database infrastructure."

Configuring availability groups in SQL Server on Linux

In this section, we provide a summary of how to configure availability groups with SQL Server on Linux. Red Hat Enterprise Linux (RHEL), Ubuntu, and SUSE Linux Enterprise Server (SLES) are all supported platforms; however, this section focuses specifically on the Microsoft-recommended RHEL, using Pacemaker for the cluster manager, and setting up an availability group.

> ➤ You can read how to create a read-scale availability group that does not require a cluster manager at *https://docs.microsoft.com/sql/linux/sql-server-linux-availability-group-configure-rs*.

In this section we make the assumption that you have some limited knowledge of Linux. This chapter builds on Linux concepts introduced in Chapter 5, "Installing and configuring SQL Server on Linux." All commands provided should be run in the bash shell.

Understanding the differences between Windows and Linux clustering

SQL Server is not cluster-aware when running on Linux. This is the first key difference from the Windows world. You can configure an availability group in SQL Server on Linux to be clustered or clusterless. For an availability group with a cluster in SQL Server on Linux, Pacemaker is the cluster provider, but is much more limited than Windows Failover Cluster Manager. You can also configure a clusterless or read-scale availability group, just as you can with SQL Server on Windows. The rest of this section will be discussing a cluster-based availability group in SQL Server on Linux.

Second, because we are not creating a Windows FCI (nor extending a Windows availability group to a Linux replica), virtual network names do not exist, so you will need to manually add the listener name yourself to DNS, with the virtual IP you create.

Third, you will need to configure a *fencing agent* for your cluster, which ensures that misbehaving nodes in the cluster are returned to a known state (which might include forcing it to shut down and restart).

> ➤ **For more information about STONITH, refer to Chapter 2, "Introducing database server components." To read more on how to configure an appropriate fencing agent, visit** *https://access.redhat.com/documentation/Red_Hat_Enterprise_Linux/7/html/High_ Availability_Add-On_Reference/ch-fencing-HAAR.html.*

To set up an availability group on Linux, you must do the following:

1. Create the availability group (from within SQL Server).

2. Configure the cluster resource manager (Pacemaker).

3. Add the availability group to the cluster.

To reiterate, you must create the availability group *before* the you create the cluster create. This is the opposite order of operations for SQL Server on Windows.

> ➤ **A step-by-step walkthrough is available at** *https://docs.microsoft.com/sql/linux/sql-server-linux-create-availability-group.*

Setting up an availability group in SQL Server on Linux

Linux clusters require at least two synchronous replicas to guarantee HA, but at least three replicas for automatic recovery. We recommend that you set up your availability group on at least three nodes. Each node can be physical or virtual, but Red Hat requires that VMs use the same hypervisor, to keep the platform-specific fencing agents happy. One of these replicas could be in a configuration only role, running any edition including SQL Server Express for Linux. We'll discuss this more in detail.

Configuring the server

Each node must have a unique name on the network, which can be no more than 15 characters in length. (This 15-character limit is a legacy requirement dating back to the old NetBIOS service.) To set the server name, edit the entry in the file /etc/hostname (remember to do this on all nodes).

If you are making use of a DNS server (which we recommend), you do not need to add entries to each node's hosts file. Otherwise, you will need to add entries for each node that will be in the availability group, including the node on which you edit each hosts file. You can find the hosts file at /etc/hosts.

Once you have installed SQL Server and opened TCP port 1433 on the firewall, you can connect to it by using Azure Data Studio or SSMS.

Turning on availability groups

Now, you need to turn on availability groups on each node using mssql-conf. The following two commands configure the instance for availability groups and then restarts SQL Server:

```
sudo /opt/mssql/bin/mssql-conf set hadr.hadrenabled 1
sudo systemctl restart mssql-server
```

Optionally, you can set up the familiar AlwaysOn_health extended events session, which will aid with troubleshooting availability group issues. We discuss this more in depth later in this chapter, in the section "Analyzing extended events for availability groups."

To start the session, execute:

```
ALTER EVENT SESSION AvailabilityGroupHealth ON SERVER
WITH (STARTUP_STATE = ON);
```

Creating the availability group

To create the availability group, you need to set up the database mirroring endpoints first (see the Inside OUT box below).

This is where things are closer to how Windows works (but remember that the cluster has not been set up yet). You can use the New Availability Group Wizard in SSMS to configure your primary and secondary replicas just as you would on Windows. But because Pacemaker is an external cluster resource manager, you must create the availability group with the cluster type and failover mode set to EXTERNAL.

Inside OUT

How do you set up the database mirroring endpoints in Linux?

You need to create a user on each replica, being sure to use a strong password, using CREATE LOGIN, then CREATE USER.

Then, you create a certificate to allow the nodes to communicate securely with one another, using CREATE MASTER KEY ENCRYPTION, followed by CREATE CERTIFICATE. Copy the certificate and the private key that you generated to the same location on each availability replica, and run the commands again, remembering to use the same password and certificate files. Remember to back up your certificate using BACKUP CERTIFICATE.

Finally, you create the database mirroring endpoints on all replicas using CREATE ENDPOINT. Note that 0.0.0.0 is the only IP address you can use for the availability group listener. For more information on crediting the certificate, visit: *https://docs.microsoft.com/sql/linux/sql-server-linux-availability-group-configure-ha#create-a-certificate.*

Adding a database

On the primary replica, ensure that the database you want to add to the availability group is in the full recovery model and take a full backup of it.

When the backup is complete, you can add the database to the availability group by using the following T-SQL command:

```
ALTER AVAILABILITY GROUP [LinuxAG1] ADD DATABASE [<dbname>];
```

To check whether the database has been created on the secondary replicas, you can run the statements that follow. Note that the second statement is checking the synchronization status, make sure it is "SYNCHRONIZING" or "SYNCHRONIZED".

```
SELECT * FROM sys.databases WHERE name = '<dbname>';
SELECT DB_NAME(database_id) AS 'database', synchronization_state_desc
FROM sys.dm_hadr_database_replica_states;
```

Congratulations! You have created an availability group on Linux. The next step is to create the cluster so that your availability group is highly available.

Setting up the cluster

Each node in the cluster must have an appropriate subscription for the HA components in RHEL.

> ➤ To read more about subscriptions, visit
> *http://web.archive.org/web/20170912203244/http://www.opensourcerers.org/pacemaker-the-open-source-high-availability-cluster/*

After you have registered each replica and configured the subscription, you can configure Pacemaker.

As discussed in Chapter 2 and earlier in this chapter, WSFC uses quorum votes to decide on how to manage resources in the cluster. Pacemaker uses a scoring system, which is calculated per resource. We'll discuss more about the scoring system and the constraints to control it later in this chapter, in the section "Create colocation constraint and ordering constraint."

Pacemaker does not provide for a witness functionality like in a WSFC, instead, you have the option to use a third SQL Server as a configuration only replica, which does not act as a node in the availability group, only an extra copy of the availability group configuration information. First introduced with SQL Server 2017 CU1, the configuration only replica type only applies to availability groups that aren't based on WSFC and helps provide additional coverage for replica loss scenarios for a two-node cluster. The configuration only replica can be a SQL server of any edition, including SQL Server Express for Linux. As with the various witness types in a WSFC, you can only have one configuration only replica, and it does not contain the synchronized databases, only cluster configuration metadata.

Various scenarios and guidance around the use of the configuration only replica is available here: *https://docs.microsoft.com/sql/linux/sql-server-linux-availability-group-ha#two-synchronous-replicas-and-a-configuration-only-replica*.

Configure the cluster resource manager (Pacemaker)

Pacemaker requires the following ports to be opened on the firewall. You can use the same method as described in Chapter 5.

- **TCP.** 2224, 3121, and 21064

- **UDP.** 5405

On each node, install Pacemaker from the command line:

```
sudo yum install pacemaker pcs fence-agents-all resource-agents
```

Pacemaker creates a user name called hacluster by default, which requires a proper password. Make sure it is the same one for all nodes:

```
sudo passwd hacluster
```

The pcsd service is required to allow nodes to rejoin the cluster after a restart. You should run this on all nodes for the cluster:

```
sudo systemctl enable pcsd
sudo systemctl start pcsd
sudo systemctl enable pacemaker
```

Create the cluster (Pacemaker)

The commands that follow create the cluster. Note that the nodes must have the correct names, and you must use the hacluster password you set previously. This is where you get to choose the cluster name (not the same as your availability group name, but it can be):

```
sudo pcs cluster auth server1 server2 server3 -u hacluster -p <password>
sudo pcs cluster setup --name <clusterName> server1 server2 server3
sudo pcs cluster start --all
```

Now install the SQL Server resource agent:

```
sudo yum install mssql-server-ha
```

Pacemaker is installed, so now you will use the pcs command-line tool to manage it. You can run all commands from a single node.

Remember to configure node-level fencing with STONITH, based on your organizational requirements.

> ➤ **For more information about how to set up node fencing, refer to the Red Hat documentation at** *https://docs.microsoft.com/sql/linux/ sql-server-linux-availability-group-cluster-rhel#configure-fencing-stonith.*

Restarting nodes after failure

What you don't want is a node that never restarts after a failure. Turning off this feature relies on a more sensible failure count and associated threshold, which you can do by using the following command on each server:

```
sudo pcs property set start-failure-is-fatal=false
```

Now when a failover occurs, the restarted instance will be demoted to a secondary and automatically rejoins it to the availability group.

Create the Pacemaker login in SQL Server

You must create a SQL Server login for Pacemaker on each server so that it can manage the availability group in the event of a failover. First CREATE LOGIN, then grant permissions for ALTER, CONTROL, and VIEW DEFINITION of the AG to that login.

For safety, save the credentials on the file system on all servers:

```
echo 'pacemakerLogin' >> ~/pacemaker-passwd
echo 'UseAReallyStrongMasterKeyPassword' >> ~/pacemaker-passwd
sudo mv ~/pacemaker-passwd /var/opt/mssql/secrets/passwd
sudo chown root:root /var/opt/mssql/secrets/passwd
sudo chmod 400 /var/opt/mssql/secrets/passwd
```

These passwords will be accessible only by root. You can see the ownership change (chown) and access permission (chmod) commands in the preceding example.

Creating an availability group resource and virtual IP resource

The following command (which spans two lines) creates a primary/replica type *availability group resource* (the "master" terminology is unfortunate; it doesn't refer to the master database):

```
sudo pcs resource create ag_cluster ocf:mssql:ag ag_name=LinuxAG1 \
--master meta notify=true
```

In the example of three synchronous replicas, the Pacemaker agent sets REQUIRED_SYNCHRONIZED_SECONDARIES_TO_COMMIT to 1, which ensures that the primary replica will not accept transactions without an online, synchronized secondary replica. By default, this value is 0. We discuss this setting in more detail earlier in this chapter in the section "Configuring the minimum synchronized required nodes."

> ➤ You can read more about data protection for availability group configurations specific to SQL Server on Linux at
> *https://docs.microsoft.com/sql/linux/sql-server-linux-availability-group-ha*.

To create the virtual IP resource, run the following command on one of the nodes (use your own valid IP address here):

```
sudo pcs resource create virtualip ocf:heartbeat:IPaddr2 ip=172.8.0.120
```

Remember that there is no virtual server name equivalent, so ensure that you have DNS configured with the virtual IP resource and virtual server name. Remember to do this in your DR environment, as well.

Create colocation constraint and ordering constraint

As discussed in Chapter 2 and earlier in this chapter, WSFC uses quorum votes to decide on how to manage resources in the cluster. Pacemaker uses a scoring system, which is calculated per resource. You can manipulate the scoring system by using *constraints*.

To make sure that the *virtual IP resource* runs on the same host as the primary replica, for instance, you can create a constraint with a score of INFINITY. Anything lower than INFINITY is simply taken as a recommendation.

To create a *colocation constraint* to have the virtual IP and primary replica on the same host, run the following command on one node (note that it again spans two lines):

```
sudo pcs constraint colocation add virtualip ag_cluster-master \
INFINITY with-rsc-role=Master
```

A colocation constraint is implicitly ordered. In the previous example, if a failover occurs, the virtual IP will point to a secondary node before the first node is demoted to secondary, and the second node it is promoted to the primary replica.

To resolve this, you can create an ordering constraint, which will wait for the promotion before pointing the virtual IP resource to the new node; here's how to do it:

```
sudo pcs constraint order promote ag_cluster-master then start virtualip
```

That concludes the content strictly specific to availability groups on SQL Server on Linux. Now we will discuss management and monitoring of availability groups across all platforms.

Administering availability groups

Although the built-in availability groups dashboards in SSMS provide a base amount of information about overall availability group health, they do not provide much in the way of monitoring the performance, current latency, or throughput of the availability groups cluster.

In this section, we review the insights to be had in monitoring availability groups in three main categories: DMVs, wait types, and extended events. In all three categories, *most* of the data to be had will be on the primary replicas.

> ➤ For more scripts to automate the management of availability groups, including failover, see Chapter 9.

Analyzing DMVs for availability groups

In this section, we review a few scenarios for which using DMVs to retrieve availability group information is useful. You either won't see data or will see incomplete data when viewing HADR DMVs on secondary replicas.

Monitoring availability group health and status

You can view dashboards for individual availability groups within SSMS or by using the script that follows, which uses three different DMVs. Both methods provide a complete snapshot of data only when run on a SQL Server instance that serves as the primary replica for an availability group, but the script will show information for all replicas, for all availability groups in which the instance is the primary replica. This sample is a good foundation script for monitoring.

```
/*Monitor availability group Health

On a secondary replica, this query returns a row for every secondary database on the
server instance. On the primary replica, this query returns a row for each primary
database and an additional row for the corresponding secondary database. Recommended
executing on the primary replica. */

IF NOT EXISTS (SELECT @@SERVERNAME

    FROM sys.dm_hadr_availability_replica_states rs

    WHERE rs.is_local = 1
```

```
    and rs.role_desc = 'PRIMARY')
SELECT 'Recommend: Run script on Primary, incomplete data on Secondary.';
SELECT AG = ag.name
, Instance = ar.replica_server_name + ' ' +
CASE WHEN is_local = 1 THEN '(local)' ELSE '' END
, DB = db_name(dm.database_id)
, Replica_Role = CASE WHEN last_received_time IS NULL THEN
'PRIMARY (Connections: '+ar.primary_role_allow_connections_desc+')'
ELSE 'SECONDARY (Connections: '+ar.secondary_role_allow_connections_desc+')' END
, dm.synchronization_state_desc, dm.synchronization_health_desc
, ar.availability_mode_desc, ar.failover_mode_desc
, Suspended = CASE is_suspended WHEN 1 THEN suspend_reason_desc ELSE 'NO' END
, last_received_time, last_commit_time, dm.secondary_lag_seconds
, Redo_queue_size_MB = redo_queue_size/1024.
, dm.secondary_lag_seconds
, ar.backup_priority
, ar.endpoint_url, ar.read_only_routing_url, ar.session_timeout
FROM sys.dm_hadr_database_replica_states dm
INNER JOIN sys.availability_replicas ar
on dm.replica_id = ar.replica_id and dm.group_id = ar.group_id
INNER JOIN sys.availability_groups ag on ag.group_id = dm.group_id
ORDER BY AG, Instance, DB, Replica_Role;
```

> ➤ For more information on the data returned in this DMV, read on
> to the next code sample and reference *https://docs.microsoft.com/*
> *sql/relational-databases/system-dynamic-management-views/*
> *sys-dm-hadr-database-replica-cluster-states-transact-sql.*

Monitoring for suspect pages and database automatic page repair events

Availability groups, and the database mirroring feature that came before them, used the
replicas to automatically repair any corrupted, unreadable data pages on one replica with data
from a replica with a readable copy of the data page. This is different from the behavior of DBCC
CHECKDB and REPAIR_ALLOW_DATA_LOSS, which could result in lost data when repairing pages.

The automatic page repair is a background process that occurs after the operation that discovered the corrupted page data. Transactions will still fail with an error code 823, 824, or 829 in the SQL Server error log.

You should monitor the system table `msdb.dbo.suspect_pages` and the DMV `sys.dm_hadr_auto_page_repair`, which will contain entries of these events; for example:

```
--Check for suspect pages (hopefully 0 rows returned)

SELECT * FROM msdb.dbo.suspect_pages WHERE (event_type <= 3);

--Check for autorepair events (hopefully 0 rows returned)

SELECT db = db_name(database_id), * FROM sys.dm_hadr_auto_page_repair;
```

Monitoring live availability group performance

Typically, the gap between the primary and an asynchronous replica is mere seconds. You can measure the backlog of transactions waiting to be committed to an asynchronous replica using the `sys.dm_hadr_database_replica_states` DMV, which provides a wealth of information of interest to tracking how far behind a secondary replica is:

- **log_send_queue_size.**   Expressed in kilobytes, this is the amount of log data not yet sent to the secondary replicas.

- **log_send_rate.**   Expressed in kilobytes per second, this is the average of data sent to secondary replicas. Values only present for primary replicas.

- **redo_queue_size.**   Expressed in kilobytes, this is the amount of log data not yet committed on of the secondary replica. This data must be committed before the secondary replica can become primary in a failover, a part of RTO.

- **redo_rate.**   Expressed in kilobytes per second, this is the average amount of data committed on the secondary replica.

- **secondary_lag_seconds.**   Expressed in seconds, this is a more accurate amount of time the secondary replica is "behind." It does not express how long it would take the secondary replica to "catch up."

Dividing `log_send_queue_size` (KB) by `log_send_rate` (KB/s) provides a rough estimate for the amount of time it will take to send all data from the primary to secondary replicas. Similarly, dividing `redo_queue_size` (KB) by `redo_rate` (KB/s) provides an estimate for the number of seconds it will take a secondary replica to "catch up" to the primary.

You can combine what we've learned about the DMVs `sys.dm_hadr_database_replica_states` and `sys.dm_os_performance_counters` to create a script, which you can see in the code sample that follows. This code returns a significant amount of availability groups performance data. As usual, you should run this on the primary replica of an availability group. This script (which is three pages long) is available for download under this chapter's sample scripts, named "Monitoring availability group health and status", at *https://www.MicrosoftPressStore.com/SQLServer2019InsideOut/downloads*.

Analyzing wait types for availability groups

You should baseline these wait types and take action on increases in this wait type, whether they be sudden or gradual. In this section, we look at some wait types to take note of when administering availability groups.

> ➤ **For more information on wait statistics, such as how to monitor and trend them, see Chapter 8, "Maintaining and monitoring SQL Server."**

There are 60-plus wait types in SQL Server that are prefixed with HADR_*. Many are background tasks that are expected or will rise when the SQL Server is idle. The following wait types are those of which you should be wary, and when:

- The HADR_SYNC_COMMIT wait type is the transaction delay present when using synchronous mode secondary replicas. It is associated with the wait that primary replicas experience when sending log data to synchronous replicas, and then waiting on the acknowledgement of the synchronous replicas. An increase of HADR_SYNC_COMMIT on the primary replica will be due to performance constraints on the secondary replica. This wait type, and many others, will not be present when running only with asynchronous secondary replicas. This wait type does not include the time spent on the secondary replicas processing the redo log data. The secondary replica might be experiencing WRITELOG.

- A sudden spike in the HADR_SYNCHRONIZING_THROTTLE wait type would indicate that synchronous secondary replicas are trying to get caught up and indicates that transactions are waiting on secondary replicas to commit. You should expect to see this wait on synchronous, secondary replicas when they are still in the SYNCRONIZING state. (Correspondingly, on the primary, you'll see HADR_SYNC_COMMIT.)

- The WRITELOG wait type is likely to appear on any SQL Server instance, including availability group primary and secondary replicas, when there is heavy write activity. The WRITELOG wait is time spent flushing the local SQL Server instance log to the drive and is due to physical I/O subsystem performance.

- The ASYNC_NETWORK_IO wait is not usually associated with network transport speed for availability groups; rather, it measures the communication via the network stack to remote clients or storage systems. Misconfigured networks, such as routing problems inside the data center, or malfunctioning network cards could explain this wait, but more likely it is not related to availability group communication and is caused instead by excessive data sent to remote clients, especially long-running report applications.

There are some common wait types you will see that are not a cause for concern. For example, the HADR_WORK_QUEUE and WAIT_XTP_OFFLINE_CKPT_NEW_LOG wait types are an indication of worker threads waiting; you do not need to worry about them. The HADR_TIMER_TASK and HADR_CLUSAPI_CALL wait types are also not indicative of a problem, and thus you can ignore them. If it is among the top waits, it generally indicates a lack of activity, not performance problems. The HADR_GROUP_COMMIT wait indicates that log records are waiting for a sufficient quantity to be grouped together and is also not indicative of any performance issue.

Analyzing extended events for availability groups

SQL Server includes an extended event session called AlwaysOn_health. By default, this session collects Data Definition Language (DDL) events, failover and state changes, and more than 30 SQL Server errors by number. You can view the details of what the session collected by scripting it.

The AlwaysOn_health session is actually used by the dashboard, but it can also be queried in aggregate, and by default keeps up to four 5-MB rolling .xel files in the *Instancepath*\MSSQL\ Log folder. This extended events session is always present in SQL Server, but not enabled unless you have configured availability groups.

Look for the log_flush_complete event duration in your extended events sessions; it includes the duration (in milliseconds) which will indicate the amount of time it took for I/O to complete the log flush on any replica.

The ucs_connection_send_msg event signals the communication between replicas. This occurs after the hardening of the block of transaction log data on the secondary replica, and in the case of synchronous replication, occurs before the hardening of the block on the primary replica.

The hadr_log_block_group_commit and hadr_db_commit_mgr_harden events on the primary node are the start and end of the log block replication. The hadr_db_commit_mgr_harden event follows the acknowledgement from any synchronous secondary replicas and the hardening of the primary transaction log.

You might consider creating an extended events session to watch the timing of synchronization events on your primary and secondary instances. Here is a script to get you started:

> ➤ **For more information on extended events, see Chapter 8.**

> ➤ **For more information on the syntax configuring alerts that follow, see Chapter 9.**

```
--Create extended events session to monitor availability group synchronization

--Recommended for diagnostic purposes only

--For monitoring events on Primary Replica
```

CHAPTER 11

```
CREATE EVENT SESSION [AG_Synchronization_Events_Primary] ON SERVER

ADD EVENT sqlserver.hadr_log_block_group_commit,

ADD EVENT sqlserver.log_flush_start,

ADD EVENT sqlserver.hadr_log_block_send_complete,

ADD EVENT sqlserver.log_flush_complete,

ADD EVENT ucs.ucs_connection_send_msg,

ADD EVENT sqlserver.hadr_receive_harden_lsn_message,

ADD EVENT sqlserver.hadr_db_commit_mgr_harden

ADD TARGET package0.event_file

    (SET filename=N'Synchronization_Events_Primary.xel',

    max_file_size=(5),max_rollover_files=(2))

WITH (STARTUP_STATE=ON);

GO

--Recommended for diagnostic purposes only

--For monitoring events on a Secondary Replica

CREATE EVENT SESSION [AG_Synchronization_Events_Secondary] ON SERVER

ADD EVENT sqlserver.hadr_transport_receive_log_block_message,

ADD EVENT sqlserver.log_flush_start,

ADD EVENT sqlserver.log_flush_complete,

ADD EVENT sqlserver.hadr_send_harden_lsn_message,

ADD EVENT ucs.ucs_connection_send_msg

ADD TARGET package0.event_file

    (SET filename=N'Synchronization_Events_Secondary.xel',

    max_file_size=(5),max_rollover_files=(2))

WITH (STARTUP_STATE=ON);

GO

ALTER EVENT SESSION [AG_Synchronization_Events_Secondary] ON SERVER STATE=START

ALTER EVENT SESSION [AG_Synchronization_Events_Primary] ON SERVER STATE=START
```

Alerting for availability groups

Consider placing alerts for a list of errors that are specific to availability groups, which should trigger nontrivial, actionable emails to be sent to your SQL DBA team. If you are not already using SQL Server Agent Alerts for error events to send emails to your SQL DBA team via Database Mail, see Chapter 9. If you are using an external error log monitoring application, be sure to trigger high priority alarms for the following error messages, each of which is significant:

- **35264.** Database movement for a database has been suspended.

- **35265.** Database movement for a database has resumed; informational only.

- **35273, 35274.** Indicate database failure during recovery at failover.

- **35276.** Synchronization of database has stopped and cannot be resumed.

- **41418.** A secondary replica has become disconnected from the primary and will need to be reconnected.

PART IV

Security

Administering security and permissions

In this chapter, we are going to look at how to implement security when it comes to accessing the data in your databases, starting with authenticating who you are, what you can access, and what you can do with the data once you have access. Many of these principles will apply equally to SQL Server and Microsoft Azure SQL based offerings; but there are some differences due to the fundamental nature of each services.

The chapter will start out covering the modes of authenticating who the entity is that is trying to access the database. There are several authentication modes that you can use to access the server, from on-premises Windows Active Directory, to Azure offerings, to standalone security using SQL Server's built in authentication.

After authenticating to the server where the data is located, the accessing entity is assigned to security principals. A security principal is an entity that can be authenticated, and then be given access to some resource. Principals will be used to get access to system activities at the server level, and database objects at the database level.

Once authenticated and sorted into security principals, we will cover permissions that we can give to principals to see and make changes to our servers, databases, structures, and data in tables.

Lastly, we will look at common security administration tasks that DBAs need to handle security tasks, including handling orphaned security identifiers (SIDs), security migration, service account permissions, and more.

Authentication modes

When it comes to security, you should focus on connecting to the database where your data is stored. This section covers an overview of the modes of authentication to a SQL Server instance, or one of the Azure SQL database types. You will see the types of authentication modes when you first open SQL Server Management Studio (SSMS) as shown in Figure 12-1.

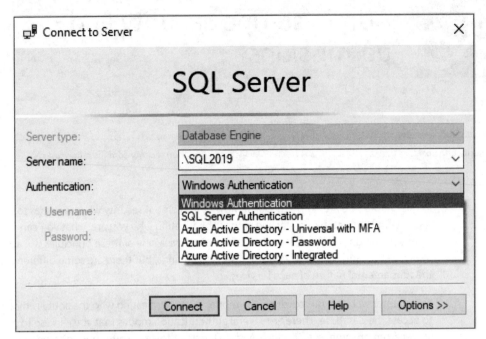

Figure 12-1 The Connect To Server dialog box in SSMS.

Let's start with the authentication methods with which DBAs are most familiar when working with the on-premises versions of SQL Server, since they are still the most typical. Azure continues, however, to become more and more prevalent to use for new and existing applications, so it is important as a DBA to maintain your current expertise.

Windows authentication

Windows-authenticated logins take advantage of authentication that's built into Windows clients to seamlessly pass credentials in a Windows or domain environment. This is the only authentication method that is turned on by default during installation of the on-premises version, and we strongly recommend it for use in most applications where possible. This will help alleviate the need to manage multiple logins for most users. Windows Authentication only works with on-premises versions of SQL Server. Azure Active Directory authentication will be covered in a following section.

For Windows-authenticated logins, the Windows SID for the account or group is used as the reference value in the SQL Server. For domain accounts, this SID will be the same from Windows server to Windows server, making it easy to move security data around.

In a typical business environment, using Windows Authentication means that account creation/ termination, Active Directory security group membership, and password policy are handled by an existing corporate security administration infrastructure. In fact, using Active Directory security groups is a best practice for centrally managed role-based authentication (RBA).

SQL Server Authentication

SQL Server Authentication is a method that stores usernames and passwords in the master database of the SQL Server instance. SQL DBAs must manage password complexity policy, password resets, locked-out passwords, password expiration, and changing passwords on each instance that uses SQL Server Authentication.

The SID assigned to a newly created SQL Server–authenticated login is generated by the SQL Server. Two logins with the same name and password on two SQL Server instances will seem as if they are the same to the DBA, but they will have different SIDs, which will cause some complexities in managing your databases (this is covered in the "Common security administration tasks" section later in this chapter).

You can use SQL Server Authentication to connect to on-premises SQL Server instances, Azure virtual machine–based SQL Server instances, and databases in Azure SQL Database, but other methods of authentication are preferred in all cases when possible. It is certainly something that should be considered when surveying your instances, as it may have been turned on for legacy reasons. A good time to question the value of the use of SQL Server Authentication is during upgrades as well.

In the most common usage, SQL Server Authentication authenticates you to the server. However, the same concept can be used for contained databases, which is covered later in the Authentication Modes section.

Azure Active Directory universal authentication

The next three authentication types are exclusive to Azure-based resources, specifically Azure SQL Database or Azure Synapse Analytics, using Azure Active Directory (Azure AD) credentials.

In the Connect To Server dialog (as seen in Figure 12-1) is the "Azure Active Directory – Universal with MFA support" selection. MFA is multi-factor authentication. Universal Authentication uses Azure two-factor authentication, and you can use it for connecting to Azure SQL Database or Azure Synapse Analytics resources. SSMS and ADS can use the Azure Authenticator application or other two-factor methods.

In addition to the password, users will be prompted initially to log in with the universal login client, asking for your domain account, and whatever extra authentication it requires, for example a pin or smart card. As is true for any account on the Internet, it is always better to use two-factor authentication whenever possible. It can be more burdensome to the users, but someone who gets your password cannot then log in without the second factor in their possession.

Azure Active Directory password authentication

Azure AD accounts can be used for authentication with a username and password, using users that have been created in the Azure tenant and granted access to the Azure SQL Database or Azure Synapse Analytics.

This authentication method makes it possible for you to use your Azure account to sign into SQL Server via a username and password. This is more secure than SQL Server–based authentication because it is linked to an Azure AD account that is, in theory, managed by an existing Enterprise Security group.

You can use this method, for example, to grant an Azure AD account with a Microsoft Office 365 license direct access to a database in Azure SQL Database over the web.

Azure Active Directory integrated authentication

This mode is analogous to Windows Authentication, using an Azure AD account rather than a Windows Server AD account. Once logged into a Windows machine with your Azure AD account, you can use the Azure AD account to authenticate to the database very similar to Windows Authentication. No username or password is requested; instead, your profile's local connections are used to connect to the SQL Server.

For example, you can use this authentication method when connected via Remote Desktop to an Azure AD–authenticated session on a virtual machine (VM) in Azure.

Advanced types of server principals

You can create another type of server principal aside from Windows or SQL Server authentication; it has limited uses, but it is good to understand.

You can create a server principal that is mapped directly to a certificate or to an asymmetric key. Secure access to the SQL Server instance is then possible by any client with the public key of the certificate, using a nondefault endpoint that you create specifically for this type of access.

The Service Broker feature of SQL Server, used for asynchronous messaging and queueing, supports Certificate-Based Authentication.

As examples, the ##MS_PolicyEventProcessingLogin## and ##MS_PolicyTsqlExecutionLogin## login principals, created automatically with SQL Server, are certificate-based.

You can list out the server principals using the following query, including the certificate mapped ones.

```
SELECT name, type_desc, is_disabled

FROM    sys.server_principals

ORDER BY type_desc;
```

Authentication to SQL Server on Linux

You can make SQL Server connections to instances running on the Linux operating system by using Windows Authentication and SQL Authentication.

In the case of SQL Authentication, there are no differences when connecting to a SQL Server instance running on Linux with SSMS and ADS.

NOTE

There are otherwise very few significant differences between SQL Server on Linux and SQL Server on Windows Server for the purposes of the rest of this chapter, and indeed, for most of the chapters in this book.

It is also possible to join the Linux server to the domain, using Kerberos (with the realm join command), and then connecting to the SQL Server instance on Linux just as you would connect to a SQL Server instance on Windows Server. The steps necessary are detailed in the SQL Server on Linux documentation at *https://docs.microsoft.com/sql/linux/sql-server-linux-active-directory-authentication*.

Inside OUT

You've created a SQL Server instance on a Linux VM in Azure. How do you connect to it?

If you are using a Linux VM running Azure, you need a Network Security Group inbound security rule to allow connections to the SQL instance. Without it, your authentication attempt will wait and eventually fail with Error 1225, "The remote computer refused the network connection."

After allowing network connections to your Azure VM, you must then do an initial configuration of the SQL Server. Connecting via Bash on Ubuntu on Windows or PuTTY, or similar tool, run the following command:

```
sudo /opt/mssql/bin/mssql-conf setup
```

You will be asked to accept the license terms and to provide the "sa" password. You then will be able to connect to the SQL Instance in Azure via SSMS with SQL Authentication using the "sa" account and the password you provided.

You can make connections to the Linux operating system itself via the Windows 10 built-in Bash shell (a feature introduced with the Windows Creators Update). Windows Server 2016 build 1709 and later have been updated to include the Windows Subsystem for Linux feature. For more information, visit *https://msdn.microsoft.com/commandline/wsl/install-on-server*.

Contained database authentication

Contained databases are a partially implemented feature that encourages the database programmer to think of their on-premises database in the same way an independent Azure SQL Database does, as a fully independent container, rather than a member of a collection of databases with an external server. The idea is to shift many server-level concepts to the database level in a move that allows databases to be more mobile between server environments. This has advantages specific to high availability and cloud-based designs, in that other than connectivity to a server, everything else behaves in the same manner.

We cover containment more in the section on "Configuring Database Principals," but suffice it to say that at this point you can use this feature to authenticate users to just a single database on the server, which gives them some access to TempDB and master.

There are two types of contained database authentication: Contained Users From Windows and Contained Users with Password. They both behave similarly to their cousins Windows Authentication and SQL Server Authentication, except how data is stored for connecting to the server itself.

Security principals

In security terminology, a security principal is an entity that can be authenticated, and then be given access to some resource. In SQL Server, a principal is given access though several layers of abstractions, covered in this section.

Once you have decided the authentication mode you are going to use to authenticate to your server/database, the next step is to start building your layers of security. For SQL Servers implemented on the Windows OS (Or Azure SQL Database managed instances), the next step is to configure the security context of the entity you are authenticating.

> ### NOTE
> There is one concept in database-scoped security that we initially ignore: containment. Contained databases have users that can be accessed directly, without a server login to tie back to. In practice they are rarely used, and complicate discussions beyond their value. Contained database users will be discussed later in the chapter.

Given that we're starting on the ground floor of security, let's begin by establishing some important terminology:

- The *scope* of a principal depends on that to which it can be given access. SQL Server has two scopes of principals:

  - **Server** – This allows principals to access SQL Server from the outside of the system. This will include access by people and services.

- **Database** – Once a principal has accessed the server, each individual database has a security system of its own to determine what can be done with the contents of the database.

- The primary server principal used to access resources is commonly called a *login*.

- The primary database principal used to access database resources are commonly referred to as a *user*.

- Another type of principal that is available at either scope is a *role*, which allows you to bundle privileges to grant to another principal (a user, or even another role).

In each database, a user can be associated with a maximum of one server login. Logins might not be associated with users in all databases, and it is possible for users to exist without any association to a login, though oftentimes this occurs accidentally. (We talk about this scenario more later in the chapter in the "Preventing orphaned SIDs" section.)

Logins and users are not associated by their names that you see in SSMS; instead, they are associated by a binary value known as a SID (Security Identification Number). How the SID is generated for each login is based on the type of authentication used by the login. You can view the SID for a login in the `sys.server_principals` view. For example, the following query will return the name, SID, and type of the server principals that have been created on the server:

```
SELECT name, sid, type_desc

FROM   sys.server_principals;
```

Table 6-1 presents a quick comparison of the purpose of the database and server principals.

Table 6-1 Comparison of users and logins

Server Login	Database User
• Authenticates sessions to a SQL Server instance	• Identifies the login's context within a database
• Can be linked to Active Directory (Windows Authentication) or have a password stored in SQL Server's Master databases	• Generally linked to a server login to access data after authenticated
• Assigned to server roles to obtain packaged rights over the server, as well as all databases if desired	• Does not have a password
	• Assigned to database roles to obtain packages of rights to use the database
• Not affected by the restore of any user database	• Stored in the user database, and is brought along with a User DB Restore
• Used to allow server operations such as RESTORE, CONNECT, CREATE DATABASE, DROP DATABASE, or even viewing data in any database.	• Used to allow database operations such as SELECT, UPDATE, EXECUTE, CREATE TABLE, and so on.

It is important to understand this terminology and the differences between these objects, not just for interacting with SQL Server, but for communicating with fellow SQL administrators and developers.

Understanding the basics of privileges

In order to move much deeper into the discussion of setting up and configuring server and database principals, we need to cover the basics of privileges in SQL Server. Most "things" in SQL Server have privileges that you can give to some principal for giving or taking away rights to do things. For example, for a table, there are privileges to INSERT, UPDATE, DELETE, and SELECT which are typically used. There is also a REFERENCES privilege that allows you to use a FOREIGN KEY constraint against the table, which is infrequently used, but allows objects managed by one user to reference objects managed by another.

Then there are privileges that pertain to the entirety of a server or database. Such as ALTER TABLE, CREATE TABLE, BACKUP, and CONTROL.

> ➤ You can see the more complete list of possible permissions in the Microsoft Docs at *https://docs.microsoft.com/sql/relational-databases/security/permissions-database-engine*.

We don't cover most of the permission types, nor will you ever likely use a great number of them, but it is important to know they exist in case you have a specific purpose that doesn't match the commonly used permissions that we cover. In order to give or take away permissions, there are three statements that can be used:

- GRANT – Gives a user access to a resource, if they have not also been denied access

- DENY – Disallows access to a resource

- REVOKE – Basically the delete statement of security, will delete a GRANT or DENY that has been applied

Here is the basic syntax of the security statements:

```
GRANT   permission(s) ON objecttype::Securable TO principal;

DENY   permission(s)  ON objecttype::Securable TO principal;

REVOKE permission(s) ON objecttype::Securable  FROM | TO principal;
```

The ON portion of the permission statement may be optional depending on whether you are applying permission to a specific resource, or to the container. For example, you can omit the ON portion to grant a permission to a principal for the current database by doing this:

```
GRANT EXECUTE TO [domain\katie.sql];
```

Keep in mind that this statement would grant EXECUTE permissions for any stored procedure in the database, but not to each individual stored procedure. Any stored procedures created in the future could also be run by the principal.

Where permissions get complex are when you start having access to a resource through multiple paths. Roles will be discussed in more depth later in the chapter, but roles will allow you to group together permissions. You may be a member of multiple roles.

Hence, you may be granted access to read some data, for example in a schema named `Sales`, through multiple methods. You may also be denied via another path. GRANT and DENY oppose each other, with DENY taking precedence. To demonstrate, consider the following opposing GRANT and DENY statements run from an administrative account on the WideWorldImporters sample database:

```
GRANT SELECT ON SCHEMA::Sales TO [domain\katie.sql];

DENY SELECT ON OBJECT::Sales.InvoiceLines TO [domain\katie.sql];
```

Or you can grant `[Domain\Katie_sql]` access TO insert, update, and delete data using:

```
GRANT INSERT, UPDATE, DELETE ON SCHEMA::Sales TO [domain\katie.sql];
```

After applying this GRANT statement, user `[domain\katie_sql]` can query all tables in the `Sales` schema that exist, or later get created, other that the `Sales.InvoiceLines` table.

It doesn't matter how many times you are granted access to a resource, DENY overrides it. You can delete the DENY using:

```
REVOKE SELECT ON OBJECT::Sales.InvoiceLines TO [domain\katie.sql];
```

And then delete the original GRANT using the following statements (which can be condensed into one statement, if desired, they needn't match the GRANT):

```
REVOKE SELECT ON SCHEMA::Sales TO [domain\katie.sql];

REVOKE INSERT, UPDATE, DELETE ON SCHEMA::Sales TO [domain\katie.sql];
```

Now `[domain\katie_sql]` will have no access to the `Sales` schema, based on the permissions we originally granted, and will not be denied them either since we revoked that on the `Sales.Invoice` table.

NOTE

You can use the syntax REVOKE *permission* TO or REVOKE *permission* FROM syntax interchangeably. This is to make the syntax a little easier to write and generate.

CHAPTER 12

Configuring login server principals

In this section, we cover some important topics for configuring the logins to your SQL Server instance. Including authentication mode, special logins, server roles (built-in and user-created), and how to best set up a login for your administrative users.

Choosing Server Authentication mode

In this section, when discussing server authentication mode, we are working with SQL Server on a Windows or Linux instance. There are two modes of security that your SQL Server can operate in: Windows Authentication mode and Mixed mode (or as the user interface states it: "SQL Server And Windows Authentication Mode").

The goal is to use Windows Authentication mode for your access whenever possible. If the content of this chapter refers to SQL Server Authentication as redundant, often unnecessary, and problematic for administrators, that's intentional: using SQL Server Authentication (aka configuring the SQL Server instance in mixed mode) creates additional administrative overhead and possible security holes, which DBAs need to be aware.

As the DBA of a SQL instance, be sure to emphasize to developers and application administrators that Windows Authentication, via named domain accounts or service accounts, is always preferred to SQL Server Authentication.

If, however, you are in a situation where this is not possible (for example, when Windows-authenticated accounts are impossible to use or for network scenarios involving double-hop authentication when Kerberos is not available) it is important to configure your server properly. Make sure to enforce password length, changing passwords, and more.

> **NOTE**
>
> **What comprises a strong password is a complex topic. Microsoft SQL Server documentation has the following document outlining some of additional characteristics as a starting point:** *https://docs.microsoft.com/sql/relational-databases/security/strong-passwords,* **though we generally suggest a truly secure password ought to be at least 15 characters.**

Since SQL Server 2005, usernames and passwords of SQL Server–authenticated logins are no longer transmitted as plain text during the login process. And, unlike early versions of SQL Server, passwords are not stored in plain text in the database. Any SQL Server–authenticated login can potentially have its password reverse-engineered by a malicious actor who has access to or a copy of the master database .mdf file. In fact, the tools to do so are part of SQL Server's code:

```
--Create a login with a password
```

```
CREATE LOGIN BadPassword WITH PASSWORD = 'Password';

--find all logins with this password using the PWDCOMPARE function

SELECT Name

FROM    sys.sql_logins

WHERE PWDCOMPARE ( 'Password', password_hash) = 1;

--Drop the login

DROP LOGIN BadPassword;
```

Given enough time, and even one password that is commonly used, P@ssw0rd, or a birthdate, and it can be easily figured out. For these reasons and more, Windows-authenticated accounts are far more secure because the passwords are not stored in this fairly arcane manner.

If you are using an Azure SQL Database managed instance, you will continue to have mixed mode available, with the ability to create SQL logins with passwords, and you can use the Azure Active Directory Authentication modes covered in the first section of this chapter.

Enforcing password policies

As stated earlier, one of the problems with SQL Server Authentication is that it is a redundant security system within each SQL Server. Included in each server, and in each user, is whether a SQL login must adhere to the machine's password policy. It is not required to be enforced.

The policies applied from the machine's local security policy, inherited from the domain if applicable, include minimum length and complexity requirements.

The Enforce Password Policy check box is selected by default when you open the Login – New dialog box (Figure 12-2) in SQL Server Management Studio, but you can clear the check box to turn off this option. So, with SQL Server Management Studio it is possible to create a login with a noncomplex (or even blank) password.

> ### NOTE
> If you try to create a login with a blank password in SSMS, it pops up a warning that asks if you are sure, but it does ultimately allow it if you override the good advice from the user interface.

When you create a login in T-SQL code, the CHECK_POLICY option is not required, but it defaults to ON (According to *https://docs.microsoft.com/powershell/module/sqlserver/add-sqllogin*, there is no default for the -EnforcePasswordPolicy when using Add-SqlLogin in Powershell).

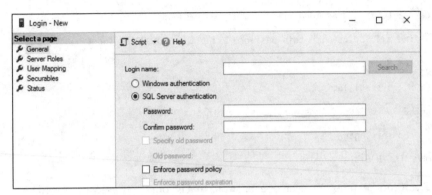

Figure 12-2   The blank Login – New dialog box in SSMS.

You should keep in mind that if you turn on the CHECK_POLICY option on an existing login that did not already have it on, the existing password is not affected. The policy, though, will be enforced the next time the password is changed. Applications and end users can still sign into the SQL instance by using the existing, potentially noncomplex password. Subsequent DBAs might assume that the password policy is enforced on the existing password. Therefore, do not turn on CHECK_POLICY on a login without then immediately changing the password, or at least setting the MUST_CHANGE option at the same time so that the user must change her password on the next login.

In addition to enforcing password policy, you can optionally enforce a maximum password age by selecting the Enforce Password Expiration check box. You also can force a user to change their password on their next login, but keep in mind that although SQL Server Management Studio has built-in behavior to allow for this password to be changed with a simple dialog box, other applications might not have the ability for users to change their passwords interactively, and they will instead see only a failed login.

The bar is raised for the Azure SQL Database managed instance, which requires enforce password policy.

Setting the login default database

Each login includes a default database option, which you should set appropriately depending on how the login principal is to be used. It is convenient to be able to simply log in to a server and be in a desired database without specifying it at login, but it is not without a few concerns.

Authentication of the server principal will fail if its default database is not accessible, including if the database is restoring, offline, or dropped from the instance. Authentication to the server will fail even for a member of the sysadmin server role, so you should rarely if ever change the default database of a known administrator login. The sysadmin role has all permissions to the SQL Server instance. We will talk more about the sysadmin role and other server-level roles later in this chapter.

What to set administrator logins to is an interesting choice between two databases, master or TempDb, which both will always be there when the server comes up by definition. Either the master (the default setting) or TempDb should be set as the default database, In our experience, using TempDb can be a safer choice, as very often you go to a server to create some code. If the USE statement is left off, or misspelled, you end up with objects in your TempDb instead of master.

NOTE

Ending up with stray objects in your master databases due to a combination of not specifying a database and forgetting to set the database during execution is a very common occurrence. While it does not excuse scripts not specifically directing you to the proper database, it does happen, particularly on DEV or TEST environment servers. It is best to start in a safe place like TempDb for your logins regardless.

This guidance generally follows even for logins that are not a member of the sysadmin server role. There might be some cases for which a default database set to a user database is appropriate; for example, for a login that will be used only for a single database. In this way, the default database setting might be helpful because the login will be denied new connections if that single database is inaccessible, moved to another instance, or dropped from the instance.

Configuring and setting up server roles

A *role* in SQL Server is similar to a group in Windows terminology. It is a grouping that allows other principals to be assigned to it, referred to as *members of the role*. This grouping can then have permissions assigned to it, which every member of the role is granted by membership.

Roles are foundational to a solid security scheme and should be used to grant almost all rights on a SQL Server. Granting rights to an individual login or user means that over time it is seemingly impossible to remove these rights due to how complicated they become. If you have 10 DBAs on your team, and 100 users, for example, could end up in 1000s of permissions to grant, and each user could end up slightly different over time.

Building up a group of roles that match the tasks you desire to be accessible to your logins and users, then applying and removing them as needed, lets you keep security in well-defined chunks of code that can be far easier audited. If you need a person to be able to manage databases, back up databases, or view three tables in a database, you can create a role, give it a name, and test that it does only what you desire it to.

There are two kinds of roles you will work with: built-in roles, and user-defined roles. Built in roles are groups of permissions that someone at Microsoft concocted as basic roles that people may need. Full power, access to drop/create databases, read all the data in a database (or all databases,) and many other administrative level tasks that have permissions that generally go together for common tasks.

We start by reviewing the server roles built into SQL Server, with a focus on when and why they should (and should not) be granted. Several server roles are built into SQL Server, including the one you are likely most familiar with, the all-powerful sysadmin. We will also cover how you can create your own user-defined server roles, if the ones set up by Microsoft aren't granular enough (and they often are not).

Understanding the built-in server roles

Server roles are used to bundle together one or more privileges that you want to give to a login. The built-in server roles are generally used to grant administrative logins access to do certain tasks. Most of these are quite powerful in nature and need to be given out cautiously, if at all.

A common concern is that vendor specifications or developers request inappropriate permissions to be given to end users and service accounts via fixed server roles to run their applications. It is essential to understand what you are allowing an application to have access to. While it is not our assertation that any reputable third-party software is malicious, the bigger concern is if they are well built to avoid issues like SQL injection.

> **NOTE**
>
> Server roles are not a feature of Azure SQL Database, though database roles (covered later in this chapter) are provided. This will be analogous to how a contained user behaves in SQL Server.

To manage a user assignment to server roles, SQL Server Management Studio provides the membership page in the Login Properties dialog box (Figure 12-3). By default, only the Public check box is selected (you cannot clear it). Initially, a new login is assigned to only the public built-in server role, from which that login cannot be removed.

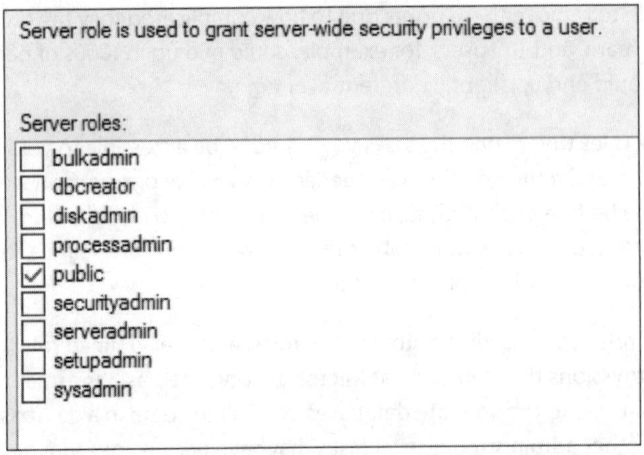

Figure 12-3   The server role membership page from the Login Properties dialog box in SQL Server Management Studio. By default, only the public role is selected (and cannot be cleared).

You also can use T-SQL to add and remove members from server roles, as shown in this example:

```
--Katie is made a domain admin on 2019-01-01, because she is a DBA in good standing
ALTER SERVER ROLE serveradmin ADD MEMBER [domain\katie.sql];

GO

ALTER SERVER ROLE processadmin DROP MEMBER [domain\katie.sql];

GO
```

We would generally suggest that whether you create your principals using the GUI or by script, that you generate scripts for your logins and roles (other than passwords) so you can know what is supposed to be on any server. Security sprawl frequently happens when multiple administrators just give out rights to people as they ask, but you can add comments and perhaps reference documentation as to who authorized access in the script you have created.

Security can get complicated quite fast, because a role can be a member of a role, and that role the member of another role. This will be discussed in greater detail later in the section specifically on roles. The key here is that you need to clearly understand what a role can do, and don't just add system roles to user defined ones without understanding what they do and why you are doing it.

CHAPTER 12

Inside OUT

Once you get security right, how can you test it to make sure without asking for the user to try it, or even to give you their password?

If you wish to test security, all you need is IMPERSONATE rights to an account. This is sometimes done in an application to let an application or user account impersonate the other principal, but the most typical application is to test security for a login or user. For example, say you have a login named Login1 and you just gave the access to a table, you can check using EXECUTE AS LOGIN (you can also execute as a user in a database), and then execute the statement. You can revert to your original context using REVERT, and you can see who you are acting as using SUSER_SNAME() and the original security context using ORIGINAL_LOGIN().

```
--For a domain account, do not include square brackets or the account will not
be found

EXECUTE AS LOGIN = 'Login1';

SELECT SUSER_SNAME() AS ActingAs, ORIGINAL_LOGIN() AS ActuallyAre;

SELECT * FROM dbo.Table1;
```

> REVERT;
>
> **For all intents and purposes, you will behave like the security principal you are impersonating. If Login1 has no access to dbo.Table1, there will be an error returned by the batch.**

Let's explore the list of built-in server roles, beginning with the unlimited sysadmin role.

- **sysadmin.** The sysadmin server role has unrestricted access to all operations where there is not code to check for names (for example, row-level security may exclude sysadmin, if the function it is based on doesn't spell it out.) It is appropriate for properly vetted DBA administrative accounts only. Although software vendors or other accounts can request membership to the sysadmin server role to simplify their security configuration, this is not appropriate. A responsible DBA should push back on granting membership to this role, or since this is often impossible to beat politically, test the application on another server before allowing access to your live database.

  When granting the sysadmin role, it is unnecessary to grant membership to any other server role (unless needed for row-level security). Granting membership to every server role is redundant because sysadmin doesn't just have rights to do everything, the server basically ignores security for its members.

  The sysadmin role is also granted certain other permissions, often in the code of SQL Server Management Studio. The privileges of the sysadmin role is nearly the equivalent of the GRANT CONTROL SERVER permission, with some slight differences. The most notable is the fact that the sysadmin role is unaffected by any DENY permissions; for example:

```
USE Master;

GO

--using standard security for simplicity

CREATE LOGIN TestSysadminDeny WITH PASSWORD = 'S3cure1$'

GO

GRANT CONTROL SERVER TO TestSysadminDeny;

DENY VIEW SERVER STATE TO  TestSysadminDeny;

GO

EXECUTE AS LOGIN = 'TestSysadminDeny';

SELECT * FROM sys.dm_exec_cached_plans;

GO
```

```
REVERT;

GO
```

The result is an error:

```
Msg 300, Level 14, State 1, Line 7

VIEW SERVER STATE permission was denied on object 'server', database 'master'.

Msg 297, Level 16, State 1, Line 7
```

The user does not have permission to perform this action.

But if you execute the following and add them as a member of the sysadmin role, re-execute the statement and it will succeed.

```
ALTER SERVER ROLE sysadmin ADD MEMBER TestSysadminDeny;
```

- **bulkadmin**.   The bulkadmin server role has been granted permissions to perform BULK INSERT operations from local files. It can be suitable for service accounts for unattended processes that perform automated mass data movement. Bulk operations from any local folders are allowed; this is the main difference between granting membership to this role and granting the ADMINISTER BULK OPERATIONS permission.

    Principals that are members of this role can use bcp, SQL Server Integration Services, or T-SQL to perform BULK INSERT statements.

NOTE

To perform BULK INSERT operations, permissions to access the target database, and INSERT into the destination tables are additionally required, and permissions to ALTER TABLE for the destination table might also be required, depending on the exact settings used, as it can be set to ignore constraints, which is technically a change to the table.

- **dbcreator.**   Service accounts for applications that generate databases automatically, such as on-premises Microsoft SharePoint, can be granted membership to this server role instead of sysadmin, to allow databases to be created. You can create new databases directly or via the restore from a backup.

    The dbcreator server role has the CREATE ANY DATABASE permission. Keep in mind that this permission also gives the user the capability to ALTER and DROP any database. This is quite a powerful role. For example, consider the following script. In it, we will create a new database owned by sa, then one by a new principal named TestDbcreator. The only thing this login will not be able to do with the database is change the owner, but it can drop the database, and make important setting changes.

```
USE Master;

GO
```

```
--using standard security for simplicity
```

```
CREATE LOGIN TestDbcreator WITH PASSWORD = 'S3cure1$'
```

```
GO
```

```
ALTER SERVER ROLE dbcreator ADD MEMBER TestDbcreator;
```

```
GO
```

Now, still as the `sysadmin` enabled login you are using to administer your test instance, create a database and make it owned by the `sa` built in login.

```
CREATE DATABASE TestDropSa;
```

```
ALTER AUTHORIZATION ON DATABASE::TestDropSa TO sa;
```

```
GO
```

Now, impersonating the `TestDbcreator` principal, attempt to create, alter, and drop databases.

```
EXECUTE AS LOGIN = 'TestDbcreator';
```

```
CREATE DATABASE TestDrop;
```

```
ALTER AUTHORIZATION ON DATABASE::TestDrop TO sa;
```

This command fails with the following error, indicating that it does not have permissions to change the owner.

```
Msg 15151, Level 16, State 1, Line 17
```

```
Cannot find the principal 'sa', because it does not exist or you do not have
permission.
```

You can, however, change very important settings:

```
ALTER DATABASE TestDropSa SET SINGLE_USER;
```

```
ALTER DATABASE TestDropSa SET READ_COMMITTED_SNAPSHOT ON;
```

And you can drop the databases:

```
DROP DATABASE TestDrop;
```

```
DROP DATABASE TestDropSa;
```

```
REVERT;
```

- **processadmin.**   This role grants admin-level visibility to sessions and requests, and to view and reset server performance information. These permissions can prove useful to non-administrators who monitor activity.

  The role is granted the ALTER ANY CONNECTION permissions, allowing members of this role to view and stop (KILL) sessions. The role is also granted VIEW and ALTER SERVER STATE, making it possible for members to view a wide array of helpful Dynamic Management Objects (DMOs).

Any connection can view its own sessions in the sys.dm_exec_sessions, but with the ALTER ANY CONNECTION permission, a connection can view all sessions and requests active on the server, including system sessions below session_id 50.

The ALTER SERVER STATE allows access to DBCC SQLPERF, a well-documented command that can view and reset wait and latch statistics that you can view via the DMOs, as well as view space utilization data from transaction log files. In Azure SQL Database, resetting wait and latch statistics is not supported.

- **public.** The public role allows you to give access to any authenticated user of your server. Which is to say, under only extremely rare occasions should permissions be granted to the public server role.

  Every login is a member of the public server role. Unless you have considered all of the downfalls of doing it, do not grant any additional permissions to the public role, because they will be granted to all current and future logins and users. We hasten to say "never," because there are use cases for every tool, but most of the time, using the public role is just taking the easy route, much like adding application logins to the sysadmin role.

- **securityadmin.** The securityadmin role should be considered as close to sysadmin as it gets. The ability to create logins at the server level and users in each database, to grant and revoke permissions at the server and database level, should not be granted lightly. Members of the securityadmin role can create and add logins to the sysadmin role, so membership should be given scrutiny equivalent to the sysadmin role.

  Membership in the securityadmin role is required by some service accounts to delegate the management of security to applications, especially those that create databases procedurally and thus need to provision security for them; for example, we have the setup and farm accounts for Microsoft SharePoint On-Premises installations.

  The securityadmin role possesses the ALTER ANY LOGIN permission and more, including security permissions inside each database, plus management of account status and passwords for SQL Server–authenticated logins.

- **Serveradmin.** Membership in the serveradmin server role grants the ability to alter and create endpoints, sp_configure settings, and to shutdown the SQL Server instance. The role is also granted VIEW and ALTER SERVER STATE, allowing the permission to view a wide array of helpful DMOs.

  The ALTER SERVER STATE allows access to DBCC SQLPERF, a well-documented command that can view and reset wait and latch statistics as well as view space utilization data from transaction log files. In Azure SQL Database, resetting wait and latch statistics is not supported.

  The serveradmin has no access to data or database-level settings or security-related permissions, and so is often combined with other roles to provide a subset of administrative capability.

- **diskadmin.**　A subset of the serveradmin fixed server role, the diskadmin server role has rights to affect drive resources; for example, to create and drop backup devices.

  In addition to other permissions, diskadmin has been granted the ALTER RESOURCES permission, which is fairly limited, poorly documented, and is not recommended to grant individually. Instead, grant membership only to the diskadmin role.

- **setupadmin.**　The setupadmin role only grants permissions to deal with linked servers using T-SQL statements. To use SQL Server Management Studio to set up linked servers, the sysadmin role is required.

Creating custom server roles

Beginning with SQL Server 2012, you are able to create custom server roles to help you further define the roles that various administrators and non-administrators can serve. This can be especially helpful when crafting a package of less-than-sysadmin permissions for deployment managers, security administrators, auditors, developers, integration testers, or external access.

Inside a DBA team, we might seek to break down duties and grant permissions to suit, for example, junior administrators or high availability administrators, who should not need full sysadmin rights, but do need advanced rights that are not packaged together in the built-in roles. The key to creating custom server roles is to have a good understanding of the permissions involved to perform certain tasks and then divvying up permissions. You also can make custom server roles to be members of any built-in server role except for sysadmin.

Similarly, you have the ability to create custom database roles in each database. We discuss that later in this chapter.

Following is an example of a potentially useful custom server role. You can create it to allow read-only access to administrators to an instance. In the next section "Providing logins to the DBA team", we discuss separating the Windows credentials used by DBAs into an "everyday" account and an administrative account. This custom server role is useful to provide read-only access to a DBA's "everyday" account.

```
--Create a new custom server role

CREATE SERVER ROLE SupportViewServer;

GO

--Grant permissions to the custom server role

--Run DMOs, see server information

GRANT VIEW SERVER STATE to SupportViewServer;

--See metadata of any database

GRANT VIEW ANY DATABASE to SupportViewServer;
```

```
--Set context to any database

GRANT CONNECT ANY DATABASE to SupportViewServer;

--Permission to SELECT from any data object in any databases

GRANT SELECT ALL USER SECURABLES to SupportViewServer;

GO

--Add the DBA team's accounts

ALTER SERVER ROLE SupportViewServer ADD MEMBER [domain\DBATeamGroup];
```

Granting commonly used server privileges

Granting a domain account membership to the sysadmin role is appropriate only for administrator accounts who absolutely need them; it is inappropriate for developers, power users, and
analysts. What permissions might they need, short of "all of them?"

As a DBA, you should be aware of permissions that your IT colleagues can be granted short of
the server sysadmin role or database db_owner roles to give them access to advanced activities
they need, but avoid giving out super powers except for DBAs who truly need them.

These common securables are server-level and so are not supported (or necessary) in Azure
SQL Database. They are not supported even when run in the master database of the Azure
SQL Database server.

The following subsections present some examples of permissions that you can grant users to do
certain tasks, or in one case all tasks. Hence, it is not only important to know what you can do,
but also understand what privileges mean when you do an audit.

It is not a simple task to determine exactly how a server principal obtained the privileges they
have, but it is very simple to determine what effective rights a user has at the server level using
fn_my_permissions, which you can use at the server or database level to see what the current
security context has access to. If you run this as a sysadmin, you will see every privilege listed.

```
USE master

CREATE LOGIN ListEffectivePermissions WITH PASSWORD = 'S3cure#';

GRANT CONNECT ANY DATABASE TO ListEffectivePermissions;
```

Next, we check the login's effective permissions by passing SERVER to the function (the first
parameter is for the object to check permissions), which we will use at the database level.

```
EXECUTE AS LOGIN = 'ListEffectivePermissions';

SELECT permissions.permission_name

FROM    fn_my_permissions(NULL, 'SERVER') AS permissions
```

```
REVERT;
```

From this you will see:

```
permission_name
-----------------------------------------------------------
CONNECT SQL
VIEW ANY DATABASE
CONNECT ANY DATABASE
```

One of these we granted, but two others have appeared that we did not grant. Every login has one privilege granted on create CONNECT SQL. VIEW ANY DATABASE is inherited from the public group, which allows all server principals to see all databases, unless you DENY this privilege.

VIEW SERVER STATE

```
GRANT VIEW SERVER STATE TO [server_principal];
```

This permission at the server level allows the principal to view a large number of server metadata objects, system views, and DMOs, many of which are essential to a developer who is looking to troubleshoot, analyze, or performance tune.

Most of the DMOs mentioned here in Chapter 12 need only the VIEW SERVER STATE permission.

This is a relatively safe permission to grant in terms of damage that can be done, or data that can be seen. With VIEW SERVER STATE, the principal still has no access to data (other than some values that might show up in a query plans), database objects, logins, or passwords. This is a read-only permission at the server level and provides a lot of diagnostic information for someone doing support without the ability to affect major changes.

CONNECT ANY DATABASE

```
GRANT CONNECT ANY DATABASE TO [server_principal];
```

Introduced in SQL Server 2014, this is a quick way to allow a login to set its context to any current or future database on the server. It grants no other permissions. Although it does not create a user in each database for the login, it behaves as if a user had been granted in each database for login and has been given no other rights (or basically what the CONNECT right confers to a user in a database).

This permission alone doesn't seem very useful, but it could be handy for setting up a DBA's "everyday" account or, rather, granting this securable to a Windows-authenticated group to which all DBA "everyday" accounts belong. Consider granting this permission and the next, as well, SELECT ALL USER SECURABLES, to grant read-only access to a server, including each database on the server.

SELECT ALL USER SECURABLES

```
GRANT SELECT ALL USER SECURABLES TO [server_principal];
```

Introduced in SQL Server 2014, this permission grants the ability to select from all readable database objects in all user databases. The object types include tables, views, table-valued functions. It does not give the user access to execute stored procedures. This is a fast way to give administrators access to read from all current and future databases and their objects but is not appropriate for non-administrative end users or application logins.

Keep in mind that production data could contain sensitive, personally identifiable, personal health information, etc, that should not be accessible to even typical support people. In some regulatory environments, granting this permission would not be appropriate and might fail regulatory audit, unless SELECT permission on sensitive tables was denied, masked, or those columns were encrypted, perhaps with the Always Encrypted feature.

Similarly, you could also use this permission to DENY read access to all data on a server by denying this right. This could ensure that administrators can accomplish a variety of other server-level tasks in production systems with safe assurance that they cannot casually access data using their "everyday" accounts. Keep in mind that members of the sysadmin server role would not be affected by any DENY permission.

> ➤ For more information on encryption of sensitive data, including Always Encrypted, see Chapter 13.

CONTROL SERVER

```
GRANT CONTROL SERVER TO [server_principal];
```

This effectively grants all permissions on a server or database and is not appropriate for developers or non-administrators.

Granting the CONTROL permission is not exactly the same as granting membership to the sysadmin server role, but it has a very similar effect. Members of the sysadmin role are not affected by DENY permissions, but owners of the CONTROL permission might be.

IMPERSONATE

```
GRANT IMPERSONATE ON LOGIN::[server_principal] TO [server_principal];
```

The IMPERSONATE permission allows the server principal to use the EXECUTE AS statement, the EXECUTE AS clause on a coded object like a stored procedure, or the EXECUTE statement to execute T-SQL code in the security context of another server principal.

This permission can create a complicated administrative environment and should be granted only after you understand the implications and potential inappropriate or malicious use. With this permission, it is possible to configure a login to impersonate a member of the sysadmin role and assume those permissions, so this permission should be granted in controlled scenarios, and perhaps only temporarily.

Other than for support persons doing testing, this permission is most commonly granted for applications that use EXECUTE AS to change their connection security context. You can grant the IMPERSONATE permission on logins or users.

Logins with the CONTROL SERVER permission already have IMPERSONATE ANY LOGIN permission, which should be limited only to administrators. It is unlikely that any application that uses EXECUTE AS would need its service account to have permission to IMPERSONATE any login that currently or ever will exist. Instead, service accounts should be granted IMPERSONATE permissions only for known, appropriate, and approved principals that have been created for the explicit purpose of being impersonated temporarily.

ALTER ANY EVENT SESSION

GRANT ALTER ANY EVENT SESSION TO [*server_principal*];

A developer might need this permission to trace the SQL Server as part of a troubleshooting expedition, after you tell them about extended events. This will grant them access to create extended events sessions with T-SQL commands, but will not give them access to view server metadata in the New Extended Events Session Wizard in SQL Server Management Studio. For that, they will need one further commonly granted developer permission: VIEW SERVER STATE.

Similar to traces, extended events sessions can capture events on the server from all databases and processes. You cannot trace certain sensitive events; for example, the T-SQL statement of CREATE LOGIN for a SQL authenticated login.

However, as of Azure SQL Database v12, for developers to view extended events sessions, you must grant them an ownership-level permission CONTROL DATABASE (discussed later in this chapter in "Granting commonly used database level privileges"). In production environments, this isn't recommended for developers or non-administrators.

ALTER TRACE

GRANT ALTER TRACE TO [*server_principal*];

A developer might need this permission to trace the SQL Server as part of a troubleshooting expedition into the SQL Server. (Though you should remind them after granting this permission that traces are deprecated, and extended events are a much better diagnostic tool.)

➤ For more information, see Chapter 8, "Maintaining and monitoring SQL Server."

Because ALTER TRACE is a server-level permission developers can trace all events on the server, from all databases and processes. Certain sensitive events cannot be traced; the T-SQL statement of CREATE LOGIN for a SQL authenticated login is an example.

Understanding special logins

Here we discuss some important special logins to be aware of, including special administrative access, which you should tightly control.

The sa login

The sa login is a special SQL Server–authenticated login that is, simply put, all powerful. It is a known member of the sysadmin server role with a unique SID value of 0x01, and you can use it for all administrative access. If your instance is in mixed mode (in which both Windows Authorization and SQL Server Authentication are turned on), and the sa password is known, it can be used to do anything on the server.

Even if you never use the sa account for authentication, it has utility as the authorization (aka owner) of databases on a server for many configurations, such as a general corporate server where all of the databases are used by the enterprise. In cases where a server is used for multiple customers, you may wish to have each customer's login own their own database(s). When two databases are owned by the same user, you can turn on the DB_CHAINING database setting to allow cross database queries in some circumstances (*https://docs.microsoft.com/dotnet/ framework/data/adonet/sql/enabling-cross-database-access-in-sql-server*).

This known administrator account, however, has obvious potential consequences if used for typical access, much as any sysadmin level login will with the addition of not being able to tell one user of the account from another. This means it could serve as an anonymous backdoor for malicious or noncompliant activity by current or former employees. In the best case, the sa account should have a wickedly complex password that is locked away for safe keeping.

Applications, application developers, and end users should never use the sa account. This much should be obvious. The sa account, like any SQL Server–authenticated account, can potentially have its password reverse-engineered by a malicious actor who has access to or a copy of the master database .mdf file.

The sa account is a common vector for brute-force attacks to compromise a SQL Server. For this reason, if your SQL Server is exposed to the Internet, we recommend that you rename and/or disable this account.

The BUILTIN\Administrators Windows group

If you have experience administering SQL Server 2005 or older, you'll remember the BUILTIN\ Administrators group, which was created by default to grant access to the sysadmin server role to any account that is also a member of the local Windows Administrator group. This was a convenience that might seem logical. Should anyone that has admin rights to a server, have admin rights by default to everything that server has on it? The answer is no.

Beginning with SQL Server 2008, this group was no longer added to SQL Server instances by default, because it is an obvious and serious security back door. Although it was potentially convenient for administrators, it was also targeted by malicious actors.

Service accounts

In Chapter 4, "Installing and configuring SQL Server instances and features," we discuss service accounts in greater depth, but it is worth pointing out that service accounts for a server are simply server logins. They are usually given the minimal permissions needed to run the services to which they are assigned by SQL Server Configuration Manager. For this reason, do not use the Windows Services (services.msc) to change SQL Server feature service accounts. Changing the instance's service account with the Windows Services administrative page will likely result in the service's failure to start.

It is not necessary to grant any additional SQL Server permissions to SQL Server service accounts. (You might need to grant additional NT File System (NTFS)–level permissions to file locations) Although the SQL Server Agent service account likely needs to be a member of the sysadmin role (though this can be debatable if you take the time to change jobs to use specific credentials for the jobs they execute using Credentials and Proxies), the SQL Server service account does not. For these reasons and more, different service accounts for different services is very desirable.

You also should never grant the NT AUTHORITY\SYSTEM account, which is present by default in a SQL Server instance, any additional permissions. Many Windows applications run under this system account and should not have any nonstandard permissions.

> ## Inside OUT
>
> *What about service accounts for instances in your Always On availability group?*
>
> For SQL Servers in an Always On availability group, the SQL Server service on each replica instance does not need to have the same domain service account, though this is the simplest approach.
>
> If each replica SQL Server service account is different, you must create a login for each other replica's domain service account on each replica.
>
> Though not recommended, if you choose to use nondomain service accounts for each SQL Server instance, you must create the database mirroring endpoint (not to be confused with the deprecated database mirroring feature) using an encrypted certificate for the instance.

We also recommend that you do not use local or built-in service accounts, including the machine account, though it is also possible to do by granting each machine's network service account a login on each other's replica. This is definitely not a secure approach.

For more on Always On availability groups, see Chapter 11, "Implementing high availability and disaster recovery."

Providing logins to the DBA team

The first logins you will need to create is for the database administrators, so they have access to do everything they need to do. In all but the most rudimentary IT departments, SQL DBAs need access to production SQL Server instances, but need their access governed and constrained to certain uses and privileges, at least most of the time. By this we mean that during your normal duties, it is better if you don't have rights to drop the primary sales database because you "thought you were on your local machine." A day of lost sales, plus the need to creatively explain to potential employers why you left your previous employer is not worth avoiding a few extra steps to apply upgrades to your production server.

Assuming you are primarily using Windows Authentication for your server access, this generally means that SQL DBAs will sign into a Windows instance using the domain credentials they use to access their email account, the timesheet application, and so on. Then, they connect to the SQL Server instance with Windows Authentication on that same account and begin their work. DBAs often use this same method whether they are connecting to a production environment SQL Server or a preproduction (often used for development) environment SQL Server, though next we'll talk about using different credentials for each.

Inside OUT

What is a "production" environment, and how is it different?

In the upcoming section, we talk about "production" versus "preproduction." What does that mean? Let's take a look at what each environment actually is:

- **Production.** This is the main system of record. It might, for example, connect to the actual instruments or machines, or control life-critical systems, or customer-facing applications, or contain the business's valuable data. It is subject to disaster recovery plans, needs high availability, and is "the server" to which the CEO of your company refers.

- **Preproduction.** This is a class of systems that may resemble the production environment but aren't visible to the actual machinery (physically or metaphorically

> speaking) of the business. They go by many names including Development, Test, Quality Assurance (QA), User Acceptance Testing (UAT), Business Acceptance Testing (BAT), and many others. Very often this environment will simply be referred to as dev or test. The key is that we are not talking about the user data that the business relies on.
>
> Preproduction servers should generally not contain actual customer or patient information (other than a true testing system such as a UAT or BAT system where the customer must see their actual data in action; and in such cases the system may actually need to be treated similar to production).
>
> Developers, report writers, and quality assurance testers should ideally have access only to preproduction systems. If they need to troubleshoot a production problem, only trusted developers are given access, and even then, only temporarily.
>
> DBAs need to have access to SQL Server instances in all environments, but, still, we need to discuss how best to arrange for access to production systems.

To illustrate, let's consider the following scenario: tasked with backing up and restoring a database from the production environment to the development environment, the DBA uses the connections already open in SQL Server Management Studio, copies the backup to a network share, and then begins the restore. The restore is 50 percent complete when a user calls to ask, "Is the SQL Server down?"

What do you think has happened? And it happens to the best of us when we have too much access. At a conference recently, the speaker asked how many SQL Servers people managed. Well over half of the people managed 50+ servers. If 1/3 of them are production, the other 2/3s look just like those servers, just in a preproduction configuration.

If your DBA team isn't already using *two or more* Windows-authenticated accounts, you should consider segmenting each DBA's production database access from the account they use for the rest of their day-to-day activities, including preproduction systems, but also email, office applications, Office 365, and more.

Consider creating "admin-level" accounts for each DBA that have no preproduction access, office applications or Office 365 access, Virtual Private Network (VPN), or even Internet access. The idea is to encourage your DBA team to use its admin accounts only for administrative activities.

For example, Katherine is a DBA and uses Domain\Katherine to access her "everyday" activities such as email, instant messaging, preproduction SQL instances, source control, Office 365, VPN, and more. But this domain account has limited access to production SQL Servers—for example, she can access server-level DMV's, activity levels, SQL Agent job history, and the SQL Server error log. But she cannot create logins, read or update live production data, alter databases, and so on.

To perform any of those tasks, Katherine starts SSMS using Run AS another user, or opens a remote desktop session to another computer using Domain\admin-Katherine. This activity is deliberate and requires heightened awareness—the production databases are important! Starting SQL Server Management Studio from within the remote desktop session, Domain\admin-Katherine is a member of the sysadmin server role and can accomplish anything she needs to in the production environment. When she's done, she logs out.

Domain\admin-Katherine also has no VPN access; thus if it is compromised, it cannot be used to both gain access to the corporate network remotely and access SQL Servers.

In the end, you might have good regulatory, corporate policy, security, or private reasons to separate a DBA's "everyday" access from production SQL Server instance access. However, access to the production servers using their "admin-" account (many other naming conventions are common) requires deliberate steps and mental awareness of the task at hand, so the risk of accidentally running intended-for-development tasks in production is considerably reduced.

Later in this chapter, in the "Creating custom server roles" section, we talk about fixed server roles that you can use to separate duties among a team of DBAs, and a custom server role that you can create to set up read-only access to an entire server.

Configuring database principals

A database security principal is a part of the database and is the anchor in which you can obtain access to data and coded objects in the database. There are two major types of database principals: users and roles.

Each of these are in some ways considered the same in that you can grant and deny access to database resources using them. Users will be the hook to obtain access to a database, whereas a role will be a way to group together one or more users to give them a common set of permissions.

Configuring and setting up database users

There are four major types of database users: users mapped to logins, users mapped to Windows Authentication principals directly, users that cannot authenticate at all, and contained users, which we have covered earlier in this chapter.

Users mapped to logins and groups

Users mapped to logins are by and far the most common type you will come in contact with. For example, if you had created a standard login named Bob and a Windows authenticated login named [Domain\Fred], using the following code:

```
CREATE LOGIN Bob WITH PASSWORD = 'Bob Is A Graat Guy'; --Misspellings in passwords can
--be helpful!
```

```
CREATE LOGIN [Domain\Fred] FROM WINDOWS;
```

Then you could create users for these logins using:

```
CREATE USER [Domain\Fred] FOR LOGIN [Domain\Fred];
```

```
CREATE USER Bob FOR LOGIN Bob;
```

There is nothing stating that the name of the login must match the domain name, but it is a very typical way to create users, and definitely helps to document your database users and where they come from. The following is perfectly legal syntax as well:

```
CREATE USER fred FOR LOGIN [Domain\Fred];
```

The Windows principal that the login and the database user it references needn't be a Windows based login. It can be a Windows group, for example, which will allow every member of that group to access the database without being named individually.

Users mapped to Windows Authentication principals directly

In the previous section, we created the login for [Domain\Fred], so the CREATE USER statement referenced that login. However, a user could be created for that login regardless of the existence of the explicit login principal.

```
CREATE USER [Domain\Fred] FOR LOGIN [Domain\Sam];
```

In a non-contained database, this user can be used by Domain\Sam, if and only if Domain\Sam can authenticate to the server. So, if Sam was a member of Domain\DatabaseUsers, and there was a login mapped to Domain\DatabaseUsers, creating the user Domain\Sam in the database would give just Domain\Sam access to the database, but all members of Domain\DatabaseUsers rights to access the server (and as we discussed in the server principal section earlier, rights to see the existence of the database, but not access it).

Users that cannot be authenticated to at all

A user does not have to have a login at all, even in a non-contained database. This means it cannot be authenticated to, but it can still exist and have rights assigned. In this scenario, the user will not have a SID assigned.

> **NOTE**
> Another way a user cannot be authenticated at all is from a broken connection to a SID on the server, often from restoring a database on a new server. This scenario, and how to handle it will be covered later in the chapter in the "Solving orphaned SIDs" section.

While the user principal cannot be authenticated to, it can be impersonated using EXECUTE AS, and is a very useful tool for testing security, as well be used frequently in the Permissions section later in this chapter. The syntax for creating a login-less user is simply:

```
CREATE USER Sally WITHOUT LOGIN;

ALTER RoleYouWantToTest ADD MEMBER Sally;

EXECUTE AS USER = 'Sally';
```

Then you can test the role all you want to, without connecting to the server, or creating unneeded logins. Roles will be covered in more details later in the chapter.

Users contained in the database

Databases created or altered on a SQL Server instance by using CONTAINMENT = PARTIAL allow the creation of database principals referred to as "Contained Users." Contained users can be Contained Users with Password or Contained Windows Authentication Users. Contained Users with Password behave like SQL Server Authentication principals, and can be used directly, bypassing the server's authentication.

> **NOTE**
>
> Currently, only partially contained databases are offered by SQL Server 2019 because some objects still cross the database boundary, such as management of the SQL instance's endpoints. When fully contained databases are implemented, they would have no external dependencies even for metadata, temporary objects, configuration, and even SQL Agent Jobs. This level of containment is not available in SQL Server 2019.

You can move contained databases from SQL Server instance to instance without the need to re-create server-level objects, such as server-level security (logins). Some features are only partially contained. Use the views sys.dm_db_uncontained_entities and sys.sql_modules to return information about uncontained objects or features. By determining the containment status of the elements of your database, you can discover what objects or features must be replaced or altered to promote containment.

A significant security factor to be aware of with contained databases is that any user with the ALTER ANY USER permission, and of course any user who is a member of the db_owner fixed database role, can grant access to the database and therefore the server's computing and storage resources. Users with this permission can grant access to new users and applications independently of the SQL Server instance's administrators.

Though the concept of creating databases with the specific CONTAINMENT option does not exist in Azure SQL Database (in v12), contained databases are specifically developed to assist with the concept of a cloud-based database as a service, to allow Azure SQL databases to be mobile between different cloud hosts, and to assure very high levels of availability.

Table 6-2 compares contained database users to database users and server logins (previously shown in Table 6-1).

Table 6-2 Comparing users, logins, and contained users

Server Login	Database User	Contained database user
• Authenticates sessions to a SQL Server • Can be linked to Active Directory (Windows Authentication) or have a password stored in SQL Server's Master databases • Assigned to server roles to obtain packaged rights over the server, as well as all databases if desired • Not affected by the restore of any user database • Used to allow server operations such as RESTORE, CONNECT, CREATE DATABASE, DROP DATABASE, or even viewing data in any database	• Identifies the login's context within a database • Generally linked to a server login to access data after authenticated • Does not have a password • Assigned to database roles to obtained packages of rights to use the database • Stored in the user database, and is brought along with a User DB Restore • Used to allow database operations such as SELECT, UPDATE, EXECUTE, CREATE TABLE, and so on	• Authenticates to a SQL Server, and the database they are contained in (plus TempDB) • May have a password or be linked to Active Directory • Stored in the database they are contained to • Brought along with a User DB Restore • Given access to database-level permissions typically granted to both logins and users • Contained users cannot be given access to external databases directly

Configuring and setting up database roles

Database roles, much like server roles discussed in the section earlier in this chapter titled "Configuring login server principals", allow you to provide packages of permissions to ease the provisioning of database users. You also can create your own user-defined database roles to further customize the packages of permissions granted to users.

In this section, we review the database roles, both built-in and custom, with a focus on when and why they should be granted. The same list of roles applies to SQL Server and Azure SQL Database.

Understanding the built-in database Roles

Let's examine the list of built-in database roles, their permissions, and appropriate use. These roles have some utility when setting up your security, but in a well configured database, most users will not be a member of any of these roles, but rather will be made a member of a custom role, which we cover in the next section.

- **db_owner.** The db_owner database role's name is a bit misleading because it can have many members. It provides unrestricted access to the database to make any/all changes to the database and contained objects. This is not the same as being identified as the login that owns the database (represented by the owner_sid in sys.databases). Changing the AUTHORIZATION for the database to a principal confers the same rights as db_owner because the server principal will be mapped to the dbo built-in user when accessing the database, which is a member of the db_owner role.

The db_owner role does not grant the CONTROL DATABASE permission but is equivalent. Different from the sysadmin server role, the db_owner role does not bypass DENY permissions. Hence, in the following code, the output would be an error that SELECT permissions were denied:

```
CREATE USER fred WITHOUT LOGIN;

ALTER ROLE db_owner ADD MEMBER fred;

DENY SELECT ON Sales.BuyingGroups TO fred;

GO

EXECUTE AS USER = 'fred';

SELECT *

FROM test;
```

However, note that while you can deny members of the db_owner group access to some resource, the actual owner of the database will not be subject to the deny, and as a member of the db_owner role, the user will be able to impersonate the dbo user, unless you deny them that ability.

```
EXECUTE AS USER = 'dbo'

SELECT *

FROM test;

GO

REVERT; REVERT;
--Revert twice, once to get back to fred, and another to get back to your security
context.
```

The only users in the database who can add or remove members from built-in database roles are members of the db_owner role and the principal that holds AUTHORIZATION for the database. (Authorization is covered later in the chapter in the "Understanding authorization" section.) However, a loophole to this is a database role such as:

```
CREATE ROLE ALLPowerful;

ALTER ROLE db_owner ADD MEMBER allPowerful;
```

This is why the general prescription is to avoid adding the fixed database roles to custom roles unless it makes perfect sense for your purpose and you understand the implications.

➤ **For more on AUTHORIZATION, the equivalent of "ownership" terminology, see the section "Understanding authorization."**

- **db_accessadmin.**   The db_accessadmin role not only has the right to create and manage database users and custom database roles, but to create schemas and grant permissions on all database objects. Among other permissions, the db_accessadmin has the ALTER ANY LOGIN and CREATE SCHEMA permissions.

  Members of the db_accessadmin role can create users with or without an association to existing logins. However, members of the db_accessadmin database role cannot fix orphaned users or change the login that a user is assigned to, because they do not have the CONTROL DATABASE permission.

  Even though members of the db_accessadmin role can create schemas, they cannot change the authorization for schemas, because they do not have the ALTER ANY SCHEMA permission.

  In a contained database, members of the db_accessadmin role (and the db_owner role) can create users with passwords, allowing new access to the SQL Server. Because of the high level of control over permissions and membership in the database, this role should be considered as important as the db_owner role and not given out lightly especially for contained databases.

- **db_backupoperator.**   The db_backupoperator role has permissions to BACKUP DATABASE (including full and differential backups), BACKUP LOG, and to CHECKPOINT the database. Note that this role has no rights to RESTORE the database, because that requires server-level permissions found in the sysadmin and dbcreator fixed server roles, or the owner of the database. So while this is generally safe in terms of harm that can be done to the server, it does give the user rights to back up the database and do with it what they want to.

- **db_datareader.**   The db_datareader role given rights to SELECT from any object in the database, including tables, views, and table-valued functions. This is a heavy-handed and brute-force way to give access to application accounts, and it ignores the ability for views to abstract the permissions necessary to read from tables. It is preferable to add permissions to individual objects or schemas instead of granting SELECT access the entire database (note that there is a database level SELECT privilege that can be granted as well). There may come a time when you need to add a table, view, or function you don't want user to have access to by default, and placing this in a schema that you have not granted rights to typical users is a very easy way to accomplish this.

- **db_datawriter.**   The db_datawriter permission can execute INSERT, UPDATE, or DELETE statements on any table in the database. This is a heavy-handed and brute-force way to give access to application accounts, and it ignores the ability for stored procedures to provide approved or audited methods for data changes by abstracting the permissions necessary to write to tables. You should instead grant write permissions on specific objects to specific principals or use stored procedures to accomplish writes. In the same way there was a SELECT database privilege, there are also full database INSERT, UPDATE, and DELETE privileges, which are similar to this role.

- **db_ddladmin.**   The db_ddladmin role has the rights to perform DDL statements to alter any object in the database, but it has no permission to create or modify permissions, users, roles, or role membership. This role also does not have the permission to EXECUTE objects in the database, even objects that members of this role create. There is no built-in database role that provides EXECUTE permissions, which you should grant more granularly than at the database level (Note that there is an EXECUTE privilege at the database level that will allow you to convey execute permission to every object at the database level.)

- **db_denydatareader.**   Kind of the inverse to, db_datareader, the db_denydatareader role denies SELECT on all objects. We will discuss this later in the "Understanding ownership chaining" section, but this does not stop certain kinds of access, such as access through a stored procedure.

- **db_denydatawriter.**   Kind of the inverse of db_datawriter, the db_denydatawriter role denies INSERT, UPDATE, and DELETE on all objects.

- **db_securityadmin.**   Members of the db_securityadmin role can manage fixed database roles (but not change the membership of the db_owner role), create and manage custom roles, role membership, and GRANT, REVOKE, and DENY permissions on database objects in the database.

  Note that members of the db_accessadmin role can create and manage users, but members of the db_securityadmin cannot.

- **public.**   Every database user is a member of the public database role. Under almost all circumstances, do not grant any additional permissions to the public roles in any database, because they will be granted to all current and future users.

Inside OUT

What are common security antipatterns that you should look out for?

Here are two common worst practices in the wild from software vendors:

- Grant EXECUTE on stored procedures, or to the entire database context, to public to ensure that all users have the ability to call all current and future stored procedures.

- Grant SELECT on the entire database context to public to ensure that all users aren't blocked from the ability to read data from views and tables.

This public-permissioned strategy belies a fundamental arrogance about the relationship between the end user and the vendor application. Software developers should never assume that their application's security apparatus will be the only way to access the database.

In reality, an enterprise's power users, analysts, and developers will access the vendor's database with other applications, including but not limited to Azure Data Studio, SQL Server Management Studio; Microsoft Office applications, including Excel and Access; or ad hoc business intelligence tools such as Microsoft Power BI. Users will have unrestricted access to all data and procedures in the database when connecting to the database with other tools.

In this day and age of multiplatform devices and data access, it's wise to assume that users can connect to your data outside of the primary application. Database security should be enforced in the database, as well, not solely at the application layer. Instead of ever granting permissions to public roles, grant only appropriate EXECUTE | SELECT | INSERT | UPDATE | DELETE permissions to specific principals linked to domain security groups.

Creating custom database roles

You can create custom database roles to define the permissions that various application users or service accounts need for proper data access. Unlike server roles, roles will not just be for administrative purposes. Ideally, you assign packages of data access and database object permissions, and most likely only assign access to roles, and then users to roles. Custom database roles can own schemas and objects, just like database user principals.

As with server roles, the key to creating custom database roles is to have a good understanding of the tasks you wish the members of the role should be able to do, the permissions involved, and the appropriateness of data access. It is unlikely that all users in a database will need the same data access, and not all read-only access will be the same.

```
--Create a new custom database role

USE WideWorldImporters;

GO

--Create the database role

CREATE ROLE WebsiteExecute AUTHORIZATION dbo;
```

```
GO

--Grant access rights to a specific schema in the database

GRANT EXECUTE ON SCHEMA::Website TO WebsiteExecute;

GO
```

Like users, custom database roles can themselves be made members of other database roles. Be careful with putting built-in database roles as members of custom role, as you may end up giving users more rights than you expect. Keep in mind that it is critical to use proper naming of roles so that you don't have a role like:

```
CREATE ROLE ReadOneTable AUTHORIZATION dbo;
```

And it actually has db_owner rights:

```
ALTER ROLE db_owner ADD MEMBER ReadOneTable;
```

Remember too that while members of the db_securityadmin built-in role cannot change membership in db_owner, they can change membership in the ReadOneTable role, which then conveys db_owner level rights.

You should create domain security groups for access roles based around job function, levels of oversight, zones of control, and so on. Your Active Directory environment might already have groups for different job functions, including SQL DBAs (for both their "everyday" and administrative accounts). If not, request that a smart list of groups be created so that you can implement proper security in your SQL Server.

Using role membership to handle environment differences

Security is definitely one of the most complicated parts of the DBA's job. Most of the code and objects in a database will be of the sort where you strive to have your preproduction servers (DEV, TEST, QA, and so on), look exactly the same. There is obviously lifecycle involved, and DEV will have changes in progress, QA will have changes you believe are ready to release, and PROD will have the least up to date code, because this is the environment for well tested code. But over time, version by version, the code will be the same.

In security, no two environments will look even somewhat alike. Perhaps the DBA may be the same, if you can't do what we suggested earlier and make DBAs use one login for normal work, and one for production modifications. But you will not want the sales clerk to have the same access on your development server as the production server where they are making point of sale actions (which is likely done in another security context).

This is where roles come into play. If you only ever grant and deny privileges to roles, you will be able to put that security code into your source control system, and test it in DEV, QA, and then apply it to production. You might create the following role:

```
CREATE ROLE SalesSchemaRead;
```

And grant it rights:

```
GRANT SELECT ON SCHEMA::Sales TO SalesSchemaRead;
```

Then in DEV, you can test this schema with user [Domain\TestUser], and it will have the same access as the [Domain\RealUser] does in production if you make them a member of the SalesSchemaRead group. Then the only thing you need to manage outside of source control is which users are members of which roles in the different environments.

Granting commonly used database level privileges

Much like was said at the server level, it is rare that we want to just give a user complete, db_owner level access to the database. Often you will find that none of the database roles match your desires well enough. In this section, we are going to go through several permissions that are commonly useful to grant to users and programmers at the database level.

VIEW DEFINTION

```
GRANT VIEW DEFINTION ON schema.objectname TO [database_principal];
```

This provides permission to the developer to view the T-SQL code of database objects, without the rights to read or change the objects. This is known as the metadata of the objects.

Developers might need access to verify that code changes have deployed to production; for example, to compare the code of a stored procedure in production to what is in source control. This is also a safe permission to grant developers because it does not confer any read or modification permissions.

Instead of going through each object in a database, you might instead want to GRANT VIEW ANY DEFINITION TO [principal]. This applies the permission to all objects in the current database context. You can revoke it easily.

SHOWPLAN

```
GRANT SHOWPLAN TO [server_principal];
```

As part of performance tuning, developers almost certainly need access to view a specific query's runtime plan, for queries against any database on the server. Seeing the execution plan is not possible even if the developer has the appropriate SELECT or EXECUTE permissions on the database objects in the query. This applies to both estimated and actual runtime plans.

The SHOWPLAN permission, however, is not enough: developers also must have the appropriate read or read/write permissions to run the query that generates the plan.

Non-administrators and developers can still view *aggregate* cached runtime plan statistics via the DMO sys.dm_exec_cached_plans without the SHOWPLAN permission, if they have the VIEW SERVER STATE permission.

IMPERSONATE

```
GRANT IMPERSONATE ON USER::[database_principal] TO [database_principal];
```

The IMPERSONATE permission allows the user of the EXECUTE AS statement and also the EXECUTE AS clause to run a stored procedure. This permission can create a complicated administrative environment and should be granted only after you have an understanding of the implications and potential inappropriate or malicious use. With this permission, it is possible to impersonate a member of the sysadmin role and assume those permissions, so this permission should be granted in controlled scenarios, and perhaps only on a temporary basis.

This permission is most commonly granted for applications that use EXECUTE AS to change their connection security context. You can grant the IMPERSONATE permission on logins or users.

Logins with the CONTROL SERVER permission already have IMPERSONATE ANY LOGIN permission, which should be limited to administrators only. It is unlikely that any application that uses EXECUTE AS needs its service account to have permission to IMPERSONATE any login that currently or ever will exist. Instead, service accounts should be granted IMPERSONATE permissions only for known, appropriate, and approved principals that have been created for the explicit purpose of being impersonated temporarily.

CONTROL DATABASE

```
GRANT CONTROL ON DATABASE::[Database_Name] TO [database_principal];
```

This effectively grants all permissions on a database and is not appropriate for most developers or pretty much any non-administrators.

Granting the CONTROL permission is not exactly the same as granting membership to the db_owner database role, but it generally has the same effect. Members of the sysadmin role or logins mapped to the dbo database user are not affected by DENY permissions, but members of a database role (even db_owner) or users that have been granted the CONTROL permission will be affected by a DENY.

Because ALTER TRACE is a server-level securable, developers can trace all events on the server, from all databases and processes. Certain sensitive events cannot be traced; for example, the T-SQL statement of CREATE LOGIN for a SQL authenticated login.

➤ **For more information about using traces, see Chapter 8.**

Permissions

Let's examine the basics of SQL Server permissions as it pertains to creating objects in a database and then giving access to users. Previously we covered the basics of using GRANT, REVOKE, and DENY, as well as setting up database roles. Now we want to start getting down to giving users access to do things with our database objects.

Understanding permissions for Data Definition Language and Data Manipulation Language

Statements in Transact-SQL (T-SQL), and the permissions that can be applied to them, can be sorted into two basic categories of actions:

- **Data Definition Language** (DDL) – DDL statements are used to define structures in the database, such as creating tables, stored procedures, or functions.

- **Data Manipulation Language** (DML) – DML statements are used to fetch data from a table, or to modify the contents of a table.

Each of the types of statements have very different purposes. DDL is typically done by an administrator or developer in preproduction environments, and by a select few or automated processes in production. It is also not atypical to allow a user to store results and data permanently in a database, with very tight control as to where they can create new objects. DML is the statements that most users of a database use to view and modify data.

The goal of a proper security plan is to allow the user access to do what you want them to (create and drop their own tables), but not what they should not (drop tables of other users, or worse perhaps, the application).

DDL

Example DDL statements are things like CREATE TABLE, ALTER TABLE, UPDATE STATISTICS, CREATE PROCEDURE, CREATE OR ALTER PROCEDURE, and so on. Pretty much any statement that is used to modify the code or settings of the database is considered DDL.

The security needed to execute these statements include the following base categories:

- ALTER – used to grant the ability to change the properties (except ownership) of a specific named object

- ALTER ANY – used to give a user the right to change any database securable

- CREATE <securable type> - used to give a user the right to create a given type of securable

- VIEW DEFINITION – used to allow the database principal the right to look at the code of any object in the database

You can tell from the list of statements listed that it is important to be careful with these permissions. We have worked with people who built applications, requiring the application to have permissions to disable triggers in a special scenario, but then used it to disable other triggers to make the application seem faster. Most of the security concerns will not be that blatant, but are more likely to be accidental in nature, like an application generating code drops an object by accident.

DML

DML statements manipulate data in the tables. The following statements access and modify data in tables and are commonly used BULK INSERT, DELETE, INSERT, MERGE, SELECT, UPDATE, TRUNCATE TABLE, EXECUTE PROCEDURE. The rights given to do these statements include the following:

- SELECT, INSERT, UPDATE, DELETE – These four permissions are the foundational ones. They give the user the right to either view, change, create, and delete data from a certain securable, or, if no securable is included in the call, the entire database.

- EXECUTE – Used to let a user execute a stored procedure or scalar function.

TRUNCATE TABLE is the odd item in the list. It is technically DML based on Microsoft's documentation, since the net effect is the table is emptied. However, it requires ALTER permissions to the table because of how it works.

> ## Inside OUT
>
> **You thought TRUNCATE was DDL. Is it really a DML command?**
>
> For the job of removing all rows from a table, the TRUNCATE TABLE command accomplishes the task faster than a DELETE statement without a WHERE clause, if it is allowed. (You cannot use TRUNCATE TABLE, for example if you have FOREIGN KEY constraints that reference your table.)
>
> This is because individual rows are not logged as deleted, rather the data pages are deallocated. The TRUNCATE operation is written to the transaction log and can be rolled back within of an explicit transaction because the pages are not fully deallocated until the transaction commits. TRUNCATE is a deallocation of data pages, as opposed to a DELETE, which removes rows from a table.

CHAPTER 12

> If this sounds like something closer to a DROP than a DELETE, you're right! You will find that TRUNCATE TABLE actually requires rights to modify the structure of the table, but it is still classified by Microsoft as a DML statement, even though you will often find it classified as a DDL, as it was in the prior edition of the book.
>
> *https://docs.microsoft.com/sql/t-sql/statements/statements*

Three more DML statements are deprecated and are needed to modify permissions for the deprecated text, ntext, and image data types. Do not use them, except for legacy support.

- READTEXT
- UPDATETEXT
- WRITETEXT

Understanding overlapping permissions

When building a complete security solution, as we have discussed, it is best to use roles to provide a security interface that we can keep the same in each of our environments. Each of these roles should be distinct in purpose from one another, but generally should be able to work together. It is not at all unreasonable to say you might have two roles, one that allows a user to view sales data, and another to view warehouse data. The purpose of each of these may overlap slightly, for example, both may need access to the Sales.Customer table.

Giving two roles similar, but different in nature, permissions generally will make perfect sense to a proper security configuration. A database principal's access is based on the summation of all the roles they are members of, and any privileges they are directly given. Order doesn't matter, but as introduced earlier in the chapter, GRANT and DENY oppose each other, and even one DENY wins out over 100s of GRANTs.

Where things get complicated is when you want to say users in Role X should have absolutely no access to a certain table, but users in Role Y should. You may be tempted to use a DENY on that table for Role X, and this may make sense or not, depending on the desired effect.

To demonstrate, consider the following opposing GRANT and DENY statements run from an administrative account on the WideWorldImporters sample database:

```
CREATE ROLE SalesSchemaRead GRANT SELECT on SCHEMA::sales to SalesSchemaRead;

DENY SELECT on OBJECT::sales.InvoiceLines to SalesSchemaRead;
```

Next, create a login-less user to test with.

```
CREATE USER TestPermissions WITHOUT LOGIN;

ALTER ROLE SalesSchemaRead ADD MEMBER TestPermissions;
```

As a result, assuming the database user TestPermissions is only a member of this single role SalesSchemaRead, it would have permissions to execute SELECT statements on every object in the sales schema, except for the Sales.SalesInvoice table. Let's assume that no other permissions or role memberships have been granted to the database user TestPermissions. If this is run by user TestPermissions:

```
USE WideWorldImporters;

GO

EXECUTE AS USER = 'TestPermissions';

SELECT TOP 100 * FROM Sales.Invoices;
SELECT TOP 100 * FROM Sales.InvoiceLines;

REVERT;
```

The result is this:

```
Msg 229, Level 14, State 5, Line 4

The SELECT permission was denied on the object 'InvoiceLines', database
'WideWorldImporters', schema 'SALES'.
```

And 100 rows are returned from the Invoices table. The Sales.Invoices table was still accessible to TestPermissions because it was in the sales schema, even though the user was denied access to Sales.InvoiceLines.

Now, let's add another role, that has the specific purpose of not allowing access to the Sales schema:

```
CREATE ROLE SalesSchemaDeny;

DENY SELECT on SCHEMA::SALES to SalesSchemaDeny;

ALTER ROLE SalesSchemaDeny ADD MEMBER TestPermissions;
```

This results in the following when TestPermissions runs the same pair of SELECT statements:

```
Msg 229, Level 14, State 5, Line 4

The SELECT permission was denied on the object 'Invoices', database
'WideWorldImporters', schema 'SALES'.

Msg 229, Level 14, State 5, Line 5

The SELECT permission was denied on the object 'InvoiceLines', database
'WideWorldImporters', schema 'SALES'.
```

CHAPTER 12

The DENY on the entire sales schema overlapped and won.

If you execute the following:

```
REVOKE SELECT on SCHEMA::SALES to SalesSchemaDeny;
```

Now, the only thing that will be denied to `TestPermissions` is access to `Sales.InvoiceLines`.

NOTE

In the previous sample code snippets, for simplicity, we're granting access to an individual named user, `TestPermissions`. When possible, you should avoid this as a practice. As previously mentioned in the "Assigning database role membership appropriately" section, make roles for job responsibilities, and keep them the same in DEV, PROD, etc. You can then even test with a login-less user like `TestPermissions` and it will be no different than using any other user in the system, in term of their database access.

Understanding authorization

In this section, we cover the topic of database "ownership" and its impact on the overall security of a database. Beginning with SQL Server 2008, "ownership" was redefined as "authorization." Ownership is now a casual term, whereas *authorization* is the concept that establishes this relationship between an object and a principal that has primary responsibility for it.

Changing the AUTHORIZATION for any object, including a database, is the preferred, unified terminology rather than describing and maintaining object ownership with a variety of syntax and management objects. In the case of a database, however, although AUTHORIZATION does not imply membership in the db_owner role, it does grant the equivalent highest level of permissions to the server principal that owns it.

For this reason, named individual accounts (for example, your own [domain\firstname.lastname]) should generally not be the AUTHORIZATION of a database (this may vary for certain types of community/shared servers with many databases, but for most enterprise servers, it is not going to be desirable.)

The problem—which many developers and administrators do not realize—is that when a user creates a database, that user is the "owner" of the database, and that user principal's SID is listed as the owner_sid in sys.databases.

First, this gives this user access to everything in this database, even the ability to drop the database, even if they have no other server rights. Secondly, if the database's "owner_sid" principal account was ever to be turned off or removed in Active Directory, or you move the database to another server without that principal, you will encounter problems with IMPERSONATION and AUTHORIZATION of child objects, which could surface as a wide variety of errors or application failures. This is because the owner_sid is the account used as the root for authorization for the database. It must exist and be a valid principal.

For this reason, DBAs should change the AUTHORIZATION of databases to either a known high-level, noninteractive service account or to the built-in sa principal (sid 0x01). It is a standard item on any good SQL Server health check.

If there are databases with sensitive data that should not allow any access from other databases, they should not have the same owner_sid as less-secure databases, and/or you should not turn on Cross Database Ownership Chaining at the server level (it is not by default).

Changing database authorization

When "ownership" was redefined as "authorization," the stored procedure sp_changedbowner was deprecated in favor of the ALTER AUTHORIZATION syntax; for example:

```
ALTER AUTHORIZATION ON DATABASE::[databasename] TO [server_principal];
```

In SQL Server databases, the new owner can be a SQL Server–authenticated login or a Windows-authenticated login. To change the ownership of a database by running the ALTER AUTHORIZATION statement, the principal that's running needs the TAKE OWNERSHIP permission and the IMPERSONATE permission for the new owner.

The new owner of the database must not already exist as a user in the database. If it does, the ALTER will fail with the error message: "The proposed new database owner is already a user or aliased in the database." You will need to drop the user before you can run the ALTER AUTHORIZATION statement. The login, when they access the database, will have db_owner rights because they are the owner of the database.

For Azure SQL Database, the new owner can be a SQL Server–authenticated login or a user object federated or managed in Azure AD, though groups are not supported.

To change the ownership of a database in Azure SQL Database, there is no sysadmin role of which to be a member. The principal that alters the owner must either be the current database owner, the administrator account specified upon creation, or the Azure AD account associated as the administrator of the database. As with any permission in Azure SQL Database, only Azure AD accounts can manage other Azure AD accounts. You can manage SQL Server–authenticated accounts by SQL Server–authenticated or Azure AD accounts.

Understanding and using ownership chaining

Views, stored procedures, triggers, and functions abstract the permissions necessary to read and write from tables and other views. They do this using a concept known as *ownership chaining* (though perhaps it might be more clearly thought of as authorization chaining, with the change of terms). Ownership chaining says that if the owner of a coded object is the same as the owner of all referenced objects, all a caller needs is access to the coded object. In this section, we explore how coded objects can simplify the minimum permissions you need to assign.

This is an important concept to understand, so that you as a DBA can follow a principle of least privilege and grant only the minimum rights necessary for an application or end user to access data. We could even go so far as to DENY SELECT access on base table objects to application users and still provide them with data access via the stored procedures, view, and functions we have designed for appropriate data access.

Users accessing the database with minimal rights would only need EXECUTE permissions on stored procedures and scalar functions; and SELECT permissions on views and table-valued functions. No permissions are needed for triggers, other than rights to change the table.

There are several important caveats that can break this ownership chaining abstraction and require that whoever is accessing data via a coded object also have permissions to the underlying database objects:

- The procedure cannot perform any ALTER operations, which are not abstracted by the stored procedure. This includes turning on IDENTITY_INSERT.

- The procedure does not perform any dynamic SQL Server command such as sp_executesql or EXEC ('SQL statements') to access object. This is a built-in safeguard against SQL Server injection attacks.

- The underlying database objects referenced by the object have the same authorization. User A cannot confer rights to User B based on what it has access to via privileges, only rights that have been obtained by being the authorization principal on the objects.

- If the referenced objects are in a different databases, the databases need to have the same authorization, and cross database chaining turned on at the server level with sp_configure 'cross db ownership chaining', or at the database level using ALTER DATABASE <databaseName> SET DB_CHAINING ON;

Not violating any of those conditions, thanks to the intact database permission chain, you can GRANT EXECUTE permission to a principal and *no other permissions,* and you can run a procedure successfully that accesses many objects, owned by the same principal that owns the procedure. Now, the database principal has no way to access the database objects outside of your stored procedure.

A demonstration of permissions with views, stored procedures, and functions

Let's demonstrate with a simple exercise, in which we will create a testing user and a testing table in the TempDb database (you can use any database where you have rights to create objects.) Run the code in this demonstration section while logged in as a member of the sysadmin role:

```
USE tempdb;

GO

CREATE USER TestOwnershipChaining WITHOUT LOGIN;

GO

CREATE SCHEMA Demo;

GO

CREATE TABLE Demo.Sample (

SampleId INT IDENTITY (1,1) NOT NULL CONSTRAINT PKOwnershipChain PRIMARY KEY,

Value NVARCHAR(10) );

GO

INSERT INTO Demo.Sample (Value) VALUES ('Value');

GO 2 --runs this batch 2 times so we get two rows
```

We've inserted two rows into the Demo.SampleTable.

Now let's test various ways to access this table, without granting any permissions to it.

Inside OUT

When testing with EXECUTE AS, how can you determine what your current security context is?

The section that follows uses the EXECUTE AS statement, which makes it possible for you to simulate the permissions of another principal. If you are using SQL Server Management Studio, this will affect only the current query window.

Be sure to always follow an EXECUTE AS with a REVERT, which stops the impersonation and restores your own permissions. Each execution of REVERT affects only one EXECUTE AS.

If you run into issues, you can always find out what principal you are running by using this statement:

```
SELECT ORIGINAL_LOGIN(), CURRENT_USER;
```

It will provide you with two values:

- **ORIGINAL_LOGIN().** The name of the login with which you actually connected. This will not change even after you use EXECUTE AS USER or EXECUTE AS LOGIN. This is the not the name of the user you originally connected with, but could be helpful to remember how you originally connected.
- **CURRENT_USER.** The name of the user whose security content you have assumed, and is the equivalent of USER_NAME(). The result similar to SUSER_NAME() and SUSER_SNAME() on SQL Server instances, but on Azure SQL Database v12, SUSER_NAME() results an SID and SUSER_SNAME() is not supported in Azure SQL Database v12.

Test permissions using a view

Now, we will create a view on the table Demo.Sample and try to access it. Note that we just created the TestOwnershipChaining database principal and have not granted it any other permissions. Outside of what is granted to the public role, TestOwnershipChaiing has no permissions. Execute this and all following code in this section while logged in as a member of the db_owner database role (or simply with your administrator login that is a member of the sysadmin role):

```
CREATE VIEW Demo.SampleView

AS

        SELECT Value AS ValueFromView

        FROM Demo.Sample;

GO

GRANT SELECT ON Demo.SampleView TO TestOwnershipChaining;

GO
```

The TestOwndershipChaining principal now has access to the view Demo.SampleView, but not to the Demo.Sample table.

Now, attempt to read data from the table:

```
EXECUTE AS USER = 'TestOwnershipChaining';

SELECT * FROM Demo.Sample;

REVERT;
```

This results in the following error:

```
Msg 229, Level 14, State 5, Line 26
```

The SELECT permission was denied on the object 'Sample', database 'tempdb', schema 'Demo'.

Why? Remember that we have granted no permissions to the table Demo.Sample. This is as intended.

But the user TestOwnershipChaining can still access the data in column Value via the view:

```
EXECUTE AS USER = 'TestOwnershipChaining';

SELECT * FROM Demo.SampleView;

REVERT;
```

Here are the results:

```
ValueFromView

----------------------------

Value

Value
```

Note also that database principal TestOwnershipChaining has access only to the columns (and if desired by using a WHERE clause, the rows) that the view Demo.SampleView provides. Applications can use views and stored procedures to provide appropriate SELECT, INSERT, UPDATE and DELETE access to underlying table data by blocking access to rows and columns and no SELECT access directly to the table.

> ➤ For more information on techniques to grant appropriate data access, including Always Encrypted, see Chapter 13.

NOTE

Single statement table valued functions behave essentially like a view, and identically when it comes to security.

Test permissions using a stored procedure

Let's demonstrate the same abstraction of permissions by using a stored procedure, and then also demonstrate a case when it fails. Start with creating the procedure:

```
CREATE PROCEDURE Demo.SampleProcedure AS

BEGIN

SELECT Value AS ValueFromProcedure

FROM Demo.Sample;

END;
```

```
GO
```

```
GRANT EXECUTE ON Demo.SampleProcedure to TestOwnershipChaining;
```

Now try to run as our TestOwnershipChaining principal:

```
EXECUTE AS USER = 'TestOwnershipChaining';
```

```
EXEC Demo.SampleProcedure;
```

```
REVERT;
```

You will now see the output from the procedure shows the rows of the table:

```
ValueFromProcedure
```

```
----------------------------
```

```
Value
```

```
Value
```

It works without any access to the Demo.Sample table. The user TestOwnershipChaining was able to access the data in the table due to ownership chaining.

Now, let's break a stored procedure's ability to abstract the permissions using dynamic SQL:

```
CREATE PROC Demo.SampleProcedure_Dynamic AS
```

```
BEGIN
```

```
DECLARE @sql nvarchar(max);
```

```
SELECT @sql = 'SELECT Value as ValueFromProcedureDynamic
```

```
                        FROM Demo.Sample;';
```

```
EXEC sp_executesql @SQL;
```

```
END;
```

```
GO
```

```
GRANT EXECUTE ON Demo.SampleProcedure_Dynamic to TestOwnershipChaining;
```

Then when you execute this version of the procedure:

```
EXECUTE AS USER = 'TestOwnershipChaining';
```

```
EXEC Demo.SampleProcedure_Dynamic;
```

```
REVERT;
```

Here are the results:

```
Msg 229, Level 14, State 5, Line 63
```

The SELECT permission was denied on the object 'Sample', database 'tempdb', schema 'Demo'.

> ## NOTE
>
> Though generally not a large issue, errors messages may actually be a security hole, in that running an object may not allow you to access the data in the table, but it does tell the user of the existence of a table named Demo.Sample in tempdb. Use proper error handling with a THROW…CATCH block to stop this in a procedure. You cannot use dynamic SQL in a VIEW object, but if the ownership chain is broken (for example, the authorization is different on the schemas that you are using in the query), it would have the same behavior.

Note that we used the dynamic SQL command sp_executesql, passing in a string of T-SQL, which as a security feature automatically breaks the permission abstraction. It is possible to get around this issue by using the EXECUTE AS setting on the stored procedure. With EXECUTE AS, you can have the code in the procedure behave as a different principal. The same can be said of using the AS clause of the EXECUTE statement:

```
EXECUTE ('<Statements>') AS USER = '<UserName>';
```

The largest issue that people make with EXECUTE AS is they default to the all powerful dbo user, and then let the user pass in any string to execute to a dynamic SQL statement. A far safer way is to create a user principal without login, that you can grant access to some resource. Note that this does require the user be in all environments with the same rights, so may require extra scripts for your general deployment processes.

In this case, we create a database principal named ElevatedRights and grant it select rights to Demo.Sample, then execute the code as that user.

```
CREATE USER ElevatedRights WITHOUT LOGIN;

GRANT SELECT ON OBJECT::Demo.Sample TO ElevatedRights;

GO

CREATE OR ALTER PROC Demo.SampleProcedure_Dynamic

WITH EXECUTE AS 'ElevatedRights'

AS

BEGIN

DECLARE @sql nvarchar(1000)

SELECT @sql = 'SELECT Value as ValueFromProcedureDynamic

              FROM Demo.Sample;';

EXEC sp_executesql @SQL;
```

```
END

GO
```

Now, executing the procedure, access to the data is possible and data is returned.

```
EXECUTE AS USER = 'TestOwnershipChaining';

EXEC Demo.SampleProcedure_Dynamic;

REVERT;
```

The fact is: security is hard. And sometimes it can make a good deal more work for you as an administrator to get it right but keeping information away from the wrong eyes is worth it.

NOTE

Multi-statement and scalar table valued functions behave like stored procedures when it comes to ownership chaining security.

Access a table even when SELECT is denied

Let's take it one step further and DENY SELECT permissions to TestOwnershipChaining. Will we still be able to access the underlying table data via a view and stored procedure?

```
DENY SELECT ON Demo.Sample TO TestOwnershipChaining;

GO

EXECUTE AS USER = 'TestOwnershipChaining';

SELECT * FROM Demo.SampleView --test the view

GO

EXEC Demo.SampleProcedure; --test the stored procedure

GO

EXEC Demo.SampleProcedure_Dynamic; --test the stored procedure

GO

REVERT;

GO
```

Executing this code, you will see three blocks of output, with column headings ValueFromView, ValueFromProcedure, and ValueFromProcedureDynamic. We should note that this is both a good thing and a bad thing at times. For example, say you really wanted to keep people out of the Demo.SampleTable. Is there any simple, straightforward method to make your existing code fail? One such method that could be kind of complex, depending on your configuration is to rename your table, and replace it with a view with the same name.

```
--rename the table, with may be complicated by things like

--schemabound views

EXEC sp_rename 'Demo.Sample', 'SampleNewName';

GO


CREATE VIEW Demo.Sample

AS

    SELECT SampleId, Value

    FROM    Demo.SampleNewName

    WHERE IS_MEMBER('db_owner') = 1;
```

Now, any user that isn't in the db_owner role will not get back any data.

Common security administration tasks

Beyond the tasks we have covered so far: creating server and database security principals such as logins, users, and roles, there are several common security tasks that a DBA will need to handle when something isn't right. We will cover several such task in this section.

Solving orphaned SIDs

An orphaned SID is a user who is no longer associated with its intended login. The user's SID no longer matches, even if the user name and login name do.

Any time you restore a (noncontained) database from one SQL Server to another, the database users transfer, but the server logins in the master database do not. This will cause SQL Server–authenticated logins and Windows accounts that are local to the host computer to break, but Windows-authenticated logins (the ones that have access to the server, at least) will still work.

Why? The key to this common problem that many SQL DBAs face early in their careers is the SID and, particularly, how the SID is generated. For SQL Authenticated accounts, the SID is generated by the host SQL Server upon creation, and doesn't automatically match when the login is recreated. For local Windows accounts, they will only be known to the local machine, and even a login with the same name will have a different SID. Both of these are exceptionally important for the security of your data, but equally problematic for the DBA.

The SID for the login is associated with the user in each database based on the matching SID. The names of the login and user do not need to match, but they almost certainly will, unless you are a SQL DBA intent on confusing your successors. But know that it is the SID, assigned to the login and then applied to the user, that creates the association.

The most common problem scenario is as follows:

1. A database is restored from one SQL Server instance to another.

2. The SIDs for the Windows-authenticated logins and their associated users in the restored database will not be different, so Windows-authenticated logins will continue to authenticate successfully and grant data access to end users via the database users in each database, assuming the login has access to the server.

    Whether or not there is a login that matches previously existing SQL Server-authenticated logins by name, the SIDs will be different on each server. When restoring the database from one server to another, the SIDs for the server logins and database users no longer match. Their *names will still match*, but data access cannot be granted to end users.

3. The SID must now be re-matched before SQL Server–authenticated logins will be allowed access to the restore database.

Problem scenario

A database exists on Server1 but does not exist on Server2.

Original state

Server1

SQL Login = Katherine

SID = 0x5931F5B9C157464EA244B9D381DC5CCC

Database User = Katherine

SID = 0x5931F5B9C157464EA244B9D381DC5CCC

Server2

SQL Login = Katherine

SID = 0x08BE0F16AFA7A24DA6473C99E1DAADDC

Then, the database is restored from Server1 to Server2. Now, we find ourselves in this problem scenario:

Orphaned SID

Server1

SQL Login = Katherine

SID = 0x5931F5B9C157464EA244B9D381DC5CCC

Database User = Katherine

SID = 0x5931F5B9C157464EA244B9D381DC5CCC

Server2

SQL Login = Katherine

SID = 0x08BE0F16AFA7A24DA6473C99E1DAADDC

Database User = Katherine

SID = 0x5931F5B9C157464EA244B9D381DC5CCC ▫ Orphaned SID

The resolution

The resolution for the preceding example issue is quite simple:

```
ALTER USER Katherine WITH LOGIN = Katherine;
```

The SID of the user is now changed to match the SID of the login on Server2; in this case, 0x08BE0F16AFA7A24DA6473C99E1DAADDC. Again, the relationship between the Server Login and the Database User has nothing to do with the name.

You can use the script on the source database, which will generate the ALTER USER script for all of your SQL Login based database principals and will map them to server logins. The script will handle all of the logins, including ones that have a different name on the source server (assuming you have created the logins on the new server, naturally.)

> **NOTE**
>
> Are you accustomed to using sp_change_users_login to fix orphaned SIDs? That stored procedure has been deprecated and replaced by the ALTER USER ... WITH LOGIN statement.

```
SELECT    'ALTER USER [' + dp.name COLLATE DATABASE_DEFAULT + ']' +

          ' WITH LOGIN = [' + sp.name + ']; ' AS SQLText

FROM      sys.database_principals AS dp

          LEFT OUTER JOIN sys.server_principals AS sp

              ON dp.sid = sp.sid

WHERE     dp.is_fixed_role = 0
```

CHAPTER 12

```
        AND dp.sid NOT IN ( 0x01, 0x00 ) --dbo and guest

        AND sp.name IS NOT NULL --skip users without logins

        AND dp.type_desc = 'SQL_USER'
ORDER BY dp.name;
```

You should handle orphaned SIDs every time you finish a restore that brings a database from one server to another; for example, when refreshing a preproduction environment (ideally from another preproduction type database, not live data from your production server).

Preventing orphaned SIDs

In the case where you are transferring all of the logins for a server, you can actually prevent orphaned SIDS. You can re-create SQL Server–authenticated logins on multiple servers, each having the same SID. This is not possible using SSMS user interface; instead, you must accomplish this by using the CREATE LOGIN command, as shown here (or using tools we will look at later in this chapter):

```
CREATE LOGIN [Katherine] WITH PASSWORD=N'strongpassword', SID =
0x5931F5B9C157464EA244B9D381DC5CCC;
```

Using the SID option, you can manually create a SQL login with a known SID so that your SQL Server–authenticated logins on multiple servers will share the same SID. Obviously, the SID must be unique on each instance.

In the previous code example we used sys.server_principals to identify orphaned SIDs. You can also use sys.server_principals to identify the SID for any SQL Server–authenticated login. Creating SQL Server–authenticated logins with a known SID is not only helpful to prevent orphaned SIDs, but it can be crucially timesaving for migrations involving large numbers of databases, each with many users linked to SQL Server–authenticated logins, without unnecessary outage or administrative effort.

We'll look more closely at this topic later in this chapter when we examine SQL Server security migrations.

Moving SQL Server logins and permissions

Moving SQL Server logins from one SQL Server instance to another instance is a typical task that most any SQL Server DBA will need to do.

Moving Windows-authenticated logins, SQL Server–authenticated logins, and all server-level permissions are three discrete steps that are accomplished via different methods. The end goal of your maturity as a DBA is to use SQL Server Management Studio's dialog boxes as little as possible, because GUI-driven solutions to this scenario are the most time consuming and could result in an unagreeable amount of button-clicking. T-SQL scripts are superior in terms of manageability, repeatability, and deepening your understanding of the underlying security objects.

In a server migration, keep in mind that all database-level permissions, database roles, and users will be moved with the backup/restore of each database.

In this section, we discuss various methods of migrating security, some of which apply to either SQL Server instances or Azure SQL Database.

Inside OUT

Should you have scripts of principals and passwords?

It is always good to have scripts available to recreate special system objects/users. and so on. This is certainly true for system accounts where you need to be able to recreate the account with its password.

However, be extra careful to store such data in a VERY safe location, ideally itself encrypted with a secure password. What if, for example, you have a server where you are using a Standard Login that has sysadmin rights and you have a file on a DBA's computer with the account name and password in clear text? If this gets in the wrong hands, it can be the key to a lot more access than you probably desire.

Moving logins by using SQL Server Integration Services (SQL Server only)

Since SQL Server 2008 R2, SQL Server Integration Services has shipped with a Transfer Logins task that you can use to move logins from one server to another, including between different versions of SQL Server.

You use SQL Server Data Tools to create a new SQL Server Integration Services project. As Figure 12-4 shows, this provides an in-the-box, do-it-yourself alternative to the steps that follow, which involve custom scripts to migrate permissions from one server to another. The task is highly configurable, allowing for both Windows- and SQL Server–authenticated logins to be created on the target instance, with their original SIDs if desired. A Fail/Replace/Skip option is provided for login names that already exist on the destination.

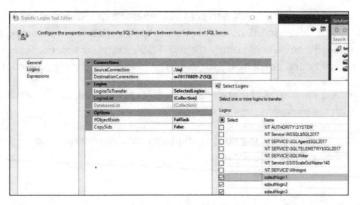

Figure 12-4 The Transfer Logins Task Editor dialog box in SQL Server Integration Services.

Logins created by the Transfer Logins task arrive at the destination disabled; you must turn them on again before you can use them. You can re-enable a login using the Security\Logins node in SSMS, or via the ALTER LOGIN statement as in:

```
ALTER LOGIN [Login1] ENABLE;
```

And can also generate a script to re-enable logins using:

```
--Script to reenable logins

SELECT 'ALTER LOGIN ' + QUOTENAME(name) + ' ENABLE;'

FROM   sys.sql_logins

WHERE  sql_logins.is_disabled = 1

AND name NOT LIKE 'NT SERVICE\%' --refine criteria as needed

AND is_disabled = 0;

--Beware: You should not necessarily enable all logins on a server. Make sure

-- to know the accounts you are enabling…
```

Keep in mind that this SQL Server Integration Services task does not move any of the role memberships or server permissions that these logins might have been granted on the source instance. Ideally these should be scripted and stored in source control to be able to recreate a server quickly (unlike Standard accounts, where you need passwords).

➤ To read more, see the sections "Moving server roles by using T-SQL (SQL Server only)" and "Moving server permissions by using T-SQL (SQL Server only)" later in this chapter.

Moving Windows-authenticated logins by using T-SQL (SQL Server only)

This is the easiest of the steps, assuming that the source and target SQL Server instance are in the same domain. Moving Windows-authenticated logins is as easy as scripting out the CREATE LOGIN statements for each login.

You do not necessarily need to use Object Explorer in SQL Server Management Studio for this operation. The system catalog view sys.server_principals contains the list of Windows-authenticated logins (types 'U' for Windows user, and 'G' for Windows group). The default_database_name and default_language_name are also provided and you can script them with the login.

Here's a sample script:

```
--Create script for windows logins to transfer

SELECT CONCAT('CREATE LOGIN ', QUOTENAME(name) +

    ' FROM WINDOWS WITH DEFAULT_DATABASE =' + QUOTENAME(default_database_name)+

    ', DEFAULT_LANGUAGE = '+ QUOTENAME(default_language_name)) + ';'
    AS CreateTSQL_Source

FROM sys.server_principals

WHERE type_desc in ('WINDOWS_LOGIN','WINDOWS_GROUP')

AND name NOT LIKE 'NT SERVICE\%'

AND is_disabled = 0

ORDER BY name, type_desc;
```

As in the previous section, keep in mind that this script does not generate T-SQL for any of the role memberships or server permissions that these logins might have been granted on the source instance. These should be maintained in a script in source control

Moving SQL Server–authenticated logins by using T-SQL (SQL Server only)

A time-honored reference for this task has been made available by Microsoft for years yet was never implemented with the SQL Server product itself. Since roughly 2000, many DBAs have referenced Microsoft support article 918992, "How to transfer logins and passwords between instances of SQL Server" (*https://support.microsoft.com/help/918992/*), which provides scripts to create a pair of stored procedures, sp_hexadecimal and sp_help_revlogin.

> ### NOTE
> Keep in mind if you can script out logins with passwords that someone with a copy of your database can do the same, giving them all they need to access your server.

With the aid of these stored procedures, it is possible to generate a hash of a SQL Server–authenticated password with its login and then re-create the SQL Server–authenticated login on another server with the same password. It is not possible to reverse-engineer the SQL Server–authenticated login password, but you can re-create it without the need to change dependent application connection strings.

But don't stop there! These stored procedures only re-create the SQL Server–authenticated logins; they do not re-create any of the role memberships or server permissions that those logins might have been granted on the source instance. In the next two sections, we discuss moving server roles and server permissions.

Moving server roles by using T-SQL (SQL Server only)

If you do not keep your server role permissions managed in a script, you ought to. And if you need to build that script, or need to move accounts to a new server you can use the following script instead of clicking through the dialog boxes for each role.

The following script retrieves server role membership via SQL Server catalog views. Here's a sample script, note that it includes options to add logins to server roles.

```
--SERVER LEVEL ROLES

SELECT DISTINCT

 CONCAT('ALTER SERVER ROLE ',  QUOTENAME(R.NAME) , ' ADD MEMBER ' , QUOTENAME(M.NAME) )
AS CREATETSQL

FROM SYS.SERVER_ROLE_MEMBERS AS RM

INNER JOIN SYS.SERVER_PRINCIPALS R ON RM.ROLE_PRINCIPAL_ID = R.PRINCIPAL_ID

INNER JOIN SYS.SERVER_PRINCIPALS M ON RM.MEMBER_PRINCIPAL_ID = M.PRINCIPAL_ID

WHERE R.IS_DISABLED = 0 AND M.IS_DISABLED = 0 -- IGNORE DISABLED ACCOUNTS

AND M.NAME NOT IN ('DBO', 'SA'); -- IGNORE BUILT-IN ACCOUNTS
```

Moving server permissions by using T-SQL (SQL Server only)

Moving server permissions can be extremely time consuming if you choose to do so by identifying them on the Securables page of each SQL Server Login Properties dialog box.

Instead, we advise that you script the permissions to re-create on the destination server by using catalog views. Ideally, too, the output of this script should be a placed in source control. Security should not be given out without some minimal review process to make sure that security matches what the agreed upon security says it should be.

Here is a script that will output a script of your permissions to groups:

```
--SERVER LEVEL SECURITY

SELECT    RM.state_desc + N' ' + RM.permission_name + CASE WHEN E.name IS NOT NULL

                                        THEN 'ON ENDPOINT::[' + E.name + '] '

                                                ELSE "

                                        END + N' TO '

        + CAST(QUOTENAME(U.name COLLATE DATABASE_DEFAULT) AS nvarchar(256)) + ';'
                        AS CREATETSQL

FROM      sys.server_permissions AS RM

        INNER JOIN sys.server_principals AS U

            ON RM.grantee_principal_id = U.principal_id

        LEFT OUTER JOIN sys.endpoints AS E

            ON E.endpoint_id = RM.major_id

                AND RM.class_desc = 'ENDPOINT'

--NOTE: this ignores many of the built in accounts, but if you have made changes to
--these accounts you may need to make changes to the WHERE clause

WHERE     U.name NOT LIKE '##%' -- IGNORE SYSTEM ACCOUNTS

    AND U.name NOT IN ( 'DBO', 'SA','public' ) -- IGNORE BUILT-IN ACCOUNTS

    AND U.name NOT LIKE 'NT SERVICE%'

    AND U.name NOT LIKE 'NT AUTHORITY%'

ORDER BY RM.permission_name, U.name;
```

Moving Azure SQL Database logins

It is not possible to use sp_hexadecimal and sp_help_revlogin against a Azure SQL Database server for SQL Server–authenticated logins. Scripting an Azure SQL Database login from SQL Server Management Studio obfuscates any password information, just as it does on a SQL Server instance.

And because you do not have access to sys.server_principals, sys.server_role_members, or sys.server_permissions, scripting these server-level permissions in Azure SQL Database isn't possible. (The system catalog view sys.server_principals is a dependent of sp_help_revlogin.)

Further, creating a login with a password HASH is not supported in Azure SQL Database.

The solution for migrating Azure SQL Database password-based logins from one server to another is to have a script for your special logins, and to re-create other logins on the destination server with a new secure password and have the users change the password when they use them.

The three types of Azure-authenticated principals are actually stored in the Azure SQL database, not at the Azure SQL server level, and are administered via the Azure portal. Like other database users and permissions, you can move those principals to a destination server along with the database itself.

Other security objects to move

Do not forget to move other server-level objects to the destination server, as appropriate.

Other security objects include Linked Server connections and SQL Server Audits, for which you can generate scripts, albeit without passwords in the case of linked servers. Given this, it is definitely advantageous to securely store your linked server creation scripts with their passwords.

You also should re-create SQL Server credentials and any corresponding proxies in use by SQL Server Agent on the destination server, although you cannot script credentials (thankfully, in terms of security, you must re-create them manually). You can script proxies in SQL Server Agent by using SQL Server Management Studio, and you should re-create them, including their assigned subsystems.

Alternative migration approaches

There is no easy way to accomplish this goal within the SQL Server Management Studio dialog boxes or to "generate scripts" of all SQL Server server-level security.

There are some third-party products available to accomplish the task. There is also a free package of Windows PowerShell cmdlets available, including some designed to assist with security migrations. You can find these in the dbatools free open source GPL-licensed Windows PowerShell project, which is available at *http://www.dbatools.io*.

If your SQL Server resides on a VM, performing a clone of the instance at the VM level might provide some transportability for the VM from one environment to another, to bypass the process of rebuilding a SQL Server instance altogether. For version upgrades, hardware changes, or partial migrations, a VM-level clone is obviously not a solution.

As has been previously, and can't be said enough, the number one method of being ready for a migration is having idempotent scripts to recreate pretty much all of your security at the server level, rather than trying to recreate a server from the 1000s of independent changes that were made over time.

Moving the master database

There is also one more potential SQL Server-based method of server login information migration that is no less complex or troublesome. If you are moving from the exact same version of SQL Server to another, a backup and restore of the master database from one SQL Server instance to another is a potential, albeit not particularly recommended, solution. (This obviously does not apply to Azure SQL Database.)

Restoring a master database from one server to another involves myriad potential changes to server-specific encryption keys, service account, user permissions, and server identification information. These changes might or might not be supported configuration changes. The process is not outlined in any support documentation, and we do not recommend it.

Keep in mind that a migration of the master database is advisable only when the destination server of the restored database has the identical volume letters and NTFS permissions, access to the same service accounts, in addition to the same SQL Server version and edition.

Saving the day with the Dedicated Administrator Connection

The Dedicated Administrator Connection (DAC) is an admin-only reserved connection into the SQL Server instance or Azure SQL Database for use as an emergency method to authenticate to the server when some problematic condition is otherwise preventing authentication.

Example uses include misconfiguration of security, misconfiguration of the Resource Governor, misconfiguration of prompts created FOR LOGON, or other interesting conditions that block even members of the sysadmin server role.

Only one member at a time of the server sysadmin role can connect using the DAC, similar to a database in single-user mode. Do not attempt to connect to the DAC via Object Explorer in SQL Server Management Studio. (Object Explorer cannot connect to the DAC, by design.)

The DAC also has resource limitations intended to limit the impact of DAC commands. You will not be able to perform all administrative tasks through the DAC; for example, you cannot issue BACKUP or RESTORE commands from the DAC. You should instead use the DAC only for diagnostic and remediation of the issues that prevent normal access, and then return to a normal connection. Do not use the DAC to carry out long-running queries against user data, DBCC CHECKDB, or to query the dm_db_index_physical_stats DMO.

When connecting to a database in Azure SQL Database with the DAC, you must specify the database name in your connection string or connection dialog box. Because you cannot change database contexts with the USE syntax in Azure SQL Database, you should always make connections directly to the desired database in Azure SQL Database, via the database or initial catalog parameters of the connection string.

There are several ways to sign in to a SQL Server instance or Azure SQL Database using the DAC via a login that is a member of the sysadmin role:

- In SQL Server Management Studio, open a new query or change the connection of a query, providing the servername as usual, but preceded by `ADMIN:`

  For example:

  ```
  ADMIN:servername
  ```

  Or, for a named instance (ensure that the SQL browser is running):

  ```
  ADMIN:servername\instancename
  ```

- From a command prompt, you can connect to the DAC via `sqlcmd` with the parameter `-A`; for example:

  ```
  C:\Users\Katie>sqlcmd -S servername -A
  ```

  Or, for a named instance (ensure that the SQL Browser Service is running):

  ```
  C:\Users\Katie>sqlcmd -S servername\instancename -A
  ```

- In SQL Server Management Studio, change a query window to SQLCMD mode, and then use the following query:

  ```
  :CONNECT ADMIN:servername
  ```

  Or, for a named instance (ensure that the SQL browser is running):

  ```
  :CONNECT ADMIN:servername\instancename
  ```

- In Windows PowerShell, the `DedicatedAdministratorConnection` parameter of the `Invoke-SQLCMD` cmdlet provides a connection to the DAC. For example:

  ```
  Invoke-SQLCmd -ServerInstance servername -Database master -Query
  "Select @@Servername" -DedicatedAdministratorConnection
  ```

  Or, for a named instance (ensure that the SQL browser is running):

  ```
  Invoke-SQLCmd -ServerInstance servername\instnacename -Database master -Query
  "Select @@Servername" -DedicatedAdministratorConnection
  ```

Allowing remote DAC connections

By default, DAC connections are only allowed locally. You can use the Surface Area Configuration dialog box in the Facets section of SQL Server Management Studio to allow remote DAC connections via the `RemoteDacEnabled` setting. You also can use `sp_configure` to turn on the Remote Admin Connections option.

We recommend that you do so because it proves invaluable to gain access to a SQL Server when remote desktop protocol or similar technologies are unable to connect to the Windows host of the SQL Server instance. Turning on the Remote DAC does not require a service restart.

The endpoint port that SQL Server uses to listen to DACs is announced in the SQL Server error log upon startup; for example, you will see this shortly after the SQL Server service starts: "Dedicated admin connection support was established for listening locally on port 1434." This is the default port for default instances, whereas named instances will use a randomly-assigned port, changed each time the service is started.

Connecting to the DAC remotely with SQL Server Management Studio is also possible by addressing the port number of the DAC instead of the ADMIN: syntax. For example, providing a connection string in SQL Server Management Studio to *servername\instancename*,49902 connects to the DAC endpoint.

Protecting data through encryption, privacy and auditing

Security has become incredibly important to private industry and the public sector. The news shows that the number of leaks and hacks of sensitive information is increasing almost daily, and we data professionals are at the forefront of securing this information. Along with the technical features built into SQL Server and Azure SQL Database, organizations should embrace the guidelines in privacy laws worldwide for handling and managing customer information.

Continuing on from Chapter 12, "Administering security and permissions," which focuses on authorization, this chapter covers features in the Database Engine and the underlying operating system (OS) that help you to secure your server and the databases that reside on it.

We begin with privacy, and how it guides the responsibilities of the data professional. Then we get into the technical details of what it means to encrypt data, looking at the different features in SQL Server and Azure SQL Database that help you achieve and maintain a more secure environment. We also look at securing the network, the OS, and the database itself right down to the column and row level.

Throughout the chapter you should be thinking about *defense in depth*, by combining different features and strategies to protect your data and minimize the fallout if your data is stolen.

Sample scripts in this chapter, and all scripts for this book, are all available for download at *https://www.MicrosoftPressStore.com/SQLServer2019InsideOut/downloads*.

Privacy in the modern era

A chapter about protecting your data estate is incomplete without discussing external policies and procedures to ensure that protection. This section is provided as a reminder to keep abreast of current local and international legislation, using one particular regulation as a reference.

CAUTION

This section does not constitute legal advice. Consult your own legal counsel for more information.

General Data Protection Regulation (GDPR)

On May 25th, 2018, the General Data Protection Regulation (GDPR) came into effect in the European Union (EU). It provides for the protection of any *personal data* associated with *data subjects* (EU residents) located in the EU. Organizations across the world may be affected if they process personal data belonging to EU residents.

Any time your organization deals with an EU resident's personal data, you are responsible for ensuring it is managed according to that legislation. The good news is, this is a business problem, not a technical one. Your organization must develop policies and procedures to enforce the requirements of the GDPR, and you as a data professional can create technical solutions to satisfy those procedures.

Responsibility of data professionals

What follows are highlights of these procedures as they might apply to data professionals. This is not an exhaustive list.

Pseudonymization

- **Problem statement.**   Personal data must be transformed in a way that the resulting data cannot be attributed to a data subject without additional information.

- **Proposed solution.**   This can be implemented through encryption. We cover this in detail in the next section, "Introducing security principles and protocols," including the various methods to ensure that sensitive data is not made available to privileged users and administrators.

Right of access

- **Problem statement.**   A data subject may request access to their personal data.

- **Proposed solution.**   This can be achieved through standard Transact-SQL (T-SQL) queries, assuming that you have taken measures to handle encryption of the data and authentication of the data subject appropriately. We cover *authentication* and *authorization* in Chapter 2, "Introducing database server components."

Right to erasure

- **Problem statement.**   A data subject may request erasure of their personal data.

- **Proposed solution.**   In order to erase personal data, you need to identify it. This can become arduous with more than a few databases. Organizations may not appreciate the numerous environments in which they store personal data, including scaled out applications, data warehouses, data marts, data lakes, and email. Fortunately, you can catalog and tag sensitive data in SQL Server and Azure SQL Database.

> ## Inside OUT
>
> *Is there an easy way to identify sensitive data?*
>
> You can use the Data Discovery and Classification feature in SQL Server Management Studio to identify columns that should be encrypted.
>
> Once the classification engine has scanned your database, you can apply these classifications using Always Encrypted or dynamic data masking, and also give columns persistent labels (such as Confidential).
>
> Read more in Microsoft Docs about Data and Classification for SQL Server at *https://docs.microsoft.com/sql/relational-databases/security/sql-data-discovery-and-classification*. For Azure, including SQL Database and Synapse (previously known as Data Warehouse) you can read more at *https://docs.microsoft.com/azure/sql-database/sql-database-data-discovery-and-classification*.

Introducing security principles and protocols

Information security is about finding a balance between the value of your data and the cost of protecting it. Ultimately the business and technical decisionmakers in your organization make this call, but at least you have the technical tools available to undertake these measures to protect yourself. In other words, you should not leave security solely to the IT department.

SQL Server implements a number of security principles through cryptography and other means, which you can use to build up layers of security to protect your environment.

Computer cryptography is implemented through some intense mathematics that use very large prime numbers, though we won't delve deeply into specifics. This section explains various security principles and goes into some detail about encryption. It also covers network protocols and how cryptography works. This will aid your understanding of how SQL Server and network security protect your data. Keep in mind that encryption is *not* the only way to protect data.

Securing your environment with defense in depth

Securing a SQL Server or Azure SQL Database environment requires a number of protections that work together to make it difficult for an attacker to get in, snoop around, steal or modify data, and then get out.

Defense in depth is about building layers of protection around your data and environment. These measures might not be completely effective on their own, but work well as part of an overall strategy, because each layer helps weaken and isolate an attack long enough to allow you to respond.

Perimeter security should include logical and physical segmentation; for example, keeping sensitive servers and applications on a separate part of the network, perhaps off-premises in a separate datacenter or in the Azure cloud. You would then want to protect these connections; for example, by using a Virtual Private Network (VPN).

You should have a firewall and other network defenses to protect against *external network attacks*. From a physical aspect, don't let just anyone plug a laptop into an unattended network point, or allow them to connect to your corporate wireless network and have access to the production environment.

From within the network, you need to implement *authentication* (who you are) and *authorization* (what you can do), preferably through Active Directory, which is available on both Windows and Linux.

On the servers themselves, you should ensure that the file system is locked down with a policy that does at least the following:

- Enforce permissions and modern protocols for files, folders, and network shares

  ➤ **SMB 1.0 (also known as CIFS) is a deprecated file sharing protocol which Microsoft recommends removing from your environment. For more information about disabling SMB 1, visit** *https://techcommunity.microsoft.com/t5/Storage-at-Microsoft/Stop-using-SMB1/ba-p/425858.* **SMB 2.0 and higher are still supported.**

- Deny access to unauthorized users

- Deny access to untrusted storage devices

- Ensure service accounts do not have system administrator privileges

- Encrypt the file system (optional but recommended)

SQL Server permissions should be set correctly so that the service account does not have administrative privileges on the server, and database files, transaction logs, and backups cannot be accessed by unauthorized users.

On the *application* side, you can implement coding practices that protect against things like SQL injection attacks, and you can implement encryption in your database (and backup files).

  ➤ **The SQL Vulnerability Assessment tool in SQL Server Management Studio can help identify possible security vulnerabilities. Read more about it in Chapter 12, or on Microsoft Docs at** *https://docs.microsoft.com/sql/relational-databases/security/sql-vulnerability-assessment.*

CHAPTER 13

Inside OUT

What is SQL injection?

One of the most prevalent attack vectors for a database is to manipulate the software application or website to attack the underlying database.

SQL injection is a technique that exploits applications that do not *sanitize* input data. A carefully crafted Uniform Resource Identifier (URI) in a web application, for example, can manipulate the database in ways that a naïve application developer is not expecting.

If a web application exposes database keys in the Uniform Resource Locator (URL), for example, an industrious person can craft a URL to read protected information from a table by changing the key value. An attacker might be able to access sensitive data or modify the database itself by appending Transact-SQL (T-SQL) commands to the end of a string to perform malicious actions on a table or database.

In a worst-case scenario, a SQL injection attack would take a few seconds, the entire database could be *exfiltrated* (data removed without your knowledge), and you might hear about it only when your organization is blackmailed, or sensitive data is leaked.

You can avoid SQL injection by ensuring that all data input is escaped, sanitized, and validated. To be very safe, all SQL Server queries should use parameterization.

You can read more about defending against SQL injection attacks on Microsoft Docs at *https://docs.microsoft.com/sql/relational-databases/security/sql-injection*.

The Open Web Application Security Project (OWASP) is also an excellent resource to identify and defend against potential vulnerabilities, including SQL injection. You can visit the OWASP website at *https://www.owasp.org*.

CHAPTER 13

The difference between hashing and encryption

In a security context, data that is converted in a repeatable manner to an unreadable, fixed-length format using a cryptographic algorithm and that *cannot* be converted back to its original form is said to be *hashed*.

Data that is converted to an unreadable form that *can* be converted back to its original form using a *cryptographic key* is said to be *encrypted*.

Cryptographic algorithms can be defeated in certain ways, the most common being *brute-force* and *dictionary* attacks. Let's take a quick look at each one:

- **Brute-force attack.**   In a brute-force attack, the attacking code checks every possible combination of a password, passphrase, or encryption key against the hashing or encryption service, until it finally arrives at the correct value. Depending on the type of algorithm and the length of the password, passphrase, or key, this can take anywhere from a few milliseconds to many years.

- **Dictionary attack.**   A dictionary attack is a lot faster to perform, so an attacker would attempt this first. Dictionary attacks take a list of words from a dictionary (which can include common words, passwords, and phrases) and use these against the hashing or encryption service. Dictionary attacks take advantage of the fact that we are bad at remembering passwords and tend to use common words.

As computers become more powerful and parallelized, the length of time to run a brute-force attack continues to decrease. Countermeasures do exist to protect against some of these attacks, and some encryption systems cannot be defeated by a brute-force attack. These countermeasures are beyond the scope of this book, but it is safe to say that sufficiently complex algorithms and long encryption keys will take several years to compromise.

> ➤ Security expert Bruce Schneier suggests that an algorithm with a 512-bit block and key size, and 128 rounds, will be sufficiently complex for the foreseeable future. Schneier's essay "Cryptography after the Aliens Land" is available at https://www.schneier.com/essays/archives/2018/09/cryptography_after_t.html.

Hashing

A *cryptographic hash function* (an algorithm) takes *variable-length data* (usually a password) and applies a mathematical formula to convert it to a fixed size, or *hash value*.

This is the recommended method of securing passwords. When a password has been hashed correctly, it cannot be decrypted into its original form. Used with a random *salt* (a random string applied along with the hash function), this results in passwords that are impossible to reconstruct, even if the same password is used by different people.

To validate a password, it must be hashed using the same hash function again, with the same salt, and compared against the stored hash value.

Because hash values have a fixed size (the length depends on the algorithm used), there is a possibility that two sets of data (two different passwords) can result in the same hash value. This is called a *hash collision*, and it is more likely to occur with shorter hash value lengths. This is why longer hashes are better.

NOTE

Make sure that you use passwords that are at least 15 characters in length and, preferably, more than 20 characters. You should use a password manager so that you don't need to memorize multiple passwords. Brute-force attacks take exponentially longer for each additional character you choose, so don't be shy about using phrases or sentences either (with spaces). Password length matters more than its complexity.

Inside OUT

Why should you use a salt, and what is a rainbow table?

If you don't use a random salt, the same hash value will be created each time the hash function is applied against a particular password. Additionally, if more than one person uses the same password, the same hash value will be repeated.

Imagine that an attacker has a list of commonly used passwords and knows which hash function you used to hash the passwords in your database. This person could build a catalog of possible hash values for each password in that list. This catalog is called a *rainbow table*.

It becomes very simple to just look up the hash values in your database against the rainbow table and deduce which password was used. Thus, you should always use a random salt when hashing passwords in your database. Rainbow tables become all but useless in this case.

Encryption

Data encryption is the process of converting human-readable data, or *plain text*, into an encrypted form by applying a cryptographic algorithm called a key (the *cipher*) to the data. This process makes the encrypted data (the *ciphertext*) unreadable without the appropriate key to unlock it. Encryption facilitates both the secure *transmission* and *storage* of data.

Over the years, many ciphers have been created and subsequently defeated (*cracked*) because those algorithms were considered weak. In many cases, this is because both CPUs and Graphics Processing Units (GPUs) have become faster and more powerful, reducing the length of time it takes to perform brute-force and other attacks. In other cases, the implementation of the cryptographic function was flawed, and attacks on the implementation itself have been successful.

Inside OUT

Why are GPUs used for cracking passwords?

A GPU is designed to process identical instructions (but not necessarily the same data) in parallel across hundreds or thousands of cores, ostensibly for rendering images on a display many times per second.

This coincides with the type of work required to crack passwords through brute force, because those thousands of cores can each perform a single arithmetic operation per clock cycle through a method called *pipelining*.

Because GPUs can operate at billions of cycles per second (GHz), this results in hundreds of millions of hashes per second. Without a salt, many password hashes can be cracked in a few milliseconds, regardless of the algorithm used.

A primer on protocols and transmitting data

Accessing a database involves the transmission of data over a network interface, which you need to do in a secure manner. A *protocol* is a set of instructions for transmitting that information over a specific network *port*.

A port is one of 65,535 possible connections per protocol that can be made to a networked device. The most common protocol for SQL Server is *Transmission Control Protocol* (TCP). It is always associated with an IP address and a port number.

Inside OUT

What's with all these protocols and ports?

Official and unofficial standards over the years have resulted in a set of commonly used protocols and ports. Aside from TCP, a common protocol is User Datagram Protocol, or UDP. A majority of current network traffic makes use of these two protocols.

For example:

- TCP ports 1433 and 1434 – SQL Server
- TCP ports 2382 and 2383 – SQL Server Analysis Services
- TCP port 80 – HTTP
- TCP port 443 – HTTPS

- TCP port 22 – Secure Shell (SSH)
- UDP port 53 – Domain Name System (DNS)

The Internet protocol suite

To discuss security on a network, you need to understand cryptographic protocols. To discuss the network itself, you need to discuss the biggest network of them all: the Internet.

The Internet is a network of networks (it literally means "between networks") that transmits data using a suite of protocols, including TCP, which sits on top of Internet Protocol (IP). TCP/IP is the most common network protocol stack in use today. Most of the services on the Internet, as well as local networks, rely on TCP/IP.

NOTE

The full Internet protocol suite comprises TCP, IP, Address Resolution Protocol (ARP), Internet Control Message Protocol (ICMP), UDP, and Internet Group Management Protocol (IGMP). All of these are required to implement the full TCP/IP stack.

IP is a connectionless protocol, meaning that each individual unit of transfer, also known as a network packet or *datagram*, contains the data itself (the *payload*) and a *header* that indicates where it came from and where it needs to go (the routing information).

IP network packets might be delivered out of order, with no delivery guarantee at all. This low overhead makes the protocol fast and allows packets to be sent to several recipients at once (*multicast* or *broadcast*).

To mitigate this, TCP provides the necessary instructions for reliability, sequencing (the order of packets), and data integrity. If a packet is not received by the recipient, or a packet is received out of order, TCP can resubmit the data again using IP as its delivery mechanism.

Versions of IP in use today

Version 4 of the Internet Protocol (IPv4) has a 32-bit address space, which provides nearly 4.3 billion addresses (2^{32}, or approximately 4.3×10^9). Unfortunately, when this version was first proposed in September 1981, very few people predicted that the Internet would be as large and important as it is today. With billions of humans online, and billions of devices connected, the available IPv4 address space is all but depleted.

➤ **You can read the Internet Protocol, Version 4 Specification, known as Internet Engineering Task Force Request For Comments #791, at *https://tools.ietf.org/html/rfc791*.**

Tricks like Network Address Translation (NAT), which uses private IP addresses behind a router with a single valid public IP address representing that entire network, have held off the depletion over the years, but time and address space has run out.

Version 6 of the Internet Protocol (IPv6) has an address space of 128 bits which provides more than 340 undecillion (340 trillion trillion) addresses (2^{128}, or approximately 3.4×10^{38}). This number is so staggeringly huge that, even with networks and devices being added every minute, including the upward trend of the Internet of Things, each of these devices can have its own unique address on the Internet without ever running out of addresses.

➤ You can read the Internet Protocol, Version 6 Specification, known as Internet Engineering Task Force Request For Comments #8200, at *https://tools.ietf.org/html/rfc8200*.

Inside OUT

What is the Internet of Things?

Until a few years ago, computing devices such as servers, desktop computers, laptops, and mobile devices have been the only devices connected to the Internet.

Today, millions of objects embedded with electronics have found their way online, including coffee machines, security cameras, home automation systems, vehicle trackers, heart monitors, industrial measurement devices, and many, many more.

Ignoring the fact that many of these devices should not have publicly accessible Internet addresses in the first place, the growth trend is exponential, with IPv6 making this massive growth possible.

Hybrid cloud platforms such as Azure have services dedicated to managing the communication and data requirements of these devices, including Azure SQL Database.

In fact, SQL Server itself can now run on an IoT edge device. For more information about Azure SQL Database Edge, visit *https://azure.microsoft.com/services/sql-database-edge*.

Making sense of an IP address

An IP address is displayed in a human-readable notation but is binary under the hood:

- **IPv4.** The address is broken up into four subclasses of decimal numbers, each subclass ranging from 0 to 255, and separated by a decimal point. For example, 52.178.167.109 is a valid IPv4 address.

- **IPv6.** The address is broken up into eight subclasses of hexadecimal numerals, each subclass being four digits wide, and separated by a colon. If a subclass contains all zeroes, it can be omitted. For example, 2001:d74f:e211:9840:0000:0000:0000:0000 is a valid IPv6 address that can be simplified to 2001:d74f:e211:9840:: with the zeroes omitted (note the double-colon at the end to indicate the omission).

➤ **You can read more about IPv6 address representation at** *http://www.ciscopress.com/articles/article.asp?p=2803866.*

NOTE

Hexadecimal is a counting system that uses all the decimal numbers plus the first six letters of the Latin alphabet, to represent the sixteen values between 0 and 15 (10 = A, 11 = B, 12 = C, 13 = D, 14 = E, 15 = F). Hex is used as a convenient way to describe binary values that would otherwise take up a lot of space to display.

Adoption of IPv6 across the Internet is taking decades, so a hybrid solution is currently in place by which IPv4 and IPv6 traffic is shared across compatible devices. If that doesn't sound like enough of a headache, let's add routing into the mix.

Finding your way around the Internet

Routing between networks on the Internet is performed by the Border Gateway Protocol (BGP), which sits on top of TCP/IP.

BGP is necessary because there is no map of the Internet. Devices and entire networks appear and disappear all the time. BGP routes billions of network packets through millions of routers based on a best-guess scenario. Packets are routed based on trust: routers provide information to one another about the networks they control, and BGP implicitly trusts that information.

BGP is thus not secure, because it was designed solely to fix the scalability of the Internet, which was (and still is) growing exponentially. It was a "quick fix" that became part of the fabric of the infrastructure long before security was a concern.

Efforts to secure BGP have been slow. It is therefore critical to assume that your own Internet traffic will be hijacked at some point. When this happens, proper cryptography can prevent third parties from reading your data.

A brief overview of the World Wide Web

A lot of people conflate the World Wide Web (the web) with the Internet, but the web is a single component of the greater Internet, along with email and other services that are still very much in use today (such as File Transfer Protocol and Voice over IP).

NOTE

Based on publicly available information, Microsoft processes more than 500 billion emails per month through its various services.

The web uses the Hypertext Transport Protocol (HTTP), which sits on top of TCP/IP. A web server provides mixed media content (text, graphics, video, and other media) in Hypertext Markup Language (HTML) format, which is transmitted using HTTP and then interpreted and rendered by a web browser.

The web grew quickly for two reasons. First, the Internet became commercialized after originally being an academic and military project for several decades. The web itself then became wildly popular because of the introduction of the first graphical web browser, NCSA Mosaic, in the 1990s. The spiritual successors to Mosaic were Netscape Navigator and Microsoft Internet Explorer, during a period of internet history known as the "browser wars."

➤ You can learn more about the commercial beginnings of the web and the so-called "Internet Era," in McCullough, B, *How the Internet Happened: From Netscape to the iPhone* (Liveright, 2018), or by listening to the Internet History Podcast, available at *http://www. internethistorypodcast.com*.

Modern web browsers include Microsoft Edge, Google Chrome, Mozilla Firefox, and Apple Safari.

NOTE

The modern web browser is hugely complex, doing a lot more than rendering HTML, but for the purposes of this discussion and in the interest of brevity, we gloss over those extras.

How does protocol encryption fit into this?

The explosive adoption of the web in the 1990s prompted public-facing organizations to start moving their sales online into electronic commerce, or *e-commerce*, ventures, which created the need for secure transactions. Consumers wanted to use their credit cards safely and securely so that they could shop and purchase goods without leaving the comfort of their homes.

Remember that the Internet is built on the Internet Protocol, which is stateless and has routing information in the header of every single packet. This means that anyone can place a hardware device (or software) in the packet stream, do something with the packet, and then pass it on (modified or not) to the destination without the sender or recipient having any knowledge of this interaction. Because this is a fundamental building block of a packet-switching network, it's very difficult to secure properly.

As we discussed earlier, encryption transforms your data into an unreadable format. Now, if someone connected to the same network were to intercept encrypted packets, that person couldn't see what you're doing. The payload of each packet would appear garbled and unreadable, unless this person has the key to decrypt it.

A secure version of HTTP was created by Netscape Communications in 1994—called HTTPS—which stands for HTTP Secure, or HTTP over Secure Sockets Layer (SSL). Over the years, the moniker of HTTPS has remained, but it has come to be known as HTTP over Transport Layer Security (TLS) as standards improved.

When we talk about data moving over the network, that usually means TCP/IP is involved, and we need to transmit that data securely.

Symmetric and asymmetric encryption

You can encrypt data in two ways: symmetric and asymmetric. Each has its advantages and disadvantages.

Symmetric encryption (shared secret)

A secret key—usually a password, passphrase, or random string of characters—is used to encrypt data with a particular cryptographic algorithm. This secret key is shared between the sender and the recipient, and both parties can encrypt and decrypt all content by using this secret key.

If the key is accidentally leaked to a third party, the encrypted data could be intercepted, decrypted, modified, and re-encrypted again, without either the sender or recipient being aware of this. This type of attack is known as a *man-in-the-middle* attack.

Asymmetric encryption (public key)

Also known as public key encryption (PKE). A key–pair is generated, comprising a private key and a public key, and the public key can be widely distributed. The *public key* is used to encrypt data, and the *private key* is used to decrypt that data.

The advantage is that the private key never needs to be shared, which makes this method far more secure because only you can use your private key to decrypt the data. Unfortunately, asymmetric encryption requires a lot more processing power, plus both parties need their own key–pairs.

Inside OUT

What encryption method should you use for SQL Server?

For practical purposes, SQL Server manages the keys internally for both symmetric and asymmetric encryption.

Owing to the much larger overhead of asymmetric encryption however, you should encrypt any data in SQL Server that you want to protect by using symmetric key encryption.

Using the encryption hierarchy, layers above the data can be protected using passwords or asymmetric keys (we discuss this in the next section).

Digital certificates

Public keys require discoverability, which means that they need to be made publicly available. If a sending party wants to sign a message for the receiving party, the burden is on the sender to locate the recipient's public key in order to sign a message.

For small-scale communications between two private entities, this might be done by sharing their public keys between each other.

For larger-scale communications with many senders and one recipient (such as a web or database server, for example), a certificate authority can provide the public key through a digital certificate, which the recipient (the website or database administrator) can install directly on the server.

This certificate serves as an electronic signature for the recipient, which includes its public key. The authority, known as a Certification Authority, is trusted by both the sender and the recipient, and the sender can verify that the recipient is indeed who it claims to be.

Digital certificates, also known as *Public Key Certificates*, are defined by the X.509 standard. Many protocols use this standard, including TLS and its predecessor, SSL.

> ➤ You can read more about how digital certificates and TLS relate to SQL Server and Azure SQL Database later in this chapter. The X.509 standard is available at *https://www.itu.int/rec/T-REC-X.509*.

Certification Authority

A Certification Authority (CA) is an organization or entity that issues digital certificates, which include the name of the owner, the owner's public key, and start and expiration dates.

The certificate is automatically revoked after it expires, and the CA can revoke any certificate before then.

For the certificate to be trusted, the CA itself must be trustworthy. It is the responsibility of the CA to verify the owner's identity so that any certificates issued in that owner's name can be trusted.

In recent years, several CAs have lost their trustworthy status, either because their verification process was flawed, or their signing algorithms were weak. Take care when choosing a CA for your digital certificates.

Protecting the data platform

You will use multiple layers of defense as you go down the stack of your data environment. Even if you are using virtual machines and containers in a cloud environment, the same principles apply.

Each layer protects the layer below it by using a combination of encryption keys (asymmetric and symmetric), certificates, and other obfuscation techniques. SQL Server provides features that protect sensitive data from unauthorized users, even if they manage the data. Azure SQL Database shares a lot in common with SQL Server, and it also has unique protections which we mention where applicable.

This section breaks down each layer into network, OS, the SQL Server instance, and finally the database itself, including columns and rows. Much of this hierarchy is encrypted by SQL Server, starting at the OS layer and working all the way down to individual cells in a table. Figure 13-1 shows this hierarchy.

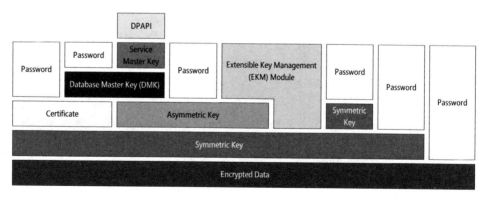

Figure 13-1   The SQL Server encryption hierarchy.

Securing the network with TLS

Data is in motion from the moment it is read from, or written to, the buffer pool in SQL Server or Azure SQL Database. *Data in motion* is data that the Database Engine provides over a network interface. Protecting data in motion requires a number of considerations, from perimeter security, to cryptographic protocols for the communication itself, and the authorization of the application or process accessing the data.

SQL Server protects data during transmission over a network connection using Transport Layer Security (TLS). Any network protocols and APIs involved must support encrypting and decrypting the data as it moves in and out of the buffer pool.

We touched briefly on TLS in the discussion about TCP/IP earlier in this chapter, but we did not go into much detail. TLS is a security layer on top of a transport layer, or *cryptographic protocol*. Most networks use the TCP/IP protocol stack, and TLS is designed to secure the traffic on TCP/IP-based networks.

Inside OUT

How do you import certificates into SQL Server?

SQL Server 2019 allows you to import your TLS certificates using SQL Server Configuration Manager.

Once you have opened Configuration Manager and expanded the SQL Server Network Configuration branch for your instance, right click on Protocols for `<InstanceName>` and select Properties. You will see an Import button, which will open the certificate import wizard. Follow the prompts and enter the appropriate credentials, confirm the addition of the certificate, and restart the instance.

After the restart, you can go back into the Properties to see your imported certificate. You can see the details by clicking the View button. You can then select the Force Encryption option on the Flags tab to force all traffic to use this certificate. Remember that changing the flag requires another SQL Server restart.

For more information about installing certificates in an availability group and a step by step guide, visit *https://docs.microsoft.com/sql/database-engine/configure-windows/manage-certificates*.

How TLS works?

With TLS protection, before two parties can exchange information, they need to mutually agree on the encryption key and the cryptographic algorithm to use, which is called a *key exchange* or *handshake*. TLS works with both symmetric and asymmetric encryption, which means that the encryption key could be a shared secret or a public key (usually with a certificate).

After the key exchange is done, the handshake is complete, and a secured communication channel allows traffic between the two parties to flow. This is how data in motion is protected from external attacks.

NOTE

Remember that longer keys mean better security. Public keys of 1,024 bits (128 bytes) are considered short these days, so some organizations now prefer 2,048-bit, or even 4,096-bit public key certificates for TLS.

A brief history of TLS

Just as earlier cryptographic protocols have been defeated or considered weak enough that they will eventually be defeated, so too have SSL and TLS had their challenges:

- The prohibition of SSL 2.0 is covered at *https://tools.ietf.org/html/rfc6176*.

- Known attacks on TLS are available at *https://tools.ietf.org/html/rfc7457*.

TLS 1.2 was defined in 2008 and is the latest commonly available public version (TLS 1.3 was only approved in March 2018). TLS 1.2 is vulnerable to certain attacks like its predecessors, but as long as older encryption algorithms are not used (for instance 3DES, RC4, and IDEA), it is good enough while we wait for TLS 1.3 to propagate.

Where possible, you should be using TLS 1.2 everywhere. SQL Server ships with TLS 1.0, 1.1, and 1.2 support out of the box, so you will need to turn off 1.0 and 1.1 at the OS level to ensure that you use TLS 1.2.

> ➤ You can see how to turn off older versions of TLS in the Microsoft Knowledge Base article at *https://support.microsoft.com/help/3135244*.

Data protection from the OS

At the top of the encryption hierarchy on a server, protecting everything below it, is the OS. Windows Server provides an Application Programming Interface (API) for system-level and user-level processes to take advantage of data protection (encryption) on the file system.

In other words, SQL Server and other applications can make use of this data protection API to have Windows automatically encrypt data on the drive without having to encrypt data through other means.

SQL Server uses the Data Protection API (DPAPI) for Transparent Data Encryption (TDE).

Inside OUT

How does data protection work for SQL Server on Linux?

The mechanism that Microsoft created for getting SQL Server to run on Linux and Docker containers, is called the Platform Abstraction Layer (PAL). It aligns all code specific to the OS in one place, forming a bridge with the underlying platform.

All APIs, including file system and DPAPIs, are included in the PAL. This makes SQL Server 2019 entirely platform-agnostic.

To read more about the PAL, visit the official SQL Server Blog at *https://cloudblogs. microsoft.com/sqlserver/2016/12/16/sql-server-on-linux-how-introduction*.

The encryption hierarchy in detail

Each layer of the hierarchy protects the layer below it by using a combination of keys (asymmetric and symmetric) and certificates (refer to Figure 13-1).

Individual layers in the hierarchy can be accessed by a password at the very least, unless an Extensible Key Management (EKM) module is being used. The EKM module is a standalone device that holds symmetric and asymmetric keys outside of SQL Server.

The Database Master Key (DMK) is protected by the Service Master Key (SMK), and both of these are symmetric keys. The SMK is created when you install SQL Server and is protected by the DPAPI.

If you want to use TDE on your database (see the "Configuring TDE on a user database" section later in this chapter), it requires a symmetric key called the Database Encryption Key (DEK), which is protected by an asymmetric key in the EKM module or by a certificate through the DMK.

NOTE

Although we do not recommend 3DES for TLS, you can still use 3DES lower in the SQL Server security hierarchy for securing DEKs because these are protected by the SMK, the DMK, and a Certificate, or entirely by an HSM/EKM module like Key Vault (see "Using EKM modules with SQL Server" in the next section).

This layered approach helps to protect your data from falling into the wrong hands.

There are two considerations when deciding how to secure a SQL Server environment, which you can implement independently.

- **Data at rest.**   In the case of TDE, this is decrypting the data on a drive as it is read into the buffer pool and encrypting the data as it is flushed to a drive from the buffer pool. (You can also encrypt your storage layer independently from SQL Server, but this does not form part of the encryption hierarchy.)

- **Data in motion.**   Protecting the data during transmission over a network connection. Any network protocols and APIs involved must support encrypting and decrypting the data as it moves in and out of the buffer pool.

As mentioned previously, data is *in motion* from the moment it is read from or written to the buffer pool. Between the buffer pool and the underlying storage, data is considered to be *at rest*.

NOTE

TDE encrypts database backup files along with the data and transaction log files. The TDE feature is available with SQL Server Enterprise and Standard editions and Azure SQL Database.

Using EKM modules with SQL Server

Organizations might choose to take advantage of a separate security appliance called a Hardware Security Module (HSM) or EKM device to generate, manage, and store encryption keys for the network infrastructure outside of a SQL Server environment.

SQL Server can make use of these keys for internal use. The HSM/EKM device can be a hardware appliance, a USB device, a smart card, or even software, as long as it implements the Microsoft Cryptographic Application Programming Interface (MCAPI) provider.

EKM is an advanced SQL Server setting and is turned off by default. To use the key or keys from an HSM/EKM device, you need to turn on EKM by using the `sp_execute 'EKM provider enabled'` command with the appropriate parameter. Then, the device must be registered as an EKM module for use by SQL Server.

After the HSM/EKM device creates a key for use by SQL Server (for TDE, for instance), the device exports it securely into SQL Server via the MCAPI provider.

The module might support different types of authentication (Basic or Other), but only one of these types can be registered with SQL Server for that provider.

If the module supports Basic authentication (a user name and password combination), SQL Server uses a credential to provide transparent authentication to the module.

Inside OUT

What is a credential?

In SQL Server, a credential is a record of authentication information that the Database Engine uses to connect to external resources.

Credentials provide security details for processes to impersonate Windows users on a network, though they can also be used to connect to other services like Azure Storage and, of course, an HSM/EKM device.

Credentials that will be used by all databases can be created in the master database by using the CREATE CREDENTIAL command, or per individual database using the CREATE DATABASE SCOPED CREDENTIAL command.

Chapter 12 contains more information on logins, and Chapter 8, "Maintaining and monitoring SQL Server," goes into more detail about credentials.

> ➤ To read more about EKM in SQL Server, visit Microsoft Docs at *https://docs.microsoft.com/ sql/relational-databases/security/encryption/extensible-key-management-ekm*.

Cloud security with Azure Key Vault

You can use Azure Key Vault in addition to, or as a drop-in replacement of, a traditional HSM/ EKM device. Your SQL Server instance (whether on-premises or on a VM in the cloud) would require Internet access to the Key Vault.

Key Vault is implemented as an EKM provider inside SQL Server, using the SQL Server Connector (a standalone Windows application) as a bridge between Key Vault and the SQL Server instance. To make use of Key Vault, you must create the vault and associate it with a valid Azure Active Directory (Azure AD).

Begin by registering the SQL Server service principal name in Azure AD. After the service principal name is registered, you can install the SQL Server Connector and turn on EKM in SQL Server.

➤ You can read more about service principal names and Kerberos in Chapter 2.

You must then create a login that SQL Server will use for accessing Key Vault, and then map that login to a new credential that contains the Key Vault authentication information.

A step-by-step guide for this process is available on Microsoft Docs at *https://docs.microsoft.com/sql/relational-databases/security/encryption/ setup-steps-for-extensible-key-management-using-the-azure-key-vault.*

Master keys in the encryption hierarchy

Since SQL Server 2012, both the SMK and DMK are symmetric keys encrypted using the Advanced Encryption Standard (AES) cryptographic algorithm. AES is faster and more secure than Triple Data Encryption Standard (3DES), which was used in SQL Server prior to 2012.

NOTE

When you upgrade from an older version of SQL Server that was encrypted using 3DES, you must regenerate both the SMK and DMK to upgrade them to AES.

The SMK

The SMK is at the top of the encryption hierarchy in SQL Server. It is automatically generated the first time the SQL Server instance starts, and it is encrypted by the DPAPI in combination with the local machine key (which itself is created when Windows Server is installed). The key is based on the Windows credentials of the SQL Server service account and the computer credentials. (On Linux, the local machine key is part of the PAL used by SQL Server.)

NOTE

You will get a new SMK if you change the service account that runs SQL Server, but it is considered "self-healing," meaning that you don't have to do anything else once it has changed.

Inside OUT

What is the difference between DES, 3DES, and AES?

Data Encryption Standard (DES) is a symmetric key algorithm developed in the 1970s, with a key length of 56 bits. It has been considered cryptographically broken since 1998. In 2012 it was possible to recover a DES key in less than 24 hours if both a plain-text and cipher-text pair were known.

> Its successor, 3DES, applies the DES algorithm three times (each time with a different DES key) to each block of data being encrypted. However, with current consumer hardware, the entire 3DES key space can be searched, making it cryptographically weak.
>
> AES (Advanced Encryption Standard) uses keys that are 128, 192, or 256 bits in length. Longer keys are much more difficult to crack using brute-force methods, so AES is considered safe for the foreseeable future. It also happens to be much faster than 3DES.

If you need to restore or regenerate an SMK, you first must decrypt the entire SQL Server encryption hierarchy, which is a resource-intensive operation. You should perform this activity only in a scheduled maintenance window. If the key has been compromised, however, you shouldn't wait for that maintenance window.

CAUTION

It is essential that you back up the SMK to a file and then copy it securely to an off-premises location. Losing this key will result in total data loss if you need to recover a database or environment.

To back up the SMK, you can use the T-SQL script shown that follows, but be sure to choose a randomly generated password. The password will be required for restoring or regenerating the key at a later stage. Keep the password separate from the SMK backup file so that they cannot be used together if your secure backup location is compromised. Ensure that the folder on the drive is adequately secured. After you back up the key, transfer and store it securely in an off-premises location.

```
BACKUP SERVICE MASTER KEY TO FILE = 'c:\SecureLocation\service_master_key'

    ENCRYPTION BY PASSWORD = '<UseAReallyStrongPassword>';

GO
```

The DMK

The DMK is used to protect asymmetric keys and private keys for digital certificates stored in the database. A copy of the DMK is stored in the database for which it is used as well as in the master database. The copy is automatically updated by default if the DMK changes. This allows SQL Server to automatically decrypt information as required. A DMK is required for each user database that will make use of TDE.

Refer back to Figure 13-1 to see how the DMK is protected by the SMK.

> **CAUTION**
>
> Don't forget to back up the DMK to a file, as well, and copy it securely to an off-premises location.

It is considered a security best practice to regenerate the DMK periodically to protect the server from brute-force attacks. The idea is that it will take longer for a brute-force attack to break the key than the length of time for which the key is in use.

For example, suppose that you encrypt your database with a DMK in January of this year. In the following July you regenerate the DMK, which will cause all keys for digital certificates to be re-encrypted with the new key. If anyone had begun a brute-force attack on data encrypted with the previous DMK, all results from that attack will be rendered useless by the new DMK.

You can back up the DMK by using the T-SQL script that follows. The same rules apply as with backing up the SMK (choose a random password, store the file off-premises, and keep the password and backup file separately). This script assumes that the master key exists.

```
USE WideWorldImporters;

GO

BACKUP MASTER KEY TO FILE = 'c:\SecureLocation\wwi_database_master_key'

    ENCRYPTION BY PASSWORD = '<UseAReallyStrongPassword>';

GO
```

> ➤ You can read more about the SMK and DMK on Microsoft Docs at
> *https://docs.microsoft.com/sql/relational-databases/security/encryption/*
> *sql-server-and-database-encryption-keys-database-engine*.

Encrypting data by using TDE

Continuing with our defense-in-depth discussion, an additional way to protect your environment is to encrypt data at rest, namely the database files (and when TDE is turned on, all backups of that database).

Third-party providers, including storage vendors, provide excellent on-disk encryption for your Direct-Attached Storage (DAS) or Storage-Area Network (SAN), as a file system solution or at the physical storage layer. Provided that your data and backups are localized to this particular solution, and no files are copied to machines that are not encrypted at the file-system level, this might be an acceptable solution for you.

If you have either the Enterprise or Standard edition of SQL Server, you can use TDE, which encrypts the data, transaction log, and backup files at the file-system level by using a DEK.

If someone manages to acquire these files via a backup server, Azure Storage archive, or by gaining access to your production environment, that person will not be able to simply attach the files or restore the database without the DEK.

The DEK is a symmetric key (shared secret) that is secured by a certificate stored in the master database. If using HSM/EKM or Key Vault, the DEK is protected by an asymmetric key in the EKM module, instead. The DEK is stored in the boot record of the protected database (page 0 of file 1) so that it is easily available during the recovery process.

> **NOTE**
>
> **TDE is invisible to any applications that use it. No changes are required in those applications to take advantage of TDE for the database.**

In the data file, TDE operates at the page level, because all data files are stored as 8-KB pages. Before being flushed from the buffer pool, the contents of the page are encrypted, the checksum is calculated, and then the page is written to the drive. When reading data, the 8-KB page is read from the drive, decrypted, and then the contents are placed into the buffer pool.

> **NOTE**
>
> **Even though encryption might to some degree increase the physical size of the data it is protecting, the size and structure of data pages is not affected. Instead, the number of pages in the data file might increase.**

For log files, the contents of the log cache are also encrypted before writing to and reading from the drive.

> ➤ **To read more about checkpoint operations and active virtual log files (VLFs) in the transaction log, refer to Chapter 3, "Designing and implementing an on-premises database infrastructure."**

Backup files are simply the contents of the data file, plus enough transaction log records to ensure that the database restore is consistent (redo and undo records of active transactions when the backup is taken). Practically speaking, this means that the contents of new backup files are encrypted by default after TDE is turned on.

> **NOTE**
>
> **Files associated with the buffer pool extension are not encrypted if you use TDE.**

Configuring TDE on a user database

To use TDE on SQL Server, you need to create a DMK if you don't already have one.

Verify that it is safely backed up and securely stored off-premises. If you have never backed up the DMK, you will be warned by the Database Engine after using it that it has not yet been backed up. If you don't know where that backup is, back it up again. This is a crucial detail to using TDE (or any encryption technology).

Next, you will create a digital certificate or use one that you have acquired from a CA. In the next example, the certificate is created on the server directly.

Then, you create the DEK, which is signed by the certificate and encrypted using a cryptographic algorithm of your choice.

Although you do have a choice of algorithm, we recommend AES over 3DES for performance and security reasons, and you have a choice of three AES key sizes: 128, 192, or 256 bits. Remember that larger keys are more secure but will add additional overhead when encrypting data. If you plan to rotate your keys every few months, you can safely use 128-bit AES encryption because no brute-force attack (using current computing power) should be able to attack a 128-bit key in the months between key rotations.

After you create the DEK, you turn on encryption on the database. The command completes immediately, but the process will take place in the background because each page in the database will need to be read into the buffer pool, encrypted, and flushed to the drive.

Inside OUT

How does TDE affect TempDB?

Turning on TDE on a user database will automatically turn on TDE for TempDB as well, if it is not already enabled. This can add overhead that adversely affects performance for unencrypted databases that make use of TempDB. If you want to turn off TDE on TempDB, all user databases must have it turned off first.

The script that follows provides a summary of the steps to turn on TDE:

```
USE master;

GO

-- Remember to back up this Database Master Key once it is created

CREATE MASTER KEY ENCRYPTION BY PASSWORD = '<UseAReallyStrongPassword>';

GO

CREATE CERTIFICATE WideWorldServerCert WITH SUBJECT = ' WWI DEK Certificate';

GO
```

```
USE WideWorldImporters;

GO

CREATE DATABASE ENCRYPTION KEY

    WITH ALGORITHM = AES_128

    ENCRYPTION BY SERVER CERTIFICATE WideWorldServerCert;

GO

ALTER DATABASE WideWorldImporters SET ENCRYPTION ON;

GO
```

Verifying whether TDE is turned on for a database

To determine which databases are encrypted with TDE, you can issue the following T-SQL query:

```
SELECT name, is_encrypted FROM sys.databases;
```

If a user database is encrypted, the is_encrypted column value for that database will be set to 1. TempDB will also show a value of 1 in this column.

Managing and monitoring the TDE scan

Enabling TDE on a database requires each data page to be read into the buffer pool before being encrypted and written back out to the drive. If the database instance is under a heavy workload, you can pause the scan and resume it at a later stage.

To pause the scan on the WideWorldImporters database, issue the following command:

```
ALTER DATABASE WideWorldImporters SET ENCRYPTION SUSPEND;
```

To resume the scan on the same database, issue the following command:

```
ALTER DATABASE WideWorldImporters SET ENCRYPTION RESUME;
```

You can also check the progress of the TDE scan using the new encryption_scan_state column in the sys.dm_database_encryption_keys DMV. To see when the state was last modified, refer to the encryption_scan_modify_date column in the same DMV.

Protecting sensitive columns with Always Encrypted

Although Transparent Data Encryption (TDE) is really useful for encrypting the entire database at the file-system level, it doesn't prevent database administrators and other users from having access to sensitive information within the database.

The first rule of storing sensitive data is that you should avoid storing it altogether when possible. Credit card information makes sense in a banking system, but not for instance in a sales database.

> ## NOTE
>
> **Many third-party systems can encrypt your data securely but are beyond the scope of this chapter. It is good to keep in mind that there is a small but inherent risk in storing encryption keys with data, as SQL Server does. Your organization must balance that risk against the ease of managing and maintaining those keys.**

➤ To learn about column-level encryption, which uses a symmetric key, visit *https://docs.microsoft.com/sql/relational-databases/security/encryption/encrypt-a-column-of-data*.

If you must store sensitive data, Always Encrypted protects how data is *viewed* at the column level. It works with applications that use particular connection types (*client drivers*; see the next section) to interact with SQL Server. These client drivers are protected by a digital certificate so that only specific applications can view the protected data.

Always Encrypted was introduced in SQL Server 2016 and has been available on all editions since SQL Server 2016 Service Pack 1. With SQL Server 2019, Always Encrypted can also be combined with secure enclaves to provide additional functionality. Secure enclaves leverage virtualization-based security (VBS) to isolate a region of memory inside the SQL Server process.

To use Always Encrypted, the database makes use of two types of keys: *column encryption keys* and *column master keys* (discussed shortly).

The encryption used by Always Encrypted is one of two types.

- **Deterministic encryption.**   This is the same as generating a hash value without a salt. The same encrypted value will always be generated for a given plain-text value. Without secure enclaves, this is useful for joins, indexes, searching, and grouping, but makes it possible for people to guess what the hash values represent.

- **Randomized encryption.**   This is the same as generating a hash value with a salt. No two of the same plain-text values will generate the same encrypted value. Without secure enclaves, this does not permit joins, indexes, searching, and grouping for those encrypted columns.

As you can see in Table 7-1, secure enclaves provide a much richer experience when protecting data with Always Encrypted.

Table 7-1   Functionality available with Always Encrypted encryption

Operation	Without enclave		With enclave	
	Randomized	Deterministic	Randomized	Deterministic
In-place encryption	No	No	Yes	Yes
Equality comparison	No	Yes (external)	Yes (internal)	Yes (external)
Beyond equality	No	No	Yes	No
LIKE predicate	No	No	Yes	No

Without secure enclaves, you can use randomized encryption for values that are not expected to participate in joins or searches, while deterministic encryption is useful for values like social security numbers and other government-issued values because it helps for searching and grouping. With secure enclaves, randomized encryption is useful for both of these scenarios.

Inside OUT

What is a secure enclave?

Prior to SQL Server 2019, operations on Always Encrypted data were limited to certain equality operations inside the Database Engine, and only with data protected by deterministic encryption. Any other operations required that the data be moved out of the database and operated on at the client side.

A secure enclave is a trusted region of memory inside the SQL Server process. It is not possible to view the data inside the enclave, even with a debugger. Now operations can be performed on encrypted data without moving the data outside of the Database Engine.

To read more about the virtualization-based security underlying secure enclaves, visit *https://www.microsoft.com/security/blog/2018/06/05/ virtualization-based-security-vbs-memory-enclaves-data-protection-through-isolation.*

Because the whole intent of Always Encrypted is to prevent unauthorized persons from viewing data (including database administrators), you should generate the keys elsewhere and store them in a trusted key store (in the operating system's key store for the database server and the application server, or an EKM module such as Azure Key Vault), away from the database server. To maintain the chain of trust, the person who generates the keys should not be the same person who is administering the database.

Client application providers that support Always Encrypted

The following providers currently support Always Encrypted:

- .NET Framework 4.6 or higher

- Microsoft JDBC Driver 6.0 or higher

- ODBC Driver 13.1 for SQL Server or higher

- Microsoft Drivers 5.2 for PHP for SQL Server or higher

CAUTION

Neither .NET Core, nor the Microsoft OLE DB Driver for SQL Server, are currently supported.

The connection between the Database Engine and application is made by using a client-side encrypted connection. Each provider has its own appropriate method to control this setting:

- **.NET Framework.**   Set the Column Encryption Setting in the connection string to enabled, or configure the `SqlConnectionStringBuilder.ColumnEncryption` Setting property to `SqlConnectionColumnEncryptionSetting.Enabled`.

- **JDBC.**   Set the `columnEncryptionSetting` to Enabled in the connection string, or configure the `SQLServerDataSource()` object with the `setColumnEncryptionSetting("Enabled")` property.

- **ODBC.**   Set the `ColumnEncryption` connection string keyword to Enabled, use the `SQL_COPT_SS_COLUMN_ENCRYPTION` pre-connection attribute, or through the Data Source Name (DSN) using the `SQL_COLUMN_ENCRYPTION_ENABLE` setting.

- **PHP.**   Set the `ColumnEncryption` connection string keyword to Enabled. Note that the PHP drivers use the ODBC drivers for encryption.

Additionally, the application must have the `VIEW ANY COLUMN MASTER KEY DEFINITION` and `VIEW ANY COLUMN ENCRYPTION KEY DEFINITION` database permissions in order to view the Column Master Key and Column Encryption Key.

The Column Master Key and Column Encryption Key

The Column Master Key (CMK) protects one or more Column Encryption Keys (CEK).

The CEK is encrypted using AES encryption and is used to encrypt the actual column data. You can use the same CEK to encrypt multiple columns, or you can create a CEK for each column that needs to be encrypted.

Inside OUT

Can you add indexes to columns protected by a secure enclave?

Indexes are permitted on enclave-enabled columns protected with randomized encryption. The enclave needs access to the column encryption key for all operations involving the index.

Microsoft recommends that your database has Accelerated Database Recovery enabled before creating your first index on an enclave-enabled column using randomized encryption. This ensures that your encrypted data is immediately available after a database is restored.

You can read more about Accelerated Database Recovery in Chapter 3.

Metadata about the keys (but not the keys themselves) is stored in the database's system catalog views:

- `sys.column_master_keys`
- `sys.column_encryption_keys`

This metadata includes the *type* of encryption and *location* of the keys, plus their *encrypted values*. Even if a database is compromised, the data in the protected columns cannot be read without access to the secure key store.

> ➤ To read more about considerations for key management on Microsoft Docs, visit *https://docs.microsoft.com/sql/relational-databases/security/encryption/ overview-of-key-management-for-always-encrypted*.

Using the Always Encrypted Wizard

The easiest way to configure Always Encrypted is by using the Always Encrypted Wizard in SQL Server Management Studio (SSMS). As noted previously, you need to have the following permissions before you begin:

- VIEW ANY COLUMN MASTER KEY DEFINITION

- VIEW ANY COLUMN ENCRYPTION KEY

If you plan on creating new keys, you also need the following permissions:

- ALTER ANY COLUMN MASTER KEY

- ALTER ANY COLUMN ENCRYPTION KEY

In SSMS, in **Object Explorer**, right-click the name of the database that you want to configure. Click **Tasks**, then **Encrypt Columns**. This brings up the Always Encrypted wizard.

On the Column Selection page, choose the column that you want to encrypt, and then select the encryption type (deterministic or randomized). If you want to decrypt a previously encrypted column, you can choose **Plaintext**.

On the Master Key Configuration page, you can create a new key by using the local OS certificate store or by using a centralized store like Key Vault or an HSM/EKM device. If you already have a CMK in your database, you can use it instead. You must also choose the master key source, which is either Current User or Local Machine.

NOTE

Memory-optimized and temporal tables are not supported by this wizard, but you can still encrypt them by using Always Encrypted.

Limitations in Always Encrypted

Certain column types are not supported by Always Encrypted, including:

- image, (n)text, xml, sql_variant, and timestamp / rowversion datatypes

- string columns with non-BIN2 collations

- FILESTREAM columns

- columns with IDENTITY or ROWGUIDCOL properties

- columns with default constraints or referenced by check constraints

➤ **You can read the full list of limitations and find out more about Always Encrypted on Microsoft Docs at** *https://docs.microsoft.com/sql/relational-databases/security/encryption/ always-encrypted-database-engine.*

Configuring Always Encrypted with secure enclaves

Always Encrypted with secure enclaves requires a fairly complex environment in order to guarantee the security it offers.

- **Host Guardian Service (HGS).**   Install HGS in a Windows Server 2019 failover cluster with three computers in its own Active Directory forest. These computers must not be connected to an existing Active Directory, and none of these computers must be used for the SQL Server installation. Microsoft suggests that this cluster be isolated from the rest of your network, and that different administrators manage this environment. The only access to HGS will be through HTTP (TCP port 80) and HTTPS (TCP port 443).

- **SQL Server 2019.**   Install SQL Server 2019 on Windows Server 2019, on its own physical hardware. Virtual machines do not support the recommended Trusted Platform Module (TPM) enclave attestation, which is hardware-based.

> ➤ You can read more about TPM attestation at *https://docs.microsoft.com/windows-server/identity/ad-ds/manage/component-updates/tpm-key-attestation*.

- **Tools for client and development.**   Install the requisite tools on your client machine:

  - .NET Framework 4.7.2 or later

  - SQL Server Management Studio (SSMS) 18.0 or later

  - SQL Server PowerShell module version 21.1 or later

  - Visual Studio 2017 or later

  - Developer pack (SDK) for .NET Framework 4.7.2

  - `Microsoft.SqlServer.Management.AlwaysEncrypted.EnclaveProviders` NuGet package

  - `Microsoft.SqlServer.Management.AlwaysEncrypted.AzureKeyVaultProvider` NuGet package version 2.2.0 or later, if you plan to use Azure Key Vault for storing your column master keys

- **Configure the enclave.**   From the client/development machine, you will enable the enclave type using SSMS. Rich computations are disabled by default for performance reasons. If you wish to use this feature, you must enable it after every SQL Server instance restart using Trace Flag 127. Make sure you test the performance impact on your environment before enabling this feature in production.

- **Provision enclave-enabled keys.**   This works in a similar way to regular Always Encrypted keys, except that the column master keys provisioned through HGS are marked as enclave-enabled. You can use SSMS or PowerShell to provision these keys, and store them either in the Windows Certificate Store, or an Azure Key Vault.

- **Encrypt sensitive columns.**   Finally, you will use the same methods to encrypt data as before.

➤ **A step-by-step walkthrough of this process is available at** *https://docs.microsoft.com/sql/ relational-databases/security/encryption/configure-always-encrypted-enclaves.*

Row-level security

Protecting the network and database instance is good and proper, but this does not protect assets within the environment from, for example, curious people snooping on salaries in the Human Resources database. Or, perhaps you have a customer database and you want to restrict the data those customers can access.

Row-level security, which does not use encryption, operates at the database level to restrict access to a table through a security policy, based on group membership or execution context. It is functionally equivalent to a WHERE clause.

Access to the rows in a table is protected by an inline table-valued function, which is invoked and enforced by the security policy.

The function checks whether the user is allowed to access a particular row, while the security policy attaches this function to the table. So, when you run a query against a table, the security policy applies the predicate function.

There are two types of security policies supported by row-level security, both of which you can apply simultaneously:

- Filter predicates, which limit the data that can be seen

- Block predicates, which limits the actions a user can take on data

Hence, a user might be able to see rows, but cannot insert, update, or delete rows that look like rows they can see. This concept is covered in more detail in the next section.

CAUTION

There is a risk of information leakage if an attacker writes a query with a specially crafted WHERE clause and, for example, a divide-by-zero error, to force an exception if the WHERE condition is true. This is known as a *side-channel attack*. It is wise to limit the ability of users to run ad hoc queries when using row-level security.

CHAPTER 13

Filtering predicates for read operations

You can silently filter rows that are available through read operations. The application then has no knowledge of the other data that is filtered out.

Filter predicates affect all read operations. This list is taken directly from the official documentation at *https://docs.microsoft.com/sql/relational-databases/security/row-level-security*:

- **SELECT.** Cannot view rows that are filtered.

- **DELETE.** Cannot delete rows that are filtered.

- **UPDATE.** Cannot update rows that are filtered. It is possible to update rows that will be subsequently filtered. (The next section covers ways to prevent this.)

- **INSERT.** No effect (inserting is not a read operation). Note, however, that a trigger could cause unexpected side effects in this case.

Blocking predicates for write operations

These predicates block access to write (or *modification*) operations that violate the predicate. Block predicates affect all write operations:

- **AFTER INSERT.** Prevents inserting rows with values that violate the predicate. Also applies to bulk insert operations.

- **AFTER UPDATE.** Prevents updating rows to values that violate the predicate. Does not run if no columns in the predicate were changed.

- **BEFORE UPDATE.** Prevents updating rows that currently violate the predicate.

- **BEFORE DELETE.** Blocks delete operations if the row violates the predicate.

Dynamic data masking

Data masking works on the principle of limiting exposure to data by *obfuscation*. It does not use encryption. Without requiring too many changes to the application or database, you can mask *portions* of columns to prevent lower-privilege users from seeing them, such as with full credit card numbers and other sensitive information.

The mask is defined in the column definition of the table, using MASKED WITH (FUNCTION = [type]) syntax, and you can add masking after table creation by using ALTER COLUMN syntax.

There are four types of masks that are available:

- **Default.** The column is masked according to the data type (not its default value). Strings will use "XXXX" (fewer if the length is less than four characters); numerics will use a zero value; dates will use midnight on January 1st, 1900; and binary will use a single byte binary equivalent of zero. If a string is too short to complete the entire mask, part of the prefix or suffix will not be exposed.

- **Email.** Only the first letter and the trailing domain suffix is not masked; for example, "aXXX@XXXXXXX.com."

- **Random.** This replaces a numeric data type with a random value within a range you specify.

- **Custom String.** Only the first and last letters are not masked. There is a custom padding string in the middle, which you specify.

➤ You can read more about dynamic data masking, including samples of how to set it up, at *https://docs.microsoft.com/sql/relational-databases/security/dynamic-data-masking*.

Limitations with masking data

Dynamic data masking has some limitations. It does not work on Always Encrypted columns, nor FILESTREAM or COLUMN_SET column types. Computed columns are also excluded, but if the computed column depends on a masked column, the computed column inherits that mask and returns masked data.

If a column has dependencies, you cannot perform dynamic data masking on it without removing the dependency first, adding the dynamic data mask, and then recreating the dependency.

Finally, a masked column cannot be a used as a FULLTEXT index key.

CAUTION

It is possible to expose masked data with carefully crafted queries. This can be performed by using a brute-force attack or by using inference based on the results. If you are using data masking, you should also limit the ability of the user to run ad hoc queries and ensure that their permissions are sound.

Protecting Azure SQL Database

All of the security features discussed thus far work equally on SQL Server and Azure SQL Database, namely TDE, Always Encrypted, row-level security and dynamic data masking.

That's great if you're just comparing SQL Server to Azure SQL Database, but there are some features unique to Azure SQL Database that are worth looking at, which we cover in the next section. Keep in mind that because Azure features and products are always changing, this is only a brief overview.

CHAPTER 13

Azure SQL Database Advanced Threat Protection (ATP)

The risks of having a publicly accessible database in the cloud are numerous. To help protect against attacks, you can activate ATP, which runs 24 hours per day on each of your Azure SQL Database servers (called nodes) for a monthly fee. This service notifies you by email whenever atypical behavior is detected.

Some of the interesting threats include SQL injection attacks and potential vulnerabilities as well as unfamiliar database access patterns, including unfamiliar logins or access from unusual locations. Each notification includes possible causes and recommendations to deal with the event.

ATP ties into the Azure SQL Audit log (discussed in the next section); thus, you can review events in a single place and decide whether each one was expected or malicious.

Although this does not prevent malicious attacks (over and above your existing protections), you are given the necessary tools to mitigate and defend against future events. Given how prevalent attacks like SQL injection are, this feature is very useful in letting you know if that type of event has been detected.

You can turn on ATP using the Azure portal, PowerShell, or with Azure CLI.

> ➤ To read more on configuring Azure SQL Database ATP with PowerShell, go to *https://docs.microsoft.com/azure/sql-database/scripts/ sql-database-auditing-and-threat-detection-powershell.*

Managed instance security features

Managed instances provide similar security features to SQL Server Enterprise edition. However, because the instance is isolated on an independent virtual network, it can only be accessed through Azure Active Directory (Azure AD), and not Windows authentication.

Otherwise it provides the same protections as on-premises instance, including TDE, Always Encrypted, row-level security, dynamic data masking, and its own flavor of auditing.

Built-in firewall protection

Azure SQL Database is secure by default. All connections to your database environment pass through a firewall. No connections to the database are possible until you add a rule to the firewall to allow access.

To provide access to all databases on an Azure SQL server, you must add a server-level firewall rule through the Azure portal (or indeed using PowerShell or Azure CLI) with your IP address as a range. This does not apply to managed instances because you access the instance through a private IP address inside the virtual network.

➤ To read more about protecting your Azure SQL Database, see Chapter 17, "Provisioning Azure SQL Database."

Auditing with SQL Server and Azure SQL Database

Auditing is the act of tracking and recording events that occur in the Database Engine. Since SQL Server 2016 Service Pack 1, the Audit feature is available in all editions, as well as in Azure SQL Database. Chapter 17 covers configuring auditing in Azure SQL Database in depth.

SQL Server Audit

There is a lot going on in the Database Engine. SQL Server Audit uses extended events to give you the ability to track and record those actions at both the instance and database level.

> NOTE
>
> Although extended events carry minimal overhead, it is important that you carefully balance auditing against performance impact. Use targeted auditing by only capturing the events that are necessary to fulfil your audit requirements.

➤ You can read more about extended events in Chapter 8, "Maintaining and monitoring SQL Server."

Audits are logged to event logs or audit files. An event is initiated and logged every time the audit action is encountered, but for performance reasons, the audit target is written to asynchronously.

The permissions required for SQL Server auditing are complex and varied, owing to the different requirements for reading from and writing to the Windows Event Log, the file system, and SQL Server itself.

Requirements for creating an audit

To keep track of events (called actions), you need to define a collection, or *audit*. The actions you want to track are collected according to an *audit specification*. Recording those actions is done by the *target* (destination).

- **Audit.**   The SQL Server audit object is a collection of server actions or database actions (these actions might also be grouped together). Defining an audit creates it in the *off* state. After it is turned on, the destination receives the data from the audit.

- **Server audit specification.**   This audit object defines the actions to collect at the instance level or database level (for all databases on the instance). You can have multiple Server Audits per instance.

- **Database audit specification.** You can monitor audit events and audit action groups. Only one database audit can be created per database per audit. Server-scoped objects must not be monitored in a database audit specification.

- **Target.** You can send audit results to the Windows Security event log, the Windows Application event log, or an audit file on the file system. You must ensure that there is always sufficient space for the target. Keep in mind that the permissions required to read the Windows Application event log are lower than the Windows Security event log, if you are using the Windows Application event log.

An audit specification can be created only if an audit already exists.

➤ To read more about audit action groups and audit actions, visit *https://docs.microsoft.com/sql/relational-databases/security/auditing/sql-server-audit-action-groups-and-actions.*

Inside OUT

What if an audit shuts down the instance or prevents SQL Server from starting?

SQL Server can be shut down by a failure in the audit. You will find an entry in the log saying MSG_AUDIT_FORCED_SHUTDOWN. You can start SQL Server in single-user mode using the −m option at the command line, which will write an entry to the log saying MSG_AUDIT_SHUTDOWN_BYPASSED.

An audit initiation failure also can prevent SQL Server from starting. In this case, you can use the −f command-line option to start SQL Server with minimal configuration (which is also single-user mode).

In minimal configuration or single-user mode, you will be able to remove the offending audit that caused the failure.

Creating a server audit in SQL Server Management Studio (SSMS)

Verify that you are connected to the correct instance in SSMS. Then, in **Object Explorer**, expand the **Security** folder. Right-click the **Audits** folder, and then, on the shortcut menu that opens, select **New Audit** (see Figure 13-2).

In the Create Audit dialog box that opens, configure the settings to your requirements, or you can leave the defaults as is. Just be sure to enter in a valid file path if you select File in the Audit Destination list box. We also recommend that you choose an appropriate name to enter into the Audit Name box (the default name is based on the current date and time).

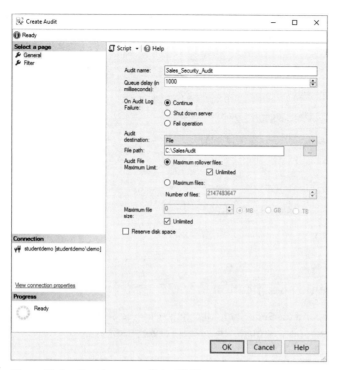

Figure 13-2   Creating an audit in SSMS.

Remember to turn on the audit after it is created. It will appear in the Audit folder, which is within the Security folder in Object Explorer. To do so, right-click the newly created audit, and then, on the shortcut menu, click **Enable Audit**.

Create a server audit by using T-SQL

The server audit creation process can be quite complex, depending on the destination, file options, audit options, and predicates. As just demonstrated, you can configure a new audit by using SSMS, and then create a script of the settings before clicking OK, which produces a T-SQL script. You can also do this manually.

> ➤ **To read more about creating a server audit in T-SQL visit** *https://docs.microsoft.com/ sql/t-sql/statements/create-server-audit-transact-sql*.

To create a server audit in T-SQL, verify that you are connected to the appropriate instance, and then run the next code sample. (You'll need to change the audit name and file path accordingly.) Note that the next example also sets the audit state to ON. It is created in the OFF state by default.

This audit will not have any effect until an audit specification and target are also created.

```
USE master;
GO
-- Create the server audit.
CREATE SERVER AUDIT Sales_Security_Audit
    TO FILE (FILEPATH = 'C:\SalesAudit');
GO
-- Enable the server audit.
ALTER SERVER AUDIT Sales_Security_Audit
    WITH (STATE = ON);
GO
```

Create a server audit specification in SSMS

In Object Explorer, expand the **Security** folder. Right-click the **Server Audit Specification** folder, and then, on the shortcut menu, click **New Server Audit Specification**.

In the Create Server Audit Specification dialog box (Figure 13-3), in the **Name** box, type a name of your choosing for the audit specification. In the **Audit** list box, select the previously created server audit. If you type a different value in the Audit box, a new audit will be created by that name.

Now you can choose one or more audit actions, or audit action groups.

> ➤ A full list of audit actions and audit action groups is available at
> *https://docs.microsoft.com/sql/relational-databases/security/auditing/*
> *sql-server-audit-action-groups-and-actions.*

NOTE

If you have selected an audit group action, you cannot select Object Class, Object Schema, Object Name, and Principal Name, because the group represents multiple actions.

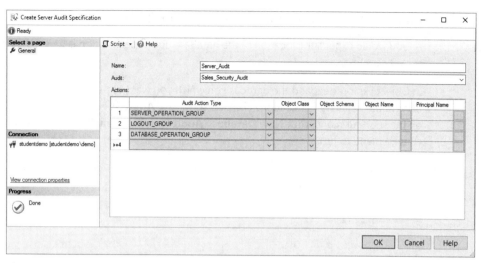

Figure 13-3 Creating a Server Audit Specification in SSMS.

Remember to turn on the server audit specification after you create it by using the context menu.

Create a server audit specification by using T-SQL

In much the same way as you create the audit itself, you can create a script of the configuration from a dialog box in SSMS, or you can create the specification manually, as shown in the script that follows. Note that the server audit specification refers to a previously created audit.

```
USE [master];

GO

-- Create the server audit specification.

CREATE SERVER AUDIT SPECIFICATION Server_Audit

FOR SERVER AUDIT Sales_Security_Audit

    ADD (SERVER_OPERATION_GROUP),

    ADD (LOGOUT_GROUP),

    ADD (DATABASE_OPERATION_GROUP)

WITH (STATE = ON);

GO
```

CHAPTER 13

Creating a database audit specification in SSMS

As you would expect, the location of the database audit specification is under the database security context.

In Object Explorer, expand the database on which you want to perform auditing, and then expand the **Security** folder. Right-click the **Database Audit Specifications** folder, and then, on the shortcut menu, click **New Database Audit Specification**. Remember again to use the context menu to turn it on.

Figure 13-4 shows an example of capturing SELECT and INSERT operations on the Sales.CustomerTransactions table by the dbo user.

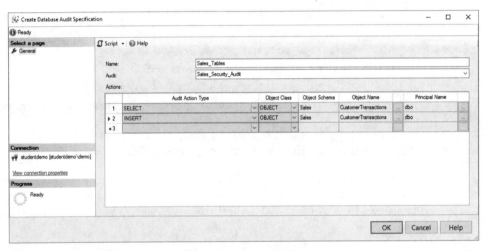

Figure 13-4   Creating a database audit specification in SSMS.

Creating a database audit specification by using T-SQL

Again, verify that you are in the correct database context. Create the database audit specification by referring to the server audit that was previously created, and then specify which database actions you want to monitor, as demonstrated in the next example.

The destination is already specified in the server audit, so as soon as this is turned on, the destination will begin logging the events as expected.

```
USE WideWorldImporters;

GO

-- Create the database audit specification.

CREATE DATABASE AUDIT SPECIFICATION Sales_Tables
```

```
FOR SERVER AUDIT Sales_Security_Audit

ADD (SELECT, INSERT ON Sales.CustomerTransactions BY dbo)

WITH (STATE = ON);
```

GO

Viewing an audit log

You can view audit logs either in SSMS or in the Security Log in the Windows Event Viewer. This section describes how to do it by using SSMS.

NOTE

To view any audit logs, you must have CONTROL SERVER **permission.**

In Object Explorer, expand the **Security** folder, and then expand the **Audits** folder. Right-click the audit log that you want to view, and then, on the shortcut menu, select **View Audit Logs**.

Note that the Event Time is in UTC format. This is to avoid issues regarding time zones and daylight saving time.

Figure 13-5 shows two audit events that have been logged. In the first, the audit itself has been changed (it was turned on). The second event is a SELECT statement that was run against the table specified in the database audit specification example presented earlier.

Figure 13-5   File Viewer dialog box for viewing a SQL Server audit.

There are many columns in the audit that you cannot see in Figure 13-5, notable among them are Server Principal ID (SPID), Session Server Principal Name (the logged-in user), and the

Statement (the command that was run). The point here is that you can capture a wealth of information.

> **NOTE**
>
> **You can also view the audit log in an automated manner by using the built-in T-SQL system function** sys.fn_get_audit_file**, though the data is not formatted the same way as it is through the File Viewer in SSMS. See more at** *https://docs.microsoft.com/sql/relational-databases/system-functions/sys-fn-get-audit-file-transact-sql*.

Auditing with Azure SQL Database

With Azure SQL Database auditing, you can track database activity and write it to an audit log in a container in your Azure Storage account (you are charged for storage accordingly).

This helps you to remain compliant with auditing regulations as well as see anomalies (as discussed earlier in the section "Azure SQL Database Threat Detection") to give you greater insight into your Azure SQL Database environment.

Auditing gives you the ability to retain an audit trail, report on activity in each database, and analyze reports, which includes trend analysis and security-related events. You can define server-level and database-level policies. Server policies automatically cover new and existing databases.

If you turn on server auditing, that policy applies to any databases on the server. Thus, if you also turn on database auditing for a particular database, that database will be audited by both policies. You should avoid this unless retention periods are different, or you want to audit for different event types.

> ➤ **You can read more about Azure SQL Database auditing in Chapter 17.**

Securing Azure infrastructure as a service

Infrastructure as a service (IaaS), or SQL Server running on an Azure VM, is secured in much the same way as the on-premises product. Depending on the edition, you can use TDE, Always Encrypted, row-level security, and dynamic data masking.

With Azure IaaS, setting up a VM in a resource group is secure by default. If you want to allow connections from outside of your Azure virtual network, you need to allow not only the connection through the OS firewall (which is on by default in Windows Server), but you also can control connections through a Network Security Group.

In addition to that, you can control access through a network appliance, such as a firewall or NAT device. This provides finer-grained control over the flow of network traffic in your virtual network, which is needed to set up Azure ExpressRoute, for example (Chapter 3 covers this in some detail).

Network Security Group

A Network Security Group (NSG) controls the flow of traffic in and out of the entirety (or part) of an Azure virtual network *subnet*.

Inside OUT

What is a subnet?

A subnet, short for subnetwork, is a logical separation of a larger network into smaller sections, making the network easier to manage and secure.

Subnetting can be complex and is beyond the scope of this book. There are subnet calculators online that you should refer to if you're doing this yourself. Because Azure Virtual Networks make use of subnets, here is a high-level overview.

Subnets are identified by a *network ID*, which is rendered in *network prefix notation* (also known as CIDR, or Classless Interdomain Routing). You will recognize this as a network address in IPv4 format followed by a prefix of /8, /16, or /24, and so on. The lower (*shorter*) the prefix, the more addresses are available.

This is a shorthand for the IP addresses that are available in that subnet, with the network address as the starting value. For example, 192.168.1.0/24 means that there are 256 possible addresses, starting at 192.168.1.1, up to and including 192.168.1.254. All subnets reserve the first address (in this case, 192.168.1.0) for the network identifier, and the last address (in this case, 192.168.1.255) for the broadcast address.

An NSG provides security for an entire subnet by default, which affects all the resources in that subnet (see Figure 13-6). If you require more control, you can associate the NSG with an individual network interface card (NIC), thus further restricting traffic.

NOTE

When creating a VM using the Azure Resource Manager, it will come with at least one virtual NIC, which you manage through an NSG. This is an important, because individual NICs can belong to different NSGs, which provides finer control over the flow of network traffic on individual VMs.

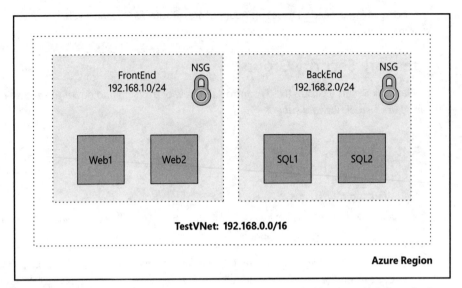

Figure 13-6   A typical virtual network, with each subnet secured by a Network Security Group.

As with typical firewalls, the NSG has rules for incoming and outgoing traffic. When a packet hits a port on the virtual network or subnet, the NSG intercepts the packet and checks whether it matches one of the rules. If the packet does not qualify for processing, it is discarded (dropped).

Rules are classified according to source address (or range) and destination address (or range). Depending on the direction of traffic, the source address can refer to inside the network or outside on the public Internet.

This becomes cumbersome with more complex networks, so to simplify administration and provide flexibility, you can use service tags to define rules by service name instead of IP address.

You can also use default categories, namely VirtualNetwork (the IP range of all addresses in the network), AzureLoadBalancer (the Azure infrastructure load balancer), and Internet (IP addresses outside the range of the Azure Virtual Network).

> ➤ You can read more about Azure Virtual Network security and get a full list of service tags at *https://docs.microsoft.com/azure/virtual-network/security-overview.*

User-defined routes and IP forwarding

As a convenience to Azure customers, all VMs in an Azure Virtual Network are able to communicate with one another by default, irrespective of the subnet in which they reside. This also holds true for virtual networks connected to your on-premises network by a VPN, and for Azure VMs communicating with the public Internet (including those running SQL Server).

➤ You can read more about **Virtual Private Networks** in Chapter 3.

In a traditional network, communication across subnets like this requires a gateway to control (route) the traffic. Azure provides these *system routes* for you automatically.

You might decide that this free-for-all communication is against your network policy and that all traffic from your VMs should first be channeled through a network appliance (such as a firewall or NAT device). Virtual appliances are available in the Azure Marketplace at an additional cost, or you could configure a VM yourself to run as a firewall.

A user-defined route with IP forwarding makes this happen. With a user-defined route, you create a subnet for the virtual appliance and force traffic from your existing subnets or VMs through the virtual appliance.

You must enable IP forwarding for the VM in order for that VM to receive traffic addressed to other destinations. This is an Azure setting, not a setting in the guest OS. (*https://docs.microsoft. com/azure/virtual-network/virtual-network-scenario-udr-gw-nva*)

You may also have to enable IP forwarding in the VM itself in certain circumstances.

CAUTION

With user-defined routes, you cannot control how traffic *enters* the network from the public Internet. They only control how traffic *leaves* a subnet, which means that your virtual appliance must be in its own subnet. If you want to control traffic flow from the public Internet as it enters a subnet, use a Network Security Group.

Until you create a routing table (by user-defined route), subnets in your Virtual Network rely on system routes. A user-defined route adds another entry in the routing table, so a technique called Longest Prefix Match (LPM) kicks in to decide which is the better route to take, by selecting the most specific route (the one with the longest prefix). As seen earlier in Figure 13-6, a /24 prefix is longer than a /16 prefix, and a route entry with a higher prefix takes precedence.

If two entries have the same LPM match, the order of precedence is as follows:

- User-defined route

- BGP route

- System route

Remember BGP? It's used for ExpressRoute. As we mentioned in Chapter 3, ExpressRoute is a VPN service by which you can connect your Azure Virtual Network to your on-premises network, without going over the public Internet. You can specify BGP routes to direct traffic between your network and the Azure Virtual Network.

CHAPTER 13

Additional security features in Azure networking

There are additional features for improving the management and security of an Azure Virtual Network, as it relates to SQL Server or Azure SQL Database, which are worth discussing here. As of this writing, some of these features are still in preview.

Virtual network service endpoints

Service endpoints make it possible for you to restrict access to certain Azure services that were traditionally open to the public Internet so that they are available only to your Azure Virtual Network, as illustrated in Figure 13-7.

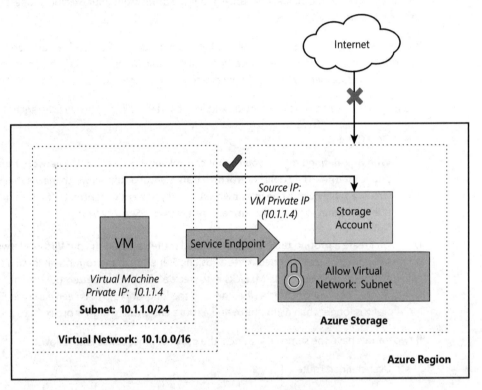

Figure 13-7   A service endpoint protecting an Azure Storage account.

Configurable through the Azure portal, PowerShell, or Azure CLI, you can block public Internet access to your Azure Storage and Azure SQL Database resources. Additional service endpoints are available, and more will be introduced in the future.

➤ **To read more about Virtual Network service endpoints, go to** *https://docs.microsoft.com/ azure/virtual-network/virtual-network-service-endpoints-overview.*

Distributed-denial-of-service protection

Azure provides protection against distributed-denial-of-service (DDoS) attacks for Virtual Networks, which is helpful given that attacks against publicly accessible resources are increasing in number and complexity. The basic service included in your subscription provides real-time protection by using the scale and capacity of the Azure infrastructure to mitigate attacks (see Figure 13-8).

For an additional cost, you can take advantage of built-in machine learning algorithms to protect against targeted attacks, with added configuration, alerting, and telemetry.

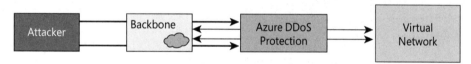

Figure 13-8   Azure DDoS protection defending a virtual network against attacks.

You also can use the Azure Application Gateway web application firewall to help protect against more sophisticated attacks.

Combined with Azure SQL Database auditing and NSGs, these features provide a comprehensive suite of protection against the latest threats.

➤ **To read more about Azure DDoS protection, go to** *https://azure.microsoft.com/services/ddos-protection.*

PART V

Performance

Performance tuning SQL Server

In this chapter, we review the database concepts and objects most associated with tuning the performance of queries and coded objects within Microsoft SQL Server and Azure SQL DB. We will not be looking at performance tuning queries that make use of the PolyBase feature, as tuning these queries will go beyond tuning SQL Server into tuning the external systems that they access.

➤ For more details on PolyBase, see Chapter 20, "Leveraging Big Data and Machine Learning."

In the first two sections of the chapter we will look at isolation levels and durability, which will touch on three of the ACID properties of an RDBMS (Relational Database Management System). These correspond to settings and configurations that let your code affect performance. The ACID properties are:

- **Atomicity.** Transactions, which make multiple step processes behave as one operation

- **Isolation.** Dealing with how multiple connections interact with one another

- **Durability.** When a transaction is committed, we have certain expectations on what happens if the server stops working.

- **Consistency.** Making sure data meets business rules in the database at the end of a transaction

Of these, we will cover the first three, but not consistency, as this is more of a database design task, which is covered in Chapter 7, "Understanding table features."

Then, we explore the process of how SQL Server executes queries, including understanding the execution plans that the query processor creates to execute your query, including how they are used in the Query Store feature. We discuss execution plans in some detail, what to look for when performance tuning, and how to control when they go parallel, meaning SQL Server can use multiple processors to execute your query, without the code changing at all.

Inside OUT

Is this all there is to performance tuning?

Entire books have been written on some of the sections in this chapter—we can't go into that degree of detail here in a single chapter, but we do provide a deep enough discussion to jumpstart and accelerate your learning toward SQL Server performance tuning, including the newest features added in SQL Server 2019, of which some are quite amazing.

However, optimizing queries is not the end of it either. Throughout the book, most of the topics will pertain to the performance of your queries, from the hardware and OS software you use, as well as how it is configured for SQL Server's needs.

Performance tuning can be a daunting task as organizations want to process more and more data, but the engineers at Microsoft are adding more and more features to the product in every version. The fundamentals of great database solutions don't change much, but the underlying software makes leaps and bounds in each new version.

The examples that in this chapter behave identically in SQL Server instances and databases in Azure SQL Database unless otherwise noted. All sample scripts in this book are available for download at *https://MicrosoftPressStore.com/SQLServer2019InsideOut/downloads*.

Understanding isolation levels and concurrency

The fundamental problem when we are working on a multi-user computing system is how to handle the problem that frequently users need access to the same resources. So, if there is a row, say Row X, and User 1 and User 2 both want to do something with this row, what is the effect? If they both want to read the row, one set of concerns exists, and if one wishes to read it, and the other write it, there is another is set of issues. Finally, if both want to write to the row, still another set of concerns arises. This is where the concept of isolation comes in, including how to isolate one connection from the other.

This is all related to the concept of atomicity, and as such, transactions containing one or more statements, because we need to isolate logical atomic operations from one another. Even a single statement in a declarative programming system like Transact-SQL provides will be hundreds and thousands of steps behind the scenes.

Isolation isn't only a matter of physical access to resources (a disk drive is fetching data from a row, so the next reader must wait for that to complete). This is a different problem for the hardware. Instead, it is a matter that while one transaction is doing its operations, others need to be as isolated from the data the user has used as needed. The performance implications are large, because the more isolated the operations need to be, the slower processing can be, but the less isolated transactions are, the greater the chance for loss of data.

The types of things that can occur between two transactions are generally referred to as phenomenon. They are:

- **Dirty Read**. Reading data that another connection is in the process of changing. The problem is much like trying to read a post-it note that your boss is writing your new salary on. Read too early, and it looks like you are getting a $1 raise annually, or $100000, because the decimal point has not been added.

- **Non-Repeatable Read.** Reading the same data over again that has changed or gone away. This problem is like when you check the box of doughnuts and see there is one left. While you are standing there, in control of the box, no one can take that last doughnut. But step away to get coffee, and when you come back it has a bite taken out of it. A repeatable read will always give you back rows with the same content as you first read (but may include more rows that did not exists when you first read a set of rows).

- **Phantom Read.** A phantom read is when you read a set of data, but then come back and read it again and get new rows that did not previously exist. In the previous doughnut example, this is the happiest day of your life since there are now more doughnuts. However, this can be bad if your query needs to get back the same answer every time you ask the same question.

- **Reading a Previous Committed Version of Data.** In some cases, you may be able to eliminate blocking by allowing connections to read a previously committed version of data that another connection is in the process of changing after your transaction started. A real-world example of this regularly happens in personal banking. You and your partner see you have $N in your account, and you both withdraw $N, not realizing the intentions of the other connection. Your ATM may even say you have $0 after both transactions, using stale information. This does not change the fees you will be receiving, but often it is perfectly acceptable for the task at hand to see how the data was at the start of the transaction.

Where this gets complicated is that many operations in a database system will be bundled into multi-step operations that need to be treated as one atomic operation. Reading data and getting back different results when executing the same query again, during what you expect to be an atomic operation, greatly increases the likelihood of returning incorrect results.

You can't control which individual phenomenon you will allow your transaction to be affected by, but they are bundled into *isolation levels* that allow certain effects to occur. For example, the default isolation level, READ COMMITTED, is subject to nonrepeatable reads and phantom rows, but not dirty reads. This provides adequate protection and performance in most situations, but definitely not all.

It is important to have a fundamental understanding of these effects because these aren't just arcane keywords you study only when it is certification time; they can have a profound effect on application performance, stability, and absolutely the most important thing for any RDBMS: data integrity.

For example, consider you are writing software to control the trains that are using track T. Two trains wish to use track T, and both conductors ask if the track is vacant, so both see it is vacant and put their trains on the track heading toward each other. Not good.

Understanding the differing impact of isolation levels on locking and blocking, and therefore on concurrency, is the key to understanding when you should use an isolation level different from the default of READ COMMITTED. Table 14-1 presents the isolation levels available in SQL Server along with the phenomena that are allowed.

Table 14-1   Isolation levels and phenomena that can be incurred

Transaction isolation level	Dirty reads	Nonrepeatable reads	Phantom rows	Reading a Previous Committed Version of Data
READ UNCOMMITTED	X	X	X	
READ COMMITTED		X	X	
REPEATABLE READ			X	
SERIALIZABLE				
READ COMMITTED SNAPSHOT (RCSI)		X	X	X
SNAPSHOT				X

Inside OUT

Should you always just use SERIALIZABLE and be completely safe?

At this point in the process, it probably seems like you need to protect your data with SERIALIZABLE isolation level in every case. But read on, as most of the real world scenarios you deal with will not require strict isolation between connections, in fact the default isolation level (READ COMMITTED) will generally suffice for most user's needs.

Note the use of the word "most". READ COMMITTED works in most cases, but not all. Why this is the case is covered in the rest of this section.

When you are choosing an isolation level for a transaction in an application, you should consider primarily the transactional safety and business requirements of the transaction in a highly concurrent multiuser environment. The performance of the transaction should be a distant second priority (yet still a priority) when choosing an isolation level.

Locking, which SQL Server uses for normal isolation of processes is not bad, it is the way that every transaction in SQL Server cooperates with others when dealing with disk-based tables.

The default isolation level of READ COMMITTED is generally a safe isolation level because it only allows connection to access data that has been committed by other transactions. Dirty reads are generally the only modification phenomenon that is almost universally bad. With READ COMMITTED, modifications to a row blocks reads from other connections to that same row. This is especially important during multi-statement transactions, such as when parent and child rows in a foreign key relationship must be created in the same transaction. In that scenario, reads should not access either row in either table until both changes are updated.

Since READ COMMITTED isolation level allows nonrepeatable reads and phantom rows, it does not ensure that row data and row count won't change between two SELECT queries on the same data in a transaction. READ COMMITTED isolation levels allow SQL Server to release locks from objects it has read and lets other users have any access, holding only locks on resources that it has changed.

For some application scenarios, this might be acceptable or desired, but not for others. To avoid these two problematic scenarios (which we talk more about soon), you need to choose the proper, more stringent isolation level for the transaction.

For scenarios in which transactions must have a higher degree of isolation from other transactions, escalating the isolation level of a transaction is appropriate. For example, if a transaction must write multiple rows, even in multiple tables and statements, it cannot allow other transactions to change data it has read during the transaction, where escalating the isolation level of a transaction is appropriate. Here are two examples.

In this example, the REPEATABLE READ isolation level blocks other transactions from changing or deleting rows needed during a multistep transaction. Unlike READ COMMITTED, REPEATABLE READ has the effect of holding locks on resources and preventing any other readers from changing them until it has completed, thus avoiding non-repeatable reads.

If the transaction in this example needs to ensure that the same exact rows in a result set is returned throughout a multistep transaction, the SERIALIZABLE isolation is necessary. It is the only isolation level that prevents other transactions from inserting new rows inside of a range of rows . It prevents other connections from adding new rows by not only locking rows it has accessed, but ranges of rows that it would have accessed had they existed. For example, say you queried for rows LIKE 'A%' in a SERIALIZABLE transaction and got back Apple and

Annie. If another user tries to insert Aardvark, it is prevented until the LIKE 'A%' transaction is completed.

Lastly, it is essential to understand that every statement is a transaction. UPDATE TableName SET column = 1; operates in a transaction, as does a statement like SELECT 1;. When you do not manually start a transaction, it is referred to as an implicit transaction. An explicit transaction is one where you start with BEGIN TRANSACTION and end with COMMIT TRANSACTION or ROLLBACK TRANSACTION. The REPEATABLE READ and SERIALIZABLE isolation levels can gather a lot of locks, more so with explicit transactions of multiple statements, if they are not quickly closed. The more locks are present, the more likely your connection might be stuck indefinitely waiting.

> ➤ For more on monitoring database locking and blocking, see Chapter 8, "Maintaining and monitoring SQL Server."

Inside OUT

When blocked, do your connections wait indefinitely? Can you control this?

By default, the time-out for a request that is being blocked in SQL Server is indefinite, and it is rarely set to anything different. Many applications implement a time out when a query run time surpasses their own time-out limitations.

There is a knob you can use to tune this behavior. You can change this for the current session by using the following statement:

```
SET LOCK_TIMEOUT n;
```

Where n is the number of milliseconds before a request is cancelled by SQL Server. You can determine the current setting of the lock timeout using the global variable @@LOCK_TIMEOUT. The default is -1, indicating that there is no time-out. When the value is positive, and a connection waits on a lock longer than the timeout, error 1222 is raised, with the message: "Lock request time out period exceeded. The statement has been terminated."

Take caution in implementing this change to SQL's default lock time-out and try to first understand the cause of the blocking. If you change the lock time-out in code, ensure that any applications creating the sessions are prepared to handle the errors gracefully and retry. (Something you should do for every application you are creating because errors can happen!)

SQL Server does have a configuration setting for a time-out for outgoing remote connections called Remote Query Timeout, which defaults to 600 seconds. This time-out applies only to connections to remote data providers, not to requests run on the SQL Server instance. It specifies the number of seconds that the query can execute, not how long it can be blocked, before it is terminated.

The most complex of the phenomena concerns reading data that is not the committed version that was initially accessed. There are two main places where this comes into a concern.

- **Reading previous versions of data.** Using SNAPSHOT or READ COMMITTED SNAPSHOT (RCSI), your query will see how data looked at the start of the query (RCSI) or once the transaction accesses data in the database. This means that the data you have may not match the data as it exists in the database.

  A side effect of this is that in SNAPSHOT isolation level if two transactions try to modify or delete the same row, you will get an update conflict, requiring you to restart the transaction.

- **Reading new versions of data.** In any isolation level that allows phantoms and non-repeatable reads, running the same statement twice can return entirely different results. It is incumbent on the programmer to recognize if this matters. For example, if you try to implement a foreign key construct in READ COMMITTED isolation level, after you check to see if the row exists, another transaction could have deleted the row.

All the topics in this introduction will be covered in greater detail in the following sections. Isolation levels are very important and can be difficult to get right. This is mostly because it is very hard to test your code to see what happens when two connections try to make incompatible reads and modifications to data simultaneously.

Understanding how concurrent sessions become blocked

In this section, we review a series of examples of how concurrency works in a multiuser application interacting with SQL Server tables. First, let's discuss how to diagnose whether a request is being blocked or if it is blocking another request. Note that in these initial examples, we will be assuming that SQL Server has been configured in the default manner for concurrency. We will be adjusting that later in the chapter to give you more ways to tune performance.

What causes blocking?

We have alluded to it already, and the answer is that when you use resources, they are locked. These locks can be on several different levels and types of resources, as seen in Table 14-2.

Table 14-2   Lockable Resources (Not every type of resource)

Type of Lock	Granularity
Row or row identifier (RID)	A single row in a heap table
Key	A single value in an index (Note that a clustered table is represented as an index in all physical structures.)
Key Range	A range of key values (for example, to lock rows with values from A–M, even if no rows currently exist). Used for SERIALIZABLE isolation level.
Extent	A contiguous group of 8, 8-KB pages
Page	An 8-KB index or data page
HoBT	An entire heap or B-tree structure
Object	An entire table, including all rows and indexes; view, stored procedure, etc.
Application	A special type of lock that is user defined
Metadata	Metadata about the schema, such as catalog objects
Database	An entire database
Allocation unit	A set of related pages that are used as a unit
File	A data or log file in the database

Locks on a given resource are of a mode. In Table 14-3 is the list of modes that an index may be in. Two of the most important ones are shared (indicating a row is being read only), and exclusive (indicating a row should not be accessible by any other connection.)

Table 14-3   Lock Modes

Lock Mode	Definition
Shared	This lock mode grants access for reads only. It's generally used when users are looking at but not editing the data. It's called "shared" because multiple processes can have a shared lock on the same resource, allowing read-only access to the resource. However, sharing resources prevents other processes from modifying the resource.
Exclusive	This mode gives exclusive access to a resource and is used during modification of data also. Only one process may have an active exclusive lock on a resource.
Update	This mode is used to inform other processes that you're planning to modify the data. Other connections may also issue shared, but not update or exclusive, locks while you're still preparing to do the modification. Update locks are used to prevent deadlocks (covered later in this section) by marking rows that a statement will possibly update, rather than upgrading directly from a shared lock to an exclusive one.

Intent	This mode communicates to other processes that taking one of the previously listed modes might be necessary. It establishes a lock hierarchy with taken locks, allowing processes that are trying to take a lock on a resource (like a table), that there are other connections with locks at a lower level such as a page. You might see this mode as intent shared, intent exclusive, or shared with intent exclusive.
Schema	This mode is used to lock the structure of a resource when it's in use, so you cannot alter a structure (like a table) when a user is reading data from it. (Note that schema locks show up as part of the mode in many views)

As queries are doing different operations, querying data, modifying data, or changing objects; resources are locked in a given mode. Blocking comes when one connection has a resource locked in a certain mode, and another connection needs to lock a resource in an incompatible mode. In Table 14-4, the compatibility of different modes is presented.

To read this table, pick the lock mode in one axis, then an X will be in any compatible column in the other. For example, an update lock is compatible with an intent shared and a shared lock, but not another update lock, or any of the exclusive variants.

Table 14-4   Lock Modes

Mode	IS	S	U	IX	SIX	X
Intent shared (IS)	X	X	X	X	X	
Shared (S)	X	X	X			
Update (U)	X	X				
Intent exclusive (IX)	X					
Shared Intent Exclusive (SIX)		X				
Exclusive (X)						

If a connection is reading data, it will take a shared lock, allowing other readers to also take a shared lock, which will not cause a blocked situation. However, if another connection is modifying data, it will get an exclusive lock, which will prevent the connection (and any other connections) from accessing the exclusively locked resources in any manner (other than ignoring the locks, which will be discussed later in this section).

How to observe locks and blocking

It's easy to find out live whether a request is being blocked. The dynamic management object (DMO) `sys.dm_db_requests`, when combined with `sys_dm_db_sessions` on the `session_id` column, provides data about blocking and the state of sessions on the server. This provides much more information than the legacy sp_who or sp_who2 commands, as you can see displayed from this query:

```
--this query will return a plethora of information in addition to just the session that
--is blocked
SELECT r.session_id, r.blocking_session_id, *
FROM sys.dm_exec_sessions s
LEFT OUTER JOIN sys.dm_exec_requests r ON r.session_id = s.session_id;
--note: requests represent actions that are executing, sessions are connections, hence
--LEFT OUTER JOIN
```

You can see details of what objects are locked by using the sys.dm_tran_locks DMO, or what locks are involved in blocking using this query:

```
SELECT
        t1.resource_type,
        t1.resource_database_id,
        t1.resource_associated_entity_id,
        t1.request_mode,
        t1.request_session_id,
        t2.blocking_session_id
    FROM sys.dm_tran_locks as t1
    INNER JOIN sys.dm_os_waiting_tasks as t2
        ON t1.lock_owner_address = t2.resource_address;
```

You can see in the output of this query, the type of resource that is locked, listed in table 14-3 and the modes listed in table 14-4, with a few exceptions. A lock on a schema is mixed with the mode of the lock, for example, you may have an object that is executing, like a stored procedure where the object is locked with executing, with a request mode of Sch-S, which indicates that it is a shared mode, because it is in use. This prevents the schema of the procedure from being changed, but it can be executed by more than one connection.

➤ You can find more details about locks and sys.dm_tran_locks at: *https://docs.microsoft.com/sql/relational-databases/system-dynamic-management-views/ sys-dm-tran-locks-transact-sql*

Now, let's review some example scenarios to detail exactly why and how requests can block one another in the real world when using disk-based tables. This is the foundation of concurrency in

SQL Server and helps you understand the reason why the NOLOCK query hint appears to make queries perform faster.

Changing the isolation level

As mentioned, by default, connections use the READ COMMITTED isolation level. If you need to change that for a session, there are two methods, using the SET TRANSACTION ISOLATION LEVEL statement, and using hints. In this manner, the isolation level can be changed for an entire transaction, one statement, or one object in a statement.

Using the SET TRANSACTION ISOLATION LEVEL statement

You can change the isolation level of a connection any time, even when already executing in the context of a transaction that is uncommitted. You are not allowed to swap to and from the SNAPSHOT isolation level because, as we'll will discuss later in the chapter, this isolation level works very differently.

For example, the following code snippet is technically valid, to change from READ COMMITTED to SERIALIZABLE isolation levels. For example, if one statement in your batch required the protection of SERIALIZABLE, but not others, you can execute:

```
SET TRANSACTION ISOLATION LEVEL READ COMMITTED;

BEGIN TRAN;

SET TRANSACTION ISOLATION LEVEL SERIALIZABLE;

SELECT...;

SET TRANSACTION ISOLATION LEVEL READ COMMITTED;

COMMIT TRAN;
```

This code snippet is trying to change from READ COMMITTED to the SNAPSHOT isolation level:

```
SET TRANSACTION ISOLATION LEVEL READ COMMITTED;

BEGIN TRAN;

SET TRANSACTION ISOLATION LEVEL SNAPSHOT;

SELECT...
```

Attempting this results in the following error:

```
Msg 3951, Level 16, State 1, Line 4

Transaction failed in database 'databasename' because the statement was run under snap-
shot isolation but the transaction did not start in snapshot isolation. You cannot
change the isolation level of the transaction after the transaction has started.
```

In .NET applications, you should change the isolation level of each transaction when it is created as it may not be in READ COMMITTED by default, which is far better for performance.

Using table hints to change isolation

You also can use isolation level hints to change the isolation level at the individual object level. This is an advanced type of coding that you shouldn't use frequently, because it generally increases the complexity of maintenance and muddies architectural decisions with respect to enterprise concurrency. Just as in the previous session, however, we may wish to hold locks at a SERIALIZABLE level for one table, but not others in the query.

For example, you might have seen developers use NOLOCK at the end of a table, effectively (and dangerously) dropping access to that table into the READ UNCOMMITTED isolation level:

```
SELECT col1 FROM dbo.Table (NOLOCK);
```

> ### NOTE
> Aside from the inadvisable use of NOLOCK in the preceding example, using a table hint without WITH is deprecated syntax (since SQL Server 2008). It should be written like this, if you needed to ignore locks.
>
> SELECT col1 FROM dbo.TableName WITH (READUNCOMMITTED);

Aside from the generally undesirable use of the NOLOCK query hint, there are 20-plus other table hints that can be useful, including the ability for a query to use a certain index, to force a seek or scan on an index, or to override the query optimizer's locking strategy. We discuss how to use UPDLOCK later in this chapter; for example, to force a use of the SERIALIZABLE isolation level.

In almost every case, table hints should be considered for temporary and/or highly situational purposes. They can make maintenance of these queries problematic in the future. For example, using the INDEX or FORCESEEK table hints could result in poor query performance or even cause the query to fail if the table's indexes are changed.

> ➤ For detailed information on all possible table hints, see the SQL Server documentation at *https://docs.microsoft.com/sql/t-sql/queries/hints-transact-sql-table*.

Inside OUT

What value is the READPAST table hint for concurrency?

Isolation is generally a matter of keeping one connection from corrupting or seeing another connection's changes. Sometimes though, you may wish to just get any row (or rows) that no other user has a hold on. READPAST is a table hint, not an isolation level, that will allow you to return only rows that meet a criteria that can be fetched without causing a blocking scenario.

READPAST can be useful in very specific circumstances, limited to when there are SQL Server tables used as "stack" or "queue," with a loose "first in, first out" architecture. READPAST allows a query to skip over rows that are currently being locked — it skips them. User transactions can fetch the "first" row in the stack that isn't locked in an incompatible lock mode.

The process typically works like this: Each process that is working this structure, updates 1 row that it will work on. This locks it from other processes. Now, other processes can't read that row, but can then update the next row and process it. When they are complete with the task, they write a status of done, so the next user doesn't see that row in the pop or push from the structure.

In this way, a multithreaded process that is regularly looping through a table can read rows, afford to skip the rows currently being written to, and read them on the "next pass." Outside of these limited scenarios, READPAST is not appropriate because it will likely return incomplete data.

Understanding and handling common concurrency scenarios

Here we look at some common concurrency scenarios and discuss/demonstrate how SQL Server will process the rows affected by the scenario.

NOTE

In Chapter 7, the concepts around memory-optimized tables will be covered, and their concurrency model is very different from disk-based tables, though similar to how row versioned concurrency is implemented, particularly the SNAPSHOT isolation level. Later in this chapter the differences for memory optimized tables will be discussed.

Understanding concurrency: two requests updating the same rows

Two users attempting to modify the same resource is possibly the most obvious concurrency issue. As an example, one user wants to add $100 to the total, and another wants to add $50. If both processes happen simultaneously, only one row may be modified (or if we take it to the absurd level, data corruption could occur to the physical structures holding the data if pointers are mixed up by multiple modifications.)

Consider the following steps involving two writes, with each transaction coming from a different session. The transactions are explicitly declared using the BEGIN/COMMIT TRANSACTION syntax. In this example, the transactions are not overriding the default isolation level of READ COMMITTED.

All examples will have these two rows simply so it isn't just a single row, though we will only manipulate the row where Type = 1. When testing more complex concurrency scenarios, it is best to have large quantities of data to work with as indexing, server resources, etc. do come into play. These examples illustrate simple, fundamental concurrency examples.

1.   A table contains only two rows with a column Type containing values of 0 and 1.

```
CREATE SCHEMA Demo;

GO

CREATE TABLE Demo.RC_Test (Type int);

INSERT INTO Demo.RC_Test VALUES (0),(1);
```

2.   Transaction 1 begins and updates all rows from Type = 1 to Type = 2.

```
--Transaction 1

SET TRANSACTION ISOLATION LEVEL READ COMMITTED;

BEGIN TRANSACTION;

UPDATE Demo.RC_Test SET Type = 2

WHERE  Type = 1;
```

3.   Before Transaction 1 commits, Transaction 2 begins and issues a statement to update Type = 2 to Type = 3. Transaction 2 is blocked and will wait for Transaction 1 to commit.

```
--Transaction 2

SET TRANSACTION ISOLATION LEVEL READ COMMITTED;

UPDATE Demo.RC_Test SET Type = 3

WHERE  Type = 2;
```

4.   Transaction 1 commits.

```
--Transaction 1

COMMIT;
```

5.   Transaction 2 is no longer blocked and processes its update statement. Transaction 2 then commits.

The resulting table will contain a row of Type = 3, and one of Type = 0, as the second transaction will have updated the row after the block was ended. This is because when Transaction 2 started, it waited for the exclusive lock to be removed after Transaction 1 committed.

Inside OUT

When two connections try to update the same row, how do you pick which connection's changes are actually saved?

Consider the case where two connections start transactions, read in the same row, then try to update the same row simultaneously. The reads can be done simultaneously, but one update is blocked until the other completes. Then the second update executes and completes, potentially overwriting the changes from the first update (assuming they are updating the same columns.)

This is what is known as the "Lost Update" problem. In the default isolation level, the rows would be overwritten. Using REPEATABLE READ, the second transactions would be unable to change the data the other connection had read in, preventing lost data but causing a deadlock.

While elevating the isolation level is one way, using optimistic locking schemes is another. Using a column of type rowversion (which changes on every change to the row) when you fetch data to read, you fetch the rowversion and compare it to the row's value on update or delete. If it doesn't match, you fail your operation and try again (after seeing what has changed).

Understanding concurrency: a write blocks a read

One of the most painful parts of blocking comes when users are trying to write data that other users are blocked from reading. What can even be more problematic is that some modification statements may actually touch and lock rows in the table even if they don't make any changes (typically due to poorly written where clauses or lack of indexing causing full table scans.)

Next, consider the following steps involving a write and a read, with each transaction coming from a different session. In this scenario, an uncommitted write in transaction 1 blocks a read in Transaction 2. The transactions are explicitly started using the BEGIN/COMMIT TRANSACTION syntax. In this example, the transactions are not overriding the default isolation level of READ COMMITTED:

1.   A table contains only two rows with a column Type value of 0 and 1.

```
CREATE TABLE Demo.RC_Test_Write_V_Read (Type int);
```

```
INSERT INTO Demo.RC_Test_Write_V_Read VALUES (0),(1);
```

2. Transaction 1 begins and updates all rows from Type = 1 to Type = 2.

```
--Transaction 1

SET TRANSACTION ISOLATION LEVEL READ COMMITTED;

BEGIN TRANSACTION;

UPDATE Demo.RC_Test_Write_V_Read SET Type = 2

WHERE  Type = 1;
```

3. Before Transaction 1 commits, Transaction 2 begins and issues a SELECT statement for rows of Type = 2. Transaction 2 is blocked and waits for Transaction 1 to commit.

```
--Transaction 2

SET TRANSACTION ISOLATION LEVEL READ COMMITTED;

SELECT Type

FROM   Demo.RC_Test_Write_V_Read

WHERE  Type = 2;
```

4. Transaction 1 commits.

```
--Transaction 1

COMMIT;
```

5. Transaction 2 is no longer blocked and processes its SELECT statement.

Transaction 2 returns 1 row where Type = 2. This is because when Transaction 2 started, it waited for committed data until after Transaction 1 committed.

Understanding concurrency: nonrepeatable reads

There are certain scenarios where you need to have the same row values returned every time you issue a SELECT statement (or read data in any modification DML), A prime example is the case where you look for the existence of a some data before allowing some other action to occur. Like insert an order row, but only if a payment exists. If that payment is changed or deleted while you are creating the order, free products may be shipped.

Consider the following steps involving a read and a write. In this example, the transactions are not overriding the default isolation level of READ COMMITTED: Each transaction is started from a different session. In this scenario, Transaction 1 will suffer a nonrepeatable read when it reads in rows that are change by a different connection, as the default READ COMMITTED does not offer any protection against phantom or nonrepeatable reads. The transactions are explicitly declared using the BEGIN/COMMIT TRANSACTION syntax.

1. A table contains only two rows with a column Type value of 0 and 1.

```
CREATE TABLE Demo.RR_Test (Type int);

INSERT INTO Demo.RR_Test VALUES (0),(1);
```

2. Transaction 1 starts and retrieves rows where Type = 1. One row is returned for Type = 1.

```
--Transaction 1

SET TRANSACTION ISOLATION LEVEL READ COMMITTED

BEGIN TRANSACTION

SELECT Type

FROM    Demo.RR_Test

WHERE   Type = 1;
```

3. Before Transaction 1 commits, Transaction 2 starts and issues an UPDATE statement, setting rows of Type = 1 to Type = 2. Transaction 2 is not blocked and is immediately processed.

```
--Transaction 2

BEGIN TRANSACTION;

UPDATE Demo.RR_Test

SET  Type = 2

WHERE Type = 1;
```

4. Transaction 1 again selects rows where Type = 1 and is blocked.

```
--Transaction 1

SELECT Type

FROM    Demo.RR_Test

WHERE   Type = 1;
```

5. Transaction 2 commits.

```
--Transaction 2

COMMIT;
```

6. Transaction 1 is immediately unblocked. No rows are returned, which is different than the one row returned earlier, since no committed rows now exist where Type=1. Transaction 1 commits.

```
--Transaction 1
```

```
COMMIT;
```

The resulting table now contains a row where Type = 2, because the second transaction has modified the row. When Transaction 2 started, Transaction 1 had not placed any locks on the data, allowing for writes to happen. Because it is doing only reads, Transaction 1 would never have placed any exclusive locks on the data. Transaction 1 suffered from a nonrepeatable read: the same SELECT statement returned different data during the same multistep transaction.

Understanding concurrency: preventing a nonrepeatable read

Consider the following steps involving a read and a write, with each transaction coming from a different session. This time, we protect Transaction 1 from dirty reads and nonrepeatable reads by using the REPEATABLE READ isolation level. A read in the REPEATABLE READ isolation level will block a write. The transactions are explicitly declared by using the BEGIN/COMMIT TRANSACTION syntax:

1. A table contains only rows with a column Type value of 0 and 1.

```
CREATE TABLE Demo.RR_Test_Prevent (Type int);

INSERT INTO Demo.RR_Test_Prevent VALUES (0),(1);
```

2. Transaction 1 starts and selects rows where Type = 1 in the REPEATABLE READ isolation level. 1 row with Type = 1 is returned.

```
--Transaction 1

SET TRANSACTION ISOLATION LEVEL REPEATABLE READ;

BEGIN TRANSACTION;

SELECT Type

FROM   Demo.RR_Test_Prevent

WHERE  TYPE = 1;
```

3. Before Transaction 1 commits, Transaction 2 starts and issues an UPDATE statement, setting rows of Type = 1 to Type = 2. Transaction 2 is blocked by Transaction 1.

```
--Transaction 2

BEGIN TRANSACTION;

UPDATE Demo.RR_Test_Prevent

SET  Type = 2

WHERE Type = 1;
```

4. Transaction 1 again selects rows where Type = 1. The same rows are returned as in step 2.

5. Transaction 1 commits.

```
--Transaction 1

COMMIT TRANSACTION;
```

6. Transaction 2 is immediately unblocked and processes its update. Transaction 2 commits.

```
--Transaction 2

COMMIT TRANSACTION;
```

The resulting table will now contain 2 rows, one Type = 2, and the original row of Type = 0. This is because when Transaction 2 started, Transaction 1 had placed read locks on the data it was selecting, blocking writes to happening until it had committed. Transaction 1 returned the same rows each time and did not suffer a nonrepeatable read. Transaction 2 processed its updates only when it could place exclusive locks on the rows it needed.

Understanding concurrency: experiencing phantom rows

Phantom rows cause issues for transactions when you expect the exact same result back from a query. For example, say you were writing a value to a table that summed up 100 other values (flaunting the fundamentals of database design's normalization rules!), for example a financial transactions ledger table that calculates the current balance. You sum the 100 rows, then write the value. If it is important that the total of the 100 rows matches perfectly, you cannot allow nonrepeatable reads, nor phantom rows.

Consider the following steps involving a read and a write, with each transaction coming from a different session. In this scenario, we describe a phantom read:

1. A table contains only two rows, with Type values 0 and 1

```
CREATE TABLE Demo.PR_Test (Type int);

INSERT INTO Demo.PR_Test VALUES (0),(1);
```

2. Transaction 1 starts and selects rows where Type = 1 in the REPEATABLE READ isolation level. Rows are returned.

```
--Transaction 1

SET TRANSACTION ISOLATION LEVEL REPEATABLE READ;

BEGIN TRANSACTION;

SELECT Type

FROM    Demo.PR_Test

WHERE   Type = 1;
```

3. Before Transaction 1 commits, Transaction 2 starts and issues an INSERT statement, adding another row where Type = 1. Transaction 2 is not blocked by Transaction 1.

```
--Transaction 2

INSERT INTO Demo.PR_Test(Type)

VALUES(1);
```

4. Transaction 1 again selects rows where Type = 1. An additional row is returned compared to the first time the select was run in Transaction 1.

```
--Transaction 1

SELECT Type

FROM    Demo.PR_Test

WHERE   Type = 1;
```

5. Transaction 1 commits.

```
--Transaction 1

COMMIT TRANSACTION;
```

Transaction 1 experienced a phantom read when it returned a different number of rows the second time it selected from the table inside the same transaction. Transaction 1 had not placed any locks on the range of data it needed, allowing for writes in another transaction to happen within the same dataset. The phantom read would have occurred to Transaction 1 in any isolation level, except for SERIALIZABLE. Let's look at that next.

It is important to understand that in some scenarios, a phantom row can have the same effect as a non-repeatable read. For example, consider a query summing the payment amounts for a customer's invoice. In order to ship a product, the invoice needs to be paid in full. An initial read of the data could show the invoice to be paid. But before the order is processed, the same query could indicate the customer had not been paid because a new row arrives with a reversal activity with a negative amount.

Understanding concurrency: preventing phantom rows

Consider the following steps involving a read and a write, with each transaction coming from a different session. In this scenario, we protect Transaction 1 from a phantom read.

1. A table contains two rows with Type values 0 and 1

```
CREATE TABLE Demo.PR_Test_Prevent (Type int);

INSERT INTO Demo.PR_Test_Prevent VALUES (0),(1);
```

2. Transaction 1 starts and selects rows where Type = 1 in the SERIALIZABLE isolation level. The one row where Type = 1 is returned.

```
--Transaction 1

SET TRANSACTION ISOLATION LEVEL SERIALIZABLE;

BEGIN TRANSACTION;

SELECT Type

FROM    Demo.PR_Test_Prevent

WHERE   Type = 1;
```

1. Before Transaction 1 commits, Transaction 2 starts and issues an INSERT statement, adding a row of Type = 1. Transaction 2 is blocked by Transaction 1.

```
--Transaction 2

INSERT INTO Demo.PR_Test_Prevent(Type)

VALUES(1);
```

2. Transaction 1 again selects rows where Type = 1. The same result set is returned as it was in step 2, the one row where Type = 1.

3. Transaction 1 executes COMMIT TRANSACTION.

4. Transaction 2 is immediately unblocked and processes its insert. Transaction 2 commits. Query the table again and there are now 2 rows where Type = 1.

Transaction 1 did not suffer from a phantom read the second time it selected from the table, because it had placed a lock on the range of rows it needed. The table now contains additional rows for Type = 1, but they were not inserted until after Transaction 1 had committed.

The case against READ UNCOMMITTED isolation level

This also pertains to using the NOLOCK hint on your queries.

If locks take time, ignoring those locks will make things go faster. This is true, but this logic is like saying: if the weight of airbags, seat belts, bumpers, and collapsible steering wheels brings down gas mileage, remove them...what could happen? Mix a little lie with the truth, it is easier to take. It is true that these things have weight, but they may save your life one day.

Locks are similar in nature. Locks coordinate our access to resources, allowing multiple users to do multiple things in the database without crushing the other users' changes. The READ COMMITTED isolation level (and an extension we will discuss in the section on SNAPSHOT isolation level called READ COMMITTED SNAPSHOT) does the best to balance locks with performance.

Locks are still held for dirty resources (exclusively locked data that has been changed by the user) but held only long enough to perform reads on a row, and then released after resources are read. The basic process:

- Grab a lock on a resource

- Read that resource

- Release the lock on the resource

- Repeat until you are out of resources to read

No one can dirty (modify) the row we are reading because of the lock, but when we are done, we move on and release the lock. Locks on modifications to on-disk tables work the same way in all isolation levels, even READ UNCOMMITTED, and are held until the transaction is committed.

The effect of the table hint NOLOCK or the READ UNCOMMITTED isolation level is that no locks are taken inside the database for reads, save for schema stability locks. (A query using NOLOCK could still be blocked by Data Definition Language [DDL] commands, such as an offline indexing operation.) The basic thinking is that: you turn on READ UNCOMMITTED isolation level for your connection and things will go faster.

This is strategy that many DBA programmers have all tried before: "We had performance problems, but we've been putting NOLOCK in all our stored procedures to fix it." It will improve performance, but it can easily be detrimental to the integrity of your data.

The biggest issue is that a query may be reading a set of data and see data that doesn't even meet the constraints of the system. So, a transaction for $1,000,000 may be seen in a query, and then when the transaction is rolled back later in the transaction (perhaps because the payment details for the transaction don't meet a constraint or trigger requirement), who knows what celebratory alarms may have gone off thinking we have a million dollars in sales today.

The case against using the READ UNCOMMITTED isolation level is deeper than performance and more than simply reading dirty data, however, the counter argument a developer might make is that data is rarely ever rolled back, or that the data is for reporting only. In production environments, these are not enough to justify the potential problems.

A query in READ UNCOMMITTED isolation level could return invalid data in the following real-world, provable ways:

- Read uncommitted data (dirty reads)

- Read committed data twice

- Skip committed data

- Return corrupted data

- Or the query could fail altogether with error "Could not continue scan with NOLOCK due to data movement." This is a scenario, where since you ignored locks, the structure that was to be scanned is no longer there when you reach it, like in a page split that occurs as you read the page. The solution to this problem is the solution to a lot of concurrency issues. Be prepared to re-execute your batch on this failure.

One final caveat: in SQL Server you cannot apply NOLOCK to tables when used in modification statements, and it ignores the declaration of the READ UNCOMMITTED isolation level in a batch that includes modification statements; for example:

```
INSERT INTO dbo.testnolock1 WITH (NOLOCK)

SELECT * FROM dbo.testnolock2;
```

SQL Server knows that it will use locks for the INSERT, and makes it clear by way of the following error being thrown:

```
Msg 1065, Level 15, State 1, Line 17

The NOLOCK and READUNCOMMITTED lock hints are not allowed for target tables of INSERT,

UPDATE, DELETE or MERGE statements.
```

This protection doesn't apply to the *source* of any writes, hence yet another danger. This following code *is* allowed and is dangerous because it could write invalid data:

```
INSERT INTO testnolock1

SELECT * FROM testnolock2 WITH (NOLOCK);
```

The bottom line is to not use READ COMMITTED isolation level unless you really understand the implications of reading dirty data and have an ironclad reason for doing so (for example, it is an invaluable tool as a DBA to be able to see the changes to data being made in another connection. For example SELECT COUNT(*) FROM dbo.TableName WITH (NOLOCK); can allow you to see the count of rows being inserted into dbo.TableName.) Using it for performance gains is rather short-sighted. However, continue reading for the real way to increase performance without the chance of seeing dirty data as we introduce version-based concurrency techniques in the next section.

Inside OUT

Which isolation level does your .NET application use?

By default, if the programmer has not changed any settings, the .NET System.Transaction infrastructure uses the SERIALIZABLE isolation level, the safest but least practical

CHAPTER 14

choice. SERIALIZABLE provides the most isolation for transactions, so by default .NET transactions do not suffer from dirty reads, nonrepeatable reads, or phantom rows.

You might find, however, that queries from your application using SERIALIZABLE isolation level are being frequently blocked or are the source of blocking, and that reducing the isolation of certain transactions would result in better performance. Evaluate the potential risk of nonrepeatable reads and phantom rows for each new .NET transaction, and reduce the isolation level to REPEATABLE READ or READ COMMITTED only where appropriate. And following guidance throughout this chapter, rarely use the READ UNCOMMITTED isolation level in any production code, without full understanding of why you are doing this.

For applications with high transactional volume, consider also using the SNAPSHOT isolation level to increase concurrency.

You can set the isolation level of any transaction when it is begun by setting the IsolationLevel property of the TransactionScope class. You can also default a new database connection's isolation level upon creation. Remember, however, that you cannot change the isolation level of a transaction after it has begun.

Understanding the enterprise solution to concurrency: row version-based concurrency

In the interest of performance, application developers too often seek to solve concurrency concerns (reduce blocking, limit access to locked objects) by trying to avoid the problem with the tantalizingly named NOLOCK. At first and at scale, the performance gains are too large to consider other alternatives. Since the problems we have mentioned only happen "occasionally," even if it takes 30 hours of meetings, coding, or testing to try to figure out the issues since they seem random, and non-repeatable. There is a far safer option, without the significant drawbacks and potential for invalid data and errors, which allows you to read a previously committed version of data. Using row versioning techniques that give the user a view of a version of the data that was properly committed, you can get tremendous gains that never let the user see dirty data.

Version based concurrency is available in the SNAPSHOT isolation level, or altering the implementation of READ COMMITTED (This will often be referred to as READ_COMMITTED_SNAPSHOT isolation (RCSI) as a shortcut, even in this book, but it is not an isolation level, rather it is a setting at the database level.)

Row versioning allows queries to read from the same rows that might be locked by other queries by storing previous version(s) of a row and reading that when the other is locked. The SQL Server instance's TempDB keeps a copy of committed data, and this data can be served to concurrent requests. In this way, row versioning allows access only to committed data, without blocking access to data locked by writes. By increasing the utilization and workload of TempDB for disk-based tables, performance is dramatically improved by increasing concurrency without the dangers of accessing uncommitted data.

The SNAPSHOT isolation level works at the transaction level. Once you start a transaction, and access any data in the transaction, such as the third statement in the following snippet:

```
SET TRANSACTION ISOLATION LEVEL SNAPSHOT;

BEGIN TRANSACTION;

SELECT * FROM dbo.Table1;

--Note: COMMIT or ROLLBACK this transaction if you execute this code, with a real table
```

Your queries will see a transactionally consistent view of the database. No matter what someone does to the data in dbo.Table1 (or any other table in the same database), you will always see how the data looked as of the start of the first statement executed in that database in your transaction (in this case the SELECT statement). This is great for some things such as reporting. SNAPSHOT gives you the same level of consistency to the data you are reading as does SERIALIZABLE, except that work can continue and things changing. It is not susceptible to nonrepeatable reads and phantom rows, only that you can view expired data.).

The SNAPSHOT isolation level can be problematic for certain types of code because if you need to check if a row exists to do some action, you can't see if the row was created or deleted after you started your transaction context. And as discussed earlier, you can't switch out of SNAPSHOT temporarily, then apply locks to prevent non-repeatable reads, and go back to seeing a consistent, yet possibly expired view of the database.

While SNAPSHOT isolation level works at the transaction level, READ COMMITTED SNAPSHOT works at the statement level. This means that while data is blocked, you will see the previous version of those rows as you read from the table. But if you execute the same statement again, you may get nonrepeatable reads and phantom rows. So, execute a batch such as this:

```
SET TRANSACTION ISOLATION LEVEL REPEATABLE READ;

BEGIN TRANSACTION;

SELECT * FROM dbo.Table1;

SELECT * FROM dbo.Table1;

SELECT * FROM dbo.Table1;
```

And you may get back 1 row the first time, and 1000000 the second (including a freshly modified version of the first row), and 0 the third, all depending on the number of rows when the statement started

Understanding concurrency: accessing data in SNAPSHOT isolation level

The beauty of the SNAPSHOT isolation level is the effect on readers of the data. If you want to go in and query the database, you generally want to see it in a consistent state. And you don't want to block others. A typical problem comes in when you are writing an operational report, and you query a child table, and you get back 100 rows with distinct parentId values, but querying the parent table indicates there are only 50 parentId values (because between queries, another process deleted the other 50). When using SNAPSHOT isolation for read write processes, it is important to consider the techniques mentioned for optimistic locking in the Inside OUT sidebar in the "Understanding concurrency: two requests updating the same rows" section above.

Consider the following steps involving a read and a write, with each transaction coming from a different session. In this scenario, we see that Transaction 2 has access to previously committed row data, even though those rows are being updated concurrently.

1. A table contains only rows with a column Type value of 0 and 1.

```
CREATE TABLE Demo.SS_Test (Type int);

INSERT INTO Demo.SS_Test VALUES (0),(1);
```

2. Transaction 1 starts and updates rows where Type = 1 to Type = 2.

```
--Transaction 1

BEGIN TRANSACTION;

UPDATE Demo.SS_Test

SET  Type = 2

WHERE Type = 1;
```

3. Before Transaction 1 commits, Transaction 2 sets its session isolation level to SNAPSHOT and executes BEGIN TRANSACTION.

```
--Transaction 2

SET TRANSACTION ISOLATION LEVEL SNAPSHOT;

BEGIN TRANSACTION;
```

4. Transaction 2 issues a SELECT statement WHERE Type = 1. Transaction 2 is not blocked by Transaction 1. A row where Type = 1 is returned.

```
--Transaction 2

SELECT Type

FROM   Demo.SS_Test

WHERE  Type = 1;
```

5. Transaction 1 executes a COMMIT TRANSACTION.

6. Transaction 2 again issues a SELECT statement WHERE Type = 1. The same rows from step 3 are returned. Even if the table has all of its data deleted, the results will always be the same for the same query while in the SNAPSHOT level transaction. Once Transaction 2 is committed or rolled back, then queries on that connection will see the changes that have occurred since the transaction started.

Transaction 2 was not blocked when it attempted to query rows that Transaction 1 was updating. It had access to previously committed data, thanks to row versioning.

Implementing row-versioned concurrency

You can implement row versioned isolation levels in a database in two different ways. Turning on SNAPSHOT isolation simply allows for the use of SNAPSHOT isolation and begins the process of row versioning. Alternatively, turning on RCSI changes the default isolation level to READ COMMITTED SNAPSHOT. You can implement both or either. It's important to understand the differences between these two settings, because they are not the same:

- READ COMMITTED SNAPSHOT configures optimistic concurrency for reads by overriding the default isolation level of the database. When turned on, all queries will use RCSI unless overridden.

- SNAPSHOT isolation mode configures optimistic concurrency for reads and writes. You must then specify the SNAPSHOT isolation level for any transaction to use SNAPSHOT isolation level. It is possible to have update conflicts with SNAPSHOT isolation mode that will not occur with READ COMMITTED SNAPSHOT. The concept of an update conflict will be covered in the next section.

The statements to implement SNAPSHOT isolation in the database are simple enough but is not without consequence. Even if no transactions or statements use the SNAPSHOT isolation level, behind the scenes, TempDB begins storing row version data for disk-based tables, minimally for the length of the transaction that modifies the row. This way, if a row-versioned transaction starts while rows are being modified, the previous versions are available.

> ### NOTE
>
> **Memory-optimized tables share properties with** SNAPSHOT **isolation level but are implemented in an extremely different manner that is based completely on row-versioning and do not use** TempDB. **They will be covered in Chapter 15.**

Here's how to allow transactions in a database to start transactions in the SNAPSHOT isolation level:

```
ALTER DATABASE databasename SET ALLOW_SNAPSHOT_ISOLATION ON;
```

CHAPTER 14

After executing only the above statement, all transactions will continue to use the default READ COMMITTED isolation level, but you now can specify the use of *SNAPSHOT* isolation level at the session level or in table hints, as shown in the following example:

```
SET TRANSACTION ISOLATION LEVEL SNAPSHOT;
```

Using SNAPSHOT isolation level on an existing database can be a lot of work, and as we cover in the next session, it changes some very important ways we handle executing queries, since what once was write blocking becomes an error message for you to try again. Alternatively, if you want to apply the "go faster" solution that mostly works with existing code, you need to alter the meaning of READ COMMITTED to read row-versions instead of waiting for locks to clear.

You can use READ_COMMITTED_SNAPSHOT independently of ALLOW_SNAPSHOT_ISOLATION. Similarly, these settings are not tied to the MEMORY_OPTIMIZED_ELEVATE_TO_SNAPSHOT database setting to promote memory-optimized table access to SNAPSHOT isolation.

Here's how to turn on RCSI:

```
ALTER DATABASE databasename SET READ_COMMITTED_SNAPSHOT ON;
```

> ### NOTE
>
> Changing the READ_COMMITTED_SNAPSHOT database option on a live database where you have memory-optimized tables set to DURABILITY = SCHEMA_ONLY will empty those tables. You need to move the contents of the table to a more durable table before changing READ_COMMITTED_SNAPSHOT to ON or OFF.

➤ We discussed memory-optimized tables in greater detail in Chapter 7, "Understanding table features."

For either of the previous ALTER DATABASE statements to succeed, no other transactions can be open in the database. It might be necessary to close other connections manually or to put the database in SINGLE_USER mode. Either way, we do not recommend that you perform this change during production activity.

Inside OUT

If changing to READ COMMITTED SNAPSHOT is so much faster, why is this not the default?

In most cases, the settings that are the default in SQL Server are historic in nature. The default collation for an instance is never what you should choose when setting up a new server but is rather what was set many years ago and left alone for backward compatibility.

However, this is not the case with READ COMMITTED SNAPSHOT. Care must be taken to question what this change in fundamentals means to your system, because decisions will be made on how the table looks at the start of a read query, not how it looks in a committed state. This is generally okay, but this change in timing of what data your queries see may be important to the integrity of the data (not applicable for how constraints operate, but the change in timing will affect triggers or other coded integrity methods.)

It is essential to be aware and prepared for the increased utilization in the TempDB, both in activity and space requirements. To avoid autogrowth events, consider increasing the size of the TempDB data and log files and monitor their size. Although you should try to avoid autogrowth events by growing the TempDB data file(s) yourself, you should also verify that your TempDB file autogrowth settings are appropriate in case things grow larger than expected.

> For more information on file autogrowth settings, see Chapter 8.

Should the TempDB exhaust all available space on its volume, SQL will be unable to row-version rows for transactions and will terminate them with SQL Server error 3958. SQL Server will also issue errors 3967 and 3966 as the oldest row versions are removed from the TempDB to make room for new row versions needed by newer transactions.

NOTE

Prior to SQL Server 2016, READ COMMITTED SNAPSHOT and SNAPSHOT isolation levels were not supported with columnstore indexes. Beginning with SQL Server 2016, SNAPSHOT isolation and columnstore indexes are fully compatible.

Understanding update operations in SNAPSHOT isolation level

Transactions that read data in SNAPSHOT isolation or RCSI will have access to previously committed data instead of being blocked, when data needed is being changed. This is important to understand and could result in an update statement experiencing a concurrency error when you start to change data. Update conflicts change how systems behave; you need to understand it before deciding to implement your code in SNAPSHOT isolation level.

One of the keys to understanding how modifying data in the SNAPSHOT isolation level behaves is to understand that you can only have one "dirty" version of a physical resource. So, if another connection modifies a row and you only read the row, you see previous versions. But you change a row that another connection has also modified, your update was based on out of data information and will be rolled back.

For example, consider the following steps, with each transaction coming from a different session. In this example, Transaction 2 fails due to a concurrency conflict or "write-write error:"

CHAPTER 14

1. A table contains multiple rows, each with a unique Type value.

```
CREATE TABLE Demo.SS_Update_Test

(Type int CONSTRAINT PKSS_Update_Test PRIMARY KEY,

 Value nvarchar(10));

INSERT INTO Demo.SS_Update_Test VALUES (0,'Zero'),(1,'One'),(2,'Two'),(3,'Three');
```

2. Transaction 1 begins a transaction in the READ COMMITTED isolation level and performs an update on the row where ID = 1.

```
--Transaction 1

BEGIN TRANSACTION ;

UPDATE Demo.SS_Update_Test

SET  Value = 'Won'

WHERE Type = 1;
```

3. Transaction 2 sets its session isolation level to SNAPSHOT and issues a statement to update the row where ID = 1, this connection is blocked, waiting on the modification locks to clear.

```
--Transaction 2

SET TRANSACTION ISOLATION LEVEL SNAPSHOT;

BEGIN TRANSACTION

UPDATE Demo.SS_Update_Test

SET  Value = 'Wun'

WHERE Type = 1;
```

4. Transaction 1 commits, using a COMMIT TRANSACTION statement. The update succeeds.

5. Transaction 2 then immediately fails with SQL error 3960.

```
Msg 3960, Level 16, State 2, Line 8
```

Snapshot isolation transaction aborted due to update conflict. You cannot use snapshot isolation to access table 'dbo.AnyTable' directly or indirectly in database 'DatabaseName' to update, delete, or insert the row that has been modified or deleted by another transaction. Retry the transaction or change the isolation level for the update/delete statement.

NOTE

SNAPSHOT isolation level with disk-based tables in SQL Server is not pure row-versioned concurrency, which is why in the previous example, Transaction 2 was blocked by

Transaction 1. Using memory optimized tables, which are based on pure row-versioned concurrency, the transaction would have failed immediately, rather than having been blocked.

Transaction 2 was rolled back. Let's try to understand why this error occurred, what to do, and how to prevent it.

In SQL Server, SNAPSHOT isolation uses locks to create blocking but doesn't block updates from colliding for disk-based tables. It is possible for a statement to fail when committing changes from an UPDATE statement, if another transaction has changed the data needed for an update during a transaction in SNAPSHOT isolation level.

For disk-based tables, the update conflict error will look like the Msg 3960 that we saw a moment ago. For queries on memory-optimized tables, the update conflict error will look like this:

```
Msg 41302, Level 16, State 110, Line 8
The current transaction attempted to update a record that has been updated since this
transaction started. The transaction was aborted.
```

What this means for you is that if you decide to use SNAPSHOT isolation level for your modification query's isolation level, you must be ready to handle an error that isn't really an error. It is just warning to re-execute your statements, after checking to see if anything has changed since you started your query. This is 100% the same answer for handling deadlock conditions and will be the same answer for handling all modification conflicts using memory optimized tables.

Even though optimistic concurrency of snapshot isolation level increases the potential for update conflicts, you can mitigate these by doing the following if you need to specifically attempt to avoid update conflicts:

- Minimize the length of transactions that modify data. While it seems like this would be less of an issue because readers aren't blocked, it does increase the likelihood of modification conflicts.

- When running a modification in SNAPSHOT isolation level, try to avoid using any statements that place update locks to disk-based tables inside multistep explicit transactions.

- Specifying the UPDLOCK table hint can have utility at preventing update conflict errors for long-running SELECT statements. The UPDLOCK table hints places locks on rows needed for the multistep transaction to complete. The use of UPDLOCK on SELECT statements with SNAPSHOT isolation level is not a panacea for update conflicts, and it could in fact create them. Frequent SELECT statements with UPDLOCK could increase the number of update conflicts with updates. Regardless, your application should handle errors and initiate retries when appropriate.

CHAPTER 14

If two concurrent statements use UPDLOCK, with one updating and one reading the same data, even in implicit transactions, an update conflict failure is possible if not likely.

- Consider avoiding writes altogether while in SNAPSHOT isolation mode. Use it only to do reads where you do not plan to write the data in the same transaction you have fetched it in.

Specifying table granularity hints such as ROWLOCK or TABLOCK can prevent update conflicts, although at the cost of concurrency. The second update transaction must be blocked while the first update transaction is running—essentially bypassing SNAPSHOT isolation for the write. If two concurrent statements are both updating the same data in SNAPSHOT isolation level, an update conflict failure is likely for the statement that started second.

Understanding on-disk versus memory-optimized concurrency

Queries using memory-optimized tables (also referred to as in-memory OLTP tables) can perform significantly faster than queries based on the same data in disk-based tables. Memory-optimized tables can improve the performance of frequently written-to tables by up to 40 times over disk-based tables.

However, this almost magical performance improvement comes at a price, not just in the need for extra memory, but also in that they way they implement concurrency controls is rather different than disk-based tables. When in the concurrency scenarios previously introduced, all the concurrency protections provided were based on locking, or in other words, waiting until the other connection has completed, and then applying the changes. However, locking only applies only to on-disk tables, not memory-optimized tables.

In the case of memory-optimized tables, locking isn't the mechanism that ensures isolation. Instead, the in-memory engine uses pure row versioning to provide row content to each transaction. In pure row versioning, an UPDATE statement is an insert of a new row, and an update to the effective ending timestamp on the previous row. A DELETE statement only updates the effective ending timestamp on the current row. If you are familiar with the data warehousing concept of a Slowly Changing Dimension (SCD), this is similar to an SCD Type II. It is equally similar to how temporal tables work, though both the current and historical data are in the same physical structure.

➤ **For more explanation of temporal tables, see Chapter 7.**

Previous versions hang around as long as they are needed by transactions and are then cleaned up as they can be (data is also hardened to what is referred to as the delta file for durability purposes, as well as the transaction log.)

If two transactions attempt to modify the same physical data resource at the same time, one transaction will immediately fail due to a concurrency error, rather than being blocked and waiting. Only one transaction can be in the process of modifying or removing simultaneously. The other will fail with a concurrency conflict (SQL error 41302). However, if two transactions insert the same value for the primary key, it will not fail until the transaction is committed, as it is not the same physical resource.

This is the key difference between the behavior of pessimistic and optimistic concurrency. Pessimistic concurrency uses locks to prevent write conflict errors, whereas optimistic concurrency uses row versions with acceptable risk of write conflict errors. On-disk tables offer isolation levels that use pessimistic concurrency to block conflicting transactions, forcing them to wait. Memory-optimized tables offer optimistic concurrency that will cause a conflicting transaction to fail.

Memory optimized tables allow you to use SNAPSHOT, REPEATABLE READ, and SERIALIZABLE isolation levels and provide the same types of protections by definition. In the case of a nonrepeatable read, SQL error 41305 will be raised. In the case of a phantom read, a SQL error 41325 will be raised. Because of these errors, applications that write to memory-optimized tables must include logic that gracefully handles and automatically retries transactions. They should already handle and retry in the case of deadlocks or other fatal database errors.

> ➤ **For more information on configuring memory-optimized tables, see Chapter 7.**

> ➤ **We discuss more about indexes for memory-optimized tables in Chapter 15.**

Understanding reading memory optimized data in other than SNAPSHOT isolation level

All data that is read by a statement in memory-optimized tables behaves like SNAPSHOT isolation level. Once your transaction starts and you access any memory optimized data in the database, further reads from memory-optimized tables will be from a consistent view of those objects (note that the memory optimized and on-disk table are in different "containers", so your consistent view of the memory optimized data doesn't start if you read only on-disk tables.)

However, what makes your work more interesting is that when in REPEATABLE READ or SERIALIZABLE isolation levels, the scan for phantom and non-repeatable read rows is done during commit rather than as they occur.

For example, consider the following steps, with each transaction coming from a different session. A typical scenario might be running a report of some data. You read in a set of data, perform some operation on it, and then read another set of rows, and your process requires the data to all stay the same.

1. A table contains many rows, each with a unique ID. Transaction 1 begins a transaction in the SERIALIZABLE isolation level and reads all the rows in the table.

2. Transaction 2 update on the row where ID = 1. This transaction commits successfully

3. Transaction 1 again reads rows in this same table. No error is raised, and rows are returned as normal.

4. Transaction 1 commits. An error is raised (41305), alerting you to a non-repeatable read. (Even though this was in SERIALIZABLE isolation level, the check for a non-repeatable read is done first, since this is a reasonably easy operation, whereas the scan for phantom rows requires the engine to run a query on the data to see if extra rows are returned.

Generally speaking, most use of the isolation levels other than SNAPSHOT with memory-optimized data should be limited to operations like data integrity checks, where you want to make sure that one row exists before you insert the next row.

➤ For more details on conflict detection and retry logic with memory optimized tables, see *https://docs.microsoft.com/sql/relational-databases/in-memory-oltp/transactions-with-memory-optimized-tables#conflict-detection-and-retry-logic*

Specifying isolation level for memory-optimized tables in queries

Isolation level is specified in a few, mildly confusing ways for memory optimized tables. The first method is in an ad-hoc query, not in an existing transaction context, you can simply query the table as you always have, and it will be accessed in SNAPSHOT isolation level.

If you are in the context of a transaction, it will not automatically default to SNAPSHOT isolation level. Rather you need to specify the isolation level as a hint, such as:

```
BEGIN TRANSACTION;

SELECT *
FROM    dbo.MemoryOptimizedTable WITH (SNAPSHOT);
```

You can make it default to SNAPSHOT isolation level by turning on the MEMORY_OPTIMIZED_ELEVATE_TO_SNAPSHOT database option. This promotes access to all memory-optimized tables in the database up to SNAPHOT isolation level if the current isolation level is not REPEATABLE READ or SERIALIZABLE. It will promote the isolation level to SNAPSHOT from isolation levels such as READ UNCOMMITTED and READ COMMITTED. This option is off by default, but you should consider it because you otherwise cannot use the READ UNCOMMITTED or SNAPSHOT isolation levels for a session including memory-optimized tables.

If you need to use REPEATABLE READ or SERIALIZABLE, or your scenario will not meet the criteria for automatically choosing SNAPSHOT isolation level, you can specify the isolation level using table concurrency hints. (See the section "Using table hints to change isolation" earlier in this chapter). Note that only memory-optimized tables can use this SNAPSHOT table hint, not disk-based tables.

Finally, note that you cannot mix disk-based SNAPSHOT isolation level with memory-optimized SNAPSHOT isolation level. For example, you cannot include memory-optimized tables in a session that begins with SET TRANSACTION ISOLATION LEVEL SNAPSHOT, even if MEMORY_OPTIMIZED_ ELEVATE_TO_SNAPSHOT = ON or you specify the SNAPSHOT table hint.

➤ For more information on configuring memory-optimized tables, see Chapter 7.

➤ We discuss more about indexes for memory-optimized tables in Chapter 15.

Understanding durability settings for performance

One of the base requirements for a relational database management system is that data saved is durable, meaning that once you believe it is saved in the database, it is permanent and cannot be lost (short of losing the entire server, and your backups). This requirement is a very important requirement of relational databases, but it is certainly a detriment to performance. When data is saved to a table via a DML statement, by default, three steps are required, both for on-disk and in-memory tables. Data is synchronously saved to memory and the transaction log, then control is returned to the user. The third step is done asynchronously, which is to save the data to a disk file, hardening the data and releasing the corresponding transaction log records to be deleted.

For performance's sake, there are two configurations that we can use to increase performance at the detriment of durability. The first is to use memory-optimized tables, setting the durability setting on the table to SCHEMA_ONLY. This creates a logless memory-based object that will be empty, with only the schema remaining when you restart the server. This is a tool that can be useful in certain scenarios and will provide amazing performance, even hundreds of times faster than on-disk tables. It is not, however, a universally applicable tool to increase application performance because it makes the table completely non-durable.

NOTE

The process of writing data to disk and memory is changing as new technologies arrive. In SQL Server 2019, a new feature call Hybrid Buffer Pool can use Persistent Memory modules (PMEM) and just write data to disk, and access it from the disk instead of RAM. For more details on Hybrid Buffer Pool, check Chapter 2, in the Hybrid Buffer Pool section, as well as: *https://docs.microsoft.com/sql/database-engine/configure-windows/hybrid-buffer-pool*.

In this section, we will look at a way you can alter how durability is handled in SQL Server, in a manner that can be useful on very small departmental servers as well as enterprise servers. The other tool you can use is delayed durability, which alters the durability of your data slightly, but enough to make possibly a tremendous difference in how long it takes to return control to your server's clients when it makes sense.

Delayed durability database options

Delayed durability allows for transactions to avoid synchronously committing to a disk; instead, synchronously committing only to memory, but synchronously committing to a disk. This opens the possibility of losing data in the event of a server shutdown before the log has been written, so it does have dangers. This engine feature was first introduced in SQL Server 2014 and works basically the same today.

While this sounds concerning, it is good to note that unless your SQL Server instance's databases are running in a synchronous availability group data loss it technically possible in some cases (and even then, chance exists for the databases to drop into asynchronous under pressure), so you already face the possibility of losing recently written rows in the event of a sudden server or drive failure where you lose the log and data files.

Databases in Azure SQL Database also support delayed durability transactions, with the same caveat and expectations for data recovery. Some data loss is possible, and you should only use this feature if you can recreate important transactions on a server crash.

> **NOTE**
>
> **Distributed (DTC) and cross-database transactions are always durable.**

At the database level, you can set the DELAYED_DURABILITY option to DISABLED (default), ALLOWED, or FORCED.

ALLOWED allows any explicit transaction to be coded to be optionally set to delayed durability, using:

```
COMMIT TRANSACTION WITH ( DELAYED_DURABILITY = ON );
```

Additionally, for natively compiled procedures, you can specify DELAYED_DURABILITY in the BEGIN ATOMIC block. Take, for example, this header of a procedure in the WideWorldImporters database:

```
CREATE PROCEDURE [Website].[RecordColdRoomTemperatures_DD]

@SensorReadings Website.SensorDataList READONLY

WITH NATIVE_COMPILATION, SCHEMABINDING, EXECUTE AS OWNER

AS

BEGIN ATOMIC WITH

    (

        TRANSACTION ISOLATION LEVEL = SNAPSHOT,

        LANGUAGE = N'English',
```

```
DELAYED_DURABILITY = ON
)

    BEGIN TRY

        …
```

The FORCED option means that every transaction, regardless of what the person writing the COMMIT statement wishes, will have asynchronous log writes. This obviously has implications on the entirety of the users of the database, and you should consider it carefully with existing applications.

The delayed durability options, implemented either at the database level or at the transaction level, has use in very-high-performance workloads for which the bottleneck to write performance is the transaction log itself. By trading the possibility for new rows to be written only to memory and lost in the event of a shutdown, you can gain a significant performance increase, especially with write-heavy workloads.

Even if you cannot employ delayed durability in your normal day-to-day operations, it can be a very useful setting when loading a database, particularly for test data. Because log writes are done asynchronously, instead of every transaction waiting for small log writes to complete, log writes are batched together in an efficient manner.

NOTE

While delayed durability does apply to memory optimized tables, the DELAYED_DURABILITY database option is not related to the DURABILITY option when creating optimized tables.

A transaction that changes data under delayed durability will be flushed to the disk as soon as possible, whenever any other durable transaction commits in the same database, or whenever a threshold of delayed durability transactions builds up, You also can force a flush of the transaction log with the system stored procedure sp_flush_log. Otherwise, the transactions are written to a buffer in memory until a log flush event. SQL Server manages the buffer but makes no guarantees as to the amount of time a transaction can remain in buffer.

It's important to note that delayed durability is simply about reducing the I/O bottleneck of committing a massive quantity of writes to the transaction log. This has no effect on isolation (locking, blocking) or access to any data in the database that must be read to perform the write. Otherwise, delayed durability transactions follow the same rules as other transactions.

NOTE

Any SQL Server instance service shutdown, whether it be a planned restart or sudden failure, could result in delayed durability transactions being lost. This also applies to the failover of a failover cluster instance (FCI), availability group, or database mirror.

Transaction log backups and log shipping will similarly contain only transactions made durable. You must be aware of this potential when implementing delayed durability.

Understanding how SQL Server executes your query

The internal process to execute a query in SQL Server is *very* complex. It is, however, something that the engineers at Microsoft are working very hard for you to be able to ignore one day. This day has not yet arrived, but in SQL Server 2019, this future is inching ever closer with new and smarter query optimization features. In the next major section, entitled "Understanding advanced engine features for tuning queries," we will spend time looking at the kind of strides they are making to help the DBA deal with more important things.

However, as a DBA, it will remain essential to understand how queries are executed for many years to come, as this informs how you write queries, and how you know when SQL Server's optimizer has made an incorrect choice. The reality is that they will likely never reach the place where every query runs perfectly regardless of how it is written, but the number of cases that need manual intervention decreases over time. What it also means is that instead of a lot of easy tuning issues and several complex ones, you will instead have only complex issues to work on.

Inside OUT

What if you upgrade and SQL Server starts executing queries poorly?

A very common problem in complex systems is that people exploit how something works to their advantage. The query optimizer is no different. Often you will write a very complex query and, due to what is actually a flaw, you get good performance. Then you upgrade and your query works poorly.

Ideally you rewrite your queries and make them work with the new optimizer. But if this is not immediately possible for one or more queries, you can use the QUERY_OPTIMIZER_COMPATIBILITY_LEVEL_n query hint (where N is 100 – 150, depending on the version you want your query to behave as).

Understanding the overall query execution process

A user writes a query, which could be 1 line of code like `SELECT * FROM dbo.TableName;` or it could be a statement that contains 1,000 lines. This query could be a batch of multiple statements, use temporary objects, other coded objects such as user defined functions, not to mention table variables, and perhaps a cursor thrown in for good measure. After writing a query, the user tries to execute it.

First, the code is parsed and translated to structures in the native language of the query processor. If the query is a technically correct SQL syntax (well or poor written, either way), it will pass this phase. If there are syntax errors like SLECT * FROM dbo.TableName; then it fails with a syntax error. If you reference tables that don't exist like: SELECT * FROM dbr.TableName; (should have been dbo.), that will also fail.

Once the code is parsed and prepared for execution, the query optimizer tries to calculate the best way to run your code, and run it again using the same process, by saving what is referred to as the Query Plan, or the Execution Plan/Explain Plan depending on which tool you are using. Getting the right query plan for different parameters, or server load is where the real rocket science comes in for the engineers. That engine work is why a person with no understanding of how computers work can write a query in less than 30 seconds that will access 100 million rows, aggregating the values of one or more columns, and filtering out values that they don't want to see, and get back results in just a few seconds.

There are three kinds of execution plans you will deal with: estimated, actual, and live. The estimated plan is something you can ask for, to show you what the execution plan will probably look like. The actual query plan has more details about what actually occurred, which can vary from the estimated plan for multiple reasons, including SQL Server's Intelligent Query Processing features, which we will discuss more later in the chapter. There is another version of a plan you can see as well, referred to as the live execution plan, which basically lets you see the query plan that was chosen, with the rows of data flowing through as it is executing.

The execution plan that is created is a detailed blueprint of the query optimizer's plan for processing any statement. Each time you run a statement, including batches with multiple statements, an execution plan is generated. Query plans share with you the plan of execution for queries, inform you of the steps the Database Engine will take to retrieve data, through the various transformation steps to sort, join, and filter data, and finally return or affect data. All statements you execute will create an execution plan, including Data Manipulation Language (DML) and Data Definition Language (DDL).

The plan will contain the estimated costs and other metadata of each piece that it takes to process a query and finally the DML or DDL operation itself. This data can be invaluable to developers and database administrators for tuning query performance. When you look at the query plan, you will be able to see some of the estimates that were made, compared to the actual values.

Execution plans are placed in the procedure cache, which is stored in active memory, that SQL Server uses when a statement is executed again. The procedure cache can be cleared manually, and it is reset when you restart a server. Plans from the procedure cache are reused for a query when that exact same query text is called again. Queries will reuse the same plan only if every character of the query statement matches, including capitalization, whitespace, line breaks, and text in comments. There is one exception to this rule of query reuse, and that is when SQL Server parameterizes a query or stored procedure statement. Parameterization will allow some values, like literals or variables to be treated as having a different value on each execution, a concept we will see later in the chapter.

Retrieving execution plans in SQL Server Management Studio

Let's now look at how you can see the different types of execution plans in Management Studio in some detail, and how you can view them.

Displaying the estimated execution plan

You can generate the estimated execution plan quickly and view it graphically from within SQL Server Management Studio by choosing the Display Estimated Execution Plan option in the Query menu, or by pressing Ctrl+L. An estimated execution plan will return for the highlighted region, or for the entire file if no text is selected.

You can also retrieve an estimated execution plan in T-SQL code by running the following statement. It will be presented in an XML format:

```
SET SHOWPLAN_XML ON;
```

In SSMS, in Grid mode, the results are displayed as a link as for any XML output, but SSMS knows that this is a plan, so click the link to open the plan graphically in SSMS. You can save the execution plan as a .sqlplan file by right-clicking in the neutral space of the plan window.

You can also configure the estimated text execution plan in code by running one of the following statements, which return the execution plan in one result set or two, respectively:

```
SET SHOWPLAN_ALL ON;
```

```
SET SHOWPLAN_TEXT ON;
```

The text plan of the query using one of these two statements can be useful if you want to send the plan to someone in an email in a compact manner.

> **NOTE**
>
> Be aware that when any of the aforementioned SET options are turned on for a connection, SQL Server will not run statements, it only returns estimated execution plans. Remember to turn off the SET SHOWPLAN_ option before you reuse the same session for other queries.

As expected, the estimated execution plan is not guaranteed to match the actual plan used when you run the statement, but it is usually a very reliable approximation you can use to see if a query looks like it will execute well enough. The query optimizer uses the same information for the estimate as it does for the actual plan when you run it.

To display information for individual steps, hover over a step in the execution plan. You can also click an object, and then open the Properties window by pressing F4 or, in the View menu, by clicking Properties Window. After you have a bit of experience with plans, you'll notice the estimated execution plan is missing some information that the actual plan returns. The missing fields are generally self-explanatory in that they are values you would not have until the query has actually executed; for example, Actual Number Of Rows, Actual Number Of Batches, and Number of Executions.

As an example, consider the following query in the WideWorldImporters database:

```
SELECT *

FROM Sales.Invoices

        JOIN Sales.Customers

                on Customers.CustomerId = Invoices.CustomerId

WHERE Invoices.InvoiceID like '1%';
```

In Figure 14-1, we have part of the plan for this query, which looks pretty simple, but the full query plan takes up a good bit more space, due to a security policy (Application.FilterCustomersBySalesTerritoryRole) that implements row-level security that you wouldn't even notice without looking at the Query Plan.

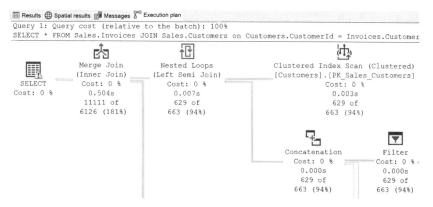

Figure 14-1   Example query plan, showing a portion of the plan for the query from the text

Displaying the actual execution plan

You can view the actual execution plan used to execute the query along with the statement's result set from within SSMS by choosing the Include Actual Execution Plan option in the Query menu, or by pressing Ctrl+M to turn on the setting. After turning on this setting, when you run a statement, you will see an additional tab appear along with the execution results after the results of statements have completed.

NOTE

Turning on the actual execution plan feature will add extra time to the execution of your query. If you are comparing runs of a query, this could skew the results.

You can also return the actual execution plan as a result set using T-SQL code, returning XML that can be viewed graphically in SSMS, by running the following statement:

```
SET STATISTICS XML ON;
```

The actual execution plan is returned as an XML string. In SSMS, in Grid mode, the results display as a link which can be viewed graphically by clicking on the link. Remember to turn off the SET STATISTICS option before you reuse the same session, if you don't want to get back the actual plan for every query you run on this connection.

You can save both estimated and actual execution plans as a .sqlplan file by right-clicking the neutral space of the plan window.

You might see that the total rows to be processed does not match total estimated number of rows for that step; rather, the multiple of that step's estimated number of rows and a preceding step's estimated number of rows. Back in Figure 14-1, on the Merge Join (Inner Join) operator, you can see that 11111 of 6654 rows were processed. The 6654 was the estimate, and 11111 was the actual number of rows.

Inside OUT

What's the difference between "Number Of Rows Read" and "Actual Number Of Rows"?

This is an important distinction, and it can tip you off to a significant performance issue.

Both are "Actual" values, but Actual Number Of Rows contains the number of values in the range of rows we expect to retrieve, and Number Of Rows Read contains the number of rows that were actually read, based on the number of rows that needed to be accessed to filter the rows for a predicate you have included.

The difference could be significant to performance, and the solution is likely to change the query so that the predicate is narrower and/or better aligned with indexes on the table. Alternatively, you can add indexes to better fit the query predicates and make for more efficient searches.

One of the easiest ways to reproduce this behavior is with a wildcard search, for example in the WideWorldImporters sample database:

```
SELECT Invoices.InvoiceID

FROM Sales.Invoices

WHERE Invoices.InvoiceID like '1%';
```

In the XML, in the node for the Index Scan, you see:

```
<RunTimeInformation>

<RunTimeCountersPerThread Thread="0" ActualRows="11111" ActualRowsRead="70510"

...
```

Defined as "ActualRowsRead" in the XML of the plan, this value is displayed as "Number of Rows Read" in SQL Server Management Studio. Similarly, "ActualRows" is displayed as "Actual Number of Rows."

Displaying live query statistics

Live query statistics are an excellent feature that was introduced in SQL Server 2016 Management Studio. You can generate and display a "live" version of the execution plan by using SQL Server Management Studio. You can access live statistics on versions of SQL Server starting with SQL Server 2014.

You turn on the Live Execution Statistics option for a connection via the Query menu of SQL Server Management Studio, as demonstrated in Figure 14-2.

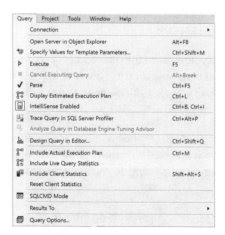

Figure 14-2 The Include Live Query Statistics option

Executing the query we used back in the previous section, you will see something like the following in Figure 14-3.

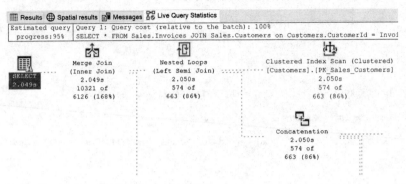

Figure 14-3   Example Live Query Statistics

In Figure 14-3, you can see that 10231 of the estimated 6126 rows have been processed by the Merge Join Operator, and 574 rows had been processed by the Nested Loops (Left Semi Join) operator.

The Live Query Statistics window initially displays the execution plan more or less like the estimated plan but fills out the details of how the query is being executed as it is processing it. If your query runs quickly, you'll miss the dotted, moving lines and the various progress metrics including the duration for each step and overall percentage completion. The percentage is based on the Actual rows processed currently incurred versus a total number of rows processed for that step.

The Live Query Statistics contains more information than the Estimated query plan, such as Actual Number Of Rows and Number Of Executions, but less than the Actual query plan. The Live Query Statistics does not display some data from the Actual Execution Plan, Actual Execution Mode, Number Of Rows Read, and Actual Rebinds.

Returning a live execution plan will noticeably slow down the query processing, so be aware that the individual and overall execution durations measured will often be longer than when the query is run without the option to display Live Query Statistics. However, it can be worth it to see where a query is hung up in processing.

If your server is configured correctly to do so, you can see the live query plan of executing queries in action by using Activity Monitor, which is accessed by right-clicking on a server in SSMS. Then you can access the live execution plan by right-clicking any query in the Processes or Active Expensive Queries panes.

To understand the details of setting up your server's Query Profiling Infrastructure, go to *https://docs.microsoft.com/sql/relational-databases/performance/query-profiling-infrastructure*.

Just note that it is not free to add the ability to capture live query execution statistics, so determine if it is worth it first.

Permissions necessary to view execution plans

Not just anyone can view the execution plans of a query. There are two ways you can view plans, and they require different kinds of permissions.

If you wish to generate and view a query plan, you will first need permissions to execute the query, even to get the estimated plan. Additionally, retrieving the Estimated or Actual execution plan requires the SHOWPLAN permission in each database referenced by the query. The Live Query Statistics feature requires SHOWPLAN in each database, plus the VIEW SERVER STATE permission to see live statistics, so it cannot (and should not) be done by just any user.

It might be appropriate in your environment to grant SHOWPLAN and VIEW SERVER STATE permissions to developers. However, the permission to execute queries against the production database may not be appropriate in your regularly environment. If that is the case, there are alternatives to providing valuable execution plan data to developers without production access:

- Consider providing database developers with saved execution plan (.sqlplan) files for offline analysis.

- Consider also configuring the dynamic data masking feature, which may already be appropriate in your environment for hiding sensitive or personally identifying information for users who are not sysadmins on the server. Do not provide UNMASK permission to developers; assign that only to application users.

- Sometimes, an administrator may need to execute queries on a production server due to differences in environment/hardware, but be cautioned on all of what that means in terms of privacy, etc.

> ➤ **For more information on dynamic data masking, see Chapter 7.**

Providing the ability to see already generated and used execution plans can be done using several tools. SQL Server Extended Events and Profiler have ways to capture execution plans. Activity Monitor, in query reports such as Recent Expensive Queries, will allow you to right click and see the plan if it is still available in cache. Finally, there the DMVs that provide access to queries that executed (such as sys.dm_exec_cached_plans), or requests (sys.dm_exec_requests) will have a column named plan_handle that you can use to pass to the sys.dm_exec_query_plan DMV to retrieve the plan. In order to access plans in this manner, the server principal will need the VIEW SERVER STATE permission or be a member of sysadmin.

Finally, you can see execution plans in Query Store, which is covered later in the chapter, and for it you need VIEW DATABASE STATE, or you must be a member of the db_owner fixed role.

Understanding execution plans

At this point, we have established the basics of what an execution plan is, where to find it, and what permissions you need to see it. After you have a graphical execution plan in front of you, it is important to have a basic understanding of how to read how the statement was processed, and how future queries that use this same plan will operate.

Interpreting graphical execution plans

In the next list, we review some of the most common things to look for as you review execution plans in SSMS.

> **NOTE**
>
> You can also choose to review execution plans with a well-known third-party tool called **Plan Explorer**, which is a free download from *https://www.sentryone.com/*. It provides a number of additional features that are often helpful when working with very large query plans.

First, start an execution plan. For our purposes, a simple one like for the following query:

```
SELECT Invoices.InvoiceID

FROM Sales.Invoices

WHERE Invoices.InvoiceID like '1%';
```

Click Ctrl+L, and you will be presented with the following estimated query plan shown in Figure 14-4.

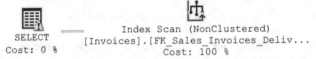

```
Query 1: Query cost (relative to the batch): 100%
SELECT Invoices.InvoiceID FROM Sales.Invoices WHERE Invoices.InvoiceID LIKE '1%'
```

Figure 14-4   Simple query plan

To display details for individual steps, position your pointer over a step in the execution plan. A detailed tooltip style window will appear, much like you can see in Figure 14-5. An interesting detail immediately should come to you when you look at the plan. It doesn't say it is scanning the `Sales.Invoices` table, but rather an index. This is because the index is set up for not only searching for data, but if an index has all the data needed to execute the query, the index "covers" the needs of the query and the table's data structures are not touched.

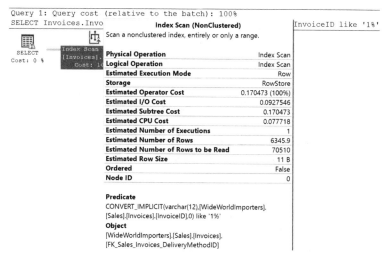

Figure 14-5   Simple query plan with statistics

You can also click an object, and then open the Properties window by pressing F4 or, in the View menu, clicking Properties Window. You will see the same estimated details in the properties pane. Now, let's get the Actual Execution Plan, by using Ctrl-M, or one of the other methods discussed earlier. Execute the query, and you will see the actual plan, as seen in Figure 14-6.

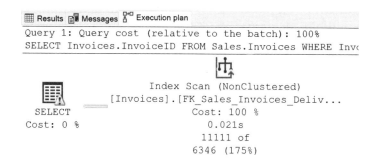

Figure 14-6   Actual Execution Plan for Example Query

The first thing you should notice is that we have a few more details on our query plan. In particular, that 11111 rows were processed, of 6346. You can see that the 6346 is the estimated number of rows that would be returned by the query. This guess was based on statistics, which do not give perfect answers, and when you are tuning larger queries, very large disparities of such guesses need to be investigated.

Open the properties pane and you'll notice the returned estimate and actual values for some metrics, including Number of Rows, Executions, IO Statistics, etc. Look for differences in estimates that were made, and actual numbers here; they can indicate an inefficient execution plan and the source of a poor performing query. Your query might be suffering from a poorly chosen plan because of the impact of parameter sniffing or stale, inaccurate index statistics. (We discuss parameter sniffing later in this chapter and discuss index statistics in Chapter 15)

Notice that some values, like cost information, contain only estimated values, even when you are viewing the actual execution plan. This is because the operator costs aren't sourced separately, they are generated the same way for both estimated and actual plans, and do not change based on statement execution. Furthermore, cost is not just comprised entirely of duration. You might find that some statements far exceed others in terms of duration, but not in cost.

Start with the upper left operator

The upper-left operator will reflect the basic operation that the statement performed. For example, SELECT, DELETE, UPDATE, INSERT, or any of the DML statements (if your query created an index, you might see CREATE INDEX.) This operator might contain warnings or other items that require your immediate attention. These can show up with a small yellow triangle warning icon, with additional detail when you position your pointer on the operator.

For example, in our example plan, the SELECT operator was the far left, and it has a triangle over it. You can see in the ToolTip, that it is due to: "Type conversion in expression (CONVERT_IMPLICIT(varchar(12),[WideWorldImporters].[Sales].[Invoices].[InvoiceID],0)) may affect "CardinalityEstimate" in query plan choice, Type conversion in expression (CONVERT_IMPLICIT(varchar(12),[WideWorldImporters].[Sales].[Invoices].[InvoiceID],0)>='1') may affect "SeekPlan" in query plan choice."

In other words, we used a LIKE on an integer value, so the query plan is warning us that it cannot estimate the number of rows as well as it can if our WHERE clause employed integer comparisons to integers.

Click the upper-left operator, and then press F4 to open the Properties window, or open the Properties window from the View menu in SQL Server Management Studio. In this list are some other things to look for. You'll see warnings repeated in here, along with additional aggregate information.

> ### NOTE
> Yellow triangles on an operator indicate something that should grab your attention. The alert could tip you off to an implicit conversion—a data type mismatch that could be costly. Investigate any warnings reported before moving on.

Look also for the Optimization Level, which typically says FULL. If the Optimization Level was TRIVIAL, the query optimizer bypassed optimization of the query altogether because it was straightforward enough. For example, if the plan for the query only needed to contain a simple

Scan or Seek operation along with the operation operator, like SELECT. If the Optimization Level is not FULL or TRIVIAL, this is something to investigate.

Look next for the presence of a value for Reason For Early Termination, which indicates the query optimizer did not spend as much time as it could have picking the best plan.

- It may have determined that the plan it had picked was good enough to not need to keep optimizing, so a value of "Good Enough Plan Found" is returned.

- If the reason is "Time Out," the optimizer tried as many times as it could to find the best plan before taking the best plan available, which might not be good enough. If you see this case, consider simplifying the query, especially reducing the use of functions, and by potentially modifying the underlying indexes.

- If the reason is "Memory Limit Exceeded," this is a rare and critical error indicating severe memory pressure on the SQL Server instance.

Next, look right, then read from right to left

Graphical execution plans build from sources (rightmost objects), and apply operators to join, sort, and filter data from right to left, eventually arriving at the leftmost operator. In the rightmost objects, you'll see Scans, Seeks, and Lookups of different types. You might find some quick, straightforward insight into how the query is using indexes.

Each of the items in the query plan are referred to as operators. Each of these is a module of code that does a certain task to process data. Reading the query plan, the rightmost operators are acquiring data, possibly filtering it, then passing it off to the left until it reaches the single operator leftmost operator that represents the action of the query. Two of the main types of operators for fetching data from a table or index are seeks and scans.

A seek operator is used to find a portion of a set of data, through the index structure. For example, if you wanted to find Chapter 7 in this book, you would go to the table of contents, find the page number, and go to that page. They are generally the most efficient operators to see and can rarely be improved by additional indexes. The seek operation will find the leaf page in the index, which contains the keys of the index, plus any included column data (which in the case of a clustered table, will be all the data for the row).

Once you have the leaf data, if it contains everything you need, the operation was covered by the index. However, when you need more data than the index contains, you will see a lookup operator joined to the seek operator using a join operator. This means that although the optimizer used a seek, it needed a second pass at the table in the form of a lookup on another object, typically the clustered index, using a second seek operator. Key lookups (on clustered indexes) and RID lookups (on heaps) are expensive and inefficient, particularly when a large number of rows are being accessed. These lookups can tally up to a very large percentage of the cost of a query.

If key lookup operators are needed frequently, they can usually be eliminated from the execution plan with the modification to an existing nonclustered index with included columns for the data that needed to be looked up.

> ➤ **For an example, see the section "Designing nonclustered indexes" in Chapter 15.**

The other typical data source operator is a scan. Scan operations aren't great unless your query is intentionally performing a query that returns a large number of rows out of a table or index. Scans read all rows from the table or index, which can be very inefficient when you need to return only a few rows, or more efficient when you need a large number of rows. Without a nonclustered index with a well-designed key (if one can be found) to enable a seek for the query, a scan might be the query optimizer's only option. Scans can be ordered if the source data is sorted, which is useful for some joins and aggregation options.

Scans on nonclustered indexes are often better than scans of clustered indexes, in part due to what is likely a smaller leaf page size (though they suffer from the same issues with key lookups), in fact it is generally worse because the optimizer will likely expect to return many rows from the object. If you are expecting to return a low number of rows, test and compare the performance of a new or updated nonclustered index, created based on the predicates and outputs of Index Scans and Clustered Index Scans.

NOTE

Very few queries are important enough to deserve their own indexes. Think "big picture" when creating indexes. If you try to cover every query's needs with an index, you may discover more and more issues creating data. More than one query should benefit from any nonclustered indexes you create. Avoid redundant or overlapping nonclustered indexes. See Chapter 15 for more information on creating nonclustered indexes, including "missing" indexes.

Other types of scans include the following:

- **Table Scans.**   These indicate that the table has no clustered index. We discuss why this is probably not a good idea in Chapter 15.

- **Index scan.**   Scan the rows of an index, even the included columns of the index, for values.

- **Remote Scans.**   This includes any object that is preceded by "remote," which is the same operation but over a linked server connection. Troubleshoot them the same way, but potentially by making changes to the remote server instead. For more details on PolyBase, see Chapter 20, "Leveraging Big Data and Machine Learning" as an alternative to linked server connections that may be superior in many usages.

- **Constant Scans.**   These appear when the query optimizer deals with scalar values, repeated numbers, and other "constants." These are necessary operators for certain tasks and generally not actionable from a performance standpoint.

- **Columnstore Index Scans.**   These are incredibly efficient operators when you are working with lots of rows, but relatively few columns, and likely will outperform a Clustered Index Scan or Index Seek where millions of rows, for example, must be aggregated. No need to create a nonclustered index to replace this operator, unless your query is searching for a few rows.

NOTE

Since SQL Server 2016, columnstore indexes are a viable option for read-write tables in a transactional system. In previous versions of SQL Server, nonclustered columnstore indexes did not allow writes to the table, and so couldn't easily be adopted in transactional databases. If you aren't using them already to optimize large row count queries, consider adding them to your toolbelt.

Furthermore, since SQL Server 2016 SP1, columnstore indexes are even available to all edition licenses of SQL Server, even Express edition, though editions below Enterprise edition have limits to the amount of columnstore cache in memory. For more information, see Chapter 15, as well as *https://docs.microsoft.com/sql/sql-server/ editions-and-components-of-sql-server-version-15.*

The weight of the lines connecting operators tells part of the story, but isn't the full story

SQL Server dynamically changes the thickness of the gray lines to reflect the actual number of rows. You can get a visual idea of where the bulk of data is coming from by observing the pipes, drawing your attention to the places where performance tuning could have the biggest impact. If you hover over the line in your query plan, you can see the rows transmitted in each step, as you can see in Figure 14-7.

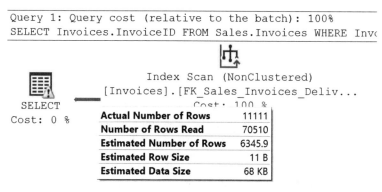

Figure 14-7   Showing number of rows read and estimated in query plan.

The visual weight and the sheer number of rows does not, however, directly translate to cost. Look for where the pipe weight changes from light to heavy, or vice versa. Be aware of when thick pipes are joined or sorted.

Operator cost share isn't the full story either

When you run multiple queries, the cost of the query relative to the batch is displayed in the query execution plan header, and within each plan, the batch cost relative to the rest of the operators in the statement is displayed. SQL Server uses a cost-based process to decide which query plan to use.

When optimizing a query, it is usually going to be useful to start with the costliest operators. But deciding to address only the highest-cost single operator in the execution plan might be a dead end, as there are definitely examples where this will not be the case.

In Figure 14-8, we can see an example of when operator cost might not align with the amount of data. You should investigate performance tuning this execution plan using all the information provided.

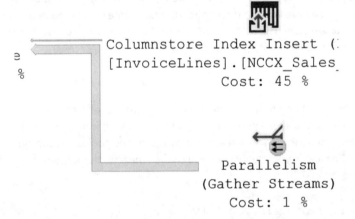

Figure 14-8   Plan snippet showing cost and relative data amounts

Look for Join operators and understand the different algorithms

As you read from right to left, in a query of any complexity, you'll likely see the paths meet at a join operator. Two tables, indexes, or the output from another operator can be joined together. There are three types of join operators to be aware of, particularly as this is where you will often find a large portion of the cost of an execution plan.

The types are hash match, merge join, and nested loop, and each can be the fastest way to join two sets of data, depending on the size of the sets, if they are indexed, and if they are sorted already or it won't be too costly to sort with a sort operator. (There is an adaptive join operator, new to SQL Server 2019, which allows the optimizer to situationally choose between hash match or nested loop. This will be mentioned again in the "Intelligent Query Processing" section later in the chapter.)

A merge join operator takes two large sorted sets of data and merges the sets together. The query processor can scan each set, in order, matching row from each table with a single pass through the sets. This can be quite fast, but the requirement for ordered sets is where the cost comes in. If you are joining two sets that are keyed on the same column, they are then sorted, so two ordered scans can be merged. The optimizer can choose to sort one or both inputs to the merge join, but this is often costly.

Hash match is the join operator that is used to join two large sets to one another, generally when there is no index to easily use and sorting is too costly. As such, it has the most overhead, with a temporary "index" created based on an internal hashing algorithm to bucketize values to make it easier to match one row to another. This hash structure is in memory if possible but may spill onto disk. The presence of a hash join is not necessarily a bad thing, but just know that it is the least efficient algorithm to join two data sets together, precisely because they are not suited for the other two operators.

> ## NOTE
>
> Understand that usually when the optimizer does something that seems weird, like sort sets of data for an internal operation like a join, it is usually doing this because it has calculated that for the design of your database, this is the best way to do it.
>
> As we discussed earlier, sometimes complex queries take too long to find the absolute best way to process your query, and sometimes the plans are just horribly wrong, like where statistics are not up to date, for example. This is one reason to watch for plans that have full optimization.

> ➤ Later in the section named "Analyzing cached execution plans" we will look at a technique to analyze cached plans for different scenarios like partial optimization.

Finally, the most efficient join algorithm is the least optimized sounding one. The nested loops join algorithm is the basic row-by-row processing that people preach about you as a programmer never doing. It takes one row in one input and searches the other input for values that meet the join criteria. When you are joining two sets together, one is indexed on the join key, and doesn't need to go fetch additional data using a key lookup, nested loops are very fast. The additional operators were implemented to support larger, ideally reporting-style workloads.

Each of the following could reduce the cost of a join operator.

- There may be an opportunity to improve the indexing on the columns being joined, or perhaps, you have a join on a compound key that is incompletely defined.

- In the case of a merge join, you may see a preceding sort operator. This can be an opportunity to present the data already sorted according to how the Merge Join requires the data to be sorted. If this is a composite key, perhaps changing the ASC/DESC property or the order of an index key column in a composite index could remove the sort operator. As usual, test to make sure that the original sort order isn't used in other places as well.

- Make sure you that are filtering at the lowest level possible. Perhaps a WHERE clause could exist in a subquery instead of at the top level of the query, or in the definition of a derived table or common table expression (CTE) instead of in the subsequent query.

- Hash operators are the most expensive. Reducing the row counts going into a hash match or hash join could allow the query optimizer to use a less memory-intensive and less costly join operator.

- Nested loops are often necessitated by key lookups and sometimes quite costly. They too are no longer necessary if a new nonclustered index is added to address the Key Lookup or to make an accompanying Index Seek more capable.

Inside OUT

If it is bad for you to write looping code, why is this usually the best way for SQL Server to perform the task?

This really comes down to the type of code that is executing the different code elements. T-SQL is an interpreted, declarative language. There is a fairly significant cost to executing a statement. This cost does not show up when you are running a few statements, but when you run 100s of statements, it becomes obvious.

The query processor runs in very efficient, machine code, and is highly optimized to process our joins in just three ways. While you may write FROM Table1 JOIN Table2 ON... the resulting amount of code that is executed to pull data from disk, to memory, and then do the comparisons is astonishing.

As such, the architects of SQL Server's engine did not optimize for you to go row by row with a cursor, but to leave it to the engine.

Look for Parallel icons

The left-pointing pair of arrows in a yellow circle shown in Figure 14-9 indicate that your query has been run with a parallel-processing execution plan. We talk more about Parallelism later in this chapter, but the important thing here is to be aware that your query has gone parallel.

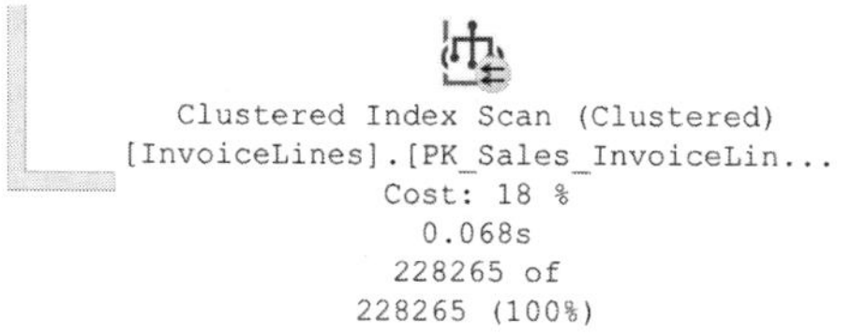

```
Clustered Index Scan (Clustered)
[InvoiceLines].[PK_Sales_InvoiceLin...
           Cost: 18 %
             0.068s
           228265 of
        228265 (100%)
```

Figure 14-9 The parallel indicator on a Clustered Index Scan operator.

This doesn't mean that multiple sources or pipes are being read in parallel; rather, the work for individual tasks has been broken up behind the scenes. The query optimizer decided it was faster if your workload was split up and run into multiple parallel streams of rows.

You might see one of the three different parallelism operators—the distribute streams, gather streams, and repartition streams operators—each of which appear only for parallel execution plans.

Cardinality estimation

When a query plan is being generated, one of the most important factors you will deal with is the cardinality estimation. Cardinality is defined as the number of items in a set (hence, a cardinal number is a non-negative integer). The importance of cardinality estimation cannot be overstated and is analogous to how you might do a task. If you run a store and ship 3 products a week, you may just have a stack of products, and walk 2 miles to the post office and be efficient enough. If you have to ship 300,000 products a day, the net effect of each product being shipped needs to be the same, but the way you will achieve this must be far more optimized and include more than just one person.

SQL Server makes the same choices. You join table X with table Y on column Id. If X has 1000 rows, and Y 10, the solution is easy. If they each have a billion, and you are looking for a specific value in table X, say `value = 'Test'`, there are many choices to make. How may rows in X have a value of `'Test'`? Then, once you know that value, how many values of Id in X will match Id values in Y.

This estimation is done in two ways. First: with guesses based on histograms of the data. The table is scanned when creating statistics (for example, by executing UPDATE STATISTICS, or by automatic statistics gathering that happens as data changes, based on the database setting AUTO_UPDATE_STATISTICS). Take the first case where the tables are small. The engine stores a histogram that has something like the following:

RANGE_HI_KEY	RANGE_ROWS	EQ_ROWS	DISTINCT_ RANGE_ROWS	AVERAGE_ RANGE_ROWS...
Smith	400	200	20	10
Tests	200	120	23	5

CHAPTER 14

From this, the number of rows that are equal to `'Test'` can be guessed to be < 400 (since Test is between Smith and Tests), less than 200, since approximately 200 rows matched Smith, and there are approximately 20 distinct values, so it might be guessed that there are 10 matches. Exactly how this estimation is done is proprietary, but it is definitely important to keep your statistics up to date using maintenance methods (see Chapter 8 for more details on proper upkeep of SQL Server).

For many versions of SQL Server, the same cardinality estimation algorithms were pretty much used. However, starting in SQL Server 2014 and continuing in SQL Server 2019, Microsoft has been tweaking the cardinality estimation significantly with pretty much every release. Example changes for recent versions of SQL Server are that the cardinality estimator understands the number of rows may have increased since the samples were taken. Or that certain column values may be related (searching for names of automobiles, like auto maker and model, go together.) While SQL Server 2014 was now 3 releases and 5 years ago, there are still very large amounts of the user base that are on earlier versions (at this year's PASS Summit, a big focus from Microsoft was to get people to upgrade from SQL Server 2008 and 2008 R2 which are no longer supported.)

The problem with cardinality estimation is that it is a very inexact science. The guesses made are frequently imperfect enough to be bad for performance, sometimes due to the changes made version to version, particularly with very large, very complex queries. In order to control which cardinality estimator is used, there are a few methods. The first is to use the database compatibility level, like this to use the SQL Server 2016 cardinality estimator (and everything else that this limits to 2016 rules too):

```
ALTER DATABASE database_name

SET COMPATIBILITY_LEVEL = 130;
```

To use the SQL Server 7.0 legacy cardinality estimator (with a database set in 120 compatibility level, which was SQL Server 2014), you can use the following database configuration value:

```
ALTER DATABASE SCOPED CONFIGURATION
    SET LEGACY_CARDINALITY_ESTIMATION = ON;
```

In compatibility level 130 and higher (SQL Server 2016 SP1), there is a query hint you can use:

```
SELECT …
FROM …
OPTION (USE HINT ('FORCE_LEGACY_CARDINALITY_ESTIMATION'));
```

Alternatively, you can use the compatibility level to use the cardinality estimator of that previous version in all your queries. For the most part, we suggest using the latest cardinality estimator possible, and addressing issues in your queries if possible, but realize this is not always a feasible solution.

➤ For more information, including how to tell which version of cardinality estimation was used, see Microsoft Docs: *https://docs.microsoft.com/sql/relational-databases/ performance/cardinality-estimation-sql-server.*

Understanding parameterization and "parameter sniffing"

SQL Server parameterization occurs when the query optimizer detects values (such as the search criteria of a WHERE clause statement) that can be parameterized. For example, the statements in a stored procedures are parameterized from the stored procedure declaration. A query can be parameterized when it meets certain conditions.

For example, a query may have values that could take on multiple values. A query such as:

```
SELECT Value From TableName WHERE Value = 'X';
```

A simple query such as this can be parameterized and the literal 'X' replaced by a parameter, much like if you were writing a stored procedure. By default, a query where you reference more than one table will not be parameterized, but you can change the database setting of PARAMETERIZATION to FORCED and more complex queries will be parameterized. Finally, you can get a parameterized plan by using a variable:

```
DECLARE @Value varchar(10) = 'X';
SELECT Value From TableName WHERE Value = @Value;
```

This query will be parameterized no matter how complex it is. There are additional ways that a query will be parameterized through client APIs, but the best way to parameterize your queries is with stored procedures.

With parameterization, it's possible that two potentially helpful or potentially problematic conditions can occur:

- You can reuse a query plan for multiple queries for which the query text is exactly the same, except for parameterized values.

- The same query could use the same execution plan for two different values of a parameter, resulting in vastly different performance.

For example, you might create the following stored procedure to fetch the orders that have been placed for goods from a certain supplier:

```
CREATE OR ALTER PROCEDURE Purchasing.PurchaseOrders_BySupplierId

    @SupplierId int

AS

SELECT PurchaseOrders.PurchaseOrderID,

    PurchaseOrders.SupplierID,
```

CHAPTER 14

```
           PurchaseOrders.OrderDate

   FROM    Purchasing.PurchaseOrders

   WHERE   PurchaseOrders.SupplierID = @SupplierId;
```

> **NOTE**
>
> **The CREATE OR ALTER statement is a relatively new improvement that either creates to object if it doesn't exist, or alters it if it does. For more detail, see: *https://blogs.msdn.microsoft.com/sqlserverstorageengine/2016/11/17/ create-or-alter-another-great-language-enhancement-in-sql-server-2016-sp1***

Now, the plan of this procedure will depend on what value is passed in on the first compilation. For example, if the larger rowcount query (@SupplierID = 5) is used first and has its query plan cached, the query plan will choose to scan the clustered index of the table, because the value of 5 has a relatively high cardinality in the table. If the smaller rowcount query (@SupplierID = 1) is run first, its version of the plan will be cached which will use an index seek and a key lookup. In this case, the plan is different, less efficient for very large row counts, and will be used for all versions of the parameterized statement.

Here are a few advanced troubleshooting avenues to alleviate this scenario:

- You can use the OPTIMIZE FOR query hint to demand that the query analyzer use a cached execution plan that substitutes a provided value for the parameters. You also can use OPTIMIZE FOR UNKNOWN, which instructs the query analyzer to optimize for the most common value, based on statistics of the underlying data object.

- The RECOMPILE query hint or procedure option does not allow the reuse of a cached plan, forcing a fresh query plan to be generated each time the query is run.

- You can use the Plan Guide feature (implemented via stored procedures) to guide the query analyzer to a plan currently in cache. You identify the plan via its plan_handle. For information on identifying and analyzing plans in sys.dm_exec_cached_plans, see the upcoming section.

- You can use the Query Store feature (implemented with a GUI in SQL Server Management Studio and via stored procedures behind the scenes) to visually look at plan performance and force a query to use a specific plan currently in cache.

  ➤ **For more information, see the section "Using the Query Store feature" later in this chapter.**

- Use the USE PLAN query hint to provide the entire XML query plan for any statement execution. This obviously is the least convenient option, and like other approaches that override the query analyzer, you should consider it an advanced and temporary performance tuning technique.

- Turn off parameter sniffing at the database level using: ALTER DATABASE SCOPED CONFIGURATION SET PARAMETER_SNIFFING = OFF;. This will cause plans to all act like OPTIMIZE FOR UNKNOWN.

Understanding the Procedure Cache

The Procedure Cache is a portion of memory that contains query plans for statements that have been executed. New execution plans enter the Procedure Cache only when a statement is run. If the procedure cache already contains a plan matching a previous run of the current statement, the execution plan is reused, saving valuable time and resources.

This is one reason that complex statements can appear to run faster the second time they are run, other than the fact that data may be cached on a second execution.

The Procedure Cache is empty when the SQL Server service starts and grows from there. SQL Server manages plans in the cache, removing them as necessary under memory pressure. The size of the Procedure Cache is managed by SQL Server and is inside the memory space configured for the server in the Max Server Memory configuration setting. Plans are removed based on their cost and how recently it has been used. Smaller, older plans and single-user plans are the first to be cleared.

CHAPTER 14

Inside OUT

If you run a statement only once, does SQL Server need to remember its plan?

By default, SQL Server adds an execution plan to the Procedure Cache the first time it is generated, because it expects that it may be executed again. You can view the number and size of cached execution plans with the dynamic management view sys.dm_exec_cached_plans. You might find that a large amount of space in the Procedure Cache is dedicated to storing execution plans that have been used only once. These single-use plans can be referred to as *ad hoc* execution plans, from the Latin, meaning "for this situation." This should not be confused with the other way that this term is used in SQL Server circles to mean all queries not contained in a stored procedure, trigger, or function.

If you find that a SQL Server instance is storing many single-use plans, as many do, selecting the server configuration option Optimize For Ad Hoc Queries will benefit performance. This option does not optimize ad hoc queries; rather, it optimizes SQL Server memory by storing an execution plan in memory only after the same query has been detected twice. Queries might then benefit from the cached plan only upon the third time they are run.

The following query provides the number of single-use versus multiuse query plans, and the space used to store both:

```
SELECT
      PlanUse = CASE WHEN p.usecounts > 1 THEN '>1' ELSE '1' END
      , PlanCount = COUNT(1)
        , SizeInMB = SUM(p.size_in_bytes/1024./1024.)
FROM sys.dm_exec_cached_plans p
GROUP BY CASE WHEN p.usecounts > 1 THEN '>1' ELSE '1' END;
```

Clearing the Procedure Cache

You might find that manually clearing the Procedure Cache is useful when performance testing or troubleshooting. Typically, you want to reserve this activity for preproduction systems.

There are a few common reasons to clear out cached plans in SQL Server. For example, one common reason is to compare two versions of a query or the performance of a query with different indexes—you can clear the cached plan for the statement to allow for proper comparison.

NOTE

While this can be a good thing to try, what you are testing is not only your query, but your hardware's ability to fetch data from the disk. When you look at the output of SET STATISTICS IO ON, the Logical Reads measurement will give you an accurate comparison of two query version's amount of reads of data from memory. The presence of Physical Reads will tell you that data the query needed was not in cache. Higher amounts of physical reads will indicate that the server's ability to hold everything needed into RAM may not be sufficient, .

You can manually flush the entire Procedure Cache, or individual plans in cache, with the following database-scoped configuration command, which affects only the current database context, as opposed to the entire instance's procedure cache:

```
ALTER DATABASE SCOPED CONFIGURATION CLEAR PROCEDURE_CACHE;
```

This command was introduced in SQL Server 2016 and is effectively the same as the command DBCC FREEPROCCACHE within the current database context. It works in both SQL Server and Azure SQL Database. DBCC FREEPROCCACHE is not supported in Azure SQL Database, and should be deprecated from your use going forward in favor of ALTER DATABASE.

CAUTION

Avoid clearing the Procedure Cache in a live production environment during normal business hours. Doing so will cause all new statements to have their execution plans compiled, dramatically increasing processor utilization and potentially dramatically slowing performance.

You can also remove a single plan from cache by identifying its plan_handle and then providing it as the parameter to the ALTER DATABASE statement. Perhaps this is a plan you would like to remove for testing or troubleshooting purposes that you have identified with the script in the previous section:

```
ALTER DATABASE SCOPED CONFIGURATION CLEAR PROCEDURE_CACHE 0x06000700CA920912307B86
7DB701000001000000000000000000000000000000000000000000000000000000;
```

You can alternatively flush the cache by object type. This command clears cached execution plans that are the result of ad hoc statements and prepared statements (from applications, using sp_prepare, typically through an API):

```
DBCC FREESYSTEMCACHE ('SQL Plans');
```

The advantage of this statement is that it does not wipe the cached plans from "Programmability" database objects such as stored procedures, multi-statement table-valued functions, scalar user-defined functions, and triggers. The following command clears the cached plans from those type of objects:

```
DBCC FREESYSTEMCACHE ('Object Plans');
```

Note that DBCC FREESYSTEMCACHE is not supported in Azure SQL Database.

You can also use DBCC FREESYSTEMCACHE to clear cached plans association to a specific Resource Governor Pool, as follows:

```
DBCC FREESYSTEMCACHE ('SQL Plans', 'poolname');
```

Analyzing cached execution plans

You can analyze execution plans in aggregate starting with the dynamic management view sys.dm_exec_cached_plans, which contains a column named plan_handle. The plan_handle column contains a system-generated varbinary(64) string that can be used with a number of other dynamic management views. As seen in the code example that follows, you can use the plan_handle to gather information about aggregate plan usage, plan statement text, and to retrieve the graphical execution plan itself.

You might be used to viewing the graphical execution plan only after a statement is run in SSMS, but you can also analyze and retrieve plans for queries executed in the past by using the following query against a handful of dynamic management objects (DMOs). These DMOs return data for all databases in SQL Server instances, and for the current database in Azure SQL Database. The following queries can be used to analyze different aspects of cached execution plans. Note that this query may take considerable amount of time as written, so you may wish to pare down what is being output for your normal usage.

```
SELECT
    p.usecounts AS UseCount,
    p.size_in_bytes / 1024 AS PlanSize_KB,
    qs.total_worker_time/1000 AS CPU_ms,
    qs.total_elapsed_time/1000 AS Duration_ms,
    p.cacheobjtype + ' (' + p.objtype + ')' as ObjectType,
    db_name(convert(int, txt.dbid )) as DatabaseName,
    txt.ObjectID,
    qs.total_physical_reads,
    qs.total_logical_writes,
    qs.total_logical_reads,
    qs.last_execution_time,
     qs.statement_start_offset as StatementStartInObject,
    SUBSTRING (txt.[text], qs.statement_start_offset/2 + 1 ,
      CASE WHEN qs.statement_end_offset = -1
           CRLF THEN LEN (CONVERT(nvarchar(max), txt.[text]))
         ELSE qs.statement_end_offset/2 - qs.statement_start_offset/2 + 1 END)
      AS StatementText,
     qp.query_plan as QueryPlan,
    aqp.query_plan as ActualQueryPlan
FROM sys.dm_exec_query_stats AS qs
INNER JOIN sys.dm_exec_cached_plans p ON p.plan_handle = qs.plan_handle
OUTER APPLY sys.dm_exec_sql_text (p.plan_handle) AS txt
OUTER APPLY sys.dm_exec_query_plan (p.plan_handle) AS qp
OUTER APPLY sys.dm_exec_query_plan_stats (p.plan_handle) AS aqp
--tqp is used for filtering on the text version of the query plan
```

```
CROSS APPLY sys.dm_exec_text_query_plan(p.plan_handle, qs.statement_start_offset,
qs.statement_end_offset) AS tqp

WHERE txt.dbid = db_id()

ORDER BY qs.total_worker_time + qs.total_elapsed_time DESC;
```

Note that the preceding query orders by a sum of the CPU time and duration, descending, returning the longest running queries first. You can adjust the ORDER BY and WHERE clauses in this query to hunt, for example, for the most CPU-intensive or most busy execution plans. Keep in mind that the Query Store feature, as detailed later in this chapter, will help you visualize the process of identifying the most expensive and longest running queries in cache.

As you will see after running in the previous query, you can retrieve a wealth of information from these DMOs, including statistics for a statement within an object that generated the query plan. The query plan appears as blue hyperlink in SQL Server Management Studio's Results To Grid mode, opening the plan as a new .sqlplan file. You can save and store the .sqlplan file for later analysis. Note too that this query may take quite a long time to execute as it will include a line for every statement in each query.

For more detailed queries, you can add some code to search only for queries that have certain details in the plan. For example, looking for plans that have a Reason For Early Termination. In the execution plan XML, the Reason For Early Termination will show in a node StatementOpt-mEarlyAbortReason. Simply add the search conditions before the ORDER BY in the script, using the following logic:

```
and tqp.query_plan LIKE '%StatementOptmEarlyAbortReason%'
```

Included in the query is sys.dm_exec_query_plan_stats, which is new in SQL Server 2019 and will return the actual plan, with the details that are added to the plan after an execution.

> ➤ **More details on sys.dm_exec_query_plan_stats are available on Microsoft Docs:**
> *https://docs.microsoft.com/sql/relational-databases/system-dynamic-management-views/*
> *sys-dm-exec-query-plan-stats-transact-sql.*

Permissions required to access cached plan metadata

The only permission needed to run the previous query in SQL Server is the server-level VIEW SERVER STATE permission, which might be appropriate for developers to have access to in a production environment because it does not give them access to any data in user databases.

In Azure SQL Database, because of the differences between the Basic/Standard and Premium tiers, different permissions are needed. In the Basic/Standard tier, you must be the server admin or Azure Active Directory Admin to access objects that would usually require VIEW SERVER STATE. In Premium tier, you can grant VIEW DATABASE STATE in the intended database in Azure SQL Database to a user who needs permission to view the above DMVs.

CHAPTER 14

Understanding parallelism

Parallelism in query processing (much less general computing) is a very complex topic, but luckily much of the complexity of parallelism in SQL Server is generally encapsulated from the DBA and programmer. A query that uses parallelism and one that doesn't can be the same query, with the same plan (other than allowing one or more operators to work in parallel.) When SQL Server decides to split and stream data needed for requests into multiple threads, it uses more than one processor to get the job done. The number of different parallel threads used for the query is called the degree of parallelism. Because parallelism can never exceed the number of logical processors, naturally the maximum degree of parallelism (MAXDOP) is capped.

The main job of the DBA is to tune the MAXDOP for the server, database, and individual queries when the defaults don't behave well. On a server with a mixed load of OLTP and analytics workloads, some larger analytics queries can overpower other active users.

The max degree of parallelism is set at the server level using the server UI in SSMS, or more commonly using the sp_configure system stored procedure. In SQL Server 2019, there is a MaxDOP tab in the Database Engine Configuration that will calculate what MaxDOP probably ought to be for your server configuration. In previous versions, the system default was 0 (allowing all processors to be used in a single statement).

Parallelism is a seemingly magical way to make queries run faster (most of the time), but even seeming like magic comes at a price. While queries may perform fastest in a vacuum going massively parallel, the overuse of parallelism creates a multithreading bottleneck at scale with multiple users. Split into too many different parts, queries slow down en masse as CPU utilization rises and SQL Server records increasing values in the *CXPACKET* wait type.

> ➤ We talk about CXPACKET here, but for more about wait type statistics, see Chapter 8.

Until SQL Server 2016, MAXDOP was only a server-level setting, a setting enforced at the query level, or a setting enforced to sessions selectively via the Resource Governor, an Enterprise edition feature. Since SQL server 2016, the MAXDOP setting is also available as a database-scoped configuration. You can also use the MAXDOP query hint in any statement to override the database or server level MAXDOP setting.

> ➤ For more details on Resource Governor, see Chapter 3: "Designing and implementing an on-premises database infrastructure" and Chapter 8.

Setting a reasonable value for MAXDOP will determine how many CPUs will be used to execute a query, but there is another setting to determine what queries to allow to use parallelism. This is the Cost Threshold for Parallelism (CTFP), which enforces a minimum bar for query cost before a query can use a parallel execution plan. The higher the threshold, the fewer queries go parallel. This setting is fairly low by default, but its proper setting in your environment is quite dependent on the workload and processor count. More expensive queries usually benefit from parallelism more than simpler queries, so limiting the use of parallelism to the worst queries in your workload can help. Similarly, setting the CTFP too high could have an opportunity impact, as performance is limited, queries are executed serially, and CPU cores go underutilized. Note that CTFP is a server-level setting only.

If large queries are already a problem for performance and multiple large queries regularly run simultaneously, raising the CTFP might not solve the problem. In addition to the obvious solutions of query tuning and index changes, it may be worth it to include the use of columnstore indexes for analytic queries and using MAXDOP as a hint instead to limit some very large queries from taking over your server.

A possible indication of parallelism being an issue is when the CXPACKET wait is a dominant wait type experienced over time by your SQL Server. You may need to adjust both MAXDOP and CTFP when performance tuning. You can also view the live and last wait types for a request using sys. dm_exec_requests. Make these changes in small, measured gestures, and don't overreact to performance problems with a small number of queries. Use Query Store to benchmark and trend the performance of high-value and high-cost queries as you change configuration settings.

Another flavor of CPU pressure, and in some ways the opposite of the CXPACKET wait type, is the SOS_SCHEDULER_YIELD wait type. The SOS_SCHEDULER_YIELD is an indicator of CPU pressure, indicating that SQL Server had to share time or "yield" to other CPU tasks, which may be normal and expected on busy servers. Whereas CXPACKET is the SQL Server complaining about too many threads in parallel, the SOS_SCHEDULER_YIELD is the acknowledgement that there were more runnable tasks for the available threads. In either case, first take a strategy of reducing CPU-intensive queries and rescheduling or optimizing CPU-intensive maintenance operations. This is more economical than simply adding CPU capacity.

Inside OUT

How can you reduce the processor utilization during maintenance operations?

If processor utilization spikes during maintenance operations such as index maintenance or integrity checks, you can force these to run serially. Although this can increase the duration of maintenance, other queries should be less negatively affected.

You can use the MAXDOP query hint at the end of index maintenance to force index rebuild steps to run serially. Combined with the ONLINE hint, an Enterprise edition feature, your scripted index maintenance might run longer but have a minimal impact of concurrent queries. You can also specify MAXDOP when creating indexes. You cannot specify a MAXDOP for the reorganize step.

```
ALTER INDEX ALL ON WideWorldImporters.Sales.Invoices REBUILD
WITH (MAXDOP = 1, ONLINE = ON);
```

> You can also turn on trace flag 2528 to disable parallelism server-wide for DBCC CHECKDB, DBCC CHECKFILEGROUP, and DBCC CHECKTABLE operations. Keep in mind these operations can take hours to complete on large databases and might run longer if single-threaded.

Forcing a parallel execution plan

Released with SQL Server 2017 (and also implemented in SQL Server 2016 CU2 and later) is a query hint that can force a statement to compile with a parallel execution plan. This can be valuable in troubleshooting, or to force a behavior in the query optimizer, but is not usually a necessary or recommended option for live code.

Appending the following hint to a query will force a parallel execution plan, which you can see using the Estimate or Actual execution plan output options:

```
OPTION(USE HINT('ENABLE_PARALLEL_PLAN_PREFERENCE'));
```

> **NOTE**
>
> The presence of certain system variables or functions can force a statement to compile to be serial, that is, without any parallelism. This behavior will override the new ENABLE_PARALLEL_PLAN_PREFERENCE option.
>
> The @@TRANCOUNT system variable will force a serial plan, as will any of the built-in error reporting functions, including ERROR_LINE(), ERROR_MESSAGE(), ERROR_NUMBER(), ERROR_PROCEDURE(), ERROR_SEVERITY(), or ERROR_STATE(). Note that this pertains only to using these objects in a query. Using them in the same batch, such as in a TRY ... CATCH handler, will not affect the execution plans of other queries in the batch.

Understanding advanced engine features for tuning queries

In the past few versions of SQL Server and Azure SQL DB, the programmers building the core relational engine have started to add especially advanced features to go from the same cost-based optimizations we have had for many years, to tools that can sense when plans need adjusted before a DBA does.

Not that any of these features will replace well written code and a DBA that understands the architecture of how queries work, but as data needs explode, the more the engine can do for you the better.

Plan Guides and Query Store

Plan Guide and Query Store are two complimentary, and slightly overlapping technologies that will help you tune your queries.

Plan Guides first existed in SQL Server 2005, and allow you to influence or set a particular plan for a certain query string. You can influence a plan by simply adding a hint (a common example would be WITH RECOMPILE) or providing an entire plan for a query. This can be very useful if you have a plan that is being chosen by SQL Server that doesn't work for you and you have no way to change the query in question. A common example is parameter sniffing, which was discussed earlier in the chapter, but other scenarios exist, like complex queries that don't work with a new version of the query optimizer, even though the rest of your system is performing better.

The Query Store feature is a more complete tuning solution, which captures the plans from the plan cache in your local database and allows you to see how a query performs over time. Where it overlaps with Plan Guides is that you can override the query plan chosen where there is a previous plan that worked well, but now does not.

In this section, we will review aspects of both tools, to help guide you as to which tool to choose. Note however, that tools that force a plan to override what the optimizer has chosen are not considered the best approach to query tuning. If you have an application where you own the source code, forcing a plan might be good to do until you can make a change to code, but should not be your primary tuning tool. If it is a third-party application, you should work with your vendor on a proper solution, but these features will help you to get past a serious issue.

Using Plan Guides

Plan Guides are often maligned because they are complex to work with, and for good reason, they can be complex to use. There was not a UI for them initially, and the UI that is in SSMS does not really guide you to how they are used. However, once you get the basics down, they help to allow you to optimize queries when you cannot change the text of a query or coded object.

What makes them powerful is that while you can change the entire plan of a query, you can also just influence the plan with a query hint, either in a coded object like a stored procedure, or a textual query that is executes outside of an object. You can also affect how an ad-hoc query parameterizes.

There are three types of Plan Guides we will cover in the following sections: Object Plan Guides, SQL Plan Guides, and Template Plan Guides.

You can create a Plan Guide using the UI in the Programmability section of the database, or with the following stored procedures, which will be demonstrated.

- sp_create_plan_guide – allows you to create the plan guide from the text of the query.

- sp_create_plan_guide_from_handle – allows you to create the plan guide from the plan handle you have retrieved from another DMV or system object.

- sp_control_plan_guide – used to drop, disable, and enable one or all plan guides in a database.

In the following examples, we tweak the plans of the queries with hints, but if you have a complete plan you can use the @hints parameter to include the entire query plan to override. However, we suggest doing this with Query Store generally, unless you are doing very advanced tuning and are taking an existing plan and tweaking it. Doing this is beyond the scope of this book.

Object Plan Guides

An object plan guide lets you override the plan of a query in an object. For example, we used in the parameterization section earlier, as the following procedure.

```
CREATE OR ALTER PROCEDURE Purchasing.PurchaseOrders_BySupplierId

@SupplierId int

AS

SELECT PurchaseOrders.PurchaseOrderID,

        PurchaseOrders.SupplierID,

        PurchaseOrders.OrderDate

  FROM    Purchasing.PurchaseOrders

WHERE  PurchaseOrders.SupplierID = @SupplierId;
```

In our example, this procedure is not changeable (it came as part of a third party system), and you want to make sure it optimizes for the lower cardinality values, such as 2. Sometimes, the procedure has optimized for a parameter value that gave us a poorly executing plan, and performance is suffering because most of your queries would benefit from the lower cardinality plan. The optimal plan will use an index seek and a lookup, which is great for a few rows, whereas it will be more costly on the few occasions that you retrieve the higher cardinality set of rows.

You apply the hint using the following call, where you provide the query to be guided, and the hint to add. The query text doesn't have to perfectly match, for example it ignores white space, but the query text itself must match (For complete details, see: *https://docs.microsoft.com/sql/ relational-databases/system-stored-procedures/sp-create-plan-guide-transact-sql*)

```
EXECUTE sp_create_plan_guide
```

```
@name = N' SP-Purchasing.PurchaseOrders_BySupplierId_AddOption',

@stmt = N'SELECT PurchaseOrders.PurchaseOrderID,

     PurchaseOrders.SupplierID,

     PurchaseOrders.OrderDate

 FROM    Purchasing.PurchaseOrders

WHERE   PurchaseOrders.SupplierID = @SupplierId',

@type = N'OBJECT',

@module_or_batch = N'Purchasing.PurchaseOrders$BySupplierId',

@params = NULL,  --null for object since it is declare in the parameters

@hints = N'OPTION (OPTIMIZE FOR (@SupplierId = 13))';
```

To drop the plan guide, you can execute:

```
EXEC sp_control_plan_guide 'DROP', N' SP-Purchasing.
PurchaseOrders_BySupplierId_AddOption';
```

You can check to see if your Plan Guide is working by looking at the properties of a query plan, In the properties you will see properties `PlanGuideDB` and `PlanGuideName` if so.

SQL Plan Guides

A SQL Plan guide works the same way as the object, except it will match any query that uses the same query in an ad-hoc fashion. For example, say the query from the stored procedure we just looked at was actually an ad-hoc SQL call. If it is a call that a user is making by typing in a query, it would be almost impossible to use a plan guide, since the query must match character for character, including white space.

But if it is an application, it will use a parameterized version of the query call, such as the following:

```
EXECUTE sp_executesql @stmt = N'SELECT PurchaseOrders.PurchaseOrderID,

             PurchaseOrders.SupplierID,

             PurchaseOrders.OrderDate

FROM    Purchasing.PurchaseOrders

WHERE PurchaseOrders.SupplierID = @SupplierId',

@params = N'@SupplierId int',

@SupplierId = 2;
```

You can easily create a plan guide to handle this query, because the application will always be sending the query with the exact same text:

```
EXECUTE sp_create_plan_guide

    @name = N'SQL-Purchasing_PurchaseOrders$BySupplierId_NoParallelism',

    @stmt =

'SELECT PurchaseOrders.PurchaseOrderID,

                PurchaseOrders.SupplierID,

                PurchaseOrders.OrderDate

FROM    Purchasing.PurchaseOrders

WHERE PurchaseOrders.SupplierID = @SupplierId',

    @type = N'SQL',

    @module_or_batch = NULL,

    @params = '@SupplierId int',

    @hints = N'OPTION (OPTIMIZE FOR (@SupplierId = 2))';
```

Template Plan Guide

Finally, you can use a template guide to apply a parameterization hint, to make a single query either parameterize or not parameterize, based on the database setting of FORCED PARAMETERIZATION. In this example, assume that that setting is turned off, so the following query will not have a parameterized plan:

```
USE WideWorldImporters;

SELECT * FROM Sales.Orders AS o

INNER JOIN Sales.OrderLines AS ol

    ON ol.OrderID = o.OrderID

WHERE o.OrderId = 679;
```

You can make queries of this form parameterized by using the following code. The sp_get_query_template procedure formats and parameterizes the query to make it easier to match. Then we create a plan guide, so further calls that do the same SELECT statement will be parameterized, instead of an individual plan for each value of OrderId, without making all complex statements parameterized.

```
DECLARE @stmt nvarchar(max);

DECLARE @params nvarchar(max);
```

```
EXEC sp_get_query_template

    N'SELECT * FROM Sales.Orders AS o

      INNER JOIN Sales.OrderLines AS ol

          ON ol.OrderID = o.OrderID

      WHERE o.OrderId = 679;  ',

    @stmt OUTPUT,

    @params OUTPUT

EXEC sp_create_plan_guide N'TemplateGuide1',

    @stmt,

    N'TEMPLATE',

    NULL,

    @params,

    N'OPTION(PARAMETERIZATION FORCED)';
```

Using the Query Store feature

The Query Store provides a practical history of execution plan performance for a single database, which persists even when the server has been restarted (unlike the plan cache itself, which is cleared, eliminating all of the interesting data that one needs for tuning queries over time.) It can be invaluable for the purposes of investigating and troubleshooting sudden negative changes in performance, by allowing the administrator or developer to identify both high-cost queries and the quality of their execution plans, and especially where the same query has multiple plans, where one performs poorly, and the other well.

The Query Store is most useful for looking back in time toward the history of statement execution. It can also assist in identifying and overriding execution plans by using a feature similar to, but different from the plan guides feature. As discussed in the previous section, Plan Guides are used to add guidance to a query's optimization, parameterization, or by even replacing the entire plan. The Query Store allows you find plans that are not working well, but only gives you the ability to force an entire plan that worked better from the history it has stored. The Query Store has a major benefit over Plan Guides, in that there is a user interface in SSMS to access it, see the benefits, and find places where you may need to apply a new plan.

You see live Query Store data as it happens from a combination of both memory-optimized and on-disk sources. Query Store minimizes overhead and performance impact by capturing cached plan information to in-memory data structure. The data is "flushed" to disk at an interval defined by Query Store, by a default of 15 minutes. The Disk Flush Interval setting defines how much Query Store data can be lost in the event of an unexpected system shutdown.

NOTE

Queries are captured in the context of the database where the query is executed. In the following code example, the query's execution is captured in the Query Store of the WideWorldImporters database.

```
USE WideWorldImporters;

GO

SELECT *

FROM

AdventureWorks.[Purchasing].[PurchaseOrders];
```

The Query Store is a feature that Microsoft delivered to the Azure SQL Database platform *first*, and then to the SQL Server product. In fact, Query Store is at the heart of the Azure SQL Database Advisor feature that provides automatic query tuning. The Query Store feature's overhead is quite manageable, tuned to avoid performance hits, and is already in place on millions of databases in Azure SQL Database.

The VIEW DATABASE STATE permission is all that is needed to view the Query Store data.

Initially configuring the query store

The Query Store feature is identical between the Azure SQL DB and SQL Server in operation, but not in how you activate the feature. Query Store is turned on automatically on Azure SQL Database, but it is not automatically on for new databases in SQL Server. While it is possible to set this on the model database so all new databases will inherit Query Store turned on, we suggest against it because it is best to think about your needs and tailor them when you create your database.

When should you enable Query Store? Enabling Query Store on all databases you have in your environment is a generally acceptable practice, as it will be useful in discovering performance issues in the future when they arise. You can turn on Query Store via the database Properties dialog box, in which Query Store is a page on the menu on the left. Or, you can turn it on via T-SQL by using the following command:

```
ALTER DATABASE [DatabaseOne] SET QUERY_STORE = ON;
```

This will turn on Query Store with the defaults and you can adjust them using the UI.

NOTE

As with pretty much any configuration task, while it is OK to use the UI the first time or two, it will always be better to have a script in T-SQL/Powershell/etc. to capture any settings in a repeatable manner. Use the Script button in most of the UIs in SSMS to output a script of what has changed when you are setting new values.

Query Store begins collecting when you activate it. You will not have any historical data when you first turn on the feature on an existing database, but you will begin to immediately see data for live database activity. You can then view plans and statistics about the plan in the Query Store reports.

In versions of SQL Server prior to 2019, the Query Store Capture Mode default setting was ALL, which included all queries that were executed. In SQL Server 2019, this default has been changed to AUTO, and for earlier versions it is best to set the same way because the additional data of one-use plans might not be useful and can reduce the amount of historical data can be retained.

NOTE

The Query Store data is stored in the user database. It is backed up and restored along with the database.

The Query Store retains data up to two limits: a Max Size (1000 MB by default in 2019, 100 MB in earlier versions), and a Stale Query Threshold time limit of Days (30 by default). If Query Store reaches its Max Size, it will clean up the oldest data. Because Query Store data is saved on a drive, its historical data is not affected by the commands we looked at earlier in this chapter to clear the Procedure Cache, such as DBCC FREEPROCACHE.

You should almost always keep the Size Based Cleanup Mode set to the default Auto. If not, when the Max Size is reached, Query Store will stop collecting data and enter Read Only mode, which does not collect new data. If you find that the Query Store is not storing more historical days of data than your Stale Query Threshold setting in days, increase the Max Size setting.

Using query store data in your troubleshooting

Query Store has several built-in dashboards, shown in Figure 14-10, to help you examine query performance and overall performance over recent history.

Figure 14-10   The SQL Server Object Explorer list of built-in dashboards available for Query Store in SQL Server Management Studio 18.

You can also write your own reports against the collection of system DMO that present Query Store data to administrators and developers by using the VIEW DATABASE STATE permission. You can view the schema of the well-documented views and their relationships at *https://docs.microsoft.com/sql/relational-databases/performance/ how-query-store-collects-data*.

On many of the dashboards, there is a button with a crosshairs symbol, as depicted in Figure 14-11. If a query seems interesting, expensive, or is of high value to the business, you can click this button to view a new screen that tracks the query when it's running as well as various plans identified for that query.

Figure 14-11   The Query Store tool bar at the top of the screen on many of the dashboards, in this example, the tool bar for the Regressed Queries report.

You can review the various plans for the same statement, compare the plans, and if necessary, force a plan that you believe is better than the optimizer will choose, into place. Compare the execution of each plan by CPU Time, Duration, Logical Reads, Logical Writes, Memory Consumption, Physical Reads, and several other metrics.

Most of all, the Query Store can be valuable by informing you when a query started using a new plan. You can see when a plan was generated and the nature of the plan; however, the cause of the plan's creation and replacement is not easily answered, especially when you cannot correlate to a specific DDL operation or system change. Query plans can become invalidated automatically due to large changes in statistics due to data inserts or deletes, changes made to other statements in the stored procedure, changes to any of the indexes used by the plan, or manual recompilation due to the RECOMPILE option.

As discussed in the Plan Guides section, forcing a statement (see Figure 14-11) to use a specific execution plan is not a recommended common activity. If you have access to the source code, work on a code change quickly, only using a forced plan temporarily. For systems where you have no code access, you can use a plan guide for specific performance cases, problematic queries demanding unusual plans, etc. Note that if the forced plan is invalid, such as an index changing or being dropped, SQL Server will move on without the forced plan and without a warning or error, although Query Store will still show that the plan is being forced for that statement.

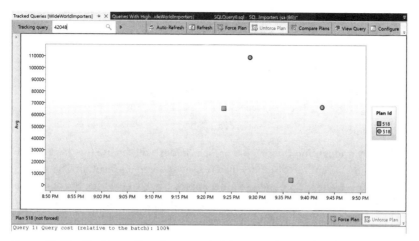

Figure 14-12   The Query Store has recorded the execution results of the query.

Note that one plan has been Forced (using the Force Plan button) for this statement and is displayed with a check mark.

Inside OUT

How should you force a statement to use a certain execution plan?

Your options for forcing a statement to follow a certain execution plan are either plan guides stored procedures (which also allow you to make slight changes to the plan by adding a hint to the plan, rather than replacing the entire plan) or the Query Store interface (and its underlying stored procedures) to force an execution plan.

Both options are advanced options for limited and/or diagnostic use only (and if at all possible, temporary use.) Overriding the query optimizer's execution plan choice is an advanced performance tuning technique. It is most often necessitated by query parameter sniffing.

It is possible to create competing plan guides or Query Store forced plans. This is certainly not recommended because it could be extremely confusing for the user. If you create competing plan guides or Query Store forced plans, you'll generally see the Query Store forced plan "win." (But this is not guaranteed or documented as far as we can determine.)

In case you are troubleshooting competing plan guides and Query Store forced plans, you can view any existing plan guides and forced query plans with the following queries of the system catalog:

```
SELECT * FROM sys.plan_guides;
SELECT *
FROM sys.query_store_query AS qsq
JOIN sys.query_store_plan AS qsp
    ON qsp.query_id = qsq.query_id
WHERE qsp.is_forced_plan = 1;
```

Finally, without using Query Store or Plan Guides, you can use the USE PLAN query hint to provide the entire XML query plan for any statement execution. This obviously is the least convenient option, and like other approaches that override the query analyzer should be considered an advanced and temporary performance tuning technique.

Automatic Plan Correction

Automatic Plan Correction is a tool that is capable of detecting and reverting plan regression. For example, a commonly executed query runs in 100 milliseconds, but then starts running in 2 minutes. Instead of just waiting on the company owner's complaints of slow performance, the engine can notice this regression and deal with it. SQL Server 2017 introduced this feature to the on-premises versions of the relational engine. The feature was originally released for the Azure SQL Database platform where the DBA is given considerably less control over tuning than what we have in SQL Server.

In SQL Server 2016, you could use Query Store to manually identify a query that regressed in performance, and then force a past execution plan into use. With Automatic Plan Correction, the database can be configured to detect plan regression and take this action automatically. The sample syntax for enabling automatic plan correction is below:

```
ALTER DATABASE WideWorldImporters SET AUTOMATIC_TUNING (FORCE_LAST_GOOD_PLAN = ON );
```

In both SQL Server 2017 and 2019, FORCE_LAST_GOOD_PLAN is the only option for automatic plan tuning.

The DMO sys.dm_db_tuning_recommendations captures plan recommendations based on query performance regression. This doesn't happen immediately–the feature has an algorithm that requires several executions before regression is identified. When a recommendation appears in sys.dm_db_tuning_recommendations, it includes a large amount of diagnostic data, including a plain-language "reason" explanation for the recommendation to be generated, and a block of JSON data containing diagnostic information. A sample query to parse this data is available at *https://docs.microsoft.com/sql/relational-databases/automatic-tuning/automatic-tuning*.

Intelligent Query Processing

Intelligent Query Processing is a somewhat random set of awesome features that make the processing of queries more efficient in some manner. Some features will help to pick or adapt a query plan to current conditions. Others are just straight up changes to how the SQL Server relational engine uses long existing query constructs. In every case though, the goal is to change the way queries are processed to give you better performance without much, if any, change in code. All of these features are available in SQL Server 2019, but only some will be available in 2017 (which is noted in each section).

Adaptive Query Processing

Adaptive Query Processing is a set of features that will allow SQL Server to adapt a given query to new conditions from when the query was originally compiled or last executed. The type of adaptations that can be made currently include:

- **Batch Mode Adaptive Joins** – In a query that is executing in batch mode (that is, dealing with more than 1 row at a time), the query can use an adaptive join operator that lets the choice of hash or nested loops join be made after one of the inputs has been scanned. So, if it is a small, selective set, the nested loops join may work better, for example. Or if the two input sets are huge, hash match may be the better choice.

- **Memory Grant Feedback** – When a query executes, it uses some amount of memory to execute. The Memory Grant Feedback feature lets future executions of the same query know if the memory granted for the execution was too much, or too little and let it adjust future executions. This was available on SQL Server 2017 for batch mode executions, and in 2019 it is available for row mode executions.

  This feature can be turned on and off for batch mode queries without breaking compatibility using the following statements:

  ```
  -- SQL Server 2017

  ALTER DATABASE SCOPED CONFIGURATION SET DISABLE_BATCH_MODE_MEMORY_GRANT_FEEDBACK =
  OFF;

  -- Azure SQL Database, SQL Server 2019

  ALTER DATABASE SCOPED CONFIGURATION SET BATCH_MODE_MEMORY_GRANT_FEEDBACK = ON;
  ```

  For row mode queries, this feature is controlled using:

  ```
  ALTER DATABASE SCOPED CONFIGURATION SET ROW_MODE_MEMORY_GRANT_FEEDBACK = ON;
  ```

- **Interleaved Execution** – Introduced in SQL Server 2017, this feature currently helps with plans that make use of Multi-Statement Table-Valued functions (MSTVF). When a plan is generated that uses as MSTVF in the query, prior to SQL Server 2014, the number or rows returned was estimated as the literal value of 1. Subsequent versions use 100 as the estimate, but neither estimate is very good unless you are actually returning very few rows. Interleaved execution lets the optimizer execute parts of the query during optimization to get better estimates, because if your MSTVF actually is going to output 100000 rows, the plan needs to be considerably different than the 100 row estimate would have provided.

Interleaved execution can be controlled using the following statements:

```
-- SQL Server 2017

ALTER DATABASE SCOPED CONFIGURATION SET DISABLE_INTERLEAVED_EXECUTION_TVF = ON;
--or OFF

-- Azure SQL Database and SQL Server 2019

ALTER DATABASE SCOPED CONFIGURATION SET INTERLEAVED_EXECUTION_TVF = OFF; --or ON
```

Table Variable Deferred Compilation

Much like Interleaved Execution of MSTVFs, Table Variable Deferred Compilation seeks to deal with the lack of statistics for a table variable at compile time, the standard guess was 1 row would the number of rows contained in the table variable. This provided poorly performing plans if the programmer had stored thousands (or more) rows in the table variable.

Table variable deferred compilation, instead of using the guess of 1 to define the query plan, waits to complete the actual plan until the table variable has been loaded the first time, and then the rest of the plan is generated. This feature may be one of the best for many DBAs who have had performance problems with very large table variables, despite the fact that they sound like they should be lightweight, highly performant tools for programmers to use.

NOTE

Just because they have improved how table variables are optimized does not make them the best choice for large numbers of rows. Table variables still lack column statistics – a key difference between them and temp tables (prefixed with # or ##) that can make temp tables far superior.

Batch Mode on Rowstore

One of the features that was added to SQL Server along with columnstore indexes was a type of processing known as Batch Mode. Typical processing in SQL Server had always used a method that sounds terrible. Row by row, now referred to as *row mode* processing. But columnstore indexes were built to process large amounts of rows so it was updated to, when the heuristics told the query processor it would be worth it, work on batches of rows at a time.

> ➤ **For more details on batch and row mode processing, see the following on Microsoft Docs:** *https://docs.microsoft.com/sql/relational-databases/query-processing-architecture-guide.*

In SQL Server 2019, this feature is extended to work for certain types of queries with row store tables and indexes as well as columnstore tables and indexes. A few examples:

- Queries that use large quantities of rows in a table, often in analytical queries touching hundreds of thousands of rows.

- Systems that are CPU bound in nature. (I/O bottlenecks are best handled with a columnstore index).

> ➤ **For more details, see the following on Microsoft Docs:** *https://docs.microsoft.com/sql/relational-databases/performance/intelligent-query-processing/#batch-mode-on-rowstore.*

The feature is enabled in SQL Server and Azure SQL DB when the compatibility level is 150, but if you find it is harming performance, you can turn it off using ALTER DATABASE.

```
ALTER DATABASE SCOPED CONFIGURATION SET BATCH_MODE_ON_ROWSTORE = OFF;
```

If you want to only then allow this feature to apply to a specific query you may need to execute that touches large number of rows, you can use the query hint ALLOW_BATCH_MODE.

```
SELECT …

FROM …

OPTION(RECOMPILE, USE HINT('ALLOW_BATCH_MODE'));
```

T-SQL scalar User Defined Functions (UDF) inlining

Of all the features to make a negative impact to performance, T-SQL UDFs have generally been the worst. Every programmer who has taken any class in programming instinctively desires to modularize their code. So if you have a scenario where you want to classify some data (say something simple like CASE WHEN 1 THEN 'True' ELSE 'False' END, it makes sense to bundle this up into a coded module). So, when user defined functions were created, there were shouts of joy. Until performance was taken into consideration.

In WideWorldImporters, we create the following, extremely simply UDF to do exactly what was described.

```
USE WideWorldImporters;

GO

CREATE SCHEMA Tools;
```

```
GO

CREATE FUNCTION Tools.Bit_Translate
(
     @value bit
)
RETURNS varchar(5)
as
 BEGIN
      RETURN (CASE WHEN @value = 1 THEN 'True' ELSE 'False' END);
 END;
```

Execute this function in the following query, once in 150 (SQL Server 2019) compatibility level, and again in 140.

```
SET STATISTICS TIME ON;

ALTER DATABASE WideWorldImporters SET COMPATIBILITY_LEVEL = 140; --SQL Server 2017
 GO

SELECT Tools.Bit_Translate(IsCompressed) AS CompressedFlag,
         CASE WHEN IsCompressed = 1 THEN 'True' ELSE 'False' END AS
CompressedFlag_Desc
 FROM   Warehouse.VehicleTemperatures;

GO

ALTER DATABASE WideWorldImporters SET COMPATIBILITY_LEVEL = 150; -- SQL Server 2019
 GO

SELECT Tools.Bit_Translate(IsCompressed) AS CompressedFlag,
         CASE WHEN IsCompressed = 1 THEN 'True' ELSE 'False' END
 FROM   Warehouse.VehicleTemperatures;
```

On the 65,998 rows that are returned, you will likely not notice a difference in performance. Checking the output from SET STATISTICS TIME ON, on my test computer it was around 450 ms for the SQL Server 2017 compatibility level version, and 500 ms for the SQL Server 2019 compatibility level version.

Looking at the actual plan CPU used for the two executions in Figure 14-13, you can see an interesting difference.

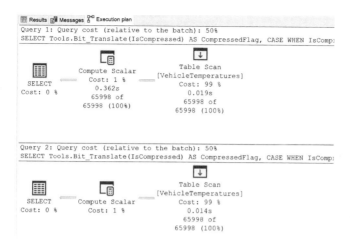

Figure 14-13   Query plan output for two runs. First in SQL Server 2019 compatibility level, the second in 2017.

The big thing to notice between these two executions is that the compute scalar in Query 2 appears as a typical Compute Scalar for any scalar expression not including a UDF. In Query 1, it shows rows passing through, and an amount of time as it calculates the scalar for each row that passes through. Even in this extremely simple case, we saved .245 seconds because instead of running the function for every execution as a separate call, it behaved as if you had written the query using the scalar expression alone.

While the function was extremely simple, without accessing tables, this is not limited to simple functions, nor does the function need to avoid accessing data in a table. There are limitations, such as not using time dependent intrinsic functions like SYSDATETIME(), not changing security context using EXECUTE AS (only EXECUTE AS CALLER, the default, is allowed), and not referencing table variables or table-valued parameters.

> **For more details and the complete list of requirements see Microsoft Docs here:** *https://docs.microsoft.com/sql/relational-databases/user-defined-functions/scalar-udf-inlining.*

This feature will have immediate value for programmers who completely ignored the common advice to not use scalar UDFs, but for most, it will be more of a change where something you have long wanted to do is now perfectly acceptable. Formatting functions, translation functions where it might be easier than creating a table, are now possible and will perform very well, as opposed to destroying your performance.

CHAPTER 14

Inside OUT

Are there tools to help you with compatibility level issues?

There is a tool called the Query Tuning Assistant that will help you find queries that might be affected by an upgrade of compatibility level. It is primarily created to handle upgrade tasks (You launch the tool in SSMS by right-clicking the database and choosing Tasks; Database Upgrade; New Database Upgrade Session), but can be used for any database that is not in the max compatibility level for a server.

Starting in an earlier compatibility level, It uses query store data, over a number of days that will represent a full business cycle of activity (not just on a holiday where the business is closed, but a full cycle that is representative of true activity. Then you set your database to a later compatibility level, and the tool will look for regressed query plans and give you advice on how to make things work better in the target compatibility level.

For more details, see Chapter 19, "Migrating to SQL Server solutions in Azure" where we discuss using Query Tuning Advisor for migrations, and also check out this following lab that Microsoft created: *https://github.com/microsoft/tigertoolbox/blob/master/Sessions/Winter-Ready-2019/Lab-QTA.md*

Approximate Query Processing

Approximate Query Processing is the primary feature of the Intelligent Query Processing family of changes that does require code changes to work. A very costly query aggregate operation is doing something like counting distinct values. Say you execute a query such as:

```
SELECT COUNT(DISTINCT(CustomerID))

FROM    Sales.Invoices;
```

This will give you an exact number of customers that have been invoiced. If this is a very large set (which it is not in this case), then it may be a very costly query to execute, using a lot of memory. To combat this, they have created a new aggregate: APPROX_COUNT_DISTINCT, which cuts out one operation from the plan, and instead of giving you the exact answer, it provides an answer that is close enough for many operations that need to be done for analysis. So the query can be rewritten as:

```
SELECT APPROX_COUNT_DISTINCT(CustomerID)

FROM Sales.Invoices;
```

If you execute these two queries in the `WideWorldImporters` database, the plans to do the APPROX_COUNT_DISTINCT will actually show to be a bit more costly at 51 to 49% in the plan, as shown in Figure 14-14.

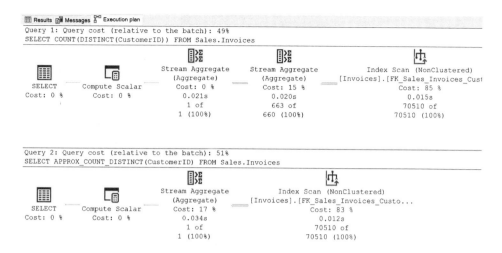

```
Results   Messages   Execution plan
Query 1: Query cost (relative to the batch): 49%
SELECT COUNT(DISTINCT(CustomerID)) FROM Sales.Invoices
```

Figure 14-14   Plans compared for COUNT(DISTINCT()) versus APPROX_COUNT_DISTINCT.

The first query will return the exact answer 663, and the second a close value (in this case 666 was returned). Execute the queries with SET STATISTICS TIME turned on and you will see an interesting cost savings, even on this smaller set. On the test machine, over several test runs,

- COUNT(DISTINCT())): CPU time = 15 ms, elapsed time = 38 ms

- APPROX_COUNT_DISTINCT: CPU time = 16 ms, elapsed time = 18 ms.

Just as in previous examples, a 20 ms difference seems inconsequential, and it generally is. But when we are working with millions or billions of rows, the amount of memory used by the second query will be far less, and the time savings not inconsequential at all.

> **NOTE**
>
> While APPROX_COUNT_DISTINCT may very well provide a tremendous increase in performance on very large sets, you need to be very clear about the differences in the value returned APPROX_COUNT_DISTINCT versus the exact answer from COUNT(DISTINCT()). It is likely largely inappropriate for most reporting queries where an approximate answer may not be acceptable to your client.
>
> However, it may be useful as a performance improvement for scenarios when counting large number of rows (in the high millions/billions) of rows where a good enough answer is acceptable.

CHAPTER 14

CHAPTER 15
Understanding and designing indexes

In this chapter, we dive into indexing of all kinds—not just clustered and nonclustered indexes—including practical development techniques for designing indexes. We spend time on memory-optimized tables throughout, including hash indexes for extreme writes, and columnstore indexes for extreme reads. We review "missing" indexes and index usage, and then introduce statistics: how they are created and updated. There are important performance-related options for statistics objects. Finally, we explain special types of indexes for niche uses.

In SQL Server you have access to a variety of indexing tools in your toolbox.

We've always had clustered and nonclustered indexes in 21st century versions of SQL Server, those two rowstore index types that are the bread and butter of SQL Server. We'll cover those in the first half of this chapter, including important new options for SQL Server 2019. Introduced in SQL server 2012, columnstore indexes presented a new and exciting way to perform analytical queries on massive amounts of compressed data. They became an essential tool of the database developer, and we'll discuss them in detail in this chapter. In SQL Server 2014, Project Hekaton brought memory-optimized tables and their uniquely powerful hash indexes for latchless querying on rapidly changing data. You can even combine the power of these two new concepts now, with columnstore index concepts on memory-optimized tables, allowing for live analytical-scale queries on streamed data.

First, we're going to dive into the index design concepts.

Inside OUT

What's the difference between rowstore and columnstore?

If the term is new to you: rowstore indexes describe the only type of clustered indexes (and nonclustered indexes) that existed before SQL Server 2012. These indexes are traditional B+tree indexes that have always existed in Microsoft SQL Server and continue

to be foundational to OLTP workloads. Rowstore also includes tables without a clustered index, known as heaps, as well as memory-optimized tables.

Columnstore indexes were introduced in SQL Server 2012, and really perfected in time for SQL Server 2016, and serve a different purpose. Columnstore indexes are superior to rowstore data storage for performance only in appropriate situations, specifically, in scans of millions of rows or more in large tables. Highly compressed, columnstore indexes take up less storage (and therefore, need less IO) to serve queries typical in enterprise reporting, data warehousing, and OLAP scenarios.

Consider both rowstore and columnstore indexes as important tools for the database designer in modern applications. In some database designs, rowstore, columnstore, and hash-based indexes on memory-optimized tables all play a role. We will discuss both at length in this chapter.

Designing clustered indexes

Let's be clear about what the clustered index is and then state the case for why every table in a relational database should have one, with very few exceptions.

We will first are discuss rowstore clustered indexes, but it is also possible to create a clustered columnstore index. We'll discuss that later in this chapter.

Whether you are inheriting and maintaining a database or designing the objects within it, there are important facts to know about clustered indexes. In the case of both rowstore and column-store indexes, the clustered index stores the data rows for all columns in the table. In the case of rowstore indexes, the table data is logically sorted by the clustered index key, while in the case of clustered columnstore indexes, there is no key. Memory-optimized tables don't have a clustered index structure inherent to their design but could have a clustered columnstore index created for them.

Choosing a proper rowstore clustered index key

When designing the clustered index key for a table, there are four marks of a good clustered index key for most OLTP applications, or in the case of a compound clustered index key, the first column listed. The column order matters.

Let's review four key factors that will help you understand what role the clustered index key serves and how best to design one:

- **Increasing sequential value.**   A value that increases (such as 1,2,3..., or an increasing point in time, or an increasing alphanumeric) is valuable from a page organization standpoint. This means that the insert pattern of the data as it comes in from the business will match the loading of rows onto the physical structures of the table.

A column with the `identity` property, or populated by a value from a sequence object, matches this perfectly. Use date and time data only if it is highly unlikely to repeat, and then strongly consider using the `datetimeoffset` data type to avoid repeated data once annually during daylight savings time changes.

- **Unique.**   A clustered index key does not need to be unique, but more often than not, it should be. (The clustered key also does not need to be the primary key of the table, or the only uniqueness enforced in the table.) A unique (or near-unique) clustered index means efficient seeks, and if your application will be searching for individual rows out of this table regularly, you and the business should know what makes those searches unique.

  Unique constraints, whether they be nonclustered or clustered, can improve performance on the same data, and create a more efficient structure. A unique constraint is the same as a unique rowstore nonclustered index.

  If a clustered index is declared without the UNIQUE property, a second key value is added in the background, a four-byte integer uniquifier column. Microsoft SQL Server must have some way to uniquely identify each row. The key from the rowstore clustered index is used as the row locator for non-clustered indexes

- **Nonchanging.**   The clustered index key idea doesn't change, and is a system—generated key that shouldn't be visible to end-user applications or reports. In general, when the end users can see data, they will eventually see fit to *change* that data. You do not want clustered index keys to ever change (much less PRIMARY KEY key values). A system-generated or surrogate key of sequential values (again, an `identity` column is perfect) is deal. A field that combines system or application-generated fields such as dates and times, or numbers, would work too.

  The negative impact of changing the clustering key includes the possibility that the first two aforementioned guidelines would be broken. If the clustered key is also a primary key, updating the key's values could also require cascading updates to enforce referential integrity. It is much easier for everyone involved if only columns with business value are exposed to end users and, therefore, could be changed by end users. In normalized data-base design, we would call these "natural keys" as opposed to "surrogate keys."

- **Narrow data type.**   This is not listed last as an indication that it is least important; quite to the contrary, the decision of data type for your clustered index key can have a large impact on table size, the cost of index maintenance, and the efficiency of queries at scale. The clustered index key value is also stored with every nonclustered index key value, meaning that an unnecessarily wide clustered index key will also cause unnecessarily wide nonclustered indexes on the table. This can have a very large impact on storage on drives and in memory at scale.

The narrow data type guidance should also steer you away from using the `uniqueidentifier` field, which is 16 bytes per row, or four times the size of an integer column per row, and twice as large as a `bigint`. It also steers away from using wide strings, such as names, addresses, or URLs.

Inside OUT

Why are `uniqueidentifiers` an overall bad choice for the clustered index key, even for the "oil rig problem"?

There is a common design challenge to store rows from multiple (perhaps disconnected) data sources in the same table; for example, oil rigs, medical devices, or a supervisory control and data acquisition (SCADA) system. Each source of the data must create unique values for itself, but those values must then be combined into a single table. The `uniqueidentifier` data type and `newid()` function appear to be an option because they will generate values uniquely across multiple servers.

This is not a good design for scale, however, because `uniqueidentifiers` are random, meaning that inserts will perfectly fragment a table with each new row. This will cause page splits (an expensive I/O operation) as the rows naturally merge into the rest with each insert in the "middle" rather than at the end, inserting sequentially. (You can mitigate this, though not significantly, by altering the fill factor of each index that uses the `uniqueidentier` as a key. However, this is also not desirable, because it will further increase the space to store the same data.)

Even the `newsequentialid()` function, which can only be used as a column default, has fatal flaws. Used to create sequential uniqueidentifier values, after a server restart, the sequence may start at a new point, meaning that eventually you will be back to writing new rows in the middle of existing rows, causing page splits again. There are numerous events that could trigger a reset to the starting point of the newsequentialid() function, which is based on the MAC of the network interface card (NIC) on the server. Therefore, any failover of a failover cluster instance (FCI) or availability group will result in a new starting point, as well as any future upgrade or migration to new hardware. Similarly, changing the tier of Azure SQL Database, reimaging an Azure VM with ephemeral OS, or a new Docker run without explicit MAC will all reset the starting point. Finally, and most importantly, the MAC of any NIC could change on startup of VM in VMWare or HyperV. Obviously, given this list, the newsequentialid() is fatally flawed and shouldn't be relied on for sequential values long-term.

This design problem usually involves these devices merging their data periodically—not continuously. A pair of int's should be a good replacement for a uniqueidentifier field in those cases. Consider instead a solution using multiple integers, one that autoincrements and one that identifies the data source, if you are considering the `uniqueidentifier` field. Even two four-byte integers are half the size of a `uniqueidentifier`, and they compress better.

In the case of continuous connected application integration into a single table, consider using the `sequence` feature of SQL Server, introduced in SQL Server 2012, instead of a `uniqueidentifier`. Using the `sequence` object will allow for multiple database connections write rows using a unique, autoincrementing, ascending, procedurally generated integer.

It is ironic that a number of Microsoft-developed platforms use `uniqueidentifiers` heavily, and sometimes to very public failures, for example, the Windows 7 RC download page. (Read Paul Randal's blog, "Why did the Windows 7 RC download failure happen?" *https://www.sqlskills.com/blogs/paul/why-did-the-windows-7-rc-download-failure-happen/*) But systems like Microsoft SharePoint and even SQL Server's own merge replication needed to be developed for utility and versatility across unlimited client environments and a wide array of user expertise. When designing your own systems, take advantage of your knowledge of the business environment to design better clustered index keys that escape the inefficiencies of the `uniqueidentifier` data type.

CHAPTER 15

The clustered index is an important decision in the structure of a new table. For the vast majority of tables designed for relational database systems, however, the decision is fairly easy. An `identity` column with an `integer` or `bigint` data type is the ideal key for a clustered index because it satisfies the aforementioned four recommended qualities of an ideal clustered index. A procedurally generated timestamp or other incrementing time-related value, combined with a unique, autoincrementing number also provides for a common albeit less-narrow clustered index key design.

When a table is created with a primary key constraint and no other mention of a clustered index, the Primary Key's columns become the clustered index's key. This is typically safe, but a table with a compound Primary Key or a Primary Key that does not begin with a sequential column could result in a suboptimal clustered index. It is important to note that the Primary Key does not need to be the clustered index key, but often should be. It is possible to create nonunique clustered indexes or to have multiple unique columns or column combinations in a table.

When combining multiple columns into the clustered index key of an index, keep in mind that the column order of an index, clustered or nonclustered, does matter. If you decide to use multiple columns to create a clustered index key, the first column should still align as closely to the other three rules, even if it alone is not unique.

In `sys.indexes`, the clustered index is always identified as `index_id = 1`. If the table is a heap, there will instead be a row with `index_id = 0`. This row represents the heap data.

The case against intentionally designing heaps

Without a clustered index, a table is known colloquially as a *heap*. In a heap, the Database Engine uses a structure known as row identifier (RID), which is set up to uniquely identify every row for internal purposes. The structure of the heap has no order when it is logically stored. RID's do not change, so when a record is updated, a forwarding pointer is usually created in the old location to point to the new. If that sounds like it is complicated or would increase the amount of I/O activity needed to retrieve the data, you're right.

Furthering the performance problems associated with heaps are that Table Scans are the only method of access to read from a heap structure, unless there is a nonclustered index created on the heap. It is not possible to perform a seek against a heap; however, it is possible to perform a seek against a nonclustered index that has been added to a heap. In this way, a nonclustered index can provide an ordered copy for some of the table data in a separate structure.

Of the edge cases for designing a table purposely without a clustered index, a case can be made for the situation in which you would only ever insert into a table. Without any order to the data, you might reap some benefits from rapid, massive data inserts into a heap. Other types of writes to the table (deletes and updates) will likely require table scans to complete and likely be far less efficient than the same writes against a table with a clustered index.

Deletes and updates will also probably leave wasted space within the heap's structure, which cannot be reclaimed even with an Index Rebuild operation. To reclaim wasted space inside of a heap without recreating it, you must ironically create a clustered index on the table then drop the clustered index.

The perceived advantage of heaps for workloads exclusively involving inserts can be easily out-weighed by the significant disadvantages whenever accessing that data—when query performance would necessitate the creation of a clustered and/or nonclustered index. Table scans and RID lookups for any significant amount of rows are likely to dominate the cost of any execution plan accessing the heap. Without a clustered index, queries reading from a table large enough to gain significant advantage from its inserts would perform poorly.

With Microsoft's expansion into modern unstructured data platforms such as SQL Server integration with Hadoop, or Microsoft Azure Data Lake, other architectures are likely to be more appropriate when rapid, massive data inserts are required. This is especially true for when you will be continuously collecting massive amounts of data and then only ever analyzing the data in aggregate. It's likely that these alternatives, integrated with the Database Engine starting with SQL Server 2016 or a focus of new Azure development, would be a superior alternative to intentionally designing a heap.

Further, adding a clustered index to optimize the eventual retrieval of data from a heap is non-trivial. Behind the scenes, the Database Engine must write the entire contents of the heap into the new clustered index structure. If any nonclustered indexes exist on the heap, they also will be re-created, using the clustered key instead of the RID. This will likely result in a large amount of transaction log activity and TempDB space consumed.

Understanding the OPTIMIZE_FOR_SEQUENTIAL_KEY feature

Earlier in this chapter we sang the praises of a clustered index key with an increasing sequential value, such as an integer based on an identity or sequence. For very frequent, multithreaded inserts into a table with an identity or sequence, the "hot spot" of the page in memory with the "next" value can provide some IO bottleneck. (Note that long term, this is still likely preferable to the pain of fragmentation-upon-insertion as explained in the previous section, and only surfaces at scale.)

A new feature of SQL Server 2019 is the OPTIMIZE_FOR_SEQUENTIAL_KEY index option, which improves the concurrency of the page needing rapid inserts for rowstore indexes from multiple threads.

You may observe a high amount of the PAGELATCH_EX wait type on sessions performing inserts into the same table. You can observe this with the dynamic management view (DMV) sys. dm_exec_session_wait_stats, or at an instance aggregate level with the sys.dm_os_wait_ stats. You should see this wait type drop when the new OPTIMIZE_FOR_SEQUENTIAL_KEY index option is enabled on indexes in tables that are written to by multiple requests simultaneously. Note that this isn't the PAGEIOLATCH_EX wait type – more associated with physical page contention, but PAGELATCH_EX, associated with memory page contention.

> ➤ For more information on observing wait types with DMVs, including the differences between the wait types PAGEIOLATCH_EX and PAGELATCH_EX, see Chapter 8, "Maintaining and monitoring SQL Server."

Let's take a look at implementing OPTIMIZE_FOR_SEQUENTIAL_KEY. With multiple TSQL threads frequently executing single-row inserting statements, the top 2 predominant wait types accrued via the DMV sys.dm_os_wait_stats were WRITELOG and PAGELATCH_EX. As Chapter 8 will explain, the WRITELOG wait type is fairly self-explanatory-sending data to the transaction log, while PAGELATCH_EX is an indication of a "hot spot" page, symptomatic of rapid concurrent inserts into a sequential key.

By enabling OPTIMIZE_FOR_SEQUENTIAL_KEY on your rowstore indexes – both clustered and nonclustered – you should see some reduction in PAGELATCH_EX and the introduction of a small amount of a new wait type, BTREE_INSERT_FLOW_CONTROL, that is associated with the new OPTIMIZE_FOR_SEQUENTIAL_KEY setting.

NOTE

The new OPTIMIZE_FOR_SEQUENTIAL_KEY option is not available when creating columnstore indexes or for any indexes on memory optimized tables.

You can query the value of the OPTIMIZE_FOR_SEQUENTIAL_KEY option with a new column added to sys.indexes of the same name. Note that this new option is not enabled by default, so would need to be enabled manually on each index. The option is retained after an index is disabled and then rebuild. For existing rowstore indexes, you can change the new OPTIMIZE_FOR_SEQUENTIAL_KEY option without a rebuild operation with the simple syntax:

```
ALTER INDEX PK_table1 on dbo.table1
SET (OPTIMIZE_FOR_SEQUENTIAL_KEY = ON);
```

NOTE

Fun fact: there are only a handful of index settings that can be set like this without a rebuild operation, so the syntax may look a little unusual. The index options ALLOW_PAGE_LOCKS, ALLOW_ROW_LOCKS, OPTIMIZE_FOR_SEQUENTIAL_KEY, IGNORE_ DUP_KEY, and STATISTICS_NORECOMPUTE can be set without a rebuild.

Designing rowstore nonclustered indexes

Each table almost always should have a clustered index that becomes the organization of the data in the table. Nonclustered indexes provide additional copies of the data in vertically-filtered sets, sorted by nonprimary columns.

You should approach the design of nonclustered indexes in response to application query usage, and then verify over time that you are benefitting from indexes (you can read more about index usage statistics later in this chapter.) You may also choose to design a unique row-store nonclustered index as part of the table's design, to enforce a business constraint. A unique constraint is the same as a unique rowstore nonclustered index. This may be a valuable part of the table's behavior even if the resulting unique rowstore nonclustered index is never queried.

Here are the properties of good nonclustered indexes:

- Broad enough serve multiple queries, not just designed to suit one query.

- Well-ordered keys that eliminate unnecessary sorting in high-value queries.

- Well-stocked INCLUDE sections prevent Lookups in high-value queries.

- Proven beneficial usage over time in the sys.dm_db_index_usage_stats dynamic management view (DMV).

- Unique when possible (keep in mind a table can have multiple uniqueness criteria).

- Key order matters, so in a compound index it is likely best for the most selective (with the most distinct values) columns to be listed first.

- The index key list doesn't overlap other nonclustered indexes.

Nonclustered indexes on disk-based tables are copies of a rowstore table that take up space on a disk and in memory (when cached). (On memory-optimized tables, indexes interact with the disk much differently. More on that later in this chapter.) You must spend time backing up and maintaining all nonclustered indexes. They are kept transactionally consistent with the data in the table, serving a limited, reordered set of the data in a table. All writes (including deletes) to the table data must also be written to the nonclustered index (in the case of updates, when any indexed column is modified), to keep it up to date. (On memory-optimized tables, this happens a little differently, with a delta store of change records.)

The positive benefit rowstore nonclustered indexes can have on SELECT queries, however, is potentially very significant. Keep in mind also that some write queries might appear to perform faster because accessing the data that is being changed can be optimized, as well, just as accessing the data in a SELECT query. It is not a rule that your applications' writes will slow with the addition of nonclustered indexes, though adding many nonclustered indexes will certainly contribute to poor write performance. You can be confident that creating any one well-designed nonclustered index will contribute to reads greatly, and not have a perceivable impact on writes.

You should not create nonclustered indexes haphazardly or clumsily; you should plan, modify, and combine them with one another when appropriate, and review them regularly to make sure they are still useful. (See the section later in this chapter on "Understanding and proving index usage.) Nonclustered indexes represent a significant source of potential performance tuning, however, that every developer and database administration should be aware of, especially in transactional databases. Remember always to create indexes when looking at the "big picture"—very rarely does a single query rise to the importance level of justifying its own indexes.

> **NOTE**
>
> Starting with SQL 2019, the RESUMEABLE syntax can also be used when creating an index with the ONLINE syntax. An ALTER INDEX and CREATE INDEX statement can be similarly paused and resumed. For more on RESUMABLE index maintenance, see Chapter 8.

Understanding nonclustered index design

Let's talk about what we meant a moment ago when we said, "you should not create indexes haphazardly or clumsily." When should you create a nonclustered index, and how should you design them? How many should you add to a table?

Even though adding nonclustered indexes on Foreign Key columns can be beneficial if those referencing columns will frequently be used in queries, it's rare that a useful nonclustered index will be properly designed with a single column in mind. This is because outside of joins on foreign keys, it is rare that queries will be designed to both seek and return a single column from a table. So while starting a database design with indexes on foreign key columns is useful, that doesn't mean they cannot be changed to have more columns at the end of the key list or in the include list.

Choosing a proper nonclustered index key

When creating new nonclustered indexes for a table you must always compare the index to existing indexes. The order of the key of the index matters. In Transact-SQL (T-SQL), this looks like this:

```
CREATE NONCLUSTERED INDEX IDX_NC_InvoiceLines_InvoiceID_StockItemID

ON [Sales].[InvoiceLines] (InvoiceID, StockItemID);
```

In this index, `InvoiceID` and `InvoiceLineID` are defined as the key. Via Object Explorer in Management Studio, you can view the index properties to see the same information. This non-clustered index represents a copy of the data of the `InvoiceLines` table, sorted by the column `InvoiceID` first, and then the `StockItemID`.

To emphasize that the order of key columns in a nonclustered index matters, the two indexes that follow are completely different structures, and will best serve different queries. It's not likely that a single query would have much use for both, though SQL Server can still choose to use a nonclustered index with less than optimal key order than to scan a clustered index:

```
CREATE INDEX IDX_NC_InvoiceLines_InvoiceID_StockItemID

ON [Sales].[InvoiceLines] (InvoiceID, StockItemID);

CREATE INDEX IDX_NC_InvoiceLines_StockItemID_InvoiceID

ON [Sales].[InvoiceLines] (StockItemID, InvoiceID);
```

The columns with the most distinct values are more selective and will best serve queries if they are listed before less-selective columns in the index order. Note, though, that the order of columns in the INCLUDE portion of a nonclustered index (more on that later) does not matter.

Remember also from the previous section on clustered indexes that the clustered index key is already inside the key of the nonclustered index. There might be scenarios when the missing indexes feature (more on this later) suggests adding a clustered key column to your nonclustered index. It does not change the size of a nonclustered index to do this—the clustered key is already in nonclustered index. The only caveat is that the order of the nonclustered index keys still determines the sort order of the index. So, having the clustered index key column(s) in your nonclustered index key won't change the index's size, but could change the sort order of the keys, creating what is essentially a different index when compared to an index that doesn't include the clustered index key column(s).

Implied in this T-SQL. the sort order of each column by default is ascending. If queries frequently call for data to be sorted by a column in descending order, which may be common for queries looking for the most recent data, you could provide that key value like this:

```
CREATE INDEX IDX_NC_InvoiceLines_InvoiceID_StockItemID

ON [Sales].[InvoiceLines] (InvoiceID DESC, StockItemID);
```

Creating the key's sort order incorrectly might not matter to some queries. For example, the nested loop operator does not require data to be sorted in a particular order, so different sort orders in the keys of a nonclustered index might not make a significant impact to the execution plan. On the other hand, a merge join operator requires data in both inputs to the operator to be sorted in the same order, however, so changing the sort order of the keys of an index, especially the first key, could simplify an execution plan by eliminating unnecessary sort operators. This is among the strategies of index tuning to consider. Remember to review the query plan performance data that the Query Store collects, to observe the impact of index changes on multiple queries.

Understanding redundant indexes

Earlier, we mentioned that nonclustered index keys shouldn't overlap with other indexes in the same table. Because index key order matters, we need to be aware of what is and what isn't an overlapping index. Consider the following two nonclustered indexes on the same table:

```
CREATE INDEX IDX_NC_InvoiceLines_InvoiceID_StockItemID_UnitPrice_Quantity

ON [Sales].[InvoiceLines] (InvoiceID, StockItemID, UnitPrice, Quantity);

CREATE INDEX IDX_NC_InvoiceLines_InvoiceID_StockItemID

ON [Sales].[InvoiceLines] (InvoiceID, StockItemID);
```

Both indexes lead with `InvoiceID` and `StockItemID`. The first index includes additional data. The second index is completely overlapped. Queries can still use the second index, but because the leading key columns match the other index, the other index will provide very similar performance gains with less to maintain. The space it requires, the space in memory it consumes when used, and the effort it takes to keep the index up-to-date and maintained could all be considered redundant. The index `IDX_NC_InvoiceLines_InvoiceID_ StockItemID` isn't needed and should be dropped, and queries that used it will use `IDX_NC_InvoiceLines_InvoiceID_StockItemID_UnitPrice_Quantity`.

Consider then the following two indexes:

```
CREATE INDEX IDX_NC_InvoiceLines_InvoiceID_StockItemID_UnitPrice_Quantity
ON [Sales].[InvoiceLines] (InvoiceID, StockItemID, UnitPrice, Quantity);
CREATE INDEX IDX_NC_InvoiceLines _StockItemID_InvoiceID
ON [Sales].[InvoiceLines] (StockItemID, InvoiceID);
```

Note that the second index's keys are in a different order. This is physically and logically a different structure than the first index.

Does that mean both of these indexes are needed? Probably. Some queries might perform best using keys in the second index's order. The query optimizer can still use an index with columns in a suboptimal order; for example, to scan the smaller structure rather than the entire table. The query optimizer might instead find that an Index Seek and a Key Lookup on a different index is faster than using an index with the columns in the wrong order.

You can prove whether or not each index is used using the DMV sys.dm_db_index_usage_stats, which we will discuss soon in this chapter, in the section "Understanding and proving index usage."

The Query Store can be an invaluable tool to discover queries that have regressed because of changes to indexes that have been dropped, reordered, or resorted.

Understanding the INCLUDE list of an index

In the B+tree structure of a rowstore nonclustered index, key columns are stored through the two major sections of the index object: the branch levels and the leaf levels. The branch levels are where the logic of seeks happen, starting at a narrow "top" where key data is stored so that it can be traversed by SQL Server using binary decisions. A seek moves "down" the B+tree structure via binary decisions. The leaf levels are where the seek ends and data is retrieved. Adding a column to the INCLUDE list of a rowstore nonclustered index adds that data only to the leaf level.

Inside OUT

How can you see the properties and storage for each level of the index's B+tree?

You can view the page_count, record_count, space_used statistics, and more for each level of a B+tree by using the DETAILED mode of the sys.dm_db_index_physical_stats dynamic management function. Only the leaf level (index_ level = 0) is visible in other modes. The mode parameter is the fifth parameter passed in, as demonstrated in the following code:

```
SELECT * FROM sys.dm_db_index_physical_stats
(DB_ID(), object_id('Sales.Invoices'), null , null, 'DETAILED');
```

Notice that the leaf level of each index has the same number of rows, but has a different number of pages (because each index has different columns). Note that the branch levels (where index_level > 0) of each index's B+tree contain less data. Indexes with more columns and on larger tables will require more levels.

The INCLUDE statement of an index allows for data to be retrievable in the leaf level only, but not stored in the branch level. This reduced the overall size and complexity needed to cover a query's need. Consider the following query and execution plan (Figure 15-1) from the WideWorldImporters database:

```
SELECT CustomerID, AccountsPersonID

FROM [Sales].[Invoices]

WHERE CustomerID = 832;
```

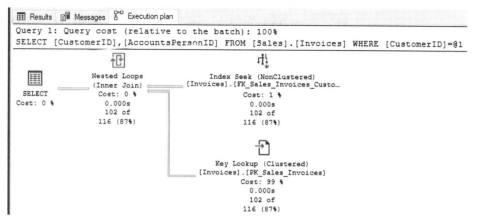

Figure 15-1 This execution plan shows an Index Seek and a Key Lookup on the same table; the Key Lookup represents 99% of the cost of the query.

Object
[WideWorldImporters].[Sales].[Invoices].
[FK_Sales_Invoices_CustomerID]
Output List
[WideWorldImporters].[Sales].[Invoices].InvoiceID,
[WideWorldImporters].[Sales].[Invoices].CustomerID
Seek Predicates
Seek Keys[1]: Prefix: [WideWorldImporters].[Sales].
[Invoices].CustomerID = Scalar Operator((832))

Figure 15-2 The properties of the Index Seek in the previous example script. Note that `CustomerID` is in the Seek Predicate and also in the Output List, but that `AccountsPersonID` is not listed in the Output List.

Note that `CustomerID` is in the Seek Predicate and also in the Output List, but that `AccountsPersonID` is not listed in the Output List. Our query is searching for and returning `CustomerID` (it appears in both the SELECT and WHERE clauses), but our query also returns `AccountsPersonID`, which is not contained in the index `FK_Sales_Invoices_ CustomerID`. Here is the code of the nonclustered index `FK_Sales_Invoices_ CustomerID`, named because it is for `CustomerID`, a foreign key reference:

```
CREATE NONCLUSTERED INDEX [FK_Sales_Invoices_CustomerID] ON [Sales].[Invoices]
```

```
( CustomerID ASC )

ON [USERDATA];
```

To remove the Key Lookup, let's add an included column to the nonclustered index, so that the query can retrieve all the data it needs from a single object:

```
CREATE NONCLUSTERED INDEX [FK_Sales_Invoices_CustomerID] ON [Sales].[Invoices]

( CustomerID ASC )

INCLUDE ( AccountsPersonID )

WITH (DROP_EXISTING = ON)

ON [USERDATA];

GO
```

Let's run our sample query again (see also Figure 15-3):

```
SELECT CustomerID, AccountsPersonID

FROM [Sales].[Invoices]

WHERE CustomerID = 832;
```

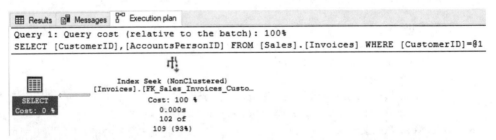

Figure 15-3 The execution plan now shows only an Index Seek; the Key Lookup that appeared in Figure 10-1 has been eliminated from the execution plan.

The Key Lookup has been eliminated. The query was able to retrieve both CustomerID and AccountsPersonID from the same index and required no second pass through the table for the column AccountsPersonID. The estimated subtree cost, in the properties of the SELECT opera-tor, is now 0.0034015, compared to 0.355919 when the Key Lookup was present. Although this query was a small example for demonstration purposes, eliminating the Key Lookup represents a significant improvement to query performance without changing the query.Just as you do not want to add too many nonclustered indexes, you also do not want to add too many columns unnecessarily to the INCLUDE list of nonclustered indexes. Columns in the INCLUDE list, as we saw in the previous code example, still require storage space. For infrequent queries that return small sets of data, the key lookup operator is probably not worth the cost of storing additional columns in the INCLUDE list of an index.

In summary, you should craft nonclustered indexes to serve many queries smartly, you should always try to avoid creating overlapping or redundant indexes, and you should regularly review to verify that indexes are still being used as applications or report queries change. Keep this guidance in mind as we move into the next section!

The previous sample script and all scripts for this book are available for download at *https://www.MicrosoftPressStore.com/SQLServer2019InsideOut/downloads.*

Creating filtered nonclustered indexes

Nonclustered indexes are a sort of vertical partition of a table, but you can also create a horizontal filter of an index. A filtered index has powerful potential uses to serve up pre-filtered data. Obviously, filtered indexes are only then suited to serve data to queries with matching WHERE clauses.

Filtered indexes could have particular use in table designs that include a soft delete flag, or a processed/unprocessed status flag, or a current/archived flag. Work with developers to identify this sort of table design usage.

Imagine a scenario where a table has millions of rows, with few rows marked "unprocessed" and the rest marked "processed". An application may query this table regularly with a query that uses WHERE processed = 0, looking for rows to process. A nonclustered index on the processed column, resulting a seek operation in the execution plan, would be much faster than scanning the entire table. But a filtered index with the same WHERE clause would only contain the few rows marked "unprocessed", resulting in a performance gain for the same query with no code changes.

A filter can be added to an index easily, for example:

```
CREATE INDEX [IX_Application_People_IsEmployee]

ON [Application].[People]([IsEmployee])

WHERE IsEmployee = 1;
```

In your database, look for potential uses of new filtered indexes in columns that are of the bit data type, or use prefix like "Is" or suffixes like "Flag", or perhaps, when a query only ever looks for data of a certain type, or whether the data is NULL or NOT NULL.. Work with developers to identify potential uses when the majority of data in the table is not needed for many queries.

Keep in mind that adding a filter to an existing index may make it unusable to queries that do not use the same query. Avoid adding a filter to an existing nonclustered index marked unique, as this will change the enforcement of the constraint and the intent of the unique index. Filtered nonclustered indexes can be created with the unique property to enforce filtered uniqueness. For example, this could have potential uses in employee ID's that are allowed to be reused, or, in data warehouse scenario where a table needs to enforce uniqueness on only the active records of a dimension.

Understanding the "missing" indexes feature

The concept of intelligently combining many similar indexes into one super-index is crucial to understanding the utility of using SQL Server's built-in Missing Indexes feature. First introduced in SQL 2005, the Missing Indexes feature revolutionized the ability to see the "big picture" when crafting nonclustered indexes. The missing indexes feature has been passively gathering information on every database since SQL Server 2005, as well as in Azure SQL Database.

The Missing Indexes feature collects information from actual query usage. SQL Server passively records when it would have been better to have a nonclustered index; for example, to replace a Scan for a Seek or to eliminate a Lookup from a query's execution plan. The Missing Indexes feature then aggregates these requests together, counts how many times they have happened, calculates the cost of the statement operations that could be improved, and estimates the percentage of that cost that would be eliminated (this percentage is labeled the "impact"). Think of the Missing Indexes feature as the database wish list of nonclustered indexes.

However, some caveats and limitations about the Missing Indexes feature. The recommendations in the output of the missing index dynamic management objects (DMOs) will likely include overlapping (but not duplicate) suggestions. Also, only rowstore nonclustered indexes can be suggested – remember this feature was introduced in SQL Server 2005 – so clustered, columnstore, and other types of indexes won't be recommended. The recommendations are lost when any DDL changes to the table occur, and also when the SQL Server instance restarts.

You can look at missing indexes any time, with no performance overhead to the server, by querying a set of DMOs dedicated to this feature. You can find the following query, which concatenates together the CREATE INDEX statement for you, according to a simple, self-explanatory naming convention. As you can see from the use of system views, this query is intended to be run in a single database:

```
SELECT mid.[statement], create_index_statement =
    CONCAT('CREATE NONCLUSTERED INDEX IDX_NC_',
     TRANSLATE(replace(mid.equality_columns, ' ',''), '],[' ,'___')
   , TRANSLATE(replace(mid.inequality_columns, ' ',''), '],[' ,'___')
   , ' ON ' , mid.[statement] , ' (' , mid.equality_columns
   , CASE WHEN mid.equality_columns IS NOT NULL
    AND mid.inequality_columns IS NOT NULL THEN ',' ELSE '' END
    , mid.inequality_columns , ')'
     , ' INCLUDE (' , mid.included_columns , ')' )
, migs.unique_compiles, migs.user_seeks, migs.user_scans
, migs.last_user_seek, migs.avg_total_user_cost
, migs.avg_user_impact, mid.equality_columns
, mid.inequality_columns, mid.included_columns
FROM sys.dm_db_missing_index_groups mig
INNER JOIN sys.dm_db_missing_index_group_stats migs
```

```
ON migs.group_handle = mig.index_group_handle
INNER JOIN sys.dm_db_missing_index_details mid
ON mig.index_handle = mid.index_handle
INNER JOIN sys.tables t ON t.object_id = mid.object_id
INNER JOIN sys.schemas s ON s.schema_id = t.schema_id
WHERE mid.database_id = DB_ID()
-- count of query compilations that needed this proposed index
--AND        migs.unique_compiles > 10
-- count of query seeks that needed this proposed index
--AND        migs.user_seeks > 10
-- average percentage of cost that could be alleviated with this proposed index
--AND        migs.avg_user_impact > 75
-- Sort by indexes that will have the most impact to the costliest queries
ORDER BY migs.avg_user_impact * migs.avg_total_user_cost desc;
```

This sample script and all scripts for this book are all available for download at *https://www. MicrosoftPressStore.com/SQLServer2019InsideOut/downloads*. At the bottom of this query are a series of filters that you can use to find only the most-used, highest-value index suggestions. If you have hundreds or thousands of rows returned by this query, consider spending an afternoon crafting together indexes to improve the performance of the actual user activity that generated this data.

Some indexes returned by the missing indexes queries might not be worth creating because they have a very low impact or have been part of only one query compilation. Others may overlap each other. For example, you might see these three index suggestions:

```
CREATE NONCLUSTERED INDEX IDX_NC_Gamelog_Team1 ON dbo.gamelog (Team1)
INCLUDE (GameYear, GameWeek, Team1Score, Team2Score);
CREATE NONCLUSTERED INDEX IDX_NC_Gamelog_Team1_GameWeek_GameYear ON dbo.gamelog (Team1,
GameWeek, GameYear) INCLUDE (Team1Score);
CREATE NONCLUSTERED INDEX IDX_NC_Gamelog_Team1_GameWeek_GameYear_Team2 ON dbo.gamelog
(Team1, GameWeek, GameYear, Team2);
```

You should not create all three of these indexes. Instead, you should combine the indexes you deem useful and worthwhile into a single index that matches the order of the needed key columns and covers all the included columns, as well. Here is the properly combined index suggestion:

```
CREATE NONCLUSTERED INDEX IDX_NC_Gamelog_Team1_GameWeek_GameYear_Team2 ON dbo.gamelog
(Team1, GameWeek, GameYear, Team2)
INCLUDE (Team1Score, Team2Score);
```

This last index is a good combination of the previous suggestions. It will deliver maximum positive benefit to the most queries, and it minimizes the negative impact to writes, storage, and maintenance. Note that the Key columns list overlaps and is in the correct order for each of the previous index suggestions, and that the TNCLUDE columns list also covers all the columns needed in the index suggestions. If a column is in the key of the index, it does not need to exist in the INCLUDE of the index.

CHAPTER 15

However, don't create this index yet. You should still review existing indexes on the table before creating any missing indexes. Perhaps you can combine a new missing index and an existing index, in the Key column list or the INCLUDE column list, further increasing the value of a single index.

Finally, after combining missing index suggestions with one another and with existing indexes, you are ready to create the index and see it in action. Remember always to create indexes when looking at the "big picture": remember, rarely does a single query rise to the importance level of justifying its own indexes. For example, in SQL Server Management Studio, you will sometimes see green text suggesting a missing index for this query, as illustrated in Figure 15-4 (note that in this figure the text is gray).

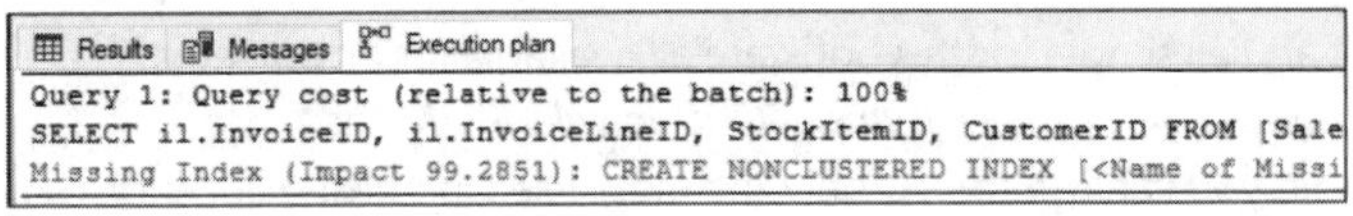

Figure 15-4 In the execution plan tab, in the header of each execution plan, text starting with "Missing Index" will alert you to the possible impact. Do not create this index on the spot!

That's valuable, but do not create that index on the spot! Always refer to the complete set of index suggestions and other existing indexes on the table, combining overlapping indexes when possible. Consider the green missing index alert in SQL Server Management Studio as only a flag that indicates you should spend time investigating new missing indexes.

So, to recap, when creating nonclustered indexes for performance tuning, you should do the following:

1. Use the Missing Indexes DMVs to identify new "big picture" nonclustered indexes:
   a. Don't create indexes that will likely only help out a single query—few queries are important enough to deserve their own indexes.
   b. Consider nonclustered columnstore indexes instead for very large rowcount tables where queries often have to scan millions of rows for aggregates. (You can read more on columnstore indexes later in this chapter.)
2. Combine Missing Index suggestions, being aware of key order and INCLUDE lists.
3. Compare new index suggestions with existing indexes; perhaps you can combine them.
4. Remember to review index usage statistics, as well, to verify whether indexes are helping you. (See the next section for more on the index usage statistics DMV.)

Inside OUT

Does the Missing Indexes feature suggest only rowstore nonclustered index?

Yes, only rowstore nonclustered indexes.

The missing indexes feature can't help you with proper clustered index design—that's up to you, the informed database designer. It can provide some insight into usage after a time, but that would mean running a typical production workload against a heap, and suffering the performance issues likely to arise.

Here's another limitation to the missing indexes feature: it is not aware of clustered or nonclustered columnstore indexes, which are incredibly powerful structures to add for massive row count queries on large tables. The Missing Indexes (introduced in SQL 2005) feature cannot suggest columnstore indexes (introduced in SQL 2012). The Missing Indexes feature will even suggest an index to replace a useful columnstore index. Be aware of all indexes in your table, including columnstore indexes, when considering new indexes.

Therefore, when you have created a columnstore index on a table, you may will need to ignore index suggestions that look like the same workloads that are currently benefitting from the columnstore. For a query that requires a scan on many rows in the table, the query optimizer is unlikely to pick a nonclustered index over a nonclustered columnstore index. The columnstore index will typically vastly outperform a nonclustered index for massive row count queries, though the missing index feature might still count this as a new nonclustered index suggestion.

CHAPTER 15

Understanding when Missing Index suggestions are removed

Missing Index suggestions are cleared out for any change to the tables; for example, if you add or remove columns, or if you add or remove indexes. Missing Index suggestions are also cleared out when the SQL Server service is started, and cannot be manually cleared easily. (You can take the database offline and back online, which would clear out the Missing Index suggestions, but this seems like overkill.)

Logically, make sure the missing index data that you have collected is also based on a significant sample actual production user activity over time spanning at least one business cycle. Missing index suggestions based on development activity might not be a useful representation of intended application activity, though suggestions based on end-user testing or training could be.

Understanding and proving index usage

You've added indexes to your database, and they are used over time, but meanwhile the query patterns of applications and reports change. Columns are added to the database, new tables are added, and although you add new indexes to suit new functionality, how does a database administrator ensure that existing indexes are still worth keeping?

SQL Server tracks this information for you automatically with yet another valuable DMV: sys. dm_db_index_usage_stats. Following is a script that measures index usage within a database, combining sys.dm_db_index_usage_stats with other system views and DMVs to return valuable information. Note that the ORDER BY clause will place indexes with the fewest read operations (seeks, scans, lookups) and the most write operations (updates) at the top of the list.

```
SELECT TableName = sc.name + '.' + o.name, IndexName = i.name
    , s.user_seeks, s.user_scans, s.user_lookups
    , s.user_updates
    , ps.row_count, SizeMb = (ps.in_row_reserved_page_count*8.)/1024.
    , s.last_user_lookup, s.last_user_scan, s.last_user_seek
    , s.last_user_update
FROM sys.dm_db_index_usage_stats AS s
  INNER JOIN sys.indexes AS i
ON i.object_id = s.object_id AND i.index_id = s.index_id
  INNER JOIN sys.objects AS o ON o.object_id=i.object_id
  INNER JOIN sys.schemas AS sc ON sc.schema_id = o.schema_id
   INNER JOIN sys.partitions AS pr
ON pr.object_id = i.object_id AND pr.index_id = i.index_id
   INNER JOIN sys.dm_db_partition_stats AS ps
ON ps.object_id = i.object_id AND ps.partition_id = pr.partition_id
WHERE o.is_ms_shipped = 0
--Don't consider dropping any constraints
AND i.is_unique = 0 AND i.is_primary_key = 0 AND i.is_unique_constraint = 0
--Order by table reads asc, table writes desc
ORDER BY user_seeks + user_scans + user_lookups asc, s.user_updates desc;
```

The previous sample script and all scripts for this book are all available for download at *https://www.MicrosoftPressStore.com/SQLServer2019InsideOut/downloads.*

Any indexes that rise to the top of the preceding query should be considered for removal or redesign, given the following caveats:

1. Before justifying dropping any indexes, you should ensure that you have collected data from the index usage stats DMV that spans at least one complete business cycle. The index usage stats DMV is cleared when the SQL Server service is restarted. You cannot manually clear it. If your applications have week-end and month-end reporting, you might have indexes present and tuned specifically for those critical performance periods.

2. Logically, verify that the index usage data that you have collected is also based on actual production user activity. Index usage data based on testing or development activity would not be a useful representation of intended application activity.

3. Note the final WHERE clause that ignores unique constraints and primary keys. Even if a nonclustered index exists and isn't used, if it is part of the uniqueness of the table, it should not be dropped.

Again, the Query Store can be an invaluable tool to monitor for query regression after indexing changes.

> ➤ For more info on the Query Store, see Chapter 14: Performance tuning SQL Server.

Like many DMVs that are cleared when the SQL Server service restarts, consider a strategy of capturing data and storing it periodically in persistent tables.

Like many server-level DMVs, the index usage stats data requires the VIEW SERVER STATE permission in SQL Server. In Azure SQL Database Premium tier, the VIEW DATABASE STATE permission is required, but only the server admin or Azure Active Directory admin accounts can access this data in standard and basic tiers.

Understanding columnstore indexes

Columnstore indexes were first introduced in SQL Server 2012, making a splash in their ability to far outperform clustered and nonclustered indexes when it comes to massive table scans. They were typically used in the scenario of nightly-refreshed data warehouses, but now they have beneficial applications on transactional systems, including on memory-optimized tables.

Columnstore indexes are superior to rowstore data storage for performance in appropriate situations.

Recent changes to columnstore indexes have greatly expanded their usefulness:

- Prior to SQL Server 2016, the presence of a nonclustered columnstore index made the table read-only. This drawback was removed in SQL Server 2016, and now nonclustered columnstore indexes are fully-featured and quite useful in a variety of applications aside from nightly-refresh databases.

- Starting with SQL Server 2016 SP1, columnstore indexes are even available below Enterprise edition licenses of SQL Server (though with a limitation on columnstore memory utilization).

- Snapshot isolation and columnstore indexes are fully compatible. Prior to SQL Server 2016, using read committed snapshot and snapshot isolation level were not supported with columnstore indexes.

- You can place a clustered columnstore index on a memory-optimized table, providing the ability to do analytics on millions of rows of live real-time Online Transaction Processing (OLTP) data.

- Starting with SQL Server 2017, a variety of batch mode features grouped under the Intelligent Query Processing label increased performance of queries with columnstore indexes.

➤ **For more about the suite of features under Intelligent Query Processing, see Chapter 14.**

- Starting with SQL Server 2019, using the WITH (ONLINE = ON) syntax is supported for creating and rebuilding columnstore indexes.

These key improvements opened columnstore indexes to be used in transactional systems, when tables with millions of rows are read, resulting in million-row result sets. This is when columnstore indexes really shine.

Columnstore indexes have two compression levels. In addition to the eponymous default COLUMNSTORE compression level, there is also a COLUMNSTORE_ARCHIVE compression option, which further compresses the data at the cost of more CPU when needing to read or write the data.

As with rowstore indexes, you can compress each partition of a table's columnstore index differently. Consider applying COLUMNSTORE_ARCHIVE compression to partitions of data that are old and rarely accessed. You can change the data compression option for rowstore and columnstore indexes by using the index rebuild operation via the DATA_COMPRESSION option. For columnstore indexes, you can specify the COLUMNSTORE or COLUMNSTORE_ARCHIVE options, whereas for rowstore indexes, you can use the NONE, ROW, and PAGE compression options.

➤ **For more detail on Data Compression, see Chapter 3: "Designing and implementing an on-premises database infrastructure".**

You cannot change the compression option of a rowstore index to either of the columnstore options, or vice versa, you must instead build a new index of the desired type.

The `sp_estimate_data_compression_savings` system stored procedure can be used to estimate the size differences between the compression options. Starting with SQL Server 2019, this stored procedure includes estimates for the two columnstore compression options.

NOTE

There is currently a three-way incompatibility between the system stored procedure `sp_estimate_data_compression_savings`, columnstore indexes, and the new SQL Server 2019 Memory-Optimized TempDB Metadata feature. You cannot use `sp_estimate_data_compression_savings` withcolumnstore indexes if the new Memory-Optimized TempDB Metadata feature is enabled. For more information visit: https://docs.microsoft.com/sql/relational-databases/system-stored-procedures/sp-estimate-data-compression-savings-transact-sql.

Designing columnstore indexes

Columnstore indexes are not a B+tree; instead, they contain highly compressed, unordered data (on disk and in memory), stored in a different architecture from the traditional clustered and nonclustered indexes. Unlike rowstore indexes, there is no "key" or "include" of a columnstore index, only a set of columns that are part of the index. The order of the columns in the definition of a columnstore index does not matter. You can create "clustered" or "nonclustered" columnstore indexes, though this terminology is used more to indicate what role the columnstore index is serving, not what it resembles behind the scenes.

You can also create nonclustered rowstore indexes on tables with a clustered columnstore index, which is potentially useful to enforce uniqueness. Columnstore indexes cannot be unique, and so cannot replace the table's unique constraint or Primary Key. Clustered columnstore indexes may also perform poorly when a table receives updates, so consider the workload for a table before adding a clustered columnstore. Tables that are only ever inserted into, but never updated or deleted from, would be an ideal candidate for a clustered columnstore index.

You can combine nonclustered rowstore and nonclustered columnstore indexes on the same table, but you can have only one columnstore index on a table, including clustered and non-clustered columnstore indexes. You can even create nonclustered rowstore and nonclustered columnstore indexes on the same columns. Perhaps you create both because you want to filter on the column value in one set of queries, and aggregate in another. Or, perhaps you create both only temporarily, for comparison.

You can also create nonclustered columnstore indexes on indexed views, another avenue to quick-updating analytical data. The stipulations and limitations regarding indexed views apply, but you would create a unique rowstore clustered index on the view, then a nonclustered columnstore view.

One significant difference when you choose columnstore index keys is that the order doesn't matter. You can add columns in any order to satisfy many different queries, greatly increasing the versatility of the columnstore index in your table. This is because the order of the data is not important to how columnstore indexes work.

The size of the key for columnstore indexes, however, could make a big difference in performance. For columnstore indexes, the columns in a columnstore index should each be limited to 8000 bytes for best performance. Data larger than 8000 bytes in a row is compressed separately outside of the columnstore compressed row group, requiring more decompression to access the complete row.

While large object data types varchar(max), nvarchar(max), and varbinary(max) are supported in the key of a columnstore index, they are not stored in-line with the rest of the compressed data, but rather in stored outside the columnstore structure. These data types are not recommended in columnstore indexes. Starting with SQL Server 2017, they are supported, but still not recommended. For more on data type restrictions and limitations for columnstore indexes, visit *https://docs.microsoft.com/sql/t-sql/statements/create-columnstore-index-transact-sql#LimitRest.*

One of the reasons that data types more than 8 bytes per row reduce columnstore performance is that they cannot be used with segment elimination. The most optimal datatypes for columns in a columnstore index are datatypes that can be stored in an 8 byte integer value, such as integers, and some date and time based datatypes. They allow you to use what is known as segment elimination. If your query includes a filter on such values, SQL Server can issue reads only those segments in row groups that contain data within a range, eliminating ranges of data outside of the request. The data is not sorted, so segment elimination may not help all filtering queries, but the more selective the value, the more likely it will be useful. Other datatypes with a size less than 8000 bytes will still compress and be useful for aggregations, but should generally not appear as a filter, because the entire table will always need to be scanned.

Understanding batch mode

Batch mode is one of the existing features lumped into the Intelligent Query Processing umbrella, a collection of performance improvements. Batch mode has actually been around since SQL Server 2014. Like many other features listed under Intelligent Query Processing, batch mode can benefit workloads automatically and without requiring code changes.

You'll see "Batch" (instead of the default "Row") in the Actual Execution Mode of an execution plan operator when this faster method is in use. Batch mode processing appears in the form of batch mode operators in execution plans, and benefits queries that process millions of rows or more.

➤ For more information on Intelligent Query Processing features, see Chapter 14.

Initially, only queries on columnstore indexes could benefit from batch mode operators. Starting with compatibility mode 150 (SQL Server 2019), batch mode for analytic workloads are available outside of columnstore indexes: the query processor may decide to use batch mode operators for queries on heaps and rowstore indexes. No changes are needed for your code in SQL Server 2019 to begin to benefit from batch mode on rowstore objects.

➤ For more information on which operators can use batch mode execution, go to *https://docs.microsoft.com/sql/relational-databases/indexes/columnstore-indexes-query-performance.*

NOTE
Batch mode has not yet been extended to in-memory OLTP tables or other types of indexes like full-text, spatial, or XML indexes. Batch mode will also not occur on sparse and XML columns.

Understanding the deltastore of columnstore indexes

The columnstore deltastore is an ephemeral location where changed data is stored in a clustered B+tree rowstore format. When certain thresholds of inserted rows are reached, typically 1,048,576 rows, or when a columnstore index is rebuilt or reorganized, a group of deltastore data is "closed". Then via a background thread called the Tuple Mover, the deltastore rowgroup is compressed into the columnstore. The number of rows SQL Server compresses into a rowgroup may be smaller under memory pressure, this happens dynamically.

The COMPRESSION_DELAY option for both nonclustered and clustered columnstore indexes has to do with how long it takes changed data to be written from the deltastore to the highly compressed columnstore.

The COMPRESSION_DELAY option does not affect the 1,048,576 number, but rather how long it takes SQL Server to move the data into columnstore. By setting the COMPRESSION_DELAY option to 10 minutes, data will remain in deltastore for at least an extra 10 minutes before SQL Server compresses it. The advantage of data remaining in the deltastore, delaying its eventual compression, could be noticeable on tables that continue to be updated and deleted. Updates and deletes are typically very resource-intensive on columnstore indexes. Delete operations in the columnstore are "soft" deleted, marked as removed, and then cleaned out eventually during index maintenance. Updates are actually processed as deletes and inserts into the deltastore.

The advantage of COMPRESSION_DELAY is noticeable for some write workloads, but not all. If the table is only ever inserted into, COMPRESSION_DELAY doesn't really help. But if a block of recent data is updated and deleted for a period before finally settling in after a time, implementing COMPRESSION_DELAY can speed up the write transactions to the data and reduce the maintenance and storage footprint of the columnstore index.

Changing the COMPRESSION_DELAY setting of the index, unlike many other index settings, does not require a rebuild of the index, and you can change it at any time; for example:

```
ALTER INDEX [NCCX_Sales_InvoiceLines]
    ON [Sales].[InvoiceLines]
    SET (COMPRESSION_DELAY = 10 MINUTES);
```

SQL Server can ignore the deltastore for inserts when you insert data in large amounts. This is called bulk loading in Microsoft documentation, but is not related to the BULK INSERT command. When you want to insert large amounts of data into a table with a columnstore index, SQL Server will bypass the deltastore for large insert. Bypassing the deltastore increases the speed of the insert and the immediate availability for the data for analytical queries, as well as reducing the amount of logged activity in the user database transaction log.

Under ideal circumstances, the best number of rows to insert in a single statement is 1,048,576, which creates a complete, compressed columnstore row group. The number of rows to trigger a bulk load is between 102,400 rows and 1,047,576 rows, depending on memory. If you specify

TABLOCK in the INSERT statement, the bulk loading of data into the columnstore in parallel. The typical caveat about TABLOCK is applicable here, as the table may block other operations at the time of the insert in parallel.

Demonstrating the power of columnstore indexes

To demonstrate the power of this fully operational columnstore index, let's review an example scenario in which more than 14 million rows are added to the `WideWorldImporters.Sales.InvoiceLines` table. About half of the rows in the table now contain `InvoiceID = 69776`.

To demonstrate, start by restoring a fresh copy of the sample WideWorldImporters database from Microsoft: *https://docs.microsoft.com/sql/samples/wide-world-importers-oltp-install-configure*.

In the below script sample, we dropped the existing WideWorldImporters-provided nonclustered columnstore index and added a new nonclustered index we've created here, which performs an Index Scan on it to return the data. Remember that `InvoiceID = 69776` is roughly half the table, so this isn't a "needle in a haystack" situation; this isn't a seek. If the query can use a seek operator, the nonclustered rowstore index would likely be better. When the query must scan, columnstore is king.

```
USE WideworldImporters;

GO

-- Fill haystack with 3+ million rows

INSERT INTO Sales.InvoiceLines (InvoiceLineID, InvoiceID

, StockItemID, Description, PackageTypeID, Quantity

, UnitPrice, TaxRate, TaxAmount, LineProfit, ExtendedPrice

, LastEditedBy, LastEditedWhen)

SELECT InvoiceLineID = NEXT VALUE FOR [Sequences].[InvoiceLineID]

, InvoiceID, StockItemID, Description, PackageTypeID, Quantity

, UnitPrice, TaxRate, TaxAmount, LineProfit

, ExtendedPrice, LastEditedBy, LastEditedWhen

FROM Sales.InvoiceLines;

GO 3 --Runs the above three times

-- Insert millions of records for InvoiceID 69776
```

```
INSERT INTO Sales.InvoiceLines (InvoiceLineID, InvoiceID

, StockItemID, Description, PackageTypeID, Quantity

, UnitPrice, TaxRate, TaxAmount, LineProfit, ExtendedPrice

, LastEditedBy, LastEditedWhen)

SELECT InvoiceLineID = NEXT VALUE FOR [Sequences].[InvoiceLineID]

, 69776, StockItemID, Description, PackageTypeID, Quantity

, UnitPrice, TaxRate, TaxAmount, LineProfit

, ExtendedPrice, LastEditedBy, LastEditedWhen

FROM Sales.InvoiceLines;

GO

--Clear cache, drop other indexes to only test our comparison scenario

DBCC FREEPROCCACHE

DROP INDEX IF EXISTS [NCCX_Sales_InvoiceLines]

ON [Sales].[InvoiceLines];

DROP INDEX IF EXISTS IDX_NC_InvoiceLines_InvoiceID_StockItemID_Quantity

ON [Sales].[InvoiceLines];

DROP INDEX IF EXISTS IDX_CS_InvoiceLines_InvoiceID_StockItemID_Quantity

ON [Sales].[InvoiceLines];

GO

--Create a rowstore nonclustered index for comparison

CREATE INDEX IDX_NC_InvoiceLines_InvoiceID_StockItemID_Quantity

    ON [Sales].[InvoiceLines] (InvoiceID, StockItemID, Quantity);

GO
```

Now that the data is loaded, you can perform the query again for testing (see Figure 15-5). Note again we are using the STATISTICS TIME option to measure both CPU and total duration.

```
SET STATISTICS TIME ON;

SELECT il.StockItemID, AvgQuantity = AVG(il.quantity)

FROM [Sales].[InvoiceLines] AS il

WHERE il.InvoiceID = 69776 --1.8million records
```

```
GROUP BY il.StockItemID;

SET STATISTICS TIME OFF;
```

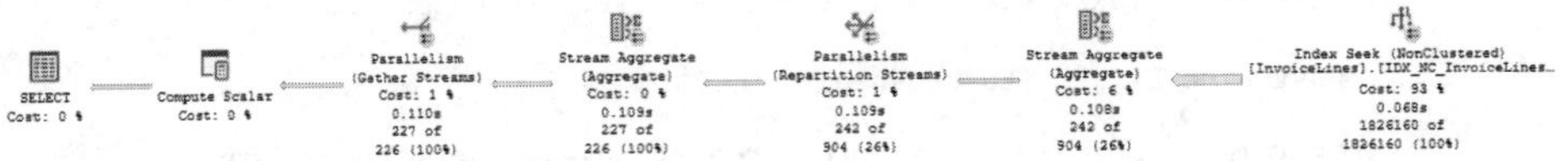

Figure 15-5 A screenshot of the execution plan of our sample query, starts with an Index Seek (NonClustered) on the rowstore nonclustered index. Note the large amount of parallelism operators along the way.

Our sample query on 69776 had to work through 1.8 million records and returned 227 rows. With the rowstore nonclustered index, the cost of the query is 4.52 and completes in 844ms of CPU time (due to parallelism), 194ms of total time. (These durations will vary from system to system, the lab environment was a four-core Intel processor with hyperthreading.)

Now, let's create a columnstore index, and watch our analytical-scale query benefit.

NOTE

Starting with SQL Server 2019, using the WITH (ONLINE = ON) syntax is supported for creating and rebuilding columnstore indexes.

```
--Create a columnstore nonclustered index for comparison

CREATE COLUMNSTORE INDEX IDX_CS_InvoiceLines_InvoiceID_StockItemID_quantity

    ON [Sales].[InvoiceLines] (InvoiceID, StockItemID, Quantity) WITH (ONLINE = ON);

GO
```

Perform the query again for testing. Note again we are using the STATISTICS TIME option to measure both CPU and total duration.

```
SET STATISTICS TIME ON;

--Run the same query as above, but now it will use the columnstore

SELECT il.StockItemID, AvgQuantity = AVG(il.quantity)

FROM [Sales].[InvoiceLines] AS il

WHERE il.InvoiceID = 69776 --1.8million records

GROUP BY il.StockItemID;

SET STATISTICS TIME OFF;
```

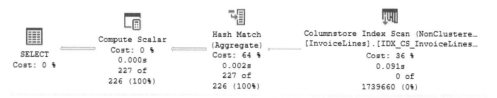

Figure 15-6 A screenshot of the execution plan of our sample query, now starting with a Columnstore Index Scan (NonClustered).

Our sample query on 69776 still returns 227 rows. With the benefit of the columnstore nonclustered index, the cost of the query is 1.54 and completes in 47ms of CPU time, 160ms of total time. This is a significant but relatively small sample of the power of a columnstore index on analytical scale queries. The previous sample script and all scripts for this book are available for download at *https://www.MicrosoftPressStore.com/SQLServer2019InsideOut/downloads.*

Understanding indexing in memory-optimized tables

Memory-optimized tables provide for table performance less bound by I/O constraints, providing high-performance, latchless writes. Memory-optimized tables don't use the locking mechanics of pessimistic concurrency, as is discussed in Chapter 14. Data rows for memory-optimized tables are not stored in pages, and so do not use the concepts of disk-based tables.

Memory-optimized tables can have two types of indexes: hash and nonclustered. Nonclustered indexes for memory-optimized tables behave similarly on memory-optimized tables as they do for disk-based tables, whereas hash indexes are better suited for high-performance seeks for individual records. You must create at least one index on a memory-optimized table. Either of the two types of indexes can be the structure behind the Primary Key of the table, if you desire both data and schema to be durable.

Indexes on in-memory tables are never durable and will be rebuilt whenever the database comes online. The schema of the memory-optimized table is always durable, but you can choose to have only the schema of the table be durable, but not the data. This has utility in certain scenarios as a staging table to receive data that will be moved to a durable disk-based or memory-optimized table. You should be aware of the potential for data loss. If only the schema of the memory-optimized table is durable, you do not need to declare a Primary Key. However, in the CREATE TABLE statement, you must still define at least one index or a Primary Key for a table by using DURABILITY = SCHEMA_ONLY. Our suggestion is that only in very rare situations should a table not have a primary key constraint, no matter the durability.

Keep in mind that adding indexes to memory-optimized tables increases the amount of server memory needed. There is otherwise no limit to the size of memory-optimized tables in Enterprise edition; however, in Standard edition you are limited to 32 GB of memory-optimized tables per database.

Earlier versions of SQL Server put a cap on the number of indexes on a memory-optimized table, that cap was raised from 8 to 999 in SQL Server 2017.

Although there is no concept of a rowstore clustered index in memory-optimized tables, you can add a clustered columnstore index to a memory-optimized table, dramatically improving your ability to perform analytical scale queries on the data, even as it is rapidly inserted. Because columnstore indexes cannot be unique, they cannot serve as the Primary Key for a memory-optimized table.

Let's go over the basics of using hash and nonclustered indexes on memory-optimized tables.

Understanding hash indexes for memory-optimized tables

Memory-optimized hash indexes are an alternative to the typical B+tree internal architecture for index data storage. Hash indexes are best for queries that look for the needle in the haystack, and are especially effective when matching exact values, but they are not effective at range lookups or queries with an ORDER BY.

One other limitation of the hash index is that if you don't query all the columns in a hash index, they are generally not as useful as a nonclustered index in a memory-optimized table (see the next section). The WHERE clause must try to seek each column in the hash index's key. Unlike B+tree–based nonclustered indexes, hash indexes also do not perform as well when there are multiple columns in the key of the indexes but not all columns, or even just the first column, are queried.

Hash indexes are currently available only for memory-optimized tables, not disk-based tables. You can declare them by using the UNIQUE keyword, but they default to a non-unique key. You can create more than one hash index.

There is an additional unique consideration for creating hash indexes. Estimating the best number for the BUCKET_COUNT parameter can have a significant impact. The number should be as close to as possible to the number of unique key values that are expected. BUCKET_COUNT should be between 1 and 2 times this number. Hash indexes always use the same amount of space for the same-sized bucket count, regardless of the rowcount within.

For example, if you expect the table to have 100,000 unique values in it, the ideal BUCKET_COUNT value would be between 100,000 and 200,000.

Having too many or too few buckets in a hash index can result in poor performance. More buckets will increase the amount of memory needed and the number of those buckets that are empty. Too few buckets will result in queries needing to access more, larger buckets in a chain to access the same information.

Ideally, a hash index is declared unique. Hash indexes work best when the key values are unique or at least highly distinct. If the ratio of total rows to unique key values is too high, a hash index is not recommended and will perform poorly. Microsoft documentation recommends a threshold of less than 10 rows per unique value for an effective hash index.   If you have data with many duplicate values, consider a nonclustered index instead.

You should periodically and proactively compare the number of unique key values to the total number of rows in the table. It is better to overestimate the number of buckets. You can change the number of buckets in a memory-optimized hash index by using the ALTER TABLE/ALTER INDEX/REBUILD commands; for example:

```
ALTER TABLE [dbo].[Transactions]

ALTER INDEX [IDX_NC_H Transactions_1]

REBUILD WITH (BUCKET_COUNT = 524288);
--will always round up to the nearest power of two
```

Understanding nonclustered indexes for memory-optimized tables

Nonclustered indexes for memory-optimized tables behave similarly on memory-optimized tables as they do for disk-based tables. Instead of a B+tree like a rowstore, disk-based nonclustered index, they are in fact a variant of the B-tree structure called the Bw-Tree, which does not use locks or latches. They will outperform hash indexes for queries that perform sorting on the key value(s) of the index, or when the index must be range scanned. Further, if you don't query all the columns in a hash index, they are generally not as useful as a nonclustered index.

You can declare nonclustered indexes on memory-optimized tables UNIQUE, however, the CREATE INDEX syntax is not supported. You must use the ALTER TABLE/ADD INDEX commands, or include them in the CREATE TABLE script.

Neither hash indexes nor nonclustered indexes can serve queries on memory-optimized tables for which the keys are sorted in the reverse order from how they are defined in the index. These types of queries simply can't be serviced efficiently right now from memory-optimized indexes.

Remember, you can also add a clustered columnstore index to a memory-optimized table, dramatically improving your ability to analyze fast-changing data.

Understanding index statistics

When we talk about statistics in SQL Server, we do not mean the term generically. Statistics on tables and views are created to describe the distribution of data within indexes and heaps; they are created as needed by the query optimizer.

Statistics are important to the query optimizer to help it make query plan decisions, and they are heavily involved in the concept of cardinality estimation. The SQL Server Cardinality

CHAPTER 15

Estimator provides accurate estimations of the number of rows that queries will return, a big part of producing query plans.

> ➤ **For more on the performance impact of statistics on cardinality estimation, see Chapter 14.**

Making sure statistics are available and up to date is essential for choosing a well-performing query plan. "Stale" statistics that have evaded updates for too long contain information that is quite different from the current state of the table and will likely cause poor execution plans.

There are a number of options in each database regarding statistics. We reviewed some in Chapter 4: "Installing and configuring SQL Server instances and features" but we present them again here in the context understanding how indexes are used for performance tuning.

Automatically creating and updating statistics

Most statistics needed for describing data to the SQL Server are created automatically, because the database option Auto Create Statistics should be enabled. This results in many automatically created indexes with the naming convention _WA_Sys_<column_name>_<object_id_hex>.

- When the database option AUTO_CREATE_STATISTICS is turned on, SQL Server can create single-column statistics objects, based on query need. These can make a big difference in performance. You can determine that a statistics object was created by the AUTO_CREATE_STATISTICS = ON behavior because it will have the name prefix _WA.

- The behavior that creates statistics for indexes (with a matching name) happens automatically, regardless of the AUTO_CREATE_STATISTICS database option.

Statistics are not automatically created for columnstore indexes, and instead will use statistics objects that exist on the heap or the clustered index of the table. Like any index, a statistics object of the same name is created; however, for columnstore indexes it is blank, and in place for logistical reasons only. This statistics object is actually populated on the fly and not persisted in storage.

As you can imagine, statistics must also be kept up to date with the data in the table. SQL Server has an option in each database for AUTO_UPDATE_STATISTICS, which is ON by default and should almost always remain on.

You should only ever turn off both AUTO_CREATE_STATISTICS and AUTO_UPDATE_STATISTICS when requested by highly complex application designs, with variable schema usage, and a separate regular process that creates and maintains statistics, such as Microsoft SharePoint. On-premises SharePoint installations include a set of stored procedures that periodically run to create and update the statistics objects for the wide, dynamically assigned table structures within. If you have not designed your application to intelligently create and update statistics using a separate process from that of the SQL Server engine, we recommend that you never turn off these options.

Inside OUT

Should you turn on the database settings Auto Update Statistics and Auto Update Statistics Asynchronously?

Yes! (Again, unless an application specifically recommends that you do not, such as SharePoint.)

Starting with compatibility mode 130, the ratio of data modifications to rows in the table that helps identify out-of-date statistics has been aggressively lowered, causing statistics to be automatically updated more frequently. This is especially evident in large tables in which many rows were regularly updated. In SQL Server 2014 and before, this more aggressive behavior was not turned on by default, but could be turned on via Trace Flag 2371, starting with SQL 2008 R2 SP1.

It is more important now than ever to turn on Auto Update Statistics Asynchronously, which can dramatically reduce the overhead involved in automatic statistics maintenance.

Manually creating statistics for on-disk tables

You can also create statistics manually during troubleshooting or performance tuning by using the CREATE STATISTICS statement.

You can consider manually creating statistics for large tables, and with design principals similar to how nonclustered indexes should be created. The order of the keys in statistics does matter, and you should choose columns that are regularly queried together to provide the most value to queries.

When venturing into creating your own statistics objects, consider using filtered statistics, which can also be helpful if you are trying to carry out advanced performance tuning on queries with a static filter or specific range of data. Like filtered indexes, which we covered earlier in this chapter, or even filtered views and queries, you can create statistics with a similar WHERE clause. Filtered statistics are never automatically created.

➤ For more information on maintaining index statistics, see Chapter 8.

Understanding statistics on memory-optimized tables

Statistics are created and updated automatically on memory-optimized tables. Memory-optimized tables require at least one index to be created, and a matching statistics object is created for that index object.

It is always recommended to create memory-optimized tables in databases with the highest compatibility level. If a memory-optimized table was created in SQL 2014 compatibility level, you must manually update the statistics object yourself by using the UPDATE STATISTICS command. Then, if the AUTO_UPDATE_STATISTICS database option is turned on, statistics will update as normal. Statistics for new memory-optimized tables are not automatically updated when the database compatibility level was below compatibility level 130 when the tables were created.

➤ **For more on memory-optimized tables, see Chapter 7: Understanding table features.**

Understanding statistics on external tables

You can also create statistics on external tables; that is, tables that do not exist in the SQL Server database but instead are transparent references to data stored in a Hadoop cluster or in Azure Blob Storage via PolyBase.

You can create statistics on external tables, but currently, you cannot update them. Creating the statistics object involves copying the external data into the SQL Server database only temporarily, and then calculating statistics. To update statistics for these datasets, you must drop them and re-create the statistics. Because of the data sizes typically involved with external tables, using the FULLSCAN method to update statistics is not recommended.

➤ **For more on external tables, see Chapter 7.**

Understanding other types of indexes

There are other types of indexes that you should be aware of, each with specific, limited uses for certain SQL Server features; for example, the Full-Text Search engine, spatial data types, and the xml data type. Thought not nearly as common as other types of indexes mentioned in this chapter, they have powerful specific uses.

Understanding full-text indexes

If you have optionally chosen to install the Full-Text Search feature of SQL Server, you can take advantage of the full-text service (fdhost.exe) and query vast amounts of data using special full-text syntax, looking for word forms, phrases, thesaurus lookups, word proximity, and more. You can of course choose to add the feature via SQL Setup if not already installed.

Because they have specific uses for particular architectures and applications, we won't spend much time on them in this reference. Developers might take advantage of powerful full-text specific functions CONTAINS or FREETEXT.

By design, full-text indexes require a unique nonclustered or clustered rowstore index on the table in which they are created, with a single column in the key. We recommend that this index have an integer key for performance reasons, such as an identity column. Full-text indexes are usually placed on varchar or nvarchar columns, often with large lengths, but you can also place them on xml and varbinary columns.

It is important to understand the two viable options to updating the full-text index. A full population of the full-text index is effective but will take more resources than an incremental load strategy. If the table receives writes frequently, you should consider the two possible incremental load strategies. By default, the CHANGE_TRACKING AUTO option enables the Change Tracking feature on the table that hosts the full-text index, which makes it possible for changes to propagate into the full-text index. This asynchronously keeps the full-text data synchronized with minimal overhead. If enabling Change Tracking is not an option for the table, another option is adding or using an existing column with the timestamp data type in the table and then periodically updating the full-text index by starting an incremental population. Consider both strategies, along with your requirements for frequency of updates to the full-text index. Both are superior to frequent full populations.

Understanding spatial indexes

A spatial index is a special B–tree index that uses a suite of special code and geometry methods to perform spatial and geometry calculations. Developers can use these data structures for non-Euclidean geometry calculations, distance and area calculations on spheres, and more. Spatial indexes can improve the performance of queries with spatial operations.

You can create these indexes only on columns that use the spatial data types geometry or geography, and you can create different types of indexes on the same spatial column to server different calculations. To create a spatial index, the table must already have a Primary Key.

You create spatial indexes by using bounding boxes or tessellation schemes for geometry and geography data types. Consult the documentation and the developers' intended use of spatial data when creating these these indexes here: *https://docs.microsoft.com/sql/relational-databases/spatial/spatial-indexes-overview*.

Understanding XML indexes

Eponymous XML indexes are created for much the same benefit for which we use nonclustered indexes: you use them to prevent the runtime shredding of XML files each time they are accessed, and to instead provide a persistent row set of the XML data's tags, values, and paths.

Because the xml data type is stored as a BLOB and has an upper limit of 2 GB of data per row, XML data can be massive, and XML indexes can be extremely beneficial to reads. Like nonclustered indexes, they also incur an overhead to writes.

Primary XML indexes prevent the on-demand shredding of the data by providing a reference to the tags, values, and paths. On large XML documents, this can be a major performance improvement. Secondary XML indexes enhance the performance of primary XML indexes. Secondary XML indexes are created on either path, value, or property data in the primary XML index and benefit a read workload that heavily uses one of those three methods of querying XML data. Consult the documentation and the developers' intended use of XML data when creating XML XML indexes here: *https://docs.microsoft.com/sql/relational-databases/xml/ xml-indexes-sql-server*.

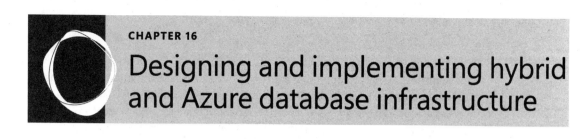

Designing and implementing hybrid and Azure database infrastructure

In this chapter, we examine the options for designing a database infrastructure where some or all your data is hosted in a public cloud, specifically the Microsoft Azure cloud. The chapter begins with an overview of cloud and Azure concepts. We then discuss the considerations for deploying SQL Server-based infrastructure using infrastructure-as-a-service (IaaS), platform-as-a-service (PaaS), or in a hybrid fashion. We end the chapter with a cursory listing of some non-SQL Server data platform services in Azure.

> ➤ Detailed coverage of several platform-as-a-service offerings, specifically Azure SQL Database and Azure SQL Database managed instance, is found in Chapter 17, "Provisioning Azure SQL Database," and 18, "Provisioning Azure SQL Database managed instance," respectively. Migrating to Azure is covered in Chapter 19, "Migrating to SQL Server solutions in Azure."

NOTE

Microsoft Azure consists of multiple "clouds," including Azure Government and the sovereign clouds in China and Germany. The content of this chapter applies to the public cloud. Service and feature availability may vary in the other environments.

Cloud computing and Microsoft Azure

You have likely already heard or read many different definitions of cloud computing. Rather than add yet one more, we will briefly discuss some key features of cloud computing and how they apply to SQL Server offerings in Azure.

- **Financial accounting.** The first concept, expenses, relates to accounting. With traditional on-premises environments, there is usually a significant initial outlay of capital. This is called capital expenditure, or "CapEx." Expenses in Azure, on the other hand, generally fall under the category of operational expenditure, or "OpEx." With OpEx, there is no initial monetary outlay and mostly no long-term financial commitment. The fees you pay are pay-per-use charges and are all-inclusive: hardware, licensing, electricity, monitoring, and more.

Under some Azure subscription models, you are incentivized for committing to a minimum annual spend in return for a reduced service cost. It is important to note that OpEx might not be cheaper than CapEx overall, depending on how efficiently cloud services are provisioned and used. Those considerations are beyond the scope of this text, but we strongly encourage you to plan early for optimizing your resource allocation.

- **Elasticity.**   The second concept in cloud computing is *elasticity*, which means that the resources you provision are not fixed in terms of capacity. In on-premises environments, you provision hardware and software (licensing) sufficient to accommodate peak demand. In Azure, elasticity gives you the ability to scale up and down or out and in as needed to accommodate demand at any given moment.

- **Control.**   Finally, *control* also becomes a discussion topic. With on-premises deployments of SQL Server, the DBA team decides which hardware to select, when to apply patches, and when to upgrade to a major new release. If you select an Azure platform-as-a-service offering, it's the team at Microsoft that makes these decisions. The team announces changes and updates using a variety of channels, and, as a cloud DBA, one of your tasks will include regularly reviewing these announcements. You will need to thoroughly understand your Azure environment to determine which changes or updates will affect your application(s).

Database-as-a-service

Azure provides many types of services, including virtual machines (VMs), web applications, and, of course, Azure SQL Database. Cloud services are often categorized in one of three types: infrastructure-as-a-service (IaaS), platform-as-a-service (PaaS), and software-as-a-service (SaaS). In this book, we often refer to Azure SQL Database as database-as-a-service (DBaaS), which is a specialized type of PaaS.

You may also choose to host SQL Server databases in the cloud using Azure VM images, which can come with a SQL Server version preinstalled. In that case, you are using IaaS. With IaaS, you gain increased control and complete feature parity with on-premises deployments. IaaS also introduces more responsibility for sizing the VM specifications appropriately and managing software updates for both the operating system (OS) and SQL Server.

Managed instance (MI) is a more recent addition to the SQL Server offerings in Azure. MI strikes a better balance between feature parity and control than IaaS. We discuss managed instance in Chapter 18.

Managing Azure: The Azure portal and PowerShell Core

When you are ready to begin using Azure, you will need to deploy, manage, and eventually tear down resources when applications are retired or upgraded. To manage on-premises Microsoft environments, you might use various GUI tools (often based on the Microsoft Management

Console) or PowerShell. The primary GUI in Azure is the Azure portal. It will help if you also become comfortable managing your resources using PowerShell. With the advent of PowerShell Core a few years ago, PowerShell scripts can now be executed on a variety of platforms: Linux, macOS, and, of course, Windows.

A third option for managing Azure is the Azure -Line Interface (CLI). You can use the Azure CLI across platforms (Windows, macOS, and Linux) and within the portal using Azure Cloud Shell.

NOTE

PowerShell Core is available cross-platform, but not all PowerShell commands are supported on non-Windows operating systems.

Unlike Windows PowerShell, PowerShell Core is not yet part of the Windows operating system, or indeed any other OS. If you need to install PowerShell Core, refer to the Microsoft Docs at *https://docs.microsoft.com/powershell/scripting/install/installing-powershell*. The GitHub releases page lists preview releases in addition to regular releases. The releases shown first might be preview releases, so scroll down to find the release marked *latest*.

For managing Azure and Azure SQL Database using PowerShell Core, you should always use the latest Azure PowerShell module. The module is updated frequently, so be sure to regularly check for updates. You can install the PowerShell module using the following PowerShell command, run with Administrator privileges:

```
Install-Module -Name Az -AllowClobber
```

NOTE

The `-AllowClobber` parameter is generally only necessary if you have the AzureRM module installed in Windows PowerShell. The AzureRM PowerShell module will be maintained through December 2020, but hasn't received feature updates since December 2018. You should plan to migrate any scripts that use the AzureRM module to the Az module.

Be patient while the module downloads all its child modules; there are quite a few of them to manage most Azure services.

If you need to update the module, use the following:

```
Update-Module Az
```

Before you can manage your Azure resources with PowerShell Core, you will need to log in. Use the `Login-AzAccount` to use the device login mechanism.

NOTE

At the time of writing, the device login mechanism, which requires you to copy and paste a code into a website to authenticate, is the only option for the Az module in PowerShell Core. Later, Microsoft will likely implement the modern authentication flow, as is the case with the AzureRM and Az modules in Windows PowerShell.

After logging in, the `Login-AzAccount` cmdlet outputs some information about the active subscription. If you need to switch the subscription, use the `Get-AzSubscription` cmdlet to see a list of all subscriptions your account can manage. You can then use the `Select-AzSubscription` cmdlet to change the active subscription to another one. This is illustrated using the commands that follow and assumes that you have a subscription with the name "Pay-As-You-Go."

```
Get-AzSubscription

# A list of subscriptions is displayed.

# You can copy and paste a subscription name on the next line.

Select-AzSubscription -SubscriptionName 'Pay-As-You-Go'
```

NOTE

This section intentionally does not cover managing Azure resources. Managing SQL resources in Azure is discussed in Chapter 17 and Chapter 18.

Finally, Azure exposes a complete REST API that third-party tools or in-house developed tools can use to perform virtually any action in the Azure environment. Developers may not even need to call the APIs directly because for many platforms, official client libraries are available. The use of the REST API is not covered in this book.

➤ The Microsoft Docs at *https://docs.microsoft.com/rest/api/azure/* discuss the use of the REST API.

Azure governance

Even relatively modest on-premises environments require governance—the organizational processes and procedures by which the environment is managed and responsibilities are delineated. Governance is also a necessity in cloud environments. In this chapter, we can't delve into all of the governance issues related to cloud operations. We do, however, discuss some features of Azure that allow governance to be formalized.

Azure resources are organized in a hierarchy of containers. The container at the top level is the subscription. The subscription is primarily a billing boundary—all resources in a single subscription appear on a single bill and have the same billing cycle. There are also life cycle consequences: should a subscription be discontinued, all resources within the subscription will stop. (Eventually, the subscription and resources will be deleted.) Security configuration is also associated with the subscription: a subscription trusts a single Azure Active Directory (Azure AD) instance. This means that all user accounts used to manage resources within the subscription must exist within the trusted Azure AD instance. Microsoft accounts, or user accounts from other Azure AD instances, can be added as external users to the trusted instance. An organization can choose to have multiple Azure subscriptions that trust the same Azure AD instance.

As Figure 16-1 illustrates, a single subscription can have many resources of several types, and Azure SQL Database is just one. *Resource groups* exist to allow organizing these resources by life cycle and to provide a security boundary. Resource groups are logical containers that have a name and a little metadata. The resources in a resource group are deleted if the resource group itself is deleted, hence the life cycle relationship between the resources and the resource group.

Using Role-Based Access Control, permissions can be granted on a resource group, and those permissions will apply to the resources within the group. Configuring permissions this way can be a huge timesaver and increase visibility into permission assignments. This is discussed in more detail in the "Security in Azure SQL Database" section in Chapter 17. Up front, you need to know that the permissions assigned to the Azure SQL Database resource don't grant permissions to login to the database itself.

NOTE

You can move resources between resource groups and subscriptions. When moving resources, the Azure region in which they are located will not change, even if the target resource group's location is different. The location of a resource group determines only where that resource group's metadata is stored, not where the actual resources are hosted.

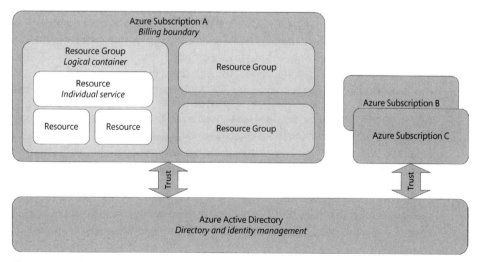

Figure 16-1   The container relationship between an Azure subscription, resource groups, and resources.

Cloud-first

If you've been working with SQL Server for more than a few years, you've likely noticed the increased release cadence. This is a direct result of the *cloud-first* approach in SQL Server product development that Microsoft adopted a few years ago. Cloud-first in this context means that new features are generally first made available in Azure SQL Database as a preview feature. Those preview features are usually opt-in and are closely monitored by the product team. The close monitoring allows the team to quickly identify usage patterns and issues. These features are then included in the next SQL Server release. Examples of features released this way for SQL Server 2019 include the SHORTEST_PATH graph function, intelligent query processing, and Unicode support. Previously, Always Encrypted, dynamic data masking, and graph tables were made available in Azure SQL Database prior to their release in SQL Server 2017.

Resource scalability

Scalability is a key feature of cloud computing, and can be considered along a vertical axis of performance (scaling up) or a horizontal axis (scaling out). Scaling up means that additional hardware resources are assigned to a server or to a database. Scaling out means that a database is either broken up into multiple databases, each holding a portion of the data (sharding), or that additional copies of the database are made available for read-only connections, such that those read-only connections are offloaded from the primary database, which will handle the writes.

Generally, scalability with PaaS resources is easier than with IaaS resources. Scaling a VM up or down causes some downtime, but it still is considerably less onerous than moving a database to different hardware as the workload changes. You can scale up or scale down an Azure SQL Database with minimal impact to applications. Depending on the size of the database and the nature of the scale operation, the operation can take several hours to complete. This scaling activity is completed while the database is online, though we must point out that at the end of the scale operation, existing connections are dropped. This benefit, and many others, of PaaS may encourage you to look at PaaS first for your cloud database needs. That is a valid strategy: choose PaaS unless it is unable to meet your requirements, in which case you fall back to IaaS.

When managing many databases, each with potentially many different scaling needs, you should also consider running these databases in an elastic pool. An elastic pool is a grouping of databases on a single logical server that share the resources available within the pool. We discuss elastic pools in depth in the "Elastic database pools" section later in this chapter.

Scaling out in Azure SQL Database (recall, that is the PaaS offering) can be accomplished using read-only replica in service tiers that support it. Read-scale replicas are discussed later in this chapter, along with elastic pools, which are ideally suited for sharding databases.

Networking in Azure

Networking in Azure is an extensive topic that cannot be fully covered in a single section of this chapter. Therefore, we focus on the aspects of Azure networking that are critical to the successful operation of the various types of SQL Server deployments.

In Azure, a virtual network is a resource type and it's appropriately called Virtual Network (VNet). A VNet defines an IP range, subnets, and more, as discussed later in this section. In some Azure deployments, you may not find a VNet: many PaaS resources don't require it and some deployments wouldn't benefit from having a VNet. However, many IaaS and some PaaS resources require a VNet to be present. These include the virtual machine and managed instance resource types.

You might not be too excited about exposing services to the public Internet. To secure your virtual network, you can use network security groups (discussed a little later) or Azure Firewall. Azure Firewall is a fully managed service that provides granular control over connections to and from the virtual network.

A VNet can be divided into multiple subnets. Each subnet might then have its own route table, network security group, and service endpoints. Brief definitions of some of these networking features follow:

- **Network security group.**   A network security group combines security rules that define the inbound and outbound traffic that is allowed or denied. A network security group can be applied to a subnet or a single VM network interface. Network security groups can define source and target IP ranges and ports, service tags, or application security groups.

- **Service tag.**   A service tag allows you to define a rule in a network security group without knowing the details about source or target IP addresses. An example service tag relevant for this book is *Sql.KoreaCentral*. This service tag defines the IP addresses of the Azure SQL Database service in the Korea Central region of Azure.

- **Application security group.**   An application security group (ASG) is essentially just a name. An ASG can be assigned to multiple network interfaces, and a network interface can have multiple ASGs assigned. The ASG can then be used instead of a source or destination IP or IP range, thus simplifying the maintenance of security rules as VMs are added or removed from your Azure infrastructure. An example of how ASGs can simplify rules is available at *https://docs.microsoft.com/azure/virtual-network/security-overview#application-security-groups*.

- **Service endpoint.**   A service endpoint is a connection between the VNet and Azure services. Using service endpoints increases security because the Azure services deployed to the VNet using a service endpoint are accessible only from the VNet. Service endpoints also provide routing benefits because the traffic between the resources in the VNet and the Azure services does not take the same route as Internet traffic. Not all Azure services support service endpoints, but Azure SQL Database does.

Private Link, which is in preview at the time of writing, is a technique that allows you to assign a private IP address from a VNet to a PaaS service. By enabling Private Link, public endpoints traditionally assigned to PaaS services can be completely ignored. Connections to the service can be established only from the same VNet, a peered VNet, a cross-region VNet-to-VNet con-nection, Express Route, or VPN. Like service endpoints, only select PaaS services support Private Link. Azure SQL DB supports it, but managed instance does not (perhaps, yet). An interesting aspect of the Private Link configuration for Azure SQL DB is that both inbound as well as out-bound access to the Internet is disabled.

> ➤ Private networking between on-premises and Azure is discussed in the "Hybrid cloud with Azure" section later in this chapter.

> ➤ Learn more about Private Link for Azure SQL Database in the Microsoft Docs at *https://docs.microsoft.com/azure/sql-database/sql-database-private-endpoint-overview*.

Cloud models and SQL Server

Azure offers several ways to consider the management and querying of data in a SQL Server or SQL Server-like environment. This section is divided into three main areas:

- **Infrastructure-as-a-Service.**   SQL Server running on an Azure Virtual Machine (VM).

- **Platform-as-a-Service.**   Azure SQL Database, including managed instance, and Azure Synapse Analytics. These services may also be referred to as Database-as-a-Service (DBaaS).

- **Hybrid cloud.**   Combines the best features of on-premises SQL Server with Azure. Specific SQL Server features that support this are Stretch Database and Backup to URL.

Azure SQL resources, whether IaaS or PaaS, can be managed in a centralized management hub. This centralized view of SQL Server VMs, Azure SQL Database logical servers and databases, and Azure SQL Database managed instances can be used to efficiently manage SQL resources at scale. In addition to managing existing SQL resources, the experience of creating new SQL resources is also streamlined.

In each section, we discuss specific terminology and configuration considerations for running an optimal SQL Server deployment in Azure. Specifics for deploying Azure SQL Database and Managed Instance are covered in the next two chapters.

Infrastructure-as-a-service

Take what you've learned in the first three chapters of the book about VMs, and that's infrastructure-as-a-service (IaaS) in a nutshell, optimized for a SQL Server environment.

As we detail in Chapter 2, "Introducing database server components," a VM shares physical resources with other VMs. In the case of Azure Virtual Machines, there are some configurations and optimizations that can make your SQL Server implementation perform well, without requiring insight into the other guest VMs.

When creating a SQL Server VM in Azure, you can choose from different templates, which provide a wide range of options for different virtual hardware configurations, OS, and, of course, versions and editions of SQL Server.

Azure VMs are priced according to a time-based usage model, which makes it easier to get started. You pay per minute or per hour, depending on the resources you need, so you can start small and scale upward. In many cases, if performance is not acceptable, moving to better virtual hardware is very easy and requires only a few minutes of downtime.

Azure VM performance optimization

Many of the same rules that we outlined for physical hardware and VMs in Chapter 3, "Designing and implementing an on-premises database infrastructure," apply also to those Azure VMs used for SQL Server. These include setting Power Saving settings to High Performance, configuring Max Server Memory usage correctly, spreading TempDB over several files, and so on.

When you deploy the VM using one of the Microsoft-provided SQL Server templates, some of these tasks have been done for you. For instance, power-saving settings are set to High Performance already, and TempDB files are configured properly when you configure a new Azure VM running SQL Server 2016 or higher.

Azure VMs have a limited selection for storage. You don't have the luxury of custom Direct-Attached Storage or Storage-Area Networks dedicated to your environment. Instead, you can choose from the following options:

- Standard hard disk drives (HDDs) or multiple solid-state storage (SSDs) types

- Unmanaged or Managed Disks

- SQL Server data files in Azure Storage

CHAPTER 16

> ## Inside OUT
>
> *What is Azure Blob Storage?*
>
> Coming from a database background, you think of a "blob" as a large object in binary format, which is stored using the data types Singular data type `varbinary(max)`.
>
> In a similar vein, Azure Blob Storage is a service for storing unstructured text or binary data as objects (or blobs), accessible using HTTP or HTTPS. You can think of these blobs conceptually as files. The blobs can contain any type of data, including SQL Server files, but the service doesn't know, care, or provide any functionality to handle structured data.
>
> As a storage service, Azure Storage focuses on high availability, performance, and disaster recovery functions. These highly desirable attributes make Azure Storage attractive for many scenarios. You'll find later in this chapter that many SQL Server-related services are beginning to take advantage of this service.

> ➤ To read more about using Azure Blob Storage with SQL Server, go to *https://docs.microsoft. com/sql/relational-databases/tutorial-use-azure-blob-storage-service-with-sql-server-2016*.

Virtual hard drives

Virtual hard drives (VHDs) in Azure are provided through several storage offerings (note that these values may change after publication):

- **Standard HDD.** Designed for backups and low-cost, latency-insensitive workloads. The maximum throughput is 500 Mbps, the maximum IOPS is 2,000.

- **Standard SSD.** Suited for low use enterprise workloads, including web servers, and development and test environments. There is a 750 Mbps maximum throughput, and 6,000 maximum IOPS.

- **Premium SSD.** Recommended for production workloads and other performance-sensitive environments, Premium SSD offers 900 Mbps max throughput, and 20,000 max IOPS.

- **Ultra SSD.** Ideal for transaction-heavy workloads, including Large scale database and analytics environments. They offer 2,000 Mbps max throughput and 160,000 max IOPS.

> ➤ You can see the disk comparison chart at
> *https://docs.microsoft.com/azure/virtual-machines/windows/disks-types*.

Given our previously stated guidance to use the fastest drive possible, SQL Server is going to make better use of Premium SSD or Ultra SSD, because SQL Server's main performance bottleneck is TempDB, followed closely by transaction log files, all of which are I/O-bound.

Inside OUT

Can you use Standard Storage for SQL Server?

Yes, you can choose Standard storage instead of solid-state drives for your SQL Server VM, but we do not recommend it unless you have a large number of Standard drives in a striped configuration.

With solid-state storage, you will pay for the entire drive, even if you use only a portion of it. With Standard storage, you pay only for what you are using. Although this is an attractive cost-saving opportunity, the storage is not dedicated and is much slower.

Standard storage has a maximum of 2,000 IOPS (500 Mbps throughput), which will negatively affect SQL Server's performance.

It is possible to choose between unmanaged and managed disks:

- **Unmanaged disks.**   VHDs are managed by you, from creating the storage account and the container, to attaching these VHDs to a VM and configuring any redundancy and scalability.

- **Managed disks.**   You specify the size and type of drive you need (Premium or Standard), and Azure handles the creation, management, and scalability for you.

Unmanaged disks give you more control over the drive, whereas managed disks are handled automatically, including resiliency and redundancy. Naturally, managed disks have a higher cost associated with them, but this comes with peace of mind.

As of this writing, there are several sizes to choose for Premium Storage, with more offerings being added all the time. Here is a selection of these offerings.

Table 3-1   Premium Storage offerings in Azure Storage

Type	Disk Size	IOPS per disk	Throughput per disk
P4	32 GB	120	25 MBps
P6	64 GB	240	50 MBps
P10	128 GB	500	100 MBps
P15	256 GB	1,100	125 MBps
P20	512 GB	2,300	150 MBps
P30	1 TB	5,000	200 MBps
P40	2 TB	7,500	250 MBps
P50	4 TB	7,500	250 MBps
P60	8 TB	16,000	500 MBps
P70	16 TB	18,000	750 MBps
P80	32 TB	20,000	900 MBps

NOTE

Maximum throughput can be limited by Azure VM bandwidth. Each Azure VM also has a maximum uncached disk throughput. What this means is that you might not be able to address disk performance issues in SQL Server Azure VMs by adding disks or selecting disks with higher throughput numbers. Instead, you might need to select a higher size VM. In many cases, you can select a higher size VM to get more I/O throughput and memory, while keeping the vCPU count the same. Increasing the vCPU count increases the number of SQL Server per-core licenses you need, so if your only bottleneck is I/O, you don't need to provision additional vCPUs with the commensurate license count increase.

We recommend a minimum of two P30 drives for SQL Server data files. The first drive is for transaction logs, and the second is for data files and TempDB.

Disk striping options

To achieve better performance (and larger drive volumes) out of your SQL Server VM, you can combine multiple drives into various RAID configurations by using Storage Spaces on Windows-based VMs, or MDADM on Linux-based VMs. Depending on the Azure VM size, you can stripe up to 64 Premium Storage drives together in an array.

An important consideration with RAID is the stripe (or block) size. A 64-KB block size is most appropriate for an OLTP SQL Server environment, as noted previously. However, large data warehousing systems can benefit from a 256-KB stripe size, due to the larger sequential reads from that type of workload.

➤ To read more about the different types of RAID, see Chapter 2.

Storage account bandwidth considerations

Azure Storage costs are dictated by three factors: bandwidth, transactions, and capacity. Bandwidth is defined as the amount of data egress from the storage account.

For Azure VMs running SQL Server, if the storage account is in the same region as the VM, there is no additional bandwidth cost. If there is any external access on the data, however, such as log shipping to a different location or using the AzCopy tool to synchronize data to another region (for example), there is a cost associated with that.

➤ For more information about AzCopy version 10, go to Microsoft Docs at *https://docs.microsoft.com/azure/storage/common/storage-use-azcopy-v10*.

Drive caching

For SQL Server workloads on Azure VMs, it is recommended that you turn on *ReadOnly* caching on the Premium Storage drive when attaching it to the VM, for data files, and TempDB. This increases the IOPS and reduces latency for your environment, and it avoids the risk of data loss that might occur due to *ReadWrite* caching.

For drives hosting transaction logs, do not turn on caching.

➤ You can read more about drive caching at *https://docs.microsoft.com/azure/ virtual-machines/windows/sql/virtual-machines-windows-sql-performance*.

SQL Server data files in Azure Storage

Instead of attaching a data drive to your machine running SQL Server, you can use Azure Storage to store your user database files directly, as blobs. This provides migration benefits (data movement is unnecessary), high availability (HA), snapshot backups, and cost savings with storage. For system databases, this feature is neither recommended nor supported. Because performance is critical, especially when accessing storage over a network, you will need to test this offering, especially for heavy workloads.

To get this to work, you need a storage account and container on Azure Storage, a Shared Access Signature, and a SQL Server Credential for each container.

There are some limitations that might affect your decision:

- FILESTREAM data is not supported, which affects memory-optimized objects, as well. If you want to make use of FILESTREAM or memory-optimized objects, you will need to use locally attached storage.

- Only .mdf, .ndf, and .ldf extensions are supported.

- Geo-replication is not supported.

➤ You can read more (including additional limitations) at *https://docs.microsoft.com/sql/ relational-databases/databases/sql-server-data-files-in-microsoft-azure.*

Virtual machine sizing

Microsoft recommends certain types, or series, of Azure VMs for SQL Server workloads, and each of these series of VMs comes with different size options.

➤ You can read more about performance best practices for SQL Server in Azure Virtual Machines at *https://docs.microsoft.com/azure/virtual-machines/windows/sql/ virtual-machines-windows-sql-performance.*

It is possible to resize your VM within the same series (going larger is as simple as choosing a bigger size in the Azure portal), and in many cases you can even move across series as the need arises.

You can also downgrade your VM to a smaller size, to scale down after running a resource-intensive process, or if you accidentally overprovisioned your server. Provided that the smaller VM can handle any additional options you might have selected (data drives and network interfaces tend to be the deciding factor here), it is equally simple to downgrade a VM to a smaller size by choosing the VM in the Azure portal.

Both growing and shrinking the VM size does require downtime, but it usually takes just a few minutes at most.

To quote directly from Microsoft Docs:

"Es, Eas, Ds and Das Series offers the optimum memory to vCPU ratio required for OLTP workload performance. M Series offers the highest memory to vCPU ratio required for mission critical performance and is ideal for data warehouse workloads." (*https://docs.microsoft.com/azure/virtual-machines/windows/sql/ virtual-machines-windows-sql-performance#quick-check-list*).

However, choosing the right series can be confusing, especially with new sizes and series coming out all the time. The ability to resize VMs makes this decision less stressful.

> ## NOTE
> You pay separately for solid-state drives attached to Azure VMs. Keep this in mind when identifying the right VM for your workload.

Locating TempDB files on the VM

Many Azure VMs come with a temporary drive, which is provisioned automatically for the Windows page file and scratch storage space. The drive is not guaranteed to survive VM restarts and does not survive a VM deallocation.

A fairly common practice with Azure VMs is to place the SQL Server TempDB on this temporary drive because it uses solid-state storage and is theoretically faster than a Standard Storage drive. However, this temporary drive is thinly provisioned. Remember in Chapter 2 how thin provisioned storage for VMs is shared among all the VMs on that host.

Placing the TempDB on this may require preparation, because it can result in high latency, especially if other guests using that underlying physical storage have done the same thing. Whether or not this issue will affect you is determined in part by the series of VM. If you created the VM using a SQL Server template from Microsoft, then no preparation is neces- sary. If you created a VM image yourself or used a generic VM image, then register the VM with the SQL VM resource provider (recommended and covered in the next section) or per- form the steps in the blog post at *https://cloudblogs.microsoft.com/sqlserver/2014/09/25/ using-ssds-in-azure-vms-to-store-sql-server-tempdb-and-buffer-pool-extensions/*.

Managing SQL Server virtual machines in the Azure Portal

The Azure Portal provides support for managing virtual machines with SQL Server installed. When creating a virtual machine (VM) from an image that includes SQL Server, the VM will be registered with the SQL VM resource provider. If you create a VM without SQL Server pre- installed and install SQL Server yourself, you can register the VM with the resource provider.

> ### CAUTION
>
> If you will be using the Azure Hybrid Benefit licensing, which is discussed later in this chapter, you **must** register the VM with this resource pro- vider. The steps to register a VM where you installed SQL Server yourself are found at *https://docs.microsoft.com/azure/virtual-machines/windows/sql/ virtual-machines-windows-sql-register-with-resource-provider*.

Beyond this compliance requirement, the SQL VM resource provider extends the default VM management options to include automated patching, automated backup, and additional moni- toring capabilities. It is important to note that you can take advantage of automated backup and patching, but you are not required to. Both automated management features are discussed in additional detail below. The automated features depend on the SQL Server IaaS Agent Exten- sion, which is installed in the VM when the SQL VM resource provider is installed in Full mode.

Inside OUT

What about the SQL Server configuration tab?

Before the availability of the SQL VM resource provider, a SQL Server configuration tab was available for managing SQL Server from the VM resource.

With the advent of the SQL VM resource provider, this tab is now deprecated. It is the only method, however, that can be used to manage SQL Server versions that have reached end of support, namely SQL Server 2008 and SQL Server 2008 R2. You must still register those VMs with the SQL VM resource provider if you are taking advantage of the Azure Hybrid Benefit.

Automated backup

There are a few requirements for the automated backup feature. Chief among those is that only specific versions of SQL Server running on specific Windows Server versions are supported. Additionally, the user databases selected for automated backup must be running in the full recovery model.

> ➤ Read more about recovery models in Chapter 10, "Developing, deploying, and managing data recovery."

Automated backup can be configured to retain the backups between 1 and 30 days in an Azure storage account of your choice. The backups can optionally be encrypted. When enabling encryption, a certificate is generated that is protected by a password. The certificate is stored in the same storage account where the backups are kept.

For SQL Server 2016 and later, Automated Backup v2 is available, which offers additional control, including the ability to include the system databases in the backups. The system databases are not required to run in the full recovery model.

In v2 as in v1, the backup schedule can be determined automatically by Azure, in which case the log growth is used to determine the frequency of backups. In addition, v2 allows the administrator to set the frequency of the full and log backups.

> ➤ More information about the automated backup service for SQL Server 2016 and later is located at *https://docs.microsoft.com/azure/virtual-machines/windows/sql/virtual-machines-windows-sql-automated-backup-v2*.

> **NOTE**
>
> In addition to this automated backup feature, which is convenient but somewhat limited, Azure also supports backing up SQL Server using Azure Backup for SQL VMs. A brief overview of this service is available at *https://docs.microsoft.com/azure/virtual-machines/windows/sql/virtual-machines-windows-sql-backup-recovery#azbackup.*

Automated patching

If you'd like the Azure infrastructure to patch Windows and SQL Server, you can enable automated patching for SQL Server VMs. You choose a day of the week, a start hour (which is in the server's time zone), and a maximum duration for the maintenance.

Every week at that time, Windows Updates marked as *Important* will be downloaded and installed while the maintenance window is active. If the maintenance window is too short for all patches to be applied, the remaining patches will be installed during the next scheduled maintenance period. After installing patches, the system may be rebooted, thus incurring downtime.

> **NOTE**
>
> SQL Server cumulative updates are not included in the automated patching; you are still responsible for installing those.

Because of the possibility of multiple periods of performance impact and downtime each month, automated patching may not be appropriate for production systems that must be highly available. On the other hand, configuring automated patching for dev and test VMs can reduce the burden on administrators allowing them to focus on the production systems' health.

> ➤ More information about the automated patching service is available at *https://docs.microsoft.com/azure/virtual-machines/windows/sql/virtual-machines-windows-sql-automated-patching.*

Platform-as-a-service

With platform-as-a-service (PaaS), you can focus on a task without having to worry about the administration and maintenance surrounding that task, which makes it a lot easier to get up and running.

You can use database-as-a-service (DBaaS), which includes Azure SQL Database, Azure Synapse Analytics, and managed instance to complement or replace your organization's data platform requirements. This section introduces the currently available PaaS SQL Server offerings in the Microsoft Azure cloud.

> ➤ Complete coverage of Azure SQL Database is found in Chapter 17. Complete coverage of Azure SQL Database managed instance is found in Chapter 18.

Azure SQL Database provides you with a single database or set of databases logically grouped in an elastic pool and the freedom not to concern yourself with resource allocation (CPU, RAM, storage, licensing, OS), installation, and configuration of that database.

You also don't need to worry about patching and upgrades at the OS or instance level, TempDB, backups, corruption, or redundancy. In fact, the built-in support for database recovery is excellent (including point-in-time restores). You can even add on long-term backup retention to keep your backups for up to 10 years.

Microsoft's Data Platform is about choosing the right component to solve a particular problem, as opposed to one offering being all things to all people.

Azure SQL Database (including managed instance) and Azure Synapse Analytics are part of a larger vision, taking the strengths of the Database Engine and combining them with other Azure components, breaking the mold of a self-contained or standalone system. The change in mindset is necessary to appreciate it for what it offers, instead of criticizing it for its perceived shortcomings.

Azure SQL Database purchase models

Azure SQL Database charges are calculated based on one of two purchasing models: by Database Transaction Units (DTUs) or by vCore. In this section, you'll learn about the meaning of DTUs and vCores and how to choose the right purchasing model for your needs.

NOTE

It is possible to convert from the DTU-based purchasing model to the vCore model and vice versa, without incurring downtime.

Database Transaction Unit

DTUs are likely the Azure SQL Database concept that new adopters struggle with the most. DBAs must comprehend what it means and come to terms with the fact that this single measure is how you determine the level of performance to expect for your database.

A DTU is a blended measure of hardware resources that are provided for the database. This blend includes CPU, memory, and data and transaction log I/O. An increase in DTU results in a linear increase in each of the hardware resources. Thus, when doubling the DTUs for a database, you are effectively doubling how much CPU, memory, and I/O is assigned to your database. The relative mix of these hardware measures was determined by Microsoft using a benchmark developed for this purpose. This benchmark is called the Azure SQL Database Benchmark. It is designed to be representative of common Online Transaction Processing (OLTP) workloads.

➤ To read a detailed description of the benchmark, go to *https://docs.microsoft.com/azure/ sql-database/sql-database-service-tiers-dtu#dtu-benchmark*.

As you'll learn in Chapter 17, when creating a database using the DTU purchasing model, you specify the number of DTUs for that database by specifying the pricing tier and service objective. Additional differences between the pricing tiers are also discussed in that section.

Inside OUT

How do you know how many DTUs to provision?

Accurately provisioning DTUs for your database workload prevents slow response times or excessive charges. There are techniques that you can use to optimize your DTU estimations. When planning for migration from on-premises to Azure SQL Database, you can use the Azure SQL Database DTU Calculator.

The DTU Calculator is a tool available as an executable or a PowerShell script that will measure processor time, drive reads and writes, and log bytes per second for your on-premises database server using performance counters. The tool creates a CSV file with the values measured over 60 minutes. This CSV file is then uploaded to the DTU Calculator website, which returns an analysis and recommendation. The DTU Calculator is not affiliated with Microsoft. You can find the DTU Calculator at *https://dtucalculator.azurewebsites.net*.

After your database is migrated to Azure SQL Database, you can review your DTU usage and identify the queries that use the most resources by using the Query Performance Insight (QPI) blade in the portal. QPI uses information from Query Store, so verify that it is turned on if you want to use QPI. For more information on QPI, go to *https://docs.microsoft.com/azure/sql-database/sql-database-query-performance*.

Selecting a DTU pricing tier and service objective

Azure SQL Database offers three service tiers in the DTU purchasing model: basic, standard, and premium.

Because Azure SQL Database is billed by the hour, the selection of a service tier and service objective determines how much you will be charged for your database. However, there are additional considerations. Specific pricing and other details might change by the time the ink on this page has dried; thus, we will discuss some general concepts that you should be aware of and how they would influence your selection of a tier.

CHAPTER 16

NOTE

You can find current pricing for Azure SQL Database at
https://azure.microsoft.com/pricing/details/sql-database/.

The Basic tier provides the lowest available DTUs. You pay significantly less for giving up some availability guarantees and performance. This tier is suitable for development purposes and perhaps very small-scale applications.

The Standard and Premium tiers are the two main choices for production databases. At first glance, you will notice that the Premium tier provides considerably more DTUs and does so at a higher cost per DTU compared to Standard. This is because of architectural differences between these tiers. The database files in Standard tier databases are stored in Azure Storage. This means that the files are not local to the Database Engine. In the Premium tier, they are stored on local solid-state drives (SSDs). This difference in locality of the database files has performance implications, as you might expect. Further, there is also a difference in how intra-region high availability (HA) is handled. HA for Standard tier databases is ensured by using replication of the Azure blobs. In the Premium tier, HA is achieved by using Always On features.

vCore

For some workloads, the DTU purchasing model may not be appropriate. The vCore model allows the administrator to select a combination of hardware generation, number of CPU cores, and memory that is assigned to a single database or elastic pool. This makes it easier to compare the capacity you pay for with on-premises capacity. But be careful about comparing performance with on-premises performance; there are a lot of factors that impact the performance of Database Engine that aren't discovered by comparing CPU and memory capacity.

NOTE

The vCore purchasing model lowest end is significantly more powerful, and therefore more expensive, than the lowest service objective when using the DTU purchasing model. For comparison purposes, a single vCore is roughly equivalent to 100 DTUs in the standard tier and 125 DTUs in the premium tier.

Another difference is that under the vCore model, no storage is included. You will be billed for the actual storage consumed at the rate of Azure premium storage in the region where your database is hosted.

Like in the DTU model, the vCore model offers different service tiers. In vCore, the service tiers are general purpose, business critical, and hyperscale. The main differences between the general purpose and business critical tiers are found in the use of remote Azure blob storage vs. local solid-state storage (resulting in 10x higher IOPS at the lowest end and about 28x at the highest end) and support for in-memory. Both differences are much like the difference between the standard and premium service tiers in the DTU purchasing model. The business critical tier also offers the option to provision additional replicas for high availability.

➤ The architecture of the hyperscale service tier is so different, it is covered the "Hyperscale service tier" subsection below.

➤ Read-scale replicas are in the "Read-scale replicas" section below.

NOTE

vCore is your only option when considering Azure SQL Database managed instance. This is also the case for the hyperscale service tier and serverless compute tier offerings, both of which are currently in preview. The serverless compute tier is discussed later in this section.

Reserved Capacity

For scenarios where you can determine a minimum amount of Azure SQL Database resources you will use, you can reduce your total cost by prepaying for capacity. Capacity is reserved for a specific region, deployment type, performance tier (confusingly, another name for service tier that is used in this context), and a term of one or three years. Once you have reserved this capacity, any database resources that meet those criteria will be billed at the reserved capacity rate, which you have prepaid. But bear in mind that the prepaid rate does not include charges that aren't ordinarily included in the normal billing rates, notably software, networking, and storage charges.

NOTE

You do not need to create reserved capacity for all your Azure SQL Database needs if you're uncertain of your requirements for certain instances, such as dev/test. You may purchase reserved capacity for those instances that you are confident you will need, and additional capacity will be billed at your normal billing rate.

NOTE

Reserved capacity is available only with the vCore purchasing model and with managed instance.

➤ Discussing the entire process of reserving capacity is outside the scope of this book. Refer to *https://docs.microsoft.com/azure/sql-database/sql-database-reserved-capacity* for complete guidance.

Serverless compute tier

At the time of writing in preview, the serverless compute tier affords the DBA the ability to select a minimum and maximum number of vCores to assign to a single database. Based on workload, the Azure Service Fabric will automatically scale up and down how many cores are assigned. Combined with the auto-scaling of vCores comes an automatic calculation of a minimum and maximum amount of memory that will be assigned. The maximum storage size is determined by the DBA and billed separately. The vCores are charged on a per vCore per second basis.

> ## NOTE
> Compute tier is another level of differentiation in Azure SQL Database and is different from the service tier or the purchasing model, though at the time of writing, the serverless compute tier (as opposed to the provisioned compute tier) is only available in the single database vCore purchasing model in the general purpose service tier.

Beyond the auto-scaling of CPU and RAM, the entire database can be paused after a configurable number of hours of inactivity. This brings Azure SQL Database even closer to the ideal of cloud computing: pay exactly for what you need when you need it.

There is however a downside to the serverless tier, especially when auto-pausing is enabled. When database activity resumes, there will be a delay due to the warm-up period required. Even when auto-pausing is not enabled, frequent memory trimming and the occasional need for the Azure fabric to load-balance databases between servers may cause delays and dropped connections. The good news is that if serverless turns out to be a poor choice for your database, you can move the database to the provisioned compute tier without downtime.

Hyperscale service tier

The Hyperscale service tier offers significantly larger database sizes combined with other benefits to ensure that managing these very large databases (VLDBs) doesn't affect availability.

Architecturally, the Hyperscale tier is quite different from the other two service tiers (general purpose and business critical). Hyperscale introduces a very different deployment style for the SQL Server Database Engine: the query processing engine is separated from the storage engine and the log service and these components run on different systems. This radical departure from how SQL Server is deployed allows storage and compute resources to scale completely independently from each other. Figure 16-2 below illustrates the architecture of the Hyperscale tier.

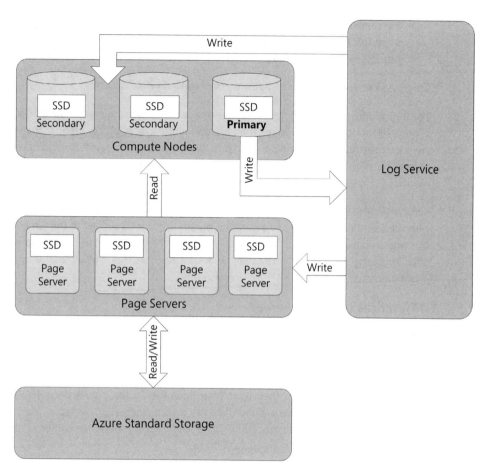

Figure 16-2   High-level overview of the Hyperscale architecture.

More than just size, the new architecture allows for several other impressive feats:

- Instantaneous backups that require no CPU or storage operations on the compute nodes (by leveraging Azure Storage snapshots)

- Warm buffer pools after startup, thanks to persisting the buffer pool using an in-memory table that is stored on fast local solid-state storage, a concept known as Resilient Buffer Pool Extensions (RBPEX)

- A recovery point objective (RPO) of 0 minutes with a recovery time objective (RTO) of less than 10 minutes. Moreover, the RTO is not affected by the size of the database

➤ For a technical deep dive into the Hyperscale architecture, refer to a paper presented by the Microsoft Azure and Microsoft Research teams at SIGMOD '19: *https://www.microsoft.com/research/uploads/prod/2019/05/socrates.pdf*.

Choosing between the DTU and vCore purchasing model

The DTU model is a good choice for low-end needs. The monthly cost of the lowest service tier in the DTU model is about 20x less than the cost of the lowest vCore offering. The vCore offering is more attractive for medium-sized databases that nevertheless have significant compute or memory requirements, because storage and compute are scaled independently in the vCore model.

Remember also that it's possible to switch from the DTU model to the vCore and back again without downtime. Switching to a different purchase model is subject to the same restrictions you would encounter while scaling down a database. Primarily, you will not be able to scale down to a service tier that allows a maximum database size that is less than the current size of your database.

Differences from SQL Server

SQL Server is a complete, standalone relational database management system designed to create and manage multiple databases and the associated processes around them. It includes a great many tools and features, including a comprehensive job scheduler.

Think of Azure SQL Database, then, as an offering at the database level. Because of this, only database-specific features are available. You can create objects such as tables, views, user-defined functions, and stored procedures, as well as memory-optimized objects. You can write queries, and, you can connect an application to it.

What you can't do with Azure SQL Database is run scheduled tasks directly. Querying other databases is extremely limited. With the exception of Azure SQL DB managed instance, you can't restore databases from a SQL Server backup. You don't have access to a file system, so importing data is more complicated. You can't manage system databases, and in particular, you can't manage TempDB.

There is currently no support for user-defined SQL Server CLR procedures. However, the native SQL CLR functions, like those necessary to support the hierarchyid and geospatial data types, are available.

On-premises environments typically use only Integrated Authentication to provide single sign-on and simplified login administration. In such environments, SQL authentication is often turned off. Turning off SQL authentication is not supported in Azure SQL Database. Instead of Integrated Authentication, there are several Azure Active Directory authentication scenarios supported. Those are discussed in more detail in Chapter 17.

Azure SQL Database does not support multiple filegroups or files. By extension, several other Database Engine features that use filegroups are unavailable, including FILESTREAM and FileTable.

> ➤ You can read more about FILESTREAM and FileTable in Chapter 7, "Understanding table features."

Database limitations

Azure SQL Database is subject to certain size limitations, such as the maximum database size. The maximum size of a database varies based on the purchase model and the pricing tier. In the DTU purchase model, the size of a database includes only the size of the data; the size of transaction logs is not counted. In the vCore purchase model, you are billed for the actual amount of storage consumed by your database, including the transaction log and backups.

If you are designing an application for the cloud, the size limitations are less of a restriction when deciding to adopt Azure SQL Database. This is because an application designed to operate at cloud-scale should shard its data across several database instances. In addition to overcoming database size limitations, the benefits of sharding also include faster disaster recovery and the ability to locate the data closer to the application if the application runs in different Azure regions.

To provide predictable performance for Azure SQL Database, there are limits to the number of concurrent requests, concurrent logins, and concurrent sessions. These limits differ by service tier and service objective. If any limit is reached, the next connection or query attempt will fail with error code 10928.

> ➤ You can find an exhaustive list of these operational limits online at *https://docs.microsoft.com/azure/sql-database/sql-database-resource-limits.*

One final limitation to be aware of is that a single server has an upper limit on the total DTUs it can host as well as on the total number of databases. For a large deployment, this might require distributing databases across servers. We recommend against operating at or near this limit because overall performance can become suboptimal. As of this writing, you should limit the number of databases per server to around 1,000.

NOTE

Any limitations discussed in this chapter are subject to change frequently, so be sure to review current limitations before deciding whether Azure SQL Database is right for you.

The resource limits, whether Database Transaction Units (DTUs) or vCores, force us to rethink how we make the best use of the service. It is easy to spend a lot of wasted money on Azure SQL Database because it requires a certain DTU service level at certain periods during the day or week, but at other times is idle.

It is possible to scale an Azure SQL database up and down as needed, but if this happens regularly, it makes the usage, and therefore the cost, unpredictable. Elastic pools (see the upcoming section on this) are a great way to get around this problem by averaging out resource usage over multiple databases with elastic DTUs or vCores.

Other SQL Server services

In addition to the Database Engine, an on-premises deployment of SQL Server might include:

- SQL Server Agent to schedule maintenance tasks or other activities

- SQL Server Integration Services to load or extract data

- SQL Server Analysis Services to support analytical workloads

- SQL Server Reporting Services to provide report functionality

These services are not included in Azure SQL Database. Instead, comparable functionality is often available through separate Azure services. A complete discussion of the available alternatives in Azure is beyond the scope of this book. The descriptions that follow are intended to merely name some of the alternatives and their high-level uses and direct you to an online starting point to learn more:

- **SQL Server Agent.**   To schedule recurring tasks for Azure SQL Database instances, DBAs should consider using Azure Automation, which is a service that makes it possible to reliably run potentially long-running PowerShell scripts. You can use Azure Automation to automate management of any Azure or third-party cloud service, including Azure SQL Database. In addition, there is a gallery of reusable scripts available.

  If you only require execution of T-SQL statements in your recurring tasks and you don't need complex job branching logic between steps, elastic database jobs might be a suitable replacement also. They are covered in the upcoming "Elastic database jobs" section.

  ➤ You can find more information about using Azure Automation with Azure SQL Database at *https://docs.microsoft.com/azure/sql-database/sql-database-manage-automation*. You can find an introduction to Azure Automation at *https://docs.microsoft.com/azure/automation/automation-intro*.

- **SQL Server Integration Services.**   Instead of SQL Server Integration Services (SSIS), use Azure Data Factory to perform tasks such as extracting data from various sources, transforming it by using a range of services, and finally publishing it to data stores for consumption by business intelligence tools or applications. Azure Data Factory includes an SSIS-compatible integration runtime, which enables running SSIS packages in Azure.

  You can use SQL Server Integration Services to extract data from and load data to Azure SQL Database, and you can use Data Factory to extract data from and load data to on-premises data stores. The decision about which service to use depends largely on where most of your data resides, which services you plan on using for transforming the data, and whether you allow a cloud service to connect to your on-premises environment using a gateway service.

➤ You can learn more about Data Factory at *https://docs.microsoft.com/azure/data-factory/*.

- **SQL Server Reporting Services.**   Microsoft Power BI is a recommended cloud-native replacement. Power BI is a powerful tool to create interactive visualizations using data from various sources. You can embed Power BI dashboards and reports in applications. You can also access them directly using a web browser or mobile app. Power BI Premium supports paginated reports. If you must have SQL Server Reporting Services, you can run it in a VM on Azure, but you'll need to pay for or provide a SQL Server license.

➤ You can learn more about Power BI at *https://docs.microsoft.com/power-bi/*.

- **SQL Server Analysis Services.**   To replace SQL Server Analysis Services, there are several alternative Azure services. Foremost, there is Azure Analysis Services. It is built on SQL Server Analysis Services and, as such, existing tabular models can be migrated from on-premises SQL Server Analysis Services deployments to the cloud. Alternatively, Power BI also includes tabular model functionality that might replace SSAS.

➤ You can learn more about Azure Analysis Services at
https://docs.microsoft.com/azure/analysis-services/analysis-services-overview.

➤ In addition to these replacements, we include a brief overview of other data services in Azure in the last section of this chapter, "Other data services in Azure."

NOTE

Some of the limitations described in this section can be addressed by using Azure SQL Database managed instance. We cover managed instance in detail in Chapter 18.

That said, Azure SQL Database is not going to completely replace SQL Server. Some systems are not designed to be moved into this type of environment, and there's nothing wrong with that. Microsoft will continue to release a standalone SQL Server product. On the other hand, Azure SQL Database is perfect for supporting web applications that can scale up as the user base grows. For new development, you can enjoy all the benefits of not having to maintain a database server, at a predictable cost.

Read scale-out

If you're thinking that a read scale-out replica is a secondary database instance that provides read-only access to your data, you would be correct. Provisioning these replicas in Azure SQL Database is supported in the following service tiers: premium, business critical, and hyperscale.

In the premium and business critical tiers, it is also enabled by default when creating a new database.

NOTE

Some features are not available on the replica database. These features are the Query Store, Extended Events, SQL Profiler, and, crucially perhaps in regulated environments, Audit. It is possible to disable the Read Scale-Out feature.

An application indicates its intent for a read-only or read-write connection using the `ApplicationIntent` property in the connection string. Specifically, a value of `ReadOnly` will cause the connection gateway to direct the connection to a read-only replica, if available. Not specifying `ApplicationIntent` or specifying a value of `ReadWrite` will direct the connect to the primary replica.

Inside OUT

What's the difference between a read-scale replica and a readable secondary?

A readable secondary database is a feature of geo-replication, which is discussed in detail in Chapter 17. As a feature of geo-replication, secondary databases are created by the DBA and generally located in a different region than the primary. Read Scale-Out is configured by the Azure infrastructure and the replicas live in the same region as the primary. Read Scale-out comes with no extra cost, unlike geo-replication.

Microsoft recommends that if read scale-out is enabled on geo-replicated databases, then it should also be enabled on the secondary database(s).

So, while there is some overlap in the functionality between the two concepts, read-scale replicas are primarily designed for load balancing, while readable secondaries are designed for high availability and disaster recovery.

Elastic pools

As noted earlier, Azure SQL Database has limits on its size and resources. Like Azure VMs, Azure SQL Database is pay-per-usage. Depending on what you need, you can spend a lot or a little on your databases.

Elastic pools increase the scalability and efficiency of your Azure SQL Database deployment by providing the ability for several databases in a pool to share resources, whether priced according to DTUs or vCores.

Without using elastic pools, each database might be provisioned with enough resources to handle its peak load. This can be inefficient. By grouping databases with different peak load times in an elastic pool, the Azure fabric will automatically balance the resources assigned to each database depending on their load. You can set limits to ensure that a single database does not starve the other databases in the pool of resources.

The best use case for elastic pools is one in which databases in the pool have low average resource utilization, with spikes that occur from time to time. This might be due to a reporting-type query that runs once a day, or a help desk system that can experience a lot of traffic at certain times of the day, for instance.

The elastic pool evens out these spikes over the full billing period, giving you a more predictable cost for an unpredictable workload across multiple databases.

NOTE
An elastic pool is tied to a single logical server. It's not possible to pool databases hosted on various logical servers in a single overarching pool.

Multitenant architecture

Azure SQL databases in an elastic pool gives you the ability to provision new databases with predictable growth and associated costs. Management of these databases is much easier in this environment because the administrative burden is lowered. Performance is also predictable because the pool is based on the combined resource utilization.

However, not all scenarios will benefit from the use of elastic pools. The most beneficial are those in which databases experience their peak load at separate times. You need to monitor the usage patterns of each customer and plan which elastic database pool they work best in.

Database consolidation

In an on-premises environment, database consolidation means finding a powerful enough server to handle the workload of many databases, each with its own workload pattern. Similarly, with elastic database pools, the number of databases is limited by the pool's size. For example, in the DTU pricing model, the current maximum pool size is 4,000 eDTUs in a Premium pool. This means that you can operate up to 160 databases (at 25 DTUs each) in that single pool, sharing their resources.

On the vCore side, the maximum pool size for a Business Critical tier gives you as many as 80 virtual cores, along with 408 GB of RAM and 4 TB data storage.

Combined with autoscale settings, depending on resource boundaries, consolidation makes a lot of sense for an organization with many small databases, just as it does with an on-premises SQL Server instance.

CHAPTER 16

Elastic database tools

Scale-Out in Azure SQL Database is also achieved using the elastic database tools client library which is available for .NET and Java applications. Applications developed using this library can save their data in different Azure SQL databases based on data-dependent routing rules while retaining the ability to run SELECT queries across all shards. This is a popular model for SaaS applications because you can assign each SaaS customer its own database.

> ➤ You can find more information on the elastic database tools at
> *https://docs.microsoft.com/azure/sql-database/sql-database-elastic-scale-get-started.*

Elastic database query

Perhaps the most surprising limitation in Azure SQL Database is that support for cross-database queries is very limited. This means that it is not possible to write a query that uses a three-part or four-part object name to reference a database object in another database or on another server. Consequently, semantic search is not available.

Elastic database query, which is a preview feature at the time of writing, aims to provide a solution. For both vertically and horizontally partitioned databases, elastic database query can provide a way to write T-SQL statements that are executed across databases. This is made possible by leveraging the external data sources and external tables feature.

There are some limitations, however. On the Standard tier, the first query can take several minutes to run because the functionality to run the query needs to be loaded first. Additionally, access is currently read-only for external data.

Performance does improve on the higher tiers as costs increase, but this is not meant to replicate home-grown systems that have many databases tightly bound together.

> ➤ Read more about elastic database queries and horizontal and vertical database partition scenarios in the Microsoft Docs at *https://docs.microsoft.com/azure/sql-database/ sql-database-elastic-query-overview.*

Elastic database jobs

SQL Server has the ability to run the same query against multiple databases from a list of registered servers, or Central Management Server. In a similar manner, the elastic database jobs feature gives you the ability to run a script written in Transact-SQL (T-SQL) For example, if your organization offers its customers a SaaS solution, each customer may receive their own database instance. Then, the schemas of all databases must be kept synchronized.

An elastic database job can target the databases that are part of a custom group of databases. A job is inserted into a job database, which is a standalone Azure SQL database on a logical server referred to as the agent server. An Azure resource called an Elastic Job Agent is created, pointed at the agent server and job database. Job credentials, which allow the agent to connect to the target databases are stored in the job database, as is the list of target databases itself. Elastic database jobs can consist out of multiple steps and can have a rudimentary schedule with simple recurrence rules. Finally, the results can be stored in the job database, and diagnostics are available from the Elastic Job Agent blade in the Azure Portal.

> ➤ You can read about Elastic Scale in Chapter 17, and find out more about elastic database jobs, such as their architecture and setup, at
> *https://docs.microsoft.com/azure/sql-database/sql-database-elastic-jobs-overview.*

NOTE

Some of the use cases for which you use the SQL Server Agent on-premises might be addressed with elastic database jobs. For other use cases, you'll need to use other Azure functions for automating tasks. See the "Other SQL Server services" section for a brief intro to Azure Automation.

Sharding databases with Split-Merge

Azure SQL Database is designed for SaaS scenarios because you can start off small and grow your system as your customer base grows. This introduces several interesting challenges, including for example what happens when a database reaches its maximum resource limit and size.

Sharding is a technique by which data is partitioned horizontally across multiple nodes, either to improve performance or the resiliency of an application. In the context of Azure SQL Database, sharding refers to distributing data across more than one database when it grows too large. (If this sounds like table partitioning, you're mostly right.)

It is all very well to add more databases (shards) to support your application, but how do you distribute your data evenly across those new databases?

The Split-Merge tool can move data from constrained databases to new ones while maintaining data integrity. It runs as an Azure web service, which means there is an associated cost. The tool uses shard map management to decide what data segments (shardlets) go into which database (shard) using a metadata store (an additional standalone Azure SQL Database) and is completely customizable.

> ➤ To read about how this process works in detail, go to *https://docs.microsoft.com/azure/sql-database/sql-database-elastic-scale-overview-split-and-merge.*

Hybrid cloud with Azure

Azure SQL Database is not designed to completely replace SQL Server. Many thousands of organizations all over the world are quite happy with the security, performance, and low latency offered by hosting their environment on-premises but would like to make use of certain components in the cloud.

The most common implementation of a hybrid cloud is with Azure Active Directory (Azure AD). Instead of having to manage user accounts in two places (on-premises and in Azure, for Microsoft Office 365, for example), you can synchronize your Active Directory Domain Service (AD DS) with Azure AD and manage it all in one place.

Mixing your on-premises and Azure environments, in whichever way you do it, falls under the definition of a hybrid cloud, and Microsoft has some interesting ways of helping you achieve this, especially around the data platform and SQL Server.

Azure Hybrid Benefit

Users can obtain significant savings on SQL Server VM or Azure SQL Database list prices if they have active Windows or SQL Server core licenses with Software Assurance. Exactly which type of licenses can be converted or re-used and how they map to Azure offerings is covered in detail in the Azure Hybrid Benefit FAQ found at *https://azure.microsoft.com/pricing/hybrid-benefit/faq/*.

> ➤ **You can calculate the expected savings using the Azure Hybrid Benefit Savings Calculator at** *https://azure.microsoft.com/pricing/hybrid-benefit/*.

Azure Hybrid Benefit is available for SQL Server VMs, Azure SQL Database using the vCore purchase model, and Azure SQL Database managed instance. In other words, Azure SQL Database in the DTU purchase model is not eligible for discounted rates using Azure Hybrid Benefit.

> ### NOTE
> **Azure Hybrid Benefit is a feature unique to Azure. It is different from the Software Assurance license mobility benefit, which may be used to reassign SQL Server core licenses to third-party providers offering unmanaged services, such as virtual machines or hosted SQL Server.**

Keeping cold data online and queryable by using Stretch Database

In larger organizations, it can be expensive to maintain historic (cold) data in a SQL Server database, when you consider not only the storage, but also the associated maintenance and administration costs. Additionally, data retention laws require organizations to store data for several years, which can be cumbersome.

Stretch Database is designed to balance the needs of keeping cold data online by reducing the cost of storing and managing that data locally and reducing RTO and RPO mandated in a Service-Level Agreement (SLA).

Because historic data can account for a large percentage of an existing database, removing cold data from an on-premises database can significantly reduce the storage, time, and other resources for necessary tasks like backups, index and statistics maintenance, data consistency checks, and so on, while still making it available to be queried.

Stretch Database is activated at the instance level, but you move rows at a database and table level. If your cold data is already stored in a separate archive table, you can move the entire table. If your cold data is in a large table that also contains active, or hot data, you can set up a filter to move only the older rows.

No application changes are needed, but there are some considerable limitations to using a Stretch Database:

- Constraints in the migrated data are not enforced for uniqueness (including primary key and unique constraints), and you cannot move tables referenced by foreign key constraints, or check and default constraints.

- You cannot perform any data modification on migrated data (updates and deletes), and you cannot insert rows directly (they must be moved in by the Stretch Database functionality).

- You cannot perform data modification on the data that is eligible for migration.

- You cannot create indexes on views that refer to Stretch-configured tables, and you cannot move tables that are used in existing indexed views.

- Filters on indexes are not propagated on migrated data, which can cause issues with unique filtered indexes.

- Tables cannot take part in replication, change tracking, or change data capture.

- Tables cannot contain more than 1,023 columns or 998 indexes.

There are also limits to the type of data and indexes that can participate in a Stretch Database:

- `text`, `ntext`, and `image` data types are not permitted.

- `timestamp` (`rowversion`), `xml`, and `sql_variant` types are not permitted.

- FILESTREAM and, by extension, FileTable is not permitted.

- CLR (Common Language Runtime, or .NET) data types are not permitted (including the built-in types `geography`, `geometry`, and `hierarchyid`).

- Computed columns are not permitted.

- Full-text, XML, and spatial indexes are not permitted. Tables cannot be referenced by indexed views.

Finally, the costs for Stretch Database are based on both storage and compute models. This means that you will pay for storage even if you never query the data. If you query the data, you will also pay for the compute costs (priced according to a Database Stretch Unit, or DSU) as well as any data transfer.

These limitations might exist for good reasons, but those reasons could be enough cause to consider alternatives. However, for ease of use, Stretch Database works as advertised.

NOTE

The Data Migration Assistant (DMA) tool can provide recommendations related to Stretch Database. Guidance on using the DMA for Stretch Database is available in the Microsoft Docs at *https://docs.microsoft.com/sql/sql-server/stretch-database/ stretch-database-databases-and-tables-stretch-database-advisor*.

Automated backups with SQL Server Managed Backups

With SQL Server on Azure VMs, you can automate SQL Server native backups that write directly to Azure Blob Storage. (This works with an on-premises version of SQL Server, as well, but latency can be an issue.)

By default, the schedule depends on the transaction workload, so a server that is idle will have fewer transaction log backups than a busy server. This reduces the total number of backup files required to restore a SQL Server database in a disaster recovery (DR) scenario.

You can also use advanced options to define a schedule. However, you must set this up before turning on Managed Backups to avoid unwanted backup operations. Additionally, the retention period is customizable, with the maximum being 30 days.

You can configure these backups at the instance or database level, providing much needed flexibility for smaller database environments that would not ordinarily have a full-time database administrator on hand.

You can fully encrypt backups through SQL Server backup encryption, and Azure Blob Storage is encrypted by default (for data at rest).

➤ You can read more about encryption in Chapter 13, "Protecting data through encryption, privacy and auditing."

There is an associated cost with the Azure Storage container required to store these database backups, but when the retention period is reached, older files will be cleared out, keeping the costs consistent. If you were building your own custom backup solution, you would incur similar costs anyway, and there is a good chance the managed backup storage costs will be lower.

➤ To read more about SQL Server Managed Backup to Microsoft Azure, go
to *https://docs.microsoft.com/sql/relational-databases/backup-restore/
sql-server-managed-backup-to-microsoft-azure*.

Azure SQL Database Edge

For the Internet of Things (IoT), a lot of effort is expended in getting sensors and other devices
to report their data to a SQL Server instance or Azure SQL Database in the cloud. Azure SQL
Database Edge (in preview) is a repackaged SQL Server instance that can run on low-power and
IoT edge computing devices, with either 64-bit ARM or Intel x64 CPUs. For example, imagine
running it on a Raspberry Pi computer.

Edge includes the full SQL Server Database Engine running on Linux, along with some analytics
features including data streaming and time-series support.

➤ You can read more about Azure SQL Database Edge (preview) at
https://azure.microsoft.com/services/sql-database-edge.

Azure Stack

This is Microsoft's version of an edge and hybrid cloud, in which you can install certain Azure
services on-premises, on Microsoft-approved hardware. This brings the power of Azure to your
own datacenter.

After you have developed the solutions that best suit your organization, you can deploy your
applications and solutions to the Azure region that makes the most sense, or just keep them on-
premises, hosted on Azure Stack.

You can expose Azure SQL databases as a service by using the SQL Server resource provider.
This gives your users the ability to create databases without having to provision a VM every
time. Think of it as an on-premises version of Azure SQL Database.

Keep in mind that certain features like elastic pools, and scaling databases, are not available at
this time.

➤ You can read more about Azure SQL databases on Azure Stack at
https://docs.microsoft.com/azure/azure-stack/azure-stack-sql-resource-provider-deploy.

Private networking between on-premises and Azure

Many organizations want to ensure a secure channel between their environments, whether that
is using Azure VNets, or their on-premises network and Azure. You can achieve this by way of a
Virtual Private Network (VPN).

A VPN encrypts traffic over any network (including the Internet), through a tunnel that it creates. All traffic that travels through that tunnel is secure, which means that no bad actors will be

able to monitor the traffic. However, there is a performance overhead with encrypting that traffic, which makes the connection slightly slower.

There are two main ways that Azure implements connections between your on-premises environment and Azure itself. One of these is through a traditional VPN service over the Internet (site-to-site), and the other is through a dedicated connection that does not use the public Internet (Azure ExpressRoute).

Site-to-site VPN

There are two different types of problems that you need to deal with when connecting systems to an Azure VNet: connecting two Azure VNets together and connecting an external network to an Azure VNet.

To connect two Azure VNets together in the same region, you can create a peering network— in other words, no part of the VNet goes out to the Internet—which is priced per gigabyte transferred.

If you want a VPN gateway, instead, which creates a connection between your on-premises network and an Azure VNet, those are priced according to the maximum bandwidth you would require (100 Mbps, 650 Mbps, 1 Gbps, and 1.25 Gbps), and charged at an hourly rate (which, depending on what you need, is also reasonably priced).

Azure ExpressRoute

If the speeds of site-to-site VPNs are not satisfactory, and you want to connect your on-premises network to your Azure VNet, you can use ExpressRoute. With its low latency, ExpressRoute expands your existing network to the virtually limitless services available in Azure, depending on your budget, of course. According to Microsoft Docs:

ExpressRoute is "...excellent for scenarios like periodic data migration, replication for business continuity, disaster recovery, and other high-availability strategies." (https://azure.microsoft.com/ services/expressroute)

This type of bandwidth gives you the flexibility of moving entire VMs from on-premises to Azure, for test environments and migrations. Your customers can use Azure web services that take data from your on-premises environment without ever going over the public Internet.

You can also use it for creating a DR site, using SQL Server Log Shipping. Perhaps you want to extend your availability group to the cloud, which you can do by using a distributed availability group (see Chapter 2). Using ExpressRoute, you can treat Azure as an extension of your own network, as illustrated in Figure 16-3.

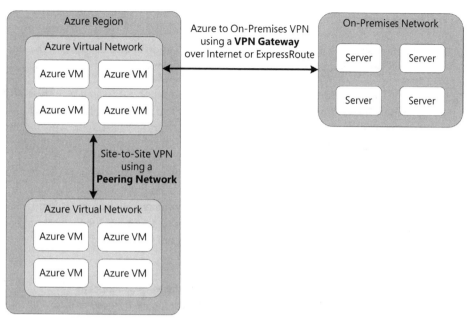

Figure 16-3 Azure virtual networks can connect to an on-premises network in various ways

Inside OUT

How fast can data be transferred over a VPN connection?

Network speed is measured in bits per second (bps). Because there are eight bits in a byte, a single byte would take eight seconds to be transmitted at 1 bps, at the theoretical maximum throughput (perfect network conditions).

For speeds in the gigabit-per-second (Gbps) range, it will take at least eight seconds to transfer 1 GB at a speed of 1 Gbps. It will take slightly longer due to latency and other overhead, like encryption.

Transferring data over large distances incurs latency. A network packet will take approximately 65 milliseconds to move across the continental United States and back again. You must consider both network speed and latency when planning migrations, as well as DR and HA scenarios.

Cloud security

Although we didn't include a comprehensive discussion of cloud security in this book, in this section we provide a few considerations for DBAs considering a cloud migration.

First, many of the SQL Server offerings in the cloud support the same security features as on-premises. This is true for SQL Server in Azure VMs and largely true for Azure SQL Database and managed instance. Specific security considerations for the PaaS offerings are included in their respective chapters: Chapter 17 and Chapter 18.

An important aspect of managing security in Azure is the Azure Security Center. Found in the Azure Portal, it provides an integrated view of the security posture for all your Azure resources. The Security Center also provides metrics and recommendations that help you improve the security of your resources, including the SQL resources. Some of the features of Security Center are available in the paid standard tier, while many are included with the cost of your existing resources.

> ➤ **Learn more about Azure Security Center in the Microsoft Docs at**
> *https://docs.microsoft.com/azure/security-center/security-center-intro.*

Among the SQL recommendations you might receive from Security Center are enabling auditing on Azure SQL Databases or enabling vulnerability assessment on an SQL Server VM.

Deploying SQL resources in Azure means that you'll need to understand security in Azure in general. As a DBA, you'll need to know who has access to view and especially manage the SQL resources. Permissions to manage resources can be given at the account, subscription, resource group, or individual resource level. You'll need to know how to monitor changes to the Azure resources. Further, you'll need to learn about networking in Azure.

Other data services in Azure

Azure offers more data services than we cover in this book. We mention these here briefly because in today's multi-platform environments, there is more to our world than SQL Server. These different offerings each have their strengths and weaknesses. Deploying a modern application may involve mixing these different services to create a single solution to a business need.

The most closely related offering is Azure Synapse Analytics, formerly known as Azure SQL Data Warehouse. Built on SQL Server, it is a PaaS service optimized for parallel query processing and large data volumes. Compared with Azure SQL Database, however, Azure Synapse can scale storage and compute independently by leveraging Azure Storage and a massively parallel processing engine that manages multiple SQL compute nodes via a control node. This makes it suitable for storing enormous amounts of data that might only occasionally need to be processed.

➤ Learn more about Synapse Analytics at
   https://docs.microsoft.com/azure/sql-data-warehouse/.

Azure also offers third-party fully managed database platforms, namely Azure Database for MariaDB, Azure Database for MySQL, and Azure Database for PostgreSQL. These offerings are all relational databases offered as PaaS.

➤ Learn more about these services at *https://azure.microsoft.com/services/mariadb/,*
   https://azure.microsoft.com/services/mysql/, and *https://azure.microsoft.com/services/*
   postgresql/, respectively.

Outside of the realm of relational DBMS, Microsoft's Cosmos DB is noteworthy. This is a globally distributed database service that supports multiple data models, including key-value, document, graph, and relational. Cosmos DB wraps multiple APIs in a single service.

➤ Learn more about Cosmos DB at *https://docs.microsoft.com/azure/cosmos-db/.*

Another data offering is Azure Data Lake Storage. The underlying storage is provided by Azure Storage and is augmented with hierarchical namespace functionality, meaning that folder and other file system semantics are native to the solution while benefitting from Azure Storage's features for scale and disaster recovery. Data Lake can store unstructured data in addition to relational data.

➤ You can learn more about Data Lake Storage at
   https://docs.microsoft.com/azure/storage/blobs/data-lake-storage-introduction.

The final data platform offering we'll include is Azure Databricks. Azure Databricks is built on Apache Spark and tightly integrates with Azure to provide a complete environment where team members with various roles on data science projects can collaborate.

➤ The documentation for Azure Databricks is located at
   https://docs.microsoft.com/azure/azure-databricks/.

CHAPTER 16

Provisioning Azure SQL Database

This chapter delves into Microsoft Azure SQL Database, a cloud database service providing compatibility with the SQL Server relational Database Engine. Azure SQL Database is designed so that cloud applications can take advantage of relational database services without most of the overhead of managing the Database Engine. Azure SQL Database is also designed to meet requirements from hosting a single database associated with an organization's line-of-business application to hosting thousands of databases for a global software-as-a-service offering. In this chapter, we look at Azure SQL Database concepts and how to provision databases and manage them.

> ➤ For an overview of cloud concepts and an introduction to the different SQL Server offerings in Microsoft Azure, see Chapter 16, "Designing and implementing hybrid and Azure database infrastructure." Managed instance is covered in Chapter 18, "Provisioning Azure SQL Database managed instance."

You'll learn how to create your first server and database. These sections include thorough coverage of the available options and why each one matters. Next, the chapter teaches the creation and management of elastic pools.

Security must be on your checklist when deploying any database, and perhaps even more so in the cloud. This chapter includes coverage of the security features specific only to Azure SQL Database. For security features common to SQL Server, refer to Chapter 12, "Administering security and permissions," and Chapter 13, "Protecting data through encryption, privacy and auditing." Finally, this chapter reviews features designed to prepare your cloud-hosted database for disaster recovery.

Throughout the chapter, you will also find many PowerShell Core samples to complete tasks. This is important because the flexibility of cloud computing offers quick setup and teardown of resources. Automation through scripting becomes a must-have skill—unless you prefer to work overtime clicking around in the web GUI. If you need an introduction to PowerShell Core, a solid place to start is *https://github.com/PowerShell/PowerShell/tree/master/docs/learning-powershell*.

> ➤ The scripts for this book are all available for download at
> *https://www.MicrosoftPressStore.com/SQLServer2019InsideOut/downloads.*

Provisioning a logical SQL server

The Azure SQL Database service introduces a concept called a *logical SQL Server*. This "server" is quite different from what you might be used to on premises. An Azure SQL Server is best described as a connection endpoint and less as an instance or a server. For example, a logical SQL Server does not provide compute or storage resources. It does not provide much configuration. And although there is a virtual master database, there is no model, TempDB, or msdb—those are abstracted away.

In addition to missing several features of an on-premises SQL Server, there are also features that are unique to logical SQL servers: firewall configuration and elastic pools to name just two.

> ➤ You can find more information about firewall configuration later in this chapter. We covered elastic pools in Chapter 16.

You should consider that your logical SQL Server determines the geographic region where your data will be stored. When a single server hosts multiple databases, these databases are collocated in the same Azure region, but they might not be hosted on the same hardware. That is of no consequence to you when using the databases, but the point serves to illustrate the purely *logical* nature of the concept.

Creating a logical SQL server (just called "server" from here on) is the first step in the process of deploying a database. The server determines the region that will host the database(s), provides the basis for access control and security configuration (more on that later), and provides the fully-qualified domain name (FQDN) of the endpoint.

NOTE

Using the Azure portal, it is possible to provision a new server while creating a new database. All other methods require two separate steps or commands, so for consistency, we will discuss each separately in this chapter. This will allow the focus to remain on each distinct element (server and database) of your provisioning process.

You'll be interested to know that provisioning a server does not incur usage charges. Azure SQL Database is billed based on the resources assigned to each database or elastic pool. The server acts only as a logical container for databases and provides the connection endpoint. This is also why there are no performance or sizing specifications attached to a server.

Inside OUT

When should you create a new logical SQL server?

The logical SQL server determines the region where the databases are located. Your databases should be in the same region as the applications or users that access them, both to avoid cross-region traffic charges as well as to have the lowest possible latency when running queries.

Security considerations can also dictate how many logical SQL servers you operate. Because the server admin login and Azure AD principal assigned as server admins have complete control and access to all databases on a server, you might set up different servers for different applications or different environments, such as development, test, and production. On the other hand, the threat detection feature (discussed in detail in the section "Security in Azure SQL Database" later in the chapter) is charged per logical server. Therefore, it's likely that you'll want to strike a balance between manageability, cost, and security.

The final factors when considering creating a new server or reusing an existing one is the database life cycle and billing aggregation. The database life cycle is tied directly to the server, so if you operate databases with very different life cycles, you could benefit from improved manageability by hosting those on different servers. As it relates to billing, because your usage is charged per database, you might find benefits in aggregating charges for specific databases. You can aggregate charges by using a resource group or by using tags. Recall that all databases are tied to the resource group of the server where they are hosted. If you want to aggregate charges for several databases, these databases could be deployed to the same server or you could assign the same tag and value to each database even if they are hosted on different servers in different resource groups.

Creating a server using the Azure portal

To provision a server using the Azure portal, use the SQL Server (logical server only) blade. You need to provide the following information to create a server:

- **Subscription.**   The subscription in which you create the server determines which Azure account will be associated with databases on this server. Database usage charges are billed to the subscription.

- **Resource group.**   The resource group where this server will reside. Review the section on Azure governance in Chapter 16 to learn about the importance of resource groups.

- **Server name.**   The server name becomes the DNS name of the server. The domain name is fixed to database.windows.net. This means that your server name must be globally unique and lowercase. There are also restrictions as to which characters are allowed, though those restrictions are comparable to on-premises server names.

- **Location.**   This is the Azure region where any databases are physically located. Azure SQL Database is available in most regions worldwide. You should carefully consider the placement of your servers and, by consequence, databases. Your data should be in the same region as the compute resources (Azure Web Apps, for example) that will read and write the data. When you locate the applications that connect to the server in the same region, you can expect latency in the order of single-digit milliseconds. Another consequence of locating resources in other regions is that you might end up paying per gigabyte for the egress from the region where the data is located. Not all services incur these charges, but you must be aware before going this route.

- **Server admin login.**   This username is best compared to the "sa" account in SQL Server. However, you cannot use "sa" or other common SQL Server identifiers for this username; they are reserved for internal purposes. You should choose a generic name rather than a name derived from your name because you cannot change the server admin login later.

- **Password.**   Unlike an on-premises SQL Server, it's not possible to turn off SQL Server Authentication. Therefore, the password associated with the server admin login should be very strong and carefully guarded. Unlike the login itself, Azure users with specific roles can change it.

> ➤ **You can read more about Role-Based Access Control to your Azure SQL Database resources later in the chapter.**

While creating a new server using the Azure portal, you can allow the new server's firewall to accept connections from all Azure resources. You can read more about the firewall in the section "Server and database-level firewall" later in the chapter. Before deploying any databases, we recommend that you either configure the firewall to only allow connections from known IP addresses or use a VNet endpoint, as described in Chapter 16.

Another decision you'll make at the server level is enabling Advanced Data Security. Advanced Data Security is covered later in this chapter.

Creating a server by using PowerShell Core

To provision a server using PowerShell, use the `New-AzSqlServer` cmdlet, as demonstrated in the code example that follows. Of course, you'll need to modify the values of the variable in line 1 to fit your needs. These commands assume that a resource group with the name SSIO2019 already exists and that the resource group name will also become the server name. The server will be created in the active Azure subscription.

```
$resourceGroupName = "SSIO2019"

$location = "southcentralus"

$serverName = $resourceGroupName.ToLower()

$Cred = Get-Credential -UserName dbadmin -Message "Pwd for server admin"

New-AzSqlServer -ResourceGroupName $resourceGroupName `

   -ServerName $serverName `

   -Location $location -SqlAdministratorCredentials $Cred
```

In this script, the Get-Credential cmdlet is used to obtain the password for the dbadmin server administrator. This cmdlet opens a dialog box that asks for the password. All values needed to create a server are provided as parameters to the New-AzSqlServer cmdlet.

NOTE

Throughout this chapter, the Azure PowerShell sample scripts all build upon the existence of a server named ssio2019 in a resource group named SSIO2019. You will need to choose your own server name because it must be globally unique. The sample scripts available for download are all cumulative and define the value just once, which makes it easy to make a single modification and run all the sample scripts.

Establishing a connection to your server

With a server created, you can establish a connection. Azure SQL Database supports only one protocol for connections: TCP. In addition, you have no control over the TCP port number; it is always 1433.

TROUBLESHOOTING

Some corporate networks might block connections to Internet IP addresses with a destination port of 1433, so if you have trouble connecting, check with your network administrators.

Using SQL Server Management Studio 18 as an example to connect to the newly created server, Figure 17-1 shows the different values entered in the Connect To Server dialog box. When you first establish the connection, you will be prompted by SQL Server Management Studio to create a firewall rule to allow this connection (see Figure 17-2). You will need to sign in with your Azure account to create the firewall rule.

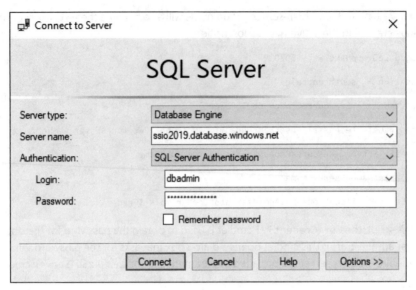

Figure 17-1 The Connect to Server dialog box, showing values to connect to the newly created logical SQL server.

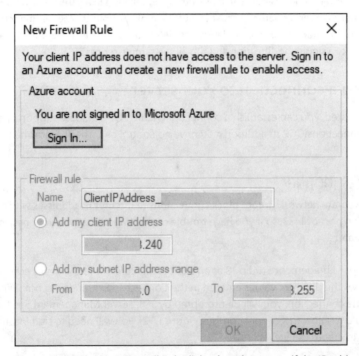

Figure 17-2 The New Firewall Rule dialog box that opens if the IP address attempting to connect is not included in any existing firewall rule.

Connections to Azure SQL Database are always encrypted, even if it is not specified in the connection string. For older client libraries, you might need to specify encryption explicitly in the connection string because these libraries might not support the automatic upgrade of the connection. If you neglect to specify it explicitly when using these older client libraries, you may receive an error message. Use `Encrypt=True` in the connection string if needed to successfully connect.

You might be tempted to look up the IP address of your server and use the IP address instead of the FQDN to connect. This is not recommended, because the IP address for the server is really the IP address of a connection gateway. This IP address is subject to change at any time as the Azure infrastructure conducts updates or failovers.

NOTE

During Azure upgrade windows or infrastructure failures, you might experience a brief period of connectivity loss while the DNS infrastructure and your client(s) retain the cached IP address. The configured time-to-live (TTL) of the DNS entries is purposefully short: five minutes.

Deleting a server

Deleting a server is a permanent, irreversible operation. You should delete a server only if the following conditions are true:

- You no longer need that server's name.

- You are confident that you will not need to restore any databases that are or were hosted on it.

- You are approaching the limit of servers permitted in a subscription.

NOTE

As of this writing, the maximum number of servers in a single subscription is 20 in a single region and 200 servers in total. You can request an increase by contacting Azure Support.

Provisioning a database in Azure SQL Database

After provisioning a server, you are ready to provision your first database. Provisioning a database incurs charges associated with the pricing tier that you select. As a reminder, pricing for Azure SQL Database is per database or elastic pool, not per server.

You can create a database from one of three sources: Blank, Sample, or Backup. A Blank database is just that: there are no user database objects. If you choose **Sample**, the new database will have the lightweight Adventure Works schema and data. If you choose **Backup**, you can restore the most recent daily backup of another Azure SQL Database in the subscription. The sections that follow discuss the process of provisioning a database using the Azure portal, PowerShell, Azure CLI, and Transact-SQL (T-SQL).

NOTE

You can provision a new logical SQL server while provisioning a new database only by using the Azure portal. All other methods require two separate steps or commands.

Creating a database using the Azure portal

There are several methods to begin creating a new database in Azure SQL Database using the Azure portal. One method is to start from the Overview blade of an existing server. You can also start from the Create New Service blade. The method you choose determines which values you will need to provide:

- **Subscription.**   Select the subscription that will be used to bill the charges for this database. The subscription you select here will narrow down the list of server choices later. This parameter is not shown when the process is started from a server.

- **Resource group.**   Here, you will choose to create a new resource group or use an existing one. If you choose to create a new resource group, you will also need to create a new server. But note that choosing an existing resource group will not narrow the list of server choices later.

- **Database name.**   The database name must be unique within the server and meet all requirements for a database name in SQL Server.

- **Server.**   You can select an existing server in the selected subscription or create a new server. The existing servers that are listed are filtered to the subscription you selected earlier, but not to the resource group. If you select a server in a different resource group than the group you selected earlier, the resource group value will be updated automatically to reflect the correct selection. That is because the life cycle of a database is tied to the life cycle of the server, and the life cycle of the server is tied to the resource group. Therefore, a database cannot exist in a different resource group than its server. This server value is locked when the process is started from a logical SQL server.

- **Elastic database pool.**   We discuss elastic pools in detail in the "Provisioning an elastic pool" section later in this chapter. From the Create SQL Database pane, you can select an existing elastic pool or create a new one.

- **Collation.**   The collation selected here becomes the database's default collation. Unlike on premises, there is no GUI to set the new database's collation name. You can type the collation name from memory or use a basic UI to search the list of valid SQL Server collation names.

- **Source.** You select one of three values that match the afore mentioned options: Blank database, Sample, or Backup.

- **Backup.** You will be prompted to provide this only when you've selected Backup as the source of the new database. The database you select will be restored to its most recent daily backup, which means it might be up to 24 hours old.

➤ You can read more about options for restoring database backups in the "Understanding default disaster recovery features" section later in this chapter.

- **Pricing tier.** When creating a standalone database, you need to select a pricing tier. The pricing tier determines the hourly usage charges and several architectural aspects of your database. We discussed pricing tiers in Chapter 16. It is possible to mix pricing tiers within a server, underscoring the notion that the server is a mere logical container for databases and has no relationship to any performance aspects. While selecting the pricing tier, you also can set a maximum database size. Your database will not be able to run INSERT or UPDATE T-SQL statements when the maximum size is reached.

Creating a database by using PowerShell Core

The script that follows illustrates how to create a new Standard-tier standalone database with the S0 service objective on an existing server named ssio2019. The database collation is set to Latin1_General_CI_AS. The -Collation, -Edition, and -RequestedService ObjectiveName parameters are optional. We show them here because they are commonly specified. Their respective defaults are SQL_Latin1_General_CP1_CI_AS (generally not desired), Standard, and S0. Pay attention to the server name: it is lowercase because the parameter value must match exactly. Logical SQL server names cannot contain uppercase characters.

```
$resourceGroupName = "SSIO2019"

$serverName = $resourceGroupName.ToLower()

$databaseName = "Contoso"

New-AzSqlDatabase -ResourceGroupName $resourceGroupName `

    -ServerName $serverName -DatabaseName $databaseName -Edition Standard `

    -RequestedServiceObjectiveName "S0" -CollationName Latin1_General_CI_AS
```

Other optional parameters include the following:

- **CatalogCollation.**   This collation parameter determines the collation of character data in the database's metadata catalog. Note that you cannot set this database property in the GUI. This value defaults to SQL_Latin1_General_CP1_CI_AS.

- **ElasticPoolName.**   When specified, this database will be added to the existing elastic pool on the server. The next section covers elastic pools.

- **MaxSizeBytes.**   Sets the maximum database size in bytes. You cannot set just any value here; there is a list of supported maximum sizes. The available maximum sizes depend on the selected pricing tier.

- **SampleName.**   Specify AdventureWorksLT if you want the database to have the available sample schema and data.

- **Tags.**   This parameter is common to many Azure cmdlets. You can use it to specify an arbitrary number of name–value pairs. Tags are used to add custom metadata to Azure resources. You can use both the Azure portal and PowerShell to filter resources based on tag values. You can also obtain a consolidated billing view for resources with the same tag values.

   A usage example is -Tags @{"Tag1"="Value 1";"Tag 2"="Value 2"}, which would associate two name–value pairs to the database. The name of the first tag is Tag1 with Value 1, and the name of the second tag is Tag 2 with Value 2.

After creating the database, you can retrieve information about it by using the Get-AzSqlDatabase cmdlet, as shown here:

```
Get-AzSqlDatabase -ResourceGroupName SSIO2019 -ServerName ssio2019 `

   -DatabaseName Contoso
```

Creating a database by using Azure CLI

The Azure CLI makes it possible for you to use the same set of commands to manage Azure resources regardless of the platform of your workstation: Windows, macOS, Linux, and even using the portal's Cloud Shell.

NOTE

Installing the Azure CLI on different operating systems is not covered in this text. Guidance for each OS is available at *https://docs.microsoft.com/cli/azure/install-azure-cli*.

The Azure CLI command that follows creates a database with the same parameters as those found in the preceding PowerShell script. After creating the database, the new database's properties are retrieved.

➤ You can find the full list of supported CLI commands for Azure SQL Database at *https://docs.microsoft.com/cli/azure/sql/db*.

```
az sql db create --resource-group SSIO2019 --server ssio2019 \

    --name Contoso --collation Latin1_General_CI_AS \

    --edition Standard --service-objective S0

az sql db show --resource-group SSIO2019 --server ssio2019 --name Contoso
```

NOTE

For clarity, the long parameter names have been used in the preceding example. Many parameters for the az command also have a shorthand version. For example, instead of using `--resource-group`, you can use `-g`. The `--help` (shorthand: `-h`) parameter shows both the long and shorthand parameter names, if a shorthand version is available.

Creating a database by using T-SQL

The T-SQL script that follows creates a new Azure SQL database with the same properties as used in both of the previous examples. To create a new database, connect to the server on which the new database will reside; for example, using SQL Server Management Studio:

```
CREATE DATABASE Contoso COLLATE Latin1_General_CI_AS

    (EDITION = 'standard', SERVICE_OBJECTIVE = 'S0');
```

Because the T-SQL command is run in the context of a server, you do not need to, nor can you, provide a server name or resource group name. You cannot use T-SQL to create a database based on the AdventureWorksLT sample, but you can use it to restore a database backup from a database on the same server using the AS COPY OF clause, as shown here:

```
CREATE DATABASE Contoso_copy AS COPY OF Contoso.
```

Scaling up or down

Azure SQL Database scale operations are conducted with minimal disruption to the availability of the database. A scale operation is performed by the service using a replica of the original database at the new service level. When the replica is ready, connections are switched over to the replica. Although this will not cause data loss and is completed in a time frame measured in seconds, active transactions might be rolled back. The application should be designed to handle such events and retry the operation.

Scaling down might not be possible if the database size exceeds the maximum allowed size for the lower service objective or pricing tier. If you know that you will likely scale down your database, you should set the maximum database size to a value equal to or less than the maximum database size for the service objective to which you might scale down.

In most tiers, scaling is initiated by an administrator. Only the serverless tier supports autoscaling. If the serverless tier does not meet your needs, you can consider deploying databases to an elastic pool (discussed in the next section) to achieve automatic balancing of resource demands for a group of databases. Another option to scale without administrator intervention would be to use Azure Automation to monitor resource usage and initiate scaling when a threshold has been reached. You can use the PowerShell Set-AzSqlDatabase cmdlet to set a new pricing tier by using the -Edition parameter, and a new service objective by using the -RequestedServiceObjectiveName parameter.

Provisioning an elastic pool

For an introduction to elastic pools, refer to Chapter 16. Elastic pools are created per server, and a single server can have more than one elastic pool. The number of eDTUs or vCores available depends upon the pricing tier, as is the case with standalone databases. Beyond the differences between tiers described in Chapter 16, which also apply to elastic pools, the relationship between the maximum pool size and the selected eDTU or vCore, and the maximum number of databases per pool are also different per tier.

You can create elastic pools in the Azure portal, by using PowerShell, the Azure CLI, or the REST API. After an elastic pool is created, you can create new databases directly in the pool. You also can add existing single databases to a pool or move databases out of pools.

In most of the next sections, no distinction is made between standalone databases or elastic pool databases. Management of standalone databases is not different from management of databases in elastic pools. Also, whether a database is in an elastic pool or standalone makes no difference for establishing a connection.

Use the following PowerShell Core script to create a new elastic pool on the ssio2019 server and move the existing Contoso database to the pool:

```
$resourceGroupName = "SSIO2019"

$serverName = $resourceGroupName.ToLower()

$databaseName = "Contoso"

$poolName = "Contoso-Pool"

# Create a new elastic pool

New-AzSqlElasticPool -ResourceGroupName $resourceGroupName `

    -ServerName $serverName -ElasticPoolName $poolName `

    -Edition "Standard" -Dtu 50 `

    -DatabaseDtuMin 10 -DatabaseDtuMax 20
```

```
# Now move the Contoso database to the pool

Set-AzSqlDatabase -ResourceGroupName $resourceGroupName `

    -ServerName $serverName -DatabaseName $databaseName `

    -ElasticPoolName $poolName
```

This script creates a new pool named Contoso-Pool in the Standard tier and provides 50 total eDTUs. A single database will be assigned no less than 10 DTUs and no more than 20 DTUs. The parameters -Dtu, -DatabaseDtuMin and -DatabaseDtuMax have a list of valid values depending on the selected tier and one another.

Managing database space

The Azure SQL Database service manages the growth of the data and log files. For log files, the service also manages shrinking the log file. Data files are not automatically shrunk because of the potential impact on performance. Each pricing tier has an included maximum database size. When your database size approaches that maximum, you can choose to pay for extra storage space (up to a certain limit, again determined by the pricing tier) or scale your database up.

In some cases, the database data space may be allocated for your database, but may no longer be in use. This effect can be especially significant in elastic pools. If many databases in a single pool have a significant amount of unused space, the pool maximum size may be reached sooner than expected.

> ➤ The Microsoft Docs at *https://docs.microsoft.com/azure/sql-database/sql-database-file-space-management#understanding-types-of-storage-space-for-an-elastic-pool* discuss how to determine the amount of unused allocated space for all databases in a pool.

If you don't expect your databases to need the unused space, you might consider reclaiming that space. Beware of the need to rebuild indexes after shrinking and the fact that rebuilding indexes will cause the data file to grow again to some extent. All other caveats related to shrinking database files and rebuilding indexes apply. If you decide to shrink the database file, use the standard T-SQL statement:

```
DBCC SHRINKDATABASE ('Contoso');

-- Rebuild all indexes!
```

> ➤ See Chapter 8, "Maintaining and monitoring SQL Server," for information on rebuilding indexes.

NOTE

As with on-premises SQL Server databases, Azure SQL Database supports auto-shrink. There are no valid reasons to enable auto-shrink.

Security in Azure SQL Database

As with many cloud services that fall in the PaaS category, there are certain security operations that are handled for you by the cloud provider. As it relates to security in Azure SQL Database, this includes patching the OS and the database service.

Other aspects of security must be managed by you, the cloud DBA. Some of these aspects, such as Transparent Data Encryption (TDE) are shared with on-premises SQL Server 2019. Others are specific to Azure SQL Database and include firewall configuration, access control, and auditing and threat detection. We discuss these features of Azure SQL Database in the upcoming sections. Microsoft's commitment regarding Azure SQL Database is to not differentiate the pricing tiers with security features. All the features discussed in this section are available in all pricing tiers, though some features incur additional charges.

Security features shared with SQL Server 2019

An important security consideration is access control. Azure SQL Database implements the same permission infrastructure that's available in SQL Server 2019. This means that database and application roles are supported, and you can set very granular permissions on database objects and operations using the Data Control Language (DCL) statements GRANT and REVOKE. Refer to Chapter 12 for more information.

TDE is on by default for any new database. This hasn't always been the case, so if your database has been around for a long time, you should verify whether it is turned on. When TDE is on for a database, not only are the database files encrypted, but the geo-replicated backups are also encrypted. You will learn more about backups in the "Preparing Azure SQL Database for disaster recovery" section later in this chapter. TDE is covered in Chapter 13.

Other security features shared with SQL Server 2019 are dynamic data masking, row-level security, and Always Encrypted. Chapter 13 looks at these features in detail.

Server and database-level firewall

A server is accessed using an FQDN, which maps to a public IP address. To maintain a secure environment, managing firewall entries to control which IP addresses can connect to the logical server or database is a requirement.

> **NOTE**
> You can associate a server with a Virtual Network offering enhanced network security when other Azure resources in the same VNet connect. Managed instances are currently always associated with a Virtual Network.

When creating a new server using the Azure portal, you might choose to allow any Azure resource through the server-level firewall. This appears convenient, but it leaves the server open to unauthorized connection attempts from an attacker who merely needs to create an Azure service such as a web app. Servers created using other methods—for example, PowerShell—do not have any default firewall rules, which means any connection attempt is refused until at least one firewall rule is created.

Database-level firewall rules take precedence over server firewall rules. After you have created database firewall rules, you can remove the server firewall rule(s) and still connect to the database. However, if one server will be hosting several databases that each need to accept connections from the same IP addresses, keeping the firewall rules at the server level might be more sensible. It is also convenient to keep server-level firewall rules in place for administrative access.

You can find server-level firewall rules in the virtual master database in the `sys.firewall_rules` catalog view. Database-level firewall rules are in the user database in the `sys.database_firewall_rules` catalog view. This makes the database more portable, which can be advantageous in combination with contained users. Especially when using geo-replication, which we discuss in the "Preparing Azure SQL Database for disaster recovery" section coming up later in this chapter, having portable databases avoids unexpected connection issues when failing-over databases to another server.

> ➤ You can learn more about contained databases in Chapter 12.

Setting the server-level firewall

You can create server-level firewall rules by using the Azure portal, PowerShell, Azure CLI, or T-SQL. As seen earlier, SQL Server Management Studio might prompt you to create a firewall rule when establishing a connection, though you would not use this method to create firewall rules for your application's infrastructure. To create a firewall rule, you need to provide the following:

- **Rule name.**   The rule name has no impact on the operation of the firewall; it exists only to create a human-friendly reminder about the rule. The rule name is limited to 128 characters. The name must be unique in the server.

- **Start IP address.**   This is the first IPv4 address of the range of allowed addresses.

- **End IP address.**   The end IPv4 address can be the same as the start IP address to create a rule that allows connections from exactly one address. The end IP address cannot be lower than the start IP address.

Inside OUT

How do you automate firewall rule management?

Managing the firewall rules in a dynamic environment can quickly become error-prone and resource intensive. For example, when databases on a server are accessed from numerous Azure Web App instances, which often scale up and down and out and in, the rules will need to be updated frequently. Rather than resorting to allowing any Azure resource to pass through the server-level firewall, you should consider automating the firewall rule management.

The first step in such an endeavor is to create a list of allowed IP addresses. This list could include static IP addresses, such as from your on-premises environment for management purposes, and dynamic IP addresses, such as from Azure Web Apps or Virtual Machines. In the case of dynamic IP addresses, you can use the Az PowerShell module to obtain the current IP addresses of Azure resources. After you build the list of allowed IP addresses, you can apply it by looping through each address, attempting to locate that IP address in the current firewall rule list, and adding it if necessary. In addition, you can remove any IP addresses in the current rule list that are not on your allowed list.

We must note that this is not always an option. There are Azure services for which it's not possible to obtain their IP addresses. One such example is Azure Data Factory, a data integration service. In those scenarios, you should review if those services can be joined to a virtual network where your server has an endpoint. If that feature is not available (yet), you will need to allow access from all Azure services or re-architect your solution to avoid using those services.

Using PowerShell, the New-AzSqlServerFirewallRule cmdlet provides the -AllowAllAzureIPs parameter as a shortcut to create a rule to allow all Azure services: you do not need to provide a rule name, start, or end IP address. Using the CLI, to create a server-level firewall rule that allows access from any Azure resource, you would create a rule using 0.0.0.0 as both the start and end IP address of the rule. You must provide a rule name for the command to work, but you'll find that in the Azure portal, the rule is not shown. Instead, the toggle switch is in the on position.

TROUBLESHOOTING

When SQL Server Management Studio offers to create a server-level firewall rule, you will need to sign in with an Azure AD user account whose default directory matches the directory that is associated with the subscription where the logical SQL server exists. If this is not the case, the creation of the firewall rule will fail with an HTTP status code 401 error.

Setting the database-level firewall

Configuring database-level firewall rules requires that you have already established a connection to the database. This means you will need to at least temporarily create a server-level firewall rule to create database-level firewall rules.

You can create and manage database-level firewall rules only by using T-SQL. Azure SQL Database provides the following stored procedures to manage the rules:

- **sp_set_database_firewall_rule.**   This stored procedure creates a new database-level firewall rule or updates an existing firewall rule.

- **sp_delete_database_firewall_rule.**   This stored procedure deletes an existing database-level firewall rule using the name of the rule.

The following T-SQL script creates a new database-level firewall rule allowing a single (fictitious) IP address and then updates the rule by expanding the single IP address to a range of addresses, and finally deletes the rule:

```
EXEC sp_set_database_firewall_rule N'Headquarters', '1.2.3.4', '1.2.3.4';

EXEC sp_set_database_firewall_rule N'Headquarters', '1.2.3.4', '1.2.3.6';

SELECT * FROM sys.database_firewall_rules;

EXEC sp_delete_database_firewall_rule N'Headquarters';
```

Integration with virtual networks

Azure SQL Database can be integrated with one or more virtual network subnets. By integrating a logical SQL server with a virtual network subnet, other resources in that subnet can connect to the server without requiring a firewall rule.

In addition to removing the need to create firewall rules, the traffic between these resources stays within the Azure backbone and does not go across public Internet connections at all, thereby providing further security and latency benefits.

Virtual network integration and the public endpoint of the Azure SQL server can simultaneously be used.

➤ Virtual networks are discussed in somewhat more detail in Chapter 16.

Access control using Azure AD

To set up single sign-on (SSO) scenarios, easier login administration, and secure authentication for application identities, you can turn on Azure AD authentication. When Azure AD authentication is turned on for a server, an Azure AD user or group is given the same permissions as the server admin login. In addition, you can create contained users referencing Azure AD principals. This means that user accounts and groups in an Azure AD domain can authenticate to the databases without needing a SQL login.

For cases in which the Azure AD domain is federated with an Active Directory Domain Services domain, you can achieve true SSO comparable to an on-premises experience. The latter case would exclude any external users or Microsoft accounts that have been added to the directory; only federated identities can take advantage of this. Furthermore, this also requires a client that supports it.

NOTE

The principal you set as the Active Directory admin for the server must reside in the directory that is associated with the subscription where the server resides. The directory that is associated with a subscription can be changed, but this might have effects on other configuration aspects, such as Role-Based Access Control, which we describe in the next section. If users from other directories need to access your SQL Server, add them as guest users in the Azure AD domain backing the subscription.

To set an Active Directory admin for a server, you can use the Azure portal, PowerShell, or Azure CLI. You use the PowerShell `Set-AzSqlServerActiveDirectoryAdministrator` cmdlet to provision the Azure AD admin. The `-DisplayName` parameter references the Azure AD principal. When you use this parameter to set a user account as the administrator, the value can be the user's display name or user principal name (UPN). When setting a group as the administrator, only the group's display name is supported.

Inside OUT

How do you set the Active Directory admin if the group's display name is not unique?

If the group you want to designate as administrator has a display name that is not unique in the directory, the optional `-ObjectID` parameter is required. You can retrieve the `ObjectID` from the group's properties in the Azure portal or via PowerShell using the `Get-AzADGroup` cmdlet.

NOTE

If you decide to configure an Azure AD principal as server administrator, it's always preferable to designate a group instead of a single user account.

After you set an Azure AD principal as the Active Directory admin for the server, you can create contained users in the server's databases. Contained users for Azure AD principals must be created by other Azure AD principals. Users authenticated with SQL authentication cannot validate the Azure AD principal names, and, as such, even the server administrator login cannot create contained users for Azure AD principals. Contained users are created by using the T-SQL CREATE USER statement with the FROM EXTERNAL PROVIDER clause. The following example statements create an external user for an Azure AD user account with UPN l.penor@contoso.com and for an Azure AD group Sales Managers:

```
CREATE USER [l.penor@contoso.com] FROM EXTERNAL PROVIDER;

CREATE USER [Sales Managers] FROM EXTERNAL PROVIDER;
```

By default, these newly created contained users will be members of the PUBLIC database role and will be granted CONNECT permission. You can add these users to additional roles or grant them additional permissions directly like any other database user. Chapter 12 has further coverage on permissions and roles.

TROUBLESHOOTING

Users are unable to connect using Azure AD credentials

The workstation from which users will connect must have .NET Framework 4.6 or later and the Microsoft Active Directory Authentication Library for Microsoft SQL Server installed. These prerequisites are installed with certain developer and DBA tools, but they might not be available on end-user workstations. If not, you can obtain them from the Microsoft Download Center.

Role-Based Access Control

All operations discussed thus far have all assumed that your user account has permission to create servers, databases, and pools and can then manage these resources. If your account is the service administrator or a co-administrator, no restrictions are placed on your ability to add, manage, and delete resources. Most enterprise deployments, however, will require more fine-grained control over permissions to create and manage resources. Using Azure Role-Based Access Control (RBAC), administrators can assign permissions to Azure AD users, groups, or service principals at the subscription, resource group, or resource level.

RBAC includes several built-in roles to which you can add Azure AD principals. The built-in roles have a fixed set of permissions. You also can create custom roles if the built-in roles do not meet your needs.

➤ You can find a comprehensive list of built-in roles and their permissions at *https://docs.microsoft.com/azure/active-directory/role-based-access-built-in-roles*.

Three of the built-in roles relate specifically to Azure SQL Database:

- **SQL DB Contributor.**   This role can primarily create and manage Azure SQL databases, but not any security-related settings. For example, this role can create a new database on an existing server and create alert rules.

- **SQL Security Manager.**   This role can primarily manage security settings of databases and servers. For example, this role can create auditing policies on an existing database, but cannot create a new database.

- **SQL Server Contributor.**   This role can primarily create and manage servers, but not databases or any security-related settings.

Note that the permissions do not relate to server or database access; instead, they relate to managing the resources in Azure. Indeed, users assigned to these RBAC roles are not granted any permissions in the database, not even the CONNECT permission.

> ### NOTE
> An Azure AD user in the SQL Server Contributor role can create a server and thus define the server administrator login's username and password. Yet, the user's Azure AD account does not get any permissions in the database at all. If you want the same Azure AD user to have permissions in the database, including creating new users and roles, you will need to use the steps in this section to set up the Azure AD integration and create an external database user for that Azure AD account.

Auditing

Azure SQL Database provides auditing and threat detection to carry out monitoring of database activity using Azure tools. In on-premises deployments, *extended events* are often used for monitoring. SQL Server builds upon extended events for its SQL Server Audit feature (discussed in Chapter 13). This feature is not present in Azure SQL Database in the same form, but a large subset of extended events is supported in Azure SQL Database.

> ➤ You can find more details about support for extended events at
> *https://docs.microsoft.com/azure/sql-database/sql-database-xevent-db-diff-from-svr.*

Azure SQL Database auditing creates a record of activities that have taken place in the database. The types of activities that can be audited include permission changes, T-SQL batch execution, and auditing changes themselves.

> ➤ Audit actions are grouped in audit action groups, and a list of audit action groups is available in the PowerShell reference for the Set-AzSqlDatabaseAudit cmdlet at
> *https://docs.microsoft.com/powershell/module/az.sql/set-azsqldatabaseaudit#parameters.*

NOTE

By default, all actions are audited. The Azure portal does not provide a user interface for selecting which audit action groups are included. Customizing the audited events requires using the PowerShell cmdlet or the REST API.

Auditing and advanced threat protection are separate but related features. Investigating alerts generated by advanced threat protection is easier if auditing is enabled. Auditing is available at no charge, but there is a monthly fee per server for activating Advanced Data Security.

You can turn on auditing at the server and database level. When auditing is turned on at the server level, all databases hosted on that server are audited. After you turn on auditing on the server, you can still turn it on at the database level, as well. This will not override any server-level settings; rather, it creates two separate audits. This is not usually desired, though in environments with specific compliance requirements that only apply to one or a few databases on a single server, this can make sense. These compliance requirements might include a longer retention periods or additional action groups that must be audited.

Auditing events are stored in an Azure storage account or sent to Azure Monitor via a Log Analytics workspace or Event Hub. The latter two options are in preview at the time of writing, and their configuration is beyond the scope of this book. When storing events in a storage account, the account must be in the same region as the server. This is a sensible requirement; you would not want to incur data transfer charges for the audit data or deal with the latency of such a transfer. Many types of storage accounts are supported, but not Premium. The storage account must also not be deployed in a VNet or behind a firewall.

Configuring auditing to a storage account

To configure auditing, you need to create or select an Azure storage account. We recommend that you aggregate logging for all databases in a single storage account. When all auditing is done in a single storage account, you will benefit from having an integrated view of audit events.

You also need to decide on an audit log retention period. You can choose to keep the audit logs indefinitely or you can select a retention period. The retention period can be at most 3,285 days, or about nine years.

The following PowerShell script sets up auditing for the Contoso database on the ssio2019 server:

```
$resourceGroupName = "SSIO2019"

$location = "southcentralus"

$serverName = $resourceGroupName.ToLower()

$databaseName = "Contoso"
```

```
# Create your own globally unique name here

$storageAccountName = "azuresqldbaudit"

# Create a new storage account

$storageAccount = New-AzStorageAccount -ResourceGroupName $resourceGroupName '

    -Name $storageAccountName -Location $location -Kind Storage '

    -SkuName Standard_LRS -EnableHttpsTrafficOnly $true

# Use the new storage account to configure auditing

$auditSettings = Set-AzSqlDatabaseAudit '

    -ResourceGroupName $resourceGroupName '

    -ServerName $serverName -DatabaseName $databaseName '

    -StorageAccountResourceId $storageAccount.Id -StorageKeyType Primary '

    -RetentionInDays 365 -BlobStorageTargetState Enabled
```

The first cmdlet in the script creates a new storage account with the name `azuresqldbaudit`. Note that this name must be globally unique, so you will need to update the script with a name of your choosing before running the script. Storage account names can contain only lowercase letters and digits.

> ➤ For more details on the `New-AzStorageAccount` cmdlet, see
> *https://docs.microsoft.com/powershell/module/az.storage/new-azstorageaccount*.

The second cmdlet, `Set-AzSqlDatabaseAudit`, configures and turns on auditing on the database using the newly created storage account. The audit log retention period is set to 365 days.

NOTE
To set auditing at the server level, use the `Set-AzSqlServerAudit` cmdlet. This cmdlet uses the same parameters, except that you'll leave out the `–DatabaseName` parameter.

Viewing audit logs from a storage account

There are several methods that you can use to access the audit logs. The method you use largely depends on your preferences as well as the tools that you have available on your workstation. We discuss some of the methods in this section in no particular order.

> ➤ You can find a full list of methods to access the audit logs at
> *https://docs.microsoft.com/azure/sql-database/sql-database-auditing#subheading-3*.

If your goal is to quickly review recent audit events, you can see the audit logs in the Azure portal. In the Auditing blade for a database, click View Audit Logs to open the Audit records blade.

This blade shows the most recent audit logs, which you can filter to restrict the events shown by the latest event time or that show only suspect SQL injection audit records. This approach is rather limited because you cannot aggregate audit logs from different databases, and the filtering capabilities are minimal.

A more advanced approach is to use SQL Server Management Studio. SQL Server Management Studio 17 and later support opening the audit logs directly from Azure storage. Alternatively, you can use the Azure Storage Explorer to download the audit logs and open them using older versions of SQL Server Management Studio or third-party tools. The audit logs are stored in the sqldbauditlogs blob container in the selected storage account. The container follows a hierarchical folder structure: logicalservername\DatabaseName\SqlDbAuditing_AuditName\ yyyymmdd. The blobs within the date folder are the audit logs for that date (in Coordinated Universal Time [UTC]). The blobs are binary extended event files (.xel).

NOTE

Azure Storage Explorer is a free and supported tool from Microsoft. You can download it from *https://azure.microsoft.com/features/storage-explorer/.*

After you have obtained the audit files, you can open them in SQL Server Management Studio. On the **File** menu, click **Open**, and then click **Merge Audit Files** to open the **Merge Audit Files** dialog box, as shown in Figure 17-3.

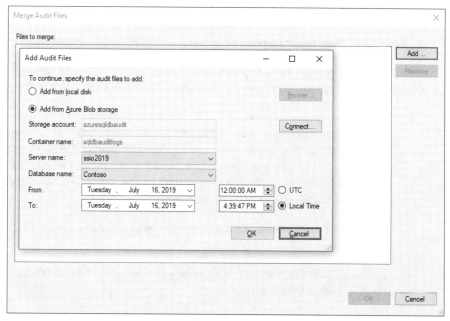

Figure 17-3   SQL Server Management Studio 17 and later support opening and merging multiple Azure SQL Database audit files directly from an Azure storage account.

A third way of examining audit logs is by using the `sys.fn_get_audit_file` T-SQL function. You can use this to perform programmatic evaluation of the audit logs. The function can work with locally downloaded files or you can obtain files directly from the Azure storage account. To obtain logs directly from the Azure storage account, you must run the query using a connection to the database whose logs are being accessed. The following T-SQL script example queries all audit events logged to the azuresqldbaudit storage account from July 16, 2019, for the Contoso database on the ssio2019 server:

```
SELECT * FROM sys.fn_get_audit_file ('https://azuresqldbaudit.blob.core.windows.net/
sqldbauditlogs/ssio2019/Contoso/SqlDbAuditing_Audit/2019-07-16/', default, default);
```

➤ You can find more information on the `sys.fn_get_audit_file` function at *https://docs. microsoft.com/sql/relational-databases/system-functions/sys-fn-get-audit-file-transact-sql*.

The output from the T-SQL function can be visualized and analyzed using Power BI. To get started, a sample Power BI dashboard template is available for download from the Microsoft Tech Community. Using the template, you only need to provide the server name, storage account name, and credentials. You can use the template as is or customize it. The template can be used directly in the free Power BI Desktop tool. You might also choose to publish it to your organization's Power BI service.

➤ The template and a walkthrough on using it are available on the Microsoft Tech Community at *https://techcommunity.microsoft.com/t5/Azure-Database-Support-Blog/ SQL-Azure-Blob-Auditing-Basic-Power-BI-Dashboard/ba-p/368895*.

Advanced Data Security

Advanced Data Security is the collective name for three services that are enabled at the logical server level and apply to all databases on that server. These three services are:

- **Data discovery and classification.**   Most databases contain sensitive data such as personally identifiable information (PII), healthcare data, or financial data. This service attempts to discover such data by examining column names and allows the DBA to classify data in any column according to a classification scheme. Provided auditing is enabled for the database, the audit log will include the classification or classifications of the columns that were accessed with each query.

- **Vulnerability assessment.**   This feature assesses your database against security best practices.

- **Advanced Threat Protection.**   This feature provides alerts when potentially malicious activity is detected in the database.

Data discovery and classification is briefly covered in Chapter 13. In the next two sections, you will learn more about vulnerability assessment and Advanced Threat Protection.

Understanding vulnerability assessment

Vulnerability assessment consists of a set of rules that are evaluated against one or more databases on the server. Optionally, you can schedule weekly automatic scans of all databases on the server. Unfortunately, at the time of writing, the schedule for these weekly scans is not customizable. This means the vulnerability scan can run at a time when your database is under heavy load. Fortunately, though the impact on compute utilization is measurable, the scan completes quickly.

Because not one size fits all when it comes to best practices, many of the rules can be configured with a custom baseline. By way of example, the rule that checks the membership in user-defined roles will fail if there is any user-defined role with any members. If your environment uses user-defined roles, you will need to review the current configuration and approve it as a baseline. Then, during the next scan, the rule will fail only if the membership is different from the baseline.

The value of vulnerability assessment is further enhanced by the actionable steps and, when appropriate, T-SQL scripts that are provided to remediate the failure. A scan itself will not modify the database or server automatically; the scan is read-only. However, with a single click, the suggested remediation script can be opened in the portal's online query editor.

CHAPTER 17

Inside OUT

Should you use SSMS or the Azure portal to conduct the vulnerability assessment?

Although SQL Server Management Studio has a built-in vulnerability assessment scanner, and the rule sets between SSMS and the Azure portal are the same, this section discusses configuring vulnerability assessment using the Azure portal as part of Advanced Data Security.

There is a difference in the evaluation that is conducted between both. In addition to examining the user databases, the periodic recurring scans that can be configured in the Azure portal also include the virtual master system database. Further, when configuring custom baselines for rules using SSMS, the baselines are stored in a folder local to the computer where SSMS is installed. Custom baselines approved in the portal are stored in the portal with the database metadata and are thus available to any user who runs or reviews vulnerability assessment scans.

Our recommendation is to take advantage of the periodic recurring scans in the Azure portal and examine the weekly reports. Customize the baselines as needed. In addition, administrators in highly regulated environments should consider running the vulnerability analysis also from SSMS, where the baselines can be stored locally or potentially in a source control system, for enhanced control.

➤ For directions on how to run a vulnerability assessment scan using SSMS, see *https://docs. microsoft.com/sql/relational-databases/security/sql-vulnerability-assessment*.

Configuring Advanced Threat Protection

Advanced Treat Protection examines the database activity for anomalies and alerts the Azure service administrators and co-administrators or a list of configured email addresses. There are five types of threats that can be detected:

- **SQL injection.**   This threat type detects the possible occurrence of a SQL injection attack.

- **SQL injection vulnerability.**   This type detects the possible existence of a SQL injection vulnerability due to faulty queries.

- **Data exfiltration.**   This type of threat is detected if an anomalous amount of data is extracted within an hour or using a single query, or if a database is backed up to an unusual location.

- **Unsafe action.**   Unsafe actions includes execution of potentially malicious SQL commands, such as xp_cmdshell.

- **Anomalous client login.**   This type detects logins that are unusual, such as from a geographic location from which a user has not previously signed in. This type also includes logins from unusual Azure data centers or logins from unfamiliar principals.

➤ Additional information about these threats is at *https://docs.microsoft.com/azure/ sql-database/sql-database-threat-detection-overview#advanced-threat-protection-alerts*.

You can turn off these threat types individually if you do not want to detect them.

The configuration of Advanced Threat Protection allows the DBA to specify one or more email addresses that should receive alerts. Optionally, subscription administrators and owners can also receive the alerts via email. DBAs should consider including the enterprise security team's alert address in the list for rapid triage and response.

➤ The Microsoft Docs at *https://docs.microsoft.com/azure/security-center/security-center- incident-response* provide elementary guidance on using the Azure Security Center for incident response.

Inside OUT

Which audit action groups should be turned on for Advanced Threat Protection to work?

Advanced Threat Protection no longer requires that auditing is turned on for the database or server, but auditing records will still provide for a better experiencing investigating detected threats. The audit records are used to provide context when Advanced Threat Protection raises an alert.

To effectively analyze threat detections, the following audit action groups are recommended: BATCH_COMPLETED_GROUP, SUCCESSFUL_DATABASE_ AUTHENTICATION_ GROUP, and FAILED_DATABASE_AUTHENTICATION_GROUP.

Turning on these groups will provide details about the events that caused the threat detection to alert.

Preparing Azure SQL Database for disaster recovery

Hosting your data on Microsoft's infrastructure does not mean that you can avoid preparing for disasters. Even though Azure has high levels of availability, your data can still be at risk due to human error and significant adverse events. Azure SQL Database provides default and optional features that will ensure HA for your databases when properly configured.

Understanding default disaster recovery features

Without taking any further action after provisioning a database, the Azure infrastructure takes care of several basic disaster recovery (DR) preparations. First among these is the replication of data files across fault and upgrade domains within the regional datacenters. This replication is not something you see or control, but it is there. This would be comparable to the on-premises use of Always On availability groups or storage tier replication. The exact method of replication of the database files within a datacenter depends on the chosen tier. We discussed this in Chapter 16 in the "Selecting a pricing tier and service objective" section. As Azure SQL Database evolves, the methods Microsoft employs to achieve local HA are of course subject to change.

Regularly scheduled backups are also configured by default. A full backup is scheduled weekly, differential backups take place every few hours, and transaction log backups every 5 to 10 minutes. The exact timing of backups is managed by the Azure fabric based on overall system workload and the database's activity levels. These backups are retained for a period of seven days (by default, and the maximum for the Basic service tier) to 35 days (maximum).

You can use these backups to restore the database to a point-in-time within the retention period. You also can restore a database that was accidentally deleted to the same server from which it was deleted. Remember: deleting a server irreversibly deletes all databases and backups. You should generally not delete a server until the backup retention period has expired, just in case. After all, if Advanced Data Security is turned off, there is no cost associated with a server without databases.

You also can restore databases to another Azure region. This is referred to as a geo-restore. This restores databases from backups that are geo-replicated to other regions using Azure Storage replication. If your database has TDE turned on, the backups are also encrypted.

Although these default features provide valuable DR options, they are likely not adequate for production workloads. For example, the Estimated Recovery Time (ERT) for a geo-restore is less than 12 hours with a Recovery Point Objective (RPO) of less than one hour. Further, the maximum backup retention period is 35 days for the Standard and Premium tiers, and only seven days for the Basic tier. Some of these values are likely unsuitable for mission-critical databases, so you should review the optional DR features in the next sections and configure those as needed to achieve an acceptable level of risk for your environment.

Manually backing up a database

In addition to the automatic, built-in backup discussed in the preceding section, you might have a need to back up a database manually. This might be necessary if you need to restore a database in an on-premises or IaaS environment. You might also need to keep database backups for longer than the automatic backups' retention period, though we encourage you to read the "Using Azure Backup for long-term backup retention" section later in the chapter to understand all options for long-term archival.

The term "backup" is inappropriate because the method to create a manual backup is exporting the database to a BACPAC file. (You can read more about BACPAC files in Chapter 4, "Installing and configuring SQL Server instances and features." A significant difference between a database backup and an export is that the export is not transactionally consistent. During the data export, Data Manipulation Language (DML) statements in a single transaction might have completed before and after the data in different tables that were extracted. This can have unintended consequences and can even prevent you from restoring the export without dropping foreign key constraints.

Azure SQL Database can, however, provide you with a transactionally consistent export using a three-step procedure: first, make a copy of the database. The copy is guaranteed to be transactionally consistent. Then, export the copy. Because no applications are accessing this copy, no data manipulation is taking place during the export. Finally, delete the copy to avoid incurring continued charges. You can perform this procedure by using the Azure portal, but because it involves multiple steps, and some steps can be long-running, it lends itself perfectly to using a PowerShell script.

A database export's destination is an Azure blob, so a storage account is required. The following script determines a name for the database copy based on the existing database and the current time:

```
# Set variables

$resourceGroupName = "SSIO2019"

$location = "southcentralus"

$serverName = $resourceGroupName.ToLower()

$databaseName = "Contoso"

# Create a name for the database copy

$d = (Get-Date).ToUniversalTime()

$databaseCopyName = "$databaseName-Copy-" + ($d.ToString("yyyyMMddHHmmss"))

# The storage account name must be globally unique; replace it with your own name

$storageAccountName = "azuresqldbexport"

# Ask interactively for the server admin login username and password

$cred = Get-Credential

# Create a new Azure storage account

$storAcct = New-AzStorageAccount -ResourceGroupName $resourceGroupName `

-Name $storageAccountName -Location $location `

-SkuName Standard_LRS

# Get the access keys for the newly created storage account

$storageKey = Get-AzStorageAccountKey -ResourceGroupName $resourceGroupName `

   -Name $storageAccountName

# Create a database copy - this copy will have the same tier as the original

# If your database is an elastic pool, add the -ElasticPoolName parameter

$newDB = New-AzSqlDatabaseCopy -ResourceGroupName $resourceGroupName `

   -ServerName $serverName -DatabaseName $databaseName `

   -CopyDatabaseName $databaseCopyName

# Prepare additional variables to use as the storage location for the BACPAC
```

```
$containerName = "mydbbak"

$container = New-AzStorageContainer -Context $storAcct.Context -Name $containerName

$bacpacUri = $container.CloudBlobContainer.StorageUri.PrimaryUri.ToString() + "/" + `
    $databaseCopyName + ".bacpac"
# Initiate a database export of the database copy - see Firewall troubleshooting
$exportRequest = New-AzSqlDatabaseExport -ResourceGroupName $resourceGroupName `
    -ServerName $NewDB.ServerName -DatabaseName $databaseCopyName `
    -StorageKeytype StorageAccessKey -StorageKey $storageKey[0].Value `
    -StorageUri $bacpacUri `
    -AdministratorLogin $cred.UserName -AdministratorLoginPassword $cred.Password
# Run a loop while the export is progressing
Do {
    $exportStatus = Get-AzSqlDatabaseImportExportStatus `
        -OperationStatusLink $ExportRequest.OperationStatusLink
    Write-Host "Exporting... sleeping for 5 seconds..."
    Start-Sleep -Seconds 5
} While ($exportStatus.Status -eq "InProgress")
# Delete the copied database to avoid further charges
Remove-AzSqlDatabase -ResourceGroupName $resourceGroupName `
    -ServerName $serverName -DatabaseName $databaseCopyName
```

First, a new storage account is created in the same Azure region as the database server to avoid cross-region traffic charges. The script then creates the database copy on the same database server. Next, the new storage account is used for the export of the database copy. The export operation is asynchronous, so a loop is used to wait for completion of the export. Finally, when the export is completed, the database copy is deleted. As in previous scripts, the storage account name you create must be globally unique, so change the value of the variable in the script before running it.

This script produces several lines of output. At the end of the script, if everything was successful, you can use the Azure Storage Explorer to access the new storage account and download the BACPAC file for further use. Alternatively, you can leave the BACPAC file in Azure Storage and use related commands to import the database file later, should a restore become necessary.

TROUBLESHOOTING

BACPAC exports require a firewall rule to allow all Azure services

The Azure SQL Database Export Service, which is used to export to a BACPAC file, can run anywhere in the Azure region of the source database server. Because the IP address of the host running the service is not known in advance, you will need to open the server firewall to allow all Azure IP addresses to access the server. For more information, review the "Server and database-level firewall" section earlier in this chapter.

Enabling zone redundant configuration

Applicable only to the Premium and Business Critical (with Gen5 hardware) tiers, zone redundant configuration is an optional setting that will distribute the default high availability nodes between different data centers in the same region. Zone redundant configuration provides fault tolerance for several classes of failures that would otherwise require geo-replication to handle.

Unlike geo-replication, which is discussed in the next section, there is no change to the connection string required if a single data center suffers an outage.

There is no additional cost associated with this feature, so your decision to enable it is entirely based on the workload's ability to accept a few extra milliseconds of latency before transactions commit.

> ➤ Additional information about zone redundant configuration is in the Microsoft Docs at *https://docs.microsoft.com/azure/sql-database/ sql-database-high-availability#zone-redundant-configuration.*

Zone redundant deployments increase the service-level agreement's availability guarantee from the normal 99.99% to at least 99.995%.

Configuring geo-replication

If your disaster recovery needs are such that your data cannot be unavailable for a period of up to 12 hours, you will likely need to configure geo-replication. When you geo-replicate a database, there are one or more active secondary databases to which all transactions are replicated. Geo-replication takes advantage of the Always On feature also found in on-premises SQL Server.

You can configure geo-replication in any pricing tier and any region. To configure geo-replication, you will need to provision a server in another region, though you can do this as part of the configuration process if you are using the Azure portal.

In the event of a disaster, you would be alerted via the Azure portal of reliability issues in the datacenter hosting your primary database. You would then need to manually failover to a secondary database. Using geo-replication only, there is no automatic failover (but keep reading to learn about failover groups, which do provide automatic failover capability). Failover is accomplished by selecting (one of) the secondary database(s) to be the primary.

Because the replication from primary to secondary is asynchronous, an unplanned failover can lead to data loss. The RPO for geo-replication, which is an indicator of the maximum amount of data loss expressed as a unit of time, is five seconds. Although no more than five seconds of data loss during an actual disaster is a sound objective, when conducting DR drills, no data loss is acceptable. A planned change to another region, such as during a DR drill or to migrate to another region permanently, can be initiated as a planned failover. A planned failover will not lead to data loss because the selected secondary will not become primary until replication is completed.

Unfortunately, a planned failover cannot be initiated from the Azure portal. The PowerShell cmdlet Set-AzSqlDatabaseSecondary with the -Failover parameter and without the -AllowDataLoss parameter will initiate a planned failover. If the primary is not available due to an incident, you can use the portal (see Figure 17-4) or PowerShell to initiate a failover with the potential for some data loss, as just described. If you have multiple secondaries, after a failover, the new primary will begin replicating to the remaining available secondaries without a need for further manual configuration.

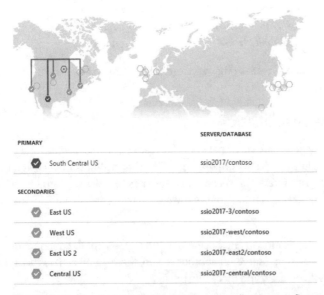

PRIMARY		SERVER/DATABASE
✓	South Central US	ssio2017/contoso

SECONDARIES		
✓	East US	ssio2017-3/contoso
✓	West US	ssio2017-west/contoso
✓	East US 2	ssio2017-east2/contoso
✓	Central US	ssio2017-central/contoso

Figure 17-4   The Azure portal showing geo-replication configured with the maximum of four secondaries. The recommended region for geo-replication, North Central US, is indicated using the purple hexagon. There is no replica hosted in that region.

CHAPTER 17

NOTE

When you first configure geo-replication using the Azure portal, the UI will inform you of the recommended region for the geo-replicated database. You are not required to configure the secondary in the recommended region, but doing so will provide optimal performance for the replication between regions. The recommendation is based on Microsoft's knowledge of connectivity between its datacenters in different regions.

For each secondary database, you will be charged the same hourly charges as a primary database, with the same pricing tier and service objective. A secondary database must have the same pricing tier as its primary, but it does not need to have the same service objective or performance level. For example, a primary database in the Standard tier with service objective S2 can be geo-replicated to a secondary in the Standard tier with service objective S1 or S3, but it cannot be geo-replicated to a secondary in the Basic or Premium tier.

To decide whether your service objective for secondaries can be lower than that of the primary, you will need to consider the read-write activity ratio. If the primary is write-heavy—that is, most database operations are writes—the secondary will likely need the same service objective to be able to keep up with the primary. However, if the primary's utilization is mostly toward read operations, you could consider lowering the service objective for the secondary. You can monitor the replication status in the Azure portal or use the PowerShell `Get-AzSqlDatabaseReplicationLink` cmdlet to ensure that the secondary can keep up with the primary.

CAUTION

If one or more secondary databases cannot keep up with the rate of change at the primary database, the primary database will be throttled to allow all secondaries to catch up.

As of this writing, geo-replication introduces a limitation on the scalability of databases. When a primary database is in a geo-replication relationship, its pricing tier cannot be upgraded (for example, from Standard to Premium) without first upgrading all secondaries. To downgrade, you must downgrade the primary before any secondaries can be downgraded. As a best practice, when scaling up or down, you should make sure that the secondary database has the higher service objective longer than the primary. In other words, when scaling up, scale up secondary databases first; when scaling down, scale down secondary databases second.

Inside OUT

What are other uses for geo-replication?

The judicious configuration of geo-replication and application programming can make it possible for you to downgrade your primary Azure SQL database to a lower service objective. Because secondaries are readable, you can use them to run read-only queries. By directing some of the read queries, such as for reporting or data integration purposes, to secondary databases, fewer resources may be used by the primary.

In addition to potentially lowering service objective requirements, you also can use active geo-replication during application upgrades and to move a database to another server or region with minimal downtime.

Setting up failover groups

As discussed in the previous section, geo-replication represents a very capable option for DR planning. Geographically distributing relational data with an RPO of five seconds or less is a goal that not many on-premises environments can achieve. However, the lack of automatic failover and the need to configure failover on each database individually creates overhead in any deployment, whether it has a single database in a shop with a single DBA or many hundreds or thousands of databases. Further, because a failover causes the writable database to be hosted on a different logical server with a different DNS name, connection strings must be updated, or the application must be modified to try a different connection.

Failover groups build on top of geo-replication to address these shortcomings. Configured at the server level, a failover group can include one, multiple, or all databases hosted on that server. All databases in a group are recovered simultaneously. By default, failover groups are set to automatically recover the databases in case of an outage, though you can turn this off. With automatic recovery turned on, you need to configure a grace period. This grace period offers a way to direct the Azure infrastructure to emphasize either availability or data guarantees. By increasing the grace period, you are emphasizing data guarantees because the automatic failover will not occur if it would result in data loss until the outage has lasted as long as the grace period. By decreasing the grace period, you are emphasizing availability. In practical terms, this means that if the secondary database in the failover group is not up to date after the grace period expires, the failover will occur, resulting in data loss.

When you configure a failover group, two new DNS CNAME records are created. The first CNAME record refers to the read-write listener and it points to the primary server. During a failover, this record is updated automatically so that it always points to the writable replica. The read-write listener's FQDN is the name of the failover group prepended to database.windows. net. This means that your failover group name must be globally unique. The second CNAME record points to the read-only listener, which is the secondary server. The read-only listener's DNS name is the name of the failover group prepended to secondary.database.windows.net. If the failover group name is ssio2019, the FQDN of the read-write listener will be ssio2019. database.windows.net and the FQDN of the secondary will be ssio2019.secondary.database.windows.net.

NOTE

As of this writing, a failover group can have only one secondary. For high-value databases, you should still configure additional secondaries to ensure that HA isn't lost in case of a failover.

You can create failover groups with existing geo-replication already in place. If the failover group's secondary server is in the same region as an existing geo-replication secondary, the existing secondary will be used for the failover group. If you select a region for the failover secondary server where no replica is yet configured, a new secondary server and database will be created during the deployment process. If a new secondary database is created, it will be created in the same tier and with the same service objective as the primary. You will recall that these replicas incur service charges.

Unlike with geo-replication, the Azure portal supports initiating a planned failover for failover groups. You can also initiate a planned failover by using PowerShell. Planned failovers will not cause data loss. Both interfaces also support initiating a forced failover, which, as with geo-replication's unplanned failover, can lead to data loss within the five-second RPO window.

Inside OUT

How can you effectively provision auditing and Advanced Data Security with geo-replication?

When configuring auditing for geo-replicated databases, you should configure auditing at the server level on both the primary and secondary server. You should not turn on auditing at the database level. By configuring auditing at the server level, the audit logs will be stored in the same region as the server, thereby avoiding cross-region traffic.

As a side effect of configuring auditing on the secondary databases' server, you can set a different retention period, though we do not recommend this configuration, because valuable correlations between events on the primary and secondary can be lost. As described in the security section, you can use SQL Server Management Studio to merge audit files from different servers and databases to analyze them together.

You should apply the same configuration for Advanced Data Protection.

NOTE

DR and business continuity planning should not just consider the Azure SQL Database resources, but also other Azure services your application uses. These other services might include Azure Web Apps, Virtual Machines, DNS, storage accounts, and more. You can find more information on designing highly available services that include Azure SQL Database at *https://docs.microsoft.com/azure/sql-database/ sql-database-designing-cloud-solutions-for-disaster-recovery*.

Using Azure Backup for long-term backup retention

To meet compliance and regulatory requirements, you might need to maintain a series of long-term database backups. Azure SQL Database can provide a solution using long-term retention (LTR). You can elect to have full backups retained for a maximum of ten years. The retained backups are stored in Azure blob storage, which is created for you; you don't need to provide a storage account.

Long-term backup retention is configured at the server level, but databases on the server can be selectively included or excluded. To begin, you create a retention policy. As its name indicates, the retention policy determines how long the backups are retained. After you configure retention, the next full backups meeting the criteria for weekly, monthly or yearly will be retained. In other words, existing backups are not included in the long-term retention. A different retention period can be specified for weekly, monthly, and yearly full backups. You can also choose a simpler configuration, choosing to keep only some of the backups.

NOTE

For more information on creating a vault as well as step-by-step guidance, see *https://docs.microsoft.com/azure/sql-database/ sql-database-long-term-backup-retention-configure*.

When a database is deleted, you will continue to be charged for the backups contents; however, the charges will decrease over time as backup files older than the retention period are deleted.

You can configure long-term backup retention by using the Azure portal or PowerShell. Although only primary or standalone databases are backed up, and will therefore be the only databases that have backups added to storage, you should also configure long-term backup retention on geo-replicated secondaries. This ensures that in case of a failover, backups from the new primary database will be added to its vault, without further intervention. After a failover, a full backup is immediately taken and that backup is added to long-term storage. Until a failover takes place, no additional costs are incurred for configuring retention on the secondary server.

NOTE

When the server hosting a database is deleted, the database backups are immediately and irrevocably lost. This also applies to long-term backup retention. For as long as the logical SQL server is around, you will be able to restore a database up to the retention period, even if the database itself was deleted. We should stress again that there is no cost to keeping a logical SQL server around, so exercise restraint and caution before deleting servers.

Provisioning Azure SQL Database managed instance

Azure SQL Database managed instance is a managed instance of SQL Server running in Azure. It is designed with almost full compatibility with the latest SQL Server engine. It offers easy migration from on-premises installations. Designed specifically to offer 99.99% availability with minimal management, this offering fills a space in Azure that is not available to organizations using strictly on-premise solutions.

What is a Managed Instance?

A Managed Instance is a Platform as a Service (PaaS) offering for SQL Server. It has nearly a 100% compatibility with the current Enterprise edition of the Database Engine. Azure SQL Database managed instance includes benefits such as automatic patching, version updates, automated backups, and high availability that come with a PaaS offering. This allows for an easy lift and shift from on-premises to the cloud with minimal to no application or database changes. The isolation and security of your Managed Instance is protected with native VNET and Private IP addresses.

It is also important when choosing a managed instance to understand what it is not. Managed instance is not an alternative for the SQL Server services. SQL Server Integration Services (SSIS) cannot be used in a managed instance in the traditional way. SSIS packages can be used with an integration run time in conjunction with Azure Data Factory, a PaaS offering, to create the same functionality. SQL Server Analysis Services (SSAS) needs to be a separate PaaS, and SQL Server Reporting Services (SSRS) needs to be replaced with either Power BI or SSRS IaaS. A managed Instance is intended for a traditional OLTP workload, but not to replace the other SQL Server services.

Although the majority of items that make up a managed instance are similar to the latest version of SQL Server, there are a few things that make it different as well.

Differences between SQL Server on-premises and in a Managed Instance

When assessing the benefits of a Managed Instance, it is important to compare like servers and services. The Managed Instance benefits from always being up to date in the cloud, which means that some features in on-premises SQL Server may be either unnecessary or have alternatives. There are also specific cases when a particular feature works in a slightly different way.

High Availability

High availability is built in and pre-configured using technology similar to Always On Availability Groups. If you currently use Always On you will find there are a number of statements that are not supported including:

- Create Endpoint for database Mirroring

- Create Availability group

- Alter Availability group

- Drop Availability group

- Set HDR clause of the Alter database statement

There are a few features used in Managed instances to ensure high availability that are different from on-premises.

- INSTANCE_LOG_GOVERNOR wait is a resource governor constraint that slows down logging to ensure replicas do not get out of sync. Index rebuilds, for example, are an activity that can be affected by this governor.

- HADR_DATABASE_FLOW_CONTROL and HADR_THROTTLE_LOG_RATE_SEND_RECV are waits that you will see if the secondary's get behind. They will slow the primary to prevent data loss.

SSIS, SSRS, and SSAS usage

Managed instance supports SQL Server Integration Services (SSIS) and can host SSIS catalog (SSISDB) that store SSIS packages, but they are executed on a managed Azure-SSIS Integration Runtime in Azure Data Factory (ADF). For details on how to use this see the Microsoft docs at *https://docs.microsoft.com/azure/data-factory/create-azure-ssis-integration-runtime*.

- To compare the SSIS features in Azure SQL Database at *https://docs.microsoft.com/azure/data-factory/create-azure-ssis-integration-runtime#comparison-of-a-sql-database-single-database-elastic-pool-and-managed-instance*.

- SQL Server Analysis Services (SSAS) needs to be a separate PaaS and SQL Server Reporting Services (SSRS) needs to be replaced with either Power BI or SSRS IaaS. A managed Instance is intended for a traditional OLTP workload and not to replace the other SQL Server services.

General Differences

Managed instance and an on-premises SQL Server have a few general differences that should be considered. These are behavior changes that can affect your decision on using a managed instance or how you use it.

- All Managed Instance databases use full recovery model to guarantee high availability and no data loss. If you're on-premises database is in simple or bulk logged mode, you may find the Managed Instance slower for bulk logged operations.

- Transparent Data Encryption is on by default with a Managed Instance and that will affect performance. This can be turned off, but if any of the database in an instance is encrypted, tempdb will still be encrypted, so there will be at least some impact to all databases.

Time to provision

One of the limitations we see with Managed Instance is the delay in provisioning. It can take many hours to provision a Managed Instance. This can be reduced by using the same subnet when provisioning additional Managed Instances, since a large portion of the time to create the Managed Instance is in the provisioning of the subnet. There is no way to save that time when you first provision an instance. However, the limitations on how many Managed Instances you can have in a subnet can be an issue as well.

Backups and Restores

Backups from a Managed Instance can only be restored to another Managed Instance, not to an on-premises SQL Server, a single database, or an elastic pool without using a workaround method. There is no backup and restore to an on-premise native option in a managed instance. Managed Instances have automatic backups, which means the Managed Instance takes care of the backup for you, but it also means that you cannot take your own Differential, Log, File, Tape, or file snapshot backup. There are a couple of ways to get data back to an on-premises database for testing. The work arounds for this are to take a copy only backup or backup to a URL. In addition to this you can use the copy activity in Azure Data Factory. It has a number of supported data stores and formats. They are all listed at *https://docs.microsoft.com/azure/data-factory/copy-activity-overview#supported-data-stores-and-formats*.

There is a limitation of 32 stripes for the Managed Instance backup and a stripe size of 195GB. Your backup will not be restored when using the restore method for managed instance if your

.bak file has any features that are not supported by Managed Instance. Backups containing databases that have active In-memory objects cannot, for example, be restored to a General-Purpose managed instance.

Managed Instance does not allow specifying full physical paths, so all corresponding scenarios have to be supported differently: RESTORE DB does not support WITH MOVE, CREATE DB doesn't allow physical paths, and BULK INSERT works with Azure Blobs only. The limitations on Managed Instance are related to the specific use case of how they are intended to be used and what the managed instance was designed to do. For example, the Restore DB command does not support WITH Move because it should never be needed. The location of the database is handled by the Managed Instance.

Security

Managed Instance provides most of the same security features of the latest SQL Server on-premises Enterprise edition. It limits access in an isolated environment and uses identity authentication (Azure AD and SQL Authentication). Additional security features can be enabled, such as data masking and encryption, as well as additional authorization with role-based memberships and permissions enforced. There are a few items to draw your attention to, which may determine if a managed solution will work for your solution. The "Security" section in this chapter has more information on the details of the security options, but there are some limitations that may determine if the product is a fit for your architectural needs. Additional information about managing instances and database security can be found in Chapter 12, "Administering security and permissions."

Certificates

Managed instances do not access file shares or Windows folders. So you cannot create from, or backup to a file share for certificates, nor can you backup or create from a file or assembly. Details on how to handle certificates can be found at *https://docs.microsoft.com/sql/t-sql/ statements/create-certificate-transact-sql?view=sql-server-ver15*.

Azure Active Directory access

A managed instance needs permissions to read Azure Active Directory (AAD) to do tasks, such as authenticate users in security groups or create new users. Each managed instance starts with a single server administrator account that is the administrator of the managed instance. This is set up during or after provisioning, with an admin SQLServer account. It is called the Azure AD admin and has sysadmin permissions and creates AAD and SQL logins in the master database for the managed instance.

A second SQL Server administrator must be created, which is an Azure AD account. This account is called the Azure AD server principal and it's created as a contained database user in the master database. As administrators, the server administrator accounts are members of the db_owner role in every user database, entering each user database as the dbo user.

For additional information on how to create Azure AD server principal logins for managed instances see the detailed instructions in Microsoft docs at *https://docs.microsoft.com/azure/sql-database/sql-database-managed-instance-aad-security-tutorial#create-an-azure-ad-server-principal-login-for-a-managed-instance-using-ssms.*

NOTE

The Azure Active Directory principle is relatively new and only shows in SSMS at version 18.0.

Azure Active Directory Database principals are created at the database level. This account can be either a user or a group. It does not have to be an administrator, but it must be configured to use Azure Active Directory to connect Azure Active Directory accounts to the Azure SQL Database. Windows logins are not supported, and Azure Active Directory users should be used instead. Both server principals and admin accounts can overlap in permissions. The server principal takes precedence in the event of a conflict.

Additional details can be found later in this chapter in the "Security of Managed Instance" section.

Configurations differences

There are several configurations to note with Managed Instances that are different from the latest SQL Server engine:

- Buffer pool extensions are not supported.

- Compatibility levels below 100 are not supported.

- Database mirroring is not supported.

- Instant file initialization is not supported.

- Multiple log files are not supported.

- In memory is a Business-Critical tier only feature.

- SQL Server Agent is always running.

- *FILESTREAM* and FileTable are not supported.

- DBCC undocumented statements that are enabled in SQL Server do not function.

- Session level trace flags are not supported.

- Elastic Transactions are not supported.

- PolyBase, R, and Python external libraries and tables are not supported.

- Linked server is supported for SQL Server and Azure SQL Database targets only.

- Cross instance service broker is not supported.

- Extended stored procedures are not supported.

- Managed instance automatically manages XTP filegroup and files for databases containing In-Memory OLTP objects.

- Xp_cmdshell is not supported.

- TempDB on the General tier cannot exceed 24GB.

- TempDB is always split into 12 data files; the size per file cannot be changed and new files cannot be added.

There are several features and syntax that cannot be used in a managed instance, because those features are handled by the instance automatically and therefore are not relevant and can't be changed. A list of them can be found here:

- *https://docs.microsoft.com/azure/sql-database/ sql-database-features#sql-server-feature-support-in-azure-sql-database.*

- *https://docs.microsoft.com/azure/sql-database/sql-database-managed-instance-transact- sql-information#stored-procedures-functions-and-triggers.*

As of the writing of this book, there are a number of known issues with managed instances and they are being resolved quickly by the Microsoft engineering team. This is normal with any product, and one of the values of using a product like Managed Instance is that Microsoft's impetus is to correct and then apply bug fixes rapidly for its large customer base.

You can keep up with the latest bugs and workarounds in Microsoft Docs at *https://docs.microsoft.com/azure/sql-database/ sql-database-managed-instance-transact-sql-information#Issues.*

Creating a managed instance

A managed instance can be created either through the portal or by using PowerShell, but they can only be created in supported regions. When creating a managed instance (MI) for the first time it is highly recommended that you use the portal. The portal steps make it simple, directing you in which v-nets to use and to ensure you have all of the necessary items before starting the deployment. A list of those regions can be found at *https://azure.microsoft.com/global-infrastructure/services/?products=sql-database&regions=all.*

An additional managed instance limitation is subscription types. A managed instance is supported only for the following subscription types.

- Enterprise Agreement (EA)

- Pay-as-you-go

- Cloud Service Provider (CSP)

- Enterprise Dev/Test

- Pay-As-You-Go Dev/Test

- Subscriptions with monthly Azure credit for Visual Studio subscribers

Selecting a pricing tier and service objective

Managed Instance is based on the VCore purchasing model. The intent of it is to make for an easier transition from on-premises machines, or IaaS in Azure, to independently choose to scale out compute and storage. There are two different service tiers for managed instances: General Purpose and Business Critical.

1. *General Purpose* tiers are for balanced usage with scalable compute and storage options. High availability is built in based on Azure blob storage and Azure Service Fabric.

2. *Business Critical* tiers are typically for applications with high I/O requirements that offer minimal impact due to maintenance operations. It offers the highest resilience to failures by using isolated replicas. High availability is built-in and is based on a technology similar to Always On availability groups and Azure Service Fabric. It has additional read-only replicas that can be used for reporting or other read-only workloads. Additional features include In-memory OLTP and SSD storage for increased performance.

All service tiers guarantee 99.99 % availability and independently scale size and compute.

NOTE

If you need guaranteed high availability higher than 99.99%, with no impact on maintenance operations and outages, there are other options beyond managed instances. Additionally, if the ability to handle critical servicing tasks, planned, and unplanned events is critical to your business, you should look at Chapter 17, "Provisioning Azure SQL Database," for options outside of managed instance.

All options have hardware choices where you can choose the generation of hardware, and your options as of the writing of this book are:

- **Gen4**:   Up to 24 logical CPUs based on Intel E5-2673 v3 (Haswell) 2.4-GHz processors, vCore = 1 PP (physical core), 7 GB per core, attached SSD.

- **Gen5**:   Up to 80 logical CPUs based on Intel E5-2673 v4 (Broadwell) 2.3-GHz processors, vCore = 1 LP (hyper-thread), 5.1 GB per core, fast eNVM SSD.

For additional details on the different service-tiers, go to *https://docs.microsoft.com/azure/sql-database/sql-database-managed-instance-resource-limits#service-tier-characteristics.*

With software assurance from your on-premises offering, you can exchange existing licenses for discounted rates on a managed instance using Azure Hybrid Benefit for SQL Server at *https://azure.microsoft.com/pricing/hybrid-benefit.*

Provisioning a managed instance from the portal

Once the decision is made that Managed Instance is the best platform for your needs, the next step is provisioning. It is highly recommended that you use the portal for provisioning until you fully understand the experience, particularly the networking aspects because the portal automates much of it for you and limits the number of issues that can arise.

The following instructions can help you complete the task of creating a managed instance through the portal:

- From the show portal menu, choose + Create A Resource.

- In the search box type **managed instance** and choose the Azure SQL Instance option when displayed.

- Select the create box, displaying the steps necessary to complete the creation of the managed instance.

- The basics step includes all of the minimum required information to provision a managed instance. It requires a subscription (see previous note on available subscriptions) and a resource group. There is an option to create a new resource group.

- Further down the page are the details that are needed, including the managed instance name, region, compute and storage. The portal guides you in the requirements for naming but not in what you will need for compute and storage. If you choose Configure Managed Instance inside the compute and storage section, you will go to another screen that will allow for customization of options and additional choices. This is also where you note you have your own license, an option that can save you money as the license is automatically included in a managed instance.

- The final section of the basics is setting up the Administrator account. This can be any valid name, which is checked for in the portal, however the name "serveradmin" is a reserved server-level role and cannot be used as an administrator account here.

- The next section is networking. This section defines the level of access and connection type. You can define your virtual network and public end points here.

- Start by creating a virtual network. If you have a compliant virtual network it can be found in the list. Otherwise it is recommended to create a new one.

- Choose a connection type to accelerate application access. The default value is proxy, however, it is recommended to use redirect. With proxy all connections are proxied via the Azure SQL Database gateways, which means to enable connectivity the client must have outbound firewall rules that allow only the IP address of the Azure SQL Database gateway port 1433. Although it is easier to set up, it is recommended that the redirect option is used for improved performance. The improvement comes with extra set up. The clients establish connections directly to the node hosting the database, which requires outbound firewall rules to all Azure IP address in the region using Network Security Groups (NSG) with service tags for ports 11000-11999, not just the Azure SQL Database gateway. This allows packets to go to the database directly and reduces latency and improves through-put and therefore performance.

- The last part of networking is the public end point option. By default for security, the public endpoint is not enabled, as it allows access to the managed instance without a VPN and there can be a security risk. Once enabled you get the option of choosing from Azure Services, Internet, and no access. Ideally you would use the no access and enable only specific endpoints as needed. See these options for scenarios that may benefit from enabling a public end point at *https://docs.microsoft.com/azure/sql-database/sql-database-managed-instance-public-endpoint-securely*.

- Additional Settings on the next tab is where you choose a collation if you need to change the default, change the time zone, or setup geo-replication. Geo-replication is used to create a secondary managed instance as the failover group secondary. This step allows you to choose an already setup Primary to use and will allow the new instance to join the DNS of the primary you picked. After the secondary the following steps still need to be completed. Create a VPN between the primary and secondary. Setup inbound and out-bound NSG rules and create an auto failover group between the two instances.

NOTE

Creating a Managed Instance can take many hours. On average you can expect six hours for the first instance with subsequent instances in the same pool being quicker. The VNet set up is usually what takes the time. If you have errors in your setup it has been known to take up to 24 hours to notify you of the issue. Don't cancel the operation simply because it takes longer than you expect. Regardless of how long a process takes it is best to let the process fail on its own if it is going to fail, given how it makes the following steps simpler. If provisioning takes longer than 36 hours it is likely because the process failed and it is doing a roll back. Allowing the process to roll back will save many hours fixing, troubleshooting, and determining how to get back to a clean start.

Provisioning a managed instance using PowerShell

Creating a Managed Instance using PowerShell and the Azure Resource Manager template (ARM) requires you to have pre-created a valid v-net and subnet where you can deploy your

Managed Instance. It is beneficial to use PowerShell or ARM templates if you are deploying more than one managed instance and it's only recommended once you have some experience with it. It can take a long time for the process to complete and for you to find out you have missed a step or made a mistake. At minimum, it is highly recommended to complete at least one managed instance deployment in a test environment before attempting this to ensure you understand all the steps and pieces that are needed for the deployment.

V-net and subnet creation

Networking and specifically the v-net and subnet configuration have been a challenge for Managed Instance users. Often times it is the missed configuration of the v-net that causes the managed instance to not provision. To remedy this, managed instance is transitioning from manual to service-aided subnet configuration. The subnet configuration is now automated for you and will reduce many of the issues previously encountered. Managed instance now has service-aided subnet configuration, giving users full control of data traffic while managed instance takes full responsibility to ensure uninterrupted flow of the management traffic to ensure it can meet its SLA. This noted it is still possible to create your own subnet inside the virtual network. If you choose to do this, ensure you use a dedicated subnet. The subnet can't contain any other cloud services associated with it, and it can't be a gateway subnet. The subnet can't contain any resource other than the managed instance, and you can't later add other types of resources in the subnet. The managed instance's subnet needs to be delegated to the Microsoft.SQL/managedInstance resource provider. For additional details about virtual networks see *https://docs.microsoft.com/azure/sql-database/ sql-database-managed-instance-create-vnet-subnet*.

Delegating a subnet to an Azure service allows that service to establish basic network configuration rules for that subnet, which help operate their instances in a stable manner. It also provides full control to the customer on managing the integration of the Azure services into their virtual networks. A network security group (NSG) needs to be associated with the managed instance's subnet. You can use an NSG to control access to the managed instance's data endpoint by filtering traffic on port 1433 and ports 11000-11999 when managed instance is configured for redirect connections. Services will automatically add rules required to allow uninterrupted flow of management traffic. A list of these can be found at *https://docs.microsoft.com/azure/sql-database/sql-database-managed-instance-connectivity- architecture#mandatory-inbound-security-rules-with-service-aided-subnet-configuration*. A user defined route table (UDR) needs to be associated with the managed instance's subnet. You can add entries to the route table to route traffic that has on-premises private IP ranges as a destination through the virtual network gateway or virtual network appliance (NVA). You will need to ensure entries are added to allow an uninterrupted flow of management traffic. You can see the entries needed at *https://docs.microsoft.com/azure/sql-database/sql-database- managed-instance-connectivity-architecture#user-defined-routes-with-service-aided-subnet- configuration*. Service endpoints can be used to configure virtual network rules and storage accounts that keep backups and audit logs.

➤ Pre-creating the VNet requires you to properly size the subnet for the Managed Instance because it cannot be resized after you put resources inside it.

Once the VNet is installed, you can complete the installation using the Azure cloud shell as described at *https://docs.microsoft.com/azure/sql-database/scripts/sql-managed-instance-create-powershell-azure-resource-manager-template#open-azure-cloud-shell*.

Once you have the pre-requisites and networking set up you can create a Managed Instance either with PowerShell or an ARM Template. For PowerShell: *https://docs.microsoft.com/azure/sql-database/scripts/sql-database-create-configure-managed-instance-powershell*.

To create the managed instance using ARM templates: *https://docs.microsoft.com/azure/sql-database/scripts/sql-managed-instance-create-powershell-azure-resource-manager-template*.

Here are instructions for creating a Managed Instance using the portal: *https://docs.microsoft.com/azure/sql-database/sql-database-managed-instance-get-started*.

Establishing a connection

Once you have created your Managed Instance, consider how you will connect to it. The most secure and common way of connecting to the managed instance is via a subnet, whether that is a Gateway subnet for your on-premises solutions, web app frontend subnet, or IaaS apps subnet. Figure 18-1 provides an overview of the more common communication architectures.

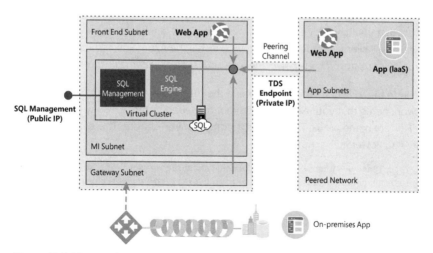

Figure 18-1 Managed Instance Connections Diagram.

Creating the endpoints via the portal

The recommended way to create the Public and Private endpoints shown in Figure 18-1 is to do it during the creation of the Managed instance itself. It was briefly mentioned in the section on "Provisioning a Managed Instance from the Portal" that you can define your Public and Private endpoints in the networking section. It is in that section on networking that you can define the Public endpoint under the section called "Connection type." The default, Proxy, is recommended to use redirect mode because this enables direct connectivity to managed instance resulting in improved latency and throughput. This is ideal for peer-to-peer networking and use with other Azure services. The Public endpoint is the step directly after the connection type, allowing you to enable a public end point for the ability to connect to your managed instance from the Internet without using a VPN. It uses TDS only.

If you did not choose these during your managed instance you can still do it manually following the direction in the Microsoft docs at *https://docs.microsoft.com/azure/sql-database/sql-database-managed-instance-public-endpoint-configure*.

Creating the VPN Gateway via PowerShell

Native virtual network implementation and connectivity to your on-premises environment will need a VPN Gateway. To complete this Microsoft has a handy PowerShell script available at *https://docs.microsoft.com/azure/sql-database/sql-database-managed-instance-configure-p2s#attach-a-vpn-gateway-to-your-managed-instance-virtual-network*.

Creating a VPN Gateway to the managed instance VNet is best done from your client machine.

Ensure that you have PowerShell 5.1 and Azure PowerShell 1.4.0 or newer installed on your on-premises client. Instructions for how to install the Azure PowerShell module can be found at *https://docs.microsoft.com/powershell/azure/install-az-ps#install-the-azure-powershell-module*.

To create the VPN gateway, you will need the subscription Id, resource group, and a virtual network name that you used to create your managed instance. You will also need to create a certificate name prefix. The prefix is a string that you choose. These items are used in the following PowerShell script:

```
$scriptUrlBase = 'https://raw.githubusercontent.com/Microsoft/sql-server-samples/master/
samples/manage/azure-sql-db-managed-instance/attach-vpn-gateway'
$parameters = @

{

  subscriptionId = '<subscriptionId>'
  resourceGroupName = '<resourceGroupName>'
  virtualNetworkName = '<virtualNetworkName>'
  certificateNamePrefix  = '<certificateNamePrefix>'
  }
```

```
Invoke- -ScriptBlock ([Scriptblock]::Create((iwr ($scriptUrlBase+'/attachVPNGateway.
ps1?t='+ [DateTime]::Now.Ticks)).Content)) -ArgumentList $parameters, $scriptUrlBase
```

This code will create and install the required certificates on the client machine. It will calculate the IP subnet range needed for the gateway and then create the gateway. Finally, the script will deploy the Azure Resource Manager template that attaches the VPN Gateway to the VPN subnet.

If you prefer to create the VPN using the portal you can find those instructions in the Microsoft docs at *https://docs.microsoft.com/azure/sql-database/sql-database-managed-instance-configure-p2s#create-a-vpn-connection-to-your-managed-instance.*

Once you have completed the VPN connection and your TDS endpoints are ready to use, there are three main ways to connect to it.

1. Connect from an on-premises computer, sometimes called a point-to-site connection.

2. Connect from a Virtual Machine (VM); the process is different if your VM is an Azure VM or an on-premises VM.

3. Connect applications from any location.

Connect from an on-premises computer

Connecting from an on-premises computer is sometimes called a point-to-site connection. To connect using SSMS (most recent version) start with making a connection to the VPN from your on-premises machine. From the network and Internet go to VPN, then choose your managed instance Vnet to choose the connection. If prompted for an elevated privilege, choose to elevate and continue to make the connection.

When connecting using SSMS remember to use the fully qualified host name of the Managed Instance in the Server name box (see Figure 18-2).

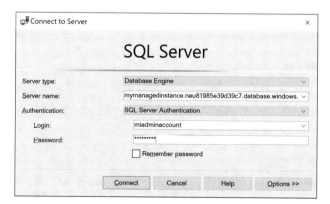

Figure 18-2 Creating the VPN Gateway.

Connect from a Virtual Machine (VM)

When connecting to a Managed Instance from a Virtual Machine (VM), the process is different if your VM is an Azure VM or an on-premises VM.

Azure VM connections

For an Azure VM connection the connection is over a private IP to the TDS using a VM in a subnet separate to the one created for the managed instance. The VNet used to create the managed instance cannot be used, because it is dedicated to the managed instance. You will need to create an additional subnet in the managed instance VNet to put the VM in if you do not already have one. Direction on how to do this can be found at *https://docs.microsoft.com/ azure/sql-database/sql-database-managed-instance-configure-vm#create-a-virtual-machine-in-the-new-subnet-in-the-vnet.*

Once you have the subnet details, create a VM in this subnet. Direction on how to add the virtual machine can be found at *https://docs.microsoft.com/azure/sql-database/sql-database-managed-instance-configure-vm#create-a-virtual-machine-in-the-new-subnet-in-the-vnet.*

Wait until the connection is completed, then you will need to ensure the VM is set up to allow a remote desktop connection, as shown at *https://docs.microsoft.com/azure/sql-database/ sql-database-managed-instance-configure-vm#connect-to-virtual-machine.*

VM from on-premises

For the VM on-premises the method of connection is a bit different because you need to attach a VPN gateway to the managed instance. This is easily done with the script in the previous section, "Creating the VPN Gateway via PowerShell." This script creates and installs the certificates on the client machine, calculates the VPN gateway subnet range, creates the subnet for the gateway, and deploys the ARM (Azure Resource Manager) template that attaches the VPN gateway to the VPN subnet that you need for access. You can also find the instructions on Microsoft docs at *https://docs.microsoft.com/azure/sql-database/sql-database-managed-instance-configure-p2s#attach-a-vpn-gateway-to-your-managed-instance-virtual-network.*

Connect to applications

Applications can be connected to managed instances regardless of where they are hosted. In the cloud, on-premise, or a hybrid option, with Managed Instance you can choose what is best for your application. There are many options to choose from to connect.

Applications in the Cloud

- An application inside the same V-net is the simplest, since even if they are in separate subnets, they can connect with the correct connection string making this the simplest way.

- An application inside a different VNet is useful if you have VNets in different subscriptions because this method works for that scenario. This has two options: Azure Virtual Network peering is the preferable method because it uses the backbone Microsoft network so there are no latency issues between the peered VNets. The draw back to this is that the VNets have to be in the same region. If that is not an option, there is always the VNet to VNet using a VPN gateway.

Applications on-premises

- An on-premises application can be done through a private IP using either a site-to-site VPN connection or ExpressRoute. An ExpressRoute is a service that lets you create a private connection to your on-premises location. More information on Express Routes can be found at *https://docs.microsoft.com/azure/expressroute/expressroute-introduction*.

- An application on a developer's machine is the same as the point-to-site connection and was covered earlier in the "Creating the VPN Gateway via PowerShell" section, and in the "Connect from an on-premises computer" section.

- On-premises with Vnet peering can work when the VPN gateway is installed in a separate virtual network and a subscription from the managed instance where the networks are peered. This should be used only in special cases and details on how to set it up can be found in Microsoft docs at *https://docs.microsoft.com/azure/sql-database/sql-database-managed-instance-connect-app#connect-from-on-premises-with-vnet-peering*.

- An Azure app service hosted application is accessed using a private IP. If using your app service requires a gateway, that gateway subnet must be created outside the Managed Instance Vnet. This is different from the classic set up for on-premises gateways. In this situation the gateway must go through the peering channel.

Review the networking options and connections needed here to find the option that is best for your organization: *https://docs.microsoft.com/azure/sql-database/sql-database-managed-instance-connect-app*.

Migrating data to managed instance

Managed Instance targets the migration scenario, from Infrastructure as a Service (IaaS), or from on-premises. In both cases you will want to bulk move your data. There are two options for you to choose from the backup and restore method or Data Migration Service. Each has their own benefits as outlined in this section.

Data Migration Service

The Azure Database Migration Service is a managed service designed to enable migrations to Azure Data platforms with minimal downtime. This includes managed instance, but is not limited to it, so it can also be used for third party databases, and SQL Server databases to be

CHAPTER 18

moved to Azure SQL Database (single databases, or pooled databases in elastic pools) and SQL Server in an Azure VM. The third party databases that are supported for the online migration method are RDS SQL and Oracle.

There are online and offline migrations, depending on your business' tolerance for down time. It is recommended you do a trial run with the offline migration to determine what your downtime will be before you decide on which method to use. Keep in mind that using the Azure Database Migration Service for online migrations requires using the Premium pricing tier.

Whether you use online or offline migration, be sure to create your Azure Database Migration Service in the same region as the Managed Instance you are migrating to. This will prevent errors, cut down the down time or migration time, and limit any movement of data across regions or geographies.

To do an offline migration you can follow the steps at
https://docs.microsoft.com/azure/dms/tutorial-sql-server-to-managed-instance.

To do an online migration you can follow these steps at
https://docs.microsoft.com/azure/dms/tutorial-sql-server-managed-instance-online.

There are several prerequisites. It is recommended that you review them before you begin. They can be found within the tutorial or directly at *https://docs.microsoft.com/azure/dms/ tutorial-sql-server-managed-instance-online#prerequisites*.

➤ Chapter 19, "Migrating to SQL Server solutions in Azure" has a section on Data Migration Service.

NOTE

For online migrations using Azure Database Migration Service do not append multiple backups into a single backup media. Ensure instead that each backup is on a separate backup file. You will need both a backup and a subsequent log backup on the share that is used.

Backup and restore

The backup and restore method of migration leverages the simplicity of moving SQL backups to Azure Blob storage or backup directly to it. Backups in Azure blob storage can be directly restored into a managed instance using the traditional T-SQL restore command. The important part to remember is that the backup file must have been previously uploaded and secured with a Shared access signature (SAS) key. Details on how to do this are covered in Chapter 10, "Developing, deploying, and managing data recovery."

```
RESTORE DATABASE { database_name | @database_name_var }
FROM URL = { 'physical_device_name' | @physical_device_name_var } [ ,...n ] ;
```

Here n can be up to 64 backup devices separated in a comma delimited list.

NOTE

The restore option on Managed Instance is asynchronous. Should your connection to your managed instance be lost or your Internet connection to it goes down, your operation continues. You can check the status of the operations with sys.dm_operation_status:

```
SELECT * FROM sys.dm_operation_status
            WHERE major_resource_id = 'myddb'
 ORDER BY start_time DESC;
```

Backups from a Managed Instance can only be restored to another Managed Instance, not to an on-premises SQL Server, a single database, or an elastic pool.

The version of SQL Server you take your backup from is important as well. Backups from SQL 2012 SP1 CU2 and prior can only be directly uploaded as .bak files. For those greater than SQL 2012 SP1 CU2 a direct backup using the depreciated "WITH CREDENTIAL" syntax will work, and for 2016 and above you will want to backup direct using the "WITH SAS CREDENTIAL."

If you are restoring a Transparent Data Encryption database using native restore, make sure you migrate the certificate first before you do the restore. This is done the same way should you have to move your certificate on-premises.

Inside OUT

Can you use backup and restore to get the settings from the system databases?

System database restores are not supported with Managed Instance. It is recommended that you script out the system databases out and run them on the destination instance independently of your backup and restore processes if needed.

Deleting a managed instance

Deleting a managed instance is a basic command: DELETE. *https://management.azure.com/ subscriptions/{subscriptionId}/resourceGroups/{resourceGroupName}/providers/Microsoft.Sql/ managedInstances/{managedInstanceName}?api-version=2015-05-01-preview.*

Use Delete followed by a space and then the URL above with all the items in the curly braces resolved with the names of your managed instance items. This is simple when the Managed instance is working correctly. Issues arise when a Managed Instance is not correctly created, and you want to begin again. To avoid issues with deleting the instance, ensure you do not cancel a deployment. Complex challenges arise when deployments are only partially complete, and they are far more difficult to fix after the fact.

CHAPTER 18

If the above does not resolve your issue, review your networking. Check the "Networking Provisioning" section in this chapter to confirm that you have the requirements set up correctly. Then try again. Do not try to delete a subnet before the Managed Instance.

Network requirements for managed instances

The dedicated subnet has already been mentioned for the managed instance in the "Establishing a connection" section, however, it is important enough to mention separately as it is an area that commonly causes issues. The network architecture is for connectivity as well as directing traffic to the managed instance. The important parts to remember are that the managed instances must be inside a subnet that is dedicated to managed instances and provides that ability to make the connections you need.

NOTE

Subnets can take a long time to create or configure. It is not uncommon for this process to take 24 hours or more if an issue arises as it needs to roll back the process before you are notified. To prevent issues when creating managed instances, do not cancel a creation. Let the creation fail on its own if there is an issue; do not cancel it.

One of the most common challenges with a managed instance are those related to networking. You can prevent these by ensuring you meet the requirements in the following sections before you begin provisioning any instances.

Subnet

Managed instances need a dedicated subnet that is not a gateway subnet. The subnet can only house managed instances. The subnet cannot be shared with other resources.

Network Security Group

The Network Security Group (NSG) that is associated with the managed instance must define the inbound and outbound security rules before any other rules. If you are doing transactional replication in your managed instance and have a publisher or distributor, you will need to open port 445 (outbound) as well to allow access to the Azure file share.

NOTE

It is important to note that there should be only one inbound rule for ports 9000, 9003, 1438, 1440, 1452, and one outbound rule for ports 80, 443, 12000. These are TCP management endpoint ports. Managed instance provisioning through Azure Resource Manager deployments will fail if inbound and outbound rules are configured separately for each port. If these ports are in separate rules, the deployment will fail with a "VnetSubnetConflictWithIntendedPolicy" error. Although these ports are open for Manager end points for NSG, they have a Managed Instance built in firewall at the network level for security.

User Defined Route table

A User Defined Route (UDR) table that's associated with the virtual network must include specific entries at *https://docs.microsoft.com/azure/sql-database/ sql-database-managed-instance-connectivity-architecture#user-defined-routes.*

Endpoints

Managed instances should not have service end points. Make sure this option is disabled when you create the virtual network.

IP addresses

Managed instances require 16 IP addresses, and a minimum (does not allow for scale out) of 32 are recommended. As Managed Instance VNet can use up to 256 IP addresses, the number of Managed Instances that can be deployed in a single subnet depends on the subnet range. A subnet with the prefix /27 or below is recommended.

Inside OUT

Why do Managed Instances need so many IP addresses?

When a Managed Instance is created, a number of virtual machines are created in addition to your primary instance during provisioning. How many depends on the tier you choose. They are used to ensure high availability during regular operations as well as service maintenance. This is all done behind the scenes for you, but they require the IP addresses to complete.

Managed Instance administration features

It is the Managed Instances services that enable Database administrator to spend less time on administrative tasks that make the Managed Instance such an attractive option. The following services are either simplified for the administrator or handled completely, saving time and the need for the expertise.

High Availability

Managed Instance offers 99.99% up time without concern for maintenance and upgrade outages. This is accomplished by using something called retry logic in your apps. Retry logic essentially is code that can retry the call when a transient fault occurs. A transient fault occurs when Azure dynamically reconfigures servers for a heavy workload and can cause clients to lose their connection. It is recommended that the client program have retry logic so that it can reestablish the connection (ideally with a 5 second delay, growing up to 60 with each retry). This delay is called back-off logic and is to ensure that the database does not get overwhelmed in a retry situation with many connections.

High Availability for managed instance is achieved by employing two models for price options based on your tolerance for degradation during maintenance. If you can tolerate some degradation, then there is a model that uses a simple separation of compute and storage. For workloads that can not have that type of impact there is a cluster model that uses a quorum of engine nodes and can guarantee very minimal impact during maintenance. As with many PaaS instances there are continuous upgrades, and this potential impact is something to strongly consider when choosing tiers when installing the managed instance.

General purpose tier

This tier leverages the separation of compute and storage. This contains two layers: the stateless compute layer runs the SQL Server engine process and contains the cached data on SSD for things like TempDB, Plan cache, and buffer pool. This is operated by the Azure Service Fabric and controls the health of the node and performs any failovers. The stateful layer contains the database files that are stored in blob storage with built-in redundancy to guarantee the data in case of a failure.

When a failure or upgrade occurs the Azure Service Fabric moves the stateless process to a different node. The blob storage in the stateful layer is not affected. The data and log files are attached to the newly initialized SQL Server. This is when this tier can experience degradation as this transition occurs and the instance starts with an initialized cache. As mentioned earlier Managed Instance does not use instant file initialization, so it is important to understand all the aspects that can affect your degradations.

Business critical tier

This tier integrates the SQLServer engine and the storage into a single node and uses replication to additional nodes to create a three or four node cluster. The database files are on SSD storage to improve IO and high availability is achieved by using technology similar to the Always On Availability Groups seen on-premise. For more information on Always On Availability Groups see Chapter 11, " Implementing high availability and disaster recovery."

The cluster includes a single primary, and up to three secondary replicas. To ensure durability the primary writes each transaction to at least one secondary before committing the transaction. This durability grantees there is always a node to fail over to incase of a crash on the primary. Should a crash occur, the failover is initiated by the Azure Service Fabric. When a new primary is created another node is set and an additional replica is created to ensure quorum and the connections are redirected to the new primary.

> ## Inside OUT
>
> ### Can you have your Managed Instance in multiple zones?
>
> Zone redundancy can be achieved by placing replicas in different availability zones in the same region to eliminate a single point of failure from a control ring or datacenter outage without making changes to your applications. This can also be useful for regular reporting if you are using one of the secondary replicas as a read scale-out and place a replica closer to the users that will need it. Note that the added distance in the replicas can increase the latency and commit time so there may be an impact to performance. This feature has no added cost and can be changed with an online operation.

Replication

Managed Instance uses transactional replication to replicate data to another instance database, a SQL Server, database, a single database in Azure, or a pooled database in an Azure SQL database elastic pool. A managed instance can host a publisher, distributor and subscriber database. Common configurations can be found at *https://docs.microsoft.com/azure/sql-database/sql-database-managed-instance-transactional-replication#common-configurations*.

For the Managed Instance to be a publisher and or distributor there are a few requirements.

- The instance cannot participate in geo-replication.

- The publisher, distributor, and subscriber all must be on the same virtual network or have VNet peering set up between all three networks.

- The authentication used between all parties must be SQL Authentication and the replication working directory must be an Azure Storage Account share and set up using TCP outbound port 445 in the security rules of NSG.

- Bidirectional or one-way replication are both supported; however, updatable subscriptions are not.

> **NOTE**
>
> Single databases and pooled databases in Azure SQL Database can only be subscribers.
>
> Details on how to set up replication set by step can be found at *https://docs.microsoft.com/azure/sql-database/ replication-with-sql-database-managed-instance#1---create-a-resource-group*.

Scaling up or down

Manage Instances use vCores that allow you to define the CPU cores and configure the storage capacity you need for your instance within each tier. All databases in the managed instance share these resources. The storage and CPU can be scaled up or down as needed within the limits of the service tier, however, it does cause a downtime, and for this reason it is important to scale your resources appropriately. Keep in mind that managed instances cannot be turned off and on like other resources at will, and over provisioning will be an added cost.

Note that as you change tiers there are differences between the tiers that can affect the change. For example, if downgrading from critical to standard, the backup retention period is different. If a database exceeds the threshold database size, then extra storage costs will apply. If you are upgrading to a higher tier, you must explicitly increase the size.

Automated backups

Managed Instance uses automated backups. This service creates full backups every week, differential backups every 12 hours, and transaction log backups every 5-10 minutes. The specific frequency is based on the compute size and amount of database activity. The backups are stored in storage blogs and replicated to another data center for protection against data center outages or disasters. The default backup retention is 7 days for the general-purpose tier and up to 35 days for Business Critical.

> **NOTE**
>
> If you reduce your retention period by changing tiers or modifying them, then all backups older than the new retention period are no longer available.

The options to restore are:

Restore to a point in time.   This can be a copy in the same or a different managed instance, but must be under the same subscription.

Restore a deleted database.   This must be restored to the managed instance the backup was taken from.

Restore to a new region.   This creates a new database in any existing server anywhere in the world and is used in case of a geographic disaster.

Restore from a specific long-term backup.   This works only if a long-term policy has been set.

Azure SQL Analytics

Managed Instance is included in the services that access Azure SQL Analytics. Azure SQL Analytics is a monitoring tool for performance. It collects and visualizes performance metrics and has built-in intelligence for trouble shooting. The metrics help you customize monitoring rules, alerts and identify issues. This cloud-only solution can be used in conjunction with other single or pooled databases to be looked at individually or collectively and across subscriptions. The service is found in the Log Analytics workspace. Details on how to set it up can be found at *https://docs.microsoft.com/azure/sql-database/sql-database-metrics-diag-logging#configure-streaming-of-diagnostics-telemetry-for-managed-instances.*

Security of Managed Instance

Security for Managed Instance is provided by a number of different features, including Azure Active Directory, multifactor authentication, and authorization.

Azure Active Directory (Azure AD)

Azure AD enables Microsoft services to integrate with centrally managed identities and permissions to enhance security. Combined with Multi-factor authentication you can increase data security and still support a single sign-on process for easy use. For details on how to set up Multi-factor authentication see this link at *https://docs.microsoft.com/azure/sql-database/sql-database-ssms-mfa-authentication-configure*. If using a hybrid option or you need to connect to legacy or on-premises applications, Azure AD can also be an on-premises Active Directory Domain Service that is federated with the Azure AD. The benefits of this centralized authentication include:

1. Provides an alternative to native SQL Server authentication.

2. Discourages the creation of multiple user identities across database servers.

3. Allows centralized and simple password changes.

4. Allows for external (Azure AD) groups.

5. Enables integrated Windows authentication and other forms of authentication supported by Azure Active Directory.

CHAPTER 18

6. Azure AD authentication uses contained database users to authenticate identities at the database level.

7. Azure AD supports token-based authentication for applications connecting to Azure SQL Database.

8. Azure AD authentication supports ADFS (domain federation) or native user/password authentication for a local Azure Active Directory without domain synchronization.

9. Azure AD supports Multi-Factor Authentication (MFA) when using SSMS.

10. Azure AD supports Active Directory Interactive Authentication when using SQL Server Data Tools (SSDT). Active Directory Integrated Authentication connects to the Managed Instance by using identities. This is similar to the connection from a federated domain.

Access control using Azure AD

Azure Active Directory (AAD) is slightly different for Managed Instances compared to Azure Data Warehouse or Azure SQL database. It is critical that the subscription associated with Active directory and the Managed Instance are the same. An Azure Active Directory (AAD) administrator is needed to read AAD. This also allows the administrator to complete authentication of users through security group membership, or creation of new users, a task that can only be executed by Global/Company administrator in Azure AD. Once you have provisioned an Azure AD admin for your Managed Instance, you can create Azure AD server logins.

Detailed steps to complete this can be found at *https://docs.microsoft.com/azure/sql-database/sql-database-aad-authentication-configure#provision-an-azure-active-directory-administrator-for-your-managed-instance.*

Azure Active Directory set-up

Managed Instance is most often used to replace a traditional SQL Server installation, so it is natural that it supports the traditional SQL server Database engine logins and logins integrated with Azure Active Directory (AAD). Azure Active Directory server principals, previously called logins, are the Azure version of on-premises database logins in your SQL Server. These let you specify users and groups from your Azure Active Directory tenant (think AD Groups on-premises). They are capable of any instance-level operation, including cross-database queries within the same managed instance. To create the login for these specific server-level principals in conjunction with the Azure AD, a new option has been created for the CREATE LOGIN syntax that is relevant for server-level principals mapped to Azure AD accounts only and when left out creates the traditional SQL login. The new option is (FROM EXTERNAL PROVIDER).

When FROM EXTERNAL PROVIDER is specified the login_name must represent an existing Azure AD account that is accessible in Azure AD by the current Managed Instance.

> ## Inside OUT
>
> ### How do you know which logins in your Managed Instance are Azure AD users?
>
> Azure AD logins are signified with a value of EXTERNAL_LOGIN, or EXTERNAL_
> GROUP in the type_desc column in the sys.server_principals table with the type
> column set to E for login or X for groups in the type_desc value.

Data protection features

Managed instances secure your data by providing built-in security features to make administering it easier. Some of them you should be familiar with are listed here in this section.

Isolation

Security Isolation is achieved in Managed Instance by the use of VNet implementations and using VPNs and express gateways to connect to your on-premises machines. The only endpoints exposed are through private IP addresses. The underlying infrastructure is always dedicated ensuring a single-tenant infrastructure completes the trifecta of isolation security.

Auditing

Managed Instance auditing is used to track events in the audit log file of the Azure storage account. The audit file is used to maintain regulatory compliance, gain insight into discrepancies, or review for suspected security violations using threat detection. Threat detection is built-in and used to detect unusual attempts to access databases. There are alerts regarding suspicious activities, potential vulnerabilities, SQL injection attracts, and anomalous database access patterns. These alerts can be viewed from Azure Security Center and provide details of suspicious activity, offering recommendations on how to resolve the issues.

Data encryption

Data encryption is provided in motion using Transport Layer Security (TLS). Always Encrypted is offered for protection of data in flight, at rest, and during query processing. Although not strictly encryption, Dynamic data masking is used to limit exposure by masking the data. This allows an added layer of protection and the ability to determine who has access to sensitive data. This allows the data to look different to specific users without actually changing the underlaying data. Data at rest is encrypted with Transparent data encryption (TDE). TDE encrypts the data and log files, using real-time I/O encryption and decryption when it is accessed.

Row-level security

Row-level security is used to control the access to specific rows of data in a table based on the user executing a query. Row-level security simplifies design and coding by enabling you to implement restrictions on the user and not on other factors. Combined with an Azure Active Directory, this can be a powerful security feature.

Migrating to SQL Server solutions in Azure

Migration Services Options

There are a number of migration services available from Microsoft to help you migrate to newer versions of SQL Server or to an Azure IaaS or PaaS offering. This chapter looks at the different migration services options, helping you choose the best option for your particular project.

Microsoft has many different tools they have created, to get you from point A to point B in your migration journey. These tools have been evolving over the last few years as the tools become more specific in what they handle. Let's begin with an introduction to the Microsoft players in this realm and then we can decipher how they should each be best used, and for what:

- **Database Experimentation assistant (DEA).** An experimentation solution for SQL Server upgrades. It gives feedback on potential issues with an upgrade.

- **Azure Data Migration Assistant (DMA).** Helps you upgrade to a modern data platform by detecting compatibility issues that can impact database functionality in your new version of SQL Server or Azure SQL Database.

- **Database Migration Service (DMS).** A managed service used to do online and offline migrations.

- **SQL Server Migration Assistant (SSMA).** A tool designed to automate database migration to SQL Server from Microsoft Access, DB2, MySQL, Oracle, and SAP ASE.

As you can see from the descriptions of each migration service, they are similar and can overlap in use cases. Table 19-1 may help compare them.

Table 19-1   Features and descriptions of migration services.

Feature	DEA - Database Experimentation Assistant	DMA Azure Data Migration Assistant	DMS Database Migration Service	SSMA SQL Server Migration Assistant
Deficiency reporting	X	X	X	X
Used for Upgrade	X			
Used for Analysis	X	X	Uses DMA in the service for this feature	X
Used for Migration		X	X	X
Migration issues		X	X	X
Feature issues		X		
Compatibility issues	X	X		
Performance issues	X			
Source Versions	SQL Server 2005 and later	SQL Server 2005 and later, Amazon RDS SQL Server	SQL Server 2005 and later on Windows, AWS RDS for SQL Server	Access, DB2, MySQL, Oracle, and SAP ASE
Target Versions	SQL Server 2008 and later, on premise	SQL Server 2012 and later on Windows, SQL Server 2017 on Linux, Azure SQL Database and Azure SQL Database managed instance	SQL Server 2012 and later on Windows, SQL Server 2017 on Linux, Azure SQL Database and Azure SQL Database managed instance	SQL Server 2008 and later on Windows, SQL Server 2017 and 2019 on both Windows and Linux, Azure SQL Database

➤ Note: This table was current at the time of writing this chapter, however, these tools are evolving quickly, and they are expected to change. Please see the Microsoft documentation here for the latest list of source and targets: *https://docs.microsoft.com/azure/dms/dms-tools-matrix#pre-migration-phase.*

Database Experimentation Assistant (DEA)

The Database Experimentation Assistant (DEA) is a tool for evaluating upgrades of SQL Server with specific workloads. The tool can test workloads coming from SQL Server as early as 2005.

The purpose of it is to give the user confidence in a successful upgrade. This would be a first step in your analysis to determine the types of issues if any you would encounter in an upgrade scenario with on premises servers. This tool can be instrumental in creating a baseline for testing upgrades and comparing workloads. The Database Experimentation Assistant looks for:

1. SQL code that has compatibility issues.

2. SQL code that may run slower.

3. Query plans that may run slower.

4. Work load comparisons between the different versions.

These issues and comparisons are found using a solution first introduced in SQL Server 2012 that was originally a command line only tool called Distributed Replay. It has since been expanded to have a Graphical User Interface (GUI) and simpler set up. The tool collects data in a similar manner to SQL Server profiler. You run a workload on a machine and collect the workload, then you can "replay" that workload on other versions, configurations, or setups of SQL Server.

Once the analysis is run, the tool provides a report showing the performance implications based on a threshold you choose. For example, if you deem a 7% improvement to be a notable amount, set the threshold to 7% and the report will reflect any improvement as better than 7%, and any degradation as worse. These are shown in a pie chart that allows you to drill into each section to get further details. Summary statistics for individual queries are shown in graphs displaying how many queries have degraded, errored, improved, stayed the same, or did not have enough information to make a determination.

This tool can be run multiple times, and once set up with a workload it is relatively easy to use that workload to compare many different setups, configurations, and versions.

CHAPTER 19

InsideOUT

Can the Data Experimentation Assistant be used only for version comparison?

The Data Experimentation Assistant can be used for hardware changes, configuration changes, and feature comparisons between different versions of SQL Server, you can also use this feature to test other changes. For example, you can test the performance of a different index would have on the work load you run by not changing anything other than the index

The Database Experimentation Assistant can be downloaded from: *https://www.microsoft.com/ download/details.aspx?id=54090.*

Azure Data Migration Assistant (DMA)

The Data Migration Assistant (DMA) is used to find compatibility issues and other migration challenges when targeting SQL Server on a variety of platforms. The Data Migration Assistant can recommend performance improvements and allows you to move a schema, data, and uncontained objects from a source to a target server.

This would be a first step in your analysis to determine the types of issues you encounter in an upgrade scenario or migration to Azure SQL database. When targeting an Azure PaaS (Platform as a Service) database, the Database Migration Assistant does the following:

- Finds compatibility issues with the Azure version.

- Finds partially supported or unsupported features.

- Benefits from new features

- Provides recommendations on how to resolve issues.

When targeting SQL Server on premises or in an Azure VM, the Database Migration Assistant:

- Detects compatibility issues for upgrades.

- Recommends potential benefits for performance, security and storage.

In migrations to Azure or to an on-premises SQL Server, the migration assistant can help migrate:

- Database Schemas

- Data and users

- Server roles

- Logins (Windows and SQL Server)

The Data Migration Assistant can be downloaded from the download center here: *https://www.microsoft.com/download/details.aspx?id=53595.*

The Data Migration Assistant runs on both production and non-production databases. If you intend to run it on production databases, it is recommended that you run it during non-peak workload times and run each piece for the assessment separately. For example, run the compatibility issues and new features recommendations at different times to avoid consuming too many resources. To reduce performance impact, it is best to run the DMA on a machine other than the SQL Server host.

If you are migrating logins or data, ensure you are using a secure Intranet connection or SSL. This will slow your migration but is worth the added overhead. Be sure your test run is encrypted so your estimates are accurate.

The Data Migration Assistant can be run multiple times without issue. It is recommended to run it as often as needed to resolve all issues before migration. It is also useful for informational purposes when running upgrades as well. Even if you are not migrating to another server or the cloud, this tool can ensure you are aware of potential issues in performing an in-place upgrade.

InsideOut

How do you handle agent jobs when using Data Migration Assistant?

The Data Migration Assistant (DMA) will not copy linked servers, agent jobs or service broker end points. Check out the open source tools at the end of this section for options to recreate what is needed after migration.

Specifics for Linux migrations

While the overall migration workflow for Windows and Linux is the same, the move to Linux from Windows, requires a couple of additional considerations. Linux and Windows use different path formats. As a result, migrating to SQL Server on Linux requires that the user provide both the Windows and Linux versions of the path to the location of the physical file. You can provide both versions of the path in different ways depending on the location of the physical file. Use Samba to share the file with other computers on the network. On Windows, use the 'mount' command to mount the share onto the computer running Linux.

While the migration of Active Directory logins is officially supported by SQL Server on Linux, it requires additional configuration to work successfully. The details are outside the scope of this chapter, but can be found at *https://docs.microsoft.com/sql/linux/sql-server-linux-active-directory-authentication*. After performing the required configuration, the setup is complete, and you can migrate Active Directory logins as usual. Standard SQL authentication works as expected without any additional setup.

Features of Data Migration Assistant

The most recent releases of the migration assistant contain a few more specific features that may be of particular interest as you plan your migration. Here is an overview of a few:

- **Version 4.5.**   Assessment of the migration of SQL Server Integration Services (SSIS) packages hosted in file system to Azure SQL Database or Azure Managed Instance.

- **Version 4.4**   Supports the uploading of assessments to Azure Migrate.

- **Version 4.3**   Recommends SKUs for Azure SQL Database managed instances based on workload assessment. Amazon RDS for SQL Server became a source for assessment in this version. Agent job assessments for Azure SQL Database managed instances as a target became available in this version. The ability to ignore certain assessment rules was introduced. Assessment of T-SQL queries in job activity steps with appropriate recommendations was new in this version, along with improved performance for handling a large number of schema objects or complicated schemas. The extended events assessments became public preview in this version completing the list of improvements

- **Version 4.2**   line support with target readiness assessment for multiple server instances, for migration to Azure SQL Database Managed Instance became available.   line activity to collect metadata about database schemas, to detect the blockers and learn about partially or unsupported features that affect migration to Azure SQL Database managed instance with the results available for rendering in a provided Power BI template was announced and implemented.

- **Version 4.1**   The introduction of comprehensive assessment of on-premises SQL Server databases migrating to Azure SQL Database managed instance was first introduced. This was the first version to provide a comprehensive set of recommendations, and alternative approaches available in Azure along with mitigating steps to that customers can use for planning migrations.

Database Migration Service

Azure Database Migration Service (DMS) is a managed service known for the ability to do online migrations. It is designed specifically for the migration of multiple database sources. The service is a combination of the Data Migration Assistant that generates assessments and a migration service to performs the steps needed to migrate the data to the cloud. This is a service with a pricing tier, however, even the premium tier that allows for both online and off-line migration is free for 183 days after the creation of the service. This makes it a great tool for one-time migrations and to get you started.

InsideOUT

Is DMS available everywhere?

At the time of this writing DMS was not available in the following Azure regions: UAE Central, Switzerland, South Africa West, Australia Central, Australia Central 2, West

Central US, Azure Gov.China non-regional, China East, China North, China North 2,Norway, France South and all regions of Germany.

Please see the up to date list here: *https://azure.microsoft.com/global-infrastructure/services/?products=database-migration.*

Using Azure Database Migration Service to perform an online migration requires creating an instance based on the Premium pricing tier. DMS performs both online (continuous sync) and offline migrations. It is recommended that if you are doing a homogenous migration, you should access your existing database(s) using DMA. For heterogenous migration from complete sources, access your existing database with SSMA.

With an offline migration, the downtime begins at the time the migration begins. To limit your down time, it is recommended that you use the online migration options to keep things in sync for the time between migration completion and cut over. The online option allows for the down time to be limited to just the time to cut over at the end of the migration.

The Data Migration Service takes just a few steps to complete the migration. A typical simple migration consists of the following steps:

1. Create a target database(s).

2. Access your source database(s).

3. Create an instance of Azure Database Migration Service.

4. Create a migration project specifying the source database(s), target database(s) and the tables to migrate.

5. Start the full load.

6. Pick the subsequent validation.

7. Perform a manual switchover of your production environment to the new cloud-based database.

InsideOut

How do you know how long a migration will take?

Regardless of the migration method used for the live cut over, it is recommended that an offline migration be done during testing to determine the approximate length of time

> for the migration. This rough estimate will also help you determine if an offline migration is possible for your scenario.
>
> To improve your performance, you can also consider using the multi CPU General Purpose Pricing Tier when you create your service instance to allow the service to take advantage of multiple vCPUs for parallelization and faster data transfer during the migration period and change tiers when complete. Alternatively, you can temporarily scale up your Azure SQL Database target instance to the Premium tier SKU during the data migration operation to minimize Azure SQL Database throttling that may impact data transfer activities when using lower-level SKUs.

This is a relatively new service that is expanding regularly. For example, as of the writing of this chapter, a hybrid option for this service was in private preview. This service uses a migration worker hosted on-premises together with an Azure hosted worker to manage the migration lifecycle. This hybrid model of DMS is recommended for situations where the ground to cloud connectivity may be challenging.

SQL Server Migration Assistant

The SQL Server Migration Assistant (SSMA) is designed specifically for migration of non-SQL Server workloads to a SQL Server machine. This includes Access, DB2, mySQL, Oracle, and Sybase. Each of these sources has very different requirements and processes for migration. For the most current information it is recommended that you review the Microsoft documentation directly, which can be found here:

- **Access:** *https://docs.microsoft.com/sql/ssma/access/ sql-server-migration-assistant-for-access-accesstosql*

- **DB2:** *https://docs.microsoft.com/sql/ssma/db2/ migrating-db2-data-into-sql-server-db2tosql*

- **mySQL**: *https://docs.microsoft.com/sql/ssma/mysql/ sql-server-migration-assistant-for-mysql-mysqltosql*

- **Oracle:** *https://docs.microsoft.com/sql/ssma/oracle/ sql-server-migration-assistant-for-oracle-oracletosql*

- **Sybase Adaptive Server Enterprise (ASE):** *https://docs.microsoft.com/sql/ssma/sybase/ sql-server-migration-assistant-for-sybase-sybasetosql*

Common causes for migration failures

Support for online migrations to Azure SQL Database using Azure Database Migration Service extends only to the Enterprise, Standard, and Developer editions, so ensure you are using a supported edition before beginning. The majority of additional causes for migration failures come with the online migration. The most common are outlined here.

Certain datatypes are not supported. The geometry, geography and sql_variant datatypes are not currently supported in Azure SQL DB. Hierarchyid datatypes are supported but cannot be migrated. Exclude any tables with these datatypes from the configuration migration settings blade, where you specify tables for migration. Alternatively, if it is an option, change the datatype before migration or migrate these datatypes offline. You can use this code to determine which if any of your tables have columns that have an unsupported data type.

```
SELECT distinct c.TABLE_NAME,c.COLUMN_NAME,c.DATA_TYPE

from INFORMATION_SCHEMA.columns c

WHERE c.data_type in ('hierarchyid','geometry','geography', 'sql_variant' )
```

The previous sample script and all scripts for this book are all available for download at *https://www.MicrosoftPressStore.com/SQLServer2019InsideOut/downloads.*

Temporal tables are not supported for online migration. Exclude these tables from the configuration migration settings blade, where you specify tables for migration. You can use this code to determine which if any of your tables are temporal:

```
select name, temporal_type, temporal_type_desc

 from sys.tables

where temporal_type <>0
```

The previous sample script and all scripts for this book are all available for download at *https://www.MicrosoftPressStore.com/SQLServer2019InsideOut/downloads.*

Active *triggers* are not supported for online migration. All triggers must be disabled before the migration. Use this code to determine if you have any active triggers.

```
select s.name 'Schema',T.name 'Table Name',G.name 'Trigger Name'

from sys.TABLES T

join sys.triggers G

on G.parent_id = T.object_id
```

```
join sys.schemas S

on s.schema_id = t.schema_id

 where is_disabled =0
```

The previous sample script and all scripts for this book are all available for download at *https://www.MicrosoftPressStore.com/SQLServer2019InsideOut/downloads.*

Large object columns with data larger than 32KB

Large Object data types will require special handling. In this context, large-value data types are those that exceed the maximum row size of 8 KB. Columns larger than 32 KB may get truncated at the target. Exclude these tables from the configuration migration settings blade, where you specify tables for migration. You can use this code to determine which if any of your columns will be affected.

```
with infoschema_CTE (Table_name, Column_name)

as (

Select TABLE_NAME, COLUMN_NAME

from INFORMATION_SCHEMA.columns

)

select table_name, column_name,max(DATALENGTH(COLUMN_NAME)) as 'SizeInBytes',max(DATALEN
GTH(COLUMN_NAME))/1024 as 'SizeInKB'

from infoschema_CTE

group by table_name, column_name

having (max(DATALENGTH(COLUMN_NAME))/1024) > 32

order by max(DATALENGTH(COLUMN_NAME)) desc
```

The previous sample script and all scripts for this book are all available for download at: *https://www.MicrosoftPressStore.com/SQLServer2019InsideOut/downloads.*

Timestamp columns are not migrated as the source timestamp value

Azure generates a new value in the target table. If you need the source value migrated instead, contact the engineering team at *AskAzureDatabaseMigrations@service.microsoft.com*. Post-migration changes for migrations to Azure

Final notes for migration

When the migration of the data is complete, it is not the last step. There are a few items you want to include in your migration plan as it relates to connectivity error handling and security for the database and the application.

The most important thing once your data has migrated is to be able to connect to it.

To find your connection string, go to your Azure portal and choose **All Services** > **SQL Databases**. You can filter the list as needed to find the database you want to connect to. Click the database and it will take you to an overview screen where you have a list of settings. In the resource specific menu under the Settings group, choose **Connection Strings** to find the details you need based on the connection type you want. Options include ADO.NET (SQL authentication), JDBC (SQL authentication), ODBC (includes Node.js and SQL authentication), PHP (SQL authentication), and Go (SQL authentication). Each of these options provides a link to download the associated driver for SQL Server as well. Here is an example of an ODBC/Node.js connection string:

```
Driver={ODBC Driver 13 for SQL Server};

Server=tcp:insideout.database.windows.net,1433;

Database=[databasename];Uid=[userid@servername];

Pwd=[your_password_here];Encrypt=yes;

TrustServerCertificate=no;Connection Timeout=30;
```

The connection string does not come with the password in the connection string. All of the connection strings except for ADO.NET come with the userid filled in. Be sure to always verify what information to leave in the connection strings based on your security requirements. It is recommended to not store either the userid or password if possible.

Open Source PowerShell migration option

Before we get into the integration runtime options for migration services, let's take a look at open source solutions. One example of an option for migration is *https://dbatools.io*. This open source PowerShell library was created by Chrissy LeMaire, SQL Server & PowerShell MVP, and a host of people helping her expand and improve the library. This section is based on a Microsoft post to migrate an on-premises SQL Server to a PaaS SQL Database managed instance in Azure. The article can be found at *https://techcommunity.microsoft.com/t5/Azure-SQL-Database/ Automate-migration-to-SQL-Managed-Instance-using-Azure/ba-p/830801*.

It details how to create PowerShell scripts that automate migration to Managed Instance using Azure PowerShell and dbatools. This is an offline migration option. If you want an online migration you still only have the Data Migration Services option. For this offline migration process, Azure PowerShell controls and manages the Azure resources, and dbatools initiates the migration of the logins, and agent jobs. This process requires that you have version 150.18147.0 or higher of Microsoft.SqlServer.SqlManagementObjects, and that the location you are running the commands from has access to both the source SQL Server and the target managed instance.

Migration Process

The process using this open source solution requires you to ensure you have loaded the `Az.Resources, Az.Storage,` and `dbatools modules`

Migration Code

Start by populating the parameters that define the names of source/target instances and temporary Azure Blob Storage account.

```
# temporary resources needed for backups

$location = "westus"

$resourceGroup = "temp-migration-demo-rg"

$blobStorageAccount = "temp-demostorage"

$containerName = "backups"

 # source and target instances

$sourceInstance = "SOURCESQLSERVER"

$sourceDatabase = "WideWorldImporters"

 $targetInstance = "targetmi.public.920d05d7463d.database.windows.net,3342"

$targetDatabase = "WideWorldImporters"
```

The previous sample script and all scripts for this book are all available for download at *https://www.MicrosoftPressStore.com/SQLServer2019InsideOut/downloads*.

Change these parameters depending on your needs. This example uses an Azure public endpoint to connect to Managed Instance. This can be set up for a point-to-site connection or run the script from a virtual machine that is placed in the same subnet as your managed instance.

NOTE

Make sure that you use the same region where your managed instance is placed, which makes a significant difference in the speed of the database restore process.

Storage setup

In order to move your databases, you need a temporary Azure Blob Storage account. If you already have one, you can skip this step.

The following PowerShell script creates an Azure Blob Storage account that will be used in this example:

```
New-AzResourceGroup -Name $resourceGroup -Location $location
```

```
$storageAccount = New-AzStorageAccount -ResourceGroupName $resourceGroup '

-Name $blobStorageAccount '

-Location $location '

-SkuName Standard_LRS '

-Kind StorageV2


$ctx = $storageAccount.Context

New-AzStorageContainer -Name $containerName -Context $ctx -Permission Container
```

The previous sample script and all scripts for this book are all available for download at *https://www.MicrosoftPressStore.com/SQLServer2019InsideOut/downloads.*

 Execute this script to create an Azure Blob Storage account to use.

Source instance setup

Generate the SAS key, which enables your SQL Server instance to access the Azure Blob Storage account and puts the database backups in that location. This SAS key should be stored in the credential object on the source SQL Server instance:

```
$sas = (New-AzStorageAccountSASToken -Service Blob -ResourceType Object -Permission "rw"
-Context $ctx).TrimStart('?')

$sourceCred = New-DbaCredential -SqlInstance $sourceInstance '

                        -Name "https://$blobStorageAccount.blob.core.windows.
net/$containerName" '

                        -Identity "SHARED ACCESS SIGNATURE" '

                        -SecurePassword (ConvertTo-SecureString $sas -AsPlainText
-Force)
```

The previous sample script and all scripts for this book are all available for download at *https://www.MicrosoftPressStore.com/SQLServer2019InsideOut/downloads.*

Database migration

Take backups of your SQL Server databases and place them in Azure Blob Storage. The simplest way is to backup directly to a URL. Here is where dbatools comes in.

```
Backup-DbaDatabase -SqlInstance $sourceInstance -Database $sourceDatabase '

                -AzureBaseUrl "https://$blobStorageAccount.blob.core.windows.
net/$containerName" '

                -BackupFileName "WideWorldImporters.bak" '
```

```
-Type Full -Checksum -CopyOnly
```

The previous sample script and all scripts for this book are all available for download at *https://www.MicrosoftPressStore.com/SQLServer2019InsideOut/downloads*.

To migrate multiple databases, place them in the Database parameter value in a comma separated list.

If you are taking a backup of a large database you might also want to create backups on multiple URLs (striped backups) and set some of the following parameters: COMPRESSION, MAXTRANSFERSIZE = 4194304, BLOCKSIZE = 65536. For more information on striped backups review this article: *https://blogs.msdn.microsoft.com/sqlcat/2017/03/10/backing-up-a-vldb-to-azure-blob-storage/*.

Migrating databases to target instance

The migration stage requires you to create a SAS token that will enable managed instance to read a .bak file from Azure Blob Storage, create a credential with this SAS token, and restore the databases:

```
## Generate new SAS token that will read .bak file

$sas = (New-AzStorageAccountSASToken -Service Blob -ResourceType Object -Permission "r"
-Context $ctx).TrimStart('?') # -ResourceType Container,Object

$targetLogin = Get-Credential -Message "Login to target Managed Instance as:"

$target = Connect-DbaInstance -SqlInstance $targetInstance -SqlCredential $targetLogin

$targetCred = New-DbaCredential -SqlInstance $target `

                    -Name "https://$blobStorageAccount.blob.core.windows.
net/$containerName" `

                    -Identity "SHARED ACCESS SIGNATURE" `

                    -SecurePassword (ConvertTo-SecureString $sas -AsPlainText
-Force) `

                    -Force

Restore-DbaDatabase -SqlInstance $target -Database $targetDatabase `

                    -Path "https://$blobStorageAccount.blob.core.windows.
net/$containerName/WideWorldImporters.bak"
```

The previous sample script and all scripts for this book are all available for download at *https://www.MicrosoftPressStore.com/SQLServer2019InsideOut/downloads*.

This script will prompt for the SQL login details that should be used to access the managed instance.

This will result in the selected database backup being restored on the target managed instance, and your database migration will be complete.

Server-level objects migration

Once you migrate your database objects, you may still need to migrate server-level objects such as Agent jobs and operators, or logins.

Dbatools provides a set of useful scripts that you can apply to migrate these objects using Copy-Dba commands. Of the next set of commands, customize and use only those relevant to your environment. As mentioned earlier, this is where you can migrate Agent jobs, linked servers, and end points. If you do not see the command you need here, check the documentation at: *https://docs.dbatools.io*.

```
Copy-DbaSysDbUserObject -Source $sourceInstance -Destination $targetInstance
-DestinationSqlCredential $targetLogin

Copy-DbaDbMail -Source $sourceInstance -Destination $targetInstance
-DestinationSqlCredential $targetLogin

Copy-DbaAgentOperator -Source $sourceInstance -Destination $targetInstance
-DestinationSqlCredential $targetLogin

Copy-DbaAgentJobCategory -Source $sourceInstance -Destination $targetInstance
-DestinationSqlCredential $targetLogin

Copy-DbaAgentJob -Source $sourceInstance -Destination $.targetInstance
-DestinationSqlCredential $targetLogin

Copy-DbaAgentSchedule -Source $sourceInstance -Destination $targetInstance
-DestinationSqlCredential $targetLogin

Copy-DbaLogin -Source $sourceInstance -Destination $targetInstance
-DestinationSqlCredential $targetLogin -ExcludeSystemLogins

Copy-DbaLinkedServer -Source $sourceInstance -Destination $targetInstance
-DestinationSqlCredential $targetLogin -LinkedServer] <Object[]>

Copy-DbaEndpoint -Source $sourceInstance -Destination $targetInstance
-DestinationSqlCredential $targetLogin [-Endpoint] <Object[]>]
```

The previous sample script and all scripts for this book are all available for download at *https://www.MicrosoftPressStore.com/SQLServer2019InsideOut/downloads*.

Cleanup process for PoSh migration

If your Azure Blob Storage account is temporary storage that you need to use when moving databases, you can remove these resources using the following PowerShell command. It is good practice to always clean up resources you no longer need.

```
Remove-AzResourceGroup -Name $resourceGroup -Force
```

The previous sample script and all scripts for this book are all available for download at *https://www.MicrosoftPressStore.com/SQLServer2019InsideOut/downloads*.

Integration Runtime options for Migration Services

Azure Data Factory has integration tools that can be used for migrating data. An integration runtime (IR) is a service that allows integration of data across different network environments. They are used in Azure data factory (ADF) but have use outside of data factory (DF) as well. Integration Runtimes are also used for migration of data; however, they are typically not used as a full migration but as a part of an ongoing process of migrating data. If you just need to copy data to a table in azure that can be done, or data can be moved at regular intervals as well.

An IR can also be used for data that is on premises and needs to move to the cloud at regular intervals. An IR provides the compute environment where the activity either runs from or gets dispatched from. The ability to target the location of the compute activity is important for security, compliance and performance.

The data factory stores the JSON of the data movement and metadata of the database where the triggering is initiated. This is not only important for compliance, security, and performance, but for egress costs as well. Integration runtimes are a feature of ADF and as such the regional availability is found based on the ADF service. ADF has been optimized for a global service reach by allowing the location of the integration run time and as such the activity to belong to a different location than the DF it belongs to. A list of regions in which ADF is available can be found at *https://azure.microsoft.com/global-infrastructure/services/?products=data-factory*.

Azure Data Factory has 3 different types of integration runtimes that can be used separately or in combination with each other within a pipeline.

Azure Integration Runtime

The Azure Integration Runtime can be used only in Azure. This runtime is commonly used for data flows in Azure and running copy activities between different types of storage in Azure. It can also be used for dispatching transform activities in Azure such as a Databricks Notebook activity. The runtime is a fully managed compute service. There is no infrastructure or patching, and you only pay for the actual utilization. The amount of integration units used for the copy activity and the runtime is elastically scaled without the need to adjust the size of the runtime. A Data Integration Unit is a measure that represents the power (a combination of CPU, memory, and network resource allocation) of a single unit in Azure Data Factory *https://docs.microsoft.com/azure/data-factory/copy-activity-performance#data-integration-units*.

Azure IR Location

It is considered best practice to choose where possible data moves to run in the same region as the destination data store. This may require you to create a new Azure Integration Runtime in a particular region, but often this is done by the default setting. If this can potentially cause an issue due to compliance, for example the data needs to stay in a particular region, then create the runtime in the needed region and use the ConnectVia property to force the use of that runtime. This is a typical need for governments, banks and other institutions.

Self-hosted Integration Runtime

The Self-hosted Integration Runtime can be used both in the cloud and on a private network. This is a common method for moving data from on premises to the cloud on a virtual machine. An Azure Integration Runtime is used for dispatching transform activities such as Stored Procedure activity. However, we wouldn't use the Self-hosted IR for a Databricks Notebook activity. This illustrates how these Runtimes can be used collectively. The Self-hosted Integration Runtime can be used to move data to the cloud and then the Azure Runtime can be used to dispatch the transform activities from a Databricks notebook. Another typical use case for the Self-hosted Integration Runtime is the support for datastores that require you to bring your own driver. The full list of supported data stores for copy activities can be found here: *https://docs.microsoft.com/azure/data-factory/ copy-activity-overview#supported-data-stores-and-formats*.

The self-hosted Integration Runtime (self-hosted IR) only runs on Windows machines and needs to be installed on a machine inside a private network in which the source or target is located.

> ### NOTE
>
> **An Azure IaaS virtual machine is the equivalent of an on-premises machine, and if your data is stored in an Azure IaaS virtual machine you will still need to use the Self-hosted integration runtime rather than the Azure integration runtime.**

You can share a self-hosted IR across data factories, but they have to be in the same tenant. If you need to work across multiple tenants, you will need one self-hosted IR per tenant containing a data factory. There is a limit of only one self-hosted integration runtime on a machine. If you do not want to use a second machine there is the option of sharing the self-hosted IR for two different Data factories. They need to be in the same Azure Active Directory tenant and have a Managed Service Identity (MSI). The MSI is created automatically when in the portal or with a PowerShell cmdlet, however the identity property will need to be set if the self-hosted IR was created through an Azure Resource Manager (ARM) template or Software development kit (SDK).

Self-hosted IRs can be associated with multiple on-premises machines or virtual machines in Azure and are called nodes. Each self-hosted IR can have up to four nodes. The benefit of this is that the self-hosted IR is no longer the single point of failure with multiple nodes. The additional nodes can improve performance and throughput during data movement between on-premises and cloud data stores.

> ## InsideOUT
>
> **Should the Self-hosted Integration Runtime be on the same server as the data source?**
>
> It is recommended that the integration runtime be on a different server but one that is close. By being on a different server it will not compete with the data source for resources. Having the server that hosts the integration runtime close will reduce as much network overhead as possible. It is recommended that you do not co-locate a Data Factory Self-hosted Integration Runtime and a Power BI on-premises data gateway on the same machine.

Step-by-step instructions for creating a Self-hosted Integration Runtime can be found here: *https://docs.microsoft.com/azure/data-factory/tutorial-hybrid-copy-powershell*.

Potential issues with self-hosted integration runtimes

Tasks might fail in a self-hosted integration runtime that's installed on a Windows server on which FIPS-compliant encryption is enabled. You can determine if your FIPS encryption is turned on by checking the registry at this location:

```
HKLM\System\CurrentControlSet\Control\Lsa\FIPSAlgorithmPolicy\Enabled
```

If the value is 1, it is enabled, but if 0 it is disabled.

When a host machine hibernates, the self-hosted integration runtime goes offline. Check the power plan on the host machine of the integration runtime and turn the hibernation off. When considering scaling-out for the self-hosted integration runtime, here are some general guidelines:

1. When memory is low and the CPU is high, add a node.

2. When the memory and CPU are both high, increase the concurrent jobs, if the concurrency is maxed out, add a node and bring the concurrency back down.

3. If you are receiving timeouts, add a node.

4. If the execution of concurrent jobs is reaching its limit but the CPU and Memory are low, then increase the concurrent jobs per node.

When choosing runtime node certificates, do not use Subject Alternative Name (SAN) certificates since they have limitations. Do not use certificates that use CNG keys because they are not supported.

Azure-SSIS Integration Runtime

The Azure-SSIS Integration Runtime can be used both in the cloud and on-premises.This Integration Runtime is installed in Azure, and joined to a virtual network that is connected to an on-premises network to support the data access. The Azure-SSIS Integration Runtime is made up of a cluster of Azure VMs that you can scale by specifying the number of nodes in the cluster. The cost of the runtime is regulated by ensuring you stop the runtime when not being used. This runtime supports packages deployed to an SSIS Catalog (SSISDB) hosted by Azure SQL Database as well as those deployed to a file system or share in or outside of Azure. When the deployment target is an Azure SQL Database it uses a project deployment model, and when the deployment target is a file system it deploys with a package deployment model. Once the runtime is provisioned you can use either SQL Server Data Tools or SQL Server Management Studio and the command line tools (dtinstall/dtutil/dtexec) to deploy and run the SSIS packages in Azure.

SSIS integration runtime location

Location of the Azure-SSIS Integration Runtime (Azure-SSIS IR) is important to ensure the best performance of any data integration processes. Although the location of the Azure-SSIS IR does not need to be the same as the Azure Data Factory, it should be in the same region where the Azure SQL Database hosting the SSISDB is located to limit the traffic between the two regions. When possible, it is best if the location of the Azure-SSIS IR and the Azure SQL Database are in the same virtual network to minimize data movement. If the location of the SSISDB is not the same as the VNet connected to the on-premises network, create the Azure-SSIS IR using an existing Azure SQL DB and join another VNet in the same region, and configure a VNet-to-VNet connection.

For step-by-step directions on how to set up an Azure-SSIS Integration Runtime see the instructions at: *https://docs.microsoft.com/azure/data-factory/ tutorial-deploy-ssis-packages-azure*.

Best Practices for security and resiliency during migration

During migration of databases, when possible, provide a single share location. A shared folder that is accessible by the source server and the target server, to avoid a copy operation. A copy operation may introduce a delay based on the size of the backup file and the added step increases the chances of failure. It is important to provide the correct permissions to the shared folder to avoid migration failures. The permissions can be specified in the tool. If the SQL Server instance runs under Network Service credentials, give the correct permissions on the shared folder to the machine account for the SQL Server instance.

For a secure migration, enable an encrypted connection when connecting to the source and target servers. Using SSL encryption increases the security of data transmitted across the networks between Data Migration Assistant and the SQL Server instance. This is particularly important when migrating SQL logins. The SSL encryption is used to prevent the SQL logins being migrated from being intercepted and/or modified on-the-fly by an attacker. If all access involves a secure intranet configuration, encryption might not be required. Enabling encryption slows performance because the extra overhead that is required to encrypt and decrypt packets.

Once migrated it is important for all applications to understand that partial failures will occur. These are referred to transient connectivity issues and occur when a database is being moved or reconfigured and the application loses its connection to the database. These can be planned (load balancing) or unplanned (process crash) events. It is not a matter of if but when, and all applications need to be resilient to these failures, responding to them in a way that avoids downtime or data loss. Resiliency is the ability to recover from failures and to continue to function. The goal of resiliency is to return the application to a fully functioning state after a failure.

Once migrated, applications need to continue to cope with partial failures, like network outages or nodes or VMs crashing in the cloud. Even microservices or containers being moved to a different node within a cluster can cause intermittent short failures within an application.

To maximize resiliency when using asynchronous communication, such as HTTP calls, it is advisable not to create long chains of synchronous HTTP calls across the internal microservices, because that will increase the risk of outages. Other than front-end communications between the client applications and the first level of microservices or API Gateways, it is recommended to use asynchronous (message-based) communication only across the internal microservices past the initial request/response cycle, It is recommended to use event-driven architectures to enforce a higher level of microservice autonomy and prevent the problems discussed here.

Retries with exponential backoff is a technique that retries an operation, with an exponentially increasing wait time, until a maximum retry count has been reached (the exponential backoff). Exponential backoff is an algorithm that uses a feedback loop to multiplicatively decrease the rate of some processes, in order to gradually find an acceptable rate and reduce network congestion. They are used to help to avoid short and intermittent failures by performing call retries with exponentially increasing wait times, until a maximum retry count has been reached, in case the service is not available for a short time. These types of intermittent network issues often happen when a container is moved to a different node in a cluster. If these retries are not designed properly, they can create a ripple effect, ultimately even causing a denial of service (DoS).

The recommended solution to this is to design clients to always use timeouts, when waiting for a response. Using timeouts ensures that resources are not tied up indefinitely. The use of the

Circuit Breaker pattern is a method that allows the client process to track the number of failed requests. If the error rate exceeds a configured limit, a "circuit breaker" trips so that further attempts fail immediately. If a large number of requests are failing, that suggests the service is unavailable and that sending requests is pointless. After a timeout period, the client should try again and, if the new requests are successful, close the circuit breaker.

Another approach is to provide fallbacks. This is done by the client process performing fallback logic when a request fails, such as returning cached data or a default value. This approach is suitable for queries but is more complex for updates or commands.

When a service is unavailable you will want to limit the number of queued requests. Clients should also impose an upper bound on the number of outstanding requests that a client microservice can send to a particular service. If the limit has been reached, it is pointless to continue to make additional requests, and those attempts should fail immediately. There are a few ways to design for this situation. The Bulkhead Policy object in Polly (http://www.thepollyproject.org/) exposes to the client how full the bulkhead and queue is, and offers events on overflow so it can also be used to drive automated horizontal scaling. It also allows for proactively shedding excess load before execution due to a full queue. This can be faster than the circuit breaker method as it does not wait for the failure. The details of this are outside the scope of this chapter but are worth learning. You can find details on the Polly Bulkhead Isolation policy here: *https://github.com/App-vNext/Polly/wiki/Bulkhead*.

Feedback occurs when outputs of a system are routed back as inputs as part of a chain of cause-and-effect that forms a circuit or loop. The system can then be said to feed back into itself. The notion of cause-and-effect has to be handled carefully when applied to feedback systems.

Simple causal reasoning about a feedback system is difficult because the first system influences the second and second system influences the first, leading to a circular argument. This makes reasoning based upon cause and effect tricky, and it is necessary to analyze the system as a whole.

The retransmission is delayed by an amount of time derived from the slot time (for example, the time it takes to send 512 bits or 512 bit-times) and the number of attempts to retransmit.

After a number of collisions defined as c, a random number of slot times between 0 and 2c − 1 are chosen. After the first collision, each sender will wait 0 or 1 slot times. After the second collision, the senders will wait anywhere from 0 to 3 slot times (inclusive). After the third collision, the senders will wait anywhere from 0 to 7 slot times (inclusive), and so forth. As the number of retransmission attempts increases, the number of possibilities for delay increases exponentially.

Truncated simply means that after a certain number of increases, the exponentiation stops; or the retransmission timeout reaches a ceiling and thereafter does not increase any further. For example, if the ceiling is set at $i = 10$, then the maximum delay is 1023 slot times. This is useful because these delays can limit the number of other client requests that are being sent. It will reduce the number that will collide as well. There is a possibility that, on a busy network, hundreds of client requests may be caught in a single collision set.

This technique embraces the fact that cloud resources might intermittently be unavailable for more than a few seconds for any reason. For example, an orchestrator might be moving a container to another node in a cluster for load balancing. During that time, some requests might fail. Another example could be a database like Azure SQL Database, where a database can be moved to another server for load balancing, causing the database to be unavailable for a few seconds.

There are many approaches to implement retry logic with exponential back off.

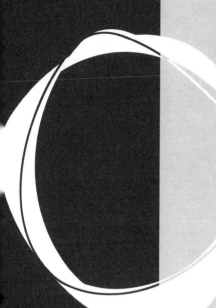

The enterprise data warehouse may be the center of the business intelligence universe in many organizations, but it does not always meet the needs of every end user. Making changes to existing data warehouse processes comes at a high cost in both time and effort. In recent years there has also been a proliferation of data across organizations in a variety of forms.

In this chapter we begin with the trends around big data. Then we delve into how those trends, along with widespread adoption of container-based deployment, have helped Microsoft build a big data solution into SQL Server 2019.

Big Data Clusters (BDC) is an exciting new introduction to the big data landscape with SQL Server. Bringing together relational and non-relational data and using T-SQL for querying, BDC allows users to perform the analysis they need while minimizing the amount of data movement needed to gain those insights. The key part of the infrastructure is built on top of Kubernetes, so having a good understanding of this modern container orchestration system is to your advantage.

➤ Refer to Chapter 3, "Designing and implementing an on-premises database infrastructure" to learn more about Kubernetes.

The next section covers operationalizing analytics with Machine Learning Server, and will detail the installation, configuration, and operationalization of machine learning models.

This chapter also provides you with information about Microsoft machine learning and other big data features that are relevant for a DBA. You can determine what services to use and when to use them based upon what you want to achieve. The goal is to understand what objects are needed and what to request to support deployments of machine learning and big data solutions.

A big data primer

Traditional data processing uses extract, transform and load (ETL) tools like SQL Server Integration Services (SSIS), and internal SQL Server tools like transactional replication or linked servers. At the same time, business users are demanding that organizations evolve rapidly into a world far beyond relational databases, whether it's JSON data from a company's mobile app going into a MongoDB database, or a data lake consisting of large pools of data running on the Hadoop Distributed File System (HDFS). This is the realm of big data. Far from being a buzzword, *big data* refers to data sets that are too large to be processed by traditional tools, including relational database systems like SQL Server. The practile effects of big data along with the question of how to integrate data from disparate systems, are a longstanding challenge across IT organizations and are the challenge being met by BDC.

Introducing MapReduce with Hadoop and HDFS

Big data systems like Hadoop and Spark reduce the effort of ETL processes by applying a schema to data only when it is read, which allows for changes without moving large volumes of data around.

The lack of data movement combined with the horizontal scale of big data systems allows for the processing of petabytes of data. Some of the common Hadoop use cases include fraud detection for banks, firms analyzing semi-structured data from social media and mobile apps, and a batch processing center for data from Internet of Things (IoT) devices. It is important to remember that Hadoop was designed as a batch processing system—for the most part, even in well-tuned systems, large scans are performed as part of Hadoop's MapReduce (shuffle and sort) processing.

Inside OUT

What is MapReduce?

MapReduce is a combination of two processes, named Map and Reduce. The *map* procedure filters and sorts data into queues. Then, a *reduce* procedure summarizes the data in each queue. MapReduce runs this process in a massive distributed system in parallel.

Architecturally, Hadoop consists of two core components: the processing power that performs the MapReduce processes, and schedules and manages work in the cluster; and Hadoop Distributed File System (HDFS), which is the storage component. HDFS is a distributed file system that provides redundant storage space for very large files. To ensure reliability, files are separated into large blocks (64 to 128 MB in size) and distributed across nodes in a given cluster. Each block is also replicated to three nodes by default (this setting is configurable), so that in the event of a node going down, data can be retrieved from the other two nodes.

NOTE

HDFS is used more broadly than in just Hadoop clusters as you will see in the following sections. It has become the *de facto* standard for big data storage.

Introducing distributed memory with Spark

Spark is another open source project and is now a part of Apache Spark, which makes use of in-memory processing on its data nodes. Hadoop clusters are designed to execute large sequential I/O operations, while Spark leverages heavier memory utilization to deliver better performance. Because of this better performance, Spark has become popular for many workloads that were formerly processed by Hadoop.

Some common use cases for Spark include processing streaming data from IoT sensors, streaming ETL processes, machine learning, and general interactive querying because of the performance Spark offers. Spark has an active community of developers and offers a rich set of libraries and APIs to execute machine learning processes using Python.

CAUTION

Managing Spark clusters has traditionally been a challenge, even for mature organizations. Offerings like Databricks aim to reduce this complexity by making Spark available in a PaaS solution using automated cluster management.

Spark supports multiple storage engines including HDFS, HBase (which runs on top of HDFS), Solr (which provides search support), and Apache Kudu (a tabular storage model).

Introducing Big Data Clusters

A major challenge facing many organizations is moving data between systems. This is because ETL processes are complicated to build, and because of this complexity they can be expensive both in terms of resources and performance to change. In recent years *data virtualization* has become a buzzword in the industry, to help mitigate the complexity of ETL efforts. Data virtualization is the process of using data, while it stays in its original location. The process minimizes and the need for complex extract, transform, load (ETL) processes. The BDC provides the tools to provide a few key elements:

- **Abstraction.** Technical details about the data are abstracted from the consumer.

- **Virtualized access.** A common data point to deliver access to an array of data sources.

CHAPTER 20

- **Transformation.**   Either prebuilt transformations or easy to use simple transforms like those built in the Excel Power Query plugin.

- **Data federation.**   Combines results from multiple sources.

- **Data delivery.**   Delivers data results as views and/or data services accessible to users or client applications.

Microsoft added the PolyBase feature to SQL Server 2016 to address some data virtualization concerns. Customers found the licensing and configuration to be complex, limiting the adoption. In the Azure Synapse, formerly Azure SQL Data Warehouse, offering it was widely adopted because it allowed users to consume text and parquet files of various formats and define external tables on them. These external tables are a *virtual schema* imposed on a file, which allows the file to be read and consumed by the Database Engine. The load pattern was to first load files to storage, create an external table on those files, and then insert the data from the virtual tables into a regular database table. In Synapse this allows for a massively parallel load process.

In an effort to increase adoption, and because the feature set of Big Data Clusters requires it, PolyBase has been revamped for SQL Server 2019. The original implementation of PolyBase for SQL Server supported Hadoop and text files in Azure Blob Storage. The new implementation builds on that support by adding Oracle, Teradata, and MongoDB support. PolyBase can also be used to connect SQL Servers to each other, with the limitation that PolyBase is not supported in Azure SQL database.

Inside OUT

How is PolyBase different from a linked server?

PolyBase is different to linked servers in a number of ways. The first is in scope: PolyBase uses External Tables, which are scoped to the database, whereas linked servers are scoped to the instance level.

PolyBase also uses ODBC drivers compared to OLE DB for linked servers, and offers scale-out options where linked servers are limited to running on the server on which they are configured.

Finally, PolyBase has been optimized for large analytic queries, it supports push-down computation for external sources, and is required for the use of Big Data Clusters.

Bringing all of these trends and information together, Microsoft started a development path of building a fully integrated data virtualization solution using PolyBase, Kubernetes, and modern scale-out architecture, resulting in Big Data Clusters.

Big Data Clusters technical overview

The Big Data Cluster (BDC) technology is designed to give users a common entry point to all data needed for analysis, and to reduce the friction of bringing in new data sources. It offers a common security layer (via SQL Server and Apache Knox) and reduces data latency, allowing users to perform analysis on more recent data. It also takes advantage of the machine learning features built into the Database Engine to support R, Python, and Java.

A look at BDC architecture

Big data clusters are built on Kubernetes, and implemented as a cluster of containers. The nodes in the cluster are divided into three logical planes: the control plane, the compute plane, and the data plane. Each of these planes serve a different set of functionalities in the cluster as shown in Figure 20-1.

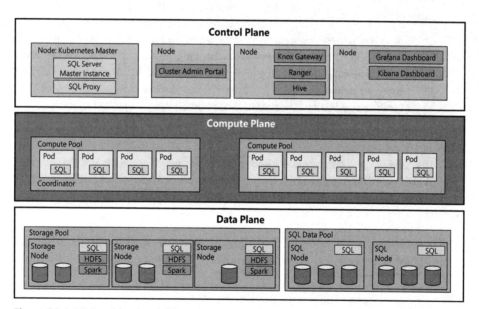

Figure 20-1 BDC architectural diagram.

The BDC control plane

The control plane performs a few functions. The first and most important is that it contains the SQL Server *master instance* and the SQL *proxy*. The master instance provides a secure endpoint (using TDS, the protocol used by SQL Server) for users to connect to using the tool of their choice. The master instance also contains the scale-out query engine that is used by PolyBase to distribute queries across all of the SQL Server instances in the compute pool(s). This instance also contains the cluster metadata, the HDFS table metadata (beyond what is stored in the Hive metastore), and a data plane shard map. SQL Server Machine Learning services are also available in the master instance, so you can execute R and Python jobs using `sp_external_script`.

BDC makes use of Hive, which is an Apache project for building tables on top of data stored in Hadoop, as well as Knox, an application gateway for interacting with Hadoop through the use of its APIs. Hive and Knox metadata are both stored in the control plane. Finally, Grafana and Kibana are both open source tools used to monitor your cluster.

Inside OUT

What is Apache Hive?

When Hadoop was originally built, users had to build their own MapReduce jobs in Java. While this was wonderful if you were a Java developer, an open source project called Hive was built to broaden the use of Hadoop. Hive imposes a structure on top of data files in Hadoop, contains deserializers for formats like JSON, and includes a metadata repository that stores all of its table information. Hive also includes a language called HiveQL that is very similar to ANSI-SQL. Hive's metadata store and table definitions are widely used across a number of tools that provide similar functionality, include Impala and Databricks.

The control plane also includes a *controller service*, which connects SQL Server, Kubernetes, Spark, and HDFS to each other. That service is deployed from a command line utility called *azdata*, which provides cluster management functions. The controller service performs the following functions:

- Manages cluster lifecycle, including cluster bootstrap, delete, and configuration updates

- Manages master SQL Server instances

- Manages compute, data, and storage pools

- Exposes monitoring tools to observe the state of the cluster

- Exposes troubleshooting tools to detect and repair unexpected issues

- Manages cluster security, ensuring secure cluster endpoints, managing users and roles, configuring and storing credentials for intra-cluster communication

- Manages the workflow of upgrades to services in the cluster so that they are implemented safely

• Manages high availability of the stateful services in the cluster

All communication using the controller is performed using a REST API over HTTPS. A self-signed certificate is created at the time of cluster creation along with the username and password for the controller.

The BDC compute plane

The compute plane, as its name suggests, provides computation resources to the cluster. It contains a number of Kubernetes pods running SQL Server on Linux and base services for cluster communications. This plane is divided into task-specific pools. The pool can act as a PolyBase scale-out group to help the performance of large PolyBase queries against sources like Oracle, Teradata, or Hadoop.

The BDC app pool

The application pool (part of the compute plane) is composed of a set of pods that hold multiple end-points for access to the overall cluster. SQL Server Integration Services is one example of an application available in this pool that can be run as a containerized application. A potential use case for a pool would be for a long-running job (for example, IoT device streaming) or machine learning endpoint. The pool could be used for scoring a model or returning an image classification.

The BDC data plane

The data plane is made up of two specific types of nodes:

• **Data pool.**   This node type runs SQL Server on Linux, and is used to ingest data from T-SQL queries or Spark jobs. To provide better performance, the data in the data pool is sharded across all of the SQL Server instances in the data pool and stored in columnstore indexes.

• **Storage pool.**   This node type is made up of SQL Server, HDFS, and Spark pods, which are all members of an HDFS cluster. It is also responsible for data ingestion through Spark and provides data access through HDFS and SQL Server endpoints.

NOTE

Sharding is a term for partitioning data across databases and is similar to the sharding feature in Azure SQL Database. It separates very large databases into smaller parts called shards. The smaller parts allow shards to be handled individually making the whole easier to manage and faster. This feature requires a shard map to be in place, which is provided by the BDC control plane.

Deploying Big Data Clusters

A Kubernetes infrastructure is a requirement for BDC deployment; however, you have several options to help you get Kubernetes in your cluster up and running. The following options are currently supported:

- A cloud platform such as Azure Kubernetes Service (AKS)

- On-prem/IAAS Kubernetes deployments using kubeadm

- Minikube for training and testing purposes

If you are using AKS for your cluster, you should have the Azure Line Interface (Azure CLI) installed on your management machine, as well as kubectl for Kubernetes administration. Additionally, management access to the cluster is provided by Azure Data Studio.

No matter which approach you take for deploying your infrastructure, building the cluster is quite easy. You have to first install the azdata utility on the administration machine (not needed to be part of the Kubernetes cluster) and then run the following command:

```
azdata bdc create
```

This command will take you through a series of prompts to choose your target Kubernetes environment, which will prompt you for a series of usernames and passwords for the following accounts listed in Table 20-1.

Table 20-1 **Accounts required for cluster services.**

Accounts	Description
DOCKER_USERNAME	The username to access the container images in case they are stored in a private repository.
DOCKER_PASSWORD	The password to access the above private repository.
CONTROLLER_USERNAME	The username for the cluster administrator.
CONTROLLER_PASSWORD	The password for the cluster administrator.
KNOX_PASSWORD	The password for Knox user.
MSSQL_SA_PASSWORD	The password of SA user for SQL master instance.

These can be setup as environment variables using either bash or PowerShell to automate this processing.

➤ If you are using AKS, Microsoft has fully automated the deployment process with a Python script available at *https://raw.githubusercontent.com/Microsoft/sql-server-samples/master/ samples/features/sql-big-data-cluster/deployment/aks/deploy-sql-big-data-aks.py*.

➤ To deploy with active directory mode, step-by-step instructions are available from books online at *https://docs.microsoft.com/sql/big-data-cluster/deploy-active-directory*.

Configuring BDC storage

BDC relies on the persistent volumes feature in Kubernetes to persist data. Kubernetes also supports the Network File System (NFS), which can be used for backup storage. You can define storage classes within your Kubernetes cluster. In AKS there are multiple classes of storage based on redundancy or, you can create your own storage classes within AKS. kubeadm does have predefined storage classes and you will have to define them in order to provision volumes. You should think of these storage classes like tiers in a storage area network (SAN). You will want your actively used data to be stored on low latency storage, most likely solid-state drives (SSD), particularly in the public cloud. These classes will also be used for dynamic storage provisioning, such as when a data file is growing rapidly.

➤ Refer to Chapter 3 to learn more about types of storage.

Big Data Clusters security

One of the benefits of the BDC architecture is a seamless security implementation. Security is executed via normal SQL Server security, and access control lists (ACLs) in HDFS, which associate permissions with the users identity. HDFS supports security controls by limiting access to service APIs, HDFS files, and execution of jobs. This limitation makes the following end points important to understanding security and ensuring the access you need.

There are three key endpoints to the BDC:

- **HDFS/Knox gateway.** This is an HTTPS endpoint that is used for accessing webHDFS and other related services.

- **Controller endpoint.** This is the cluster management services that exposes APIs for cluster management and tooling.

- **Master instance.** This is the TDS endpoint for database tools and applications to connect to SQL Server.

As of this writing, there are no options for opening other ports in the cluster. Cluster endpoint passwords are stored as Kubernetes secrets. The accounts that get created at cluster deployment are detailed in Table 20-1, however, there are a number of additional SQL logins that are created. A login is created in the controller SQL instance that is system-managed and has the sysadmin role. Additionally, a sysadmin login is created in all SQL Server instances in the cluster, which is owned and managed by the controller. This login performs administrative tasks such as High Availability (HA) setup and upgrades, and it is also used for intra-cluster communication between SQL instances (see Figure 20-2).

CHAPTER 20

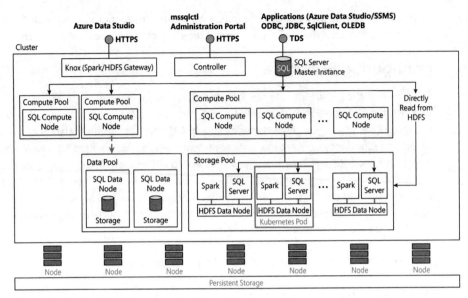

Figure 20-2   Big Data Clusters endpoint architecture.

Benefits of PolyBase

As mentioned earlier, PolyBase is a feature now expanded with the Big Data Cluster architecture. There are four key scenarios that best use PolyBase in SQL Server:

- Parallelized import of data into SQL Server

- Joining multiple data sources in a single query

- Eliminating data latency and reducing the need for multiple copies of data

- Archiving data to alternate storage

To understand the difference between PolyBase on a stand-alone server compared to a big data cluster, look at these features detailed in Figure 20-3.

Feature	Big Data Cluster	Stand Alone Instance
Create external data source for SQL Server, Oracle, Teradata, and Mongo DB	X	X
Create external data source using a compatible third-party ODBC Driver		X
Create external data source for HADOOP data source	X	X
Create external data source for Azure Blob Storage	X	X
Create external table on a SQL Server data pool	X	
Create external table on a SQL Server storage pool	X	
Scale-out query execution	X	X

Figure 20-3 Big Data Cluster Features.

Unified data platform features

Apache Spark joined SQL Server and HDFS in SQL Server 2019, and is referred to as just Spark. This was done to extend the functionality to easily integrate and analyze data of all types in a single integrated solution. This expands the surface area of SQL Server to cover more big data options. The expansion includes HDFS, Spark, Knox, Ranger, and Livy, which all come packaged together with SQL Server. They can also be deployed as Linux containers on Kubernetes.

HDFS tiering

HDFS tiering is similar to PolyBase in that it allows you to access external data. HDFS tiering allows you to mount file systems that are compatible with HDFS. This includes Azure Data Lake Storage Gen2 and Amazon S3. This feature is only available in a big data cluster.

CHAPTER 20

The benefit of tiering is that it allows seamless access to the data as though it was mounted locally. Only the metadata is copied over to your local database. The data is copied on demand when accessed. This allows Spark jobs and SQL queries to be executed as though they are being run on local HDFS systems.

The file mounts are read-only, and directories or files cannot be added or removed through the mount. If the location of a mount changes, the mount must be deleted and recreated. The mount location is not dynamic.

> ## NOTE
>
> **Detailed steps to connect to Azure Data Lake Storage can be found in the Microsoft Docs at** *https://docs.microsoft.com/sql/big-data-cluster/ hdfs-tiering-mount-adlsgen2#use-oauth-credentials-to-mount.*
>
> **Detailed steps to connect to Amazon S3 are found at** *https://docs.microsoft.com/sql/big-data-cluster/hdfs-tiering-mount-s3.*

The Spark connector

One of the more common ways of cleaning, analyzing, and processing data is in Spark. To make this process easier, two new connectors have been introduced in SQL Server 2019. The Spark to SQL connector uses JDBC to write data to the SQL Server. A sample of how this connector is used can be found at *https://github.com/microsoft/sql-server-samples/blob/master/samples/ features/sql-big-data-cluster/spark/data-virtualization/spark_to_sql_jdbc.ipynb*

The second connector is the MSSQL Spark connector. This connector uses SQL Server Bulk copy APIS to write data to SQL Server. A sample of the connector code in use can be found at *https:// github.com/microsoft/sql-server-samples/blob/master/samples/features/sql-big-data-cluster/ spark/data-virtualization/mssql_spark_connector_non_ad_pyspark.ipynb.*

Shared access signatures

As the name suggests, a shared access signature (SAS) is a way to share an object in your storage account with others without exposing your account key. This gives you granular control over the access you grant. This can be done at the account, service, or user level.

- You can set a start time and expiry time

- Blob containers, file shares, queues and tables are all resources that accept SAS policies

- You can set an optional IP address or range from which access will be accepted

- You can restrict access from HTTPS clients by specifying the accepted protocol

NOTE

It is best practice to never share your account key. Think of it like a password on your bank account. Never distribute it or leave it in plain text anywhere, and regenerate it if you believe it has been compromised, just like you would a password. It is recommended that you use Azure Active Directory (AAD) for all your blob and queue storage applications. For more details on that see the Microsoft Docs at *https://docs.microsoft.com/azure/storage/common/storage-auth-aad*.

Shared access signatures (SAS) are used to allow clients to read, write, or delete data in your storage account without access to your account key. This is typically needed when a client wants to upload large amounts of data or high-volume transactions to your storage account, and creating a service to scale and match demand is too difficult or expensive. The SAS is a signed URI that points to resources and includes a token that contains a set of query parameters (token) that indicate how the resource can be accessed. Azure Storage checks both the storage piece and the provided token piece of the SAS URI to verify the request. If for any reason the SAS is not valid, it receives an error code 403 (Forbidden) and access is denied.

There are two different types of SAS:

1. The Service SAS delegates access to a resource in a single storage service (blob, queue, table, or file service).

2. The Account-level SAS delegates access to resources in one or more storage services within a storage account. This also includes the option to apply access to services such as Get/Set Service Properties and Get Service Stats.

For details on all the parameters that can be set with Shared access signatures at *https://docs.microsoft.com/azure/storage/common/ storage-dotnet-shared-access-signature-part-1#shared-access-signature-parameters*.

An ad hoc SAS can be created either as an account SAS or service SAS, and the start time, expiry time, and permissions are all specified in the SAS URI. An SAS with a stored access policy is defined on a resource container and can be used to manage constraints on one or more SAS. When the SAS is associated with a stored access policy, it inherits the constraints defined for the stored access policy.

Inside OUT

Are there any risks to using a SAS URI?

Yes, a SAS URI is a URL, so anyone who has it can access your storage account. If a client application expires and the application is unable to retrieve a new SAS from your service, then the applications functionality is diminished.

> To mitigate these issues, we recommended that you:
>
> - Always use HTTPS to create or distribute a SAS.
> - Use storage access policies.
> - Set the expiration on an account SAS far in the future and regularly monitor and move if necessary, for regularly used SAS.
> - Set the expiration on ad hoc SAS shorter to reduce the risk if compromised.
> - Ensure clients renew with enough time to avoid disruption.
> - Ensure you use the principle of least privilege when creating SAS URIs to reduce risk.

Any SAS access attributes egress costs to your Azure Subscription. The data that is uploaded with a SAS is not validated in any way, so a middle tier that performs rule validation, authentication and auditing may still be the better option. Regardless of what you choose, monitor your storage for spikes in authentication failures.

Examples of how to create account and service SAS can be found at *https://docs.microsoft.com/azure/storage/common/storage-dotnet-shared-access-signature-part-1#sas-examples.*

NOTE

Machine Learning Services and PolyBase are the key features of this section that have specific installation needs or prerequisites before starting. Azure Machine Learning Service is used to build, train, write code, or manage deployed models. The key to this is the Azure Machine Learning service workspace. The details on how to install it based on different methods can be found at
https://docs.microsoft.com/azure/machine-learning/service/setup-create-workspace.

The Azure Machine Learning SDK for Python method is used in the accompanying example available for download at
https://www.MicrosoftPressStore.com/SQLServer2019InsideOut/downloads

PolyBase installation is now available on Linux in SQL Server 2019, and the details for installing it on either Windows or Linux is in Chapter 5: "Installing and configuring SQL Server on Linux."

Installation

With SQL Server 2019, PolyBase is available on Linux as well as Windows. The virtues and architecture of big data clusters were discussed earlier in this chapter. In this section we look at the installation and application of the PolyBase concepts.

Installation instructions for Windows can be found at *https://docs.microsoft.com/sql/ relational-databases/polybase/polybase-installation.*

When installing on a Windows machine keep these items top of mind:

1. PolyBase can be installed on only one instance per machine

2. To use PolyBase you need to be assigned the sysadmin role or Control Server permission

3. All nodes in a scale-out group need to run under the same domain account

4. You must enable the PolyBase feature after installation

5. If the Windows firewall service is running during installation, the necessary firewall rules will be set up automatically

For step-by-step instructions on how to install PolyBase on Linux (Red Hat, Ubuntu, or SUSE) at *https://docs.microsoft.com/sql/relational-databases/polybase/polybase-linux-setup.*

As with Windows, you must enable the PolyBase feature after installation on Linux.

NOTE

The only way to change the service accounts for the PolyBase Engine Service and Data Movement Service is to uninstall and reinstall the PolyBase feature.

If you are connecting to Hadoop specifically, there are a few additional steps needed for configuration and security. Please follow the steps listed at *https://docs.microsoft.com/sql/ relational-databases/polybase/polybase-configure-sql-server.*

With the installation complete the next steps are:

- Configure sources

- Enable access

- Create External Tables

CHAPTER 20

Configure and enable

A master key is a symmetric key used to protect other keys and certificates in the database. It is encrypted with both an algorithm and password. A master key is needed for protecting the credentials of the external tables. Details on how to create and update a master key, and the instructions to set it up, can be found in this chapter in the section called External Tables.

Along with the master key you will need to configure PolyBase globally using `sp_configure`. The `configvalue` can range from 0 to 7 with 1 through 6 dealing with the older versions of Hortonworks. Setting 7 allows for connectivity with more recent versions on both Windows and Linux as well as Azure Blob Storage. As you usually do after running the `sp_configure` command, RECONFIGURE needs to be run and a restart of SQL Server service needs to be completed. The PolyBase services will both have to be started manually as they are automatically turned off during this process and do not start automatically.

This can be done with these commands:

```
exec sp_configure @configname = 'polybase enabled', @configvalue = 1;

exec sp_configure @configname = 'hadoop connectivity', @configvalue = 7;

RECONFIGURE [ WITH OVERRIDE ]  ;
```

You can find details on the command on Microsoft Docs at *https://docs.microsoft.com/sql/database-engine/configure-windows/polybase-connectivity-configuration-transact-sql*.

Database scoped credential

Scoped credentials are used to access non-public Azure blob storage accounts from SQL Server or Azure Synapse with PolyBase. Hadoop clusters secured with Kerberos that are accessed from SQL Server with PolyBase also require scoped credentials.

Syntax for creation of scoped credentials can be found in the Microsoft Docs at *https://docs.microsoft.com/sql/t-sql/statements/create-database-scoped-credential-transact-sql*.

> ## Inside OUT
>
> *Can you just use system credentials for my scoped credentials?*
>
> System credentials start with ##. Database scoped credentials cannot start with the pound sign (#). This means system credentials are not eligible to be scoped credentials.

NOTE

If your SAS key value begins with a '?' be sure to remove the leading '?' because it is not recognized. Ensure you have already set up a master key. The master key will be used to protect these credentials. If you do not yet have a master key, the instructions to set it up can be found in the section called External Tables.

External data source

External data sources are used to establish connectivity to systems outside of SQL Server for data virtualization or loading data using PolyBase. The most common use cases are loading data with bulk insert or openrowset activities or access to data that would otherwise not be available in SQL Server because it resides on another system such as Hadoop.

The following example shows how to load data from a CSV file in an Azure blob storage location, which has been configured as an external data source. This requires a database-scoped credential using a shared access signature.

```
-- Create the External Data Source

-- Remove the ? from the beginning of the SAS token

-- Do not put a trailing /, file name, or shared access signature parameters at the end
of the LOCATION URL when configuring an external data sources for bulk operations.

CREATE DATABASE SCOPED CREDENTIAL AccessPurchaseOrder
WITH
        IDENTITY = 'SHARED ACCESS SIGNATURE'
, SECRET = '******srt=sco&sp=rwac&se=2017-02-01T00:55:34Z&st=2016-12-
29T16:55:34Z***************'
;
CREATE EXTERNAL DATA SOURCE ExternalPurchaseOrder
WITH
(LOCATION    = 'https://newinvoices.blob.core.windows.net/week3'
,CREDENTIAL = AccessPurchaseOrder, TYPE = BLOB_STORAGE)
;
--Insert into

BULK INSERT Sales.Orders
FROM 'order-2019-11-04.csv'
WITH (DATA_SOURCE = ' ExternalPurchaseOrder');
```

NOTE

Ensure you have at least read permission on the object that is being loaded, and that the expiration period is valid (all dates are in UTC time). A credential is not needed if the Blob storage has public access.

External file format

The external file format is required before you can create the external table. As suggested, the file format specifies the layout of the data to be referenced by the external table. Hadoop, Azure Blob Storage, and Azure Data Lake Storage all need an external file format object defined for PolyBase. Delimited text files, Parquet, and both RCFile and ORC Hive files are supported.

An example is:

```
CREATE EXTERNAL FILE FORMAT skipHeader_CSV
WITH (FORMAT_TYPE = DELIMITEDTEXT,
      FORMAT_OPTIONS(
          FIELD_TERMINATOR = ',',
          STRING_DELIMITER = '"',
          FIRST_ROW = 2,
          USE_TYPE_DEFAULT = True)
)
```

Syntax for this command can be found at *https://docs.microsoft.com/sql/t-sql/statements/create-external-file-format-transact-sql.*

Inside OUT

Can any format be used as an external file?

Delimited text files, RCFile, parquet and ORC Hive files are supported but have some limitations. Hive ORC offers better compression and performance than the RCFile. Delimited text has some limitations on the field terminators, string delimiters, and date formats.

External table

External tables are used to read specific external data and to import data into SQL Server. No actual data is moved to SQL Server during the creation of an external table, only the metadata along with basic statistics about the folder and file are stored. The intent of the external table is to be the link connecting the external data to SQL Server to create the data virtualization. The external table looks much like a regular SQL Server table in format and has a similar syntax as you see here with this external Oracle table.

```
-- Create a Master Key

  CREATE MASTER KEY ENCRYPTION BY PASSWORD = 'password';
  CREATE DATABASE SCOPED CREDENTIAL credential_name
  WITH IDENTITY = 'username', Secret = 'password';
-- LOCATION: Location string for data
  CREATE EXTERNAL DATA SOURCE external_data_source_name
```

```
    WITH ( LOCATION = 'oracle://<server address>[:<port>]',   CREDENTIAL =
  credential_name)
--Create table
  CREATE EXTERNAL TABLE customers(
  [O_ORDERKEY] DECIMAL(38) NOT NULL,
  [O_CUSTKEY] DECIMAL(38) NOT NULL,
  [O_ORDERSTATUS] CHAR COLLATE Latin1_General_BIN NOT NULL,
  [O_TOTALPRICE] DECIMAL(15,2) NOT NULL,
  [O_ORDERDATE] DATETIME2(0) NOT NULL,
  [O_ORDERPRIORITY] CHAR(15) COLLATE Latin1_General_BIN NOT NULL,
  [O_CLERK] CHAR(15) COLLATE Latin1_General_BIN NOT NULL,
  [O_SHIPPRIORITY] DECIMAL(38) NOT NULL,
  [O_COMMENT] VARCHAR(79) COLLATE Latin1_General_BIN NOT NULL
  )
  WITH ( LOCATION='customer', DATA_SOURCE= external_data_source_name   );
```

NOTE

It is important to remember that external tables can be affected by schema drift. If the external source changes, that does not automagically change in the external table definition. Any change to the external source will need to be reflected in the external table definition.

In ad-hoc query scenarios, such as querying Hadoop data, PolyBase stores the rows that are retrieved from the external data source in a temporary table. After the query completes, PolyBase removes and deletes the temporary table. No permanent data is stored in SQL tables. Connect to an employee.tbl file in blob storage on a Hadoop cluster. The query looks similar to a standard T-SQL query. Once the external table is defined the data is retrieved from Hadoop and displayed.

```
CREATE EXTERNAL DATA SOURCE mydatasource
WITH (
    TYPE = HADOOP,
    LOCATION = 'hdfs://xxx.xxx.xxx.xxx:8020'
)
CREATE EXTERNAL FILE FORMAT myfileformat
WITH (
    FORMAT_TYPE = DELIMITEDTEXT,
    FORMAT_OPTIONS (FIELD_TERMINATOR ='|')
);
CREATE EXTERNAL TABLE ClickStream (
    url varchar(50),
    event_date date,
    user_IP varchar(50)
)
WITH (
        LOCATION='/webdata/employee.tbl',
        DATA_SOURCE = mydatasource,
        FILE_FORMAT = myfileformat
    )
```

CHAPTER 20

```
;
SELECT TOP 10 (url) FROM ClickStream WHERE user_ip = 'xxx.xxx.xxx.xxx' ;
```

In an import scenario, such as `select into` from external table, PolyBase stores the rows that are returned as permanent data in the SQL table. The new table is created during query execution when PolyBase retrieves the external data.

PolyBase can push some of the query computation to Hadoop to improve query performance. This action is called predicate pushdown. It is used by specifying the Hadoop resource manager location option when creating the external data source, and turning the pushdown on using these parameters:

```
PUSHDOWN                  = [ON | OFF]
, RESOURCE_MANAGER_LOCATION = '<resource_manager>[:<port>]'
```

You can create many external tables that reference the same or different external data sources.

NOTE

Elastic query also uses external tables, but the same table cannot be used for both elastic queries and PolyBase. Although they have the same name, they are not the same.

Statistics

Statistics on external tables is done the same as other tables.

Syntax for this command can be found at *https://docs.microsoft.com/sql/t-sql/statements/create-statistics-transact-sql*.

NOTE

If you are unsure if PolyBase is installed, you can check its SERVERPROPERTY with this command

```
SELECT SERVERPROPERTY ('IsPolyBaseInstalled') AS IsPolyBaseInstalled;
```

It returns 1 if it is installed and 0 if it is not.

Catalog views

There are catalog views for the installation and running of PolyBase.

sys.external_data_sources

Sys.external_data_sources is used to identify external data_sources and gives visibility into the metadata about it. This includes the source, type, name of the remote database, and in the case of Hadoop the IP and port of the resource manager, which can be very helpful.

Sys.external_file_formats

Sys.external_file_formats is used to get details on the external file format for the sources. Along with the file format type it includes details about the delimiters, general format, encoding, and compression.

Sys.external_tables

Sys.external_tables contains a row for each external table in the current database, detailing information needed about the tables such as id links to the above tables. The majority of the columns give details about external tables over the shard map manager. The shard map manager is a special database that maintains global mapping information about all shards (databases) in a shard set. The metadata allows an application to connect to the correct database based upon the value of the sharding key. Every shard in the set contains maps that track the local shard data (known as shardlets).

Dynamic management views

There are a number of dynamic management views that can be used with PolyBase. The list of relevant views can be found in the Microsoft Docs at *https://docs.microsoft.com/sql/relational-databases/polybase/polybase-troubleshooting#dynamic-management-views*.

They can be used to troubleshoot issues such as finding long running queries and to monitor nodes in a PolyBase group.

Operationalizing analytics with Machine Learning Server

It often falls to a data engineer or DBA to operationalize and deploy machine learning models to production for the Data Scientist or other data professionals in our organization. In this section, we review the installation and configuration of Machine Learning Services and the best practices for operationalization of models and their code to allow for client applications and users to access them.

Regardless of the program or IDE used to create the scripts, model, functions and algorithms used to create them, Machine Learning Services can be used to operationalize them.

The mrsdeploy package for R and/or the azureml-model-management-sdk package for Python are used to deploy the packages. These R and Python analytics packages are often deployed as web services to a production environment.

Once deployed, the web service is available to a broader audience that can then consume the service. Machine Learning Server provides the operationalizing tools to deploy R and Python inside web, desktop, mobile, and dashboard applications as well as backend systems. Machine Learning Server turns your scripts into web services, so R and Python code can be easily executed by applications.

Architecture

There are two main configurations for the operationalization of Machine Learning Services. Single Server is used for easy and quick processes like proof-of-concepts. Enterprise scales to support complex production usage.

1. Single Server – A single web and compute note run on a single machine along with a database (see Figure 20-4). It is ideal for development, proof-of-concepts, prototyping and very small implementations.

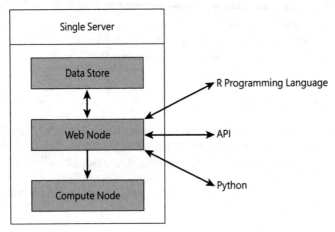

Figure 20-4 One-box Architecture, ideal for development and prototyping.

Supported platforms can be found at *https://docs.microsoft.com/machine-learning-server/operationalize/configure-start-for-administrators#supported-platforms*.

2. Enterprise.   Enterprise-size installations are designed for production usage. This configuration uses multiple web and compute nodes configured on multiple machines with an active-active configuration to allow you to load balance the API requests and scale out as needed. Nodes can be scaled independently. They use SQL Server or PostgreSQL to share data. The web nodes are stateless; therefore, there is no need for session stickiness when using a load balancer. It is recommended you configure SSL and authenticate against Active Directory (LDAP) or Azure Active Directory for this configuration. A visual of the installation is shown in Figure 20-5.

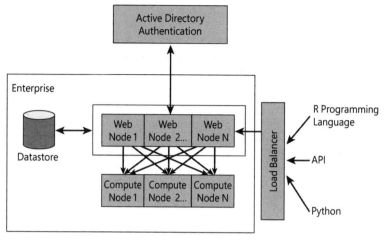

Figure 20-5 Enterprise Architecture, ideal for production usage.

Detailed instructions on how to install the components for ML Server can be found in these locations:

- **Windows:** *https://docs.microsoft.com/machine-learning-server/install/ machine-learning-server-windows-install*

- **Linux:** *https://docs.microsoft.com/machine-learning-server/install/ machine-learning-server-linux-install*

- **CLI:** *https://docs.microsoft.com/machine-learning-server/ operationalize/configure-admin-cli-launch*

If you prefer to use Azure Resource Management (ARM) templates, they are available on GitHub at *https://github.com/microsoft/microsoft-r/tree/master/mlserver-arm-templates*.

Inside OUT

Does Machine Learning use IIS (Internet Information Services)?

Machine Learning Server uses Kestrel as the web server for its operationalization web nodes. Therefore, if you expose your application to the Internet, we recommend that you review the guidelines for Kestrel at *https://docs.microsoft.com/aspnet/core/fundamentals/servers/kestrel* regarding reverse proxy setup.

Machine Learning Server

Machine Learning Server, formerly called Microsoft R Server, had its name changed when Python was released as part of the offering. Sometimes referred to as ML Server, it is used to operationalize and deploy models. When a cluster is deployed on HDInsight it is referred to as Machine Learning Services or ML Services. It can be deployed for use in a batch or real-time scoring scenario.

Machine Learning Services can be deployed on premises or in the cloud. An on-premises Machine Learning Server runs on Windows, Linux, Hadoop Spark, and SQL Server. In the cloud your options expand to:

1. Azure Machine Learning Server VMs

2. SQL Server VMs

3. Data Science VMs

4. Azure HDInsight for Hadoop and Spark

5. Azure Machine Learning

6. Azure SQL Database

Inside OUT

Can you run Machine Learning Server on a 32-bit operating system?

When choosing VMs keep in mind that Machine Learning Server will only run on 64-bit operating systems with x86-compatible Intel chips for all platforms. Itanium-architecture chips (IA-64) are not supported. Only commercial distributions of the ML Server from Apache Hadoop are available for support.

For specific versions and platforms for running ML Server please see the Microsoft Docs at *https://docs.microsoft.com/machine-learning-server/install/machine-learning-server-install*.

NOTE

When installing Machine Learning Server, be sure to use elevated permissions to ensure all components can install. MLS is currently not supported on Windows 2019, please use Windows 2016.

How to operationalize your models

The job of a database administrator varies from organization to organization and when it comes to models it often includes the task of operationalizing them. In this section we are starting the operationalization of a model based on the model being already completed, tested and handed off with all its supporting libraries and files.

Once you have all the supporting libraries and files, you will need to install a few additional items on the client from which you will deploy. Complete the following based on whether you are deploying R or Python code.

R will require an IDE such as R Tools for Visual Studio or Azure notebooks. This will be used to develop your R analytics in your local R IDE using the functions in the mrsdeploy package that can be installed with R Client and R Server. It allows for you to connect from your local machine to deploy the models as web services. With the ML Server configured for operationalization, you can connect to the server from your local machine and deploy your models as a web service, which will allow users to consume them.

Configure ML Server for operationalization of models and analytics

All deployments must consist of at least a single web node, single compute node, and a database.

Web nodes are HTTP REST endpoints that users interact directly with to make API calls. They are used to access the data and send requests to the compute node. One web node can route multiple requests at the same time.

Commute nodes are used to execute the code. Each node needs its own pool of R or Python shells and can therefore execute multiple requests at the same time.

CHAPTER 20

> ## Inside OUT
>
> *What are some of the best practices for architecture for production?*
>
> Additional web nodes are recommended to avoid a single point of failure.
>
> A SQLite 3.7 database is installed by default, so using a SQL Server or PostgreSQL database is recommended.

Security for operationalizing models

Machine Learning Server allows for seamless integration with Active Directory LDAP or Azure Active Directory. For more details on how to do this see the Microsoft Docs at *https://docs. microsoft.com/machine-learning-server/operationalize/configure-authentication*.

Configuring the server to use a trust relationship between the users and the operational engine will allow the use of username/password combination for verification. Once the user is verified, a token is issued to the authenticated user. More details on how to manage tokens can be found on Microsoft Docs at *https://docs.microsoft.com/machine-learning-server/operationalize/ how-to-manage-access-tokens*.

In addition to authenticating the user, it is important to secure the tokens from interception during transmission and storage. This should be done using transport layer security (HTTPS), as shown in Figure 20-6. More details on how to enable SSL or TLS can be found on Microsoft Docs at *https://docs.microsoft.com/machine-learning-server/operationalize/configure-https*.

Role-based access control for web services is also recommended. Role-based access control (RBAC) is used to grant minimum security required for a user's role. More details on how to set up the roles can be found in MS Docs at *https://docs.microsoft.com/machine-learning-server/ operationalize/configure-roles*.

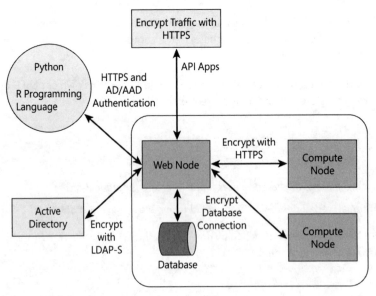

Figure 20-6 Deployment security.

Inside OUT

Does Machine Learning Server inherit Azure roles?

RBAC in Machine Learning Server is not the same as it is in Azure even though they have the same name. The roles from Azure cannot be inherited and must be set up again in Machine Learning Server.

Cross-Origin Resource Sharing

Cross-Origin Resource sharing (CORS) is used to request resources from a domain different than the one your web node is in. This is typical when using a government or third-party data source.

CORS is a mechanism that uses additional HTTP headers to tell a browser to let a web application running at one origin (your domain) have permission to access selected resources from a server at a different origin (a government site with data on how many people voted in the last election). A web application executes a cross-origin HTTP request when it requests a resource that has a different origin (domain, protocol, or port) than its own origin.

Here is an example of a cross-origin request: The frontend JavaScript code for a web application served from *http://mydomain.com* uses XMLHttpRequest to make a request for *http://api.stats.gov.ca/data.json*.

For security reasons, browsers restrict cross-origin HTTP requests initiated from within scripts. For example, XMLHttpRequest and the Fetch API follow the same-origin policy. This means that a web application using those APIs can only request HTTP resources from the same origin the application was loaded from, unless the response from the other origin includes the right CORS headers.

By default, Cross-Origin Resource sharing (CORS) is disabled and can be enabled by following the instructions in MS Docs at *https://docs.microsoft.com/machine-learning-server/operationalize/configure-cors*.

Packages for R and Python

When R or Python are installed with either SQL Server or with Machine Learning Services, a distribution of open source libraries are included. These libraries may vary with each version and can only be upgraded by upgrading your installation, regular service pack, or cumulative upgrades. An example would be upgrading from SQL Server 2016 to SQL Server 2019. The libraries should never be manually upgraded and may destabilize your installation should you do so.

Operationalizing and deploying code may often mean including additional packages in addition to the default ones included in an installation. These packages are publicly available, but due to enterprise restrictions on Internet access, it can sometimes be viable to have a repository inside the enterprise firewall. Note that all dependent packages need to be available to all nodes at runtime.

R package management options are available at *https://docs.microsoft.com/ machine-learning-server/operationalize/configure-manage-r-packages*.

The Python package list can be found at *https://docs.microsoft.com/sql/advanced-analytics/ python/install-additional-python-packages-on-sql-server?view=sql-server-ver15#add-a-new- python-package*.

Deploy model as a web service

Both R and Python models can be deployed as a web service. Using the mrsdeploy or azureml- model-management-sdk package that ships with Machine Learning Server, you can develop, test, and ultimately deploy these analytics as web services in your production environment.

Python uses the azureml-model-management-sdk Python package that ships with the Machine Learning Server to deploy the web services and manage the web service from a Python script. A set of RESTful APIs are also available for direct access. Details on how to deploy the service can be found at *https://docs.microsoft.com/machine-learning-server/operationalize/python/ quickstart-deploy-python-web-service*.

R uses the functions in the mrsdeploy package to gain access to the web service from an R script, and then uses a set of RESTful APIs to provide access to the web service directly. Publish the model as a web service to Machine Learning Server using the `publishService()` function from the mrsdeploy package.

Details on how to deploy the service can be found at *https://docs.microsoft.com/ machine-learning-server/operationalize/quickstart-publish-r-web-service*.

API libraries

Machine Learning Server uses Swagger for the creation of both Python and R APIs. Swagger is an open source tool used to build and enable APIs. Using core APIs, R, and Python code can be published as a Machine Learning Server hosted analytics Web service. Swagger offers templates to simplify this process, which are available at *https://swagger. io*. Swagger-based JSON files define the list of calls and resources available in the REST APIs. These are defined as either Core APIs or Service Consumption APIs. More details on the different APIs can be found at *https://docs.microsoft.com/machine-learning-server/ operationalize/concept-api*. An API library is needed to access the RESTful APIs outside of R/Python. This library can be built with Swagger and will simplify the calls, the encoding of data, and a markup response handling on the API. Programming language options for the library are: C#, Java, JS, Python, or Node.js. Details on the swagger template files for APIs can be found at *https://docs.microsoft.com/machine-learning-server/operationalize/how-to-build-api-clients-from-swagger-for-app-integration#get-the-swagger-file.*

> **NOTE**
>
> **For R applications, Swagger is not required if you use the mrsdeploy package directly, giving you two different options for deployment.**

Steps for Deployment

Depending on the type of deployment you are doing and to what configuration, the steps are very different, however a simple practice example that follows the basic steps in a Python notebook can be found in the accompanying sample. This script and all scripts for this book are available for download at *https://www.MicrosoftPressStore.com/SQLServer2019InsideOut/downloads.*

1. Configuration

    a. Workspace

    b. Notebook

    c. Access

2. Ensure you have data and a trained model

3. Save the package

4. Deploy

5. Run and test the deployed model

Launchpad service

The launchpad service is an NT service, added by the extensibility framework. It can be found with the other SQL Server services in the instance. It is used to execute external scripts for R and Python. An external script is the launching of a separate host for processing. This is similar to the way that the full-text indexing and query service launches a separate host for processing full-text queries. The Launchpad service has been redesigned in SQL Server 2019 to utilize AppContainer Isolation instead of the previous SQLRUserGroup (SQL restricted user group). This isolation layer removes the need to manage accounts and passwords of workers in the group for security. The SQLRUserGroup now has only one member, which is the service account instead of the multiple worker accounts.

The launch pad services used to create a separate process that runs under a low-privilege Windows account that is separate from SQL Server, the service, or the user that launched the query. This low-privilege account is a part of the SQLRUserGroup group (SQL restricted user group), which is the cornerstone of the isolation and security model for R and Python running on SQL Server. This is displayed in Figure 20-7.

Inside Out

How many Python or R queries can be run at once?

There is one launch pad service for each SQL Server instance and each instance has by default 20 worker accounts in the SQLRUserGroup to service the instance. This does not affect the parallelization within a task. For example, if a worker account is launched to run a scoring task and that task is run in parallel, the same worker account is used for all threads of the parallel process.

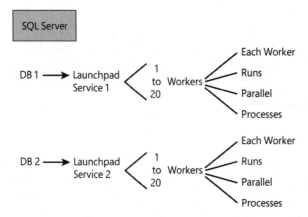

Figure 20-7 Launch Pad.

The number of worker accounts in the pool can be modified in the SQL Server Configuration Manager by right-clicking on the Launchpad and choosing properties.

NOTE

Any configuration changes to the server must be done in the SQL Server Configuration Manager. The ability to make changes in the ML Services configuration is no longer available.

Security

The Launchpad service maintains the worker accounts used to run the R or Python queries. If you need to change the passwords on a regular basis, this must be done by regenerating them for all workers. This is done in the SQL Server Configuration Manager by right-clicking on the Launchpad and choosing Properties. Choose Advanced and then change Reset External Users Password to Yes. This will change all worker passwords, and you must restart the service before running any queries to ensure the service reads the new passwords.

The security is not just a one-way process to the workers, launchpad also tracks the identity of the user that launched the process and maps that user back to SQL Server. In situations where a script, or piece of code, needs to request more data or perform additional operations in SQL Server, the Launchpad will manage the identity transfer for the request.

Index

A

AAD, 858, 878
Aardvark, 662
Aaron Swartz, 49
abreast, 605
absurd, 669
academic, 312, 616
accelerate, 658
Accelerated Database, 233, 234, 318, 634
acceleration, 68
accent, 224
Access, 51, 54, 60, 68, 69, 339, 341, 360, 637
Access Control, 123
AccessPurchaseOrder, 921
accesstosql, 888
Account Cloud, 496
Account Retry Attempts, 383
Account Retry Delay, 383
AccountsPersonID, 753, 754
accrued, 747
accumulate, 334, 407
ACID, 657
ACLs, 123, 239, 913
acronym, 125, 483, 514
Active Expensive, 37, 39, 700
actively, 37, 331, 481, 913
ActiveX, 389
Activity Monitor, 36, 37, 38, 39, 40, 41, 391, 700, 701
Actual Execution, 697, 700, 703, 764
ActualQueryPlan, 718
Actual Rebinds, 700
ActualRows, 699
ActualRowsRead, 699

acute, 455
Add Connection, 417
Add Database, 508
AddDays, 428
Add Login, 30
AddOption, 725
Add Replica, 521
Address Resolution, 613
Add Server, 30
ADF, 896
adhere, 260, 549
Advanced Cluster, 489, 490
Advanced Data, xvi, 822, 839, 842, 843, 846, 853
Advanced Encryption, 448, 625, 626
Advanced Format, 124
Advanced Package, 193
Advanced Policies, 504
Advanced Services, 147, 164
adverse, 330, 433, 438, 444, 463, 505, 845
affiliated, 797
Agent Extension, 793
Agent Job, 182, 410, 419
aggravating, 31
aging, 250
agonizing, 435
Ahead Logging, 97
Ain, 125
airbags, 677
akin, 73
Alert Definition, 42
Alert System, 384, 398
Aliens Land, 610
All Automatic, 211
All Database, 211

All Services, 891
Alphanumeric, 244
AMD, 59
ample, 317, 363
Analysis Server, 173, 174
Analytics Solution, 371
Anatomy, 95
ancestor, 234, 258
anchor, 567
annotations, 133
anomalies, 648, 844
Anomalous, 844
anticipate, 86, 503
Antimalware, 117
antipatterns, 573
antivirus, 152, 172, 179, 180, 458
Any Counter, 42
AnyTable, 686
Apache Hive, 910
Apache Knox, 909
Apache Kudu, 907
Apache Spark, 817, 907, 915
apiVersion, 133, 134, 135
apparatus, 401, 574
AppContainer, 933
Append Output, 394
Application event, 642
Application Insights, 369
ApplicationName, 19
Application Programming, 622, 623
aptitude, 193
aptly, 206
arcane, 549, 660
archaeology, 336
architectural, 226, 668, 798, 827, 858, 909

Plug into learning at

MicrosoftPressStore.com

The Microsoft Press Store by Pearson offers:

- Free U.S. shipping

- Buy an eBook, get three formats – Includes PDF, EPUB, and MOBI to use with your computer, tablet, and mobile devices

- Print & eBook Best Value Packs

- eBook Deal of the Week – Save up to 50% on featured title

- Newsletter – Be the first to hear about new releases, announcements, special offers, and more

- Register your book – Find companion files, errata, and product updates, plus receive a special coupon* to save on your next purchase

 Pearson